CHURCHILL'S
GRAND ALLIANCE

ALSO BY JOHN CHARMLEY

Duff Cooper: The Authorised Biography
Lord Lloyd and the Decline of the British Empire
Descent to Suez: The Diaries of Sir Evelyn Shuckburgh 1951–6 (ed.)
Chamberlain and the Lost Peace
Churchill: The End of Glory

CHURCHILL'S
GRAND ALLIANCE

THE ANGLO-AMERICAN SPECIAL RELATIONSHIP 1940–57

JOHN CHARMLEY

HARCOURT BRACE & COMPANY

New York   San Diego   London

Library of Congress Cataloging-in-Publication Data
Charmley, John, 1955–
Churchill's grand alliance: the Anglo-American special
relationship, 1940–57/John Charmley.
p.   cm.
Includes bibliographical references and index.
Originally published: London: Hodder & Stoughton, 1995.
ISBN 0-15-127581-5
1. Churchill, Winston, Sir, 1874–1965—Views on international
relations. 2. Great Britain—Foreign relations—United States.
3. United States—Foreign relations—Great Britain. 4. United
States—Foreign relations—20th century.   5. Great Britain—Foreign
relations—1936–1945. 6. Great Britain—Foreign relations—1945–
I. Title
DA566.9.C5C413   1995
327.41073'09'044—dc20   95-24245

Type was set in Pegasus.
Printed in the United States of America
First U.S. edition   A B C D E

To Gervase, Gerard and Kit

Contents

vii

Illustrations

Churchill with Ambassador Kennedy in 1940. (*Associated Press*)
Churchill and Ambassador J. G. Winant sign the 'bases for destroyers deal', 1941.
(*Associated Press*)
Roosevelt using a Churchillian 'V' sign as Churchill signs the Atlantic Charter,
1941. (*Franklin D. Roosevelt Library*)
Churchill and Roosevelt on board *The Prince of Wales* with Elliott Roosevelt
standing by. (*Franklin D. Roosevelt Library*)
Churchill greets Harry Hopkins in Quebec in 1943. (*Franklin D. Roosevelt Library*)
General Henri Honoré Giraud and General Charles de Gaulle with Churchill and
Roosevelt at Casablanca in 1943. (*Franklin D. Roosevelt Library*)
Roosevelt and Churchill, Casablanca, 1943.
Churchill, Roosevelt and the Sultan of Morocco at Casablanca, 1943.
Roosevelt and Churchill, Casablanca, 1943.
Talking to the press, Casablanca.
Talking to the Chiefs of Staff.
Churchill and Eisenhower in 1944. (*Copyright 1967 Screengems Inc.*)
Churchill, Roosevelt and the Canadian Prime Minister, Mackenzie King, at Château
Frontenac in Quebec, 1944. (*Copyright 1967 Screengems Inc.*)
FDR at Yalta in February 1945. (*Copyright 1967 Screengems Inc.*)

Churchill, Truman and Stalin at Potsdam.
Churchill returns to power, 1951. (*Keystone photo*)
Adulation of the Grand Old Man. Churchill receives yet another American award
in 1946. (*Illustrated London News*)
Churchill on the hills of old Missouri, 5 March 1946.
The end of Truman, 1952. (*Harry S. Truman Presidential Library: US Navy*)
Churchill with President Eisenhower in 1953. (*US National Park Service.
Photo: Abbie Rowe*)

Eden, Truman and Acheson. (*Harry S. Truman Presidential Library: US Navy*)
Ambassador Winthrop Aldrich gives Churchill an award on his 81st birthday.
(*Associated Press*)
Churchill and Eden leaving for Washington, 1954. (*Associated Press*)
Churchill calling for *détente* in Washington, June 1954. (*Associated Press*)
Churchill and the French Prime Minister, Joseph Laniel, with Eisenhower in
Bermuda, 1953. (*Associated Press*)
Churchill gets his honorary US citizenship, 1963. (*Associated Press*)

All the photographs are from: Winston Churchill Memorial and Library,
Westminster College, Fulton, Missouri. (Photographic prints by Jay E. Kish, Jr.)

Acknowledgments

In the course of the research on this volume I have incurred a number of debts which it is my pleasure to acknowledge – although the usual disclaimer, that only the author is to be held responsible for his conclusions, applies more than ever in this case.

I owe an immense debt of gratitude to my dear friend Warren M. Hollrah, archivist at the Churchill Memorial and Library in Fulton, Missouri. Although that staunch upholder of the Anglo-American special relationship will disagree with most of what is in this book, his enthusiasm, his kindness and his help almost persuaded me that I was wrong; as it is, I am willing to admit that at least in one area there will always be a 'special relationship'. The unsurpassed archive at the Memorial is, like its archivist, unique. My second debt is to my former research assistant, Kevin S. Mathis, who accompanied me to Independence and Abilene as well as to the microfilm copier in Reeves Library at Westminster College; in all these places he did sterling service – even if none of our research trips brings back quite as many memories as our sixteen-hour journey through the Cumberland Gap from Tennessee to Fulton. Like Warren, he will disagree with much that follows, but again I hope that a 'special relationship' has not been too badly damaged. I also owe thanks to Judi Bell and Randy Hendrix at the Churchill Memorial for making it such a congenial place to work. I would also like to thank the staff of the Reeves Library, especially Liz Hauer, for all their help. President Traer of Westminster College and the then Acting President, Jack Marshall, did all anyone could have asked to make my stay on their campus a most pleasant experience; anyone contemplating taking up the Fulbright Chair has my earnest encouragement to do so.

I am deeply indebted to Westminster College and to the Fulbright Commission in London for appointing me to the Robertson Founder's Chair at Westminster, which enabled me to conduct so much research in America. I cannot imagine, given its purpose, that the Fulbright Commission will feel quite as warmly towards me as I do to its selection panel for appointing me despite my views on Anglo-American relations. I should also like to extend my thanks to the Harris family and the Callaway Bank in Fulton, Missouri, who not only gave my wife a job, but also allowed her time off to help me with my researches; why can't we have banks like that in England?

To the staff of the Truman Library in Independence, Missouri, the Roosevelt Library in New York State and the Eisenhower Library at Abilene, I would like to extend my thanks; if only British archives could be as good. There is, of course, one British archive which can (almost) match the level of the American Presidential library, and that is the Special Collections Room at Birmingham University Library, presided over (though not, alas, for much longer) by that prince amongst archivists, Ben Benediktz. I am also grateful to the staffs of the following libraries and archives: the British Library; Churchill College, Cambridge; and Cambridge University Library.

My agent, Felicity Bryan, Perry Knowlton in America, and my publisher, John Curtis, have all provided aid beyond the call of duty, and I am very grateful to them all. I am grateful, as ever, for John's wise advice. I would like to thank Linda Osband for, yet again, getting me to explain myself more clearly – even if the result will distress some people!

Portions of the typescript were read and commented upon by my colleague in the School of History at the University of East Anglia, Geoff Searle, who did his best to dissuade me. I am also grateful to Heather Yasamee of the Foreign and Commonwealth Office, who provided me with documentation concerning plan 'Alpha'. It will be evident from the bibliography how much I owe to other scholars who have worked in this area. If I have not always agreed with them, I have found their books and articles stimulating.

My sons, Gervase, Gerard and Kit, all provided distractions from the word-processor and greatly added, as always, to my *joie de vivre*.

But I hope that everyone named above will understand if I say that my greatest and unpayable debt is to my wife, Lorraine, who not only provided the encouragement, understanding and endless cups of coffee necessary for the whole process to continue, but also accompanied me on many of my research trips, doing yeoman service in Abilene, Hyde Park and Birmingham when time pressed hard. It is more than convention which makes me say that without her I could not have accomplished the research and writing of this book. Inshallah!

John Charmley
Fulton Mo. and East Tuddenham 1993–4

Foreword

This book brings to an end the task I set myself nearly a decade ago. With *Chamberlain and the Lost Peace* (1989) and *Churchill: The End of Glory* (1993), it completes a triptych on British foreign and imperial policy in the mid-twentieth century. The aim was not to write a complete history – that task still awaits its chronicler – but rather to clear away the lush undergrowth laid down by Churchill and his admirers, and to try to look at the period afresh.

Contrary to some of the allegations levelled by reviewers of the other two books, I did not set out to write 'revisionist' history, save in so far as the existing version seemed to me unsatisfactory. The epilogue attempts to deal with some of the difficulties and problems attendant upon the task of 'revisionism', but for those readers joining the story at this point for the first time, a word or two of warning might be in order.

This book is about Churchill and the American alliance. It is not a history of the Second World War, or the origins of the Cold War, or even of Anglo-American relations in a wider sphere. Although all these things find their place in this book, they are not what it is about. Thus, when the Cold War creates a simulacrum of Churchill's 'Grand Alliance', the narrative passes quickly over it in order to get to the point at which Churchill himself was once more in a position to try to implement his vision. Churchill was not content with a mere alliance, he wanted something more. So from the point of view of this book NATO, the Berlin airlift and even the Korean War are of peripheral interest; in a complete history of Anglo-American relations things would be different.

The second thing to get straight is the author's motives. This would hardly be necessary save for the tendency of some critics to invent ingenious ones. It is some sort of comment on reviewing that none of the scores of commentators on *Churchill* reproached me with having written two books, *Duff Cooper* (1986) and *Lord Lloyd and the Decline of the British Empire* (1987), which took an impeccably Churchillian line on 'appeasement', Chamberlain and British foreign policy during this period. Instead of wild speculations that *Churchill* had something to do with my admiration for Lady Thatcher (I never quite saw how this one worked), reviewers might have called me to account for changing my mind. I plead entirely guilty to this charge.

The more work I did in the archives, the more dissatisfied I became with the orthodoxy which I had accepted. This may have been something to do with the fact that the archives contain the papers which led Ministers and their advisers to follow the policy of appeasement and, therefore, provide a convincing explanation of it; but it was more than that. Historians of the British Empire, especially Jack Gallagher, had long outlined a version of imperial policy in the 1930s which was not the nerveless folly which Chamberlain's critics depicted; how did British foreign policy look through Gallagherite spectacles? The same men who formulated the subtle and flexible policy designed to hold on to as much of the reality of power in India as possible also had charge of Britain's destiny in the late 1930s, and they reacted to Hitler much as they had to Gandhi; the same was true, but in reverse, of Churchill. Churchill saw Gandhi as a major threat to the Empire and wanted him, and Hitler, crushed. Chamberlain and company saw both of them as challenges which had to be met. Conscious of the fragility of British power, they preferred not to project it militarily until there was no other course. In Gandhi's case diplomacy did the trick, although Churchill nearly ruined things. With Hitler, matters did not have such a happy outcome. Britain was still a Great Power, and at the end of the day leaders decided that the point had been reached where in order to remain one she had to mobilise. Chamberlain had always feared that a war to remain a Great Power would prove to be self-defeating – and so it proved. Rather like the Habsburg Empire, Britain could remain a Great Power only by avoiding the war which her more Romantic statesmen imagined would re-establish her in that position.

It had always seemed that Britain came out of the Second World War with remarkably little reward for her immense sacrifices. The Americans had risen to global eminence, the Soviets likewise, but the British had nothing save the aim articulated by Churchill in 1940: victory over Nazi Germany. That was a great achievement, but it buttered no parsnips. In trying to understand this phenomenon it became clear that the main reason for it lay not in the weakness of Britain in 1945, but in the myopia of Churchill in 1941 and 1942. To leave the formulation of war aims until the war is won is good strategy only if you are the strongest partner in an alliance; it behoves the weakest partner to manoeuvre for war aims as early as possible. When a Great Power not only fails to do this, but fails even to formulate aims beyond 'victory', it is hardly surprising that its partners should come better out of the conflict – especially if they have formulated their own war aims. It was the attempt to explain Churchill's myopia which led to the writing of *Churchill: The End of Glory*. Whilst not blaming the Prime Minister for everything which went wrong, it seemed that his characteristic defects – impulsiveness, sentimentality, myopia and lack of judgment – all contributed in a major way to Britain's plight.

The main line of the counterblast to this gentle suggestion was that whatever Churchill may or may not have done wrong, he had won the war, obtained the American alliance and helped save us all from the Soviets. This book attempts to deal with this curious line of reasoning. Churchill did not win the war; the Russians did so – with some help, mainly from the Americans. Churchill did not bring the Americans into the war, the Japanese and the Germans did that. Indeed, Churchill's first ally was the Soviet Union, an unlooked-for one who provided the western allies with a real problem when it came to claiming that their war was some sort of crusade against totalitarianism. Nor did Churchill get the Americans involved in the Cold War. So what were the effects of Churchill's misplaced sentimentalism with regard to America? The following pages attempt to provide an answer to this question. Old and new readers begin here.

I

Churchill's American Alliance

I

Special Relationships

In the beginning was the word, and the word was Churchill's and he pronounced it good. The Anglo-American special relationship has been such a marked feature of the last fifty years that a generation which has the attention span of a television commercial is apt to regard it with awe as an ancient phenomenon. Yet in very large measure it was an artefact created by one of the greatest literary and political artists of the century, Winston Churchill. He not only acted as fugleman and midwife for the Anglo-American alliance, he was conscious of embodying it in his person. As he told Congress in 1942, had his father been American and his mother English, he might have stood amongst them in his own right. From the point of view of Franklin D. Roosevelt and America's manifest destiny, it was a good thing that Churchill's father had been English.

Churchill's attitudes towards America reflected not only his own parentage, but also the 'Anglo-Saxonism' which was intellectually and socially fashionable in the 1890s – a decade which shaped many of Churchill's ideas. A mixture of popular racial theories about the inherent superiority of the 'English-speaking peoples' and of the imperialism which often accompanied them, 'Anglo-Saxonism' enjoyed a vogue which was just durable enough to offset what might have been British fears about American rivalry.

Relatively few British statesmen were able to take the detached view of Lord Salisbury, that a Power of Britain's eminence had to get used to challenges and should not be too worried about them. Salisbury, Prime Minister and Foreign Secretary for most of the last two decades of the nineteenth century, cultivated an imperturbable style of diplomacy, which, by the end of his period of ascendancy, was an object of some annoyance to the rising generation. On the one hand came ardent Conservative imperialists like the Viceroy of India, Lord Curzon, who wanted Salisbury to pursue a firm line with those who, like the Russians, presumed to challenge Britannia's imperium; on the other hand came criticism from equally ardent Liberal imperialists, like the young Churchill himself, who objected to Salisbury's pragmatic line on what would now be called matters of human rights.[1]

Russia was far from being the only Power to attract unfavourable attention from British politicians. Germany was another Power whose activities were thought to give cause for concern, particularly after the turn of the century. The United States, on the other hand, benefited from the fashionable notion that the 'civilization of the English-speaking nations was superior to that of any other nation on the planet'.[2] In this view of the world, America was not really 'foreign' in the way that Russia, or even Germany, was. It was taken for granted, at least by those like Churchill who imbibed the gospel of 'Anglo-Saxonism', that there was a community of interests between Britain and the United States founded upon the possession of common characteristics – most notably democracy, industry, intelligence, and a shared cultural and legal heritage. The notion of Anglo-Saxon superiority provided its believers with a 'sense of shared racial heritage and a vision of a common destiny'.[3]

Where the activities of Russia in central Asia or Germany almost anywhere were matters for concern, when America despoiled Spain of her remaining Empire in the Spanish-American war, *The Times* loftily proclaimed: 'We do not ... reproach the American people in the least, with their interest in the Cuban sufferers by Spanish misgovernment.'[4] It was understood to be insupportable for an 'imperial race' like the Anglo-Saxons to tolerate the 'misgovernment' practised by others; America's easy victory over Spain was taken to be another sign of the 'innate superiority' of the English-speaking peoples.[5] The young Winston Churchill wrote to his mother, Lady Randolph Churchill, that the Americans, despite their 'unattractive side', were 'right and deep down in the heart of a great democracy there is a very noble spirit'.[6] Nor was Churchill writing without experience, for as a twenty-year-old he had visited Cuba and had written sympathetically of the American-assisted revolt against Spanish rule.[7]

Although 'Anglo-Saxonism' had had its vogue by about 1904 (with Lady Randolph Churchill exhibiting her family's usual financial acumen by starting up a short-lived magazine, *The Anglo-Saxon Review*, just in time to lose money on it), through its influence on Churchill and other British politicians it was to remain a powerful part of the unspoken assumptions which many Britons brought to bear on Anglo-American relations. The decision by the Committee of Imperial Defence in 1904 that America 'need not be taken into consideration' in defence planning placed that country in a category apart from any other Great, or potentially Great, Power. Indeed, when the Anglo-Japanese alliance was renegotiated in 1912, an escape clause was added which would prevent Britain from being involved in a war with America on Japan's behalf.[8]

Churchill's Americanophilia proved more durable than that of many of his contemporaries. The Great War placed Anglo-American relations under tremendous strain. American neutrality and President Woodrow Wilson's moralising proved quite as unpalatable to the British as Britain's searching of American vessels and her Irish policy did to Americans. By 1917 Britain was able to carry on the war only courtesy of American financial aid, a situation which many British politicians found intolerable given the fact that American help did not come without strings.[9] Even once America had entered the war, it was as an 'associated power' rather than as an ally. President Wilson was not only aware that his war aims differed from those of his partners, but he was also determined to 'force them to our way of thinking when the war was over'. By that time, he calculated, 'they will . . . be financially in our hands'; it was a shrewd assessment.[10]

Wilson's attempts to forge a new world order were not only disastrous in themselves, but they created a legacy of distrust of American moralising which a generation of British politicians, fortified by further experience of American diplomacy, was to find it difficult to discard. Wilson's belief in the virtues of democracy, nationalism and the American way, shared as they were by men like his Assistant Undersecretary for the Navy, Franklin D. Roosevelt, were to become the common currency of politically correct thought in the twentieth century; but repetition of their virtues did not make his ideas sensible. An ancient continent, criss-crossed by the racial and dynastic wars and by the folk-wanderings of a millennium, was not the best laboratory in which to experiment with the idea of national boundaries based on 'nationality'. In North America the problem of the indigenous inhabitants had been solved by the application of the sort of brutality which, had it been practised elsewhere, would have aroused fervent condemnation from Washington; Europe could not be dealt with so summarily.

Like many Liberals, Wilson assumed the best about human nature – and like many Liberals, he was doomed to disappointment. The seventeenth-century Marquess of Halifax once described party politics as a sort of conspiracy against the state. In like wise might liberalism be regarded as a conspiracy of the intellect against human nature; a true triumph of hope over experience. At the Versailles conference which constructed the new world order, it was the French Premier, Georges Clemenceau, who saw this most clearly when he said: 'God has his ten commandments, Wilson his fourteen points – we shall see.' Europe did see. Wilson's greatest contribution (sanctimony apart) to the new world order, the League of Nations, was crippled from the start by America's refusal to join,* and became a talking-shop of the worst sort. The map of Europe so painstakingly created at the peace conferences was to prove so unstable that it provided the breeding ground out of which a fresh conflict was to engulf the world.

Wilson at Versailles, American sanctimony, arrogance and vacillation, all left their mark on the generation of politicians who were to rule Britain between the wars. The debt settlement imposed on the British in 1923 was sufficiently onerous for the Prime Minister, Andrew Bonar Law, to be reduced to the expedient of writing under an assumed name to *The Times* to protest at his Chancellor's acceptance of it.[11] The imperialist wing of Stanley Baldwin's

---

* The Senate refused to ratify American membership of the League in a fit of isolationist pique.

1924–9 Cabinet came to have strong views on America's attempts to muscle in on Britain's predominance.

Nowhere was that threat more apparent than at sea, where 'anti-British sentiments among the Navy's top leadership contributed to the postwar deterioration in Anglo-American naval relations. . . . Anglo-American rivalry during this period was rooted in the belief that the US posed yet another challenge to the long-standing maritime predominance of Great Britain.'[12] American naval arrogance led to one of Churchill's infrequent bouts of anger with the United States. Writing to the First Lord of the Admiralty, William Bridgeman, on 22 December 1927, Churchill, who was then Chancellor, exploded angrily that, 'I am no longer prepared to take dictation from the U.S. and if they attempt to bully us by threatening a large programme [of ship building] I hope I shall be able to range myself with you'; he dismissed American policy as nothing more than 'bluff and bluster'.[13]

The Geneva naval conference of 1927 did little to improve the state of Anglo-American relations, with Bridgeman privately characterising American policy as wanting to 'get a good election cry for [President] Coolidge by saying they had not only made a further peace move, but also twisted the British Lion's tail by making him reduce his cruiser strength'.[14] If Bridgeman thought that the American delegates were 'not only very conceited, but often very stupid',[15] then the Cabinet Secretary, Sir Maurice Hankey, went one better. Characterising British policy towards America as one of constant 'concession', Hankey told the former British Prime Minister, Lord Balfour, that the only consequence had been that 'we are less popular and more abused in America than ever before, because they think us weak'; his own remedy was simple: 'I would refuse to be blackmailed or browbeaten.'[16] Nor was Hankey the only one to feel this way. Lord Cushenden, acting Foreign Secretary for much of 1928, wrote in a Cabinet paper that 'except as a figure of speech war is *not* unthinkable' between Britain and America.[17] Churchill took the same view, writing in November 1928 that war with America, 'however foolish and disastrous', was not really 'unthinkable'. He believed that 'the great mass of the British public do not desire to see England obsequious to the United States', and he did not think that England would 'submit' to having her imperial policy dictated from Washington; that would mean that her 'day' as a Great Power was 'over' – a situation which had not yet arrived.[18] It is as well that the ironies of history are hidden from participants.

The extent of British antipathy to America should not be exaggerated, but there can be little doubt that the experiences of the decade after 1919 imbued many British politicians with a healthy distrust of her ambitions. Baldwin was said to be so disgusted with Americans that he had no desire ever to talk with one again, whilst his heir-apparent, Neville Chamberlain, opined that it was always 'best and safest to count on *nothing* from the Americans except words'.[19] In the post Second World War period it was easy to characterise such comments as anti-American, and equally easy for Churchill to wax both indignant and lyrical about the extent of the opportunity lost by Chamberlain when he rejected Roosevelt's suggestion in January 1938 of holding an international conference.[20] It is easy to dismiss such comments with the epithet 'anti-American', but this was no more than the voice of bitter experience talking. The years 1940–5 were a real watershed in Anglo-American relations, and comments made by Churchill about it after 1945 are usually the product of hindsight and political calculation. In the period when Churchill was writing his memoirs he was once more in search of a suitable America. At Westminster College, Fulton, Missouri, in March 1946, Churchill had propounded the case for the 'two workmen' of Britain and America once again to co-operate to save the world, so he was not averse to using his memoirs to point out what had happened last time they had failed to co-operate. However, in the circumstances of the late 1930s Chamberlain was right to be sceptical about Roosevelt's grandiose but inchoate ideas.

Roosevelt was good at talking – indeed, he did it better than he did anything else – but behind his words were the spectres of an isolationist Congress and an indifferent public opinion. His fatuous offer of an international conference in early 1938 was taken seriously only by desperate men like Churchill and Anthony Eden; Chamberlain looked at it and found nothing in it. Even when Americans in China were insulted by the Japanese, the President could not be persuaded to do anything more than make speeches. In retrospect, the 1930s were to be presented (not least by Churchill) as a decade of lost opportunities for forging an alliance against Germany; in fact, it was a decade in which the last opportunity to save the civilisation of western Europe was lost. Chamberlain's instincts were sound: seek diplomatic solutions to problems created by Versailles, but rearm just in case. He correctly divined that Poland was not, as it never had been, a vital British interest, but he made the mistake of assuming that he could get involved as an 'honest broker' in the affairs of Czechoslovakia. For this he received abuse from Hitler and Churchill and obloquy from History; the irony was that if he deserved abuse, it was for thinking that Hitler would forgive him for intervening.[21]

Chamberlain did not pursue the policy of appeasement in order to gain more time for British rearmament or because circumstances dictated it – even if both statements are correct. Appeasement was the only road open to a statesman who wished to preserve the power of the United Kingdom and its Empire. Britain in the 1930s was like the Austrian Empire a century earlier – an Empire with everything to lose and nothing to gain from the arbitrament of war. It may be true that in the final resort all Empires rest upon the possession of superior force, but, as A. J. P. Taylor remarked long ago, 'it is perhaps a mistake to make the final argument the only one'.[22] The notion of comparing the provincial Mr Chamberlain with the cosmopolitan Prince Metternich, although in all other respects far-fetched, has the singular merit

7

of underlining the fact that both of them supervised the affairs of Empires suffering from 'imperial overstretch'. One of Chamberlain's concerns in trying to avoid war was his conviction that a repetition of the Great War would complete the process of undermining the foundations of British power. His foreign policy, like the imperial policy of his predecessor, was marked by an acknowledgment of the limits of British strength; it was better to conserve it, for an effort to use it would expend it at a ruinous rate. Another war carried with it the spectre not only of imperial bankruptcy, but also of the Americans reprising the role of arbitrator which Wilson had adopted in 1917, and Chamberlain did not want to pay the price which Roosevelt would exact. Churchill's advent to power, and his decision to fight on at 'all costs', transformed the situation. One of the few logical arguments in Churchill's armoury in 1940 was the belief that America was bound to intervene in the war soon.[23] But although it was a more reasonable assumption than his mystic faith in the martial virtues of an ancient people, it was equally an act of faith. If war with America had long been unthinkable, then at least as far as many Americans were concerned war alongside Britain was just as inconceivable.

The American Ambassador to the Court of St James, Joseph P. Kennedy, had warned in March 1938 in his first speech in London that Americans had little interest in foreign affairs. What interest they did have, he said, was confined largely to staying out of foreign wars. Kennedy emphasised that it was not impossible that, in the event of a European war, America might remain completely neutral.[24] The new Ambassador's Boston-Irish heritage may have played a part in his determination to present himself as a most un-Anglophile figure, but his words owed more to his isolationist beliefs, and whilst, in the long day of the ascendancy of the Churchillian version of the 1930s, Kennedy was excoriated as a craven appeaser, his views were by no means out of line with those of many of his fellow Americans.[25] In his preference for Chamberlain's policies towards Hitler and his distrust of the Prime Minister's opponents, Kennedy provided a steady stream of despatches to Washington which preached the pure milk of the Chamberlainite doctrine. He repeated to Roosevelt, with clear relish, Chamberlain's grounds for keeping Churchill out of the Government: 'He does not believe, in the first place, that he could deliver nearly one-tenth as much as people think he could; he has developed into a fine two-handed drinker and his judgement has never been proven to be good.'[26]

Kennedy's opinions did not change during the 'phoney war', except that his pessimism about Britain's chances of winning became more marked. Nor did the advent of Churchill to power in May 1940 fill the Ambassador with any more optimistic thoughts. Indeed, as the war went from bad in May to worse in June, one of Kennedy's main fears became the growth of 'definite anti-American feeling' in Britain, 'based primarily on the fact that the majority of the English people feel that America should be in this fight'; this was not a belief held by Kennedy.[27] Whatever Roosevelt's opinion of Kennedy's views, the President could hardly deny that his desire to stay out of the war was shared by millions of Americans and in election year that fact bulked large in Roosevelt's mind. In view of this, Churchill's fervent hopes that America was about to enter the war were, to put it at its mildest, fantastical.

Although Kennedy was accused by subsequent historians of defeatism, his real 'crime' was to have reported unsentimentally on one of the most sentimentalised moments in recent British history. He was clear-eyed about British criticism of America's incapacity and inability to help, and he was equally accurate in his reporting of the actualities of Britain's military situation. It is hard to quarrel in retrospect with his pithy statement that 'outside of some air defence the real defence of England is with courage and not with arms'. He also correctly summed up Churchill's hopes of America, reporting to the President on 12 June that the Prime Minister had said 'definitely to me he expects the United States will be in right after the election'.[28] This was indeed Churchill's rod and staff in troublous times. In a dramatic meeting with the French Prime Minister on 31 May Churchill had tried to stiffen Paul Reynaud's resolve with the reflection that he was sure that when the Germans started to bomb historic English towns and cities, their American namesakes would be moved, even unto war.[29] He clung in desperation to Roosevelt's speech at Charlottesville on 10 June in which the President spoke of extending aid 'full speed ahead' to the allies.[30] When Roosevelt urged Reynaud to fight on, Churchill, taking the message as a sign of imminent American aid, wanted to publish it at once.[31] By this stage Churchill seems to have expected the President to act even before the election in November. A horrified Roosevelt told Kennedy to make it plain to the overenthusiastic Prime Minister that his message was 'in no sense intended to commit this Government to the slightest military activities in support of the Allies'.[32]

What Churchill's fevered hopes of imminent American involvement in the war ignored were the realities of American politics. Whatever Roosevelt's private objectives (and these remain open to doubt), he did not possess the power to commit America. As he pointed out to Ambassador Kennedy, only Congress had the constitutional authority 'to make any commitment of [a military] ... nature'.[33] And few knew better than Roosevelt how unlikely that was to be forthcoming. Indeed, when he tried to introduce an element of bipartisanship into his administration on 19 June by inviting two prominent Republicans, Frank Knox and Henry Stimson, to join it, the Republicans promptly expelled both men.[34] Roosevelt was a Democratic President facing a Congress dominated by Republicans and an election in November; for Churchill to expect him to act dramatically revealed only how desperate he was.

All the moral arguments which justified entry into the war were as valid as they were to be eighteen months later, but American policy was decided by considerations of American national interests. During the summer of 1940 the President was to question whether those interests were best served by continuing to support Churchill and the British, but once he had so decided, Roosevelt was prepared to do whatever was practical to help. America would fight to the last Briton – or the last cache of British gold.

2

Churchill's Roosevelt

Ambiguity was part of Roosevelt's character, something his various biographers have long recognised as they have undertaken the thankless but vital task of trying to explain him to posterity. He was the 'Lion and the Fox' before he was the 'soldier of freedom', and most recently he has been called 'the juggler'.[1] This last epithet was one he used himself, telling his Secretary of the Treasury, Henry Morgenthau: 'You know I am a juggler, and I never let my right hand know what my left hand does.'[2] Described by one distinguished jurist as a 'first-class temperament' with a 'second-class intellect', Roosevelt was a man who baffled, infuriated and charmed contemporaries in much the way that he has posterity. The story is told of how, on the evening of the inauguration of the Roosevelt Library, the President was in high good humour, and when asked why he responded: 'I'm thinking of all the historians who will come here thinking that they'll find the answers to their questions.' Any historian who has worked at the Library will appreciate the President's comment.[3]

For those with a taste for psychological speculation, Roosevelt's early life, as the only child of an elderly father and a young, strong-willed mother, provides fertile territory. 'FDR' was sheltered from the rough ways of the world as a boy, but he was encouraged always to keep what the British would call a 'stiff upper lip'. Emotion and emotionalism were not encouraged by Sarah Delano Roosevelt, and her only son proved an adept pupil. Even to his own wife and family, FDR was to prove an enigma. As his daughter Anna once said, 'none of us ever knows what father feels'; her grandmother would have considered that a testimony to her handiwork. But there was more to it than this.[4]

It is tempting to apply to FDR the aphorism used about Lloyd George – that when he was alone in a room there was no one there – but such a comment would only catch part of the truth. Roosevelt certainly needed an audience, and he wanted to be liked, but he was not so lacking in confidence and a sense of self that these things assumed overriding importance. Dismissed early in his political career as an aristocratic milksop, FDR had shown how inaccurate such assessments were. Any man with less determination, self-confidence and ambition than Roosevelt would have let his political career end with the attack of polio which nearly killed him in 1921. With extraordinary determination and with a willpower which belied earlier criticisms, Roosevelt came back to forge a career in which the fact that he was a cripple was never mentioned; indeed, he went to great lengths to ensure that this was the case.⁵

Some have argued that Roosevelt's devastating illness gave him a new vulnerability, and that with it came a new ability to empathise with the poor and disadvantaged, but FDR was not the sort of man to admit to such a sea-change, even if it happened – and the evidence for it seems scanty. Roosevelt remained, as a political operator, recognisably the same man.

The *New York Herald Tribune* wrote of Roosevelt that 'the role of a true executive, functioning through able subordinates possessing both power and responsibility, has never appealed to him'; nor did it.⁶ FDR functioned like a Byzantine emperor, and as Bob Sherwood, who experienced the adminis-tration as well as writing the biography of the one-time court favourite, Harry Hopkins, put it, 'History will achieve no complete understanding of Franklin Roosevelt's Administration without knowledge of the intramural feuds which so frequently beset it.' Indeed, Sherwood did not 'believe that even history will be able to understand why he tolerated them to the extent that he did'.⁷ The explanation lies within Roosevelt's psyche. The feuds came in part from the President's way of working and in part because one of his chief weaknesses was an unwillingness to face unpleasantness until there was no option but to do so. As Ed Flynn, a leading Democrat and long-time associate of FDR's, put it, 'The Boss either appoints four men to do the job of one man, or one man to do the job of four.'⁸ Thus, at the State Department where the Tennessee Democrat, Cordell Hull, reigned as Secretary of State, FDR had the WASP patrician, Sumner Welles, as his eyes and ears, precipitating a slow-burning feud between the two men which lasted until 1943. At the War Department, before 1940, the non-interventionist Secretary of War, Harry Woodring, was balanced by his Undersecretary, Louis Johnson, who often reported to Roosevelt directly. At the Department of the Interior, Harold Ickes was balanced by the more radical Hopkins, who was given a job which encroached upon his territory.

This often looked like organised confusion, which, up to a point, it was; but it was also a means of keeping control. Like a medieval king, Roosevelt ensured that none of his barons was able to create for himself a fiefdom from which he could challenge the king; at the end of the day, the vital decisions would have to come to the President. If the President had then taken the vital decisions, things might not have looked so confused; but FDR hated taking decisions. In part this may have been because one could not both take decisions and remain universally liked, but this implies a weakness which was not really in the President's character. Henry Stimson, Roosevelt's chosen successor to Woodring as Secretary of War, was puzzled by the President's approach: 'His mind does not follow easily a consecutive train of thought but he is full of stories and incidents and hops about in his discussions from suggestion to suggestion and it is very much like chasing a vagrant beam of sunlight around a vacant room.'[9] But the question arises of how much of Stimson's perception was a genuine insight into the enigmatic FDR and how much it was the result of FDR wishing to keep his Secretary of War at arm's length during a period, late December 1940, when he had every reason to conceal his own thoughts. Any successful politician pays close attention to circumstance and timing, and FDR, as a master politician, paid more attention to these than most.

This applied no less to the war in Europe than it did to American domestic politics; indeed, FDR was more aware than anyone that the war was a factor in American political life. Stimson's bafflement may well have been deliberate – Roosevelt had, after all, every reason in late 1940 to play his cards so close to his chest that the ink rubbed off on to his shirt.[10] Roosevelt's badinage was, in any event, part of a political style which meant that no one was ever given his full confidence. Roosevelt preferred to use several channels in making his wishes known; no one was able to claim that he was speaking for the President. As one commentator has perceptively remarked, 'His approach to each subject was that of the politician – concerned with the total effect of his actions upon the situation and in particular upon his position with the American electorate rather than with individual goals.'[11] In the field of foreign affairs the same dictum holds true. FDR was concerned with the total effect of his actions upon the situation, in particular with the long-term goal of an American peace. Whether this would involve America's entry into the war as a fighting power was still something which, in late 1940, FDR was willing to leave open. As the British watched their hopes of the summer of 1940 fade, they had the excuse of the election to comfort themselves with; but as the election receded into history with still no action from the sphinx of Pennsylvania Avenue, it was not surprising that some of them began to conclude that 'FDR means to keep out of the war and dictate the peace if he can'; nor was it surprising if the fear arose in the Foreign Office that he was 'a consummate politician, much quicker than Winston'.[12]

It was not only Churchill, however, who was to find himself out-manoeuvred by the squire of Hyde Park. Roosevelt's indirect approach to political grand strategy frequently baffled his supporters as much as it enraged his opponents; it also created an impression of a man who had no 'individual goals'. But in democratic politics there are too many facets to the political process for the will of one man to be able to shape policy – and this was particularly true of the American variety of Democratic politics. No President knew better than Roosevelt that he had to carry Congress and the public with him, and that being too definite too early about goals could impede this process. But that did not mean that he had no objectives; he did. What it meant was an almost infinite plasticity about the means by which those goals were achieved. Oliver Cromwell once said that the man who did not know where he was going went furthest; on the surface it is tempting to apply this aphorism to FDR, but the temptation should be resisted. Roosevelt knew the direction in which he wished to travel, but he was not too worried about how he reached his destination. Infinitely flexible about means, the new Machiavel was less so about ends. If Machiavelli had never written, then FDR could have provided posterity with much of his message – except, of course, that FDR would never have been so unwise as to have committed himself to paper. Tactical concessions do not always imply a lack of strategy; indeed, they may be made more easily by a man with a strategy. Such a political style demanded immense reserves of self-confidence, but no one ever accused FDR of being shy and retiring; if he could not walk on water, he was quite prepared to wheelchair on thin ice. Behind and underpinning Roosevelt's diplomacy was not only massive self-confidence, but also a boundless optimism.

It must not be concluded from this that FDR had a sort of 'hidden agenda'; all that was hidden was the route by which he would achieve what he wanted. In domestic affairs, which had occupied most of his time, FDR had improvised the 'New Deal', but even as he twisted and turned, he drove forward with a belief that it was the duty of the state to intervene in the economy to help the poorer sections of society. Accused by his enemies of being a 'socialist' or even a 'communist', Roosevelt simply believed in what a later generation would call 'big Government'; it would never have occurred to him that Government was part of the problem. His views on foreign policy were less easily discerned. He had entered politics as a follower of Woodrow Wilson, and much of his rhetoric partook of the elevated nature of that of his mentor. He had supported the League of Nations, but as Governor of the Empire State and President at the nadir of the Depression, he had spent most of his career on domestic problems and had come to accept if not the tenets of the prevalent isolationism, then at least to respect its political force.

Roosevelt was concerned about fascist aggression in Europe and Japanese aggression in Asia, but that concern failed to manifest itself in any concrete form before 1940. Thereafter, he trod a line between being nice enough to the British to give them hope that he might enter the war (which would encourage them to stay in it) and avoiding doing anything which might bring the wrath of the isolationists down upon his vulnerable head. Even for so practised a magician as FDR, this was far from easy.

His long-serving Secretary of War and long-time supporter, Harry Woodring, had become increasingly worried during the early part of 1940 that the President was crossing this line too often. Woodring, who was no isolationist and who had been forthright in his warnings to the dictator Powers, was nevertheless anxious to keep America from becoming involved in a war in Europe which was none of her concern and for which she was not ready. Ironically, Woodring and FDR clashed in early 1940 over the latter's refusal to accede to the army's requests for $1,500 million. Roosevelt, for all his rhetoric, was only willing to ask Congress for a budget of $853 million. The irony lay in the fact that it was Woodring who wanted to remain strictly neutral whilst it was the President who was willing to bend the rules. There was no contradiction here; FDR did not believe that Congress would accept Woodring's requests.[13] This did not stop Roosevelt from sacking Woodring in June when he wanted to bring the more *simpatico* Stimson in as Secretary for War. Woodring had been in sympathy on tactics, but not on aims, and his tactics had been, in Roosevelt's eyes, unrealistic. Roosevelt's words, if not his actions, helped to convince an already desperate Churchill that the Americans would soon intervene; the fact that they had precisely the opposite effect on the American electorate is some witness to Roosevelt's talents as a democratic politician. Indeed, Roosevelt's words went further than this: they helped to convince Churchill to place all his eggs in the basket of the Democrats. Only if the Democrats, and in particular Roosevelt, remained in power, could Britain be saved.[14] This was to lead Churchill to ignore much of the evidence which suggested that Roosevelt's ideas on foreign and imperial policy differed widely from his own.

Although there were times when it seemed that FDR had elevated procrastination to an art form, as the summer of 1940 passed into autumn and winter with no American commitments, the President's hesitations were understandable – and to some extent understood in London. Roosevelt, whilst facing some problems within his own coalition, had the problem specific to the American situation of having to deal with a Congress in which 'isolationist' sentiment was widely represented.

Recently some historians have cast doubt on the notion that American foreign policy between the wars can accurately be described as 'isolationist'.[15] In so far as this draws attention to the complex nature of 'isolationism', such caveats are a good thing, but they must not lead us to neglect the fact that, in the eyes of most Americans, their Government's foreign policy was, in the broad sense implied by George Washington's farewell address, 'isolationist'. As one commentator has put it, 'There was never during these times any isolation economically, diplomatically, or culturally, but any act or word which might lead America into the arena of world conflict was strongly opposed.'[16] Even once the war in Europe had broken out, such sentiments continued to be strongly felt. Senator Arthur H. Vandenberg, the senior Senator from Michigan and one of the leading isolationists, summed up the fears of many of his ilk in his diary in September 1939 when he wrote:

Pressure and propaganda are at work to drive us into the new World War ... the same emotions which demand the repeal of the embargo [on the sale of arms] will subsequently demand still more effective aid for Britain, France and Poland.... It is a tribute to the American *heart*, but not to the American *head*. Oh yes, all these good people abhor the thought of our entry into the war; they are all opposed to that. President Roosevelt has given them their cue, however, in his use of the treacherous idea that we can help these countries by methods 'short of war'.[17]

Fear of becoming involved in a foreign war and fear of an increase in Presidential powers were closely intermingled. For men like Senator William E. Borah from Idaho (although it is doubtful whether there were very many men like him), one of the main impulses towards isolationism was a distrust of 'executive domination over foreign affairs'.[18] Borah, who had campaigned against Wilson and the League of Nations, feared America becoming involved in a cycle of events similar to that of 1914–18 – 'this time with perhaps even more catastrophic results'.[19]

Republicans, of course, were far from sharing the British admiration for Roosevelt. To the latter the President appeared as a potential saviour, a man whose occasionally tiresome retreats from interventionism were the result of his being hamstrung by tiresome American public opinion. But to the Republicans he was their old enemy: Roosevelt of the 'New Deal' and of the 'alphabet soup' agencies; he was the man who had tried to pack the Supreme Court* and who cosied up to the unions; and now, or so it appeared, he was not only going to break with constitutional precedent by standing for a third term in office, but he was also getting dangerously close to that old warmonger, Churchill. If Roosevelt moved carefully and covered his tracks as he went, it was not without reason.

Historians are still divided about Roosevelt's 'real' intentions between 1939 and 1941. The 'orthodox' interpretation has a President whose heart was in the right place (that is anti-Hitler), but who through (according to taste) fear of Congress, or a recognition of political realities, had to proceed cautiously (too cautiously according to some critics).[20] Other 'revisionists' take the line favoured by 'isolationists' at the time, namely that Roosevelt was trying to get America into the war by the 'back door'.[21] Of course these two lines of argument are, unlike their proponents, reconcilable, but perhaps both of them give Roosevelt too much credit (or blame).[22] Roosevelt was certainly keen to keep the British and the French in the war, but his message to Reynaud lays bare his general approach. He wanted to say enough to keep the French fighting, but no more. His horrified reaction to the idea that Churchill might publish that message is revealing. In election year there must not be even the slightest hint that America might enter the war. Quite apart from Congressional opinion, there was the fact, as Kennedy put it bluntly, that 'the United States has not the equipment which would be of service to them'.[23]

The Senate Foreign Relations Committee was 'still heavily manned by isolationists' and had defeated Roosevelt's attempts in July 1939 to repeal neutrality legislation by voting to delay consideration of the issue to the next

---

* FDR had tried to select Supreme Court Justices who would be 'New Dealers'.

session of Congress.[24] When the outbreak of the war suggested to Roosevelt that he might renew his assault on the legislation, he was advised by Congressional leaders against an all-out assault, which was why he proceeded to try to secure a lifting of the embargo on selling armaments – but only on a 'cash and carry' basis. On 27 October, by an overwhelming majority, the Senate passed the Pittman Bill. Senator Vandenberg's comments were characteristically brusque: 'we have definitely taken sides with England and France. There is no longer any camouflage about it. Repealist Senators speak frankly about it. In the name of "democracy" we have taken the first step, once more, into Europe's "power politics". . . . What "suckers" our emotions make of us!'[25] But just because some of the isolationists accused Roosevelt of trying to get America into the war through the 'back door', and just because America did eventually get into the war by such a route, that does not amount to conclusive evidence that that is what the President was up to.

Perhaps Roosevelt made sense from day to day, and the search for consistency is a vain one. In the period from the outbreak of the war to Churchill's accession to the Premiership in May 1940, Roosevelt's main aim appears to have been to loosen some of the neutrality legislation, allowing America to become the (well-paid) arsenal of democracy. But, as the war shifted against the Franco-British alliance, the President concentrated on trying to keep the French and the British in the war. Once the skies began to darken for the British, Roosevelt moved towards trying to ensure that, whatever else happened, the British fleet would not fall into German hands.[26] What he did not show was any desire for America to become involved in a fighting war herself.

Although British historians have waxed indignant at the thought of Britain making peace with Hitler in 1940, the prospect appeared far from impossible at the time. Viscount Halifax, the gaunt and aristocratic Foreign Secretary, and the Foreign Office were well aware in early June of the possibility of a 'peace offensive' coming via Italian channels, whilst Roosevelt was conscious, through his Embassy in Berlin, that,

There is a considerable current of belief here that Hitler does not desire to crush Great Britain but hopes to achieve a rapid defeat of the French army which he believes will bring the British government to the point of accepting peace terms which would not destroy the empire but would prevent Great Britain from effectively rearming or undertaking any action which would limit Germany's freedom of action.[27]

Such a prospect was, of course, profoundly unappealing to Roosevelt. As common sense (not to mention its British personification, Lord Halifax) and Ambassador Kennedy suggested that Britain would have a hard time avoiding defeat, the President naturally sought to do what he could to keep the British in the war; but he also began to prepare his back-up position, which was to secure promises from the British that if they had to withdraw from the war, their fleet would be sent to the New World.

What all those who feared or hoped that a negotiated peace was around the corner were ignoring was Churchill. Whatever else May and June 1940 were, they were Churchill's finest hour. Overcoming the reluctance of many of his colleagues to fight on, the Prime Minister sought to secure some concrete signs to back up his confident predictions that American entry into the war was imminent.

Throughout the war Churchill would evince an absolute reluctance to believe that any Power would willingly stay out of the conflict. His policy towards Vichy France and French North Africa would be marked by a belief that the Pétain regime was longing to rejoin the fray at the earliest opportunity;[28] and he would pursue Turkey for two years under the same illusion. What he could not grasp, either in these two cases, or most importantly in that of America, was that most people who were not in the war wanted to stay out of it.

Even Halifax, who had thought that 'Winston talked the most frightful rot' at Cabinet on 27 May,[29] agreed that the only real hope was to try to rally America.[30] And if that was to be done, then, as one diplomat put it, 'nobody but the Prime Minister has the necessary magic or touch to achieve such an object'.[31] The North American Department of the Foreign Office held it as an article of faith that the 'Americans earnestly desire to see the Nazi regime smashed' and that the main short-term objective of British policy was to make it clear to Washington that 'we have a fighting chance'. The diplomats were even prepared to go so far in this direction as to say that 'the possibility of fighting in England itself might be admitted with a gay heart'; anything, in short, which presented a more optimistic picture than Kennedy's, and which might get some arms and equipment from America. A 'tone ... of reasoned optimism' should, it was thought, be adopted.[32] Churchill, of course, adopted a much higher 'tone', one of sustained belief in Britain's glorious destiny, and he was not to be drawn by cautious enquiries from Washington about the future of the fleet.

When the British Ambassador in Washington, Lord Lothian, made tentative enquiries about the fleet on 9 June, Churchill took the opportunity to deliver a warning meant for the President. Pointing out that 'if Great Britain broke under invasion a pro-German Government might obtain far easier terms from Germany by surrendering the Fleet thus making Germany and Japan masters of the New World'. His Government, of course, would do no such thing, but 'if [Oswald] Moseley [*sic*] were Prime Minister or some other Quisling Government set up, it is exactly what they would do'. The purpose of this scare-mongering was made clear in the last paragraph of the telegram which was despatched to Lothian on 10 June. The Ambassador was instructed to talk to Roosevelt 'in this sense and thus discourage any complacent assumption on United States' part that they will pick up the debris of the British Empire by their present policy'. He warned, in conclusion, that 'If we go down Hitler has a very good chance of conquering the world.'[33]

Churchill's Americanophilia has already been mentioned, but so too has his occasionally acerbic attitude, and it is worth asking to what extent his suspicion that Roosevelt was hoping to 'pick up the debris of the British Empire' was justified.

Like many British Americanophiles, Churchill tended to forget who had won the American War of Independence. The Americans, by virtue of their victory, had gained the right to have an economic and foreign policy all of their own; and, because of their experience as a British colony, the Americans had carried down the years an abiding dislike of imperialism. Neither in economic nor in foreign policy was the Roosevelt administration likely to be possessed of aims which coincided with those of an imperialist of Churchill's cast of mine. For Roosevelt's cautious-minded Secretary of State, Cordell Hull, the doctrine of free trade filled a place more usually occupied in Man by religious fervour. The quiet Tennessean, whose influence on The Hill and among conservative southern Democrats had kept him in office since Roosevelt's first election, believed in the eradication of barriers to free trade; tariff barriers helped to create conflict, free trade removed this danger: Cobden and Bright could not have done better. Nor is the similarity between the views of mid-nineteenth-century British entrepreneurs and their American successors a century later accidental. It is in the interests of the 'world's dominant economic power' to use its power 'as workshop and banker of the free world, to create institutions and ground rules that foster the inter-nationalization of capital'; a 'single hegemonic power has the most to gain from such a free world and the most to lose from nationalistic efforts to limit the free movement of capital, goods, and industry'.[34] Hull and Roosevelt saw the war being waged against the ultimate autarchic state, Nazi Germany, as an occasion not 'simply to vanquish their enemies, but to create the geopoliti-cal basis for a postwar world order that they would both build and lead'. This meant not only defeating Germany, and later Japan, but also 'preparing the way for the United States to replace its British ally in the Middle East and the Mediterranean'.[35] Like it or not, it was this agenda to which Churchill was subscribing by becoming totally dependent upon Roosevelt.

None of this is discernible from the portrait of Roosevelt which emerges from Churchill's memoirs. There he is portrayed as almost a god-like figure in his wisdom and benignity. But this image was the work of a high-class literary artist. In part this may be explained by Churchill's own emotional nature – writing about FDR became an act of homage to a fallen wartime comrade in arms – but there are other reasons.

No one can read Churchill's correspondence with Roosevelt without being struck by its tone. That Churchill was the suitor can hardly be doubted. His messages are longer, more exhortatory in tenor and, at times, amount to brazen sycophancy. Yet, in the Churchillian version of the war, how great were the gains brought by this effort. We are, as readers, invited to contrast Churchill's constructive attitude with the negative one displayed by Chamberlain. Where the latter threw away the 'last great opportunity' for peace in 1938, Churchill, by his patient wooing, brought America into the war. The gains appear impressive: the bases for destroyers deal; lend-lease, that 'most unsordid act'; American acquiescence in the Mediterranean strategy; and, finally, victory. The implication could hardly be clearer: was not all of this worth a little flattery on Churchill's part? The partnership with Roosevelt was, as one writer put it, one which 'saved the world', a unique relationship forged through correspondence and refined through personal meetings. Not only does the Churchill–Roosevelt relationship lie at the centre of Churchill's account of the war, but it also acts as a paradigm for the future. As Churchill was to put it in his speech at Westminster College in March 1946, 'it helps if two of the workmen are already good friends'. The moral was, as it usually was in Churchill's writing, plain and unambiguous – the hopes for the future, like the victories of the past, depended upon an Anglo-American alliance.

Precisely because Roosevelt is such a difficult figure to pin down, Churchill's portrait is a convincing one, but that does not make it accurate. Missing from it is any sense that Roosevelt's war aims were wider or differed in kind from those of Churchill himself; there is no sign of the President's anti-imperialism, still less of his ambitions for America and a new international order. On this account, the Atlantic Charter* and the United Nations are only half-explained as manifestations of American idealism; and the reality of the bases for destroyers deal and of the hard bargaining over lend-lease is ignored. Nor would one gather, from the Churchillian account, that Roosevelt's Wilsonian internationalism or his economic views played any part in American policy – or that if they did, there was nothing incompatible in them with British war aims. Yet such was the case.

Churchill's lack of interest in planning for the post-war world was notorious at the Foreign Office and in the Cabinet, which made him perhaps prone to imagine that others were as obsessed with the winning of the war as he was.[36] For a Power as perilously placed as Britain, simply getting to the end of the tunnel was a difficult enough task, but the eyes of America's leaders were not so narrowed. FDR and his acolytes did not look to merely a military victory over Germany; they wanted an ideological victory over Nazism, militarism, imperialism and the international manifestations of the domestic enemies of 'Dr New Deal'. As Roosevelt's confidant, Harry Hopkins, put it in 1941, Hitler could 'never be conclusively defeated by the old order of democracy which is the status quo'; his '"new order"' could only be 'conclusively defeated by the new order of democracy, which is the New Deal universally extended and applied'.[37] This was Roosevelt's aim. The methods by which it was imple-

* See pages 37–8.

mented would have to be improvised as the opportunities presented themselves.

Did the British want a sign that America supported them? Roosevelt would provide fifty old destroyers, for which the British would pay in the form of Caribbean bases. Churchill could read what he liked into the gesture, but the exchange was described by the new Foreign Secretary, Anthony Eden, as 'a grievous blow at our authority and ultimately . . . at our sovereignty'. The fact that by January 1941 Britain had received two out of the famous fifty destroyers might, he thought, 'be reasonably regarded as a bad deal', but he took the position that 'it has been made & we are powerless to go back upon it', and hoped that the 'goodwill' which had been purchased at so heavy a price would be worth it.[38] Churchill, of course, never doubted that it was worth buying American 'goodwill'. Roosevelt could quieten his critics by pointing out his own cleverness. He described the islands as being 'of the utmost importance to our national defence as naval and air operations bases', whilst the destroyers were 'the same type of ship which we have from time to time been striking from the naval list and selling for scrap for, I think, $4,000 or $5,000 per destroyer'; on this basis each base cost about $250,000. As one Dutchess County farmer put it, ' "Say, ain't you the Commander in Chief? If you are and you own fifty muzzle-loadin' rifles of the Civil War period, you would be a chump if you declined to exchange them for seven modern machine guns – wouldn't you?" '[39]

The same technique served Roosevelt equally well when it came to providing the British with the financial means for staying in the war. By late October, with a British supply mission already in Washington, Churchill was telling FDR that he was confident of Britain's ability to fight on successfully 'if we are given the necessary supplies'.[40] Roosevelt certainly wanted Britain to have the means of staying in the war, but he had neither the desire nor the ability to offer a free gift; Britain's necessity would, once again, be America's opportunity. Cordell Hull, who was less than convinced by Britain's cries of poverty, was under the impression that British overseas assets were in the region of $18 billion.[41] He had long denounced the tariff system which the British Empire had adopted at Ottawa in 1932, and he saw in this plea for aid an opportunity to dismantle that system.[42] As one commentator has put it, 'No American official ever stood up and crassly proclaimed that a major goal of the nation's foreign policy should be the acquisition of Britain's empire';[43] but Hull did declare that he would use 'American aid as a knife to open that oyster shell, the empire'.[44]

The final version of the British request, despatched on 7 December 1940, laid out the seriousness of Britain's economic plight. Churchill's letter was grave and unwittingly prescient. He told FDR that he believed 'you will agree that it would be wrong in principle and mutually disadvantageous in effect if, at the height of this struggle, Great Britain were to be divested of all saleable assets so that after victory was won with our blood ... we should stand stripped to the bone'.[45] It was all sonorous and moving stuff, but it did not deflect the Americans from their determination to use Britain's predicament to extract concessions from her which would ensure that she would not be able to stand in the way of the sort of peace they wanted.[46] Roosevelt's public beneficence found expression in his famous broadcast of 17 December, when he spoke about abolishing the dollar sign and lending your hose to your neighbour when his house was on fire,[47] but his private actions a few days later were more revealing of American policy, which certainly lacked any trace of the sentimentality which oozed from Churchill. On 23 December FDR told Admiral Stark that he wanted a warship 'to pick up the [British] gold [reserves] in Africa'; not only did Roosevelt intend to distrain on the last part of Britain's once vast overseas assets, but he intended to make the British pay for the insurance on the shipment.[48]

Churchill's first inclination was to tell FDR that this was like the 'sheriff collecting the last assets of a helpless debtor';[49] but beggars cannot be choosers, and calmer reflection (or the influence of the Foreign Office, which was now appeasing America on a scale which it had never managed to apply to Germany, even when that country was not directly affecting British interests) produced a more 'diplomatic' despatch.[50] It was not only Churchill who felt a sense of humiliation. His old friend and current Minister of Supply, Lord Beaverbrook, was indignant. A Canadian and an ardent Empire man, he was furious at what he saw as the appeasement of those who would liquidate the Empire by taking advantage of Britain's situation. In a furious letter to Churchill at the end of December he accused the Americans of having 'conceded nothing' and having 'exacted payment to the uttermost of all they have done for us. They have taken our bases without valuable consideration. They have taken our gold.' American supplies, as opposed to promises, were scanty, and a bankrupt Britain was in the 'extraordinary' position of having provided monies for supplies which had not yet arrived. He thought that the time had come for a 'complete understanding with the US'.[51] But, as Morgenthau had told the chief British negotiator in Washington, it all came back to Churchill saying, '"I can put myself in Mr Roosevelt's hands, and here Mr Roosevelt, this is what we have got. I have turned my pockets inside out. Now, you have got to treat me fair."'[52]

All this is absent from the Churchillian portrait, which also glosses over the way in which, from the 1943 Tehran conference onwards, Roosevelt wooed Stalin and showed every desire to act as mediator between Britain and the Soviet Union. No sense comes through that FDR did not regard Britain as America's primary ally. Emotional and impulsive himself, Churchill was apt to invest his personal relationship with the President as expressive of the Anglo-American relationship as a whole. It is hardly surprising that Churchill sought to portray his relationship with FDR in the way he did: if the reality of the bases for destroyers deal and lend-lease had been revealed and FDR's vaulting ambitions for America described, Churchill would have looked like another of the President's dupes.

Perhaps 'dupe' is too strong a word, for it implies a conscious attempt to deceive, whereas it would be more correct to say that Churchill was a man who deceived himself. When the Americans demanded a complete list of all British overseas investments and then, like a stern banker, demanded she sell some of them at once, the Chancellor, Sir Kingsley Wood, wrote to Churchill sadly that this was 'different from what we'd hoped'.[53] The question of where these forced sales would leave the British in the future was easily, if sombrely, answered. In 1937 the British had earned about £270 million from their foreign investments; without this money Britain would either have to mount an 'unheard of export drive' in the post-war period, or suffer privation on a massive scale. As Churchill's Scientific Adviser, the newly ennobled Lord Cherwell, put it, 'the fruits of victory which Roosevelt offers seem to be safety for America and virtual starvation for us'. This was not 'a very inspiring theme to set before the British people'.[54] Although the Chancellor criticised Cherwell's figures,[55] the fact remained that in the post-war period Britain was going to have to face choices which her politicians would find unpalatable.

Beaverbrook, inevitably, was numbered amongst those who found that American actions left a bitter taste in the mouth. On 19 February 1941 he gave a full list of all the concessions that Britain had made to America since the Great War, and from the partition of Ireland in 1921 and the end of the Japanese alliance in the following year, all the way to the present day, Britain had appeased America and now she was 'being told by Roosevelt and Willkie [the defeated Republican Presidential candidate] that if only we stand up to Germany all will be well. We are doing so. But we would stand up better if we knew there would be something left to provide sustenance for our people in the day of hardship.' Beaverbrook told Churchill starkly: 'If we give everything away, we gain little or no advantage over our present situation', and exhorted him to 'Stand up to the Democrats!'[56] Given Churchill's obsession with defeating Germany and his need for American aid in this task, this was like putting a spine into a jelly-fish.

3

Alliances

There must have been times when Churchill looked back with nostalgia to the dramatic days of June and July 1940, when Britain had no allies to pamper or to appease, but such freedom did not last long. The exigent Americans began to try even Churchill's patience. For all that he told Halifax on 15 March 1941 that he refused to be 'hustled and rattled',[1] he was clearly subject to both phenomena. Only five days later he complained to the Chancellor that it was clear from the terms America was insisting on that Britain was 'not only to be skinned but flayed to the bone'.[2] The Roosevelt administration was willing to allow Britain to 'lease' or be 'lent' equipment and supplies only in return for a 'consideration' – namely the abolition of imperial preference.[3] Although the British would resort to every subterfuge and fall back on any pretext to avoid making such a concession, the Americans would prove equally relentless in seeking it. If Roosevelt sometimes seemed inclined to backslide, Hull would bring him back to the point by asking what would happen to the 'more liberal postwar world' they both wanted if the British were allowed to retain the economic structures which supported imperialism and protectionism.[4]

As a non-belligerent for most of 1941, the Americans remained in a position to press for their desiderata unencumbered by the sort of considerations which obtain between allies during a war. But whilst Churchill was kept on tenterhooks by America, Fate, in the form of Herr Hitler, delivered him an ally who, enjoying none of America's advantages, was to prove equally tenacious in pursuit of her objectives. Hitler's attack on the Soviet Union on 22 June 1941 gave the British at once fresh hope and a major headache – although since the initial hopes were small, so were the headaches.

During the long ascendancy enjoyed by the Churchillian version of the 1930s, one criticism often essayed of the 'appeasers' was that they had failed to read *Mein Kampf*. Failure to read that turgid tome was not confined to any one quarter, but those who have ploughed through it will not find any evidence of enmity towards Great Britain. Indeed Hitler, like many *altekampfer*, admired the soldiery of the British Empire, and he professed his desire to live in peaceful harmony with them – provided, of course, the British stuck to their Empire and let the Germans fulfil their destiny and dominate the Eurasian land mass.[5] The objects of Hitler's hatred were the Jews and Bolsheviks, and it would be the Semites and the Slavs whom the Aryan master race would have to bring to the reckoning. British policy from 1938 onwards put a spoke in the wheel of Hitler's plans, forcing him to deal with the British and the French before he could get around to the Soviets. But the Molotov–Ribbentrop pact of 1939 was no more than a flimsy marriage of convenience.

Stalin's suspicious nature and consequent tendency to see conspiracies everywhere had already led him to purge the 'old Bolsheviks' and the high command of the Red Army, and in 1939 it drove him towards a pact with the Nazis. Unlike the British and the French, Hitler could pay Stalin's price for an agreement – the annexation of the Baltic republics – and, what was more, he could offer a fourth partition of Poland. There was nothing in Chamberlain's diplomacy to match this, and, confident that he had prevented the western Powers from directing Hitler eastwards, Stalin settled back to enjoy the rewards of totalitarian solidarity. Indeed, so attached did he become to the Nazi alliance that he refused to believe, even on 22 June 1941, that Hitler would attack him.[6] But Hitler had long intended to have a 'showdown' with the Bolsheviks; the only question remaining after June 1940 was when he would choose to do so.[7] Hitler's objectives were the Jews, international communism and the acquisition of *lebensraum*; there were few Jews and communists in Britain, and even less *lebensraum*, so it was little wonder that in the summer of 1941 Hitler turned his attention to the Soviet Union, a place which possessed an abundance of these things.

Churchill's ready embrace of the Soviets was understandable, and his speech on 22 June has been praised for its skill in reconciling his own anti-Bolshevik past and American worries about the Soviet Union with the need to allay Soviet suspicions that Britain might negotiate a separate peace with Hitler.[8] Quite why Churchill should have gone to any pains to reassure Stalin is never explained. Indeed, he might have done better to have kept him guessing; Stalin had no such qualms in 1943. From the point of view of Churchill's policy, which was to wage war until the Nazis were defeated, the Russian alliance had to be seized, even if Russia herself was expected to succumb quickly to the *Wehrmacht*; but once it became clear that this expectation would not be realised, difficult questions arose about the basis for a formal alliance.

The Churchill Government's first act towards the Soviet Union had been symptomatic of its future policy. Churchill allowed himself to be persuaded to send the left-wing socialist gad-fly, Sir Stafford Cripps, as ambassador on a special mission to Moscow. Cripps shared the illusion common on the left that all that was needed to improve relations with the Soviets was a friendly attitude; a few months in Moscow helped to dispel this illusion, but only for Cripps himself.[9] The capacity for self-delusion amongst communist sympathisers enabled them to go on extolling the virtues of the Stalinist system even during the period when Stalin was Hitler's ally, but for the general public there seemed little to choose between the two dictators; as so often, the public instinct was sounder than that of the intellectual left.

The decision to come out in support of Stalin following the Nazi invasion was Churchill's, but Eden was even more enthusiastic. Eden had seen himself as an alternative to Cripps in 1940, and he had campaigned for a Soviet alliance in early 1939, so he was being entirely consistent in wanting more definite commitments than the Prime Minister's warm, but vague, speech had promised.[10] What neither man had spent much time in considering was what response they would make in the event of the Soviets demanding a political agreement, something they did within a week of the Nazi invasion.[11]

Adopting the attitude that the 'enemy of my enemy is my friend' allowed the British to stall whilst the war in the east brought the Nazis into western Russia. But the Americans, who did have space to consider the ramifications of the Soviet entry into the war, were more aloof.[12] One of the main problems which FDR had had with lend-lease was the provision in the Bill which gave him discretion over whom to supply. Isolationists had enough problems with supplying Great Britain, but at least that was some sort of democracy; the prospect of Roosevelt supplying aid to the communist Russians was something else entirely.[13] Churchill urged FDR to follow his own generous lead, but FDR, as ever, would not be drawn. Opinion inside his own administration, let alone the country, was divided.[14] Those, like Secretary Stimson, who were keen interventionists and who were occasionally exasperated with what they took to be the President's slowness, saw this 'providential occurrence' as an opportunity to step up aid to the British, who would be, at least for the moment, reprieved; but he saw no point in sending aid to a country like the Soviet Union which was bound to be swiftly overwhelmed.[15] Ironically, when it came to the Soviets, Stimson occupied just the position that Woodring had a year earlier towards the British. Hull, on the other hand, took the view that the United States should help any country opposing Germany, one shared by the Secretary for the Interior, Harold Ickes. At the other extreme from the anti-communist isolationists was the former Ambassador to Moscow, Joseph E. Davies, who thought that the Soviets would successfully resist the Nazis and that American aid offered an opportunity to initiate three-Power co-operation which would extend to the post-war era.[16] Davies, like many of those who held this position, did explicitly something which Churchill and Eden did implicitly – namely to discount or ignore the ideological element in Soviet foreign policy; ironically, 'revisionist' historians who defended Chamberlain's foreign policy towards Germany were to be accused of doing just the same thing.

One of the leading Republican opponents of Roosevelt's whole wartime foreign policy, Senator Robert Taft of Ohio, declared that a 'Communist victory would be far more dangerous than a fascist one';[17] it was not, however, necessary to go all the way with the Senator to be worried about the fact that Roosevelt 'feared the possibility of Communist expansion far less than the fact of fascist aggression'.[18] FDR's attitude towards the Soviet Union is almost as difficult to pin down as his intentions regarding Britain, but it would be in keeping with the interpretation adopted here, namely that the President was willing to aid anyone who would really fight America's war, that he came out gradually and cautiously in favour, as he said on 24 June, of aid to the Soviets. Indeed, his actions were remarkably similar to the ones he had taken at the end of 1940. Just as he had then wished to satisfy himself that the British wanted to stay in the war by sending Hopkins to talk to Churchill, so now did he despatch his gaunt counsellor to speak with Stalin. It was only when Hopkins reported that the Soviets could and would resist the Nazis that FDR overrode Stimson's view and settled for a position somewhere near Hull's.[19]

The British and the Americans faced the same dilemmas with regard to the Soviet Union and the different ways in which they sought to resolve them spoke volumes about the differences between the two Powers – differences which were to surface and resurface throughout the war and which were, in the end, to contribute materially to the development of the Cold War. One dilemma, already partially solved by the end of July, was the question of supplies to Russia; the other dilemma, which was never really solved, was the question of whether Soviet war aims were compatible with the causes for which the democratic Powers claimed to be fighting.

British policy towards the Soviet Union was marked by the same characteristics as her American policy, but the smooth continuity was disrupted by an ironic reversal of roles where Churchill, Eden and Beaverbrook were concerned. Consistency was to be found in the desire to win 'goodwill' without enquiring too closely what political benefits that commodity could be translated into. Even before the German invasion the Foreign Office had refused to mention to Stalin the possibility that Britain might make a separate peace with Hitler,[20] and they had declined to make use of the arrival of Rudolf Hess to stimulate such suspicions.[21] When the Soviet Ambassador, Ivan Maisky, asked Eden nervously on 23 June whether Britain would sign a separate peace with Germany, the Foreign Secretary not only gave him the reassurance he was looking for, but he even promised to fulfil all Soviet supply needs.[22] When his turn came, Stalin was not to scruple to use the possibility of a separate peace to screw concessions from his allies, even though it was far less likely that Hitler would let him off the hook.[23]

If British diplomacy remained determined not to use any of the few cards it held with either the Americans or the Soviets, there was an ironic reversal of roles when it came to who led with the British hand; it was Beaverbrook and Eden, the two sceptics when it came to appeasing America, who took the lead in this direction when it came to Stalin.

It is easier to deride Eden's attitude than it is Churchill's. Eden has no legend and few defenders and the object of his appeasement was to become the enemy of the Cold War; Churchill, on the other hand, enjoys not only the benefit of the fact that few would question his actions, but also the advantage that he was appeasing the ally of the next half century: a clear case of Churchillian prescience to be contrasted with Eden's folly. But things are perhaps less black and white than they have usually appeared with hindsight.

Stalin's demands remained consistent throughout the war: he wanted the frontiers of 21 June 1941. Eden's willingness to concede these desiderata in December 1941[24] might, indeed, be evidence of his incurable short-sightedness and naïveté, just as Churchill's rejection of them may point the way to his later hard-line attitude;[25] but there are other ways of interpreting their respective positions. Churchill's rejection of Stalin's territorial ambitions owed more to his fear that acceptance of them would upset the Americans than it did to anything else, and in this light Eden's espousal of the Soviet demands may be seen as more evidence of his determination to forge a distinctly *British* foreign policy.

At the age of forty-seven Anthony Eden had just made his come-back at the post in which he had first achieved political prominence in 1935.[26] A Baldwin protégé, Eden had been brought into the Foreign Office in December 1935 after the enforced resignation of Sir Samuel Hoare in the aftermath of the infamous Hoare–Laval pact over the future of Abyssinia. Then Baldwin had used Eden's youth and glowing League of Nations credentials to bolster his flagging administration. The youthful Foreign Secretary did not share Churchill's sentiments about India, he was properly morally indignant over Hoare–Laval, and suitably liberal in his views about Soviet Russia; in short, he was the very model of a modern 'progressive' Conservative. Handsome, in the style of the romantic male leads made popular by Hollywood, Captain Eden had no problem with the electorate, but the elders of the Tory Party were not so easily charmed. Eden had at first welcomed the advent of Neville Chamberlain to the Premiership, but he quickly changed his mind as his ideas and those of the new Prime Minister did not march in unison. The parting of the ways between the two men had come in February 1938. Eden later liked to pretend that they had separated over 'appeasement', but the truth was rather more complex and amounted to a difference of opinion over the timing of talks with Mussolini.[27] But in the circumstances of the 1930s, when so many reputations went down in flames never to recover, this turned out to be enough cover for Eden to live on, politically, for a generation. That was not how it looked at the time.

Eden's resignation speech was one of the most baffling since Gladstone had resigned in 1845 over a Bill which he later voted for, and there was nothing in Eden's behaviour between 1938 and the outbreak of the war to give Chamberlain anything to worry about. It was symptomatic of what had happened to Eden's reputation that he, a former Foreign Secretary, was offered a job outside the War Cabinet, while Churchill, the long-time outcast, was brought into it. It was a crucial moment in both men's careers and in the history of the Conservative Party in this century. In the normal course of events Churchill would never have succeeded Chamberlain; indeed, had it not been for the war, Churchill's political career would have been all but over by 1941. As a younger figure Eden had every right to expect further promotion; and it may well have been this consideration which had inhibited his opposition to Chamberlain. Instead, he was to find himself in a queue behind Churchill, which resulted in an exceedingly long wait.

Churchill had borne with his nearest rival for the Premiership, Viscount Halifax, until December 1940, when he sent him as Ambassador to Washington. Since he had succeeded Eden in 1938, there was a certain symmetry in the fact that Eden took Halifax's place at the Foreign Office. It may well not have escaped Churchill's notice that a man who had failed to rebel against Neville Chamberlain was a useful character to have as your number two.

Eden has not received a good press from historians, a process to which the current author has contributed his mite.[28] Halifax once described Eden as a 'dual personality': one 'Anthony Eden' was a 'generous idealist, intolerant of baseness', who hated dictators with 'every fibre of his body'; the other was 'the Foreign Secretary', who acutely assessed 'the dangers of the present situation' and sought to 'relieve them'.[29] This made Eden an interesting mixture of the 'old' diplomacy and the 'new'; and as the war was to show there was perhaps more of the former about him than appeared to be the case. Although he seemed to be the epitome of the League of Nations man, his attitude towards it reflected that of his mentor, Sir Austen Chamberlain, who was prepared to support it, but only when it suited Britain's interests;[30] underneath the persiflage and the impeccably correct 'progressive' attitude which Eden so often struck in public, there was an old-fashioned practitioner of *realpolitik*. Eden was no more enamoured than anyone else at giving in to Stalin's demands that the Soviet Union's 1941 frontiers should be recognised, since this meant allowing him to escape with the booty which his pact with Hitler had brought. On the other hand, if the Soviets lost the war, the question would be largely irrelevant. However, if they won it, their armies would be so far west that they would already have occupied the territories which they were asking for. It might therefore be as well to grant Stalin's demands now whilst there was a chance of winning some goodwill in return. Nor was this as vacuous as it sounded, since it would be a substitute for the 'second front now' which Stalin was demanding and the British were not delivering. Moreover, in seeking an accommodation with the Soviets, Eden was preparing the way for a post-war settlement in Europe which would not be determined by American devices and desires.

Churchill's foreign policy preferences were clearly Atlanticist in orientation; Eden's were not. He was never as taken with America as Churchill was, and he was not convinced that she would be willing to break her traditional isolationism in order to become embroiled in Europe. Although Eden had little time for the fanciful notions of European union bruited abroad by men like the Belgian Foreign Minister, Paul-Henri Spaak, he did want firm alliances with France and other western European powers to contain Germany on one side and an alliance with Russia in the east; the 'old diplomacy' with a vengeance. For this there would be a price, and Eden was willing to put moral considerations on one side in order to pay it.[31] To use Halifax's terminology, 'the Foreign Secretary' triumphed over 'Anthony Eden', as the search for a latter-day Triple Entente began.

As the Foreign Office began to survey the future, differences between Churchill and Eden would become sharper – although, thanks to Eden's inability to challenge Churchill successfully, they would never surface for long. One of the things which had enabled Chamberlain to get rid of Eden with such ease was the latter's isolation in Cabinet, and it was this same feature which enabled Churchill to get his way in foreign policy. Eden's quick rise to prominence, his good looks and seeming good fortune did nothing to recommend him to the good graces of colleagues less favoured. To this was added Eden's own lack of clubbability. His early life, with an irascible, eccentric father and a promiscuous spendthrift mother, had helped inculcate into him a sense of the value of privacy. At Oxford after the war he had read the unfashionable and unusual subject of Oriental languages and had taken no part in the Union or any student political activities. As Chamberlain's Foreign Secretary he had relied much on his own coterie of confidants, but he had no wider following. Given Eden's 'lack of sympathy' with the Conservative Party and the 'men who composed it', his relative isolation is, perhaps, easy to understand.[32]

Upon his return as Foreign Secretary, Eden had reassembled his coterie. Politically the most important member of this set was Viscount Cranborne. The eldest son of the fourth Marquess of Salisbury, 'Bobbety' Cranborne, as he was known to his friends, was a formidable political intelligence. A shortish, slight man whose marriage was, in its way, as unhappy as Eden's own, Cranborne brought to the political arena an intellect as penetrating as that of his grandfather. But Cranborne was not built for democratic politics. As a future Marquess of Salisbury he could hardly hope to occupy the Premiership, even had he possessed the common touch – something in which (again like his grandfather) he was spectacularly deficient. He was no orator, and like his uncles Robert and Hugh (Viscount Cecil of Chelmswood and Baron Quickswood), he was prone to both hypochondria and excessive devotion to principle. But, unlike his uncles, Cranborne was a man whose judgment was respected. He had resigned with Eden in 1938, and it had been his speech rather than Eden's which had excoriated the Government and which had made the most impact. As a Cecil, as a major force in Hertfordshire politics and as a man of principle, Cranborne would have counted even had he not possessed great ability; the fact that he did so made him, potentially, a formidable figure. Churchill had wanted him to lead the House of Lords in late 1940, but Lord Lloyd's prior claim and insistence upon the post had prevented this. Ironically, it had been Lloyd's too early death in January 1941 which had brought Cranborne both that post and Cabinet Office as Secretary of State for the Dominions. Later in his career Cranborne would sometimes be referred to as the 'conscience of the Tory Party' (a fairly unenviable position); at this juncture he was to function more as Eden's 'conscience' – and occasionally, to Churchill's discomfort, as that of the War Cabinet.[33]

If Cranborne's judgment was usually sound, and if he could be relied upon to tell Eden disagreeable truths as and when necessary, the same could not have been said of Eden's Private Secretary, Oliver Harvey. Harvey had served Eden during his first spell at the Foreign Office and had accepted a technical demotion in rank in order to work as his Private Secretary again. The position was usually held by a young(ish) high-flyer in the diplomatic service and involved acting as a conduit between the Minister and the Office. As such, the Private Secretary can have a great deal more influence than his actual position in the hierarchy might suggest. Harvey, although usually a 'moralist', was not the person to oppose Eden's *realpolitik* on the Soviet question. Harvey shared the naïve sentimentalism of some members of the English upper-middle classes towards the Soviet Union. He prided himself upon his 'progressive' views – in this case, as so often, this amounted to a Wykehamist distaste for the bourgeoisie, especially anyone who actually made money, and a childish enthusiasm for the Soviet Union. As the diplomats were preparing for Eden's visit to Russia in December 1941, Harvey could wax lyrical about a 'Volga Charter' as 'a counterpart to the Atlantic Charter', declaring that it would 'make Stalin feel good'.[34] The implication here that the western allies (as they were by then) and the Soviets shared the same world view was, to say the least, unlikely. Harvey took the line, which seems to have been shared on occasions by Eden, that there could be a comity of interests between the Soviets and the western Powers; that was the trouble when 'moralists' took to *realpolitik*, they had to try to find something more than a temporary coincidence of interests in their own foreign policy.

Eden, who had come back to the Foreign Office with 'a keen desire to improve our relations with the Soviet Government' and flattered himself that he might be able to do so because 'the Russians profess to regard me as one who has no prejudices against them',[35] saw Russian policy as the theatre in which he could make his mark given Churchill's domination of Anglo-American relations.[36] He realised that there were bound to be difficulties in 'harmonizing day-to-day Anglo-Russian co-operation with Anglo-American co-operation' because 'Soviet policy is amoral' while 'United States policy is exaggeratedly moral, at least where non-American interests are concerned'.[37] It was against this last rock that Eden's policy recommendations were to be shipwrecked.

Eden, unlike Churchill, seemed to be willing to recognise that Soviet war aims had to be seen for what they were. Stalin had once explained to Cripps that the purpose of the Nazi–Soviet pact was 'to get rid of the old equilibrium';[38] a victorious Soviet Union would never accept the restoration of the Versailles frontiers. Soon after the Nazi invasion, Ambassador Maisky asked Eden a crucial question about the nature of Anglo-Soviet collaboration: 'Did we intend that it should be military only, or military and economic, or military, economic and political?'[39] In one sense the British never quite decided what the answer to Maisky's question was. In June 1941 Eden had been able to parry Maisky by answering that 'political collaboration . . . was a . . . difficult problem', yet when it came to paying for it with Polish and Baltic territory, Eden had few difficulties. Churchill, on the other hand, whose early messages to Stalin were criticised by Cripps as 'too frequent' and too 'emotional' and even 'sentimental',[40] was not prepared to pay up. But Churchill had no constructive alternative to offer, only compliance with American wishes. With no 'second front now' and no diplomatic agreements, Stalin could draw his own conclusions about British intentions.

There is a pretty irony in the fact that it was Eden, often portrayed as an 'idealist', who was willing to try to reconstruct the old diplomacy in Europe, whilst it was the reactionary Churchill who refused to do so in deference to the liberal world-view of Franklin D. Roosevelt. At the Atlantic Charter conference in August, FDR had made plain his dislike of making any territorial adjustments until the end of the war.[41] Assistant Secretary of State Sumner Welles described Russian demands as 'indefensible from every moral standpoint, and equally indefensible from the standpoint of the future peace and stability of Europe', and Welles likened Eden's proposed treaty to a 'Baltic Munich'.[42] Others within the State Department, including Hull and Assistant Undersecretary Adolf Berle, took the same line.[43] This did not alter the reality contained in Eden's observation that if German military power was destroyed, 'Russia's position on the Continent will be unassailable'.[44]

FDR, however, was not willing to underwrite what he considered to be a major breach of the Atlantic Charter. He was 'confident of being able to reach agreement direct' with Stalin, without resorting to such morally dubious measures.[45] This was not just evidence of the President's usual conviction that he could walk on water; it reflected his views on Soviet Russia. He was aware that Stalin wanted 'security' and was prepared to grant him it, but at the moment he preferred to let matters develop without defining too closely just what 'security' meant. He believed that the Soviet system was evolving in a manner favourable to his plans. It was, he thought, 'increasingly true that the Communism of twenty years ago has practically ceased to exist' and that the current system 'is more like a form of the older socialism'.[46] If the future held out hope, there was no point in agreeing to something which American public opinion could hardly be expected to welcome.

Welles was surely correct in his interpretation of the Soviet proposals as 'morally indefensible', at least from the point of view of the Atlantic Charter, and it was a measure of American influence on Churchill, as well as of Churchill's influence on British foreign policy, that Eden's Soviet policy was defeated. It is worth pausing to note how remarkable this was. It was the British, who had been fighting since 1939, who had opened talks with Stalin, and many Ministers took Rab Butler's view that it was a mistake to allow American policy to dictate the terms of Anglo-Soviet relations. Butler thought that having suffered greatly in the last twenty years through taking on 'wide and idealistic commitments beyond our strength', it was more than time for Britain to be more 'realistic' than the 'rarefied atmosphere of the Atlantic Charter' allowed. Like Beaverbrook (who resigned, at least in part on the issue),[47] Butler thought that 'our refusal to concede their claim to certain territories in Central Europe – the future of which without them we are unable to influence – will tend to maintain that atmosphere of suspicion which has for so many decades affected Anglo-Soviet relations'.[48] Two years earlier he had taken the same view of Hitler. Butler, who was a consistent 'realist', was not tempted to bring thoughts of 'new world orders' into an alliance of convenience.

Roosevelt liked to see himself as a 'realist', but his visions tended to occlude his perception of reality. If Chamberlain had had little comprehension of the kind of man he was dealing with in Hitler, the same was true of FDR and Stalin. Roosevelt told Churchill in March 1942: 'I think I can personally handle Stalin better than either your Foreign Office or my State Department. Stalin hates the guts of all your top people. He thinks he likes me better, and I hope he will continue to do so.'[49] What FDR never saw was that Stalin 'hated' everyone's 'guts'. His suspiciousness bordered on (if it did not pass over into) the pathological. He never believed that his allies would not serve him as he had served them in 1939 (and would have been happy to have served them again had he been afforded the chance). The man who had thought that Trotsky with a few dozen followers exiled in Mexico was more dangerous in 1940 than Hitler was the same man who had presided over the great terror and who had ruthlessly purged his General Staff. Winning Stalin's 'trust' was an enterprise fraught with peril, to say the least; it was probably one doomed to failure.[50] Eden was willing to run the risk of upsetting the same people who had protested at 'Munich' because he had learned that 'morality' was a luxury which Britain could no longer enjoy when it came to her foreign policy. But Britain's foreign policy was now subject to an American veto. Neither Eden, Beaverbrook, Butler nor Cripps[51] were able to make headway against Churchill's deference to continued American opposition. The American position was morally impeccable, but that did not help the British.

4

Uncle Sam and the Brave New World

Neither the British nor the Soviets were ideal allies for America; indeed, it is difficult to think of any Power which could have come up to the exacting standards set by American tradition and expectations. Thanks to FDR's careful policy, America had avoided becoming entangled in the 'shooting war', but given that she was underwriting the war efforts of others, it was difficult to avoid the charge, often made in accusatory tones, that she was also underwriting their war aims. British willingness to give in to Soviet territorial demands in early 1942 was only one of a number of signs that 'imperialist' and 'socialist' clients had their own agenda which they would use American money to underwrite. Although FDR was 'emphatic that he would have no discussion ... of any post-war details',[1] this did not mean that he did not have clear ideas about the broad principles of what a later generation would call a 'new world order'.

The shadow of 1917–21 lay across FDR's hopes for an American peace. He was determined that he would not suffer the fate which had befallen Woodrow Wilson. On the domestic front this meant carrying public and Congressional opinion along with him, or at least not getting too far ahead of it. The President's careful mixture of encouragement to Britain and the Soviet Union without commitments bade fair to accomplish this. As part of this process it was necessary to ensure that British, and later Soviet, war aims were compatible with the splendid vision of American foreign policy. Americans have high ideals which they expect their rulers to realise. Charles de Gaulle wrote at the beginning of his war memoirs that all his life he had had 'a certain idea' of France; this applies in even larger measure to most Americans. As one American former Ambassador recently put it, 'America ... is the place where freedom dwells ... a beacon in the darkness, an ideal that illuminates the lives of millions ... [who] believe in the ultimate goodness of America, its destiny of greatness.' From this it follows that while America 'may sometimes consort with despots', she could 'never truly be herself except when she is engaged everywhere in the struggle for human rights and democracy'. However much it might seem to foreigners that America is 'about materialism, consumerism or mercantilism', for FDR, his forebears and heirs, America 'is about the truths that make men free'.[2] Such notions are liable to attract cynical comments from foreigners, but it is unwise to ignore them or rationalise them away, for they provide an insight into the thought-world of FDR and his heirs. Unless such ideas are taken at least as seriously as they are by those who hold them (difficult though that might be), FDR's foreign policy is apt to look as though it has no main theme.

American fears about underwriting an imperialist peace were easily aroused, which was one sign of how close to the surface they rested. One of the foremost liberals in the State Department, even if his position was dependent upon FDR, or maybe because of that, was Assistant Undersecretary Adolf Berle. Of German-American stock, Berle was the sort of doctrinaire liberal whom Republicans loved to hate – and did so with relish.[3] A complex, intellectual, aloof figure with a (well-deserved) reputation for being arrogant and self-absorbed, Berle was passionately concerned that the end of the war should see the implementation of an American peace. Despite his unpopularity in many circles in Washington, FDR kept Berle on, if only because he 'explicated so well on his . . . conception of a post-war international system'.[4] In July 1941 he wrote to the President expressing his fears that Britain was entering into commitments with other allied countries, which would, in effect, pre-empt the shape of the post-war settlement and 'channelize the trade and economics . . . [of the Balkans and Middle East] through London when the war is over'.[5]

Although Berle made 'no comment' on the 'merits' of the arrangements Britain was said to be entering into with Yugoslavia, Russia and Syria, he could have had no doubts that the news would alarm the President.[6] On 14 July FDR issued what was, in effect, a warning to Churchill and the British about making the kind of secret treaties which the latter had made during the last war. It was, FDR telegraphed, 'much too early for us to make commitments'.[7] When Churchill failed to respond to this, FDR asked Hopkins, who was in London making arrangements for the forthcoming Atlantic meeting, to take the matter up with him.

It was not just the prospect of Britain making secret commitments which brought alarm to those who wanted to internationalise the 'New Deal'. The American Ambassador in London, the Lincolnesque former Governor of New Hampshire, John G. Winant, had long thought that the 'charge of imperialism against England in the United States', which hindered support for the British, 'largely focused on the Indian situation'. Winant was well aware that Churchill opposed further constitutional change for India during the war, even though the Indian Congress Party under Nehru and Gandhi was pressing for it. Winant's own favoured solution was to have the British grant India Dominion Status at once, but, as he told Roosevelt, 'unless the idea was suggested by you', he doubted that the matter would be considered.[8] This was a foretaste of things to come.

In the sturdy Churchillian mythology of the war the first meeting between the Prime Minister and the President at sea off Newfoundland in August 1941 has a special place. With both the great men meeting each other at last, singing hymns and making high-flown commitments, the special relationship was cemented and another stage reached in bringing America into the war. That was how Churchill portrayed it to the Cabinet and posterity, but then he would have put it that way considering how little he actually came away with. Viewed from FDR's perspective, it was an opportunity for trying to ensure that the British underwrote American war aims in the form of what became known as the Atlantic Charter. A study of the documents and the meeting certainly suggests such a conclusion.

The British were not expecting any document, and the Foreign Office feared that FDR had 'bowled a fast one' at the Prime Minister.[9] Halifax commented that dealing with the Roosevelt administration was like a 'disorderly day's rabbit shooting', where 'nothing comes out where you expect and you are much discouraged. And then suddenly, something emerges quite unexpectedly at the far end of the field.'[10] If by this His Lordship meant to signify that having gone through a long period of deferred and frustrated hopes, it was somewhat surprising that the Americans should suddenly come up with what amounted to a declaration of common aims, it is easy to understand his surprise; but it reflects a certain naïveté about FDR's objectives.

The Atlantic Charter was designed to meet the fears of those many Americans like Berle and Winant who were afraid that America was underwriting British war aims. Its language may have been exalted and vague, but that has always been a characteristic of liberal rhetoric; its implications were clear enough for Churchill to add caveats. In Article 1, both Powers disclaimed any territorial ambitions, Articles 2 and 3 followed on from this, declaring that there would be no territorial changes 'that do not accord with the freely expressed wishes of the people concerned'. Quite how that 'will' was to be expressed, and how this was to mesh with Soviet policy, were questions wisely passed over at the time. Article 3, however, was to cause Churchill some problems. It provided for the 'right of all peoples to choose the form of government under which they live', as well as for the restoration of self-government to those who had been deprived of it. Churchill made it plain that nothing in this applied to the British Empire – which was just as well, since if read literally it would mean the end of that Empire. Article 4 was a reflection of Hull's interests and again, if read literally, stored up trouble for the British Empire, since it provided for all nations to have 'access on equal terms, to the trade and to the raw materials of the world which are needed for their economic prosperity'. This signified that the Americans were not about to forget the 'consideration' which they required in exchange for lend-lease. Articles 5 to 8 were, at least in their final form, less likely to prove contentious, detailing, as they did, a common commitment to economic collaboration, a secure peace, freedom of the seas and the 'abandonment of the use of force'.[11]

The last Article, however, bore signs of the discussion which had preceded it. The final version, after calling for the abandonment of the use of force, stated that 'pending the establishment of a wider and more permanent system of general security' such disarmament was 'essential'. This was a disappointment to Churchill, who had wanted a statement that there would be an 'effective international organisation' to keep the peace. FDR, however, argued for 'realism'. Churchill might have affected concern that 'internationalists' would be disappointed at the lack of any reference to a League of Nations, but FDR was more concerned about Congress and American public opinion. The inclusion of anything like a League of Nations, which America had rejected in 1921, would create 'suspicion and opposition' at home, so FDR would have none of it.[12]

Other declarations which issued from the meeting equally reflected Roosevelt's consciousness that, even by taking part in it, he was perhaps pushing American opinion further than it might want to go at that moment.[13] Involvement in a war in Europe and the Middle East had not altered the worldwide nature of Britain's commitments, and given the Japanese war against China and Britain's preoccupations elsewhere, it was hardly surprising that the safety of her Empire in the Far East gave Britain's statesmen cause for concern. America's own negotiations with the Japanese seemed to be yielding few fruits, whilst US economic sanctions, if applied severely, particularly at Japan's most vulnerable point – her lack of oil – might well lead to the outbreak of a war in the Far East in which the Empire might be embroiled. If that meant America's participation in a general war against the Axis Powers, it would be a price Churchill was willing to pay, but he wanted to be sure in advance of America's commitment. He wanted the President to agree to a joint statement that in the event of further aggression by the Japanese, there might well be war between America and Japan. He told Sumner Welles that only such a declaration could restrain Japan and that, if 'this were not done, the blow to the British Government might be almost decisive'.[14]

In public, both at the time and later, Churchill claimed that the Atlantic meeting marked a decisive stage along the road of America's participation in the war – something which got FDR into trouble. The President's enemies alleged that he had made verbal commitments to help Britain against Japan and to bring America into the war against Germany; in doing so, they were following (although in very different vein) comments made by Churchill himself. Speaking in the Commons in January 1942, Churchill said that FDR had promised to come into a war in the Far East, even if America was not attacked; the President's foes naturally picked up on this as evidence for their allegation.[15] They would have been even angrier (and more convinced of their case) if they had known that Churchill told his Cabinet on 19 August that Roosevelt had said that 'he would wage war but not declare it, and that he would become more and more provocative'.[16] There are, however, grounds for believing that Churchill had overstated his case.

It is not only the fact that it would have been quite unlike FDR to tell anyone his whole mind which leads to the conclusion that Churchill, like so many others before him, was mistaking affability for agreement. FDR had plenty of reasons to be affable. He knew how long Churchill had been hoping for America's entry into the war and that hope deferred tended to make the heart sick. If he had not had the common sense to realise this, Churchill made it plain. As the Prime Minister told the Cabinet upon his return, he had 'thought it right to give the President a warning. He had told him that he would not answer for the consequences if Russia was compelled to sue for peace and, say, by the spring of next year, hope died in Britain.' It was, in fact, in response to this that FDR had talked about looking for a naval incident which might bring America into the war. Churchill also reported the President as promising to draw up detailed contingency plans for how American destroyers would escort British convoys.

It is not impossible that Churchill's impression of FDR's intentions was correct – and those conspiracy theorists who ascribe duplicity and culpability to the President can find some corroboration in the Prime Minister's comments. But a far more likely explanation lies in the impact of FDR's personality upon Churchill. Adviser to the Treasury, John Maynard Keynes, who had heard that FDR had been ill and was no longer his old self, had reported back to London in June that the President was 'calm and gay and in full possession of his own personality and of his will and purpose and clarity of mind'. He wrote of FDR's 'supreme equanimity' and of his 'extraordinary charm'.[17] Roosevelt had every reason to use the force of his personality to cheer Churchill in a way his actions were unlikely to. The fact was that the meeting had raised British expectations, but it had produced disappointingly little which could be offered to soothe the fears and anxieties of the British people.[18] Not only had the meeting not led to any American declaration of war, but FDR had made it plain to the American press that America was not about to enter the war. Churchill evidently felt that his 'warning' to FDR might not have been tough enough, for he repeated it in a telegram to Hopkins on 29 August, telling him that there had been 'a wave of depression through Cabinet and other informed circles about the President's many assurances about no commitments and no closer to war'.[19] FDR asked Hopkins to talk to him about Churchill's telegram, but there was, of course, no direct reply. Had Churchill really felt as confident about FDR's future intentions as his comments quoted above imply, it is unlikely that he would have bothered Hopkins. Bob Sherwood, Hopkins's future biographer, who was about to take a trip to England, was told by FDR and Hopkins at dinner that he 'couldn't have picked a better time for getting a cool reception'.[20]

It was never FDR's way to play his hand unambiguously, even when there was no need for deviousness, but given the context within which he was operating, the President needed all his wonted skill and more to play the hand he was dealt.

On the one side were those Senators and Congressmen who took the views most ably expressed by Senator Taft that there was nothing to choose between Hitler and Stalin when it came to international morality. Robert Taft, the son of President William H. Taft, and a rising star in the Republican Senatorial firmament, believed that, 'Even the collapse of England is to be preferred to participation for the rest of our lives in European wars. Americans ought to determine their course entirely on what they believe to be best for the United States, whether foreign nations like it or disapprove of it.'[21] Taft was not pro-German, and he 'did not contend that German victory would make no difference to the United States', but he thought that, 'if we enter the war today in order to save the British Empire, we will be involved in war for the rest of our lives. If the English Channel is our frontier, and this is our war, then we will have to defend it for years to come.'[22] Taft feared that if the United States did defeat Hitler, there would be a 'new age of American imperialism', and thought that people like Henry Luce, the newspaper proprietor, and Stimson seemed 'to contemplate an Anglo-American alliance perpetually ruling the world . . . such imperialism is wholly foreign to our ideals of democracy and freedom. It was not our manifest destiny or our natural destiny.'[23] As events were to show, Taft's views, though unpopular after December 1941, were prescient and were shared by many before Pearl Harbor.

It was clear to FDR that American opinion was shifting, but it would be simplistic to see a President bent on entering the war waiting for public opinion to catch up with him. Such a view derives largely from British sources, and it does so because that was the impression he was anxious to leave the British with. The reason for this is not far to seek. Hopkins, according to his own later account, told Roosevelt after Churchill's gloomy telegram that most British people 'believed that ultimately we will get into the war' and that it was this which kept them going; but, Hopkins warned, if they 'ever reached the conclusion that this was not to be the case', there would be 'a very critical moment in the war and the British appeasers might have some influence on Churchill'.[24] This last view reflected the widespread conviction in Washington that there were 'important groups in London and even in the Government who are still appeasers and would welcome peace talks and a negotiated peace'. Keynes found that summer that 'these ideas exist everywhere'.[25] Although such a belief was wide of the mark, the fact that it was so prevalent ensured that FDR did not take continued British participation in the war for granted. Clearly much, if not everything, depended upon Churchill's continuing leadership, so it was important that he should be bolstered and encouraged. The Prime Minister's mind was so set on the war that there could be no going back for him, but the ailing American was correct to divine that

Churchill's position, which had received a temporary boost from Russia's entry into the war, was weaker than it had been the previous year. So FDR had every motive to try to cheer up the British leader, but we should not take his comments at face value – even if Churchill did so. It is clear that even Hopkins, who was closer to the President at this time than anyone, had no notion of what his intentions were.

The auguries to be read after this were, not surprisingly, designed to reassure the British. On Labor Day FDR delivered a stern warning to Hitler, and when, three days later, a German submarine attacked an American ship, he announced that orders had been given to the navy to 'shoot on sight'. On 13 September he also declared that American warships would escort foreign shipping between Iceland and the United States. This not only took a load off British warships, but also seemed fresh evidence to Churchill of the President's benign intentions. Beaverbrook, previously one of the most vocal and 'imperially-minded' of American critics, now changed his tune, gushing to the Prime Minister that Roosevelt's 'advance' was 'the work of your genius. You have taught the Americans to take their first faltering footsteps, then to walk and shortly to run.'[26]

Beaverbrook's metaphor neatly rationalised the long period since Churchill had first expressed the hope that America was about to enter the war, but if either he or his master thought that their period of waiting was over, they could think again. It was a tribute to Roosevelt's genius as a politician that his signals over the next few months were so mixed. The British could take heart over his statements about convoys and from his action to persuade Congress to repeal parts of the Neutrality Act which conflicted with this, but when cornered by the press with the question of why he did not end the 'dishonesty' of continuing diplomatic relations with Germany, his reply was such as to reassure anyone less astute than Senator Taft: 'We don't want a declared war with Germany,' he said, 'completely off the record', 'because we are acting in self-defense.'[27] To those, like Taft, who thought that FDR had rather a wide definition of what American 'security' demanded, there might be little comfort in such a statement, but for many Americans their President's words were reassuring. He had said during his re-election campaign that their boys were not going to join in any foreign wars, and thus far he had kept his word.

There was another reason why it was obviously in FDR's interests for America to stay out of the war in Europe – and that was the threatening situation in the Far East. According to information which reached Churchill through the Canadian Premier, W. L. Mackenzie King, FDR was convinced that if America entered the war in Europe, 'Japan would enter the war on Germany's side'.[28] This, of course, would bring America and Britain into the same war simultaneously, but it would also mean grave problems for both nations in the Far East.

There is a well-established literature accusing the President of, in effect, conniving at war with Japan and hiding the fact that he had foreknowledge of the Japanese raid on Pearl Harbor. Leaving aside the sheer improbability of FDR allowing his own Pacific fleet to be decimated, such allegations display a startling ignorance of FDR's general policy – which was to avoid American entry into the war, especially a war in the Far East. Those Staff talks which he had allowed with the British had drawn up plans based upon a 'Europe first' strategy, something which would have been ruined if Japan entered the war; in that event, there were bound to be squabbles within the American Services over allocation of resources to the various theatres of operations. FDR was, in all probability, hoping to avoid a showdown with the Japanese until Hitler was out of the way. If the Japanese were going to go to war, it appeared more likely that they would take advantage of the Soviet plight in the west; there would seem little point in being part of the Axis otherwise. Moreover, the Japanese had been engaged in talks with Hull at the State Department about how they might secure some easement of American sanctions. On 28 August the Japanese, in conciliatory mood, offered to hold a conference with the Americans in order to sort out their mutual difficulties, something FDR was tempted to concede. However, given opposition from Hull and other hardliners at the State Department, he fell back upon his favourite policy and temporised, asking for some evidence of Japanese goodwill first.[29] These were hardly the actions of a man bent on war.

Roosevelt's attitude towards Japan between the late summer and Pearl Harbor in December was just as difficult to read as his intentions regarding the war in Europe, but in both cases his ambiguity seems to have stemmed from genuine doubts and difficulties rather than from some 'hidden agenda'. Having agreed to Hull's request that the Japanese provide more evidence of goodwill, FDR turned down Churchill's suggestion in early November that they should issue a joint warning to the Japanese; even demands from the Chinese leader, Chiang Kai-shek, only brought vague promises of air support.[30] The President's mind was working on the terms of a possible peace initiative rather than on the prospects of pulling British chestnuts out of the Japanese flames. His own ideas, which were not particularly focused, centred around some relaxation of the tough American sanctions in return for Japanese concessions,[31] so he did not automatically reject a proposal made by the Japanese on 20 November for a *modus vivendi*. Indeed, in a telegram to Churchill on 24 November, although FDR professed not to be 'very hopeful' and objected to parts of the Japanese proposals, he stated America's willingness to put her own proposals forward.[32]

The British Ambassador in Tokyo, Sir Robert Craigie, took the view that had the Americans accepted the Japanese offer, the subsequent attack on Pearl Harbor would not have taken place – a view sufficiently controversial for Churchill to insist that his final despatch be rewritten before being printed.[33] Craigie thought that the Japanese offer was serious and that it could have been accepted, but it was clear to Churchill, and to FDR, from MAGIC intercepts that this was only part of the story. The Japanese offer was genuine enough, but it was a last-ditch attempt by those who did not want a war to avoid it, for already the Japanese military were preparing for war in the event of the offer being refused. Churchill, whose attitude to FDR's suggestion of a *modus vivendi* had been lukewarm, told him on 30 November that only a 'firm declaration' by America and Britain would deter further Japanese aggression.[34]

Hull, who was already inclined against giving the Japanese the benefit of the doubt, was furious when he learned that there was no doubt; intercepts showed that if there was no American agreement after 29 November, Japan intended to resort to force.[35] According to Stimson, FDR 'jumped up in the air, so to speak,' when informed of the news, declaring that it was 'evidence of bad faith' on the part of the Japanese.[36] On 26 November Hull presented the Japanese with a ten-point declaration that 'restated Washington's most stringent demands', telling Stimson: 'I have washed my hands of it and it is now in the hands of you and [Frank] Knox – the Army and the Navy.'[37] The British, who would not have minded stringing the Japanese along at the negotiating table for a while longer, fell in line; after all, like the Americans themselves, they did not rate Japan's military capacity very highly.[38]

Had FDR persevered with his intentions, or had 'hawks' in the State Department not applied sanctions rather more zealously than the President had intended, then Craigie's hopes of avoiding war might well have been realised, at least for a while – and that might have been all that was necessary. By spring or summer of 1942, with Germany beginning to suffer reverses on the eastern front, the Japanese might well have decided against a showdown with America. That, however, would hardly have suited Churchill, who took the view that it was a 'blessing that Japan attacked the United States and thus brought America wholeheartedly and unitedly into the war'.[39] On the latter score the Prime Minister was correct, and his words reflect the relief he felt at the time.

Late 1941 was a bad time for Churchill and those who had believed his words back in May 1940 that American entry into the war was imminent. The Prime Minister himself told General Smuts in early November that the 'Constitutional difficulties' facing FDR should not be underrated. All that could be done now was to 'have patience and trust to the tide which is flowing in our way and to events'.[40] To those who believe in the 'conspiracy' theory, this might seem further evidence that the British Prime Minister knew what was going to happen, but as Churchill habitually used such language, and as the Japanese themselves did not know at this time exactly what they were going to do, we may leave such 'theorists' to their ineradicable suspicions.[41] Where such writings have a point is that Churchill certainly had done his level best to 'lure' America into the war, whilst FDR, despite Congressional opinion, had done things which, in a later era, would have earned him a 'special prosecutor' and a committee of enquiry. But none of this amounts to saying that both men knew in advance about Pearl Harbor; perhaps neither of them could quite believe that Churchill was finally going to get what he had wanted for so long. Certainly by this late stage the Foreign Office had given up hope of an early American intervention, and it was not easy to see quite how she was to be brought into the war.[42] FDR had brought the British along with him, America was supplying them and the Soviets with the arms necessary to resist Germany, and it was not clear, even on 7 December, that the Japanese attack on Pearl Harbor would alter this state of affairs for the better. Pearl Harbor meant that America was at war with Japan, but despite Churchill's heartfelt declaration that 'we are all in the same boat now', 'we' were not.[43] A speedy British declaration of war on Japan ensured that the 'English-speaking peoples' had one common enemy, but for a few days the horrific (from Churchill's point of view) prospect opened up of the new allies waging a common war in the Far East, but not in Europe. All the Anglo-American Staff talks had been based on a 'Europe first' strategy, but with Germany not in the war against America, there was a very real prospect that this might not come to pass. FDR could always have tried to persuade Congress to declare war on Germany, but such was the outrage in America about the nature of the Japanese attack that the pressure to ignore Germany and pursue an all-out war in the Pacific might well have proved irresistible – in which case the British and the Soviets would have found some of their supplies drying up. Indeed, far from being 'saved', as Churchill thought, Britain might have found herself in great difficulties. It is an indication of how readily the British assumed that their interests and those of the Americans coincided that such thoughts appear not to have crossed the minds of anyone in Whitehall; indeed, Churchill immediately invited himself to America to co-ordinate strategy.

The fact that the Japanese did not declare war on the Soviets did not seem to bode well for the British, as common sense seemed to suggest that unless the Japanese were helping Hitler, there was no need for him to help them. But Hitler's confidence was still immense and, given America's far from covert help to his enemies, his impatience to strike at the 'mad' President who represented the forces of international plutocracy and Jewry was understandable. Had Hitler not declared war on America, Churchill would have found himself in a most difficult position; not for the first time he had cause to thank his old antagonist. On 11 December Hitler declared war on the United States.

The old ambiguity was over. Churchill, seeing the proverbial seventh cavalry arriving in the nick of time, was suitably relieved. On his way to America, self-invited and coming whether the President wanted him to or not, the Prime Minister was going to arrive with the future strategy of the war already mapped out. 'Europe first' would be transmuted into 'Mediterranean first', which would, *inter alia*, allow the linchpin of Empire, the Suez Canal, to be saved, as well as preserving the British position in the Middle East. The fact that this was also the one area in which Britain currently had large numbers of troops was an additional advantage as well as a reason for mounting operations in the region; it would give the British the leading part in any campaign. The British also possessed another advantage when it came to deciding the grand strategy of the war: a superior organisation.

Writing to the Chancellor of the Exchequer in early June 1941, Keynes described the American governmental machine as 'almost incredibly inefficient' and wondered 'how decisions are ever reached at all'. His description was one echoed by many observers: 'There is no clear hierarchy of authority. The different departments of the Government criticise one another in public and produce rival programmes. There is perpetual internecine warfare between prominent personalities.'[44] This was a situation ripe for exploitation by an efficient British system where Churchill, as Minister of Defence and Prime Minister, dominated a Chiefs of Staff committee whose members, steeled by the experience of real war, knew when and how to say 'no' to their dominating leader. The Americans had nothing to match it, and with FDR willing to do what Churchill would not, namely overrule his Chiefs of Staff, the British Prime Minister could look forward to playing a major part in determining the strategy of the new war. This was where Churchill's priorities lay, and he was happy that it should be so. But others inside the British Government would be less happy, because the effect of this situation was to hand the creation of the diplomatic and political new world over to the Americans. Even the cry of 'leave it until the end of the war' was, given the difference in strength of the two Powers, tantamount to saying 'leave it to the Americans'. The question of whether American and British war aims were entirely compatible would take on a new dimension now that the former was, in Churchill's phrase, 'in the harem'.[45]

But the fact remained that America was now in the war. So what had Britain's lone stand since June 1940 achieved? It had not, as is sometimes alleged, 'brought about' America's entry into the war, and the argument that it had 'bought' time for America to rearm is as bogus as it was when used in a similar sense to defend appeasement. Nor yet had Churchill's stand brought Russia into the war. It is not even true to say that Britain and America had saved the Soviet Union. That the Soviets survived and turned the tide by a small margin is undeniable, but it is by no means clear that Britain and America created that margin. The aid which the western Powers sent was most welcome, but it was slow getting there, arrived in smaller quantities when it was sent, and cannot be shown to have made the difference between Soviet success and failure. Even if it could, it was hardly a precondition for aid that the aid-giver should be in the war – America, the major donor, was not in the war when the aid programme started. Nor is it the case that the divisions which Germany stationed in the west made the difference between her success and her failure. No one in the German High Command seriously expected a British invasion of France, and there is no evidence that the generals kept back forces which would have made all the difference if they had been on the eastern front. The forces Germany stationed in the west were there to keep the fruits of the conquests of 1940, and they would have been there whether or not Britain had been in the war.

Britain had not been able to save Yugoslavia, Greece or Crete. Her 'allies' amounted on the whole to governments in exile, in control of nothing. De Gaulle, from whom so much had been hoped, had rallied a few unimportant central African colonies, but failed at Dakar and in North Africa; in Indo-China he had rallied the former Governor, General Georges Catroux, but he had lost the colony. In Syria de Gaulle had had to have the aid of British and Dominion troops to fight his fellow countrymen, and he had descended into making anti-British remarks that were giving Churchill food for thought about a man who might become to him what the Monster had to Dr Frankenstein.[46]

So what had Britain achieved? She had gained the admiration of large sections of the American public and had retained her self-respect. She had fought for her independence, but she had only been able to do so with American aid and as, in effect, an American warrior-satellite. Her future had been mortgaged, her economy strained to breaking-point, her cities bombed and her people subjected to stringent rationing. This tremendous and heroic effort had gone unrewarded for eighteen months. Her politicians would talk about presenting a 'bill' for the costs incurred, and they would expect special treatment from America,[47] but they would get neither recompense nor favours; the world does not work like that, as Churchill above all people should have known. The British had certainly gained a national myth, but they had also ensured that they would need one. The ferocious Japanese assault and the supine nature of the British resistance to it demonstrated that imperial power had been stretched beyond sustainable limits, and the spectacle of over 100,000 imperial soldiers surrendering at Singapore to an Asiatic Power was one which imperial prestige could not survive. Empires in their maturity rest upon the reputation for invincibility which they acquire in their creation, and thereafter it is seldom necessary to resort to arms to maintain them. But once the myth is punctured and the 'painted veil' removed, not all the legerdemain in the world can recreate the illusion.

Churchill imagined that now America was in the war all the tortuous negotiations about a master lend-lease agreement and British 'consideration' in return would end, and there would be the complete comradeship for which he had striven.[48] These were vain hopes and as unrealistic in their way as the

Prime Minister's fantasies of American involvement in the war in 1940. Neither of Britain's allies would treat her as some sort of precious icon, to be revered and handled gently. In the harsh world of Great Power politics the wind would not be tempered to the shorn lamb. Britain's stand had been magnificent, but in the words of General Caulaincourt: 'c'est magnifique, mais ce n'est pas la guerre'; nor was it.

5

The Empire at Bay

Eden wanted Britain to have a foreign policy of her own, and he would have liked to have run it himself;[1] in neither endeavour was he successful. Instead, Churchill's Atlanticist preferences won the day. Eden wished to construct an edifice which would survive a repetition of the rejection by Congress of Wilson's idealism,[2] whilst Churchill preferred to put all his eggs in the American basket. Eden's vision of a latter-day Triple Entente foundered on his inability to challenge Churchill.

Eden's was not a foreign policy which offered easy options, but then, except for Churchill's hope that America would pull Britain's chestnuts out of the fire, there was no easy option on offer. Eden's readiness to grant Soviet territorial demands bears witness to a willingness to pay the price in the east, whilst his championing of de Gaulle against Churchill's growing suspicions bore equal witness to a desire to build for the future in the west. Eden's post-war world was not that different to the pre-war one. He envisaged, as did most diplomats and politicians, that Germany would once more, as post-1919, become the major problem to be coped with – hence his hankering after a reconstruction of a version of the old Triple Entente. Nor was it a foreign policy which excluded America. Eden envisaged some form of expanded League of Nations in which the Americans would play a major role, but his vision was one of regional superpowers, in effect keeping the peace in their own spheres of influence.[3] The question of why Eden's vision was not achieved is one which asks serious questions about Churchill's handling of British policy.

Monocausal explanations are rarely satisfying, save for the conspiracy theorist, but if there is one common thread running through the various reasons which can be essayed in answer to the question of why Eden failed, it would be Churchill. It was Churchill who vetoed the idea of granting Stalin his 1941 frontiers; it was Churchill who refused to have anything to do with recognising de Gaulle's organisation as the provisional government of France; and it was Churchill, above all, who showed so little foresight that he could, at the end of 1944, reject the option of a western European alliance with the dismissive comment that there was nothing 'save weakness' in it.[4] Running through Churchill's attitude like a leitmotif was the theme of America. America would not like it if Britain granted Stalin's demands; America would not like it if de Gaulle was recognised as the leader of France; and the

Americans would not like talk of an alliance that involved spheres of influence. In all these things Churchill accurately assessed American attitudes, but the question was not whether he was right about America, but whether he was right to allow FDR to determine the foreign policy of the British Empire. Eden spent a good deal of his time trying to bring the Prime Minister around to the creation of a truly British foreign policy, but to no effect.

Only on imperial matters, where Churchill defended India[5] and Beaverbrook, Leo Amery and many Tories did the same for imperial preference, was there sustained resistance to American pressure.

It was symptomatic of Churchill's habitual optimism about American intentions that he should have impatiently brushed aside Halifax's warnings that they would have to come to a compromise on American demands for the abolition of imperial preference.[6] He deplored 'all this fussing about what is to happen after the war',[7] and took the view that policies formulated 'in a period separated from us by the gulf which marks the US involvement in the full war' were no longer of relevance. As he told Halifax cheerfully on 10 January 1942, 'lease-lend is practically superceded now'.[8] In taking this line, Churchill could hardly have been more wrong.

Far from dropping the whole subject of lend-lease, the Americans returned to the charge on it, and they continued to insist that Britain give the commitment to end economic protectionism demanded by Article VII of the master lend-lease agreement. But when it came to a matter so closely affecting the Empire, even Labour Ministers and free traders were 'resentful at what they felt to be an American attempt at blackmail'.[9] What was at issue was not simply a dispute over free trade and protection, although for men like Amery this was of great importance, but whether Britain appeared to be accepting American 'tutelage'. The 'key-note of our relations must surely be equality', Churchill declared.[10] That, of course, was the problem; had there been 'equality' between Britain and America, there would have been no need for lend-lease and arguments about 'consideration'. Churchill's strongly held feeling that American entry into the war had made lend-lease and its associated debates obsolete was not shared by the Americans.

To Winant, those Tories who opposed accepting Article VII were 'nothing more than imperialists' and only the more progressive Eden 'really fights to support our position'.[11] Dean Acheson, the Assistant Undersecretary charged with dealing with the American side of the economic negotiations, would later accuse the American Treasury of 'envisaging a victory where both enemies and allies were prostrate – enemies by military action, allies by bankruptcy';[12] whatever truth there was in this charge, a similar one could have been levelled at the State Department. Impatient with British procrastination in early 1942, the State Department wanted FDR to push the British into a firm acceptance of the American position,[13] but the President preferred not to press matters.[14]

If the two allies disagreed about the interpretation of Article 4 of the

Atlantic Charter, which provided for free access to raw materials, they were equally far apart when it came to Article 3, which guaranteed people the right to live under governments of their own choice. Churchill insisted that it did not apply to the British colonies or to India and Burma, whilst Ambassador Winant took the view that this 'would simply intensify charges of imperialism and leave Great Britain in the position of "a do-nothing policy"'.[15] It is some measure of the difference between the Churchillian mind-set and that of the Americans that the latter should have imagined that he would be deterred by such allegations. Churchill was a cheerful imperialist and quite content to 'do nothing' in a complicated situation where it appeared that nothing could be done.

The outbreak of the war had overtaken the attempt to implement the 1935 Government of India Act, which Churchill had so strongly opposed in the early 1930s. The overweening behaviour of the Congress Party since its elec-toral success in the 1937 provincial elections had helped to create a Muslim backlash under the leadership of Mohammed Ali Jinnah, President of the Muslim League. With the Muslims opposed to any federation which gave no guarantees for minority rights, and with the Congress leaders, Gandhi and Nehru, convinced that Britain's crisis was India's opportunity, it proved impossible to make any headway towards constitutional reform. The most that the British were prepared to offer before 1942 was Dominion Status after the war, and Nehru and company were convinced that they should be able to get more out of the situation than that. With Japan's entry into the war, elements of the Congress Party collaborated with their fellow Asiatics, whilst the majority followed Gandhi's lead in a 'Quit India' campaign. Churchill stuck to the promise which he had made in August 1940 of Dominion Status after the war.

At the 'Arcadia' conference in December 1941, FDR had bluntly suggested to Churchill that the British should grant independence to India, and although, predictably, this had got him nowhere, he continued to hope that America might be able to get the British to make some sort of declaration on the subject which would strengthen their position in the sub-continent at a time when it was under threat from the Japanese and the attitude of the Congress Party.[16] In the aftermath of the fall of Singapore, in mid-February 1942, Berle pressed for an immediate American effort to 'tackle the Indian problem in a large way'.[17] He contemplated nothing less than the declaration by Churchill that British policy, in association with the United States, was to make India a full partner 'in the United Nations'. Winant from London, the Chinese Foreign Minister and the Senate Foreign Relations Committee all added their voices to the call for America to interfere in the running of the Empire.[18]

The Prime Minister's views on India were expressed most forcibly to Sir Ramsawar Mudaliar, one of India's representatives to the War Cabinet, in

September 1942: 'Why should we be apologetic or say that we are prepared to go out at the instance of some jackanapes? Tell them what we have done for India. For eighty years we have given it peace and internal security and prosperity such as has never been known in the history of that country.' He was not, he declared, 'going to be a party to a policy of scuttle'. With an' echo of his attitude towards the Government of India Act, he told Mudaliar that he would 'tell them that for the last 25 years the Conservative Party has gone on the wrong tracks, it has lost confidence in itself, and it has given way perpetually until the present state of affairs has come about. It is all wrong, thoroughly wrong. If we ever have to quit India, we shall quit it in a blaze of glory.'[19] This was not only the authentic voice of the 'diehard', it represented a frame of mind which found American interference in British India highly objectionable. The British attitude was that the Americans understood little about the real situation in India and spoke from a standpoint so far beyond reality as to preclude their playing any useful purpose.[20] For the Americans, this was further proof that the British were incorrigibly imperialist.

In one sense it was unfortunate for the British that Churchill came to personify their war effort, for his attitudes on subjects like India were far from representative. FDR saw Churchill as 'pretty much a nineteenth-century colonialist',[21] and American policy-makers took their cue from this; in any event, the idea of the British as a race of colonialists was one which fitted easily into the American stereotype. FDR's vision of the future encompassed the notion that what might be called 'Americanism' was a 'third force' between the imperialism of the British and the communism of the Soviets.[22] This idea informed American policy towards India, British protectionism and the shape of the post-war world, and in all three areas it operated against what many British Conservatives perceived to be imperial interests. The most vocal representative of this strain of American thought was the Vice-President, Henry Wallace. Wallace believed in 'political internationalism', which 'could eventuate only with the end of European imperialism and with the abandonment of balance-of-power politics'. On that account he was

especially critical of the British, particularly Winston Churchill. Continued British domination over India, in Wallace's understanding, violated the whole purpose of the war, as did Churchill's impulse for empire, his unabashed belief in Anglo-Saxon superiority, his disdain for China and distrust of Russia, his preference for secret negotiations, and his manifest intention to hold the reins of world leadership, whatever the semblance of world government, in British, American and, unavoidably, Soviet hands.[23]

On 8 June 1942 the Vice-President delivered himself of what Halifax called an 'apocalyptic version of America as "the chosen of the Lord" in whom the culture of Palestine, Rome and Britain are to be brought to a final fruition'. It was the 'most unbridled expression to date of the view of the new deal as the New Islam, divinely inspired to save the world'.[24]

This brave new world, as envisaged by FDR, Wallace, Berle, Welles and a host of publicists, publicity-seekers and self-proclaimed American messiahs, was the Democratic agenda, writ large, complete with, at least in FDR's view, a substantial increase in Presidential powers. It was, in Wallace's famous phrase, 'the century of the common man'. But this was little more than a veil for government interference in the lives of individuals on an unprecedented scale, both through 'agencies' (a favourite Rooseveltian solution for problems) and through so-called 'progressive' taxation, which deprived individuals of the opportunity to pass on their wealth and with it a measure of independence of government. In foreign affairs it meant an end to imperialism and protectionism, indeed to any barriers which stood in the way of the imposition of 'Americanism' on an unsuspecting world. This is not to say that FDR was simply after replacing the British Empire with an American one; his ideas were both more recondite and more naïve than that. The President (like all liberals) genuinely believed that his ideals were those which ought to be shared by all sensible people, and he would have regarded as wounding (as liberals do) any allegation that his policy was self-serving. Taking his Democratic/American ideas as the norm was, of course, just the sort of arrogant self-righteousness which fails to endear liberals to others, but it is that attitude which makes it so powerful. Of course, to many British officials, forced to listen to this sort of stuff with more respect than it deserved because of the quarter from whence it came, it seemed as though the 'American substitute for a colonial empire' was 'American big business', and it seemed insignificant that rhetoric about the 'abolition of colonial empires' was usually accompanied by demands for 'equal access for all democracies to raw materials'.[25]

FDR regarded colonialism as an outdated system and thought that the British needed to 'recognize a world change' which had 'taken deep root' in India and other colonial countries. Perhaps, mercifully, he had the tact not to put these patronising views in quite this form to Churchill.[26] Egged on by his special envoy, Averell Harriman, FDR did, however, decide to offer his services as adviser to Churchill, quoting at him the analogy of the American Constitutional Convention as a way out of the Indian impasse.[27] Churchill did not reply to FDR's rather fatuous suggestion, and attention switched to the Cripps mission.

Sir Stafford had returned from Moscow the hero of the hour, being popularly (and totally incorrectly) credited with having something to do with the entry into the war of the Soviet Union. His presence in the Cabinet and his standing as the second most popular man in the country were equally irritating to Churchill, whose position in the aftermath of the collapse of Britain's Far Eastern Empire was considerably weakened.[28] Thus, sending the ascetic and saintly Cripps off to negotiate with the ascetic and saintly Gandhi was, whichever way one cared to look at it, a good idea. Not only did it give the two men concerned the opportunity to play at being holier-than-thou, something each of them excelled in, but it gave the British public and the Americans the appearance that Churchill wanted to do something about India. This, as Amery, his long-suffering Secretary of State, knew only too well, was not the case. As he told the Viceroy, Lord Linlithgow, in September 1942, Churchill 'talks all the time and does not really read papers'.[29]

It had taken a great deal of time, and even more patience, to persuade Churchill to agree to the offer of immediate post-war independence which Cripps took with him to India in March,[30] so the Prime Minister was not unduly aggrieved when Congress refused to come to an agreement with the envoy; at a stroke Cripps's prestige was dented and the Americans could no longer claim that the British were doing nothing. FDR's 'Special Representative', Louis Johnson, had played a conspicuous part in helping Cripps negotiate with Congress; indeed, not only had he on occasion acted as a go-between for Cripps and Nehru, but he had helped draw up, with Roosevelt's tacit approval, the final 'British' offer made to Congress.[31] For all Harry Hopkins's tactful attempts to deny that Johnson was acting with official approval and his claim that Cripps was 'using Johnson for his own ends',[32] the 'facts of Johnson's appointment contradict' the disclaimer, and he certainly received no reprimand for using FDR's name freely in his negotiations.[33] Johnson blamed Churchill for 'sabotaging' the mission,[34] and FDR responded to the news that the talks had broken down by urging 'one more final effort'. He did not, he told Churchill on 11 April, agree with the Prime Minister's estimation of how American public opinion would react, telling him that it was almost unanimous in blaming the British Government; it could not, he wrote, understand why the British were not willing 'to permit them [the Indians] to enjoy what is tantamount to self-government during the war' if it was willing to concede this after the war. Reverting to his earlier proposal of some sort of 'Convention', FDR warned about adverse reaction in America if India was invaded by the Japanese.[35]

Hopkins, who was in England at the time negotiating over the location and timing of a 'second front', had the unenviable job of delivering this fine piece of impertinence and irrelevance to the Prime Minister, and later recalled the 'string of cuss words' lasting for 'two hours' with which Churchill greeted the message.[36] Instead of having resort to the usual furious 'draft telegram', Churchill was able to pour out his anger directly at the President's personal representative. He told Hopkins that he was 'quite ready to retire to private life if that would do any good in assuaging American opinion', but he refused to have anything to do with a policy which would throw India into confusion at such a vital moment.[37] Hopkins warned FDR that there was not much more to be done, with Churchill in such a mood and Cripps already bound for home;[38] so, for the moment, FDR responded to Churchill's plea that 'Anything like a serious disagreement between you and me would break my heart and surely deeply injure both our countries at the height of this terrible struggle.'[39]

But American interest in India gave continued encouragement to the Congress Party that it could get more out of the British than Cripps had been prepared to offer. Eden, whose hopes that the Americans would resist the temptation to interfere were doomed to disappointment,[40] had 'no doubt that the Indian political leaders are playing up to the Americans their lack of confidence in our intentions as a means of pressure on the US to intervene', and sought to find a way of deflecting this pressure.[41] Linlithgow, who found American 'pressure an intolerable nuisance', was anxious that India did not become a 'United Nations' responsibility, with America acting as a sort of mediator between the British and Gandhi.[42]

The Viceroy's fears were not without foundation, as Johnson's part in the Cripps mission had shown. 'Interventionists' had been welcome enough before America was in the war, but now that this had come to pass, there was a danger that 'American imperialism', which unlike its British counterpart was not 'territorial outside the western hemisphere', but was, rather, 'economic and commercial', would now spill over into intervention in the affairs of the European Empires.[43] Wallace's overtly anti-imperial comments worried the Foreign Office, for even at this stage of the war, with the British Empire in the Far East being conquered by the Japanese, it was clear that it would be the Americans who would have to expel the conquerors, and the fear was that 'as *they* defeat Japan and . . . force the Japanese to evacuate the British territories . . . the Americans will expect to decide, without consulting us or our interest overmuch, what is to be done with these areas'.[44] It was taken for granted in America that 'the white peoples have lost their asiatic possessions forever', and that there would be no place for a British Empire in the 'world New Deal' which so many members of the American administration seemed to want to create.[45] Where Wallace and other interventionists might have held back from criticism of Britain whilst America was out of the war because that would have played into the hands of the isolationists, now all sides of the American political spectrum could join in attacking British imperialism. Observing the development of American opinion during the first year of America's participation in the war, it was obvious that 'American conceptions of our Colonial system are crystallizing in a form prejudicial to understanding, to our interests, and to productive collaboration on post-war reconstruction'. It may have been true that the 'depth of American ignorance of our Colonial practice is impressive',[46] but that missed the point, which was that the Americans had, and held very strongly to, a marked objection to the whole concept of colonialism. The very speed with which the Japanese overran the British Empire in the Far East convinced many Americans that the British were not 'only imperialists, but bungling imperialists', whose time had passed and whose Empire would soon be at one with those of Nineveh and Tyre.[47]

According to the head of the British Joint Staff Mission in Washington, General Sir John Dill, 'many Americans' were saying that, 'if only we had treated the Indians and the Burmese as they have treated the Philippinos, we would have no anxieties about those countries today'.[48] Idealism and self-interest made a potent cocktail.

The fact that American liberals 'generally refused to admit the category "impossible"' meant that they simply disbelieved the British, when, in the aftermath of the failure of the Cripps mission, they claimed that a 'National Government could not be formed'.[49] There is something about the liberal mind, particularly in its American manifestation, which revels in 'new initiatives' and 'constructive' proposals designed to break 'deadlocks'. It is almost as though the liberal mind believes that every problem comes into the world with a twin called 'solution' and that the art of politics is to bring the two together. Such an attitude caused considerable irritation to Leo Amery, Churchill's Secretary of State for India, a good imperial Conservative, who by October was expressing his boredom with the 'continuous clamour for some "initiative"'. 'What nobody seems to face', he told Linlithgow (who had to face it every day), was that 'there can be no immediate solution'.[50] It was all very well for Amery to fulminate in this manner, and for Eden to hope that a 'campaign' of 'education' in America would help put Anglo-American relations on a more 'realistic' basis,[51] but it was quite clear that none of this would impress FDR. Increasingly American politicians referred to 'imperialism as part of the evils which the United Nations are fighting to abolish'.[52] Reports multiplied of American officials and politicians assuming that certainly the Dutch and British and probably the French colonial Empires would all be abolished by the end of the war.[53]

There were those in Britain who comforted themselves with the thought that the 'growing tendency of Americans to concern themselves, even to meddle, with other peoples' affairs' was 'nothing more sinister than an effort by a young, untried and in many ways immature, nation to come to grips with the multitude of new problems forced upon it by the logic of events',[54] whilst others deluded themselves into thinking that it might be possible, through a campaign of 'education', to 'make the American people understand that they have a responsibility towards the people of the British Commonwealth and Empire'.[55] Even those who felt that it was natural for 'the cannibal' to be 'irritated by nebulosity and unction on the part of the missionary', laboured under the illusion that it might be possible, by skilful diplomacy, to 'more closely associate America with the British Empire'.[56] The importance of future co-operation with America was obvious enough, but this approach showed a naïveté on the part of the British about the visceral nature and the depth of American anti-imperialism. Richard Law, a junior Minister at the Foreign Office and a close friend of Eden, found himself assailed by American views on imperialism during a visit to America in late 1942. Although the purpose of his mission was to assess the possibilities and opportunities for post-war co-operation with America, he found it 'impossible to get away from the British Empire'. It 'very soon became clear' to him that, 'unless we were able to remove the misunderstandings which exist in the mind of the average intelligent American, the chances of genuine Anglo-American collaboration would be small'. Experience of America, however brief, disabused Law of any notion that American anti-imperialism was a 'surface agitation'; it was a deep-rooted emotion and exercised itself in particular where India was concerned, not least because the Americans saw themselves as defending India from the Japanese. American concern for her protégé, China, also gave American policy-makers an interest in the fate of the anti-colonialist movement in the East.[57]

It was on this last point that there was another example of the chasm which divided British and American attitudes towards the Far East. Where Churchill intended to hold his own and regarded China as a weak Power, the Americans did not mean the British, French or Dutch to hold their own, and they had 'a strong and somewhat unreasoning attachment ... to China'.[58] It came as an unpleasant surprise for the British to find that 'not only do Americans place China on an equality with ourselves as partners in the present world struggle', but 'also that the underlying relationship is much warmer and more confident in the case of China'.[59] Where Britain was perceived as a symbol of the old world in decline, replete with imperial sins, protectionist economies and snobbery, China was the symbol of the new world which was being born from the struggle – post-colonialist, democratic and egalitarian, in fact, a veritable embryonic America. The Americans wanted to 'regard the war in the East as well as that in other parts of the globe as a war of liberation'. This appealed to 'the emotional idealism' which was 'at the bottom of all American thinking'.[60] Already Britain's inability to do anything to defend Australia and New Zealand from possible Japanese assault had led to the antipodeans declaring that in future they would look to America for help, something which further increased the likelihood of the Pacific becoming a gigantic American lake; what place would there be for the British Empire in the Far East in this brave new world?

With Wallace, Welles and their like declaring that the 'age of imperialism was at an end', and with America interfering in the affairs of India and demanding an end to imperial economic policies, the question arose as to Britain's exact status in the coming American peace. Leo Amery put Churchill's dilemma best, when he commented that the latter 'hated giving up all his most deeply ingrained prejudices merely to secure more American, Chinese and Left-Wing support'. Yet this was exactly what he was finding himself doing; and, as he did so, he was 'undergoing all the conflicting emotions of a virtuous maiden selling herself for really handy ready money'.[61]

It was, then, down this road that subservience to America led. Eden found the absence of 'any guiding principle' of British foreign policy a 'grave weakness', and he spent a good deal of time in late 1942 trying to supply this defect.⁶² The need for some delineation was clear to Eden when the effects of its want were considered. He thought that 'an important element in our difficulties with the Russians' was 'the suspicions [sic] which they entertain of our ultimate intentions towards them'. Similarly, when it came to Anglo-American relations, a shadow was cast by American fears of British imperialism. Whilst the two Great Powers harboured suspicions, the 'smaller allies' were 'puzzled by an apparent inability on our part to give them the kind of lead, to provide for them the kind of focus, which they have come to realise that they must have if they are to survive in a Europe which will continue to be overshadowed . . . by Germany'. At one level – the one which Churchill (and so many historians following him) concentrated upon – the main principle was to rid Europe of German domination and to 'continue to exercise the functions and to bear the responsibilities of World Power'. But this was not Britain's only war aim: 'We have to maintain our position as an Empire and a Commonwealth. If we fail to do so we cannot exist as a World Power. And we have to accept our full share of responsibility for the future of Europe.' This was what the war was being fought for, and this was the objective for which thousands of Britons were being asked to fight and die. 'If we fail to do that,' Eden warned his colleagues, 'we shall have fought this war to no purpose, and the mastery of Europe which we have refused to Germany by force of arms will pass to her by natural succession as soon as the control of our arms is removed.' Churchill's admirers like to claim that their hero was something of a visionary, but it was Eden who saw most clearly what was to be the shape of Britain's future.

That Britain was the least of the 'Big Three' was obvious to few in 1942, and since she was still contributing more troops to the common cause than the Americans, and her economy was more heavily mobilised than any other, Eden's timing in trying to make a bid for a 'British' foreign policy was impeccable; the longer the war continued, the less chance was there of Britain having major influence over the political settlement which would follow. Whether Eden's attempt to shape allied discussions on the politics of the war would have had much success can never be known, but at least he wanted to formulate ideas – something which Churchill was, to Eden's irritation and growing frustration, refusing to do.⁶³

Eden looked forward to Great Power co-operation. He was not certain (unlike the sanguine and mistaken Churchill) that America would 'be prepared to assume responsibilities towards the world at large', but he doubted whether they would be willing to do so as part of an 'exclusive' Anglo-American alliance. It was here that Eden's ideas diverged most sharply from Churchill's, for, as the latter's speech at Harvard in May the following year would show, he saw the Anglo-American alliance as the cornerstone of world peace and of continuing British influence in the world. Taking account of Soviet suspicions and of American solicitude for China, Eden envisaged a 'Four Power Plan' by which Britain, America, China and the Soviet Union would work together under the aegis of the United Nations.[64]

Churchill's thoughts on the future were largely confined to Anglo-American co-operation. He took the view that 'we shall have to work with the Americans in many ways and in the greatest ways'.[65] On the subject of Europe his ideas were of longer gestation. For some time he had been thinking of a 'council of Europe',[66] and he now told Eden that his thoughts 'rest primarily in Europe – the revival of the glory of Europe, the parent continent of the modern nations and of civilization'. It was clear, however, from the tone of Churchill's comments that he was anxious about the ultimate intentions of the Soviet Union. 'It would be', he told Eden, 'a measureless disaster if Russian barbarism overlaid the culture and independence of the ancient States of Europe.' When it came to formulating plans to avoid this situation, Churchill was barren of suggestions, weakly commenting that, 'Unhappily the war has prior claims on your attention and on mine.' With this sonorous phrase Churchill left the field of post-war planning in international affairs open to the Americans, in much the same way as he was leaving domestic politics to the left; Conservatism was to pay a high price for the Prime Minister's total absorption in the war.

Eden argued that, 'It is from every point of view bad business to have to live from hand to mouth where we can avoid it, and the only consequence of so doing is that the United States makes a policy and we follow, which I do not regard as a satisfactory role for the British Empire.'[67] Churchill's reply reflected his inadequacy in the field of post-war planning. He preferred to rely upon time and chance, telling Eden that he hoped that 'these speculative studies will be entrusted to those on whose hands time hangs heavy'; his concluding sally of wit served only to disguise the paucity of his own thought, as he told Eden not to 'overlook Mrs Glass's Cookery Book recipe for Jugged hare – "First catch your hare"'.[68] When the Cabinet touched on some of these matters on 3 November, Churchill was at his most obstreperous, and Amery's comments that Britain and Russia should 'keep out' of Europe were unhelpful.[69] Eden, furious, muttered about Churchill having to find a new Foreign Secretary. As Oliver Harvey commented in his diary, 'If allowed to, [Churchill] will win the war and lose the peace as certain as certain.'[70]

6

The 'mad house' and the Kremlin

As Eden's Private Secretary surveyed Britain's position in late 1942, he could take no comfort from what he saw: 'With Roosevelt straining to put the British Empire into liquidation and Winston pulling in the opposite direction to put it back to pre-Boer War, we are in danger of losing the Old and the New World';[1] this was, indeed, the effect of Churchill's triumph. Eden's plans were based upon the view that 'human beings are not exclusively guided by high motives or by long and wide views of their own best interests'.[2] He took into account FDR's desire to have the world 'run' by the four Great Powers as well as his desire to foist the 'New Deal dream' on everyone else, but did so in a way which set limits to Britain's dependence upon America. Eden recognised that 'a great deal of vaguely "liberal" opinion here is really directed to relieving this country of what for want of a better word may be called her Imperial responsibilities and concentrating on nothing but the "improvement of standards of living" at home', and he had scathing words for this 'unconscious defeatism based on the theory that "we have had our day" and should now "hand over the torch"'.[3] Without some 'rallying-cry which will inspire such doubters with the belief in the necessity of our fulfilling our world-wide mission', Eden warned, 'it is possible that whether we like it or not we may sink to the level of a second-class power with all that that implies'. He showed further evidence of his powers as a visionary when he commented that although this might be 'painless' and 'even profitable in the short run', in the longer term it might result in an 'agonizing collapse from which we should emerge as a European Soviet State, or the penurious outpost of an American pluto-democracy or a German gau';[4] as it happened, when Eden's prophecy came to pass, it was the second and least unpleasant of these alternatives for which Britain had to settle. The irony of his career was that he was to be the Prime Minister under whom this state of affairs was to become plain, when he, unlike the 'canonized' Churchill, had done all that he could to warn about this fate and to avert it.

Eden saw the forces, economic and political, which were pushing America into assuming an 'imperial' role, and though he did not discount the possibility of America wanting to withdraw into isolationism, he thought that the opposite was more likely; America would wish to create a 'new world' worthy of her. With regard to the Soviets, Eden characterised them as 'realists and suspicious', but he hoped that by providing them with a system which would give 'security' against 'repeated aggression from the direction of Europe', it might be possible to co-operate – if only to ensure that Germany was held down – although he did envisage the possibility that the Soviets would prefer to set up a 'Communist Government in Germany'. The only way in which Britain could hope to continue to play a 'world role' alongside two such Powers would be for her to 'control as far as possible the policies of the local powers'; the Soviets might seek to do this, peacefully, in eastern Europe, and the British could follow suit, or even precede them, in the west.[5] With co-operation from America, or the Soviets, Britain's 'European "baby" might not prove a heavier burden than the country, in an economically weakened state, could bear; but was there a realistic chance of obtaining help from the other members of the 'Grand Alliance'?

The British tended to see themselves as a 'mediator' between their allies, and both Eden and Churchill deprecated attempts by FDR and Stalin to come together.[6] There were obvious reasons why the British did not want their two allies to get too close to each other: in the first place it would make them virtually redundant; and in the second it was likely that such a combination would be unstoppable, and any decisions which it reached would leave the British in the cold. Stalin's own inability to attend an inter-allied conference before November 1943 allowed the British to continue to fantasise about a special relationship with America; but it did not stop FDR from trying to arrange a meeting *à deux* with the Soviet leader.[7] The evident division between the western Powers, plus their inability to decide upon common foreign policy goals, allowed Stalin maximum leverage in return for minimum commitment, whilst their meagre contribution to the common struggle against fascism hardened his contemptuous view that his armies were the ones fighting the real war.[8]

Churchill's assumption of a 'natural' Anglo-American alliance tended to ignore the problems created by American anti-imperialism, but other believers in the 'special relationship' took measures between 1942 and 1944 to try to overcome this obstacle. Of course, as long as Churchill made comments about not having 'become the King's First Minister to preside over the liquidation of the British Empire',[9] no amount of diplomatic ingenuity would be able to sooth completely American fears about British imperialism. But it was hoped that a long-term campaign of information designed to 'educate' the Americans about the real nature of the Empire might have some effect.[10] In pursuit of this aim a visit by Amery to America in late 1942 was put off because of fears that he was regarded as 'the apostle of Tory Imperialism';[11] a visit by Eden himself, a very different sort of Conservative, would, it was hoped, serve all sorts of useful purposes. The other prong of British strategy was to make gestures which would appease progressive opinion in the United States.[12] At the end of 1942 they agreed in principle to join in an American declaration on colonial peoples, which made plain the eventual aim of emancipation; of course, as with Article 3 of the Atlantic Charter, none of this was meant to apply to India and Burma.[13]

It was India, above all other imperial problems, which provoked the most concern for the British in their relations with the United States. Convinced as the ex-Viceroy, Halifax, was of the invincibility of American prejudice and the 'abysmal ignorance' displayed by even 'the more intellectual elements',[14] the British could not, alas, afford to leave matters there. FDR's appointment of William Phillips as American High Commissioner with the rank of Ambassador, in late 1942, had caused a fluttering in the Viceregal dovecotes. The fear was expressed that this might be seen as an American attempt to mediate a settlement to the deadlock which still existed between Congress and the British;[15] indeed, so widespread was this view that FDR himself was forced to deny it at a press conference.[16]

Despite the confidence expressed by Halifax that an experienced diplomat like Phillips would not get himself involved in Indian politics,[17] the new Ambassador's reports to FDR did nothing to lessen the President's feelings that whatever else the war was being fought for, the preservation of the British Empire was not one of them. FDR's trip to Casablanca in January 1943 via French West Africa had done nothing to convert the President to the virtues of the imperial ethic.[18] Ever sensitive to charges that he was being outsmarted by wily 'limeys' who were using American power to bolster the British Empire, Phillips's reports in February confirmed FDR's low view of the worth of that Empire. Phillips made it clear that there was tremendous pressure from Indian leaders to 'relieve the present deadlock'.[19] Although he described the British position as 'not unreasonable' from 'their viewpoint', Phillips characterised that as being one which failed to comprehend the 'great impetus' given by the Atlantic Charter to the 'new idea ... of freedom for oppressed peoples'. Naturally, any American Ambassador would range himself on the side of such an 'idea', and Phillips suggested that they should try to bring the Indian politicians together and persuade them to agree on what form of government they wanted to adopt; America should, in effect, end the British policy of divide and rule.[20] FDR thought that such suggestions were 'amazingly radical for a man like Bill', and suggested to Hopkins that he might like to show the letter to Eden, who was then in Washington on his long-awaited (and postponed) trip.[21]

Hopkins did indeed show Eden Phillips's letter, but it is doubtful it impressed the Foreign Secretary; there was little in Washington which did. Eden found the Roosevelt administration a sight amazing to behold: Hull did not talk to Welles, and *vice versa*, whilst everybody strove to catch the President's attention; it was a 'mad house'.[22] He was alarmed by the President's 'sweeping opinions' and the 'cheerful fecklessness' with which he saw himself 'disposing of the fate of many lands'. Eden likened him to 'a conjuror, skilfully juggling with balls of dynamite, whose nature he failed to understand'.[23]

Eden's visit had its origins in his desire to discuss the post-war prospects with FDR;[24] but the fact that in so doing he might be able to outflank Churchill's obstructionism was not far from his thoughts. Given American sensitivity about the British Empire, both Eden and Halifax thought that it might be a good idea if the Americans were exposed to views less reactionary than those of the Prime Minister, whose statements on Indian and other imperial matters struck even normally sympathetic Americans as 'unconstructive and even cynical'.[25] Whatever Churchill's strong points, his attitude on colonial and imperial matters did not, as Halifax put it, do 'us much good here'.[26] But the Ambassador, sensitive to American opinion, was not sure that the time was ripe for a visit by Eden.[27] Although the Foreign Office was alive to the need for more propaganda in America,[28] little had been done by the beginning of 1943 except to set up a committee headed by Dick Law to co-ordinate publicity in the States.[29]

Halifax's misgivings were as understandable as Eden's reasons for pressing on. The fact was that American co-operation was vital to the future of British power, and it was essential to discover on what terms, if any, it was to be had. Fears that America would retreat into isolationism were fading, but they were being replaced by new ones. One phenomenon in particular caused concern, and that was the fate of the pre-war isolationists and interventionists. The number in the first camp seemed to be 'progressively diminishing', but the difficulty was now likely to be 'encountered from those who have gone over since Pearl Harbour [*sic*] from isolation and "America First" to a brand of interventionism which seeks to order the world purely in the selfish interests of the U.S.'.[30] Halifax, who took the view that any kind of interventionist was preferable to an isolationist, urged the Foreign Secretary not to be 'too frightened' of such people. The fate of some of the old isolationists, however, suggested that the British might not fare too badly at their hands should they win the 1944 election.

The possibility of Roosevelt losing the next election, assuming that he chose to stand, was not one which the British could afford to ignore. Churchill may have tied himself firmly to the agenda of FDR and the internationalising of the 'New Deal', but there were those British politicians, such as Beaverbrook, who urged him not to ignore the Republicans. The possibility of a Republican administration did not necessarily imply a return to American isolationism. Many leading Republicans, Willkie being only the most vocal, recognised the need for America to play a role in the world that befitted her strength. Republicanism might mean an end to FDR's 'Hallelujah foreign policy',[31] but that was not a thing which many British Conservatives would mourn. Indeed, the possibility of a Republican administration, with someone like former President Herbert Hoover as Secretary of State, suggested, at least if Hoover himself were to be believed, some intriguing possibilities. Where the 'interventionist' Democrats who had been all out to help Britain in 1940–1 now seemed to be chary of too close a connection with Britain, fearing that this might upset the Soviets and lead to America underwriting the British Empire,[32] the former isolationists seemed quite keen, as Hoover put it, 'that the closest cooperation between the British Commonwealth and the United States should be maintained now and after the war' to avoid Russian power coming to dominate the world.[33] This intriguing turnabout raised the possibility that a skilful use of '"the Bolshevist menace" would drive the isolationist Republicans to cooperate with us – even though we hold Stalin's right hand in our left', which might make it 'worth trying to stimulate further fear of the Russians by roundabout means'.[34] Such a *realpolitik* approach aroused protests within the Foreign Office, and Eden minuted crossly that, 'We must never try any tricks of this kind.' The British 'line' on Anglo-Soviet relations would remain: 'that the Anglo-Soviet treaty is a real and important thing to us, and that we intend to try all out to the full collaboration with Russia'.[35] The question of whether the Anglo-Saxons could co-operate with each other also, of necessity, included the question of what 'full collaboration' with the Soviets might involve.

Some of FDR's 'feckless' ideas should not have come as too great a surprise to the British Foreign Secretary. As far back as October, Halifax had warned him that FDR's ideas were 'pretty inchoate' and included 'explosive' and fanciful notions such as the disarmament of Poland and France in the post-war period.[36] Oliver Lyttelton, the Minister of Production, had been treated to similar stuff when he had met the President in November. FDR told him that everyone, except the four Great Powers, ought to be disarmed and that there should be an 'international police force' to keep the peace. When it came to the Soviet Union, FDR's view seemed to be, '"if you can't lick them, join them."' And since it was evident that 'we cannot lick the Russians', it was evidently going to be necessary to 'cooperate with them in everything'.[37]

All these opinions were ventilated by the President during his freewheeling conversations with Eden.[38] This was the first time that Eden had met FDR, but he should have been prepared, not least by Halifax's warnings, for what he had coming to him. Trying to 'reproduce the kind of atmosphere and background' against which FDR's conversations took place was, he had told Eden back in October, very 'difficult', particularly since the President himself 'said that he had had hardly any time to give serious thought to it all'.[39] Eden quickly concurred in this estimate.[40] Although the Americans welcomed the chance to talk with a Briton who did not hold Churchill's antiquated views on imperial matters,[41] they were very anxious to avoid giving 'any undue significance to it [the visit]'.[42] FDR's plans for the future may have appeared 'inchoate' to anyone not familiar with his style, but as so often talk camouflaged thought. The President did not want to appear to be siding with the British against the Soviets, nor did he wish to fan any remaining embers of isolationism; on the other hand, he did want to send the British Foreign

Secretary away in an optimistic frame of mind: hence the discursive nature of his talks with Eden.[43]

FDR's views may have struck Eden as extraordinarily unformed and fluid, reflecting, as they did, the President's tendency to keep all his options open for as long as possible, but they contained interesting assumptions about the Soviets. Convinced by his own experiences that Stalin would demand eastern Poland and the Baltic states, Eden warned the President that it would be unwise to assume that the Soviets could be fobbed off with less. FDR, when pressed, agreed that this might be so, but he thought that concessions might be extracted from the Soviets in return; he did not, however, say what these were. Although Eden does not appear to have made the connection, it seemed obvious enough that the President had in mind Soviet co-operation in his ideas on the future structure of the international order. Talking on 28 March, FDR waxed voluble on his conception of the four Great Powers taking 'all the more important decisions' and wielding the 'police powers of the United Nations';[44] all the other Powers would be disarmed.

This was just the sort of 'internationalist tripe' which imperially minded Tories like Amery feared that Eden might commit the Conservatives to backing.[45] Amery was certainly correct in supposing that Eden did not share his tastes for a return to 'a healthy and constructive Empire policy'; in the Foreign Secretary's mind such ideas belonged to where Amery appeared to be – back in the days of Joseph Chamberlain. But that did not mean that he was totally enamoured either of FDR's views, or those expounded by Hull. He disliked the cavalier way which FDR had with European boundaries – perhaps because it was reminiscent of Wilson, who, at the end of the day, had failed to secure backing for his policies from the Senate. Eden went to great pains to discover exactly what the limitations on the President's powers in foreign policy were.[46] It was, after all, no use putting up with FDR's rodomontades if it was going to be the Senate which disposed of whatever he proposed. If he could find himself in broad agreement with the idea that Germany might be disarmed and partitioned, Eden had no sympathy with the idea of disarming France – or of handing over her colonial territories to some form of 'international trusteeship'.

The question of the future of France was a central one to Eden's foreign policy; indeed, along with the Soviet alliance, one with France would be the cornerstone of any new European system. American support for Admiral Darlan after the invasion of North Africa in November 1942, and then for Giraud, his equally reactionary successor, aroused fears that all the Americans wanted was a French puppet.[47] These suspicions had been increased by the way in which FDR, after putting pressure on de Gaulle and Giraud to come to an agreement during the Casablanca conference, had casually gone behind Churchill's back afterwards and signed documents which recognised Giraud as the sole French authority in North Africa.[48] Although quick action by

General Eisenhower's new political adviser, Harold Macmillan, secured the annulment of the agreement, it remained a disturbing reminder that American priorities in Europe were not those of the British; Eden received others during his visit.

It was inevitable that Hull should have raised the question of France during Eden's visit. Through February the Secretary of State had complained to Eden about the malignant anti-American propaganda emanating from de Gaulle's London headquarters; he had even gone so far as to say that 'it seemed rather difficult to reconcile British financial support for de Gaulle with his behaviour'.[49] Hull reiterated his grievances at a meeting with Eden on 15 March, but got nowhere with them.[50] This was not surprising since the Foreign Secretary could hardly express frankly his view, which was that, 'The future government of France is a much more important matter for us than it is for the Americans, and there are limits beyond which we ought not to subordinate our French policy to theirs.'[51] Eden, however, had another reason for not responding thus – Churchill. The Prime Minister's unfavourable attitude towards the General had been greatly intensified by the latter's behaviour at Casablanca.[52] Churchill would have been quite happy to have followed America's lead. He had warned Eden in early March that de Gaulle was 'our bitter foe' and begged him not to 'allow our relations with the United States to be spoiled through our supposed patronage of this man . . . whose accession to power in France would be a British disaster of the first magnitude'.[53]

If Eden's Washington trip gave him the opportunity to expound his own ideas on the future to the Americans, and to bask in remarks such as FDR's comment that, 'He loves Winston as the man for the war, but is horrified by his reactionary attitude for after the war',[54] it did not allow him to escape altogether from the shadow of the 'old 'un'. It is difficult to believe that it was entirely accidental that Churchill chose to give a major speech on 'post-war reconstruction' just as Eden was in the middle of his talks with the Americans. The views he espoused, not surprisingly, commended themselves neither to his Foreign Secretary nor to the Americans.[55] Churchill not only offended American susceptibilities by not mentioning China as one of the Great Powers, but his advocacy of a purely European 'Council of Europe', which seemed to exclude America, had had, Hopkins told Eden, 'a very unfortunate effect over here', not least because it sounded suspiciously as though the Prime Minister was thinking in terms of spheres of influence rather than global collective security.

It was ironic that Churchill, who was doing so much to subordinate British policy towards Europe to American wishes, should have incurred criticism for seeming to want to exclude her from Europe.[56] Churchill had declared himself a 'good European', which he defined in terms of 'reviving the fertile genius' and 'restoring the true greatness of Europe'. He told his listeners that he favoured the achievement of 'the largest common measure of the integrated life of Europe that is possible without destroying the individual characteristics and traditions of its many ancient and historic races'. This sort of sonorous but vague rhetoric could mean anything, but what grated in the ears of the Americans was the lack of any mention of their participation. Eden assured them that the Prime Minister had only spoken on the 'spur of the moment' and had not meant that America should be excluded; it was an ironic position for the Foreign Secretary to be in.

Churchill's speech had indeed touched an American nerve. American diplomatic tradition, as well as Democratic sensibilities, abhorred the idea of spheres of influence, and the setting up of a European Council would, Hopkins told Eden on 27 March, 'give free ammunition to the isolationists', who would gladly settle for an American 'regional council' and an end to the global commitments which FDR contemplated. Moreover, it was essential to avoid offending the Chinese and the Soviets by giving the impression that the Anglo-Americans would 'settle the future of the world'. FDR was convinced that only a 'worldwide conception' of their 'international responsibilities' would reconcile the American people to the ending of isolation. His new world order was a global one, where there would be 'international trusteeship' for parts of the Japanese and the French Empires and where the Big Four would ensure the continuation of peace.[57] To Churchill's mind, such thinking showed the 'dangers which will attend any attempt to decide these matters while the war is raging'. He felt sure, he told Eden on 30 March, that 'while listening politely you have given no countenance to such ideas'.[58]

It was doubly ironic that it should have been Churchill, the chief apostle of the union of the 'English-speaking peoples', who should have been so suspicious whenever American war aims were raised, whilst it was the more sceptical Eden who sought to find ways of accommodating those aims to Britain's own. Churchill's persistent belief that such matters could be sorted out at the end of the war was tantamount to conceding the American vision of the post-war era – but since he did not expect to play much part in that future, he was perhaps not too worried; Eden could afford no such luxuries. The problems created by Churchill's *attentisme* were already evident with regard to the Soviet Union. Having failed to conclude a territorial agreement or to deliver a 'second front now', the British found themselves at many sorts of disadvantage in dealing with the Soviets; Eden's preferred policy might have delivered a diplomatic bonus, while Churchill's delivered nothing.

Soviet successes in the war against Germany, culminating in the surrender of the German armies at Stalingrad on 3 February 1943, made the war effort of the western allies look small beer. The decisions reached at Casablanca were 'too vague' for Soviet tastes, and, as Maisky put it in late February, he was finding it 'difficult' to persuade Stalin that 'our real and ultimate intention was not to take a "train-de-luxe" from Boulogne to Berlin, at the request of a defeated German army, rather than fight our way there'.[59] With allied convoys to the Soviet Union suspended and allied units in North Africa bogged down, the Soviet leader had every right to feel that he was bearing the heat of the day, and he was not slow to tell his allies that this was the case. He expressed his disappointment at the delays in the allied campaign and complained that the Germans had been able to transfer divisions from North Africa to the eastern front.[60] To a certain extent there was nothing Churchill could do except take this sort of thing on the chin. He told the Soviets that he 'fully understood and sympathized with Premier Stalin's sentiments'.[61] But the long delay in the completion of the Tunisian campaign placed a great strain on relations between the western Powers and the Soviets.

In one sense the 'Grand Alliance' as such hardly existed. At the military level there was little contact between the supposed allies, and Churchill, mindful that if the Soviets were given a vote, they would certainly side with General Marshall and those Americans who wanted to end the operations in the Mediterranean, was not anxious for them to have one.[62] Although Soviet impatience and frustration were understandable, there were those on the British side who wondered whether there might not be something more to Stalin's incessant demands for a 'second front now'. Was Stalin trying to 'divert us from the Balkans', or was he hoping that by undertaking the 'most difficult of the alternative operations' now, 'we and the Americans should suffer very heavy casualties'?[63] Although the possibility of such motives could not be altogether discounted, the British inclined, on the whole, to accept Soviet complaints at face value. As the Tunisian campaign neared its successful, if protracted, conclusion, Churchill even tried to lighten the tone by joking with Stalin that, 'I should like him to give me a fighting Pole for every German I catch in Tunisia from now on, and a Polish dependant, woman or child, for every Italian.' Such jokes were, the Prime Minister conceded, 'in questionable taste', but there were, he thought, 'moments and situations when they have their uses'.[64] This appealed to Stalin's grim sense of humour, for the Soviet leader replied that 'no Italian was worth a Polish woman and that it would not be fair on him'.[65] The lack of speed shown by the western Powers, and their inability to do much to help the Soviets in the face of feared German counter-attacks, deprived Churchill and FDR of much in the way of leverage when evidence emerged in April of the true nature of the ally they were on crusade with.

Churchill had once comforted himself, when thinking of the Soviet alliance, with the thought that 'it is much more easy to deal with the selfish than with the lunatics and the altruists';[66] that left open the question of how easy it would be to reconcile Anglo-Saxon moralism with Stalin's brand of *realpolitik*. The most obvious point at which these two clashed was over Poland. The British had a moral obligation to the Poles going back to 1939. Before 1941 Stalin had been an active partner in the partition of Poland and in the massacre of her citizens; although the events of June 1941 had transformed him into an enemy of Germany, it had not effected much of a change in his attitude towards the Poles. The Russian attitude was best summed up by Maisky, who described the Poles as 'brave' but 'nearly all mad'.[67] The Soviets complained about the activities of the Polish press in London, and whilst Eden defended the Poles in public, he was quite prepared to sacrifice Polish territory in the wider cause of the 'Grand Alliance'. The problem with this approach was that it assumed that Stalin would, as FDR hoped, concede something in return for western concessions, which ignored the advice of the Polish leader, General Sikorski, that it was 'never safe to believe what the Soviets said'.[68]

The British attitude towards the Soviet Union rejected both the views of those who would use the 'Bolshevist menace' to try to win over right-wing support in America, and those who imputed impure motives to the Soviet demands for an immediate invasion of Europe; it was best summed up in Ambassador Clark-Kerr's comment that it was necessary to build up 'real confidence in us' so that 'we shall be able to cooperate with the Russians after the war'.[69] It was, he admitted, 'melancholy to reflect that we must willy-nilly cooperate with this man [Stalin] not only in the beating of Hitler but in the years that will follow, and that upon this cooperation depends millions of lives and to a large extent the future of the world'.[70] It was, indeed, 'melancholy', not least because whatever chance had existed of winning Stalin's confidence, had been effectively destroyed by the failure to conclude a territorial agreement or to deliver a proper second front. Those, like the Ambassador to the Poles, Sir Owen O'Malley, who warned that a 'victorious and dynamic Russia' might 'lay a heavy hand' on the peoples of eastern Europe, suffered the fate of those whose fault it is to be right too early: namely, to be disregarded as 'unhelpful', and then to watch those who ignored their warnings take the credit for having spotted the danger just in time.[71]

The notion that the Soviets should try to 'win' the 'confidence' of the western allies was not one which appears to have occurred to FDR or Churchill, although the latter did, on occasion, become irritated at the constant Soviet carping. Perhaps neither allied leader felt able to say very much to the man whose armies were taking on the major part of the German army, and whose co-operation they were both seeking to create the post-war international order, but the revelations of April 1943 ought to have suggested that optimism about such a possibility was somewhat misplaced. The Germans announced in early April that they had found the corpses of thousands of Polish officers buried in Katyn, an area which the Soviets had held until June 1941. All the evidence indicated that the bodies had been there before that date and that they were the remains of the large number of Polish officers whose fates were unaccounted for when the communists released so many of their compatriots after Russia's entry into the war against Germany.[72]

Soviet sins had returned to haunt the 'Grand Alliance'. Genocide was an acceptable practice for an ally of Hitler's, but it was hardly the sort of thing which the Anglo-Saxons were fighting to promote.

The Churchill and Eden of late 1938 or late 1948 would have had no difficulty knowing how to react to such an outrage, but the demands of the war once more forced them into the sort of squalid compromise which had so often in the past aroused their stout moral consciences to protest. Churchill appears to have had no doubt from the start that the Soviets were indeed guilty, but that did not get the British Government anywhere.[73] When the Poles announced their agreement to the German suggestion of a Red Cross enquiry into the massacre, the Soviets made their move. On 23 April Maisky formally complained to Churchill that the Poles 'were a brave but very foolish race who had always mismanaged their affairs', and warned that 'Russia's patience was not inexhaustible'. Churchill did his best to hold the ring, telling the Soviet Ambassador that the proposal about the Red Cross was 'absolutely unacceptable', but rejecting the idea that 'the Polish Government had any desire to help the Germans'; he warned, in turn, that 'if Sikorski were to go, his successor would be more unacceptable to Russia'.[74] It soon became apparent that the Russians had their own ideas about 'Sikorski's successor'.

Stalin, professing the belief that it was all a put-up job by the 'Hitlerites' and 'Polish pro-fascist elements', accused Sikorski of having contacts with the Germans, and announced that his actions had put an end to relations between his Government and that of the heroic Soviet Union.[75] It was a sign of how little the British understood Stalin that Churchill and Eden responded to this fine piece of effrontery by asking him to postpone his decision because it ran the risk of losing Sikorski.[76] The notion that consideration for the position of a man described by the communist press as a 'fascist' would cause Stalin to desist from destabilising Anglo-Polish relations, whilst having a quaint charm of its own, failed to move him. The Soviet leader's response was to tell Churchill that the decision had already been taken and would not be revoked.[77] Further entreaties and arguments from Churchill met with the same fate. Despite some fears that the 'present Russian-Polish situation may develop into a Munich in reverse',[78] the Roosevelt administration did nothing more than add its voice to the British pleas; this had no effect. All that the British could do was pretend to believe Stalin's lies and try to secure some sort of reconciliation between him and the Poles; the notion of reconciliation being foreign to Stalin, nothing save grief came of this. Sikorski's death in an aircraft accident soon afterwards was a great blow to everyone except Stalin. Those who have alleged that Churchill in some way connived at Sikorski's death ignore not only the fact that he greatly admired the Pole, but that he also saw him as the one man who could keep the more virulent anti-Soviet Poles at bay. With Sikorski being replaced by the leader of the

Peasant Party, Stanislaw Mikolajczyk, émigré politics came to bedevil (even more than they had) attempts to broker a Soviet-Polish agreement.

It had been Churchill who had played the leading role in Anglo-Soviet relations, and if he had ceded the front seat on Anglo-American relations to Eden, his own visit to Washington in May 1943 not only made it apparent that this had been a temporary state of affairs, but also revealed the extent to which his was the controlling hand on British foreign policy. Although the chief reason for the Prime Minister's visit was to try to get the Americans to agree to a fresh extension of the Mediterranean campaign, his talks with American leaders trespassed all over territory Eden regarded as his own.[79]

Unsurprisingly, given that Churchill elaborated on the ideas which he had put forward in his speech in March, both FDR and Vice-President Wallace 'seemed a little anxious lest other countries should think that Britain and the United States were trying to boss the world'; since this was what Churchill wanted, their anxiety was understandable. Churchill told Halifax at the end of his visit: 'I made it perfectly clear to them that they ought not to be put off the necessary and rightful action by such suggestions.'[80] It never occurred to him that it was exactly the apprehension that the Soviets might come to feel this way which did influence FDR; no more did it occur to him that his derogatory remarks about China and his championing of the rights of France might strike the President as not being consonant with his vision of the future. But although the Prime Minister was not prepared to make the sort of break with traditional British foreign policy which abandoning the idea of the restoration of French power would imply, he was, to Eden's anger, prepared to agree with FDR that the time had come to break with de Gaulle.

Hull's anger with de Gaulle had not been appeased by Eden's anodyne comments in March, and FDR took the opportunity of Churchill's being in Washington to put pressure on him to rid the allied cause of the pestilential General. De Gaulle stood for most of the things which were inimical to FDR's international 'New Deal'. A traditionalist, a monarchist and a military man, the General believed in the restoration of '*la gloire de la France*' with a fervour that was religious in its intensity. Churchill had supported him in 1940, recognising in the strange, tall, proud Frenchman a kindred spirit. But there was in the relationship between the two men something of the historic rivalry between their two countries. When Churchill asked de Gaulle in November 1942 why he could not bend a little when he, the Prime Minister of Great Britain, had to defer to FDR, the General's haughty response was that it was precisely because France had nothing left but her pride that he could not compromise it.[81] De Gaulle's actions in seizing the islands of St Pierre and Miquelon from Vichy, in defiance of American wishes, set the tone for his relations with '*les américains*'. Now FDR saw the chance to get rid of the man. He showed Churchill a set of documents purporting to prove that de Gaulle was no better than a fascist and that his movement was tainted with treason, sadism and corruption. On the evidence the documents offered, Churchill recommended to the Cabinet that the time had come to break with de Gaulle.

But if Eden had been unable to convince Churchill to adopt his strategic thinking when it came to inter-allied diplomacy, he was able to rally the War Cabinet in defence of one of the pillars of his foreign policy. He took the view that to try to 'break' the General now would probably be to 'make him' and to 'make an enemy' of a man who was bound to have a great influence in post-war France. Ministers were no more enamoured of FDR's odd view that France could be ruled for a year after liberation by an allied general; Eden thought that this was 'not practical politics' and found it 'disturbing' that FDR's 'mind should run on such lines'. The Minister of Labour, Ernest Bevin, who was in the Cabinet as a symbol of the whole Labour movement and who commanded a power-base second only to Churchill's, threw his considerable weight (political as well as physical) behind de Gaulle, warning Ministers that there was 'considerable fear of growing . . . [American] influence' among trades unionists. In short, the point had arrived at which Ministers were not prepared to subordinate British interests to American fancies: 'We are sorry not to be more helpful, but we are convinced that the Americans are wrong . . . and advocate a line which would not be understood here, with possible evil consequences to Anglo-American relations.'[82]

Eden's success in preventing Churchill from wrecking Anglo-French relations was not, however, followed up by taking the one measure which might have improved them, namely granting diplomatic recognition to the newly formed French Committee of National Liberation. Churchill refused to imperil Anglo-American relations for 'the sake of a Frenchman who is a bitter foe of Britain and may well bring civil war upon France'.[83] So once again, Britain was unable either to formulate or to state a clear diplomacy of her own; it was not surprising that Eden seriously considered the possibility of going off to India as Viceroy and leaving Churchill to run the foreign policy over which he cast such a baleful shadow.[84]

7

Anglo-Saxon Attitudes

The dispute over policy towards France which rumbled on over the summer of 1943 reflected a profound cleavage between Prime Minister and Foreign Secretary concerning the conduct of British foreign policy. Churchill sought to identify himself with Roosevelt, but in Eden's eyes this was not something anyone charged with the conduct of British diplomacy ought to do. Roosevelt seemed to class France 'with Spain and Italy as a Latin power with no great future in Europe', but this was not the British view. As Eden reminded Churchill on 12 July, 'our main policy will be to contain Germany', and to that end it was necessary to complement the alliance with Russia with one with France; this 'will be indispensable for our security whether or not the United States collaborates in the maintenance of peace on this side of the Atlantic. . . . Europe expects us to have a European policy of our own, and to state it.'[1]

The clearest definition of Churchill's objectives came in a speech at Harvard on 5 September 1943. There he made an eloquent plea for 'Anglo-American unity'.[2] By 'unity' Churchill did not just mean that the two western allies should co-operate closely and in the most harmonious fashion; his vision was a more splendid and ambitious one – he looked to nothing less than the healing of the breach made in the reign of George III. The 'ties of blood and history' were so strong between Britain and America that they formed the base for a union of the two states. Citing Eisenhower's headquarters as an example of what he had in mind, Churchill urged that the wartime co-operation should be continued into the peace that was to come – the foundation for the future should be the 'fraternal association of our two peoples'. This was, indeed, a far-reaching vision, but it was not one shared by many Britons or Americans.

British attitudes towards the influx of American troops 'invading' their country during the war did little to further Churchill's grandiose hopes. The old joke that there were only three things wrong with American servicemen – 'they are over-paid, over-sexed and over here' – reflected a reality found in observations of a less jocular nature: 'The average Englishman, in his own heart, views with alarm the prospect of having his country swamped with Americans, his country desecrated by them, his restaurants crammed with them, his hedges broken, his houses damaged, his shops swept clean by them.' It was not just that the American servicemen were better paid, better fed and sexually active, which irritated the 'average Englishman'; there was also the fact that 'he had been taught to think of them [Americans] as noisy, boasting people, without our regard for other people's feelings, rights and property'.[3] Despite the attempts of the Ministry of Information, the American invasion of Britain did not lead to widespread admiration of America[4] – or even of Americans. The number of half-American illegitimate babies suggests that not everyone shared the views of those who disliked the 'invaders', but both the Foreign Office and the Ministry of Information recognised the force of anti-Americanism.[5]

But if there was little sign that Churchill's vision would appeal to his own countrymen, there was even less evidence to suppose that many Americans would fall under its spell. It was a measure of the changes wrought in American public opinion by participation in the war, and in particular of the replacement of isolationism by 'globalism', that all save the 'Anglophobe' Hearst press and the *Chicago Tribune* agreed with Churchill that American power carried with it responsibilities; but there agreement ended.[6] American public opinion was not ready to mortgage the future to an exclusive Anglo-American alliance, and it tended to agree with Josephus Daniels's *Raleigh News and Observer* that it was necessary to include 'Russia and China' because 'permanent peace hopes based on narrow alliance of great powers are doomed to frustration mainly because they inspire fear and jealousy in the world outside the alliance area'; security had to be 'collective' to be effective. Whether in favour of Churchill's general ideas or not, there was no significant strand of American opinion which was satisfied with the idea of a narrow Anglo-American alliance. The Republican *New York Post* preferred 'the broader, more courageous and more international view of the world' reflected in Willkie's best-seller, *One World*, as did FDR himself. Churchill may have thought that he could have a 'special relationship' and a fairly exclusive one, but there was nothing to suggest that any prominent American was likely to give him it.

Hostility to British imperialism and suspicion of British machinations were to be expected from the Hearst press and other former isolationist organs, but they were not alone in voicing criticism of the British. Congressional scrutiny of the terms of lend-lease, and in particular British resistance to the idea of supplying America with raw materials as 'reciprocal aid', threatened to create 'political reactions adverse to British-American relations'.[7] Given the prevalence of views that America ought to 'obtain something' for lend-lease, Halifax wondered whether the offer of permanent facilities at British naval bases might not be worth making.[8] But like Churchill's speech, this showed the gulf between British ways of thinking and those common in America. Churchill and Halifax were thinking in 'balance of power' terms, but this was anathema to American public opinion.

The American press attributed victories in North Africa and Italy to the

American army, and as far as the great American public was concerned, the British were just along for the ride.[9] Senate resolutions passed during the course of 1943 confirmed the view that an exclusive alliance with the British was the last thing most Senators wanted.[10] There was also continuing suspicion that the British might have pulled a 'fast one' over lend-lease, which was stirred up again in October when five American Senators issued a report highly critical of the way in which the administration had been 'outmanoeuvred at every point by the selfish but efficient agents of Britain'.[11] The Senators did not confine their criticisms to Britain and lend-lease, although the charge that Britain was changing labels on American goods sent to Russia and other areas was obviously damaging enough by itself. There were criticisms of a lack of British operations on the Indian and Burmese fronts and of British troops taking over territory in the Pacific conquered by the Americans; the British were also accused of not wanting to help in the war against Japan because they did not want to see a strong China, 'which might insist on the return of Hong Kong'. There was also criticism that the British were not drawing enough oil from their reserves in the Middle East, preferring instead to get American oil free.[12] All these charges and the comment that surrounded them in the American press fed on what one British diplomat called the 'ancestral American belief that [the British] . . . are very far-sighted and far "smarter" than they are'.[13] Because of that the allegations had a life of their own, outside of any truth which they might (or, as the British insisted, did not) contain. The notion that the British were playing the United States for a 'global sucker' was one of the things which made Churchill's aims for Anglo-American relations unlikely to be realised; the other lay in the perceptions of Franklin D. Roosevelt.

FDR's hopes for his brave new world rested largely upon the Soviets, not upon the fading and reactionary power of the British Empire. His conception of the 'four policemen' and of a global 'United Nations' presupposed, indeed demanded, Soviet co-operation and it was towards that end that he looked. He had not liked Churchill's idea about 'regional councils', seeing in it nothing more than a variation on the spheres of interest theme which dominated the outmoded diplomacy of the old world. At Quebec in late August, Churchill accepted the draft declaration put forward by Hull which foreshadowed the creation of a 'United Nations' organisation. There were no regional councils and, in accepting Hull's draft, 'Churchill in effect surrendered whatever hopes he had once had of pursuing an independent post-war policy'. Instead of 'relying on Britain's own strength and the support of a friendly and consolidated Europe, Churchill decided to pin his hopes upon America'.[14] But American hopes were pinned on Stalin.

Roosevelt's hopes of agreement with the Soviets are easy to deride, and with the advent of the Cold War they were duly derided; even now the criticism is often made that FDR's weakness towards the Soviets resulted in the subjugation of eastern Europe for half a century.[15] Roosevelt's defenders have focused on the complex realities which FDR faced, as well as pointing out that it was Soviet actions, not FDR's, which created the situation in which his hopes looked vain. In this situation, the argument goes, it would be 'naïve' to imagine that 'confrontation with the Soviet Union in 1943 would have meant self-determination for Poles and Balts in 1945'.[16] The realities of power, as Eden had predicted back in 1941, would always have militated against that. But there was more to it than that. From the perspective of a generation rendered cynical by the swift onset of a Cold War which threatened to destroy more than any 'hot' war had ever done, FDR did, indeed, seem a naïve idealist, but 'a world in which goodwill and common sense might prevail through some form of international association did not seem a fantastic vision to those who had suffered so much from two wars within a generation'.[17] These are the authentic tones of those touched by FDR's vision.

Two main questions arise in relation to FDR's hopes of doing a deal with Stalin: was it likely that the sort of deal that Stalin wanted would be acceptable to a western public opinion nurtured on propaganda about the Atlantic Charter? And even if such a 'deal' could be made acceptable, was it likely that it would induce Stalin to co-operate in building a world safe for the principles of that Charter? Time was to answer the first question in the negative, and it appears, to put it mildly, naïve to suppose that Stalin would ever have subscribed to the Atlantic Charter and what it stood for. But the evidence suggests that Roosevelt, the great idealist, was prepared to be a good deal more cynical than Churchill when it came to paying the price necessary for securing Soviet co-operation. Back in the 1930s, when Churchill was trying to cultivate Soviet support for an anti-Nazi front, Maisky had asked Churchill why it was that such a well-known anti-communist should now be so friendly, to which he had received the reply that 'Germany is the main enemy.' Maisky had told Stalin at the time that when Germany was out of the way, Churchill would regard communism as his next challenge.[18] Certainly Churchill's attitude at this stage of the war suggests that he was beginning to be assaulted by doubts about his ally, but until the Germans were defeated, he was prepared to swallow most of the doubts; the most he would do was commit them to paper occasionally. But tension caused by Polish affairs and by the western failure to deliver an 'effective second front' ensured that the course of Anglo-Soviet affairs ran far from smoothly. Churchill liked to see himself as a mediator between Roosevelt and Stalin, but that role was one FDR coveted – and given the state of Anglo-Soviet relations, it was a good deal more likely to fall to him.

Given his own hopes, Churchill was somewhat shaken to hear from Averell Harriman on 24 June that FDR had been trying to get the Soviet dictator to agree to a bilateral meeting.[19] Anglo-Soviet relations had been strained by the continuance of the campaign in the Mediterranean, and Churchill had, himself, been seeking a meeting with Stalin. Clark-Kerr had warned Churchill not to underestimate the 'resentment' which Stalin felt: 'his faith in our intentions has been severely shaken'. The Soviets thought that 'we and the Americans are not really playing fair but are deliberately allowing the Russians to bleed themselves to death'.[20] This seemed pretty rich to Churchill, who told the Ambassador to adopt a 'robust attitude to any further complaints', reminding him that the Soviets had 'stood by watching with complete indifference what looked like our total obliteration as a nation'. He was, he concluded, 'getting rather tired of these repeated scoldings, considering that they have never been actuated by anything but cold-blooded self-interest and total disdain of our lives and fortunes'.[21]

But as so often with Churchill, private toughness was accompanied by a more conciliatory public attitude. He explained the reasons for the allied decision to Stalin in a reasonable fashion, but was greeted in response with a message which, even by Soviet standards, was rude in the extreme. Stalin criticised both the Anglo-American strategy and the manner in which it had been decided, and concluded by stating that mounting a second front was a matter of urgency because it would 'reduce the colossal sacrifices of the Soviet armies in comparison with which the losses of the Anglo-American troops must be considered as modest'.[22] It was unlikely that the crop of rumours which began to sprout at this time about a possible Soviet–Nazi armistice were entirely accidental; Stalin was not averse to giving his allies something to worry about, even if they never returned the compliment.[23] Churchill feared that 'this is probably the end of the Churchill–Stalin correspondence from which I fondly hoped some kind of personal contact might be created between our countries'.[24] Stalin's attitude was understandable. With the Soviets about to engage in the battle of Kursk, in which units were to sustain casualties of 50 per cent in a head-on collision with the best units of the German army, Anglo-American hesitations about launching a cross-Channel operation because of fear of heavy casualties must have looked like cowardice, or worse. Given Stalin's suspicious nature, it is likely that he feared that he was being 'left hanging out to dry'.[25]

If Stalin's message was 'most unpleasant', then the revelation that FDR had been seeking a meeting with Stalin without himself being present was a nasty shock to the British Prime Minister, as his response showed. Asking FDR to 'excuse me expressing myself with all the frankness that our friendship and the gravity of the situation warrant', Churchill went on in his most portentous vein to warn of the use that 'enemy propaganda would make of a meeting between the heads of Soviet Russia and the United States at this juncture with the British Empire and Commonwealth excluded'.[26]

Roosevelt's desire to meet Stalin alone had roots partly in his own belief in the power of his personal diplomacy and partly in what he could glean about Soviet attitudes towards the Anglo-Saxons. Joseph Davies, the former

Ambassador to the Soviet Union, told Hopkins in late 1942 that the Soviets profoundly distrusted the British, and especially Churchill, whom they suspected of wanting military operations in the Balkans for purely political purposes. The former Soviet Ambassador in London, Maxim Litvinov, who was married to a British woman and who was by no means an Anglophobe, had told Davies that the British had 'purposely postponed the second front so that Russia would be "bled white through fighting Germany alone". After the war Britain would then "dominate and control Europe".'[27] Davies had advised FDR to meet Stalin by himself to convince him that America was not aligning herself with such imperialist designs. Ironically, in view of Churchill's hopes of acting as 'broker' between his two allies, Davies's view was that Stalin 'distrusted the broker more than he did the other party'.[28] On the other hand, however much Stalin distrusted the British, 'he *knew* Churchill, and had a treaty with him', and he knew that it was only the Americans who had prevented the British from recognising Soviet territorial demands. Churchill was thought to be 'realistic and not sentimental when realistics had to be faced'; it was thus necessary for FDR to evince a similar willingness – and until he did, it was unlikely that Stalin would welcome a bilateral meeting.[29] The vital issue for Stalin was the American attitude towards Poland's post-war frontiers. FDR told Davies: 'Why of course we will not fight Russia for Poland.' He did, however, want to see Stalin and 'talk to him about it and see whether I cannot convince him as to the manner in which his aims could be obtained with [sic] offending democratic public opinion'.[30]

But such conversations could only be conducted in private – and without Churchill. In response to Churchill's protests about the notion of a Roosevelt/Stalin meeting, the President cheerfully lied, fostering it on to the Soviet leader; but he still put forward arguments why it should take place.[31] Although he was to be burked of his ambition, FDR followed up his meeting with Churchill at Quebec in September 1943 with two tripartite meetings, including the first gathering of the 'Big Three', and he carefully avoided any appearance of Anglo-American collaboration beforehand.

FDR's caution, and his desire for a meeting with Stalin, are both understandable in the light of the Soviet leader's suspicions of the western Powers. Maisky (whose recall to Moscow in late 1943 prompted Foreign Office speculation that this might herald a hardening of Soviet policy)[32] confided his fears for the future to Churchill's old friend and current Minister to Syria and the Lebanon, General Louis Spears. Maisky was afraid that 'Russian grievances' might well 'endanger our relations not only in the closing stages of the war, but in the post-war settlement'. The 'major grievance' was the lack of consultation over strategy in May and the resulting decision to press on with the Mediterranean campaign. Maisky warned that if the Anglo-Americans delayed their second front until the Soviets had suffered the heavy losses which an advance into German territory would entail, 'the Russians would conclude that we and the Americans were trying to capitalise the Russian victories to our own advantage'. Nor did the Russians like the arrangements which had been made to handle control of Italy. The Allied Control Commission did not have the powers which the Soviets thought it would have, and they could not help wondering if this was a way of giving the appearance of co-operation without conceding the reality. Moreover, the arrangements for the imminent conference of Foreign Ministers in Moscow inspired no more confidence; the Anglo-Saxons seemed reluctant to discuss the second front and were equally reticent – particularly the Americans – about drawing up a detailed agenda. Maisky denied that Russia had any desire to see Poland and other states go communist, but insisted that such countries should have 'democratic . . . by which he clearly meant governments of a left-wing tendency'. He discounted the possibility of America remaining in Europe after the war and thought that it would be 'for Britain and Russia to settle the fate of Europe between them'.[33] This is what Eden had been burked of in 1942 by Churchill's insistence upon bowing to American pressure; the irony was that by late 1943 it seemed as though FDR might be ready to concede what he had vetoed the previous year – provided the circumstances were right.

Stalin's conduct at Moscow, Tehran and then in the following year bears out Maisky's general view of the Soviet position. The assessment which Roosevelt and Eden both made, which was that Soviet policy was governed by suspicion of the west and considerations of *realpolitik*, does not seem to have been wide of the mark.[34] At Moscow in late October, the first thing Stalin asked was when Operation 'Overlord' would take place. When Eden, in an attempt to reassure him, said that he 'well knew my Prime Minister was just as keen on hurting Hitler as he was', Stalin responded 'with a gust of laughter that Mr Churchill had a tendency to take the easy road for himself and leave the difficult jobs to the Russians'.[35] Throughout the conference the Soviets made plain their unwillingness to allow any political interference by the western Powers in the affairs of eastern Europe, and with Hull taking the view that he did not 'want to deal with these piddling little things',[36] the Foreign Secretary was left to deal with the Polish question. Molotov, the Soviet Foreign Minister, made it clear that he regarded Soviet-Polish relations as a matter for the two countries concerned – unless, of course, the British wanted to help by getting rid of some of the more objectionable members of the émigré Polish Government.[37] The urgent question of co-operation between the soldiers of the Polish Home Army and the advancing Soviet forces was left unsettled.

Roosevelt was not unwilling to respond to the Soviet mood. Although his refusal to set a detailed agenda for the Tehran conference in November aroused Soviet suspicions, it reflected his characteristic preference for personal diplomacy. He saw the first meeting of the 'Big Three' as an opportunity to 'obtain a clear idea as to the extent to which Russian co-operation could be expected in the post-war period'. If agreement was reached about what to do with Germany, then FDR did not think that the question of Russia's western frontiers was 'insuperable'. It should be possible, Roosevelt believed, 'to speak quite frankly to Stalin' and to 'say that we could have no idea of trying to prevent Russian occupation of such territory as they thought essential to their security, but that we had considerable difficulty in making this acceptable to our peoples'.[38] Roosevelt was prepared to deal in *realpolitik* – indeed, much more so than Churchill.

It was an essential part of FDR's strategy that Stalin should be given no grounds for supposing that he was 'ganging up' with Churchill, and so he resisted British pressure for a meeting in advance of Tehran.[39] When he did give way in the face of Churchill's importunity, it was with the insistence that Chiang Kai-shek was present. Even then Roosevelt turned up in Cairo two days later than he had promised, which left Churchill no time at all to co-ordinate Anglo-American military and political strategy before the meeting with Stalin; FDR was not worried by this.[40] Harriman had reported the Soviet 'delight' at discovering during the Moscow conference that Eden and Hull had not 'come with a united front', but he had also warned of the problems which the President would encounter at Tehran. It hardly took Harriman or anyone else to predict that Stalin would want to annex the Baltic republics and the eastern third of Poland, nor that he would insist on a 'friendly' government in Warsaw. It was, perhaps, indicative of American optimism that Harriman should have told FDR in early November that 'the problem of Poland is even tougher than we believe'.[41] But it was not so 'tough' that FDR could not sort it out. He told Stalin at Tehran that America would not fight him over eastern Europe and Poland, and confined himself to warning that Soviet claims would have to be made in a way which did not upset western opinion – particularly that of six or seven million Polish Americans.[42] This was the sort of talk Stalin could understand, even if he was 'convinced that the American position was merely a ploy to throw Russia off guard'.[43]

From Roosevelt's point of view, which was to find out whether co-operation with the Soviets was likely to be practicable, Tehran was an encouraging conference. His 'primary political objective' had been to 'get Stalin's agreement for the establishment of the United Nations at the end of the war', and the Soviet leader had not only welcomed the idea, but had agreed with FDR that it should be organised on a global rather than the regional basis desired by Churchill.[44] In this, as in other areas, American-Soviet agreement left the British in the cold. Stalin had agreed with FDR that the primary military commitment of the western allies should be the invasion of France, which meant that 'Overlord' went to the top of the agenda and stayed there; it was the end of Churchill's dreams of pursuing operations in the Balkans.[45] FDR and Stalin also made common ground on the future unimportance of France and on the possible disposal of French and Italian colonial Empires. The emblematic moment for the cementing of the new diplomatic axis was on the first night of the conference, when Stalin 'needled' Churchill 'without mercy' on the subject of whether the British were really committed to 'Overlord' and accused him of being 'soft' on Germany.[46] FDR joined Stalin in suggesting that Germany should be dismembered and in his gay little joke that the entire German General Staff should be shot, although the President, less severe than the Soviet leader, was prepared to shoot only 49,000 instead of 50,000. Churchill left the room and had to be coaxed back.[47] Far from 'ganging up' on Stalin, FDR seemed to be ganging up with him, even to the point of refusing Churchill's request on 29 November that they should lunch together *tête-à-tête*.[48] Churchill later dramatised this by saying that it was at Tehran that he had realised for the first time 'what a small nation we are. There I sat with the great Russian bear on one side of me with paws outstretched, and on the other side the great American buffalo, and between the two the poor little English donkey who was the only one . . . who knew the right way home.'[49] This has usually been cited approvingly as a sign of Churchill's prescience, but it would be more accurate to take it as an indication of his limitations.

At the centre of Churchill's attitude towards the Soviet Union was a profound ambivalence. On the one hand, Churchill was presenting the Second World War as a crusade against totalitarian evil, and on the other, he was conducting it with the help of one of the most evil dictators even the twentieth century had spawned. He resolved the problem by resorting to his usual gambit of leaving political and diplomatic questions concerning the future until after the war, using *raisons de guerre* to justify any concessions to Stalin. But these tactics were productive of nothing save prolonged diplomatic arguments over Poland. Eden had warned that if the war was won, the Soviets would be in a position to take what they had asked the western Powers to concede in 1942, and now Roosevelt, recognising the truth of that observation, seemed willing to trade territorial concessions for agreement on the basic structure of the post-war world. It was a rather brutal *realpolitik*, but at least Roosevelt had an objective in mind in return for his concessions; Churchill and the British simply found themselves making concessions and getting nothing for their pains except recriminations.

During early 1944 the British pressed Mikolajczyk, the Polish leader, to accept the 'westwards' shift of Poland which Stalin had demanded at Tehran,[50] but the Poles showed no taste for concessions. The Soviets wanted the Poles to accept the Curzon line and the removal from the Government of anti-Soviet elements. Harriman's view was that as Soviet troops advanced further, Stalin's position would become increasingly intransigent, and that the sooner the London Poles agreed to his current demands, the better.[51]

The Curzon line, demanded by the Soviets, was 'an attempt to find a

Two appeasers, 1940. Ambassador Kennedy wanted to appease Hitler, Prime Minister Churchill wanted to appease Roosevelt.

Signing away part of the Empire. Churchill and Ambassador J.G.(Gil) Winant sign the 'bases for destroyers deal' 1941.

The American Peace. Roosevelt using a Churchillian 'V' sign as Churchill signs the Atlantic Charter, 1941.

Churchill and Roosevelt on board the *Prince of Wales* with Elliott Roosevelt standing by.

The man in the (crumpled) White Suit. Churchill greets Harry Hopkins in Quebec in 1943. Brendan Bracken, in the middle, avoids contemplation of his leader's attire.

The 'Bridegroom' (General Henri Honoré Giraud, under American starting orders) and the 'Bride' (General Charles de Gaulle, refusing to take orders) square up to each other at Casablanca in 1943 with their backers looking on.

Sitting pretty, Roosevelt and Churchill contemplate success. Casablanca 1943.

Eyes right for Empire. Churchill eyes Roosevelt, who in turn eyes the Sultan of Morocco at Casablanca in 1943, Hopkins (third from left) looks on.

Roosevelt contemplates his notes, Churchill makes a point, Casablanca 1943.

Talking to the press at Casablanca.

Talking to the Chiefs of Staff. Churchill with 'Pug' Ismay and Lord Louis Mountbatten behind him. General Sir Alan Brooke to the right of FDR, with Sir Peter Portal behind him (Harry Hopkins is to the right of Portal).

Churchill and Eisenhower – when the former was in command in 1944.

Pondering the future. Churchill, Roosevelt and the Canadian Prime Minister, Mackenzie King, at Château Frontenac in Quebec, 1944.

Feeling the strain. FDR looking haggard and ill at Yalta in February 1945.

reasonably close approximation to an ethnographic frontier for Poland in 1919–20'.[52] It ran along the border of East Prussia southwards to the River Bug and thence southwards across the Carpathians and the frontier of what had been Austrian Galicia. It had been subsequently modified to give the Poles the city of Lvow and the oil-bearing region of Drohobycz. But in the Polish-Russian war of 1921–3, the Poles did well enough to insist on a border well to the east, giving them 46,000 miles of former Russian territory, with a population of four million, of whom only a quarter were ethnically Polish. The Poles also picked up 18,000 square miles of former Austrian territory, with another four million people, as well as acquiring, in their war with Lithuania, the city of Vilnius (Wilno). The 1921 treaty of Riga, in which these borders had been delineated, had never been accepted by the Soviets with a good grace, and they had used the Nazi–Soviet pact to amend it drastically. Now they wished to serve the Poles as they had been served: the boot was, after all, on the other foot. The new Soviet border was far to the west even of the original Curzon line; the Soviets also claimed Vilnius, as they were occupying Lithuania.[53] Stalin wanted to keep his loot from the deal with Hitler; the London Poles, unsurprisingly, objected, claiming that they did not have the right to sacrifice half the national territory and eleven million inhabitants without the permission of the Polish people.[54]

Churchill told Mikolajczyk on 20 January that he wanted the Poles 'not only to accept' in principle the Soviet offer of compensation in the west, but to do so 'with enthusiasm'. It was, he told the Poles, 'the best that they could hope to obtain'. Neither Britain nor America was prepared to fight the Soviets on this issue, for, as Churchill told Mikolajczyk, 'we never entered the war for the eastern frontiers of Poland'.[55] This, of course, was perilously close to the language used by Neville Chamberlain in 1938 and 1939 – reality made strange bedfellows. But neither Chamberlain then nor Churchill now was prepared to take the further step which Roosevelt seemed inclined towards – of acknowledging that unless you were prepared to go to war over the issue of the frontiers of eastern Europe, it was best to sell the Poles down the river for as good a price as could be extracted in the circumstances. But even Roosevelt could not specify how he would persuade a democratic electorate weaned on the rhetoric of moralising liberalism to accept such a policy – and there were, as Churchill now discovered, plenty who would use against his new 'realism' the morally loaded arguments with which he had undermined Chamberlain.

Sir Owen O'Malley, the British Ambassador to the Poles, told Eden on 22 January that the question of the actual frontiers of Poland was secondary to the issue of principle: was Poland's independence to be accepted or not? Would any territorial changes be the result of 'the free consent and goodwill of the parties concerned, or of force'? Was the 'basis of international relations ... to be law' or would 'an exhibition of power-politics ... be covered with our approval'? And finally, could 'England . . . be relied upon to act in what was understood to be the spirit of the Atlantic Charter'? If Churchill thought, as his actions suggested, that this was simply 'a chapter in the business of winning the war', 'his perspective and his proportions' were 'faulty'. As it was already probable that the allies were going to win the war, it was 'high time to lend increased weight to things which bear primarily on international relations after the conclusion of the war'. Referring to the 'ties supposedly created between Russia and ourselves at Tehran', O'Malley described them as 'feebler than he [Churchill] thinks'. There was, the Ambassador thought, 'small warrant for the belief that the Soviet Government's actions will be determined by anything but pure *"raison d'état"'*. He did not think that the Soviet offer was 'fair', and he believed that the British offer to try to help secure a resumption of Polish-Soviet relations was probably 'illusory'. The 'real choice before us seems to me, to put it brutally, to lie between on the one hand selling the corpse of Poland to Russia and finding an alibi to be used in evidence when we are indicted for abetting a murder; and on the other hand putting the points of principle to Stalin in the clearest possible way'; he should be warned that it might become necessary to reveal his actions to allied public opinion. This might fail to move Stalin 'from violent and illegal courses, but it would be on record that we had done our utmost to do so'.[56]

This all sounded very good, but what did it amount to in practice? Lord Halifax once commented that 'perhaps the greatest difficulty in the conduct of foreign affairs, and the one least appreciated by those not actually engaged in it, is the fact that the ideal policy is scarcely ever practicable';[57] and he thought that 'we go badly wrong if we allow our judgement of practical steps to be taken to be perpetually deflected by our moral reactions against wrong that we can in no circumstances immediately redress'.[58] Churchill and Eden would both have disapproved of such *realpolitik* in 1938, but in power and with responsibility, they both now sang to its ageless tune. As Eden put it in response to O'Malley's moralising, 'the real choice surely lies between doing our best to see that a free and independent Poland emerges after this war, or seeing the Russians overrun the country'.[59] Even Churchill was driven to telling Mikolajczyk and his colleagues that if they did not come to an agreement with the Soviets, 'he must look at the matter from the British point of view and make his own agreement with Stalin'.[60] These were not very moral arguments, but they answered the case better than O'Malley's.

It could, of course, have been argued that Churchill had had little choice but to pay the price which Stalin wanted since the only alternative, pulling out of the war at an earlier date, would have been impossible. But although this line has been used by his admirers, it was not used by Churchill himself, who, when he denied rumours emanating from Russia that he was indeed interested in a separate peace,[61] told Stalin on 24 January 1944:

I am sure you know that I would never negotiate with the Germans separately.... We never thought of making a separate peace even in the years when we were all alone and could easily have made one without serious loss to the British Empire and largely at your expense.[62]

In sharp contrast to all those admirers who have strenuously denied that an honourable peace could have been made in 1940 or 1941, Churchill knew better. Peace could have been made. It would not have depended upon 'trusting' Hitler, but rather upon the presumption that he would be bound to come into conflict with Stalin. That would, of course, have meant taking a risk on the outcome of a Soviet-German war, but such a bruising encounter would have left neither side unscathed and might even have resulted in both Powers finishing up exhausted. But that was all in the past – and now 'our triple fortunes' were 'marching to victory'; but the Polish 'test case' did not suggest that it would be one in which the moral aims for which Churchill had decided to fight on would be realised.

Indeed, the implacable O'Malley, in his role as the ghost of Churchill circa 1938, accused the Prime Minister of forcing the Poles into 'a "second Munich"', warning that 'what in the international sphere is morally indefensible generally turned out in the long run to have been politically inept'.[63] Churchill hotly refuted this suggestion, denying that forcing the Poles to accept the Curzon line was 'morally indefensible'. It was, he claimed, 'no more than what is right and just for Russia'. But as so often in a Churchill memorandum, hostages to fortune given with one paragraph were retrieved in the next one: 'If of course the view is adopted that Russia is going to present herself as a new Nazi Germany ideologically inverted, we shall have to make what head we can against another tyranny.'[64] This was more easily said than done; but it had been said, and if things should turn out that way, Churchill would be able to quote himself to show how prescient he had been.

But in early 1944 Churchill was more concerned with forcing the Poles to accept the 'cold bath' designed for them. When he saw Mikolajczyk on 16 February, all pretence at morality was flung aside.[65] Churchill had prepared a telegram for Stalin in which the Poles conceded his demands, but Mikolajczyk could and would not accept the loss of Vilnius. Churchill told him bluntly that if that was the Polish position, they were abdicating all possibility of having any influence on the situation: 'We would remain in closest relations with the Russians. Poland would then be little more than a grievance and a vast echoing cry of pain.' 'Nothing', Churchill continued, 'would have been achieved', the Poles would have 'no place of their own to live in', no compensation and no agreement. All this was true enough, but the Prime Minister took leave of reality when, in an effort to secure Mikolajczyk's agreement to his draft telegram, he told him that, 'If the Russians departed from such an agreement their position would be a bad one.' Fortunately for his own credibility, he did not elaborate on this interesting prospect. Instead, he escaped back to reality, telling the Polish leader that if the Russians 'did in fact prove untrustworthy it would indeed be a bad prospect for all the world but worst of all for the Poles'. Churchill's statement that 'Britain would always fight against tyranny in what ever form it showed itself' was no comfort to the beneficiaries of the 1939 British guarantee; Mikolajczyk did not need telling that 'we would do our best but this would not save Poland'. Churchill then moved away from the issues at question by reproaching the Poles for their attack on Teschen after the Munich agreement; this, in his mind, precluded the Poles from talking about 'another Munich'. If making one mistake precluded one from having an opportunity to make others, the Prime Minister would have been put out to grass decades ago. His very bluster showed that he was no happier than Eden, Harvey or Permanent Under-Secretary at the Foreign Office, Sir Alexander Cadogan, with what Britain was having to do. Yet nowhere did Churchill approach FDR, nor did he or the Foreign Office try to enlist American support in their efforts to help the Poles. The man who had criticised Chamberlain for not enlisting the help of the 'Grand Alliance' against Hitler was committing exactly the same mistake. But like Chamberlain, he must have been aware, at least after Tehran, that he could expect little from the Americans except for words.

In the end there was only so far that bullying Mikolajczyk could take the British Government. Churchill had to agree to a compromise, and he telegraphed to Stalin on 21 February that the Poles were prepared to admit that the Riga line 'no longer corresponds to realities'. However, since the compensation which Poland was to receive could hardly be announced in advance (it would certainly have stiffened German morale yet further – and it would have made the Atlantic Charter look a little sick), Churchill suggested that the formal demarcation of the frontier be left until the end of the war; the question of the status of Lvow and Vilnius was left obscure. The Soviet demand for changes in the Polish Government was also rejected, but changes were promised.[66] Speaking in the Commons on 22 February, Churchill tried to assuage Conservative fears by pledging that both Britain and the USSR were committed to the 'creation and maintenance of a strong integral independent Poland as one of the leading Powers in Europe'.[67] However, his statement that no particular frontiers had been guaranteed upset the Poles, who regarded it as giving 'the whole Russian case to them in advance',[68] and they issued a 'semi-official statement' on 25 February in which they made it clear that they did not accept the Curzon line frontier.[69]

It was all academic. When Stalin saw Clark-Kerr on 28 February, he 'attempted to dismiss with a snigger' the position of the Polish Government as described in the Prime Minister's message.[70] When the Ambassador said that, despite the 'semi-official' statement, the Poles would not 'disavow our action', the dictator's incredulity broke through: 'Is that serious? How handsome of them.' For the man who had broken the kulaks, starved the Ukraine, seen his own wife commit suicide and left his only son to languish in a German prisoner-of-war camp, the whole thing was obviously too risible for words: the London Poles depended upon the British for everything, the British should tell them what to do and make sure they did it; after all that was what he was doing with his own Poles. He rejected with contempt any suggestion of having the United Nations set boundaries. He repeated, as was his fashion, his 'simple' demands: 'the Curzon line and reconstruction of the Polish Government'.[71]

Churchill's attempt to soften Stalin's hard line by reminding him of the broader context in which he saw the Polish affair backfired badly. In a message of 7 March 1944 Churchill told Stalin that he was being given the Curzon line frontier 'with the blessing of your Western Allies at the general settlement', which had to be worth something. Force, he reminded Stalin (who had no need of any reminder), 'can achieve much but force supported by the goodwill of the world can achieve more'.[72] The Ambassador warned that Stalin would not like the use of the word 'force', and nor did he.[73] After an ominous silence and then complaints about 'leakages' in the British press,[74] Churchill attempted to calm the approaching storm by flattering Stalin on the achievements of his army; he expressed the 'earnest hope that the breakdown which has occurred between us about Poland will not have any adverse effect upon our cooperation in other spheres'.[75] But given the importance which Stalin attached to Poland, it was hardly likely that Churchill's hopes would be realised; unlike Roosevelt, he had not seen that agreement with the Soviets must follow concessions over Poland, not precede them.

On 25 March Churchill received Stalin's response. The Soviet dictator complained that his messages and those delivered by Clark-Kerr were 'full of threats concerning the Soviet Union' and that 'the method of threats is not only incorrect in the mutual relations of allies but is also harmful and leads to contrary results'. As the Ambassador had predicted, Stalin resented the use of the word 'force' by Churchill, claiming that the British were now trying to 'qualify the Curzon line as inequitable and the struggle for it as unjust. I can on no account agree with such an attitude.' He accused Churchill of 'breaking the Tehran agreement', by which the Soviets still stood. After stating that the Soviets were 'shedding blood for the sake of the liberation of Poland', Stalin rejected any claim that there should be any United Nations interference in the delineating of the Soviet-Polish border, and he went on to condemn the 'émigré' Polish Government, which he compared to that of the Serbian General Mikhailovich.* The accusations flowed on, with the British being represented as denying the 'emancipatory character of the war of the Soviet Union against German aggression' in an effort to 'discredit' it. As for Churchill's making a statement in the Commons, 'that is your affair', but if he

---

* Mikhailovich was considered a 'fascist' by the Soviets.

did so, Stalin would 'consider that you have committed an unjust and unfriendly act towards the Soviet Union'. After the usual tortured Marxist prose style, Stalin concluded with the customary Marxist double-speak. Professing his own desire for 'collaboration' with Britain, he expressed his 'fear' that 'the method of threats and discrediting, if it continues in the future, will not conduce to our collaboration'.[76]

This was why the British could not hope to mediate with Stalin. Churchill insisted on genuinely trying to mediate on an issue where Stalin wanted compliance. As he was to tell Churchill later that year, Russia did not interfere in France or Belgium, so why did the British interfere in Poland? Churchill, taking the view that 'to argue with the Russians only infuriates them', decided that a period of dignified silence was the only practicable policy for the moment. He was 'anxious to save as many Poles as possible from being murdered', but he did not see how anything could be done to help them now. He feared that once the Anglo-American forces landed in France, the Soviets would 'have the means of blackmail, which they have not at present, by refusing to advance beyond a certain point, or even tipping the wink to the Germans that they can move more troops into the west'. This, then, was where his efforts to 'put myself in sympathy with these Communist leaders' had led: 'I cannot feel the slightest trust or confidence in them. Force and facts are their only realities.' In the face of such a prospect Churchill felt that 'every effort must be made to reach complete agreement with the United States, and Poland is an extremely good hook'.[77] However, with FDR also 'fishing' – but for Stalin – who would 'hook' whom?

II
A 'Special Relationship'?

8

A Suitable America?

Behind Churchill's American policy was the assumption that the moral credit of 1940–1 could be converted into influence upon American policy. Like many Americanophiles, Churchill imagined that as America stepped on to the global stage she would need a wise old mentor, and he had himself and his country cast for the role. This now seems a strange fantasy, but it was one which bedevilled British diplomacy towards America throughout the period dealt with here. In attempting to outline the 'essential of an American policy' in 1944, one diplomat defined this attitude perfectly. Britain's traditional desire to prevent any one Power from assuming a dominant position was suspended in the case of America: 'it must be our purpose [not] to balance our power against that of America, but to make use of American power for purposes which we regard as good'. British policy should be directed towards helping to 'steer this great unwieldy barge, the United States, into the right harbour'.[1] The idea of using the 'power of the United States to preserve the Commonwealth and the Empire' had a quaint charm of its own, given what was known about Roosevelt's attitudes towards the Empire, but it was a perfect example of the way in which the British managed to delude themselves about America. This was on a par with Harold Macmillan's famous remark in 1943 that the British should consider themselves the 'Greeks in the new Roman Empire'. This image of the British as the subtle intelligence guiding America's brainless brawn was most flattering to the egos of the British ruling elite, who, having made a pretty ghastly job of managing their own *imperium*, had the nerve to imagine that they could handle America's; but even a Balliol man should have remembered that in the Roman Empire the Greeks were slaves. This condescending attitude towards America and her inhabitants vitiated British policy towards the United States. The Foreign Office could accept, without a blush, the statement that although 'the American may feel he is more efficient in business administration, in inventiveness, in techniques and in mass production', he 'will, almost without realizing it, accept Britain in thought, in politics, and in standards generally as an exemplar of quality'.[2] This led to a discounting of any sense of 'rivalry' since it was assumed that the sense of 'community' would always prevail. But by early 1944 there was ample evidence to suggest that the Roosevelt administration had goals of its own which were inimical to Churchill's. Hopkins himself, beginning by early 1944 to play an active role in Anglo-American relations once more, warned Halifax that if FDR was 'going to run' in 1944, they would 'probably find' him 'doing things we should not like too much – lease-lend, dollar balances, trade, palling up with U[ncle] J[oe], partly in order to dispel any damaging impression that he was in our or your pocket, and partly because he will be getting a good deal of not always good advice'.[3]

Hopkins's predictions were remarkably accurate, but he had missed out one obvious explanation for FDR's actions – that the President had a policy of his own which did not involve underwriting the British Empire; but it would hardly have been tactful to have mentioned that to Halifax. There were certainly many indications that this was the case. The Labour leader and Deputy Prime Minister, Clement Attlee, wrote to Churchill in June 1944, after the meeting of Dominion Prime Ministers in London in May, to say that the Dominion High Commissioners were 'considerably exercised in their minds as to the habit of prominent Americans, including members of the Administration, of talking as if the British Empire was in process of dissolution'.[4] Attlee thought that it 'would be well for the Americans, whose knowledge of Dominion sentiment is not extensive, to be aware that the British Colonial Empire is not a kind of private possession of the old country, but is part of a larger whole in which the Dominions are also interested'. One of Churchill's motives in convening the imperial conference had been the feeling that it was 'high time that the British Empire in its collective united aspect should put itself solidly on the map' vis-à-vis the 'mighty force of the Soviet Union' and the 'great Republic of the United States'.[5] Yet having said this much, Churchill spent the rest of the conference regaling the assembled Prime Ministers with dramatic accounts of impending operations in Normandy. What seemed to escape British Ministers was the depth and sincerity of American distaste for the British Empire. They were convinced that the American attitude stemmed from their 'almost complete ignorance regarding conditions in British colonial territories', and that what was needed was a publicity campaign in the United States telling the natives about all the good things which the Empire was doing.[6] Linlithgow had a clearer view of the possibilities of being able to 'buy off [American] ill-feeling, misunderstanding and prejudice'. Back in January 1943 he had told Churchill and the War Cabinet that he did not believe 'that we shall do anything of the sort', not only because 'the element in that country which has any real understanding of ... major colonial problems is very small', but also because of the possibility that electoral changes 'may render completely out of tune a policy which we have made great sacrifices to support'.[7] The Viceroy's opposition to the Declaration on Colonial Policy, which Hull and the Americans spent much of the year trying to foist on to the British, was valuable in helping resist American pressure, but what should have been worrying Churchill was the existence of that pressure.

It was all very well fighting a rearguard action against agreeing to specific statements, but the continuing American drive towards getting the British to commit themselves to a multilateralist position on world trade and monetary policy foreshadowed the creation of an international economic order inimical to the continued existence of an imperial trading bloc. The ideology of the Atlantic Charter was a liberal one, and however much the British Government might try to construct for itself exclusion clauses, the foreign policy pursued by Churchill towards Washington, as well as the prospect of needing American help should things fail to work out with the Soviet Union, all pointed to a future as America's pensioner.

The British may have assumed that they could deploy American power to make up the deficiencies in their own armoury, but the Americans were making their own assumptions about the future of British power. From the beginning of the lend-lease programme both Hull and Morgenthau realised that 'there could be no question of the British Government's repaying us in full either in money or in goods'; repayment would come in the form of the British agreeing to enter the brave new multilateral economic system which the State Department and the Treasury saw emerging from the discussions over Article VII of the master lend-lease agreement (which called for an end to imperial preference). America wanted a Britain fit to be her junior partner in the new world order.[8] Hull felt sincerely that 'no system of security can be expected to work unless adequate measures are taken in the field of world economics to hold out hope of a tolerable standard of living to all peoples'. This meant an end to the sort of protectionist commercial and economic policies which had been pursued by European countries before the war. Bureaucratic in-fighting between the State Department and the Treasury over whether the stress in 'international economic policy' should come on the first or second word slowed down the American effort to dragoon the British into line, but by late 1943 things had moved far enough for talks to begin between British and American experts about the implications of Article VII of the master lend-lease agreement. Morgenthau and his right-hand man, Harry Dexter White, were forced to accept bilateral conversations with a British team led by Dick Law in September 1943, but they did their best to ensure that out of them came a British commitment to an international monetary fund, which would restrict British powers to control the value and flow of sterling.[9] The Americans insisted on the abolition of imperial preference as a prelude to a multilateral reduction in tariffs which was expected to follow from any conference on the subject; this last was no real concession by America since the British were being asked to give up something which large sections of the Cabinet valued in return for hypothetical promises which Congressional opinion might negate.[10] On monetary policy Keynes and White clashed bitterly over their respective and competing plans for an international bank and a fund for reconstruction. White wanted both organisations to be under effective American control and the dollar to replace sterling as the international currency of exchange.[11]

Bitter arguments over the future shape of the new world order were only part of the reason for the 'unceasing wave of isolationism and anti-Americanism' which Keynes noticed was 'passing over us' by May 1944.[12] The social strains already referred to certainly played their part in this, with some MPs complaining loudly about the lewd behaviour of American troops – especially the blacks, who were consorting with white girls who were 'the lowest of the low' and leaving 'a number of half-caste babies' behind them.[13] But added to this popular anti-Americanism was a political edge, expressed in 1944, as in 1942, most clamantly by Beaverbrook, who told Churchill that it was time 'for a change in Government policy towards the United States'.[14] Surveying the results of Law's talks in Washington as well as Anglo-American disagreements over Middle Eastern oil and post-war civil aviation, His Lordship thought that it was time for the British to stand up for themselves. He acknowledged the necessity of close Anglo-American collaboration – it would have been difficult to deny it – but 'in seeking that friendship we should aim,' he thought, 'with an equal constancy, at maintaining and strengthening our position as a world power'. It was necessary to distinguish between means and ends. American support was needed not only to secure victory over Germany, but also to support British power in the post-war period; yet it rather seemed that far from being willing to take on this burden, America might be intruding herself into parts of the world hitherto regarded as British spheres of influence, such as the Middle East. This was not what the American alliance was supposed to be about.

Anglo-American competition for Middle Eastern oil went back to the First World War. In 1920, in defiance of Wilsonian principles, the British and the French had concluded the San Remo agreement, which divided the most promising oil regions of the Balkans and the Mediterranean between them and barred other countries from seeking concessions there. The American Government had refused to recognise the agreement and Congress had protested, but oil discoveries in Oklahoma had taken the sting out of the situation. However, with allied oil reserves under pressure in the war, and with Secretary Hull wanting to bring the benefits of free trade to the whole world, it was not to be expected that the British position in the Middle East would remain untouched.[15] Basil Jackson, the Anglo-Iranian Oil Company's representative in the United States, warned Churchill as early as 1943 that the American oil companies were taking what might prove to be an unhealthy interest in the Middle East. Arguing that neither the oil companies nor the American Government had formulated clear policies on oil, Jackson wanted Britain to take the lead in pressing for a common policy. But trying to secure this proved impossible. Although Hull and some American oil companies were interested in formulating a common policy,[16] Harold Ickes at the Interior

Department wanted to use the Petroleum Reserves Committee, set up in June 1943, to help oil companies acquire their own concessions in the Middle East, eyes being cast in particular at Kuwait whose wells had been shut down by the British army in 1942.[17] This would mean America consolidating and expanding her position 'in an area hitherto dominated by the British', and an end to 'British commercial and political restrictions' on American companies;[18] it was to this that Beaverbrook objected.

There were, however, some advantages in America having an interest in the Middle East. As one diplomat put it, this would 'produce a powerful counterweight to any Russian designs by giving the United States "a highly strategic entanglement" in the area'.[19] But co-operation with a much stronger and richer Power was an enterprise not to be hazarded lightly. Whilst sympathetic to opening conversations with the Americans over oil, Eden had 'no doubt' that they 'have thoughts of usurping ... [our] place, beginning in Saudi Arabia'.[20] The American negotiating method certainly lent credence to this notion. The British had been dubious about opening talks about oil, but were willing to do so on an 'official' level if they could be held in London and classed as 'exploratory' conversations covering the general question of allied oil resources. However, in mid-February 1944 the Americans suddenly told Halifax that the talks would concern the whole Middle East and would be held in Washington with a high-level American delegation, which would include Hull and Ickes; FDR himself would chair the first session. Roosevelt, according to Halifax, 'disclaimed any idea of stripping us but said that "his single idea was that we should work together in a field that was of vital importance to us both"'.[21] Halifax disdained any notion of an 'efficient and well-oiled machine' operating to poach British interests, and correctly put down the sudden change in direction to the civil war between Hull and Ickes: 'American politics are conducted in an 18th century atmosphere of violence and lack of coherent action.'[22] But this did not reassure Eden very much since the pressures which were driving American policy would only intensify if top-level conversations were opening in Washington in election year. Moreover, even if Halifax was correct and there was no pre-concerted American plan, it was clear that the general trend was to expand American interests at the expense of Britain's. Beaverbrook, who shared this fear, was convinced that such a conference would 'prove fatal to our interests'.[23]

According to the definitive modern account of American policy in this area, the British 'had some justification for their fears'.[24] Hull and Ickes certainly wanted to secure a relaxation of those restrictions which allowed only British companies to exploit the oil resources of the Gulf. There were also ideas floating about that America should acquire British oil as payment for American lend-lease. All Churchill could do was to protest that a 'wrangle about oil' would be 'a poor prelude for the tremendous joint enterprise and sacrifice to which we have bound ourselves', and to give voice to the 'apprehension in some quarters here that the United States has a desire to deprive us of our oil assets in the Middle East'.[25]

Far from the British 'using' American power, the evidence was indeed accumulating to suggest that the Americans were taking advantage of Britain's plight to help mould the sort of post-war world FDR wanted. It was not just that the British were being pressured to join the International Monetary Fund (IMF) or to agree to the abolition of imperial preference, or even that one of their essential sources of dollar earnings was being encroached upon, but that the Americans seemed determined that the British should not acquire enough dollars to give themselves some degree of leverage against this pressure.

In late 1943 the new British Chancellor of the Exchequer, Sir John Anderson, heard 'almost accidentally' that FDR had decided that Britain's dollar reserves should be kept at below $1 billion and that Morgenthau had talked about cutting off lend-lease when they reached that figure. By November the figure had actually reached $1.2 billion, but, as Anderson explained to Churchill on 11 November, that did not mean that 'we are getting richer'; Britain's liabilities were 'increasing four or five times as fast as our reserves and we are constantly getting deeper into the pit'. Russia's gold and dollar reserves were twice Britain's, but there were no suggestions that anything should be done to their lend-lease. 'We, however,' Anderson warned, 'are thought to be easier game.'[26] FDR chose February 1944, when negotiations over oil, the IMF and Article VII were all under way, to raise with Churchill the whole question of restricting Britain's dollar reserves.[27] He followed this up with a telegram about the oil issue which has been accurately described as 'unyielding and almost peremptory'.[28] Telling Churchill that he was 'disturbed about the rumor that the British wish to horn in on Saudi Arabian oil reserves', FDR said that this just proved how necessary high-level discussions were. It was not necessary to be Beaverbrook to be worried by this. When the Americans then introduced into the debate the questions of international monetary co-operation and world free trade, anyone could have been forgiven for wondering whether they were not unveiling an iron fist inside a rather threadbare velvet glove.[29]

It was the argument of Beaverbrook and other imperialists in the Cabinet that the results of the Law/Keynes discussions with the Americans demonstrated the extent to which the latter had an agenda of their own. If the American negotiators in the oil conversations were intent on abiding by the Atlantic Charter's declaration about equal access to raw materials, their counterparts in the Treasury and State Departments had not forgotten about Article VII of the lend-lease agreement and the 'consideration' which the British were supposed to offer. This was an essential component of the multilateral trading system which Hull, Morgenthau and their respective advisers wished to create. It was not enough to force the British away from the economic protectionism of imperial preference; they had to be tied to a system which would break down the protectionism of the sterling bloc. This ignored the fact that in a world of free exchange rates the dollar would be king; or rather, it ignored how the British might be expected to react to such a situation. In 1941 Keynes had told Dean Acheson that to apply Article VII to exchange controls was to attempt the 'hopeless and impossible task' of returning to the equivalent of the gold standard, where rigid monetary devices were used to control international trade.[30] Beaverbrook used the same comparison three years later. In a paper to the Cabinet on 9 February 1944 he described the American plans as 'the Gold Standard all over again. And at a moment when the United States has all the gold, and Great Britain has none of it.'[31] Without a guaranteed sterling area, it was likely that those countries, in particular Egypt, which had run up enormous sterling balances during the war, would rush to change their pounds into dollars, with catastrophic consequences for the British economy. Combined with American pressure for the British to reduce their dollar balances, this proposal was indeed an unappetising one. Sir John Anderson spelt out the consequences to Churchill on 24 February:

> If we were to accept the President's proposal we should have lost our financial independence, in any case precarious, as soon as lend-lease comes to an end, and would emerge from the war, victorious indeed, but quite helpless financially with reserves far inferior not only to Russia but even to France and to Holland.[32]

In such a state Britain would be in no position to resist the new American world order; it would be an odd sort of independence which the war would have preserved.

The Cabinet's Committee on the External Economic Position had its doubts about abolishing imperial preference and the sterling area, but felt that discussions with the Americans could proceed if satisfactory safeguards were given. Beaverbrook, in a minority report, contested any notion of diluting 'the Sterling Area and the Economic Empire'.[33] Churchill, who took the view that the telegrams about the dollar balance were not the work of Roosevelt and had been 'put before him when he is fatigued and pushed upon us by those who are pulling him about', thought that the best policy would be 'to let it all rip for a bit'.[34] Eden and the economic experts at the Foreign Office persuaded him that this would be unwise, and the Prime Minister intervened directly with the President.[35] Churchill told FDR on 9 March that the proposals to reduce Britain's dollar balances were not consistent 'either with equal treatment of Allies or with any conception of equal sacrifice or pooling of resources'. Churchill reminded the President that 'we alone of the Allies will emerge after the war with great overseas war debts', and he warned of the political problems which would be caused by having to 'disperse our last liquid reserves'.[36] He was right about the 'equal treatment', but wrong in presupposing that the Americans were concerned about treating the British 'equally'.

Morgenthau appreciated the British arguments, but took the view that 'neither Britain's international financial position outside the United States nor its post-war needs were among the considerations which prompted Congress to pass the Lend-Lease Act'. With Congressional opinion already objecting to anything which made it seem that America was paying for Britain's war costs, the Treasury Secretary had good reason for his cautious attitude.[37] Contrary to what Churchill was hoping, the Americans were not interested in bankrolling the British Empire. FDR had not survived this long as President without a healthy instinct for how far he could push Congress, and the important thing, after all, was to secure Congressional support for an internationalist foreign policy. It was this, and not any exclusive relationship with the British, which Roosevelt wanted. All he could promise Churchill was that conversations would continue in the hope of reaching an agreement – and then let the matter drop for the moment.[38] Churchill could regard this as evidence that his 'friend' would not push matters, but that was simply another example of his propensity to delude himself where FDR was concerned.

The real American view was expressed frankly in the report which Acting Secretary of State Edward Stettinius compiled after a mission to London in April, during which he covered the whole gamut of Anglo-American concerns. 'It is clear', he commented, 'that the British attach great importance to the active participation of the United States in the world problems of the post-war era', and in order to secure this, he thought that the British 'will go far to meeting our wishes on the form and character of the machinery for international cooperation' – as they would in other matters.[39] Far from preparing themselves for the role of British cat's-paw, the Americans were preparing to use their massive economic and military strength to create an American peace of which Britain would be a small but important part.

Halifax, his old appeaser's instincts still hard at work, preferred to attribute the tough tone of American diplomacy about oil and British dollar reserves to America's 'antiquated and curious machinery'.[40] The Ambassador thought that with Hull competing with both Ickes and Morgenthau for influence over aspects of American economic diplomacy, and with Hopkins side-lined through illness and the President distracted by an election year, American policy was even less co-ordinated than usual; but that was to ignore the fact that its general impetus was towards replacing British power, not co-operating with it. Stettinius told FDR, in response to Churchill's telegram, that he was 'certainly mindful of the political dangers inherent in the accumulation by the British Government of very large dollar balances', and he did not just mean that this would create problems with the Republicans. He wanted to leave the British with enough cash to keep their war effort going, but he thought that if the balances remained at about $1 billion, 'we thereby reduce our chances to achieve the basic economic policy we want and need'.[41] As one American official put it, 'What England does about her currency and trade control determines whether the world will be one large and prosperous trading group or whether it will be broken up into conflicting economic blocs.'[42] The Roosevelt administration, like its successor, possessed the economic muscle and the will to make the economic structures which supported the British Empire and the social system it underpinned conform to the desires of the economic and social liberalism of those who wanted to internationalise the 'New Deal'.

Churchill disliked this process where he realised it was happening, and he was vocal in his protests, but at the end of the day he needed the American alliance too much to fight it. By convincing many contemporaries and posterity that Britain needed the American alliance, Churchill successfully avoided having to answer the question of whether his sacrifices brought that alliance. The sacrifices of 1940–1 did not bring America into the war against Germany, and in like manner, the sacrifices of 1944–5 did not secure American aid against what Churchill chose to characterise as Soviet expansionism. In both cases America reached the conclusion Churchill had wanted belatedly and of her own accord. Only an eye to his posthumous reputation made Churchill claim a cause-and-effect relationship between his appeasement and American involvement in Europe; and only the exigencies of the Cold War and British decline enabled him to get away with it.

In response to FDR's unyielding attitude on the oil negotiations, all Churchill could do was to protest at his pre-empting discussion, express concern at 'the apparent possibility of a wide difference opening up' and hope that matters could be sorted out.[43] In reply Roosevelt denied that he was making 'sheep's eyes at your oil fields in Iraq or Iran'. Churchill thanked him and repudiated suggestions that Britain was trying to 'horn in' on America's position in Saudi Arabia. With a flash of spirit brought on by FDR's attitude across the whole range of financial issues, Churchill declared, in terms reminiscent of his famous statement in November 1942, that Britain 'will not be deprived of anything which rightfully belongs to her . . . at least not so long as your humble servant is entrusted with the conduct of foreign affairs'.[44] But as so often with utterances of this sort, the rhetoric was belied by the reality. The Americans had already begun to talk with Iranian officials about acquiring further concessions, whilst the State Department and FDR's special representative in Tehran, Major-General Hurley, were making plans to prevent the British and the Soviets from expanding their influence in Iran.[45] When the official conversations opened over an oil agreement, the British found that the Americans were adamantly opposed to their oil interests in the Middle East being excluded from the sort of quotas which it was thought that the glut in oil production at the end of the war would require. Since oil offered the British one of their few ways of earning valuable foreign exchange, this seemed unfair; but such was the American muscle that that was the way the agreement was drawn up. It was only the opposition of the Senate, spurred on by the oil companies who objected to what they saw as government interference in their industry, which prevented the agreement being ratified.[46]

If British interests in the Middle East were temporarily safeguarded by American political deadlock, it was political opposition nearer home which prevented Churchill from committing the Government to the results of the Law/White talks. It is easy to represent the arguments between the economic multilateralists and the advocates of a sterling area and imperial preference as ones between a bright progressive future and a dark reactionary past, not least because that was how the American champions of multilateralism presented their case; but it was not that simple. In the first place those Britons who held out against American plans disliked the form which American multilateralism was taking. Those, like Amery, who argued that the sterling bloc was a fine example of a multilateral trading system, and that America's policy of reciprocal trading agreements constituted an example of multilateral theory being ignored in favour of bilateral practice, had a point.[47] Had the Americans been advocating the erection of a tariff-free system of international trade and a monetary structure which guaranteed adequate liquidity to participate in such a system, it might indeed have been possible to portray the advocates of such a scheme as children of the light; but that was not what the British were being asked to sign up to. No American President was likely to be able to win the support of the labour unions and of large portions of Congress to a reduction or elimination of American tariffs, and the results of the Congressional mid-term elections in 1942 strengthened the hand of Republicans like Taft, who wanted to ensure that American wealth was not squandered abroad. The 'pork barrel' effect in Congress and the labour unions combined to create pressure on the White House to ensure not only that the new world economic order would be run from America in America's interests – that was understandable enough – but also that the structure of that system would 'ultimately destroy America's staunchest European ally'.[48]

Britain's economic requirements for the post-war era were as simply put as they were hard to obtain: a favourable balance of trade and a surplus balance of payments; the absence of either might well spell bankruptcy and would certainly signal the end of Britain as an independent Great Power. The message which came through from the Treasury to the War Cabinet in 1944 was that after the military successes of D-Day there would need to be an economic equivalent.[49] By this stage of the war Britain had sold off some $3,000 million worth of overseas investments, and by 1945 the country would have a balance of payments deficit of nearly $3 billion. Lend-lease had enabled nearly one and a half million workers formerly engaged in the export industries to be converted to war production, which left the British economy in no position to mount the massive export drive (150 per cent more than the

1938 level) which would be needed. Imports would be required on a grand scale to begin the reconstruction of the devastated British cities and to improve the lamentably low standard of living of the population. But America was the only market where the necessary imports could be obtained and Britain simply did not possess the dollars. Her gold reserves by June 1944 stood at about $1.6 million, but offset against these were liabilities of $11 million. What the British needed was not lectures about multilateralism but rather a system which would allow them to finance economic recovery at home by supplying financial liquidity abroad. But Morgenthau and the Treasury were committed to a policy of keeping British dollar reserves low and of creating a system of freely exchangeable currencies. It was not necessary to be an economic reactionary to see that this would produce a situation where Britain's precarious dollar and gold reserves would be sucked out in the direction of the United States, not just by domestic demand, but also by those areas of the sterling bloc such as Egypt and India liquidating their large (but useless) supplies of sterling for the almighty dollar.[50] As Keynes put it when writing to Stettinius in April 1944, he had not only failed to 'emphasise the point that the U.S. Administration was very careful to take every possible precaution to see that the British were as near as possible to bankruptcy before any assistance was given', but he had also omitted to mention 'the recent recrudescence of these same standards', according to which 'lend-lease ought to be appropriately abated whenever there seems the slightest prospect that leaving things as they are might possibly result in leaving the British at the end of the war other than hopelessly insolvent';[51] quite so.

This was the real price which was being paid for the American alliance. It was not that the American administration planned to send Britain to the poor house, but that was the effect of the interaction between the conflicting impulses that passed for American policy. Morgenthau 'basically did not trust the English and was magnanimous toward them only when he felt them in his power. . . . [He] was a multilateralist, not so much for ideological or strategic reasons, but because he saw in it a mechanism that would facilitate the transfer of power.'[52] He was as mistrustful of the City of London and British financiers as he was of their American counterparts. His admiring biographer wrote that Morgenthau 'did not want to compound British economic problems, or to push England to bankruptcy',[53] but that was not much comfort when the effect of his policies was to do just that. Morgenthau had been all in favour of helping the British in 1940 and 1941 before America was fighting the war against fascism, but once America was committed to that task he allowed his habitual suspiciousness full reign. He was not going to allow any smart 'Limeys' to pull one over on him, especially not some 'smart ass' like Keynes, and especially not when 'fancy pants' State Department boys like Dean Acheson were telling him that he was underestimating the effects of the war on the British economy. In his view it was the boys at the State

Department who were doing the underestimating, and what they were under-estimating was the wiliness of guys like Keynes. As he commented in November 1943 when he was still engaged in trying to ensure that British dollar balances remained low, 'just because we were innocent in the international field, it was no reason why they should take advantage of us'.[54]

Amery and Beaverbrook, and those who supported their line, felt that it was the Americans who were taking 'advantage', and their resistance to this process in 1944 invested the 'dismal science of economics' with a 'revivalist fervour'.[55] Churchill's views on economics were neither very recondite nor typical of the Party which he led. He had broken away from the Party in 1903 over Joseph Chamberlain's tariff reform campaign, as one MP was quick to remind him in debate on 24 April. That issue had divided him from the Conservatives until 1924, when Baldwin's willingness to let the matter rest had allowed Churchill to enter his Government as Chancellor. Although his free-trade faith had been severely tested and even compromised in the early 1930s, Churchill remained out of tune with the majority of the Conservative Party.

Amery, who was the chief standard-bearer for the Chamberlainite tradition, made plain his view that if the Government brought specific proposals about multilateralism before Parliament, 'those of us who differ would have to leave the Government and make their opposition as vigorous and effective as they could'.[56] In a letter to Dick Law which he could be sure would be shown to the Prime Minister, Amery commented that 'the only chance of averting a really first-class row within our Party lies in postponing any further action with regard to the Washington discussions [over Article VII]'; in the event of the Government adopting a multilateralist position, 'it will be impossible for a good many of us to remain members of the Government, and we should all have from then on to devote all our energies to preventing such a policy ever being sanctioned by Parliament'.[57] He was more circumspect when it came to bearding Churchill himself, but he was willing to warn the Prime Minister of the dangers of 'rush[ing] things'.[58] Churchill's response was swift and brutal. Noting that the general tenor of Amery's paper was 'calculated to cause a split in the Conservative Party', he refused permission for it to be circulated to the Cabinet, although he acknowledged that he could not prevent Amery from making his points in Cabinet.[59]

The meeting of the Cabinet on 14 April 1944 was the closest the Churchill coalition came to discussing seriously the price to be paid for the American alliance. On one side were those like the Chancellor, Sir John Anderson, who argued that it would be 'very awkward to fall out with the U.S.A.' and who pointed out that, 'if ... we antagonized the U.S., the generous assistance needed from that country would not be made available'. On the other were those like Beaverbrook, who was 'strongly opposed' to accepting either the IMF or Article VII, and Amery, who thought that trade should be 'regulated in the national interest, with Great Britain first; the Empire second, and the rest of the world third'. With opposition from Conservative protectionists, there also came a note of scepticism from the bulky and powerful form of Ernest Bevin, whose hackles rose at the mention of the words 'gold standard': 'those of us who had the experience of 1925–1931 might', he warned, 'be excused for feeling uneasy'. The Cabinet ended in a compromise decision to publish accounts of the Washington talks, but to do so without any Government commitment to their conclusions.[60] In view of this decision Amery withdrew his request to circulate his paper to the full Cabinet and with it, at least for the moment, his threat to cause 'a split in the Conservative Party'.[61]

Churchill had been warned that there were limits beyond which his own Party might not follow him, and that warning had been delivered by those who saw American policy in a less beneficent light. Churchill now needed to show not only that American co-operation was necessary to winning the war – that much was obvious even to Beaverbrook – but that it could also bring about the sort of post-war world in which British power remained intact; it was not clear how he would do this, or if it was even true.

9

Seeking a Suitable Stalin

Churchill's policy towards America was easily justified during the war by reference to the need for American help, and the same thing might be said, *mutatis mutandis*, of his policy towards the Soviet Union, even though Churchill did not say it. But after Yalta,* Churchill was increasingly to resort to the argument that the American alliance was essential because Russia might be as much of a threat to British power as Hitler had been; this was to point the way to a line of argument which has been used ever since. Concessions to America were justified because they brought America into the Cold War. But this is to give Churchill and the British too much credit; neither in 1941 nor in 1947 did the Americans commit themselves to a position because the British wanted them to; in both cases American policy was determined by American interests and considerations.[1]

Indeed, during 1944, far from seeking to enlist American aid against an expansionist Soviet Union, Churchill was seeking to come to an agreement with Stalin. The Soviet connection may have developed out of expediency, but that was not how it had been portrayed to the British people. As one commentator put it,

Democracies at war seem to think themselves to be under the necessity of developing positive and highly moral war aims and, therefore, of promoting all their allies to the status of sanctity. It was not good enough that the Russians should be necessary, they must also be good.[2]

But the Soviet Union had not been 'good' before 1939, and the territorial ambitions she had evinced then had not changed, nor were they likely to now her armies were enjoying success. If the Americans wanted to internationalise the 'New Deal', the Soviets wished, at the least, to reverse the results of the Versailles settlement and to provide themselves with their own version of its *cordon sanitaire*. This conflicted with the Atlantic Charter, and, as the Polish question showed, Soviet demands could create problems for the western allies. As Henry Stimson noted, on Poland it rather looked as if Britain and America were holding 'the leg for Stalin to skin the deer'. He feared that this 'will be a dangerous situation for us at the end of the war. Stalin won't have much of an opinion of people who have done that and we

---

* The Yalta conference, January 1945; see chapters 10 and 11.

will not be able to share much of the postwar world with him.'³ But Roosevelt took a more optimistic view. At Tehran he had taken steps to remove Stalin's suspicions. He had not only made plain his determination to open a proper second front, but he had allowed Stalin to understand that the United States no longer objected to his territorial demands. FDR saw this as a sacrifice made in the interests of a greater goal, namely post-war co-operation through the United Nations.

This had left Churchill in a difficult situation. He had hoped that overt Soviet expansionism might make Poland a 'hook' with which to catch the Americans, but Tehran left him having to find his own basis upon which to deal with the Soviets. It was this which had led him to put pressure on the Poles to agree to Stalin's territorial demands. If the Polish problem could be settled through bilateral negotiation, this would provide a precedent for a larger deal on respective Anglo-Soviet spheres of influence. This was the real significance of his famous visit to Moscow in October 1944. In his memoirs Churchill presents the episode of his October visit to Stalin as something of an aberration, but in reality it had both antecedents and consequences which the circumstances of 1953 precluded the Prime Ministerial author from mentioning. Unlike Chamberlain's notorious 'piece of paper', Churchill's 'naughty document' was the product of long consideration.

On 4 May 1944 Churchill asked Eden for a short paper on 'the brute issues between us and the Soviet Government which are developing in Roumania, in Bulgaria, in Yugoslavia, and above all, in Greece'. 'Broadly speaking', Churchill thought that 'the issue' was, 'are we going to acquiesce in the Communization of the Balkans and perhaps of Italy?' From Churchill's later reputation it might seem that this was a purely rhetorical question to which the answer was obvious, but this was far from the case. Churchill told Eden that, 'I am of the opinion on the whole that we ought to come to a definite conclusion about it.'⁴ Only two days earlier Churchill had told Eden that he thought that the Russians were 'crocodiles',⁵ and later the same day he was to tell him that he thought 'we are approaching a show-down with the Russians about their Communist intrigues in Italy, Yugoslavia and Greece'.⁶ On 8 May he confided in the Foreign Secretary his 'fear' that 'very great evil may come upon the world. . . . The Russians are drunk with victory and there is no length they may not go'; the only consolation for what might become a re-run of 1938 was that 'This time at any rate we and the Americans will be heavily armed.'⁷ This might be taken as an answer to Churchill's own rhetorical question, if it was not for the fact that far from being followed up with a firm line towards the Soviets, it was the prelude to an attempt to strike a spheres of influence deal with them.

Far from concluding that the 'crocodiles' needed caging, the British were still seeking a suitable basis for co-existence with them. Eden had told the Dominion Prime Ministers only a few days earlier that 'it remained uncertain

as yet whether we could rely upon Russia to co-operate to the full'.[8] Given
the 'immense task of rehabilitation and reconstruction' in which the Soviets
would have to engage after the war, Eden thought it was 'much the more
likely' that they would 'try a policy of collaboration with ourselves' provided
'that the Kremlin is convinced of our intention to keep Germany weak and
does not become suspicious that this country and the United States are
seeking to build up a combination . . . against her'.[9] Eden now pressed Churchill to try to convert current Anglo-Soviet 'understandings' into something
more specific. Britain had 'recognised' Soviet 'predominance' in Romania, so,
in like fashion, the Soviets might care to acknowledge that Greece was in
the British sphere. With the Soviets anxious to see the Anglo-Americans
launch their long-promised second front, Stalin's only query in response was
to wonder whether the suggestion had the agreement of the Americans –
which showed that the Soviet dictator at least knew where power really lay.[10]

Churchill put the idea to FDR in a telegram at the end of May, playing
up to American prejudices by explicitly denying any intention of carving up
the Balkans into spheres of influence. He explained, rather disingenuously,
that the 'arrangement' would prejudice neither a future peace settlement nor
current tripartite co-operation; it was simply a 'useful device for preventing
any divergence of policy' between Britain and the Soviets 'in the Balkans'.[11]
It was not a particularly good moment to put such an idea before Secretary
Hull, who had already expressed annoyance at some of 'Mr Churchill's recent
utterances'.[12]

Following the troubles created by the argument over lend-lease, Article VII
of the master lend-lease agreement and the IMF, Churchill had used a Commons debate on 'Empire Unity' to rally support from within his own Party
by emphasising his imperialist credentials. Although he disdained any recan-
tation of his opposition to old-fashioned Chamberlainite tariff reform, Churchill's recital of events since his discussions with the President at
Newfoundland made plain his refusal to interpret either the Atlantic Charter
or Article VII in the sense the Americans wanted. He went on from there to
reject any notion that the British Empire was in less than excellent health
and talked about devising 'methods . . . to bring the nations of the British
Empire into intimate and secret council' not just during the war but after it
as well. He finished off by saying that there was no contradiction between
the unity of Britain and her Empire and Britain belonging to a regional
organisation to maintain post-war security.[13] It was a masterly performance
in terms of domestic politics, well-calculated to appease the Tory right and
yet to reassure the Labour Party by its support for a United Nations organisation; but it was less fortunate in its effects across the Atlantic.

Hull told Halifax crossly that the Prime Minister's speech had 'discouraged
many people in this country and in many small countries whose governments
and peoples were becoming increasingly fearful that the three great Western

nations would be drawn ever closer together and practise the worst forms of imperialism'. He warned the Ambassador in blunt mountain-man style that 'the future would indeed be dangerous unless we could have more cooperation from the British and have it now'. Striking that note of self-righteousness which sometimes seemed to go along with being an American Secretary of State, Hull 'recalled the fight which the President and I have waged in this country for more liberal commercial policies against overwhelming odds and said that if we had faltered as the Prime Minister seemed to be faltering we would have gotten exactly no-where'. He followed this up with exhortations to Ambassador Winant to 'take every opportunity to impress our views upon the British authorities'.[14] Roosevelt's response to Churchill's suggestions about 'arrangements' in the Balkans reflected the spirit of Hull's attitude, which was hardly surprising since it was concocted in the State Department.[15]

Roosevelt told the Prime Minister that any such pact would strengthen the 'natural tendency' for military decisions to have political implications, and that it would certainly 'result in the division of the Balkan region into spheres of influence despite the declared intention'. Whatever Churchill said, the Americans were convinced that the British intended to 'follow a strong policy in regard to the Eastern Mediterranean even if it means standing up and making deals with the Soviet Union'.[16] In this conviction FDR was correct, and it was not surprising that Churchill's heated response did nothing to shake it. In a telegram on 11 June Churchill protested that he was 'much concerned' at Roosevelt's attitude, and he put forth his full eloquence to convince his old friend that a three-month trial arrangement would not harm anyone.[17] Roosevelt agreed to Churchill's request, this time without consulting the State Department,[18] which caused him some embarrassment when the American Ambassador to the Greek Government, Lincoln MacVeagh, asked Hull about the arrangement in late June.[19] Although Hull had not seen FDR's reply to Churchill's impassioned pleas of 11 June, he had seen a telegram from the Prime Minister which argued strongly in favour of an arrangement with Russia, and he was convinced that the British were trying to pull a fast one.[20] He persuaded the President to send a message to Churchill on 22 June expressing concern about even a temporary arrangement between the British and the Soviets,[21] and this, not surprisingly, called forth from Churchill a puzzled protest at what appeared to be a change in American policy.[22] In typically cavalier fashion, and again without consulting the State Department, Roosevelt told Churchill that, 'It appears that both of us have inadvertently taken unilateral action in a direction that we both now agree to have been expedient for the time being.'[23] Now it was Hull's turn to protest to the President: 'From information furnished to Mr MacVeagh by the British it would appear that some change has been made in our position, although I have not been informed.'[24]

In fact, the 'position' thus created was one which suited the President's penchant for ambiguity perfectly. Churchill had been given the go-ahead for something which he himself had denied was a spheres of influence agreement, and there could be no harm in that. Churchill was saddled with the job of seeing whether an agreement could be found with the Soviets which did not upset American public opinion whilst the President was free to disown anything which did not meet that criterion. In the meantime the deadlock in Anglo-Soviet relations caused by Poland had been broken and FDR could welcome Mikolajczyk to Washington, showing the 'Polish vote' that he was a good friend of Poland. It was typical of the President that whilst garnering the seven million or so Polish voters, he should have taken pains to make it clear to Stalin that 'his visit was not connected with any attempt on my part to insert myself into the differences which exist between the Soviet Government and the Polish-Government-in-Exile'.[25] Whilst giving the American Poles the impression that he was in some way prepared to back Mikolajczyk, FDR was in no way deviating from the position he had expounded to Stalin at Tehran, which was, in turn, consistent with the green light which he had given to Churchill. Nothing would be allowed to get in the way of an agreement with the Soviets, except American public opinion.

Whilst Roosevelt had left the way open for Churchill to take the risk of seeing whether an acceptable arrangement was to be had with Stalin, there were others who, less sanguine about this possibility, were calling for a strategic reassessment of the direction of British diplomacy. The Prime Minister's old friend Duff Cooper, who had become Ambassador to France in late 1943, was among this number, and the thoughts which he put to Eden in mid-1944 showed what path might have been taken had there existed the will to follow it. A man whose political progress had been hindered by the fact that his erudition and intellect were matched only by his hedonism and disinclination for the drudgery of politics, Cooper was a man whose thoughts on the future of British foreign policy were a great deal more sophisticated than anything which Churchill imagined. Cooper's enemies accused him of laziness, and his sybaritic brilliance did nothing to conciliate those fustian souls who confounded circumspection with wisdom and mistook mental stagnation for 'soundness'. As befitted a gifted historian who had begun his career in the pre-1914 Foreign Office, Cooper brought a long perspective to bear on the subject of the future of British foreign policy. Freed from the frenetic routine which so exhausted Churchill and Eden, Cooper had the time to distinguish clearly between the wood and the trees. Taking the classic Whig position that 'traditionally' British policy had tried to 'prevent the domination of Europe by any one too powerful nation', Cooper's thoughts turned to the question of how this was to be carried on in future.[26] It would take three years, a mountain of paper and a sea of ink before Cooper's ideas entered the mainstream of British foreign policy.

There was much to be said for Cooper's Whiggish view that since Britain's traditional foreign policy had been to preserve the balance of power in Europe, she should now seek to orientate her diplomacy against Russia, and that since America could not be relied upon not to retreat into isolation, this could only be done by organising the nations of western Europe. The Chiefs of Staff, who also wished to plan for 'the worst eventuality', went even further and saw the only post-war danger to British interests coming from the Soviet Union.[27] In their view the only 'protection against Russia' would be 'for us to have either the whole of Germany on our side or alternatively as much of Germany as we could draw into our "sphere of influence"'.

The only problem with such views was that they were likely to create the very danger which they sought to avert, and that they overrated the strength available to back British diplomacy. Sir Orme Sargent, who was Deputy Under-Secretary at the Foreign Office, expressed horror at the thought that planning should proceed upon any assumption about Soviet hostility and called the idea 'a most disastrous heresy which ought to be nipped in the bud at once'. Another diplomat, Frank Roberts, declared that the Chiefs were not only 'crossing their bridge before they come to it, but even constructing their bridge in order to cross it'. Gladwyn Jebb, the Foreign Office's representative on the Chiefs of Staff Committee, thought that the notion amounted to a policy of 'building up our enemies to defeat our allies' and speculated that it derived from 'some kind of suicidal mania'; it could only lead to Britain 'losing the peace'. Far from wishing to do anything to help Germany, the Foreign Office was operating upon the assumption that a hard line towards the Germans would help the British to gain Soviet confidence.[28]

In his response to Cooper, Eden, whilst not 'of course' suggesting that there 'is no danger of the Soviet Union pursuing a policy of expansion in Europe', argued that 'the policy suggested by you would increase that danger (if it exists) rather than diminish it'. Eden thought that it would be 'fatal' if the Soviets got the idea that a western European union was being formed for any purpose other than to guard against a recrudescence of German aggression: 'We should be throwing away the considerable chances of the U.S.S.R. pursuing a policy of collaboration after the war.' Eden's hopes rested on the 'Anglo-Soviet alliance' and a 'world organization' through which it and Anglo-American co-operation would preserve the peace. Nor was it only the Soviets who would dislike the formation of a 'western bloc'; it would be anathema to the Americans and might stop them adopting an internationalist foreign policy. Hopkins had warned in March 1943, after Churchill's speech on the subject, that 'there should be no attempt to set up a European Council, for this would give free ammunition to isolationists'.[29]

There were other siren voices raised in favour of the 'western bloc' option. Since 1942 the Belgian Foreign Minister, Paul-Henri Spaak, had tried to interest the Foreign Office in ideas for a closer European union, and once the Normandy invasions had been accomplished, there was pressure from Spaak and from the French for Britain to take the lead in opening diplomatic conversations.[30] The Spanish leader, General Franco, gave the advice that, 'with Germany annihilated, and a Russia that has consolidated her ascendancy in Europe and Asia, and the United States similarly dominant in the Atlantic and Pacific Ocean as the mightiest nation of the world', the nations of Europe would 'be facing the most serious and dangerous crisis of their history'. Unable to believe 'in the good faith of Communist Russia' and 'alive to the insidious might of Bolshevism', especially in a situation where the weakness of Russia's neighbours would increase both her 'power and ambitions', some form of European union seemed essential.[31] But General Franco was even less persuasive than Duff Cooper. However attractive such schemes looked on paper, they neglected the facts of power: western Europe was ravaged and possessed no military power which could be weighed in the scales against Soviet power. With America refusing to give a firm commitment to the post-war balance of power in Europe, an agreement with the Soviets was the only practicable policy. As the Warsaw uprising in July and August showed, the path to such an understanding would be neither smooth nor pleasant, but Churchill and Eden had already discovered what Neville Chamberlain had always known – that there was little Britain could do to influence events in eastern Europe without Soviet co-operation. Chamberlain had balked at the price Stalin had demanded, but Eden and Churchill, like Roosevelt, seemed disposed to pay it. Nor did Stalin raise his price: 'Russia's claims, as Stalin made them known at the time of the Anglo-Soviet alliance, scarcely differed from those he enforced at the end of the war, when Russia was victorious beyond all expectations and controlled all the territories to which her claims referred.'[32]

Despite his loathing for Soviet action in Warsaw, despite occasional lucubrations about possible Soviet ambitions, and even despite his anxiety 'that British forces should forestall the Russians in certain areas of Central Europe',[33] Churchill was still intent on seeing whether he could arrive at a *modus vivendi* with the Soviets.[34] It is not just that in May and June he had sought American agreement to such an arrangement, but the whole thrust of his diplomacy lay in this direction. Indeed, an Anglo-Soviet agreement offered freedom from American attempts to interfere in places like Greece. Churchill did not want the 'Grand Alliance' to operate as such in areas where it conflicted with British ambitions and where he thought these could be achieved without it. At a meeting with FDR at Hyde Park after the second Quebec conference in September, Churchill raised the subject of the 'dangerous spread of Russian influence', and FDR listened sympathetically, even promising to help ferry British troops to Greece. Yet at Quebec itself Roosevelt had also spoken about withdrawing American troops from Europe within two years of the end of the war.[35] This opened up the prospect of a 'regime of triangular telegrams' by which Britain and America interfered in Romania, whilst Russia and America interfered in Greece, a notion repugnant to Churchill. It would mean that Britain would have to use military force to secure her own interests in areas like Greece, but that she would be subject to incessant diplomatic interference from her partners. Others would do the talking whilst it would be left to the British 'to try to make all things sweet', which would, Churchill told Eden, 'be a great disaster'.[36]

It may even be that it was such considerations which lay behind Churchill's hankering for an Adriatic offensive in late 1944. Although some of his admirers have portrayed his desire to continue with the Mediterranean campaign as part of a far-sighted scheme to anticipate the Cold War, it is far more likely that the 'political reasons' for it, which he cited in September 1944,[37] were those which found expression in the 'naughty document' which the Prime Minister presented to Stalin in October. It would make more sense of that document than any other interpretation. Churchill wanted '50 per cent influence' in Hungary and Yugoslavia, and it would clearly be easier to obtain this if there were British troops on the spot. The only other area in which Churchill was really interested was Greece, where he wanted '90 per cent'. This last, Churchill was already enforcing by the use of British troops by October 1944, and such was his determination that he was willing to risk a major diplomatic row with the Americans in order to ensure British predominance. The concomitant to this was that Stalin must be allowed to have his spheres of influence, and this, of course, was precisely what the 'naughty document' offered him.

The notion that the Moscow meeting was a genuine attempt to set the boundaries of real spheres of influence in Europe is strengthened by the lengths to which Churchill went to get Mikolajczyk to agree to Stalin's political and territorial demands, and by the language he employed once the Pole had been summoned to Moscow. Mikolajczyk came with compromise proposals, which would have allowed the Lublin and London Poles equal representation in a new government, but Stalin was not interested. He preferred to concentrate on the issue of Poland's frontiers. After ominously referring to the Lublin committee as a 'government' – which made explicit what the London Poles had always said was implicit in its mere existence – Stalin made plain his determination to get what he had been promised by the western allies at Tehran: the Curzon line frontier.[38] Churchill and Eden tried to emphasise the compensation which the Poles would gain at Germany's expense, but Mikolajczyk refused to budge from the position that he had no mandate to cede the national territory. This contrasted sharply with the attitude of one of the communist Poles, Boleslaw Beirut, who told Stalin and Churchill later that afternoon that, 'We are here to demand on behalf of Poland that Lvov shall belong to Russia.'[39] It was perhaps symbolically significant that just before his next meeting with Mikolajczyk on 14 October,

Churchill should have been brought a finger bowl – 'To wash your hands, Sir.'[40]

Churchill was brutal with the Poles.[41] He told Mikolajczyk that the 'three Great Powers who had expended their blood and treasure in order to liberate Poland for the second time in a generation were entitled to insist that a matter of domestic concern to the Poles should not be allowed to become the cause of friction among them'. He wanted Mikolajczyk to make the sacrifices Stalin demanded and thus pay the price necessary for an Anglo-Soviet entente, and he repeated earlier threats of withdrawing support from the London Poles if they did not agree. The notion that Churchill was behaving in this fashion because he had no alternative is not supported by his own words. Churchill told Mikolajczyk that, 'Our relations with Russia are much better than they have ever been', and far from looking forward to any Cold War, he repudiated what he called the 'crazy' notions of the Polish General Anders, who 'entertains the hope that after the defeat of Germany the Russians will be beaten . . . you cannot defeat the Russians'.[42]

But Mikolajczyk took his stand on the view which, in other circumstances, Churchill would have supported, that he could not give up Poland's national honour for anything. In any other context Churchill would have understood perfectly the reasons for Mikolajczyk's stubbornness; he was, after all, the man who had preferred the arbitrament of war to national dishonour. What drew forth the Churchillian wrath on this occasion was the knowledge that if the Poles did not concede, British public opinion and the Conservatives in the House were likely to support them. When Mikolajczyk brought the conversation back to the frontiers question, he drew forth a blast of Churchillian wrath: 'I wash my hands off [sic]: as far as I am concerned we shall give the business up. Because of quarrels between Poles we are not going to wreck the peace of Europe.' He threatened to 'tell the world how unreasonable you are. You will start another war in which 25 million lives will be lost. But you don't care.' The Polish response was: 'I know that our fate was sealed in Tehran.' Churchill's reply, that 'It was saved in Tehran', was so thin that it must be doubted whether it even convinced himself; it certainly did not prompt Mikolajczyk to 'give away half of Poland'. Churchill described him as 'absolutely crazy' and told him that 'unless you accept the frontier you are out of business forever. The Russians will sweep through your country and your people will be liquidated. You are on the verge of annihilation.' Threats having failed, Eden and Churchill tried bribery, offering the Poles Anglo-American guarantees and American loans – explaining that 'we shall be poor after this war'. It was kind of Churchill to make so free with American guarantees and money, but it might have been better if he had checked whether the Americans were, in fact, willing to make such generous offers; but then since his main purpose was to secure a 'yes' from Mikolajczyk, these matters could be dealt with later.

After a recess the Poles proved equally obstinate, and the final meeting 'was conducted by Churchill in a very violent manner'.[43] In response to Mikolajczyk's refusal to accept the Curzon line, Churchill railed that, 'You are no Government if you are incapable of taking any decision. You are callous people who want to wreck Europe. I shall leave you to your own troubles.' Accusing the London Poles of 'cowardice', he threatened to deal with the Lublin group. Recalling once more General Anders's comments, Churchill accused the Poles of being actuated by 'hatred towards the Russians'. In fact, the Poles were not being as unreasonable as Churchill's anger suggested. Mikolajczyk was willing to accept the Curzon line 'under purely formal protest' as long as the Prime Minister was willing to put forward the idea as a British suggestion; all he was refusing to do was to be seen to be proposing the Curzon line frontier himself. Since Churchill was unwilling to do this, it was rather hard for him to be accusing Mikolajczyk of 'cowardice'. According to his own account, the Polish Premier brushed aside Churchill's guarantees of Polish independence with a request to be allowed to parachute back into Poland: 'Because I prefer to die fighting for the independence of my country, than to be hanged later by the Russians in full view of your British ambassador.'[44] There was no agreement, then or later. Mikolajczyk offered to urge his colleagues to accept the Curzon line if they were allowed to keep Lwow, but there was no chance of Stalin accepting that.[45] With the London Poles all but abandoned by their British protectors, there was no reason for Stalin to concede anything, unless, of course, Mikolajczyk's appeals to Roosevelt bore fruit. But it was now that the Poles were to find out how much truth there was in Neville Chamberlain's famous comment that it was 'safest and best to rely on the Americans for nothing but words'.

Mikolajczyk appealed to FDR on 26 October for help in keeping Lwow in Poland, reminding him of his support in the summer,[46] but he did not receive an answer until after the American election, and by the time he did so its content was crucial. In a final attempt to deliver a Polish settlement to Stalin, Churchill had a stormy meeting with the London Poles on 2 November.[47]

According to the Polish account, 'the whole conversation was carried out by Churchill, who looked very fit, in a rather unpleasant and pressing manner, although he was trying to control himself in order not to lose his temper';[48] if so, he did not always succeed. Churchill made it clear that the Poles had better accept the Curzon line frontier openly or they could expect nothing more from him. Mikolajczyk wanted to leave things a little longer to see what Roosevelt's reply was, but he was told with cutting finality that unless a response was forthcoming within forty-eight hours, 'I shall consider that everything is finished.' In a passage which has the ring of truth, the Polish account describes how the 'legal intricacies' of the case 'are beyond Churchill's grasp', but the Prime Minister's attitude made plain his view that the blunt realities of the situation seemed to be beyond the grasp of the London Poles.

This was where his policy had brought him – to telling the Poles that if they did not accept an ultimatum, they would be massacred; they had known that well enough in 1939, and it was rather hard after that experience to expect them to place much reliance on a British guarantee. Churchill had insisted upon a decision and he got one; on 3 November the Polish Cabinet rejected the Curzon line frontier and elected to place their faith in Roosevelt.[49]

But the Americans were not willing to give a 'guarantee for the territory of any particular state'. They were, however, good enough to say that if the Poles reached an agreement with the British and the Soviets on their eastern frontier, they would not oppose it – which suggested obtuseness, naïveté or a very black sense of humour on the part of Charles (Chip) Bohlen, the Soviet expert in the State Department.[50] Roosevelt's eventual reply, dated 17 November, followed the same line. After proclaiming that America 'stands unequivocally for a strong, free and independent Polish state with the untrammeled right of the Polish people to order their internal existence as they see fit', FDR spent the rest of his letter qualifying this ringing declaration: the United States could not guarantee 'any specific frontiers'; the United States would 'raise no objection' to any acceptable 'proposed frontiers' and would do her best to provide aid, 'subject to legislative authority'. The United States, in short, intended to do nothing. Mikolajczyk was now prepared to compromise, but he found himself in a minority in the Polish Cabinet. He resigned his post on 24 November. At the end of the month a new government was formed led by the socialist Tomas Arciszewski, and early in January the Soviets recognised the Lublin Poles as the legitimate Government of Poland. If Polish stubbornness helped scupper Churchill's attempts to come to an entente with Stalin, then American reaction to the percentages deal completed the process.

Churchill did not mention the arrangement directly to Ambassador Harriman, preferring instead to let out 'bits and pieces, spaced over several days'.[51] Harriman had warned the President on 10 October that Churchill would probably try to 'work out some spheres of influence with the Russians'.[52] Hopkins and the ailing Hull both reacted as might have been predicted, protesting vigorously against any such deal, but FDR abided by the spirit which had prompted him to give Churchill the green light in the first place, telling Harriman that 'my active interest at the present time in the Balkan area is that such steps as are practicable should be taken to insure against the Balkans getting us into a future international war'.[53] It is some indication of how close Churchill's and Roosevelt's views on this matter were that the Prime Minister should have told the President that 'we should try to get a common mind about the Balkans, so that we may prevent civil war breaking out'.[54] But Churchill had been careful to stress (almost to the point of obsequiousness) that 'nothing will be settled except preliminary arrangements' to which he would be careful 'not to commit you'. Harriman did not learn of the percentages deal until the morning of 12 October, when Churchill, sitting up in bed, read him the draft of a letter to Stalin. He told Churchill immediately that he was 'certain both Roosevelt and Hull would repudiate the letter if it was sent'. Churchill decided not to send it and commented in his memoirs (as did Harriman) that the matter ended there.[55]

But Churchill never revoked his 'deal' with Stalin. When trouble flared up in Romania in early November, Churchill told Eden that, 'As long as the Russians leave us a free hand in Greece, we cannot do more in Roumania than be spectators', which does not suggest that he thought that all bets with Stalin were off.[56] The Foreign Office view was that although 'ultimately nothing was settled ... in fact there has been practical agreement that the Russians should lay hands off Greece while we follow their lead in Roumania'.[57] So it proved in practice when trouble erupted in Athens in December in the form of a communist-inspired coup, which the British put down with the use of armed force. It was from the Americans and not the Soviets that trouble came; as 'Uncle Joe' once boasted, 'I always keep my word.'[58]

10

'Lady Bountiful' and Uncle Sam

If Churchill appeared to have arrived at a *modus vivendi* with Stalin by the end of 1944, it could not be said that his American policy was paying the dividend he had expected. It was true that Roosevelt had won the Presidential election, but Hopkins, the most Anglophile of FDR's intimates, was not so sure that the British were right to be quite as pleased as they seemed to be. Just before the election he told a member of the British Embassy staff that 'in one way the Republicans would be better for you. They will want to intervene as little as possible in anything that goes on more than 100 miles from the shores of America.' Hopkins thought that the Republicans

will give you a free hand in India, in Europe and in the Middle East. You will have no embarrassing insistence on this or that in Saudi Arabia and all the other places where you have been accustomed to having your own way. It won't be like that with Roosevelt after the elections. You will find him right in on all these questions with his own views and you will have to pay attention to them.[1]

Roosevelt's election victory meant that he was now secure for an unprecedented fourth term, and ignoring Hopkins's prophecy, the British looked forward to continuity of policy, despite some changes in personnel. The least important of these changes for the British seemed to be the replacement of Vice-President Wallace by a Senator from Missouri, Harry S. Truman. Nothing much was known about the new Vice-President and it did not seem very important to learn what little there was to know. More intriguing was the possible effect of the retirement of Cordell Hull in November. Although Hull had never exercised any veto over American foreign policy and his influence had been limited by FDR's penchant for running his own show, the old Tennessean had been well-respected and even feared on The Hill, and he had been around so long that it seemed difficult to imagine the State Department without him. Halifax expected the disappointed Vice-Presidential aspirant, Jimmy Byrnes, to be Hull's successor, but like most other people was surprised when the President appointed the former lend-lease administrator, Ed Stettinius.[2]

But although Halifax believed that it was 'all to the good' for there to be a 'closer integration of State Department with the White House',[3] he was wide of the mark as far as British interests were concerned. Politics, like nature, abhors a vacuum, and although it is fashionable to presuppose that

FDR was already in the steady decline that was to lead to his death in April 1945, there would appear to be reason to question this. The notion that American foreign policy drifted rudderless towards Yalta is a convenient one if the agreement reached at the latter is to be written off as an aberration; but if, as is argued here, it was the natural culmination of a policy decided on at Tehran, then this will not quite do. With the election out of the way, FDR moved to try to secure the foundations for peace he wished to create – and that involved clipping British wings as well as dealing with Stalin's demands.

Hopkins had mentioned Greece and Italy as two areas where America would no longer be content to go along with British wishes, and early December provided opportunities for America to assert her interest in both regions. For most of the time since Italy changed sides in the war, the Americans had been content to leave Italian politics to the British, intervening occasionally to try to favour liberal politicians, like Count Sforza, over some of the monarchists whom Churchill preferred to support. On 6 December, countering rumours that the British were blocking the appointment of Sforza as Foreign Minister, Stettinius issued a statement criticising British policy in both Italy and Greece, and calling, in the best approved American manner, for the installation of proper democratic (and by implication republican) governments in both countries. Stettinius called this a 'reaffirmation of our policy';[4] Churchill, no doubt, had choicer ways of describing it. On 4 December there had been reports of an attempted uprising in Athens, and Churchill had ordered British troops into action; having come to a spheres of influence deal with Stalin, it was evident that he needed one with the Americans too, as American public opinion reacted badly to what was perceived as a British attempt to 'impose a specific – more or less reactionary – pattern upon Europe'.[5]

Halifax and the British Embassy correctly divined that with the war almost won and the State Department 'renovated', there was a 'desire for a brand new 100% American foreign policy, not tied to Britain's apron-strings'. This was more than 'Brit-bashing'; it sprang from 'profound and permanent causes'. These causes were both the ideological and practical differences which underlay the British and American attitudes towards foreign policy and international relations. The British view was founded upon long experience of the necessity of pragmatism, tinged with Churchill's preference for monarchy and his determination to maintain British influence in the Mediterranean. The American view, as befitted a nation with relatively little experience of foreign affairs, derived from theory, flavoured by Roosevelt's interventionism and the growing realisation of the 'vastly expanding material power' which the Americans could now command. The philosopher Isaiah Berlin, who drew up the Embassy's weekly reports, acutely observed, in a phrase which summed up the next few decades of American foreign policy, that the country was one which 'whatever it practises, thinks of itself as deeply libertarian'. This meant a correspondingly 'deep antipathy' to what was perceived of as British support 'for right-wing forces in Europe against the left'.[6] Whether in Spain or Italy or Greece, the British, especially Churchill, were seen as sympathetic to anti-democratic forces, which made it especially damaging when the American press not only printed Churchill's orders to General Scobie in Athens to fire on the Greek insurgents as though they were the enemy, but also leaked details of the correspondence between Churchill and Roosevelt in the summer concerning spheres of influence in Greece and Romania. What was particularly disturbing about the last 'leak' was that it evidently came directly from the State Department, which added to British fears that 'a good deal of the criticism of us was officially inspired'.[7] Anglo-phobe Congressmen, as well as patriotic newspapermen, took the opportunity to make unfriendly comments on 'British *Machtpolitik*', which was, of course, contrasted most unfavourably with the pure motives and clean hands of America herself;[8] nor were these the only manifestations of the new activism in the administration's foreign policy.

Stettinius attributed the crisis in Greece to Churchill's 'arbitrary' action in vetoing the appointment of the Greek socialist leader, Andreas Papandreou, as Prime Minister, and reminded Roosevelt on 13 December that British, as well as American, public opinion had been 'stirred to an unprecedented degree by the Greek crisis'.[9] Admiral King, head of the American navy, gave orders that no American vessels should be used in ferrying British troops and their supplies to Greece.[10] Churchill, worried at the schism which seemed to be growing, sought to catch Roosevelt's attention through Hopkins, to whom he expressed the view that, 'I consider we have a right to the President's support in the policy we are following.'[11] The Prime Minister drafted a vitriolic message to the President on the subject of Admiral King's decision, telling him that it might 'produce a disaster of the first magnitude, which might endanger all relations between Great Britain and the United States'; he was, however, persuaded not to send such a stark message and so telephoned Hopkins instead.[12] According to Hopkins's account, although he could not hear the Prime Minister very well, 'it sounded as though he was very angry and stirred up about something'.[13] Churchill was indeed 'very angry'. Despite his experiences at Tehran and since, Churchill had still not grasped that under FDR America was beginning to think and act like a global Power, and that although the British connection was an important one for the Americans, it was not as important to them as the American connection was to the British. Hopkins urged Halifax to try to make sure that Churchill did not send any 'strong protest' to FDR, saying that it would serve no useful purpose, and adding for good measure that 'public opinion about the whole Greek business in this country was very bad and that we felt that the British Government had messed the whole thing up pretty thoroughly'.[14]

Roosevelt's response to Churchill's agitation once more suggested that the President was taking a wider view of affairs than the British leader would like. It was a typically Rooseveltian production, starting off with a good deal of sympathetic flannel about his role being 'that of a loyal friend and ally whose one desire is to be of any help possible', before moving on to explain why it was that circumstances beyond his control prevented him from taking a stand alongside the British. Of course the President did not need to tell his old friend 'how much I dislike this state of affairs', but public opinion was what it was and Roosevelt had to reckon with it. He concluded by adding his voice to those, both British and American, who wanted a political solution to the crisis through the establishment of a regency,[15] a course of action which Churchill, after opposing for nearly a month, adopted after visiting Athens in late December.[16]

Churchill did not help his cause in America during the crisis by comments he made in the Commons on 15 December in which he seemed to criticise American policy over Poland's frontiers for lacking the 'same precision' as British policy. Those few American newspapers which had supported Churchill over Greece, because they approved of combating communism, now rounded on him over what they termed the 'betrayal' of Poland.[17] Nor was Roosevelt best pleased. Hopkins told Churchill on 16 December that 'public opinion here' was 'deteriorating rapidly because of Greek situation and your statement in Parliament about the United States and Poland', and he warned him that FDR and Stettinius might have to 'state in unequivocal terms our determination to do all that we can to seek a free and secure world'.[18] Churchill's response suggested that he was rather baffled by the final phrase; he asserted that he would welcome any such declaration since 'We seek nothing for ourselves from this struggle.'[19]

Hopkins's telegram, like Stettinius's original statement and the leaks to the American press, were not, as the British patronisingly tended to think, the consequence of American inefficiency, but rather, as Isaiah Berlin had discerned, a sign of American concern about British imperial ambitions. Far from being hastily drafted, Stettinius's declaration had been approved by three senior State Department officials and vetted carefully by the Secretary of State himself. Roosevelt's Chief of Staff, Admiral William D. Leahy, confirmed in his memoirs that it was a deliberate statement of American policy with regard to Greece and Italy.[20] Certainly the growing influence of the Admiral, whose seniority, experience and closeness to the President made him an important figure in the post-Hull era, was unlikely to redound to the benefit of the British, since Leahy entertained 'an embittered skepticism' and 'eternal suspicion' of them.[21] As Hopkins had warned, freed of the demands of electioneering, 'the United States would be right in batting all over the world'. The administration wanted 'a strong Britain but had ideas of their own on many questions which might differ from ours and were not going to be an amenable junior partner'.[22] Britain would be 'America's outpost on the European frontier, the sentinel for the New World'.[23]

This was the reality which belied all those condescending memoranda about Britain using American power to protect her own Empire and interests.[24] The assumption that superior British diplomatic experience should ensure that 'more often than not ... the Americans follow our lead more often than we follow theirs',[25] was exposed for what it was – an illusion. The December crisis suggested that it was not going to be easy for the British to 'make use of American power for purposes which we regard as good', especially when the Americans did not share the same opinion of the 'causes' in question. By late 1944 there was in America 'a widespread consciousness that the balance of strength among the leading powers of the world has been changing to Great Britain's disadvantage', and this was accompanied by a growing conviction that America was 'the natural heir to the throne of world power which Britain has thus vacated'. Naturally 'old established' fears about 'city slicker John Bull' planning to 'hornswoggle hayseed Uncle Sam' still lingered, but they were now accompanied by attitudes such as that of the right-wing Republican newspaper magnate, Colonel McCormick, who warned the British that 'they are the junior partners without the right to make final decisions'.[26] None of this boded well for Churchill's 'balance of power' diplomacy, rooted as it was in the long traditions of European foreign policy. Roosevelt was still wedded to the ideas put forth by Woodrow Wilson in his second inaugural address, that there must not be a balance but a community of power, not organised rivalries, but organised peace. The New York Times spoke for many Americans when it called Churchill a 'product of nineteenth-century thought fighting a twentieth-century war for eighteenth-century aims'.[27]

There was much to be said for this view. If Churchill's hopes that America could be enlisted to support his vision of Britain as a Great Power were unrealistic, how realistic was that vision itself? Keynes was in little doubt that the financial underpinnings of Britain's status had been shot to pieces, and that the consequences which flowed from this would be grave ones. He wrote in August 1944 that, 'whether wisely or unwisely, we have waged the war without regard to financial consequences deliberately and of set purpose. For better or for worse, it has been our own fault.'[28] Britain had begun the war 'with a net creditor position of ... £3,500 million' and was likely to end it 'with a net debtor position of ... £2,000 million'; her 'financial diplomacy' was, in consequence, 'rooted in appeasement'. In the interests of 'getting on with the war' the British had been prepared to bankrupt themselves and hope that when tomorrow came they would still be able to live as they had before. Indeed, such were the pressures of the 'Peoples' War' that through the Beveridge Report* the British were actually looking forward to a better future

---

* Published in 1942, laying down the lines for the welfare state.

rather than the one which faced them. All Britain's 'reflex actions' were 'those of a rich man'; unfortunately her finances were those of a bankrupt spendthrift.[29] It was from this basis that Churchill was planning to continue playing a major world role.

Britain's war effort was 'planned to reach its peak in 1944' and by September of that year it was 'declining'. At the same time that Churchill was indulging in fantasies about British influence in Greece and the eastern Mediterranean, the Government was facing urgent demands to deal with 'the housing shortage' and 'repairs to industrial equipment and public utilities', which, having been postponed for five years, 'cannot any longer be delayed'. By the same measure people could not 'go on running down and wearing out their stocks of pots and pans, clothes, etc., at the current rate. In short we can no longer go on living on capital.'[30] The Government's thinking on post-war domestic policy was 'based on the assumption that we shall be able to import all the raw materials and foodstuffs necessary to provide full employment and maintain (or improve) the standard of life'; but as things stood on D-Day, this was no more than 'an act of blind faith'.[31] The same was true about plans for Britain to remain a Great Power. It was taken for granted that Britain would play her part in occupying part of Germany and that she would contribute to the costs of reconstruction and relief in Europe. Moreover, economic diplomacy towards the Soviet Union was assuming that loans would be made which would help tie the Soviets firmly into their alliance with Britain. This was indeed the 'reflex' action of a 'rich man' and it drew from Keynes the caustic comment that, 'Lady Bountiful is likely, to the best of one's observation, to continue her activities until she feels the bailiff's clutch on her shoulder.' Most of the British Empire had large reserves of sterling in London: in the case of India this came to £797 million, whilst Egypt had £297 million; by the end of 1944 there would be, even at the most optimistic estimate of what could be 'written off', accumulated balances of £1,000 to £1,500 million, 'which the countries concerned will certainly seek to withdraw at the earliest opportunity'. The obvious answer to this problem was to block these balances to ensure that they could 'only be utilized to discharge sterling loans' or to buy British exports; the latter would help Britain's much needed export drive without adding to her indebtedness. The only problem with this was that it ran counter to the demands of American multilateralism. Morgenthau and the Treasury wanted an end to the sterling area, and they wanted freely convertible currencies at fixed exchange rates. It was, Keynes thought, 'an indispensable condition of our remaining master of our own situation that we should in practice convert the sterling area into the closed system which some people believe it to be already'. But since he also acknowledged that Britain would need financial help from America in the 'transition period', and since it was clear that American policy would not allow the persistence of such a system, the British had a major problem.

Similar dilemmas proliferated wherever one chose to look. The only hope that the Government had of balancing the books within three years of the end of the war would be if exports trebled the figure for 1938, but 'such expansion will certainly be impossible unless the American Administration can be persuaded to regard an unfettered export drive, beginning in 1945, as compatible with the continuance of lend-lease'. But the Americans would not allow this, and they were determined to keep Britain's dollar reserves below $1 billion. Keynes was correct to say that 'what is political play to them is a matter of life and death to us'. If the Americans continued in their policy, then at the end of the war Britain's gold reserves would be only half those of France, two or three times less than those of Russia and sixteen times less than America's; and yet Churchill and Eden were expecting Britain to play a world role greater than the first of these and comparable with the latter. Keynes's comment was again apt: 'Our position would be ludicrously out of proportion to our liabilities.'[32]

The consequences of Britain's financial position for the home front were likely to be devastating. During the war consumption levels had fallen by 21 per cent; in America they had risen by 15 per cent. The British people were looking forward to a brave new world with a national health service, full employment and an increased standard of living; but with negligible gold and dollar reserves, massive indebtedness to the sterling area, £1,000 million in overseas assets lost and the consequent diminution of 'invisible' earnings, it was difficult, if not impossible, to see how the rewards of victory were to be delivered. The domestic and foreign policies which the Government was planning to pursue were, in short, built on the most insubstantial of foundations. As Keynes put it, 'are we not, after the greatest conquest in our history, perhaps in danger of a *manie de grandeur*? . . . We cannot police half the world at our own expense when we have already gone into pawn to the other half. We cannot run for long a great programme of social amelioration on money lent from overseas', unless Britain was willing to put herself 'financially at the mercy of America and then borrow from her on her own terms and conditions sums which we cannot confidently hope to repay'.[33]

The reaction to this description of Britain's situation was mixed. The Foreign Office, shocked by the revelation of Britain's plight, concluded that 'our relations with the US must be handled with even greater care than in the past'.[34] The Cabinet was inclined to be more sanguine. Beaverbrook thought the paper 'unduly pessimistic', whilst Churchill delivered himself of the devastatingly naïve comment that the fact that Britain had stood alone against Hitler for 'eighteen months' would count in the balance when all debts came to be calculated.[35] Quite apart from the fact that he seemed to forget the date when the Soviets had been kicked into the war, Churchill gravely overestimated American beneficence. Despite the experience of the bases for destroyers deal, despite the warships to South Africa episodes and despite the forced sale of viscose,* Churchill retained a faith in American generosity which would have been touching were it not so pathetic. Nothing which had emerged from long-running Anglo-American economic conversations gave any warrant for believing that the Americans would accept British blood, toil, tears and sweat in part payment for services rendered; quite the opposite.

Accompanying the mistrust of British imperialism and 'balance of power' diplomacy was an American determination that her money should not be used to finance them. During his visit to London in April 1944, Stettinius had responded to Sir John Anderson's litany of British financial woes and need for more lend-lease by explaining that 'when the "farmer from Kansas" learns that the British had 3 billion dollars in 1939, that they have received 10 billion or more of goods under Lend-Lease, and that they are beginning to accumulate gold and dollars again, he is going to think that the British must now be very rich'.[36] Morgenthau was equally sceptical about British cries of poverty, and it was only after visiting England in August 1944 and being told by Churchill that 'England is broke', that his scepticism abated. Roosevelt found the revelation 'very interesting. I had no idea that England was broke,' he told his old friend, adding that, 'I will go over there and make a couple of talks and take over the British Empire.'[37] Perhaps the President was joking about the last part, but his ignorance of Britain's real plight was widely shared. Even amongst those who did know that Britain was 'broke', there was no willingness to see the British use American money for their own ends. Men like Adolf Berle, Hull and the chief of the Division of British Commonwealth Affairs, John D. Hickerson, wanted a sort of updated 'dollar diplomacy', using Article VII of the master lend-lease agreement and American financial strings to secure the co-operation of other Powers, specifically Britain, in creating the sort of world which America wanted to see after the war.[38] There were those, like Dean Acheson, who regarded such missionary zeal with disfavour,[39] but in the mood of self-assertiveness which began to characterise American foreign policy in 1944, his Anglophile brand of pragmatism was not regarded with much favour. The fact that Britain could not maintain a world role without American aid gave the Roosevelt administration in effect a casting vote in the way Britain would play that role.

Hopkins, like his master, acknowledged that an 'economically healthy and powerful United Kingdom' was 'in the interests of the United States', but neither he nor Morgenthau wanted Britain to become powerful enough to be able to ignore American pressure.[40] Cherwell, Churchill's scientific adviser, optimistically thought that 'there may be some [Americans] who would like us to drift into complete economic dependence on America, but I do not believe the President is aiming at this'.[41] But American conduct at the second

---

* See John Charmley, Churchill: The End of Glory (1993), pages 437–39.

Quebec conference in September, as with the December crisis, indicated that neither the President nor Morgenthau was averse to having the British over a barrel. Churchill had approached the Quebec conference with the common British view that, 'while we are both fighting Japan and maintaining security in Europe', lend-lease on the current scale could be justified.[42] Cherwell had warned him that this was 'a matter of the utmost importance not only because it will determine the scale of our effort against Japan and the part we play in Europe, but also because our whole economic and political future depends upon the arrangement we make now'.[43] But instead of getting the sort of generous lend-lease terms to which he thought that he was entitled, Churchill was offered something which showed how Britain's financial position could be exploited for American political ends.

Roosevelt was well aware, particularly after Tehran, of the importance which Stalin attached to the 'Grand Alliance' taking a hard line on the future of Germany, and the plan which Morgenthau unfolded before Churchill at Quebec certainly merited the use of that adjective. The plan called for the dismemberment, the denazification and the deindustrialisation of Germany, and Churchill's first reaction was one of horror and disaster: 'I agree with Burke. You cannot indict a whole nation'; he thought that 'the English people will not stand for the policy you are advocating'. Morgenthau asked him pointedly how he would prevent Britain from starving when her exports had fallen so low that she would be unable to pay for her imports – would it not be to her advantage to have one of her major competitors permanently out of the way? When the matter was put this way by Cherwell, Churchill's views changed. As he explained to the War Cabinet, the pastoralisation of the German economy would mean that Britain would probably earn between three and four million pounds a year by providing the goods previously supplied by Germany. He considered 'that the disarmament argument is decisive and the beneficial consequences to us follow naturally'.[44] When he detailed 'some of the financial advantages' which the Americans were promising Britain to his Private Secretary, Jock Colville, the latter commented that they were 'Beyond the dreams of avarice'; Churchill's only response was laconic and to the point: 'Beyond the dreams of justice'.[45] On the morning of 15 September Roosevelt and Churchill signed the Morgenthau plan.

Eden was horrified and told Churchill that the War Cabinet would never accept it.[46] But a more important opinion was that of Cordell Hull, who, in one of his last major acts at the State Department, firmly squashed the plan. Hull had opposed such Draconian treatment of Germany before the conference,[47] and the fact that his rival had stolen a march on him by being at the conference did nothing to change the stubborn old man's mind. Hull disliked the fact that Roosevelt and Morgenthau had traded lend-lease for such a political concession; he had wanted them to use it to force the British into making the concessions under Article VII which he had been pressing for since 1942.[48] 'This whole development at Quebec, I believe, angered me as much as anything that happened during my career as Secretary of State,' Hull wrote in his memoirs;[49] and when it came to post-war planning, Hull's voice counted for much on Capitol Hill.[50] In the face of the combined wrath of Hull and Secretary Stimson, Morgenthau tried to blame Churchill for the 'plan', and, as it became clear that public knowledge of the scheme might damage the President's re-election chances, its days were obviously numbered. FDR performed the manoeuvre he had perfected from frequent use, that of backing away from an ill-considered policy with the excuse that he had not appreciated the extent to which signing a particular document had committed him to a course of action.[51] He told Hull on 29 September that, 'Somebody has been talking not only out of turn to the papers or on facts which are not totally true', and he stated that, 'No one wants to make Germany a wholly agricultural nation again' – which was being highly economical with the truth. But to FDR 'the real nub of the situation is to keep Britain from going into complete bankruptcy at the end of the war', and he could 'not go along with the idea of seeing the British Empire collapse financially and Germany at the same time building up a potential re-armament machine'.[52] But the Morgenthau plan was dead, and Roosevelt knew it. The whole episode demonstrated the vulnerability of the British to a combination of political and economic pressure.

Halifax was not impressed with the new activism evident by the end of 1944, and when he looked at the refusal to back Mikolajczyk or the British in Greece, he was able to say with lofty condescension that the Americans 'still cling to their old preference for dodging breathlessly round the field a few feet ahead of the bull rather than make up their minds to seize it boldly by at least one horn'.[53] But this was to underestimate Roosevelt – a dangerous habit, which had been the undoing of better men than Lord Halifax.

The equivocation in which Roosevelt indulged was not simple cowardice, but rather an acknowledgment of the complexity of the task of conducting the foreign policy of a global Power. British options were limited by history and by her financial weakness. The extent of her current military effort and her historic position all helped to sustain the illusion that Britain still had options open to her as a Great Power, but even these were strictly limited to trying to hang on to as much of what she had as was possible – or in Churchill's case rather more than was possible. America, on the other hand, faced vast horizons and unlimited possibilities. If, as the Dumbarton Oaks conference in the autumn of 1944 suggested, the Soviet Union could be carried along into active membership of a United Nations organisation, then there really might exist the chance to create a balance of peace rather than a balance of power, and the Wilsonian dream might yet be realised.

But this was not something which would come easily. Roosevelt was fully aware that some of his advisers had their doubts about the Soviets, and when it came to creating a new international order it was really the Soviets who mattered; the British could always be brought, or bought, into line. Despite Republican criticism of the administration's attitude over Poland, the Soviet hard line on that issue had long worried those who dealt with the matter. Hull had been worrying in March 1944 that a continuation of what he called 'the one-sided behaviour of Russia' might have a 'disastrous effect' on public opinion in both Britain and America, and he tended to favour 'a very plain-speaking' approach to Stalin.[54] The Warsaw uprising had the effect of driving Ambassador Harriman into a similar posture. On 15 August he told Roosevelt that 'for the first time since coming to Moscow I am gravely concerned by the attitude of the Soviet Government',[55] and he added that 'my own feeling is that Stalin should be made to understand that American public belief in the chance of the success of world security and postwar cooperation would be deeply shaken' if he continued with his policy towards Poland.[56] He told Hopkins in September that 'our relations with the Soviets have evidenced a startling turn during the last two months. They have shown an unwillingness to discuss pressing problems and have held up our requests with complete indifference to our interests.' He found Molotov's response to warnings about public opinion most ominous: 'the Soviets would judge their friends by those who accept the Soviet position'. His analysis was that 'those who oppose the sort of cooperation we expect have been getting their way recently' and that Soviet policy appeared to 'be crystalising to force the British and us to accept all Soviet policies which the Army backs by strength and prestige'. The 'general attitude' appeared to be 'that since Russia has won the war for us it is our obligation to help her and accept her policy'. Even more disturbing was Harriman's view that 'our generous attitude toward them has been misinterpreted as acceptance of their policies and as a sign of weakness'. It was, Harriman thought, time to 'take a firm stand on what we expect of them in return for our goodwill. There is every indication the Soviet Union will become a "world bully" whenever their interests are involved unless we take issue with the present policy.' But although he was 'disappointed', he was not 'discouraged'. It was going to be 'more difficult than we hoped to get the Soviet Government to play a decent role in international affairs'.[57]

Harriman thought that 'our problem' was 'to show Stalin that the advice of the counselors of a tough policy is leading him into difficulties and to strengthen the hands of those around Stalin who want to play the game along our lines', but this depended on the assumption, common from Churchill's first visit to Russia in 1942, that there were 'hard' and 'soft cops' offering conflicting advice to Stalin.[58] According to the most authoritative Soviet account, Stalin himself was the guiding force behind Soviet foreign policy and, faithful to the Leninist formula, was 'thinking in terms of minimum and maximum goals'.[59] Until the western allies actually committed themselves to the second front in France, Stalin cautiously took what opportunities he could to get 'maximum leverage at the crucial moment of Europe's liberation', which meant getting a position on the Italian Control Commission and on the European Advisory Committee. Although this meant taking the risk of opening up territories which would actually be liberated by the Red Army to western influence, 'it is hard to avoid the impression that in 1943 he simply did not consider his conquest of any such countries a foregone conclusion'.[60] Moreover, at least until Tehran, he could not be sure how far his allies would be willing to go to meet his territorial aspirations – the negotiations of 1942 had not suggested that this would be very far. Roosevelt's attitude at Tehran and afterwards gave Stalin hope that he could get his way, but he still needed to exercise caution as long as the Soviets were the only Power really taking on the German army.[61] With the opening of the second front the pressure on the Soviets receded and Stalin could afford to take his time – able to deal with his allies from a much stronger position as his victorious armies rolled over Poland and eastern Europe. it was this pheno-menon which created the 'change' in the Soviet attitude noted by Harriman, and trying to appeal to some mythical 'doves' around Stalin was not going to change the Soviet dictator's perception that, to use an English metaphor, 'he was on a winning wicket'.

If tougher rhetoric was unlikely to change Stalin's perception of his chances of getting what he wanted (defining the latter by the territorial demands which he had been making since 1939), could the Americans not have employed the financial weapon which they were able to use against Churchill at Quebec? But there was clearly a difference between the way in which the Americans regarded the British and the Soviets. Halifax was prompted to wonder in January 1945: 'Why is it that although it is known that the Russians are weak to the extent of needing great assistance in rehabilitation, they are considered strong?'[62] It is a sign of the difficulty which the British were going to have in adapting to their diminished role in the world that as acute an observer as Halifax did not see the obvious answer to this: the size of the Soviet army and the nature of the influence which this gave the Soviets made them essential partners if FDR's new world order was going to come off.

The Warsaw uprising and its aftermath certainly affected Harriman and other Soviet experts in America; indeed, George Kennan, Harriman's senior adviser in Moscow, later wrote that it should have been the occasion for a 'full-fledged and realistic showdown with the Soviet leaders: when they should have been faced with the choice between changing their policy completely and agreeing to collaborate in the establishment of truly independent countries in Eastern Europe or forfeiting Western-Allied support and sponsor-ship'.[63] But this, like many of Churchill's comments in the 1930s, shows the wisdom of hindsight. Although Kennan, who had served at the Moscow Embassy in the 1930s, took a dimmer view than Harriman of the prospects of co-operation with the Soviets, he was not advocating in 1944 what his memoirs imply. When the Ambassador was still apt to believe in the possibilities of collaboration, provided America took a firmer line and perhaps used lend-lease as a lever,[64] Kennan was much more fatalistic. His view was not, in its essence, very far from the one taken by Churchill, which was that America should adopt a spheres of influence approach 'which would limit the outward thrust of Soviet power';[65] this was what happened at Yalta.

The State Department and the President were certainly well aware of the difficulties which lay ahead of them, and they were not lacking in advice to get rather tougher, but it is not difficult to divine why they did not act on this advice. With the Dumbarton Oaks conference on the United Nations coming up, with an election on the horizon and with a war against Japan to win in which Soviet assistance was deemed to be essential, it would have been rather much to expect the State Department and the President to have taken such a dramatic stand. Moreover, such a stand would only have been justifiable in retrospect, once it was clear that there was no chance of co-operating with the Soviets, and ignored the whole logic of western policy since 1941. The Soviets were not being boastful in acting as though they had won the war. The Russians suffered casualties in the order of twelve million troops killed, the Germans lost about nine million men, whilst the British and the Americans between them lost about a million; it is not necessary to enter the realms of higher mathematics to work out who killed most of the Germans. Without the Soviets, the western allies would have been thrown back into the sea on D-Day. It is difficult to see how a harder-line policy towards the Soviets could have been planned or executed in the circumstances. They were taking the lion's share of the task of defeating the German army, and they also had potential fifth columnists in every liberated country in Europe, where the communists had been the backbone of the Resistance – and it remains doubtful whether such a line would have had the effect which Kennan imagined. With Soviet troops in eastern Europe and the western allies still facing a two-front war, it was Churchill and Roosevelt who had more to lose than Stalin from a break in allied relations. Then, of course, came the crucial point – that FDR was looking towards a Soviet-American axis to create the new post-war world order. Even a man less cynical about the sufferings of the Poles than Roosevelt might have hesitated to put all these things in the balance for their sake; with him there was no doubt. As he had told Cardinal Spellman in September 1943, 'the European people will simply have to endure the Russian domination in the hope that – in ten or twenty years – the European influence would bring the Russians to become less barbarous'.[66]

Although Harriman himself began to adopt a 'somewhat firmer and more uncompromising policy' on the delivery of lend-lease supplies, neither the President nor the State Department accepted his recommendations for a firmer line. Future military and political co-operation with the Soviet Union was deemed too important to risk losing it.[67] Hull's main worry was whether the Soviet insistence at Dumbarton Oaks that the Great Powers should have a veto on the Security Council of the proposed United Nations meant that 'Stalin and the Kremlin have determined to reverse their policy of cooperation with their Western Allies decided upon at Moscow and Tehran'. Harriman thought that this was too gloomy by far and that 'recent events perhaps were now revealing what th[eir] policy goal had been all along'. Harriman's estimate was as acute as it was accurate: 'I believe the Soviets consider that we accepted at Moscow their position that although they would keep us informed they had the right to settle their problems with their western neighbours unilaterally.'[68] Indeed, he could even have added that in recognising Britain's role as mediator in the Polish dispute, Stalin was not acting unilaterally – although that looked less true after the Soviet recognition of the Lublin 'Government' in January 1945. But that was one of the questions which Roosevelt and Churchill hoped would be decided at the forthcoming Yalta conference in February.

The western leaders both approached the conference feeling that they could strike, or had struck, a deal with Stalin. From the perspective of the Cold War their hopes look as foolish as Chamberlain's hopes of Hitler in 1938 – except to that body of opinion which is still firmly of the view that the only thing wrong with western policy was that it did not repose enough faith in Stalin for long enough, which contrasts nicely with the larger body of opinion which sees 'Yalta' as shorthand for western 'betrayal' of eastern Europe.[69] But Yalta was no more than a continuation of a policy which the British had been following since 1941 and the Americans since Tehran.[70]

There was, of course, a difference in attitude between the western Powers. Churchill was, in some senses, cutting his losses and coming to just the sort of spheres of influence deal which Kennan was advocating; Roosevelt's objectives, as usual, are a little more difficult to define. The view of the President as a sort of diplomatic Mr Micawber, waiting for something to turn up, is not one which has been taken throughout this study, and it is not one which commends itself now, nor does the variant which has poor old FDR too sick and ailing to know what he was doing. Had his actions before and after Yalta been significantly at variance with his usual behaviour towards the Soviet Union, there might have been cause to resort to these excuses. Roosevelt had connived at accepting Churchill's deal with Stalin at Moscow, despite the traditional American hostility to such arrangements. Nor was he under any illusions about what was likely to happen in Poland. Stettinius had told him at the end of October that 'Postwar Poland will be under strong Soviet influence' and that Stalin would insist on a 'sympathetic' Polish government.[71] Ever since Tehran FDR had given every impression that he was willing to pay the necessary price to ensure Soviet co-operation in the post-war era. These things only look disreputable from two vantage-points, and unfortunately for our understanding of the period these have been the ones which most post-war historians have occupied. To the Cold Warriors, the position adopted by FDR was either another version of the despised 'appeasement', or else it was down to his ill-health. Such people usually exonerate Churchill from any real share in the 'blame' by pointing up the many references to fear of the Soviets which can be found in his memoranda and minutes and stitch from them a patchwork to cover their hero's naked-ness; they tend to reject the sort of interpretation offered here, usually with more heat than light. To those who refuse to believe that morality in inter-national relations is usually ineffectual, then the sort of Metternichean *realpoli-tik* which FDR and Churchill were practising is, *ipso facto*, distasteful. But the real question to be asked of Yalta is not why Churchill and Roosevelt did what they did, but why having done it Churchill tried to go back on it. And why, instead of living up to the high hopes of its protagonists, Yalta proved the prelude to a worsening of the relations between the allied Powers.

I I

Roosevelt's Last Throw

One of the messages carried away by contemporaries from Churchill's *The Second World War* was that appeasing people is wrong, and appeasing totalitarian dictators is particularly reprehensible. The problem with this otherwise pleasing picture from the point of view of Churchill and others of this persuasion was that in the shadow of the Cold War it rather looked as though Yalta was a particularly obnoxious example of the practice of appeasement. Fortunately defences against this charge were available. An early favourite was the 'sick Roosevelt' gambit, which Churchill himself employed to some effect. For those who liked their idealism served with a dash of realism, there was the 'how many divisions has the Pope?' line, which involved pointing out that the Soviets had overwhelming force in eastern Europe. This last had to be employed with some care, but as long as no one asked awkward questions about whether it had been worth helping Stalin destroy Hitler in order to leave the Soviets masters of eastern Europe, it could be done. The most remarkable trick of all, however, was the way in which one of the architects of Yalta, Churchill, managed to transform himself into a hero of the Cold Warriors who most abominated all that Yalta stood for. It was not the least remarkable of Churchill's achievements, and it was done, at least in part, by contrasting his realism with FDR's idealism.

Roosevelt's windy liberal rhetoric is an easy, and at times irresistible, target, but this study of his wartime foreign policy has attributed to him a vein of Machiavellian cunning which would not have disgraced a statesman of the old European school of Bismarck. As FDR's best biographer has put it, 'Americans have long had both moralistic and realistic traditions', the one symbolised by Woodrow Wilson, the other by tough-minded manly figures like George Washington and the two Adamses. Because Roosevelt sounded like a Wilsonian, the dualism in his foreign policy has sometimes been overlooked. Bringing the United States into a position from which it would be able to exercise its global responsibilities created a situation in which 'no American statesman could fail to reflect this dualism'.[1] *Realpolitik* of the sort Churchill fancied he practised would never have done for a statesman who had to appeal to the idealism and traditions of American democracy. Americans were not only unaccustomed to their nation playing a world role, but they were not even sure that this was something it ought to be doing; the isolationism which had characterised the inter-war years was not a phenomenon of recent growth and it was not to be put to rest easily. Bob Taft, as so often, expressed their views best when he attacked Henry Luce's idea of an 'American century'. Old-style Republicans like Taft reacted to the new 'one worlders' rather in the manner of Roman Senators witnessing Augustan imperial ambitions:

It is based on the theory that we know better what is good for the world than the world itself. It assumes that we are always right and that anyone who disagrees with us is wrong. It reminds me of the idealism of the bureaucrats in Washington who want to regulate the lives of every American along the lines that the bureaucrats think best for them. . . . Other people simply do not like to be dominated, and we would be in the same position of suppressing rebellions by force in which the British found themselves during the nineteenth century.[2]

But, as the vehemence of Taft's attack showed, Roosevelt had hit upon a winning formula to woo the American electorate to the new internationalism. It was all very well for Taft, wrapped in the mantle of Republican virtue, to declaim that Roosevelt's line 'may appeal to the nationalistic sentiment of those Americans who picture America dominating the alliance and the world', as well as to 'the do-gooders who regard it as the manifest destiny of America to confer the benefits of the New Deal on every Hottentot',[3] but in practice this amounted to a majority of the American electorate and opinion formers. As Dean Acheson, who was by no means a Wilsonian, was to put it, 'The entire relations of the United States with the world are a seamless web.'[4] Since FDR had championed the new international role to be played by America, it was only fitting that he should have been the first to attempt to bend the bow of Ulysses; the question of whether it was a bow that only Ulysses could draw will be considered in the next chapter.

To continue with the classical analogies, it was certainly at Yalta that Roosevelt became the first American President to appreciate that global power was in some respects a shirt of Nessus. Poland, Germany, Polish-Soviet relations, European colonialism, sustaining the Chinese Government, the future of liberated Europe, trying to get the Soviets to enter the war against Japan, all these were now the concern of the President of the United States, but towering above all these was the central problem upon the solution of which all else depended: how to secure Soviet participation in the new world order? These were matters which would have taxed even Roosevelt in his prime, but his tragedy, and perhaps the world's, was that he was very far from being in that condition.

No one who saw Roosevelt at Yalta could be in any doubt that he was a very sick man. Churchill's doctor, Lord Moran, casting a professional eye over the President, commented that he 'looked old and thin and drawn': he 'appeared shrunken' and 'sat looking straight ahead with his mouth open, as if he were not taking things in. Everyone was shocked by his appearance and gabbled about it afterwards.'[5] For over a quarter of a century Roosevelt had defied his paralysis with a gaiety and panache which made people forget that he was crippled; now he was paying the price. Ever since his bout of influenza at the end of 1943 he had seemed a changed man. Where he had taken a pride in doing things for himself, even transferring himself from his chair to his car, he now let himself be carried. He seemed to tire more easily and was unable to shake off a depression; worse still was the weight loss, which had left his muscular upper body and full face looking thin and wasted. An examination at Bethseda Naval Hospital in March 1944 had diagnosed him as suffering from hypertension, hypertensive heart disease and some degree of congestive heart failure. Instead of advising his patient to rest and prescribing a regime which might reduce his blood pressure, his doctor did nothing, and it was only in the face of further deterioration in the President's condition that he was put under a restrictive regime. It was characteristic of the way Roosevelt dealt with his disability that he did not ask the reason for these things.[6] He had always been a man who kept his own feelings to himself; it was the way he had been raised, and good form dictated that however you were feeling it was necessary to appear as though nothing was wrong. But he often no longer seemed quite with things, his mind appeared to wander and he had trouble concentrating. More than ever he was thrown back upon his own resources, and these were increasingly inadequate. Physically he deteriorated. It was not just weight loss – that could in part be explained by his loss of appetite – but he suffered from frequent headaches and indigestion, and from bouts of insomnia. Polio sufferers often experience a loss of motor power as they grow older, and some doctors hold that their muscles undergo a sort of premature ageing process. Be that as it may, Roosevelt's mobility certainly decreased and there were times when his hands shook so badly that he could not control them.[7] In public he could still manage the famous Roosevelt mannerisms – the upflung head, the wide grin and the jaunty air – but as he could not maintain them for long, his public appearances became fewer, which increased the shock of his appearance to those like Lord Moran who had not seen him for some months. He spent little time at the White House, preferring Hyde Park or his treatment centre at Warm Springs in Georgia. Those close to him – and no one got very close – noted that there were times when the President was a tired old man. Yet so strong was his personal magnetism and so pervasive his spirit that few could imagine a world without him.[8]

What made him go on? Probably the same demons which had driven him to disregard his wife and strong-willed mother in 1921, when they had argued that after his polio attack he should retire to live the life of a country squire. The pride, the ambition and the egotism which had driven him then still burnt on brightly in his enfeebled frame, knitting his sinews to his willpower and driving him on to achieve what other men could not. He loved being President, exercising power and being at the centre of events. Four times he had run for the highest office and four times he had triumphed, and even now he could look ahead to his retirement – as a senior statesman, head of the United Nations or something, with world leaders coming to seek his advice at Hyde Park. These are not things a man gives up easily, and Roosevelt had never given things up easily. Perhaps, too, he suffered from the 'Chatham complex': like the elder Pitt, he knew that he could save his country and that nobody else could. All that experience and political skill, all the personal contacts and the prestige, the whole Roosevelt mystique, no one else possessed these things, nor yet the massive self-confidence which went with them. Perhaps he could only function effectively for a few hours a day, but a few hours of FDR was worth a whole day of someone else. And who could take his place in the crucial months which would determine the shape of the post-war era? Not the able administrator at the State Department nor yet the warring satraps of the Cabinet, and most certainly not the homespun Vice-President from Missouri. Secretary Stimson was apt to complain about the 'President's one-man government',[9] but it was a system suited to the man who created it – and its greatest defect was that it could not work without him.

All this concentration on one frail sexagenarian may seem a curiously old-fashioned approach to history. But it does not ignore the differing ideologies of capitalism and communism, nor yet the fact that the only real cement of the Triple Alliance was the German menace, and that as that faded, so would the alliance itself. But these great themes do not alter the fact that history is a messy business – a complex interaction between underlying forces, personality and chance – and that Roosevelt's disappearance was crucial.

The state of Roosevelt's health matters for a number of reasons, none of them to do with the usual ones cited for the sudden interest historians are apt to take in it at this period of his career. Good judges like Eden did not 'believe that the President's declining health altered his judgement, though his handling of the Conference was less sure than it might have been',[10] and others, like Harriman, concurred.[11] It matters on the level of our common humanity as a remarkable exhibition of personal courage, egotism and sheer stubborn refusal to give in to reality. But it matters most because it was to deprive Roosevelt of the opportunity to play out the game he was continuing at Yalta. No one possessed his experience, subtlety, mystique and sheer unscrupulousness; and it was certain that no one could command the influence which he had over Churchill and over American public opinion. The tragedy of Roosevelt's ill-health was that he never had the opportunity to show whether he really was a latter-day 'Chatham'. Of course it may equally be said that he was fortunate in the hour of his death, since it saved him from the consequences of his own failure, but it was also to leave his reputation in the hands of others, some of whom had motives of their own for attributing the failures of Yalta to him.

Churchill also approached Yalta determined to try to reach agreement with the Soviets. After all Stalin had abided by the spirit of the percentages agreement in Greece, and although trouble was to be anticipated over Poland and over the number of seats which the Soviets were claiming on the new United Nations Organisation, Churchill was disinclined to view these things too tragically. He told Eden on 25 January 1945: 'The only hope for the world is the agreement of the three Great Powers. If they quarrel, our children are undone.'[12] The recognition by the Soviets of the Lublin Government was obviously a discouraging omen, but Churchill's belief, as he told Stalin on 5 January, was that 'much the best thing is for us three to meet together and talk all these matters over, not only as isolated problems but in relation to the whole world situation both of the war and the transition to peace'.[13] Eden argued that it 'is essential for us . . . that there should be an independent Poland' and that the 'danger' was that 'Poland will now be insulated from the outside world and to all intents and purposes run by the Russians behind a Lublin screen'.[14] But what the Foreign Secretary did not explain was why it was 'essential'. What would happen to Britain if Poland did suffer the fate he feared, and what had changed since his willingness three years earlier to give Stalin what he wanted? The answer is found, at least in part, in the discussion which Eden had with Stettinius at Malta before the conference at Yalta.

Stettinius 'stressed that failure to find a solution would greatly disturb American public opinion, and might prejudice the whole question of American participation in the World Organization'.[15] Poland herself was not an 'essential' for the Americans, but since she impinged on things which were, the problem needed to be solved. It impinged on American public perceptions of the administration's foreign policy and, therefore, affected its ability to pursue the internationalist agenda which it had set itself. Already some sections of American opinion, outraged by British actions in Greece and the furore over Italy and Poland, were saying that 'Germany had been boxed in now and there was no longer any danger to the United States and we might just as well turn the whole situation over to England and Russia'.[16] Senator Vandenberg warned Stettinius that the 'general sentiment' was that 'the President has completely turned the Polish situation over to Stalin to do anything he wants', which was beginning to create trouble on The Hill.[17] Roosevelt's internationalist ambitions may now have been more widely shared in America as people began to realise the tremendous power which the country had, but the moral conscience of American public opinion threatened to complicate the foreign policy of its Chief Executive.[18] Roosevelt was discovering that the 'ideal policy is scarcely ever practicable'.[19] What he needed to do was to create a rhetoric and a policy which would not only appeal to his natural followers, but also to those like Senator Vandenberg who had been isolationists but now 'fully accepted . . . the extensive future role of the United States in international affairs'.[20]

In the face of criticism that his administration's foreign policy was 'rudderless', FDR arranged to meet leading Democratic and Republican Senators on 11 January, but by the time he did so it was in the shadow of a 'challenge' thrown down by Vandenberg.[21] Referring to some of Churchill's decisions as 'repugnant to our ideas and our ideals', he warned Roosevelt that America would not accept that 'our only role in this global tragedy is to fight and die and pay'. He asked a question which many Britons might well have echoed: 'What are we fighting for?' He recalled Roosevelt to the recent defence which he had himself made of the principles of the Atlantic Charter: 'These basic pledges cannot be dismissed as a mere nautical nimbus. They march with our armies. They sail with our fleets. They fly with our eagles. They sleep with our martyred dead.' He called for Roosevelt to 're-light this torch'. American self-interest demanded that America did not retreat back into isolation; the technology of war would no longer allow America to shelter behind the moat with which nature had endowed her. America had to help shape a peace settlement which would guarantee collective security and convince the Soviets that they did not need to surround themselves with a *cordon sanitaire*. This 'confession', coming as it did from one who was still regarded as something of an isolationist, was met with a massive and positive response in the American press.[22] If FDR wanted to know whether his countrymen were ready to play the role he wanted, he had an answer. But what neither he nor the American people could know was whether they would be ready to pay the price which such a role would demand.

American foreign policy had about it something of the air of a revivalist meeting – a belief that all things could be made new by faith. Roosevelt's position was now almost ironic. The man who had first inched America towards her 'manifest destiny', in the face of criticism from men like Vandenberg, was now being criticised for not being Wilsonian enough; it was as though the idealism which had inspired isolationism had been transferred directly to the support of internationalism, without acquiring any common sense on the journey. Nor had it, thus far, because the journey had been relatively painless. Although there had been sacrifices in terms of lives lost, American casualties were light by European standards. America's only problem was how to maintain the unprecedented prosperity brought by war. Although the National Debt had sky-rocketed from $37 billion to $269 billion, and the war had cost $664 billion, the Gross National Product was up from $90.5 billion in 1939 to $211.9 billion in 1945. Steel production had risen from 53 million tons to 80 million in the same period, whilst the production of aeroplanes had gone from 5,856 to 48,912, in the same quinquennium, and nearly 444,000 people had moved into the Los Angeles area with its numerous aeroplane factories. Personal savings had soared from $6.85 billion to $36.41 billion, and agricultural output had risen 15 per cent.[23] Harry S. Truman was understating it when he wrote in his memoirs: 'I was thankful that the US had been spared the unbelievable devastation of this war.'[24]

Success on this scale at such a small cost was not calculated to bring with it a sense of realism; indeed, it was more likely to produce a consciousness of immense power without a corresponding sense of what the cost of maintaining it might be. FDR still hoped to be able to square the circle of world responsibility at small cost, but that meant bringing the Soviets along. As he explained to the Senate leaders the day following Vandenberg's speech, although the newspapers had been correct in reporting that spheres of influence had been discussed at Tehran and ever since, that was only because 'the occupying forces had the power in the areas where their arms were present', and each of them knew 'that the others could not force things to an issue'. The message was that FDR was not about to abandon the Atlantic Charter, but as with what he had to say about the Soviets, the sub-text was that it was something necessary to temper idealism with reality. The victories of the Red Army gave the Soviets power in eastern Europe, and since it 'was obviously impossible to have a break with them', the only thing to do was to use American influence to ameliorate the situation. He rejected Vandenberg's argument that lend-lease could be used as a weapon in this on the grounds that this would hurt America at least as much as it would hurt the Soviets. FDR knew that there was still a war to be won against Japan and a peace settlement to be constructed, and nothing in his experience of the Soviets led him to think that they could be coerced by economic pressure into doing what America wanted. Perhaps he was 'incorrigibly optimistic',[25] but it is too harsh to say that he 'continued to deal in high principles at the expense of practical bargaining'.[26] He was simply finding that Halifax had been correct in thinking that when it came to the 'practical working out of what we want to see done we find ourselves faced with harsh and obstinate realities which often turn the ideal into the Utopian'.[27]

It was not the sickness of the President which prevented him from being able to get all that he would have wanted at Yalta; it was reality. For the Americans, Yalta was at least as much about preventing the undesirable happening as it was about getting positive results. Here the British were the weak link. If the British were allowed to pursue their plans for a western European bloc, this would encourage the Russians to do the same in eastern Europe, which would help undermine the United Nations concept, as well as alienating American public opinion; it was therefore essential to promote 'understanding between Great Britain and Russia'.[28] Another hedge against America's allies trying to promote a peace settlement which would not go down well in Peoria was 'to evolve an agreed and mutually acceptable political program'. With the Soviets suspecting the British of wanting to see 'right-wing governments' installed in newly liberated countries, 'which from the Soviet point of view would be hostile to the Soviet Union', and with the British imagining that the Soviets wanted the opposite, the room for suspicion and misunderstanding was immense. The American judgment was that 'the general mood of the people of Europe is to the left and strongly in favor of far-reaching economic and social reforms, but not, however, in favor of a left-wing totalitarian regime to achieve these reforms'. This suited the Americans, who wanted to foster coalition governments which would both exclude 'reactionary elements' and yet avoid the charge of being totalitarian. It would be necessary to get Britain and the Soviet Union to agree to a declaration on liberated Europe.[29]

To a very large extent the conference delivered the things which Roosevelt wanted. Britain and the Soviets signed the declaration on liberated Europe, and the Soviets dropped their insistence on having sixteen seats on the United Nations Security Council (one for each of the constituent republics of the Soviet Union) and agreed to a date in April for a conference to set up the Organisation. Stalin even came across with a promise to join the war against Japan once the Germans were defeated. Plans were agreed to discuss the future of Germany and reparations, and agreement was reached about sending back allied personnel in German hands. This was a large measure of agreement reached in an atmosphere of high good humour, but it was not accomplished without a price.[30]

As part of his continuing effort to convince Stalin that he would not be facing a preconcerted Anglo-American front, Roosevelt resisted Churchill's pressure for a meeting at Malta beforehand; and even when he finally gave in, it was only to the extent of spending a day with the Prime Minister. Once at Yalta he did not see Churchill alone until the fifth day of the conference and he spoke openly to Stalin about his differences with the British Prime Minister.[31] This lack of western unity, as well as the want of an agreed agenda, worried Eden, who foresaw a situation in which 'the whole business will be chaotic and nothing worthwhile [would be] settled' as Stalin was the 'only one of the three who has a clear view of what he wants and is a tough negotiator', whilst Churchill was 'all emotion in these matters' and FDR was 'vague and jealous'.[32] But the British Foreign Secretary was amongst those whose scepticism about the President blinded him to Roosevelt's devious ways of getting things done. Perhaps if Eden had spent more time with Lloyd George and less with Churchill, he would have had a better understanding of FDR.

But if the final communiqués talked of co-operation and agreements reached, it was not all done with smiles and rose-water. If Roosevelt wanted co-operation and compromises from Stalin on the United Nations and the declaration on liberated Europe, then Stalin, as he made plain from the first meeting, wanted compromises from the western Powers. From the first session of the conference on 4 February, Stalin's 'attitude to small countries' struck Eden as 'grim, not to say sinister'. Stressing that 'the three Great Powers which had borne the burden of the war should be the ones to preserve the peace', Stalin stated that it was 'ridiculous to think that a country like Albania' should have an equal voice with the 'Big Three'.[33] Churchill challenged this remark, commenting that, although there could be no question of the smaller Power dictating to the 'Big Three', 'The eagle should permit the small birds to sing and care not wherefor they sang.'[34] He evidently knew little about the habits of the Russian eagle. This attitude informed Stalin's views on Poland when it came up for discussion on the third day of the conference.

In the absence of material from the Soviet archives, and perhaps even with such evidence, it is difficult to lay bare the mainsprings of Stalin's policy, but his concerns are evident in the questions he asked and the way he raised them. In the discussions of 5 February he probed to find out whether his allies would consider dealing with an 'alternative' German government – the shadow cast by Darlan was a long one.*[35] Roosevelt and Churchill calmed any fears on this point, and when discussing the future of Germany, the President made it clear that for America these were the sort of detailed problems which the Europeans were going to have to solve by themselves. Churchill was as keen to associate France with any occupation of Germany as FDR and Stalin were reluctant. Churchill pressed the matter on the grounds that Britain would need help to play the role expected of her. In the face of this FDR moderated his position, making it clear that he did not intend to keep a large army indefinitely in Europe – that was why the American occupation would be limited to two years.[36] Stalin also relented a little, but not to the extent of letting the French have a seat on the Control Commission. This was another example of the Soviet leader's brutally realistic attitude to the 'small birds'; as far as he was concerned, the fate of France in 1940 had proved that she was no longer a Great Power.[37] But Stalin would not throw any card away, and before the conference was over he made good use of Britain's concern for France and western Europe – what was good enough for Churchill in the west would suit Stalin in the east.

Roosevelt's main interest was in the discussion after lunch on 6 February, when the question of the 'international security organisation' was brought up. The first question to be decided upon was the procedure for voting on the Security Council. The Americans proposed that the Great Powers should have the right to veto any motion unless they were themselves parties to a dispute, in which case they should abstain. Stalin asked for more time to study the proposal, but Churchill backed it as it was one of the few topics which Eden and Stettinius had been able to cover at Malta. Churchill, once more in his role as advocate of the interests of the less powerful nations (perhaps an awareness of Britain's position sharpened his sensitivities on this

* In November 1942 Eisenhower had co-operated with the Vichy Admiral Darlan to the disgust of liberal opinion in Britain and America.

issue), defended the principle of giving all nations the right to ventilate their complaints. He did not want it to look as though the 'Big Three' were ruling the world, and they should, if necessary, make what he called a 'proud submission' to the views of others. Stalin asked Churchill what he had in mind when he referred to a desire to rule the world: 'He was sure Great Britain had no such desire, nor had the United States, and that left only the USSR.'[38]

Stalin's suspicions had floated to the surface not simply to test out his allies, but also to deal with the question of how to secure what he stated was the key to future peace: how to 'preserve unity' amongst the allies. He was satisfied that, 'as long as the three of them lived, none of them would involve their countries in aggressive actions', but who could tell if they would still be there in a decade? Peace needed to rest on foundations which were firmer than the lives of three ageing men. Stalin seemed divided between thinking that the United Nations might provide such a foundation and fear of it being used to gang up on Russia. Roosevelt strove to reassure the Soviet leader that his fears were as misplaced as his hopes were well-placed. For the American leader, no part of the conference was more important than this, and when Poland was discussed later that day it is hard not to believe that FDR was not influenced by the desire to assuage Stalin's fears.[39]

The problem with Poland was that both Churchill and Stalin regarded it as 'essential', but for quite different reasons. For the British, it was, as Churchill stated on several occasions with grandiloquent eloquence, a matter of honour. Here Churchill could not quite make up his mind what would satisfy 'honour'. In discussions on 6 February he concentrated on the need to save the 'face' of the London Poles, but everything he said also suggested that it was Britain's 'face' – and his own – which needed saving. On 6 February it seemed to be border concessions, particularly Lwow, which might serve this purpose, although it would also be necessary to form a Polish government which was not entirely composed of the men of Lublin. But Stalin had easy counters to this strategy. Did the Poles want more territory? Well fine, they could have it at Germany's expense in the west, which would surely save everyone's 'face'. On the question of the Polish Government Stalin hardly needed to resort to much in the way of sophistry; a little *tu quoque* would do. Stalin based his argument firmly on the fact that for the Soviets Poland was a 'matter of security'.[40] Twice in the last thirty years Poland had been 'a corridor for an enemy attacking Russia', so the Soviets had an obvious interest in a 'strong' Poland. As for the Curzon line, why that had been drawn up by an Englishman and a French Prime Minister and he, Stalin, could not be 'less Russian than Curzon and Clemenceau'. But he was perfectly prepared to 'let the war against the Germans go on a little longer' in order to provide the Poles with compensation in the west – as far west, indeed, as the western Neisse.

On the issue of the Polish Government Stalin adopted the position which he maintained throughout – that the London Poles had been given their chance when Churchill had been in Moscow in October, but had thrown it away and caused the resignation of Mikolajczyk, who had at least been prepared to negotiate. As far as he was concerned, the Government in Warsaw had as much legitimacy as de Gaulle's in Paris. When Churchill argued that the allies could themselves nominate an interim Polish government, he laid himself open to a fine example of Stalinist nerve. How, asked Stalin, 'could a Polish Government be set up without the participation of the Poles? Many people called him, Stalin, a dictator, and did not believe he was a democrat, but he had enough democratic feeling to refrain from setting up a Polish Government without the Poles.'[41] He was, he said, 'prepared to make every effort to unite the Poles, but only if it had any chance of success. What was to be done?' He was willing to invite the Lublin Poles to Moscow, or indeed to do anything his allies could suggest. But having said that, he then launched into a bitter tirade against the 'agents of the London Government' whom he accused of having killed over two hundred Soviet troops. Churchill disputed the idea that the Lublin Government was properly representative of the Polish people, but Roosevelt cut short a potential squabble between his allies with the characteristic comment that 'the Polish question had been giving the world a headache over a period of five centuries'.

This was symptomatic of Roosevelt's attitude towards Poland. He realised that opinion in America and elsewhere wanted an honourable solution to the problem, but he was not sure that one was on offer. If the need to conciliate domestic public opinion clashed with the goal of allied unity, then, 'in a crunch, he would sacrifice self-determination to maintain good relations with Stalin'.[42] If he did not call Poland a 'far away country' of which 'we know nothing', he did say that 'he took a distant point of view of the Polish question' and made it clear that his main interest was in the creation of a Polish coalition government which American public opinion would find acceptable.[43] On the border issue he was quite prepared to stand by what had been agreed at Tehran with regard to the Curzon line, but he thought that Stalin might help the Poles save 'face' by giving Lwow to them.

On the following afternoon, 7 February, Stalin made explicit the link between his highest priority – Poland – and FDR's – the United Nations. The evening before, after consultation with Churchill, FDR had suggested to Stalin that they should summon assorted Polish notables from all parties and get them to agree on a government which the 'Big Three' would guarantee,[44] but at the start of the session Stalin said that, as his response was still being typed up, they should move on and discuss the voting arrangements for the Security Council. 'Having thus unobtrusively linked the Polish question with Roosevelt's highest priority item, Stalin announced that he would accept the American voting formula.'[45] It was a clever move since, as far as the Americans were concerned, 'the Dumbarton Oaks situation was of greater importance than anything else'.[46] In return for dropping the demand they had made at Dumbarton Oaks for sixteen seats on the Security Council, the Soviets asked for only three, and when Churchill accepted that, Stalin showed how much importance he really attached to the whole subject by suggesting that America should also have three seats. But from FDR's point of view things were going as well as he could have expected and the only fly in the ointment was Churchill's cavilling at the idea of having the conference to set up the United Nations as early as March.[47]

By this time the Soviets were ready to table their suggestions about Poland. They formalised the concession which Stalin had made verbally the day before by accepting the western Neisse as Poland's western frontier and made some small concessions about the Curzon line. On the subject of the shape of the Polish Government they were willing to 'recognize as desirable' the enlargement of the Lublin Government 'through the inclusion of some democratic leaders from among the émigré Polish circles'.[48] It was suggested that the allies recognise such a government as the prelude to a 'general election'. There was not much to object to in this, unless the omission of the word 'free' is thought to be significant. Neither Churchill nor Roosevelt was willing to push the claims of the 'émigré Poles', although they did protest at the use of the adjective. More significant in Churchill's eyes was the search for territorial compensation. As he embarked upon one of his great set-piece orations, FDR, reading the signs from Churchill's manner, passed a note to Stettinius: 'Now we are for half an hour of it'[49] – as indeed they were. The Prime Minister argued to and fro the boundary question, concluding that 'it would be a great pity to stuff the Polish goose so full of German food that it died of indigestion'. In a moment which mixed the blackest comedy with the rhetoric of what might be called machismo politics, Churchill raised the subject of the 'shock' which the movement of millions of Germans would create in Britain, whilst denying, of course, that he would feel anything of the sort. Stalin's bleak response was that most of the Germans in the areas to be handed to Poland had 'run away'.

The next session between the allied leaders took place on the afternoon of 8 February, when, after a discussion about the date of the United Nations conference and who should be invited to it, matters turned once more to Poland. Neither Churchill nor FDR was happy with moving the Polish frontier as far as the western Neisse, but they both agreed that once a Polish government of national unity had been formed, they would cease to recognise the London Poles. The Soviets stuck to the position which they had established the day before: there was already a government in Warsaw and the most that could be done was to admit a few London Poles to its ranks. Once again Churchill launched into one of his oratorical flights. 'This was the question for the settlement of which the whole world was waiting,' he said, with

pardonable exaggeration. If they left Yalta still recognising two Polish governments, then it would be apparent to everyone that 'fundamental differences
existed between Russia and their British and American allies'; this would
'stamp the conference with the seal of failure'. But the problem was, as
Churchill tacitly acknowledged, that there were 'fundamental differences'
between the allies. 'Honour', the main British concern, demanded that the
150,000 Poles who had fought with the allies should not be abandoned and
that their Government could not just be disowned. Although Churchill did
not agree with the 'foolish' actions of the London Poles, it would, he told
Stalin, cause the 'gravest criticism' in Parliament if Britain was to be seen to
abandon them. Churchill would find his Government accused of 'having
given away completely on the Eastern frontier [as they in fact had]' and of
truckling to the Soviets. These fears, as Churchill was to discover, were not
misplaced.

FDR, speaking as a 'visitor from another hemisphere', stressed the need
for early elections. Perhaps he hoped that these would deliver the pro-Soviet
governments which Stalin wanted; that would have got everybody off the
hook. It would certainly have tested Stalin's roseate view of the Poles as
people who had dropped their hostility to the Russians: 'the Poles were quite
happy to see the Russians drive the Germans before them and liberate the
Polish population, and this kindled a warm feeling for them among the
Poles'.[50] Stalin admitted that it would be better to have an elected government
in Warsaw, but as he pointed out, neither de Gaulle's Government nor the
regency in Athens headed by Archbishop Damaskinos had been elected: 'Why
was more to be demanded of Poland than of France?' It was a reasonable
question, but a dangerous one for the western leaders to answer. Both Churchill and Roosevelt settled happily for Stalin's assurance that 'elections could
be held within a month'.

It was not an unreasonable conclusion, and Churchill could cheerfully
inform the War Cabinet that Stalin was a man who could be trusted.[51]
Roosevelt had done his best to create an atmosphere in which allied co-
operation might continue. Criticism of him for not securing firmer guarantees
over Poland miss the point as he saw it. His Chief of Staff, Admiral Leahy,
criticised the declaration on Poland, warning that 'this is so elastic that the
Russians can stretch it all the way from Yalta to Washington without ever
technically breaking it'. FDR responded: 'I know it, Bill – I know it. But it's
the best I can do for Poland at this time.'[52] But there was more to it than
yielding to immovable forces. Guarantees by themselves are no good; indeed,
a proliferation of guarantees, as with France's eastern European policy before
the war, often betokens only weakness and insecurity. What was important
was to create a situation in which the Soviets would feel it was worth their
while to keep their word. But FDR's plans for the United Nations fell foul
of the great dilemma which always confronts liberals on such occasions. If

there existed the spirit of friendship and co-operation which was needed to make the United Nations work, it would hardly be necessary, but if these things were absent, then it would not work. If Churchill was correct in thinking that 'the only bond of the victors is their common Hate', then both he and Roosevelt were in trouble.[53]

12

The End of FDR

Speaking on the fortieth anniversary of the Yalta conference on 5 February 1985, President Ronald Reagan declared that

Yalta has a double meaning. It recalls an episode of cooperation between the Soviet Union and free nations in a common cause. But it also recalls the reasons that this cooperation could not continue – the Soviet promises that were not kept, the elections that were not held, the two halves of Europe which have remained apart.[1]

For most of the period which Reagan was describing, it was only the second of these meanings which was remembered, yet it had been the first which had inspired the agreement. Was what went wrong as simple as Mr Reagan's speech-writers would have it? Was it just that the Soviets did not keep their promises?

But what 'promises' did the Soviets not 'keep'? Stalin had made Soviet war aims plain from 1939 onwards, and they were not ones which fitted into the Atlantic Charter. In the negotiations with Chamberlain in 1939, again in those with Eden in 1942, as at Tehran and in the percentages deal with Churchill, Stalin had set out his stall. Both Churchill and Roosevelt had shown themselves willing to grant him what he wanted; after all, the Soviets had every right to expect some reward for winning the war. Churchill would later cover his tracks by citing his post-Yalta attempts to alert FDR to the menace posed by Soviet ambitions. But the Soviet demands had not changed. What changed was Churchill's willingness to grant them. What seemed acceptable in the middle of the war, seemed less so with victory in sight. Conservative opinion was as unready to grant Stalin's desiderata as ever – and western public opinion was to prove itself equally dubious about handing over eastern Europe. Churchill's telegrams to FDR represented a belated attempt to go back on what had been implied at Tehran, Moscow and Yalta. Breaking 'promises' after Yalta was not quite as clear-cut as Mr Reagan's speech-writers seem to have imagined.

Roosevelt was wary of Churchill's attempts to pin him down to a firm line on Russia, but his Chief of Staff, Admiral Leahy, 'believed . . . that a Europe dominated by a single overwhelming power spelled danger to American security'.[2] Not all American observers of the Soviet Union took such a Churchillian view of the situation. George Kennan, who had long taken a gloomy view of the prospect of co-operation between the western Powers and the Soviets, and who was highly critical of the Yalta accords, favoured a 'decent and definitive compromise' with Stalin, which would 'divide Europe frankly into spheres of influence' and 'keep ourselves out of the Russian sphere and keep the Russians out of ours'; this would be better than failing to 'name any limit for Russian expansionism'. In so far as this was a criticism of FDR, it was one which implicitly condemned his attempts to create a post-war world revolving around a Soviet-American axis; but Kennan was not arguing for a confrontation with the Soviets. His friend and colleague, Chip Bohlen, who had kept the American diplomatic record at Yalta, shared Roosevelt's sense that the time had not yet come to foreclose on the future in this manner. He chided Kennan for taking a position which was 'utterly impossible' from a 'practical point of view'. It might seem, 'from an abstract point of view', that the best thing was to carve up Europe into spheres of influence, but 'foreign policies of that kind cannot be made in a democracy'. Like his chief, Bohlen believed that it was pointless trying to force further assurances out of the Soviets: 'Either our pals intend to limit themselves or they don't.' The answer to this riddle was not 'yet clear', and trying to force the issue was worse than pointless. Whatever anyone thought about communism, the Soviets were 'here to stay as one of the major factors in the world. Quarreling with them', Bohlen warned, 'would be so easy, but we could always come to that.'[3]

If the western allies did not like the prospects opening up before them, then they should have thought about it earlier; to accept Soviet help when Hitler needed defeating, and then to lecture the Soviets on what to do when he had been defeated, showed a certain naïveté. Churchill himself had been foremost in coming to a spheres of influence deal with Stalin over eastern Europe; and if he imagined that Stalin would maintain his 'sphere' by western democratic methods, he was wrong. Roosevelt had shown a clearer vision than Churchill here. Stalin had men on the ground in eastern Europe and his forces had destroyed the German army, which gave the western allies very little leverage. It was, of course, open to the western Powers to take what might be called the General Anders option. Anders, the commander of the Polish forces in Italy, had much irritated Churchill in late 1944 by talking about 'beating' the 'Muscovites',[4] yet the position which the British Prime Minister adopted in March 1945 carried with it precisely that risk – and all because Stalin failed to deliver the election which he had promised?

It is hard not to draw the conclusion that Churchill was seizing upon a pretext for a showdown with the Soviets. It was true that the Soviets did not hold an election in Poland, but the British had not held one in Greece; indeed, they had intervened there by force. Nor had there been an election in France, nor was there to be one in Belgium and Holland before the end of the war in Europe. It was true that where the Soviets had liberated countries like Romania and Bulgaria, the western allies were given no say in running the country, but then the Soviet place on the Italian Control Commission was worth little and the military government which had been planned for France had no place in it for the Soviets.[5] It was also true that communists were in a leading position in Yugoslavia, but that was nothing to do with the Soviets; the British had decided all on their own to back Tito and his resistance movement, realising only too late the consequences. The fact was that Churchill applied a different set of standards to the Soviets than he did to himself. It was all right for the British to intervene by force in Greece because that protected British interests, and it was fine for the British to press for a place on the German Control Commission for the French for the same reason; yet when the Soviets acted in like manner, that was spreading communism.

It was here that the lessons of Munich became relevant. Much to both his displeasure and surprise, Churchill soon found himself under attack over the provisions of the Yalta agreement as they applied to Poland. The London Poles had a well-organised and well-used set of contacts with the press and Members of Parliament, which they put into operation. Churchill found himself being attacked in Parliament with the sort of arguments he had once employed against Neville Chamberlain, and what hurt even more was that some of those pointing the finger had been loyal supporters of the former Prime Minister. Still these things were not without their advantages. Back in 1943 Churchill had referred to Poland as a possible 'hook' to keep the Americans in Europe, and FDR had made it plain at Yalta that American forces would be withdrawn from the Continent within two years of the end of the German war. Churchill had no illusions about the immediate potential of a 'western bloc' – a 'cluster of feeble states' for which Britain 'must become responsible' was how he referred to them at Yalta.[6] He and the Foreign Office had always agreed about the need to use American power to supplement Britain's weakness; the time had come to cash in the large pile of chips which Churchill's long cultivation of the Americans had given him. To this there was one obstacle: Franklin D. Roosevelt.

Roosevelt had made it clear ever since Tehran that he was not going to enter some exclusive special relationship with the British. He had always avoided going to London and doing anything which might allow Churchill to claim that he had an entrée to the President. Indeed, even at Yalta he had opposed British attempts to build up France as a Great Power because he did not want to see the British developing a sphere of influence in western Europe. For Roosevelt, the British Empire was as much to be deplored as Soviet communism, and there are no signs that he was willing to do what Churchill wanted, which was to use burgeoning American power to prevent the Soviets dominating Europe.

Churchill's position was not without parallel in British history. At the end of the Napoleonic wars, Viscount Castlereagh had sought to use Austrian power as a counterpoise to the great influence which Russian victories had given to Tsar Alexander I. But that attempt had eventually broken down when the ideological interests shared by Metternich and the Tsar got the better of the Austrian fear of the Russians.[7] This time Churchill seemed to be hoping that American fear of the Soviets would get the better of the interests which America and Russia had in common. After all, Soviet spheres of influence in eastern Europe hardly portended any danger to America. Stalin had made his demands clear all along, and even in the hour of his greatest triumph he did not demand more.

Churchill's agitation is easy to understand. Although he returned from Yalta saying, 'Poor Neville Chamberlain believed he could trust Hitler. He was wrong, but I don't think I'm wrong about Stalin',[8] he was less certain than he sometimes sounded. The same evening that he made this remark, he ruminated in rather more sombre vein to his Private Secretary: 'What will lie between the white snows of Russia and white cliffs of Dover?'[9] Although for public consumption he spoke in the Commons debate of Stalin as head of a government which 'stands to its obligations, even in its own despite',[10] in private he was telling Roosevelt that, although he was confident of winning the vote, 'there is a good deal of unease in both parties that we are letting the Poles down, etc.'.[11]

So swift was Churchill's disillusionment with Yalta that it might be expected to be the result of some new and dangerous act by Stalin, but the observer will look in vain for anything beyond the reaction of Parliamentary opinion. It is true that in Romania the Soviets set about 'intimidating the King and Government' and began the 'establishment of a Communist minority government with all the technique familiar to students of the Comintern', and that Eden was anxious at such a breach of the 'spirit' of Yalta, but Churchill told him on 28 February that there was 'nothing' he could do: 'Russia has let us go our way in Greece, she would insist on imposing her will in Roumania and Bulgaria. But as regards Poland we would have our say.'[12] When Eden returned to the Romanian problem on 5 March, Churchill took the same line, saying that he did not want to have it said that 'we have broken our faith about Roumania after taking advantage of our position in Greece'.[13] Nor did the Prime Minister shift from this position.[14] Yet on 8 March Churchill quoted Soviet behaviour in Romania in a long telegram urging Roosevelt to protest about events there. As he explained, 'having regard to my personal relations with Stalin, I am sure it would be a mistake for me at this stage to embark on the argument' – especially in view of the Greece–Romania trade-off agreed in October. Whilst FDR mounted a protest on one side, Churchill would do the same thing about Poland.[15] In the ten days following 8 March Churchill sent Roosevelt ten telegrams urging him to take a firmer line with the Soviets.

Churchill had manoeuvred himself into a position from which he could only win. If FDR accepted his advice, there would be the sort of concerted Anglo-American front which FDR had fought so hard to avoid. If this forced Stalin to back down, all would be well. If it did not have this result, at least Churchill had acted consistently with the lessons of Munich and his domestic critics would be silenced. Either way Britain would have a major international role to play. If Roosevelt did not take the bait and Stalin did break his promises at Yalta, Churchill would be in the clear with his domestic critics – he had done his best; if the worst happened, it would be the fault of the Americans. Both Churchill and Eden, their reputations 'made' by the public perception of their stand on appeasement, were conscious of the need to preserve their own 'face'. Eden told Halifax on 5 March that if the Soviets were allowed to get away with recognising the former Lublin Government and excluding the London Poles, 'we and the Americans would be accused – rightly – of having subscribed at the Crimea Conference to a formula which we knew to be unworkable'.[16] This was not far from Churchill's comment to FDR that, 'if we do not get things right now, it will soon be seen by the world that you and I by putting our signatures to the Crimea settlement have under-written a fraudulent prospectus'.[17]

As with the stream of telegrams which followed it, there was something of an air of humbug about this one. Churchill had struck a spheres of influence deal with Stalin in October, and he was abiding by it as far as being unwilling to say publicly anything about Romania or Bulgaria. It was true that there were no signs of elections in Poland and that Stalin maintained his recognition of the Lublin Poles, but even before the Yalta conference the British had been resigned to getting nothing more from the Soviets than a 'widening of the present basis of the Lublin Committee'.[18] Stalin had not proved enthusiastic about this at the conference, and the London Poles proved equally resistant to the idea. Eden minuted rather pettishly after seeing Mikolajczyk on 20 February that, although 'I have taught myself not to expect any thanks for anything we may do for other people, I must confess that I had not quite expected these gentlemen to be so sceptical of the arrangements reached at the Crimea Conference'.[19] General Anders told Eden that his army 'had given their oath to the Polish Government and constitution and they could not lightly transfer it to any other body'. He said that he would have preferred it if the western allies had 'left matters alone' at Yalta.[20] Other members of the London Government spread stories in advance of the Commons debates about 'wholesale liquidations and deportations' in Poland.[21] As Beaverbrook put it to Hopkins on 1 March, 'over Poland the opposition is strong. It is led by a powerful Tory Group who are the erstwhile champions of Munich.' These 'followers of Chamberlain' were making 'the undercover case that Churchill beat them up in 1938 for selling the Czechs down the river, and has now done to the Poles at Yalta exactly what Chamberlain did to the Czechs at Munich'.[22]

Roosevelt received the stream of Churchillian rhetoric with more circumspection and less alarm than its originator appreciated. FDR had stage-managed the favourable reception for the Yalta accords by sending the disappointed Vice-President aspirant, Jimmy Byrnes, back home as his harbinger of good news. Byrnes, whose service as Director of the Office of War Mobilisation had given him a high profile on the home front, had been bitterly disappointed at what he rightly regarded as Roosevelt's manipulation of him during the 1944 election, and had had expectations of the succession to the State Department on Hull's retirement.[23] In compensation for his renewed disappointment, Roosevelt had sought to win him over by asking him to accompany him to Yalta. Although Byrnes had been outraged at being asked to leave the first plenary session because Stalin did not want civilians present when they were discussing military matters and had threatened to go back home, he had stayed, and in return FDR had used him as 'both a private lobbyist and a public salesman of the agreements reached at Yalta'.[24] Given the reaction of American public opinion to the December crises in the Mediterranean and to Vandenberg's speech, Roosevelt was well aware that only a 'just peace' was likely to evoke the American commitment to the United Nations that he needed, and as a former Congressman, Senator and Supreme Court Justice, the loquacious and enthusiastic Irish-American was the ideal salesman, particularly since he had not attended any of the sessions at which contentious problems like Poland and Germany were discussed. At the major press conference which he held on his return, Byrnes combated initial reports that Stalin had dominated the conference and achieved all his objectives by stressing Roosevelt's 'leadership role' and emphasising that the final decisions were entirely consistent with American principles and war aims. In support of this interpretation he played up the 'Declaration on Liberated Europe' to show that there would be no spheres of influence and that there would be 'free and unfettered elections' throughout the Continent.[25] This was, of course, some distance from the regretful compromises which FDR had actually reached at Yalta, but then it would have been rather difficult to sell them to the American people. Now came Churchill's query: 'How would the matter go in the United States?'

At Yalta the details of working out a solution to the Polish problem had been delegated to a tripartite commission composed of Harriman, Clark-Kerr and the Soviet Foreign Minister, Molotov. From the start Molotov had continued in the vein which he and Stalin had adopted at the conference – it was up to the Lublin Poles to take some of the London Poles into their Government, and which 'Londoners' were invited to discuss the issue with the Commission was a matter for them. This was unacceptable to Harriman and Clark-Kerr, but the 'Londoners' whom they suggested proved equally unacceptable to the Government in Warsaw. Harriman saw the delays and stone-walling as working to the advantage of the Lublin Government, which was 'becoming more and more the Warsaw Government and the ruler of Poland'.[26] It was this situation which Churchill wanted to take up with Stalin.

Roosevelt's first reaction was that 'he thought it better for us not to have to resort to the heavy artillery of personal correspondence with Stalin but to give the thing time and allow Ambassadors time to work it out with Mr Molotov'.[27] But Churchill was not happy with the detailed instructions which had been sent to Harriman because they spoke about getting 'the rival political groups' to 'adopt a political truce'.[28] This, Churchill exhorted the President, would hardly do: 'It suits the Soviets very well to have a long period of delay so that the process of liquidation of elements unfavourable to them or their puppets may run its full course.'[29] Once again Churchill touched on the topic which more than anything else was impelling his actions: 'I have already mentioned to you that the feeling here is strong. Four Ministers have abstained from the divisions and two have already resigned.' The lessons of Munich were indeed being driven home to the man who had first adumbrated them. He followed up his telegram with a long series of examples of Soviet misbehaviour designed to persuade Roosevelt that it was time to take a tougher stance.[30]

Roosevelt's replies were drafted at the State Department, but there is no reason for supposing that they did not reflect his own mind; indeed, in their elliptical ambiguity and oblique approach to the problem, they seem a perfect reflection of that calculating intellect. Reassuring Churchill that 'our objectives are identical', FDR argued for a less confrontational approach, feeling that matters could be left to the Moscow Commission and that they should argue for Anglo-American 'observers' to be sent to Poland.[31] Those close to FDR, including Leahy, were sceptical of the long series of abuses alleged in Churchill's cable, and they argued for practicality; there was no point pressing the issue. If Stalin refused to do anything, then their last state would be worse than their first.[32] In a further despatch on 12 March drawn up by Leahy, Roosevelt reiterated that they should leave matters to the Ambassadors – but he did not rule out an appeal to Stalin if necessary.[33]

The suggestion that Churchill was acting partly because of pressure at home and partly in order to create an Anglo-American special relationship is supported by the tenor of his dissatisfied responses to Roosevelt's prevarication. He warned that although he did not want to 'reveal a divergence between the British and the United States Governments', it might become necessary 'for me to make it clear that we are in the presence of a great failure and an utter breakdown of what was settled at Yalta, but that we British have not the necessary strength to carry the matter further'. The threat was plain: Churchill was prepared to defend his own back by putting the blame on the Americans. He urged FDR not to accept Soviet demands that the Lublin Poles should be invited to the San Francisco conference on the United Nations in April.

But Roosevelt continued to play it long, denying that there was any difference in 'policy' between Britain and America over the Polish issue; there was simply one of 'tactics'. Here the blame was neatly thrown on to the British, at whose request, FDR reminded Churchill, further negotiation through Ambassadorial channels had been delayed. The President argued in favour of realism in the negotiations; there was, after all, no point in putting forward positions which the Soviets were bound to reject.[34] Roosevelt was, according to Halifax, fully conscious of the 'political difficulties that [the Polish] situation was creating for you [Churchill] in England, and was also very conscious of his own';[35] the tenor of his telegrams suggests that he regarded Churchill as helping to create the latter by striving after a clarification of the Polish situation which was unlikely to help either leader. Roosevelt was at the most delicate stage of his manoeuvrings to persuade Americans of their manifest destiny as a world Power, and he was conscious of the difficulties which still lay in his path. It was, he wrote to the banker Thomas Lamont, 'unfortunate ... that in the field of international politics so many Americans are still living in the age of innocence'.[36] He had never needed his skills as a 'juggler' as badly as he did now. Some historians have taken the view that FDR could not face up to the realisation that he had failed in his quest to create a world free of spheres of influence and balances of power, but the interpretation offered here suggests that a subtler process was at work. With the San Francisco conference coming up, Roosevelt did not want to do anything which would sabotage the chance of Soviet co-operation. As ever he was looking at the wider horizon and the broader picture, and as usual he was trying to ignore inconvenient details which did not fit into his world-view. The problem was that Churchill's agenda was more circumscribed than his own. Facing the possibility of a general election, criticism from within his own Party and the necessity of a close Anglo-American relationship, the British Prime Minister was reacting in characteristic fashion; identifying Stalin's actions as a danger to the balance of power in Europe, he was following through the logic of the position he had outlined in 1943: Poland was to be the 'hook' which snared America in Europe.

The President found himself between the proverbial rock and the hard place. Churchill's unease was shared by sections of the American press and it could not be ignored; on the other hand, any attempt to press Stalin too closely was likely to produce deadlock, which boded ill for the San Francisco conference. It was a situation which needed 'juggling' of an impressive order. FDR sought to keep Churchill in check by agreeing that the Ambassadors should attempt to persuade the Soviets to modify their stance; this would use up time and might even produce some change in the Soviet position. He refused, as he told Churchill on 15 March, to 'agree that we are confronted with a breakdown of the Yalta agreement'. He reminded the Prime Minister that the reason why negotiations had stalled was because Churchill had

requested time to co-ordinate Anglo-American policy.[37] This produced a sub-
dued response from Churchill. Anxious, perhaps, lest he should lose American
support by the clamant attitude, the Prime Minister expressed himself
'relieved that you do not feel that there is any fundamental divergence
between us'. 'Our great desire', he told FDR, 'is to keep in step with you and
we realize how hopeless the position would become for Poland if it were ever
seen that we were not in full accord'; he might have added that it was not
only Poland's 'position' which would become 'hopeless' without American
support. He still, however, refused to accept American ideas of a political
'truce' in Poland, and he urged Roosevelt to agree to a joint Anglo-American
initiative.[38]

Roosevelt had always been careful never to present Stalin with an Anglo-
American front, but faced with Churchill's persistence and the doubts of
some of his advisers, he now abandoned this position, agreeing to 'separate
but identical' messages which reiterated the British goals of introducing democratic elements into the Lublin Government, sending western observers to
Poland and holding free elections.[39] The result of the western approach on
19 March was exactly what FDR had earlier feared, namely a Soviet rejection.
This was accompanied by what looked like a calculated snub to the Americans
in the form of an announcement that Molotov would not be leading the
Soviet delegation to the United Nations conference at San Francisco. Churchill seized the opportunity to launch a full-scale bid for American support
against Stalin, heartened by the reflection that nothing was more likely to
bring them 'into line with us than any idea of the San Francisco conference
being imperilled'.[40] In Churchill's view the Soviets had not kept their pledged
word and the western allies risked becoming 'parties to imposing on Poland,
and on how much more of eastern Europe, the Russian version of democracy'.
He wanted to make the 'strongest possible appeal to Stalin' about Poland
and 'any other derogation from the harmony of the Crimea'.[41]

Churchill had not yet entirely given up hope on Stalin. When Eden wanted
him to send a strong complaint about Russian mistreatment of British prisoners of war, Churchill avoided using words which would invite a 'rough
answer', and he concluded by stating: 'We seem to have a lot of difficulties
now, since we parted at Yalta, but I am sure that all these would soon be
swept away if only we could meet together.'[42] This was a reflection of Churchill's tendency to personalise the relationships between states, and there is
no reason to doubt that at least at some level he believed it. At another level,
that which connected with the 'lessons of Munich', Churchill also believed
in the chance of preserving Great Power co-operation, but here it would be
'firmness' rather than personal understandings which would work the oracle;
if only Stalin could become convinced of Anglo-American unity and firmness
of purpose, then he would co-operate. These were dangerously simplistic
misreadings of a situation which was fraught with complexities; the river

to be navigated was filled with shoals and cross-currents, and Churchill's navigational techniques were inadequate for the task at hand.

Any expectation that the Soviets would not 'impose' the 'Russian version of democracy' on areas within her sphere of influence was setting up a standard of conduct which the Soviets were bound to fail. Those who did not follow Churchill in erecting this fence tended to be more optimistic about the prospects for the future. Clark-Kerr, whilst acknowledging that 'much has happened since [Yalta] to trouble the harmonies established ... [there] and to fortify critics', thought that 'we should make a mistake if we built up a black record from the events of the past few weeks, and if we decided that they implied that the Kremlin had turned away from the policy of cooperation with the West'. Clark-Kerr was clear-eyed about his hosts. At international conferences they came to 'sniff the air' and to 'discover how far they can go in pushing Soviet interests', and at Yalta the message had seemed to be that as far as Poland and eastern Europe were concerned, there were few limits. Moreover, there was a natural tendency to 'press ahead with their plans' whilst they had 'a relatively free hand'. Nevertheless, Clark-Kerr argued, this was essentially 'a policy of limited objectives, none of which endangers essential British interests'. When it came to Poland, he thought that the Soviets might simply 'not understand why we should insist upon having so tight a hand upon a question where no direct British interest was involved'. It was, he thought, essential to recognise that 'the word "co-operation", like the word "democracy", has different meanings in the Soviet Union and in the West. Here it seems to mean the acceptance of something like a division of the world into spheres of interest and a tacit agreement that no one of the partners will hamper or indeed criticise the actions of the other within its own sphere.'[43]

Here then was a Kennan-like view based upon the sort of *realpolitik* which Churchill himself had practised at Moscow in October. But the objections to it were those Bohlen had raised in February: could it be sold to public opinion in the west? 'Public opinion' is an imprecise term and, as wartime propaganda has shown, it is something which can be moulded, if not created, by governments. The Soviet Union was popular in both Britain and America – indeed, in view of the performance of its armed forces it would have been surprising had it not been – so could not Soviet domination over Poland have been fed to the allied public in a way which would have been palatable? What was lacking was the will to do so.

From that conscience of the Tory Party, Lord Cranborne, came a stern warning to Eden that allowing Stalin to have his way on Poland would be to make the United Nations Charter a 'fraudulent document, to which we ought not to put our name'. It would, he added, be impossible to defend any compromise 'with any shred of honesty' in Parliament.[44] His Lordship knew whereof he spoke. Although the Yalta debate had been won comfortably by the Government, it had revealed a level of discontent amongst Conservative MPs which was only likely to be assuaged by the sort of concessions over Poland which the Soviets were not making. As one of the leading lights of the Tory right, Bobby Petherick, put it to Eden on 30 March, 'my friends have been holding our hand for the time being', but given the 'most shocking reports about deportations, arrests and tortures', it was doubtful how much longer this state of affairs could continue.[45] Any policy which assumed that the Soviets were going to adopt western definitions of words like 'democracy' and 'human rights' was going to end in tears.

For others, such as the Deputy Under-Secretary at the Foreign Office, Sir Orme Sargent, the ending of the war in Europe marked the end of that period in which military necessity had dictated a need to 'propitiate our Russian ally'. It was also an occasion for recalling how ungracious the Soviets had been and how 'very little response' they had made to the diplomatic finesse shown towards them.[46] Whilst Soviet aid had still been essential to the common victory, Churchill and Roosevelt had thought it expedient to put up with incessant Soviet complaints, in particular the perpetual charge that they were not doing as much as the Soviets in the military field. Before D-Day such taunts had had to be accepted, but now when they were once more levelled, the time had come, Sargent suggested, here as in the other areas, to take a firmer line.

The latest allegations concerned informal talks which the British and American commanders had been holding with representatives of the German SS in northern Italy. When the Soviets got wind of the talks and were refused permission to send an observer, Stalin's suspicious nature got the better of any dwindling desire to keep on good terms with his partners. Throughout the war he had lived in suspense lest the capitalist powers should serve him as he had served them in 1939; for all the apologetics spouted by fellow-travellers in the west, Stalin knew that the Nazi–Soviet pact had been designed to ward off the possibility of Chamberlain directing Hitler east. Now, with Dr Goebbels talking about 'iron curtains' falling across central Europe and appealing to the western Powers not to destroy Germany but rather to ally with her against the Soviet barbarians, Soviet paranoia took flight once more. On 29 March Stalin told Roosevelt that the Germans were giving the forces of the western Powers a more or less free ride in order to reinforce the eastern front.[47] Eisenhower had been 'deeply stirred with anger' at what he considered 'most unjustified and unfounded charges about our good faith', an attitude shared by Roosevelt and by Churchill, although the latter did admit that, 'I do not see why we should break our hearts if, owing to mass surrender in the west, we get to the Elbe or even further before Stalin'.[48] The Prime Minister joined the President in a dignified rebuttal of the Soviet allegations, telling Stalin on 6 April that he had been 'astonished' by them and 'affronted' by their implication.[49]

Sargent thought that the incident showed 'clearly the deep suspicions' which the Soviets 'harbour as to the uses to which we may put our victories',[50] and like the Prime Minister, who feared that it might 'be a very sinister sign',[51] he thought that the moment had 'come to speak plainly to the Soviet Government'. But the problem with the lesson drawn by Sargent and Churchill from Munich was that it presupposed that plain speaking would produce the desired response from the dictator. Hitler had not been unwilling to put matters to the arbitrament of war in 1939, and it was not to be supposed that a triumphant Soviet Union would be deterred from seeking security on its borders by bluster from the Anglo-Americans; the problem with Churchill's strategy was that it risked stoking the very paranoia which nourished it. As Sir Alexander Cadogan put it in his cool and somewhat cynical way, 'I am not quite clear to the form and object of the showdown in the whole field.'[52]

Roosevelt was now the main obstacle to discovering what the 'form and object' of a 'showdown' would be. To those who take the view (usually with hindsight) that the Soviets were thirsting to start the Cold War, the President's actions can be explained away as those of a sick and dying man, but they were, in fact, entirely of a piece with his attitude towards the Soviets throughout the war. Roosevelt's eyes were firmly fixed on the San Francisco conference. In his last address to the nation on 1 March he had sought to warn his fellow Americans that although the final peace would rest on the principles of the Atlantic Charter, they could not expect to get everything they wanted. He had cited the agreement over Poland as an example of one of those occasions when neither party had got everything it wanted. The important thing was the United Nations Organisation; only through the co-operation of the Great Powers could the world be spared the horrors of another world war. With the last of his failing strength Roosevelt was determined to try to hold to the course he had long set himself, but the winds from London threatened to blow him off course.[53] He did not wholly agree with Churchill's definition of the commitments entered into at Yalta, and he had always been more willing to allow the Lublin Government a privileged position. He reminded Churchill on 29 March of what he had told his countrymen at the beginning of the month: the agreement had been a compromise.[54] But the problem for the ailing President was that the Soviets were doing nothing to show that they understood the meaning of the word compromise, hence his proposal to send a sterner message to Stalin. He expressed himself 'frankly puzzled' as to why there had been no progress towards carrying out the Yalta agreement on Poland, and although he mentioned Romania in passing it was on the Polish question that he dwelt, making it clear that for any settlement to enjoy the support of western public opinion, it must amount to more than a continuation of the Lublin regime.[55]

The whole tone of the document breathed sweet reasonableness, certainly in comparison with the much firmer tone which Churchill's supporting message adopted.[56] That a firmer tone did slip into Roosevelt's last correspondence about the Soviet Union is true, but it is to be doubted whether the President was responsible for this. Stalin's allegations over the 'negotiations' with the Germans allowed Churchill to rub in his message about the need for firmness. 'We must always', he told FDR, 'be anxious lest the brutality of the Russian messages does not foreshadow some deep change of policy for which they are preparing.' It was necessary 'that a firm and blunt stand should be made at this juncture by our two countries', Churchill argued, because, 'if they are ever convinced that we are afraid of them and can be bullied into submission, then indeed I should despair of our future relations with them and much else'.[57] The almost instant response from Warm Springs, Georgia, where Roosevelt was resting, was 'general agreement' with Churchill: 'We must not permit anybody to entertain a false impression that we are afraid'; in a 'few days' the armies of the western allies would be 'in a position that will permit us to become "tougher" than has heretofore appeared advantageous to the war effort'.[58]

Britain, Churchill thought, could only 'hold her own' as a Great Power in the future by 'our superior statecraft and experience'.[59] This variant on Macmillan's 'Greeks in the new Roman Empire' had been evident throughout Churchill's long series of minatory telegrams; had Roosevelt finally 'seen the light'? It seems unlikely that one hasty telegram would be the medium for a fundamental shift of American policy. Perhaps Roosevelt was doing what he often did – playing both sides of the street. But the most likely explanation is that the message reflected the views of the man who drafted it, Admiral Leahy. Leahy had been drafting most of Roosevelt's messages on the Soviet question, often with 'little or no supervision by the President'.[60] As Leahy's biographer has put it, 'one must be careful about reading [Roosevelt's] . . . intentions' into any of the telegrams sent at this time; 'many of the important exchanges are much more an indication of the thinking in the State Department or other American agencies than they are examples of FDR's policies . . . this particular cable more likely reflected Leahy's views'.[61] Roosevelt had not abandoned hope; indeed, in what was to be his penultimate exchange with Churchill on 11 April, his tone of voice came through in characteristic manner: 'I would minimize the general Soviet problem as much as possible because these problems, in one form or another, seem to arise every day and most of them straighten out.'[62] Here was the authentic voice of FDR, the man who believed in creative procrastination as both an art form and a method of governing.

This, however, was the last time that this voice would be heard in the councils of the 'Grand Alliance'. At quarter-past one on the afternoon of 12 April Roosevelt complained of a 'terrific headache', before slumping over in his chair; three and a half hours later his doctors pronounced him dead. The headaches would henceforth belong to his successor, but with his death there passed the last exponent of a diplomacy subtle enough to maintain the co-operation of the Soviet Union. Henceforth the cruder methods which Churchill dignified with the term 'superior statecraft' would prevail; the true exponent of that art had passed from the scene leaving no worthy successor.

13

Enter Mr Truman

The dispute amongst historians over the effect of Roosevelt's death on allied relations, and in particular on the development of the Cold War, has waxed fiercely almost since April 1945, and it shows no sign of abating. The view adopted here has clearly rejected the notion that FDR had decided to 'get tough' with the Soviets, and it follows that it also rejects the idea that Truman was simply continuing that policy.[1] As one commentator has it, 'Revisionists who perceive a reversal in American policy upon Truman's accession tend to attribute greater responsibility to individuals in explaining the onset of the Cold War';[2] quite so. In this instance the argument is not only that Truman was too ill-informed and unsophisticated either to appreciate or to follow through Roosevelt's subtle evasions, but that he was also vulnerable to British attempts to use the Soviet 'threat' as a 'hook' to pull America into looking after their interests in Europe and elsewhere; but that does not mean that America entered the Cold War because of Britain.

All post-war American Presidents have suffered an eclipse in popularity following their departure from office, but Harry S. Truman, the 'man from Missouri', the straight-talking honest Joe from middle America, has seen his reputation increase. In part this is nostalgia for a vanished golden age of American greatness, when the word 'decline' was never coupled with the name of America, when the economy was booming and the dollar was king, when urban riots, drugs and political correctness were all unknown and when the American dream seemed immanent. Yet it might be argued that it was under Truman that the descent from Avernus began.

In July 1917 Woodrow Wilson had written that, 'England and France have not the same views with regard to peace that we have by any means. When the war is over we can force them to our way of thinking, because by that time they will, among other things, be financially in our hands.'[3] His pride had been brought low by a combination of his own faults, Congress and Anglo-French wiliness, but there was unlikely to be a repetition of this failure. FDR had carefully nourished an American internationalism, linking it to the attainment of a new world order organised on American principles, which would make the world safe for generations to come. This, however, imposed constraints on American diplomacy, particularly in trying to practise the sort of *realpolitik* which FDR was tempted to use in his dealings with the Soviets. As that loyal 'New Dealer', Adolf Berle, had put it in September 1944, 'we cannot sacrifice the reputation of the U.S. for a large degree of moral approach to problems, as contrasted with the cynical approach of power politics'. For America's leaders to be seen to be acquiescing in 'power politics' would 'undoubtedly endanger the likelihood of the American public's adopting a plan for world organization'. Roosevelt seemed to have been relying on a combination of American military and economic might, and adroit diplomacy backed by his own massive prestige, to deal with the problems which Soviet behaviour in Poland might cause.

This was to some extent the least enviable part of Truman's legacy. If, as Berle put it, 'the United States, in respect of certain principles, is bound to assume responsibility where and to the extent that she has the power to act militarily or diplomatically',[4] then the quest for a peace in the American mould could extend over every question which remained to be settled by the members of the 'Grand Alliance'. Here too the self-confident liberalism of Berle may stand as a text and a warning:

We have ideals and ideas as to what we would like to see happen in the entire continent of Europe. Because in some measure these depart from the ideas of our allies, they have not been pressed during the period of war, lest divisions be created. Some of the powerful reasons for not pressing our point of view will disappear with the defeat of Germany.[5]

To some extent the American attitude towards her allies had always been 'a plague on both your houses'. Berle was hardly the only American who criticised Britain and America for pursuing 'power politics ... on the pattern made nauseatingly familiar by the Axis in 1935–9',[6] but if America was going to start demanding that the allies should construct a peace settlement and a world order in accordance with her own 'ideals and ideas', then the British would be the beneficiaries – provided, that is, they played their cards according to American wishes. This would be the fulfilment of Churchill's long-held vision, even if it did not come about in quite the way he would have liked. But for this to happen American policy needed to settle itself into a mode where the Soviets took Hitler's place as the great international bogey. In this process Churchill would play some role; so too would the presumed 'lessons of Munich', the actions of the Soviet Union, and misjudgments and miscalculations on all sides. But perhaps the greatest role would be played by the American determination to impose their own values on everyone else.

But this process took time, and the Second World War did not give way immediately to the Cold War. The initial impact of Roosevelt's death was, however, to deprive western diplomacy of subtlety and range at a time when both these qualities were sorely needed. It might be that there was nothing which Truman and Churchill could have done to have secured the future co-operation of Stalin, but it is certain that the sudden crudeness which overcame western diplomacy at Truman's hands can have done nothing to further the cause of three-Power co-operation for which FDR had laboured so long.

Truman may have come to the White House unprepared for the office, but he was not surprised to be there. He had noticed at FDR's final press conference that the President was in a bad way, and he had warned his mother that he 'didn't think Roosevelt would make it'; he woke up 'every morning in a cold sweat dreading that it might be today'.[7] He was not the only one in a 'cold sweat' when the news of Roosevelt's death became public. Since the whole of Churchill's foreign policy now rested upon the choices to be made by a man unknown to the British (or to anyone else much), the first need was to collect information on the new President. Harry Hopkins, although now seriously ill, remained a good source, and his judgment was that Roosevelt's death had created a 'completely new situation in which we should be starting from scratch'. He described the new President as 'honest – capable – methodical', but frightfully inexperienced. He had told Hopkins that 'he felt equipped to handle domestic issues but completely ignorant of foreign'. He had, Hopkins told Halifax, 'accepted FDR's general line without question, and no doubt felt [the] same way, but had no background'.[8]

The problem with this assessment was that FDR's foreign policy had been so personal to himself that it was doubtful whether Truman or anyone he asked really appreciated what its 'general line' had been. Truman sought advice from Hopkins, Stettinius and others as to what the President had been planning to do, particularly on the vexed question of the Soviet Union. Since FDR had not been one to share his thoughts with others, this amounted to asking them to predict what the President would have done – always a course fraught with danger and difficulty. But it was not just from Hopkins, Stettinius, Leahy and Harriman that Truman received advice. This was a situation tailor-made for Churchill to exercise that 'superior statecraft' which the existence of Roosevelt had always precluded.

The loss of Roosevelt was no doubt a personal blow to Churchill, but, leaving aside the rose-coloured spectacles and the misty memories, it offered the British opportunities for influence which they would hardly have had otherwise. Churchill had laboured, none harder, to persuade FDR of the virtues of an exclusive Anglo-American alliance, and had sought ever since Yalta to found such a relationship on a common perception of the menace posed by the Soviet Union, but this strategy had always threatened to founder on Roosevelt's preference for prevarication and his mistrust of British imperialism. Whilst Truman had the usual American attitude towards the British Empire, he had none of Roosevelt's subtlety and ambiguity. As his advisers quickly learnt, Truman was a man who had 'the capacity for seeing things in a very black and white way'. Where Roosevelt had listened to every option available and gone on to invent some more for himself, Truman did 'not want options' from his advisers; 'instead he wanted to know whether something was the "right" thing to do'.⁹ From an ordinary human point of view it was no doubt admirable that Mrs Truman could say that her husband was 'sincere and will do what's best',¹⁰ but there are many situations where it is not readily apparent what that is – and this was one of them. Wanting to carry through Roosevelt's policy towards the Soviet Union, but ignorant of the nature of that policy, Truman naturally turned towards those who had been closest to his predecessor.¹¹ But no one had been close enough to Roosevelt to have been able to divine the labyrinthine subtlety of his intentions, and men like Leahy and some of those at the State Department, who had been drafting Roosevelt's later telegrams to Churchill on the subject, clearly wished American policy to take a firmer line. Since nothing could have suited Churchill more, the only obstacle to the imposition of such a policy was the possibility that the Soviets would begin to prove more amenable; when they did not, then the 'lessons of Munich' were applied. Regardless of the fact that it had been British meddling in an area of the world where she had neither power nor influence which had helped precipitate the war which had led directly to the current situation, Churchill persisted in believing that all could be rescued by resolute action.

But is this not to blame Truman and Churchill for the advent of what became known as the Cold War, and is it not to ignore the role played by the Soviets? If it is held that Chamberlain would have been better advised to have let Hitler pursue his Teutonic crusade against the Slavs in 1938–9, then it is at least consistent (even if it might be argued that it is consistently wrong) to argue that the western Powers should have stuck to the logic of the policy they had pursued up to Yalta. A year earlier, when Sir Owen O'Malley had been expostulating about the moral shoddiness of abandoning the Poles to their fate, neither Churchill nor Eden had been very impressed; the need to keep the Soviets in the war against Nazi Germany had stilled any clamant voices which suggested that the demands of morality were being ignored. But now Hitler's Reich lay in ruins. The Soviets had always demanded, and had been led to believe they would be granted, a sphere of influence in eastern and central Europe; it was two impulses from the western side which converted this into a diplomatic and military showdown.

Truman and Churchill did not cause the Cold War, but they helped to create the conditions in which it came about. Truman would take longer than Churchill to perceive the Soviets as a menace, but that was not Churchill's doing. In Churchill's case the motivation was complex. Natural belligerency, an intellectual heritage of social Darwinism, a long imperial rivalry with Russia ('Adam-zad – the Bear that walks like a man'), an enduring concern with the balance of power in Europe and the need for an American alliance, all these, along with the fateful 'lessons of Munich', played their part in precipitating Churchill into a new Cassandra-type role. The speed of this transformation and its completeness should not be exaggerated; as long as he remained Prime Minister, and even afterwards, Churchill's moods of belligerency would be accompanied by a wistful belief that if only he and Stalin could get together, everything would be all right.

The process by which Truman would come to share Churchill's perception of the existence of a Soviet menace was longer and more complex than the one which had caused the British leader to come by such views. At the root of Truman's conversion was American liberalism made militant and internationalist. Truman inherited an America committed to playing a world role, but internationalism was predicated on the assumption that America could not stand by and see totalitarianism flourish. Given that America's most powerful ally, the Soviet Union, was a totalitarian state, then the clear implication was that either the Soviets should change their ways or they would be stigmatised as a menace to civilisation.

This is not to ignore or excuse Soviet behaviour, but the Soviets had at least been consistent. The Molotov–Ribbentrop pact was made because the western Powers were not willing to appease Soviet desires to escape from the Versailles system and because Stalin feared that Chamberlain was being clever enough to direct the Germans eastwards. He had been wrong in the latter assumption, but he remained consistent in his desire to create a world order which would give the Soviets what they wanted: land, security and power. It was hardly unreasonable of the Power which had lost the greatest number of combatants and played the major part in destroying the Nazi military machine to want the fruits which these sacrifices had brought. In the period in power left to him Churchill would do his best to frustrate Stalin's aims, whilst still hoping for a continuation of the 'Grand Alliance', a situation oddly similar to that of Chamberlain in 1939, who, whilst denying the Soviets the concessions they wanted, believed that an alliance with them might be concluded. Truman's actions, reflecting the advice he was getting and the initial experience of office, would veer from a 'hard' Leahy–Churchill line to a use of Hopkins and Joseph Davies in an attempt to open up diplomatic options threatened by his own early clumsiness. From the British Embassy in Washington, Isaiah Berlin predicted that, given Truman's inexperience and the want of a strong hand in the State Department, 'we are likely to witness missed opportunities and neglected acts';[12] and so it came to pass.

The first fruits of Truman's determination to follow Roosevelt's policy towards the Soviets was the sort of joint Anglo-American *démarche* to Stalin which FDR had always tried to avoid. Churchill readily agreed to a proposal from Truman on 14 April (only the second message to be exchanged between the two men) that Stalin should be told that the western allies could not accept that the Lublin Poles had a veto on who should and should not take part in negotiations to form a new Polish government; instead, Truman suggested, there should be talks between three Poles from Lublin and three from London, with one neutral observer.[13] Although Eden and the Foreign

Office wanted and secured amendments to Truman's proposals, Churchill saw the real significance of the American offer. On 8 April he had told Eden that, 'I think the time has come for a show-down on these points, and the British and the United States are completely aligned. We may go far and long before finding an equally good occasion.'[14] But he had been wrong then in supposing that FDR would agree to a joint protest; however, with the new President 'so stiff and strong', Churchill finally had the lead he had been waiting for, and he was not going to give it up because Eden and the diplomats were not entirely happy with Truman's ideas.[15] As he told Eden on 15 April, 'I consider it of the highest importance that immediate agreement should be reached on President Truman's proposals.... I wished ... a lead from the United States. It has now come and I am in general agreement with it.'[16] Pushing home his advantage, Churchill also expressed his anxiety about future zones of occupation in Germany and Austria to Truman. Although agreement had been reached on these matters in 1944, 'it was not foreseen that General Eisenhower's Armies would make such a mighty inroad into Germany'. Although, as Churchill was well aware, there could be no amendment of the zones without agreement with the Soviets, he did not wish to see 'our Allied troops or your American troops ... hustled back at any point by some crude assertion of a local Russian General', and he wanted to make arrangements to ensure a 'fair distribution of the food produced in Germany between all parts of Germany'.[17] He also expressed his anxiety at the 'likelihood of the Russian armies occupying large parts of Austria before any decisions are reached'.[18]

With 'Victory in Europe' now in sight, the final disposition of the allied armies was as much on Churchill's mind as the situation in Poland – and for much the same reason: the Soviet Union. When he saw Eisenhower on 17 and 18 April, he pressed the General strongly to make an all-out effort to capture Berlin.[19] Eisenhower, however, had already decided that the Soviets would be left to do that, and whatever new mood was abroad in Truman's White House, it did not extend to altering the General's plans.[20] FDR had approved of Eisenhower's decision in late March to leave the German capital to the Soviets, and Truman and Chief of Staff General George C. Marshall did nothing to alter it. Those who argue passionately that Eisenhower ought to have gone to Berlin have failed to explain what advantage would have been gained thereby. But if much of the argument over whether Eisenhower should have occupied Berlin is infused with the hindsight of the Cold War, the fact remains that Churchill advocated the policy at the time, so was he anticipating, even helping to create, the Cold War? His continuing advocacy of a western occupation of Berlin was at one with his feverish attempts to anticipate the Soviets wherever possible. It was not just in Austria that he worried; he wanted the western allies in Prague and Denmark before the Soviets. 'Our arrival in Lubeck,' he told Eden on 18 April, 'before our Russian friends from Stettin, would save a lot of argument later on.'²¹ At the same time, Eden was pointing out to the Americans the 'great political advantages' which would accrue if American forces could press forward and liberate Prague before the Soviets.²² At the very least the British seemed intent on securing their own sphere of influence whilst denying one to the Soviets except upon terms Stalin was unlikely to accept.

It would be an over-simplification amounting to error to assert that Churchill's influence was the sole reason for Truman's tougher stand, but Eden, who was in Washington for the discussions which preceded the formation of the United Nations, played his part, along with Churchill, in pressing for a harder line to be taken with Molotov and the Soviets.²³ As early as 13 April, and quite unprompted, Truman told Stettinius 'that we must stand up to the Russians at this point and that we must not be too easy with them'.²⁴ The new President was as unlike the elegant and ambiguous Hudson valley squire he had succeeded as it was possible to be. As his latest biographer puts it, Truman, 'with his Monday night poker games, his Masonic ring and snappy bow ties, the Main Street pals, the dry Missouri voice, was entirely, undeniably middle American'.²⁵ Not just 'middle American', but a Missourian. Missouri is the 'show me' state, and its inhabitants, particularly those from small towns, are proud of their reputation for plain-speaking and straight-dealing. Truman was a true Missourian.²⁶ The difference amounted to this:

> Roosevelt loved the subtleties of human relations. He was a master of the circuitous solution to problems, of the pleasing if ambiguous answer to difficult questions. He was sensitive to nuances in a way Harry Truman never was and never would be. Truman, with his rural Missouri background, and partly, too, because of the limits of his education, was inclined to see things in far simpler terms, as right or wrong, wise or foolish. He dealt little in abstractions.²⁷

His 'solid old-fashioned Americanism' was affronted by what he took to be Soviet double-dealing,²⁸ and he dealt with it as he would have dealt with a defaulting customer in the far-off days when he had been a haberdasher in Independence. Democracy is no doubt all well and good, as are plain-speaking, plain-cooking and, for that matter, plain women, but goodness is, alas, not always enough, and plainness is no substitute for talent. If Truman had any doubts about taking a harder line with the Soviets, and there is no evidence for it, his instinctive response was reinforced by what Leahy and Ambassador Harriman had to tell him.²⁹ Whatever hopes Harriman had once held about the possibility of co-operation with the Soviet Union, events since the Warsaw uprising had disillusioned him. He thought that 'we now have ample proof that the Soviet Government views all matters from the standpoint of their own selfish interests' and that it was essential that 'we and the British now adopt an independent line';³⁰ Churchill himself could not have asked for more. Harriman thought that 'Russian plans for establishing satellite states are a threat to the world and to us',[31] and he told Truman that they were faced with a 'barbarian invasion' of Europe.[32] This was language which Truman understood, and he reacted as one might have imagined he would – by getting 'tough'. Harriman wanted America to use 'our economic interests to adopt a more positive policy of using our economic influence to further our broad political ideals';[33] 'our money and our supplies', some thought, would give America 'leverage'.[34] The Americans were already enjoying great success pursuing this line with the British, but they were to discover that Stalin was not Churchill and the Soviets were not the British. Soviet troops had performed prodigies of valour and endurance against the best army the world had ever seen; Stalin thought that this entitled him to a sphere of influence in eastern and central Europe. If strong and active communist parties in France and Italy threatened to bring to power governments in western Europe sympathetic to the Soviet cause, then Stalin would not complain, but that was not where his main focus lay. Like Alexander I after the defeat of Napoleon, it was to Poland and eastern Europe that the Red Tsar's attention was drawn.

The first fruits of Missouri diplomacy came in a famous meeting between Truman and Molotov on 23 April. Although his advisers were generally of the opinion that 'the time had arrived to take a strong American attitude towards the Soviets', there was an interesting nuance between those who had been closest to FDR and the others. Secretary Stimson was rather alarmed at the 'brutal frankness' which Truman proposed to use,[35] whilst Leahy, whom later historians were to accuse of playing the role of éminence grise, told the President that the Yalta agreement on Poland was subject to more than one interpretation.[36] But the Secretary for the Navy, James Forrestal, shared Harriman's view that what was at stake was a possible Soviet takeover of eastern and central Europe.[37] Truman had no ear for the nuances of difference here; as far as he was concerned the general consensus of 'getting tough' was enough for him – and he did just that.[38]

Because of FDR's penchant for secrecy there is room for disagreement over whether Truman was or was not carrying through the dead President's policy, but there can be no doubt that his methods were as unlike Roosevelt's as it was possible for them to be. Not only had he consulted widely amongst his senior advisers, but he had also, through Stettinius, been at pains to co-ordinate his actions with the British[39] – a most un-Rooseveltian way of proceeding. At a meeting with Stettinius on 21 April, Eden had emphasised that 'some progress' on Poland was 'absolutely essential' if the San Francisco conference was to be a success, and Stettinius had concurred, even going so far as to say that 'continued failure to settle this matter satisfactorily endangered the entire position of the United States taking its place at the world table'.[40] The meeting between Eden, Stettinius and Molotov on 22 April 'got . . . nowhere at all'.[41] Molotov had wanted to discuss San Francisco first, but Eden had insisted upon linking it to Poland and dealing with that contentious issue first. Molotov, after claiming that he was not aware of the Churchill–Truman message on Poland, got to the heart of the Soviet position when he 'argued that the Soviet Government had made no difficulties about any agreements we [the British] or the United States Government might wish to conclude with either France or Belgium'. Eden, as usual, refused to accept the analogy, although it clearly existed in the Soviet mind, with Molotov arguing that Britain and America 'were not neighbours of Poland' and could 'afford to postpone decisions', a luxury not open to the Soviets. Although the argument was sophistical, it contained the germ of the Soviet position: Poland was in their sphere and was their concern; they did not interfere in France or Belgium, so why did the western Powers interfere in Poland?[42]

Eden took 'a very bad view' of the encounter and told Stettinius that he 'felt that the fate of the San Francisco conference is in jeopardy'.[43] As Cadogan put it, 'the question arises whether we can really go to San Francisco to urge the adoption of a plan admittedly based on Great Power cooperation when the Great Powers are so obviously at sixes and sevens'.[44] Eden wished to have the Soviets 'brought up sharply against realities' by postponing the United Nations conference 'while we continue to hammer at the Polish issue'.[45] It is some sign of how little the British Foreign Secretary appreciated the differences between his own priorities and those of the Americans that he should have believed that Stettinius would go along with his request. The Permanent Under-Secretary at the Foreign Office, Sir Alexander Cadogan, was more realistic: 'the Americans are so dead set on the Conference that I doubt they'll really play along those lines'. Stettinius did, however, agree that if a further meeting on the morrow enjoyed no success, he would 'mobilize the President to talk like a Dutch Uncle to Molotov'.[46]

When the three men met again on the morning of 23 April for a meeting lasting two hours, there was 'no progress whatever'.[47] As agreed, Stettinius conferred with Truman and

> further discussion with the Americans has resulted in agreement with us on the following programme. President will see Mr Molotov this evening and explain to him in blunt terms the effect of his attitude on future cooperation between the Great Powers. . . . Americans appear to have some hope that this conversation may produce a more reasonable attitude by Russia.[48]

This meant a retreat from the position that there must be a Polish settlement before the San Francisco conference could go ahead, but Eden concluded that 'we are right to fall into this programme for above all we must keep in step with the Americans'.

Truman immediately summoned his advisers. His mood was uncompromising and, before any of them could speak, he said that he intended to 'go on with the plans for San Francisco and if the Russians did not wish to join us they could go to hell'.[49] Only General Marshall and Secretary Stimson had doubts about taking a firm line. This in itself might have given the President pause for thought because Marshall and Stimson were probably the most level-headed and sensible men in the room; instead, he went straight ahead and had a meeting with the Soviet Ambassador.

It is difficult to accept the argument that Truman's language to Molotov when they met that afternoon was solely the result of Eden's prompting Stettinius, and still less does it appear sensible to suppose that Truman's purpose was limited to ensuring that the San Francisco conference could go ahead.[50] The advice tendered by Harriman, Stettinius, Leahy, Eden and Churchill all pointed along a path congenial by its nature to the President. Straight-talking did no one any harm, and Truman proceeded to give Molotov a piece of his mind, lecturing him on the need to keep to agreements.[51] As he later told a rather shocked Ambassador Joseph Davies, 'I gave it to him straight' with a 'one-two to the jaw'; Molotov was 'visibly shaken, blanched and went pale'.[52] There is, alas, no contemporary warrant for the denouement recounted by Truman in his memoirs, which had Molotov saying: 'I have never been talked to like that in my life', and Truman replying: 'Carry out your agreements and you won't get talked to like that.' As Truman's latest biographer acknowledges, there is no contemporary record for this exchange, which has about it *l'esprit de l'escalier*.[53] If it was characteristic of Truman to play up to his own image as the plain-spoken Missourian by embellishing a good story, there can be no doubt of the toughness of the tone he did take. It was, perhaps, equally characteristic of Harriman that having been 'hawkish' at the time, he should later have claimed to have been 'a little taken aback' at Truman's behaviour, even to the extent of regretting that it 'gave Molotov an excuse to tell Stalin that the Roosevelt policy was being abandoned'. This, Harriman claimed in his memoirs, was 'a mistake, though not a decisive mistake'.[54] That is a matter of opinion. It would be exceedingly foolish to place too much emphasis upon one exchange, although if Harriman was right in claiming that this gave Molotov the excuse to tell Stalin that the 'Roosevelt policy' was being 'abandoned', then it was certainly as important as Truman makes it appear. It is, indeed, in its effect upon Soviet diplomacy that the exchange was most important.

Since Yalta Soviet diplomacy had been 'erratic and inconsistent rather than premeditated and methodical'.[55] Although the leaders of the western partners in the alliance were apt to attribute almost superhuman calculation to everything Stalin did, the reality was that the situation confronting the Soviet dictator was quite as puzzling as the one they faced themselves. He faced the same Europe in ruins as they did, and he had to live with the knowledge that it was his own misreading of events in 1939–41 which had helped bring his country to the verge of defeat. Although victory was now in sight, it had been bought at immense cost, and judging his fellow leaders by his own standards, he could not be sure, as his anxiety over Anglo-American contacts with the Germans in Berne showed, that even at this late hour the capitalists would not serve him as he had served them in 1939. He was 'tired, tense, and visibly depressed', and he had good reason to be. It is unlikely that Stalin trusted anyone; nothing in his own character and experience would have commended such a course to him, but he had thought that he knew where he was with Roosevelt: 'he dips in his hand only for bigger coins', unlike Churchill, who was 'the kind who, if you don't watch him, will slip a kopeck out of your pocket!'[56] With his ideas about the 'United Nations' and his penchant for compromise, Roosevelt was a less formidable antagonist than that old Bolshevik-hater, Churchill. With FDR gone and Truman using a tone which Churchill himself could not have bettered, it was little wonder that the surly and suspicious Stalin began to 'panic'.[57] Truman may have meant his words as a warning shot across Stalin's bows, but he had, after all, said in 1941: 'If we see Germany is winning we should help Russia and if Russia is winning we ought to help Germany and that way let them kill as many as possible, although I don't want to see Hitler victorious under any circumstances';[58] since this was almost the only thing his Kremlin dossier on him contained, it was not surprising that Stalin should have begun to fear the worst.[59] It is not the least of the many ironies with which this period is replete that misperceptions and misconceptions on both sides should have stirred up the demons which the actions of Truman and Stalin were ostensibly designed to put to flight; 'in those last tense weeks of the war, perceptions often mattered more than policies'.[60]

There was, then, almost an air of anti-climax about the end of the war against Nazism – although not amongst the crowds who thronged the streets of London, or who gathered outside Buckingham Palace to cheer 'good old Winnie', nor yet amongst their counterparts in Red Square or Times Square, who all fondly imagined that 'it was all over', bar the Japanese. But in a world of flux one thing had not changed: the peace of the world seemed to hang on what happened to Poland. In 1943 Churchill had talked about not being willing to threaten the future of the 'Grand Alliance' for Poland; now he was doing just that. Truman believed that his diplomatic style would bring the Soviets to their senses, and as he began to realise that he was mistaken in this assessment, he changed tack. It is unclear whether Churchill thought that an Anglo-American *démarche* over Poland could change Stalin's policy, but as long as Truman was taking a hard line he could not lose. If Stalin held out, then further joint Anglo-American action would become necessary and the 'special relationship' would be further cemented; the dreadful day foreshadowed by FDR at Yalta when American troops would return to their own hemisphere would be postponed, and American force would do for Britain and Europe what they could not do themselves. If, on the other hand, Stalin did back down over Poland, then the possibility of a showdown with the Soviet Union receded and British interests in Poland, which were mainly of a sentimental and public relations kind, would be satisfied and Churchill would have one thing less to worry about in the forthcoming general election. Unfortunately for Churchill this happy state depended upon Truman continuing to think that talking tough to the Soviets was the right way to deal with them, but within a week of his famous showdown with Molotov he was asking Joseph Davies, 'Did I do right?'[61]

14

'Diplomatic language' or 'a baseball bat'?

'The basic and irreconcilable difference of objective between the Soviet Union and the United States ... was its urge for its own security to see Soviet concepts extend to as large an area of the world as possible.'[1] Those like Ambassador Harriman who took this view interpreted the Soviet refusal to hold free and fair elections in Bulgaria, Romania and Poland as evidence of malign intent;[2] but other interpretations were possible. Throughout the course of the war the Soviets had consistently sought to provide for their own security in the post-war era and their actions since Yalta were not necessarily inconsistent with such an objective. Ambassador Davies tried to explain the situation from the Soviet point of view when he saw Truman on 30 April. The Soviets were primarily concerned with providing themselves with security against the possibility of a revival of German power, and to this end they needed friendly states between themselves and Germany; they had not sought to interfere in areas such as France or Greece which were of importance to the British, so why were the western Powers seeking to interfere in Poland, Yugoslavia and Bulgaria?[3]

Churchill, of course, had no difficulty with such spheres of influence diplomacy, but the same was not true of many Americans who traditionally distrusted such manifestations of the 'old diplomacy'. Churchill's objections were not theoretical but practical: Soviet expansionism posed a threat to British interests, particularly in the eastern Mediterranean and the Middle East. But Britain was not able to meet that threat from her own resources, and Churchill relied upon the Americans to help. Had he presented this so bluntly, Truman would have refused any such request; but if the Soviets could be presented as interfering in the democratic 'rights' of other nations, then perhaps the American spirit would be stirred. Roosevelt had sailed skilfully between the Scylla of American public opinion and the Charybdis of the demands of the war, and he had proved immune to the siren songs of Churchill; for a moment in April 1945 it had seemed as though his inexperienced successor would set his sails in a direction where they would be filled by Churchill's wind. But Truman's conversation with Davies reinforced the doubts expressed by the level-headed Stimson and Marshall about the correctness of his 'tough' line.[4] Under FDR it had been America which had occupied the position of mediator between imperialist Britain and communist Russia; now it seemed as though Britain were acting the part of mediator – or was it, as Davies believed, almost that of *agent provocateur*?[5] Certainly Churchill's eagerness to pull Truman into a joint Anglo-American front against Stalin began to have a counter-productive effect.

The problem with those who wanted to 'speak plainly to the Soviet Union' was that they had no real answer to Sir Alec Cadogan's question: 'I am not quite clear as to the form and object of the showdown.'[6] The assumption of men like Harriman seems to have been that after a 'good talking to', the Soviets would somehow be willing to come into line with the wishes of the western Powers, but there was not only no warrant for such a belief, there was ample evidence pointing the other way. So it proved on this occasion. Stalin's response to the Anglo-American *démarche* of 18 April simply reiterated the Soviet position that the Lublin Poles must form the nucleus of a future Polish government, which would be guaranteed to be friendly towards the Soviet Union: 'the fact that Poland has a common frontier with the Soviet Union must also be taken into account. This cannot be said of Great Britain or the United States of America.' Again Stalin drew comparisons with Greece and Belgium, where he did not 'know whether a truly representative government has been set up ... the Soviet Union was not asked ... nor did ... [it] claim the right to interfere in these matters as it understands the full significance of Belgium and Greece for the security of Great Britain.'[7] With the Soviet leader unmoved, Truman faced a dilemma. His initial, simplistic approach to Soviet-American relations was not yielding the quick and easy dividend he had supposed; what should he do next?

Churchill was not slow in providing him with answers. Without waiting to see what Truman would do, Churchill drafted a purely British reply to Stalin, which he hoped Truman would support.[8] He accused Stalin of 'trying to dictate to the U.S. Government and H.M.G.', and, in a reference back to the October 1944 'agreement', commented that 'the way things have worked out in Yugoslavia certainly does not give me the feeling of a fifty-fifty interest and influence as between us'. He was 'shocked that you should suggest that I could favour a Polish Government hostile to the Soviet Union' and went on to remind Stalin that it was because of Poland that Britain had gone to war:

This British flame burns still among all classes and parties in this island, and in its self-governing Dominions, and they can never feel this war will have ended rightly unless Poland has a fair deal including a Government fully representative of all those elements, within and without Poland, who are in favour of friendly relations with Russia.

If Churchill was saying that Britain and her Dominions would not let matters rest until Poland had a fully representative and free government, he was, as one commentator realised even at the height of the Cold War, ignoring 'the fact that, in Poland at least, genuinely free democratic elections would return governments unfriendly to Russia – certainly by Stalin's definition'.[9] Quite how Churchill proposed to get what he claimed to want – a free Polish government which was not anti-Russian – he wisely did not explain, preferring instead to complain about lack of facilities accorded to western observers in those areas of Europe liberated by the Soviets. In a passage of some prescience Churchill warned:

There is not much comfort in looking into a future where you and the countries which you dominate, plus the Communist Parties in many other States, are all drawn up on one side, and those who rally to the English-speaking nations . . . are on the other. It is quite obvious that their quarrel would tear the world to pieces and that all of us leading men on either side who had anything to do with that would be shamed before history.

This was true, but coming from the man who had negotiated the percentages deal in October it must have been difficult for Stalin to take at face value.

It is tempting to wonder whether Churchill was not hoist with his own petard, for at the same time as he was attempting to convince Stalin that he should not 'underrate the divergencies which are opening about matters which you may think are small to us but which are symbolic of the way the English-speaking democracies look at life', he was bombarding Truman with telegrams designed to present Stalin with an Anglo-American front. Churchill sought to persuade him that the use of Anglo-American forces should pre-empt potentially dangerous disputes over territory by occupying as much of central Europe as possible, whether in Trieste (to deny it to the Soviet-backed Tito Government),[10] or in Czechoslovakia,[11] or even in Austria, where the announcement of the formation of a provisional government made him 'fear that the Russians are deliberately exploiting their arrival first . . . to "organize" the country before we get there'.[12] Perception, misconception and necessity all combined in a campaign designed to align Truman with Britain. It was almost as though, having for so long blinded himself to the reality of the Soviet system as revealed at Katyn or in the reaction to the Warsaw uprising, Churchill was now overreacting.[13] As one commentator has it, 'As the war drew to a close Churchill became obsessed with the view . . . that the Soviet Union was a potentially deadly enemy which posed a real threat to the British Empire.'[14] Churchill's attitude towards the Soviets had swung from suspicion to fawning whilst their help had been essential, but with the end of the war in Europe it could swing back. Just as Chamberlain had come under pressure from the Commons after the events of March 1939, so too did Churchill after Yalta. There was a 'real outburst of anger' over Poland on 2 May,[15] and the Soviet arrest on the following day of delegates from the London Poles created a situation in which Churchill decided to press for another summit conference.[16]

Now that the moment for payment had come, Churchill was loath to settle his Faustian bargain with Stalin. For all his expressed willingness to compromise, he was willing to do so only on terms which would be acceptable to the House of Commons and the British people. He was aware of the comparisons drawn between Yalta and Munich, and he did not want to suffer Chamberlain's fate. Although Churchill had been willing to conclude a private deal with Stalin, he was well aware how such an arrangement would rebound on his own fame and upon the self-image which the British had of what 'their' war was about. As the Deputy Under-Secretary at the Foreign Office, Sir Orme Sargent, put it, a spheres of influence deal with the Soviets would 'appear in the eyes of the world as the cynical abandonment of the small nations whose interest we are pledged to defend [and] . . . it would represent the abdication of our right as a Great Power to be concerned with the affairs of the whole of Europe, and not merely with those parts in which we have a special interest'.[17] It was inconceivable that a war which had cost the British so much should end in Soviet domination of central and eastern Europe and Britain's abdication as a Great Power. It had been this line of thinking which had prodded Neville Chamberlain into the war which had produced the situation Churchill was now facing; but neither the Prime Minister nor his advisers seemed to have learned anything from the experience of the last six years. Indeed, with Hitler defeated and American aid to be had, Churchill saw no reason why he should not succeed in bilking Mephistopheles.

Churchill's attitude towards the Soviet Union remained as schizophrenic as ever. In one mood he could use the language of compromise and co-operation which had permeated his telegram to Stalin of 19 April, whilst at other times a visceral anti-Bolshevism broke through, as when he told Eden, 'I fear terrible things have happened during the Russian advance through Germany to the Elbe.' At the same time as he was lecturing Stalin on the need to honour agreements, even ones where there was room for dispute about what had been agreed, Churchill himself was contemplating the possibility of not fulfilling the agreements reached at Quebec in 1943 over occupation zones for Germany. Looking at the map he realised that if the western Powers did withdraw to their agreed positions, it 'would mean the tide of Russian domination sweeping forward 120 miles on a front of 300 or 400 miles. This would be an event which, if it occurred, would be one of the most melancholy in history.'[18] But this 'event' had been one which he had contemplated with equanimity in 1943, the year when the Katyn massacre had been revealed and when the western Powers had rightly suspected Stalin of wanting a compromise peace if he could get it. Churchill now drew back from the price he had been prepared to pay when the war was yet to be won, and he recognised the need for haste. If agreement was not reached on the future shape of Europe 'before the United States Armies withdraw from Europe and the Western world folds up its war machines, there are no prospects of a satisfactory solution and very little of preventing a third World

War'.[19] The Prime Minister's agenda for the end-game of the war was clear: America would be expected to pull British chestnuts out of any fires which the Soviets might light.

Churchill hoped that Eden would show this telegram to the President,[20] and he wanted to follow it up with firm action. He intended to publish details of the 'perfidy' by which the London Poles had been 'enticed into a Russian conference and then held fast in the Russian grip', a course which he fondly imagined 'would produce a primary change in the entire structure of the world forces. We must make sure our Russian allies understand what is at stake, but also we must make sure that the United States are with us.'[21] What was 'at stake' was, as in 1938–9, the peace of Europe and the future of civilisation; now, as then, Churchill was prepared to hazard these things on his reading of the situation. He was clearly willing to contemplate a 'third world war' in order to stop the Russians from securing the Polish settlement they wanted, and he was quite prepared to break his own agreement about lines of occupation in central Europe in pursuit of the aim of forcing the Soviets to the negotiating table.

Between the wars British politicians, conscious of the fragility of Britain's position as a Great Power, had sought to use diplomacy to cover the gap left by the evaporation of power. When they had sought to renegotiate the terms upon which collaboration with the ruling elites in India and Egypt rested, Churchill had cried betrayal, and when they had sought to meet the demands of those who were discontented with the Versailles system, he had charged them with ignorance and folly. Churchill's policy was to project British power, not to preserve it. But he had soon discovered that those who had held that the only way to preserve that power was to avoid having to project it had had a point. Even when every sinew was strained to the uttermost, the British Empire did not possess the resources to meet the challenge from Hitler. However, locked into the logic of his position in 1938, and conscious that his own legend rested upon his reputation of having been 'right' then, Churchill sought to pursue his robust foreign policy – with the Americans picking up the bill.

On 6 May he told Truman that there should be a summit meeting 'as soon as possible' and that, in the meantime, 'we should hold firmly to the existing position obtained by our armies in Yugoslavia, in Austria, in Czecho-slovakia, on the main central United States front and on the British front reaching up to Lubeck including Denmark'. Once the VE-Day celebrations were over, 'we must earnestly consider out attitude towards the Soviets and show them how much we have to offer or withhold'. He asked Truman to keep the telegram confidential, especially from Stalin, since he was 'as anxious as you are to avoid the impression of "ganging up" against him';[22] even if that was what he was doing.

But Truman was not willing to go as far as Churchill wanted. He told the Prime Minister that he preferred 'to have the request for such a tripartite meeting originate from Marshal Stalin'.[23] Impatient that Eden seemed not to have shown his earlier telegram warning of the dangers to be apprehended from the Russian advance into Europe,[24] Churchill forwarded a copy of it to Truman on 11 May, stepping up both the campaign for a summit meeting and the pressure for an Anglo-American agreement.[25] Churchill thought that the Soviets were 'concerned about us on account of our civilization and various instrumentalities' and expressed himself heartened by the general tone of his correspondence thus far with Truman.[26] On 12 May the Prime Minister took the plunge. Expressing his 'profound' concern over the European situation because of Soviet behaviour, he told Truman that 'an iron curtain is drawn down upon their front', behind which the Soviets could 'in a very short time ... advance if they chose to the waters of the North Sea and the Atlantic'. It was 'vital to come to an understanding with Russia, or see where we are with her, before we weaken our Armies mortally or retire to the zones of occupation'. Although Churchill acknowledged that 'we may take the view that Russia will behave impeccably and no doubt that offers the most convenient solution', the whole tone of the message belied such a possibility.[27] Churchill followed this up by suggesting that Truman should fulfil the long-standing (but unkept) promise made by FDR to visit London.[28]

In adopting the role of mentor to Truman, Churchill was making assumptions about an identity of Anglo-American interests which were soon to be proved false. On 12 May Truman told Churchill that if there was a summit meeting, 'it appears to me that in order to avoid any suspicion of our "ganging up" it would be advantageous for us to proceed to the meeting place separately'; he offered to visit England after the conference.[29] As for Churchill's apocalyptic vision of the Soviet threat, Truman confined himself to thanking him for his 'estimate of the future situation in Europe' and to commenting that 'from the present point of view it is impossible to make a conjecture as to what the Soviet may do'. Truman was willing to meet Stalin, but not to discuss an agenda set by Churchill. His Chiefs of Staff warned him on 16 May that any 'world conflict in the foreseeable future will find Britain and Russia in opposite camps':[30]

The greatest likelihood of eventual conflict between Britain and Russia would seem to grow out of either nation initiating attempts to build up its strength, by seeking to attach to herself parts of Europe to the disadvantage and possible danger of her potential adversary. Having regard to the inherent suspicion of the Russians, to present Russia with any agreements on such matters as between the British and ourselves, prior to consultation with Russia, might well result in starting a train of events that would lead to the situation we most wish to avoid.[31]

Churchill, as ever, had underestimated the intelligence of the Americans, who were not blind to the possible uses to which the British might want to put them. The Joint Chiefs of Staff saw the building of a 'western European bloc' to counterbalance Soviet power as one of the primary objectives of British policy, but they were by no means enamoured of the idea that America should become involved in such a struggle. Whereas the recent development of 'latent Russian military and economic strength' had been 'phenomenal', by contrast 'as regards Britain several developments have combined to lessen her relative military and economic strength and gravely to impair, if not preclude, her ability to offer effective military opposition to Russia'. The Chiefs of Staff had grave doubts that the British could defeat Russia even with American help. Given the problem of 'project[ing] our strength across the oceans ... we might be able to successfully defend Britain, but we could not, under existing conditions, defeat Russia'. America, in short, should avoid being pulled by the British 'into a war which we could not win' in pursuit of dubious aims.[32] Secretary Stimson even feared that the hard line which Churchill was trying to take in disputes with Tito over the occupation of Trieste might become the pretext for a new war.[33]

Thus, far from persuading Truman of the necessity to follow his line over Russia, the very fervour of Churchill's approach raised doubts about British motives. Writing to Eleanor Roosevelt on 10 May, Truman told her that he had been 'trying very carefully to keep all my engagements with the Russians because they are touchy and suspicious of us', and he added that 'the difficulties with Churchill are very nearly as exasperating as they are with the Russians'.[34] The President responded to Churchill's hard line over Tito by telling him on 16 May that he was 'unable and unwilling to involve this country in a war with the Yugoslavs unless they should attack us'.[35] Churchill, failing to read the auguries aright, stepped up his pleas for a harder line with the Yugoslavs.[36] But whilst the argument over Trieste rumbled on, Truman's mind was already working along finding ways of breaking what appeared to be a deadlock between the western Powers and the Soviets over the interpretation of Yalta.

During his time in America Eden had been struck by Truman's 'air of quiet confidence in himself'. At one point he had told the British Foreign Secretary: '"I am here to make decisions, and whether they prove right or wrong I am going to take them."'[37] But the British were about to discover that Truman had the 'confidence' to make decisions which Churchill and Eden would not like. Now that he had had time to survey the international scene, the new President had formulated characteristically simple ideas about how to achieve a 'reasonably lasting' peace: 'the three great powers must be able to trust each other and they must themselves honestly want it'. But the Great Powers also had to 'have the confidence of the *smaller* nations. Russia hasn't the confidence of the smaller nations, nor has Britain. We have.'[38] To this end he decided to mediate between the two Powers – a return to Rooseveltian methods which would place all Churchill's hopes of acting as his mentor in jeopardy.

On 22 May the President summoned Hopkins to the White House and asked him to go to see Stalin, 'and tell him just exactly what we intended to have in the way of carrying out the agreements', and that 'I was anxious to have a fair understanding with the Russian Government'. He told Hopkins that 'he could use diplomatic language, or he could use a baseball bat if he thought that was the proper approach to Mr Stalin'.[39] At the same time as the news of the Hopkins mission was made public, so too was the fact that Truman was sending Joseph Davies to London.[40] There could have been no better demonstration of Truman's determination to act as mediator between Britain and the Soviet Union. If Hopkins had been sent to London, it might have been interpreted by the Soviets as the British and Americans beginning to 'gang up' on them, but by sending him to Moscow Truman was trading on his reputation as a proponent of FDR's Soviet policy.[41] By sending the Russophile Davies to London, Truman avoided any imputation that he was involved in some anti-Soviet intrigue.

Davies had been American Ambassador to the Soviet Union in the late 1930s and was well known for his pro-Soviet predilections. In the weeks following his conversation with Truman on 30 April he had tried to keep lines of communication open with the Soviet Foreign Minister.[42] In response to Truman's claim that 'Stalin was out of control', Davies pointed out that throughout the war the Soviets had consistently sought to provide for their own security, and that they had had to bear the brunt of fighting the German armies whilst the western Powers had planned global strategy. The Soviets were naturally suspicious, and when they saw the British and the Americans on terms of such intimacy, they feared that plots were being hatched against them. Davies went into detail, hitherto unknown to Truman, about FDR's long attempts to convince Stalin of America's *bona fides*, and he lamented the fact that where Roosevelt had been the mediator between Churchill and Stalin, 'it is now Britain which is composing differences between us and the Soviets'. Davies thought that American policy towards Moscow was now being dictated by Churchill. He warned Truman that if the Soviets came to this conclusion, they would 'not hesitate to out-tough the west'; the Nazi–Soviet pact bore witness to the rapidity with which Soviet policy could change if they felt threatened. Davies thought that Truman 'got it more clearly . . . than when I last talked to him'. Truman told him about Churchill's requests for a meeting and confessed that he did not want to meet him before he saw Stalin. Indeed, he had gone on to ask Davies if he would go to Moscow to arrange a meeting with Stalin, and it was only after Davies's refusal that he had settled on Hopkins.

Davies's views on the Soviet Union made him the natural mediator with Stalin, but his attitude towards the British made him, to put it mildly, an odd choice as envoy to London – except on the assumption that Truman was ensuring that his envoy would not be seduced politically by Churchill. Davies had 'contempt for traditional British imperialism', but had admired the way in which Churchill had seemed to be willing to 'recognize the reality of the Soviet Union as an emerging power in Europe'. However, Churchill's post-Yalta attitude suggested that his earlier complaisance had been a tactical ploy rather than a strategic decision. Davies shared the views of those who feared that Britain was trying to enlist American support to control the balance of power in Europe in her own interests, even if that meant an all-out war with Moscow.[43]

The Hopkins mission seemed to reveal that avenues of co-operation with the Soviets still existed and that the fears expressed by Ambassador Harriman and by Churchill were, at the very least, exaggerated and premature.[44] Hopkins used his reputation and experience to play the part of the honest friend, telling Stalin that there had been such a deterioration in the attitude of American public opinion towards the Soviet Union as 'to affect adversely the relations between our two countries', and that 'if present trends continued unchecked the entire structure of world cooperation and relations with the Soviet Union which the President and the Marshal had labored so hard to build would be destroyed'. It was clear from Stalin's comments to Hopkins that the Soviets feared that 'British conservatives' wished to rebuild the *cordon sanitaire* which had been erected against the Bolsheviks at Versailles, and that American clumsiness in suddenly cancelling lend-lease supplies and supporting British protests over Poland were interpreted as signs of an impending Anglo-American front. This, then, was the explanation for Soviet behaviour since Yalta: Stalin feared that the capitalists were going to cheat him out of his proper reward; no doubt he would have cheated them, so it was natural that he should have imagined that they would serve him in the same way. Hopkins tried to make Stalin see that 'the question of Poland *per se* was not so important as the fact that it had become a symbol of our ability to work out problems with the Soviet Union'. Stalin, in turn, explained why the history of Europe in the twentieth century made a 'friendly' Poland an object of vital concern for the Soviet Union. If Stalin meant it when he said that 'any talk of an intention to Sovietize Poland was stupid', then Soviet-American relations might yet be saved.[45] Stalin agreed to meet Truman and Churchill on 15 July in Germany.

In contrast to the Hopkins/Stalin meetings, those between Ambassador Davies and Churchill were something close to a disaster. Writing to Eden afterwards, Churchill commented: 'I have not formed the best opinions of this man';[46] nor is the reason far to seek. Churchill was not pleased with Truman's decision to send emissaries to London and Moscow instead of coming to England himself, and he responded badly to the news brought by Davies that Truman wanted to meet Stalin before the forthcoming conference. Things went from bad to worse as the two men moved on to the whole question of policy towards the Soviet Union:

As the Prime Minister went on, he became vehement and even violent in his criticisms of the Soviet Armies and officials in the re-occupied areas. What was more horrible to him than Communism, was the imposition of the Secret Police and Gestapo methods. He spoke with much feeling of the 'steel curtain' of the Soviets being 'clamped down' on Eastern liberated areas, the horror of such a black out, etc. etc.

What had Churchill expected to happen when what he had once called the 'foul baboonery of Bolshevism' rolled over eastern Europe? It is clear from what followed next that his comments were designed to arouse American outrage. As Davies put it to Truman, 'What he elaborated upon at length, and with great emphasis and emotion, were the grave dangers which would arise with the withdrawal of American troops from Europe.'[47]

Davies thought that Churchill was 'one of the greatest men of our time, and the greatest Englishman of this or any other time', but he was equally aware that as an Englishman, 'he was basically more concerned over preserving England's position in Europe than in preserving peace'.[48] His reiteration of the threat posed to Europe by the Red Army and of the need for America not to withdraw her troops confirmed Davies in his opinion that Churchill hoped to use 'American manpower and resources to sustain Britain's "lead" in Europe'.[49] It was a sign of the pique which Churchill felt that he should have become 'quite emotional' about the Truman/Stalin meeting, telling Davies that he was 'both surprised and hurt that he should be "excluded"', and implying that it was a 'poor return for his support of and friendship for the U.S.A.'.[50] It was a comment which revealed more than Churchill would perhaps have liked, for he went on to say that 'He had supported "unconditional surrender". He could have made peace with Hitler at any time. He could never, never consent [to a Truman–Stalin meeting]. He would carry the issue to world public opinion. Such a meeting would be tantamount to a "Deal".' There it was again, as in his telegram of 24 January 1944 to Stalin, the admission that 'he could have made peace with Hitler at any time', but now it was combined with the blatant statement that in return for all his truckling to the Americans he expected the reward of a special relationship; denied even this, the temperamental Prime Minister became over-emotional – until, that is, Davies said that he resented such an imputation on Truman's honour. But it was 'indicative of his anxiety over Europe, and the deployment of our forces, [that] at one time he turned to me suddenly and said, "Are you trying to say for the President that the U.S. is withdrawing from participation in European affairs?"' This, of course, was the ultimate nightmare for Churchill – the prospect of seeing all the sacrifices which Britain had made leading to nothing more than a continent dominated by the Red Army, with America secure across thousands of miles of ocean. The Ambassador expressed himself 'shocked beyond words' to find Churchill so 'violent and bitter' about the Soviets when the language he had held in public gave quite a different impression: 'I feared that the fears and suspicions of the Soviets as to the implacable hostility of the West, would harden into action if they knew of this attitude.'[51] Davies thought that to 'assume that we could win through a "tough" approach . . . would involve a terrific risk'.

Here was the crucial point. In the late 1930s Churchill and others had argued that the only way to dissuade Hitler was to challenge him, and in so doing they had run the 'terrific risk' of war. But they had discovered that Hitler was not bluffing and that he was quite willing and more than able to prosecute his aims by war. Thanks largely to the Red Army, the Nazis had been defeated, but now Churchill was claiming that the Soviets were a threat to the balance of power in Europe. If that was so, it was an ironic comment on the consequences of prosecuting the war to the bitter end. Davies

said that frankly, as I listened to him inveigh so violently against the threat of Soviet domination and the spread of Communism in Europe, and disclose such a lack of confidence in the professions of good faith in Soviet leadership, I had wondered whether he . . . was now willing to declare to the world that he and Britain had made a mistake in not supporting Hitler, for as I understand him, he was now expressing the doctrine which Hitler and Goebbels had been proclaiming and reiterating for the last four years in an effort to break up allied unity. . . .[52]

It was not surprising that Churchill did not warm to Davies, whose 'unusual perspective on events'[53] had exposed the fragility of the wartime achievement which had made him a legend; if Hitler had been defeated only to be replaced with Stalin, and if the Americans would not help out, then Britain's last state would indeed be worse than her first.

Truman's policy of mediation enjoyed more immediate dividends than his earlier one of 'tough-talking' had yielded, which can only have strengthened the belief that it was the correct one to follow. Hopkins's talks with Stalin brought a settlement of two of the problems bedevilling inter-allied relations. At the San Francisco conference on the United Nations there had been a deadlock on the question of the veto rights of the Great Powers; Stalin now accepted a compromise here. It even seemed as though the running sore of the Polish question had been dealt with, as Stalin agreed to let Mikolajczyk and other non-communists into the Warsaw government. Moreover, agreement was reached on the allied administration of Austria and Germany, and even the threatening dispute with Tito over Trieste was put on the back-burner.[54] All things considered, it was a remarkable record of success, prompting Truman to write: 'We may get a peace yet.'[55]

If Truman was more sanguine by the time the Potsdam conference met in mid-July, the same could hardly be said of the Prime Minister. He found Truman's desire to meet Stalin first 'wounding', and although he thought better of telling the President so,[56] he told Eden on 1 June that if the Americans insisted on abiding by existing agreements to withdraw their troops from their current positions, 'we shall rue the day, and so shall the Americans, and you may live to see the evil consequences'.[57] He struck a doleful note in a message to Truman on 4 June, where he not only failed to see any great advance in the proposed Polish settlement, but also expressed his 'profound misgivings' about the 'retreat of the American army to our line of occupation'.[58] But Truman refused to be rushed by Churchill into either changing the date of the forthcoming conference or postponing the execution of the withdrawal of American troops.[59] He thought that 'propaganda' was 'our greatest foreign relations enemy', with the Soviet and American press distributing 'lies' and misrepresentations about each other, whilst the 'British out lie and out propagandize us both'.[60] Thus, when Churchill returned to the old song, 'Would it not be better to refuse to withdraw on the main European front until a settlement has been reached about Austria?',[61] Truman responded that he was unable to oblige.[62] This was to remain the pattern for the rest of Churchill's Premiership. Instead of receiving the rewards to which, as Roosevelt's loyal lieutenant, he felt he was entitled, Churchill had to watch whilst the new President treated Britain and the Soviet Union as though there was nothing to choose between them – except for the fact that the Soviets disposed of more power than the British did.

Back in March Eden had written that 'your policy is a sad wreck',[63] and this appeared to be nowhere more accurate than in estimating Britain's position at the end of the war in Europe. Churchill took a 'very gloomy' view of events:

The Russians were farther west than they had ever been except once. They were all-powerful in Europe. At any time that it took their fancy they could march across the rest of Europe and drive us back into our island. They had a two to one superiority over our forces, and the Americans were returning home. The quicker they went home, the sooner they would be required back here again. He finished up by saying that never in his life had he been more worried by the European situation than he was at present.[64]

That 'never in his life' was a pretty devastating indictment of his wartime leadership. Back in 1940 it had been 'victory at all costs'; now it seemed that that was what it had cost – everything. His long dealings with Stalin had failed to produce an Anglo-Soviet relationship which filled him with anything save foreboding, and his long subservience to the Americans was equally failing to deliver the required result; there was neither an Anglo-American 'special relationship' nor yet was there any sign that the Americans were prepared to accept the British as the 'Greeks' in their new Roman Empire.

With the war in Europe at an end, the bonds which united the 'Big Three' were perceptibly weakening. The Americans wanted to settle Europe down after the war and then leave the United Nations to deal with the future, and for that to happen it was essential to secure Soviet co-operation – which was the American delegation's priority at Potsdam.[65] They were perfectly aware of Britain's propensity for old-style spheres of influence diplomacy and of the fears created by Russia's dominant position on the Continent, as well as of the corollary that 'since there is no longer power to balance in Europe, Britain would logically turn to the United States as the greatest potential source of support'; they had equally little intention of falling for such a policy.[66] Instead, in an explicitly Woodrow Wilsonian mode, they hoped to remove the need for spheres of influence by encouraging the two Powers to co-operate. They saw British plans for a 'western European bloc' as part of Britain's strategy to avoid being swamped by Soviet strength, but until it was clear whether the Soviets could or could not be brought to co-operate, the Americans decided not to 'take a positive stand one way or the other' on the idea.[67]

On the economic front the Americans had equally little intention of giving the British a free ride. The agreement of the British to enter in principle the brave new world of American multilateralism had not been followed through by much in the way of practice, but with the British dependent upon $5.5 billion during the next two years, the time had come to make it plain to Churchill that willingness to 'extend lend-lease aid . . . in excess of the requirements of the Pacific war will be determined largely by the steps undertaken in the next few months by the British Government to adopt a more liberal post-war commercial policy along the lines contemplated in Article VII'.[68] It was recognised that unless the British were pressed for an agreement, there was 'a serious danger that . . . Britain may not ultimately go along with our program to restore worldwide multilateralism in finance and trade'.[69] In this respect the 'failure of the gloomy British prophecies [about their dollar reserves] to materialize' placed the achievement of this long-held aim in jeopardy.[70] Indeed, the possibility that the British might renege on their commitments to an American-style world economic order was a 'most serious threat to our post-war foreign economic program'.[71]

America had emerged from the war as the world's richest Power, and her leaders felt neither the inclination nor the need to take advice from a man who, however great, led a bankrupt Power which was trying to sustain a role in the world which she could no longer afford.

15

The Great Game

From the time when Vortigern called in Horsa and Hengeist to help him against their fellow Saxons, the policy of inviting one set of barbarians to save you from another has not generally been attended by success; the events of 1941 to 1945 did nothing to encourage a more general adoption of the practice. Evidence of British unwillingness to pay the price of the Soviet alliance once the need for it was gone was plentiful – and it did not escape the Soviets.[1] Sir Orme Sargent's comment in April about the need to 'change the technique of our diplomacy towards the Soviet Union' found echo elsewhere.[2] Clark-Kerr's counsellor in Moscow, Frank Roberts, compared the Soviet leadership to the Nazis, describing one comrade as 'a plumper and perhaps more humane version of Hitler himself'.[3] Owen O'Malley, that stalwart champion of the Poles, wanted to abandon a 'conciliatory attitude' towards the Soviets and to 'criticize Soviet foreign policy publicly in the most massive fashion'.[4] By July Eden was complaining that 'Russian policy was now one of aggrandisement', and he was 'deeply concerned at the pattern of Russian policy, which becomes clearer as they become more brazen every day'.[5] As he surveyed the scene before Potsdam, he found the 'world outlook gloomy' and saw 'signs of Russian penetration everywhere'.[6] But this situation was not new: Anglo-Russian rivalry went back at least as far as the Ochakov incident in the 1790s.* Eden, the most English of Foreign Secretaries, lacked any strain of anti-communist feeling, but he possessed a keen sense of the traditional rivalry between Great Britain and Russia in the East – whether Near or Far. It is perhaps significant that Attlee, who did not accept the traditional bases of British foreign policy and wished, instead, to found it firmly on the United Nations and collective security,[7] should also have queried Eden's conclusions about the Russian threat. During the Potsdam conference he asked whether there was not a 'danger of our getting into a position where we and the Russians confront each other as rival great powers at a number of points of strategic significance'. He argued against standing 'on the basis of our own particular interests'.[8] Although Attlee's notion that 'we ought to confront the Russians with the requirements of a world organization for

---

* In 1791 Pitt the Younger tried to prevent Russia claiming the Crimean port of Ochakov, but was thwarted in his attempt by the lethargy of British opinion. This is generally held to be the start of Britain's interest in the 'Eastern Question'.

peace, not with the needs of the British Empire,' was open to ridicule from those who did not share his touching faith in such organisations, the future Prime Minister had, none the less, hit upon an important truth: much of the opposition to Russia in 1945 derived from traditional sources of imperial rivalry and concern for the balance of power.

For most of the previous century Britain had been a 'great Naval, Indian and Colonial Power'.[9] The attempt to combine this status with interference in the balance of power in Europe had imperilled the former without securing the latter. The inter-war period had seen Britain's gaze shift towards her African possessions and the Middle East, and she had played a long and not unsuccessful hand to transform her Indian presence from 'formal' to 'informal' Empire. The full range of British 'power' involved not simply military might but a complex web of diplomatic, economic and political influence. The war certainly damaged the foundations on which British power rested, but contemporaries did not think that the damage was permanent. Sir Orme Sargent was not alone in dismissing as a 'misconception' the notion that 'Great Britain is now a secondary Power and can be treated as such';[10] indeed, some modern historians have concurred in questioning the easy assumption that the Empire was 'in decline' and that the 'decline' was 'inevitable'.[11]

In the immediate aftermath of the war all the European Powers 'were squeezing themselves to the bone' in order to regain control over colonial areas which were themselves shattered by the war. Empires offered what they always had, sources of cheap raw materials and, in the case of British Malaysia and its rubber, a rare chance to earn dollars; indeed, more than that, the fashion for colonial development marked a realisation of the potential purchasing power of the colonies. To concentrate upon Palestine and India and to treat the British withdrawals from both as signs of the Empire's impending doom is to miss the point. Palestine had been a curse from beginning to end, bringing neither honour nor profit nor yet contentment; it was a commitment which the Zionism of Arthur Balfour had made even more onerous than nature had designed it to be, and it was one which was best jettisoned; although the manner of its going was to say much about the nature of the Anglo-American relationship. India, which had long ceased to be a source of profit or strength to the Empire, was, in like fashion, a liability.[12] But this was far from being the whole of British imperial policy.

The Empire was 'just the tip of the iceberg that made up the British world system ... a system of influence as well as power which, indeed, preferred to work through informal methods of influence where possible'.[13] In both the 'formal' and 'informal' modes, British influence depended heavily upon 'local collaborators'; there was no other way in which the British could have held on to the Empire and its penumbra so cheaply.[14] This whole structure had been placed under tremendous pressure by the war, and matters had not been helped by Churchill's rather simple-minded attitude towards imperial problems. His determination to intervene in the struggle for mastery in Europe for the second time in a generation had left the financial and psychological bases of imperial power shattered, whilst his assumption that the Americans would become Britain's surrogate was beginning to seem mistaken. How then was the old imperial rivalry with Russia to be carried on?

The Prime Minister was dangerously unstable on the subject of the Soviets. In some moods he would compare the Russian menace to Genghis Khan,[15] whilst at other times a few kind words from Stalin would send him into paroxysms of joy. As Eden found at Potsdam, close proximity to the Soviet dictator put Churchill under his 'spell'. Eden was 'full of admiration of Stalin's handling of him', but frustrated by Churchill's susceptibility.[16] Given the Prime Minister's influence over foreign policy, his maudlin propensities created obstacles in the way of the firm policy which Eden and the Foreign Office wanted, and the Foreign Secretary had to work hard at Potsdam to avert any concessions from Churchill.[17] With the defeat of Churchill at the election in July 1945, this element of uncertainty passed. The new Foreign Secretary and his Prime Minister may have had their differences on foreign policy, but Ernest Bevin was master in his own house in a way which Eden had never been. As his former Private Secretary, Oliver Harvey, put it, Bevin's line on Russia was 'much what Anthony's policy would have been if he had even been allowed to have one'.[18]

Bevin's record has received treatment even more favourable than that usually accorded to the Attlee Governments.[19] The view, held by some contemporaries, that 'Bevin is too much in the hands of his officials',[20] has generally been dismissed by historians, not least because it has been discounted by those officials who served Bevin.[21] Leaving aside the obvious retort that 'they would say that, wouldn't they?', there would appear to be good reasons for querying the notion that Bevin's foreign policy was determined only by the great man himself. To state that 'he was very much his own man, making up his mind for himself with many ideas of his own,'[22] begs the question of where the information which he needed to make up his own mind came from. Bevin read with no great facility and wrote with even less. Eden's path through the documents can be traced by following the trails of red ink, but Bevin's annotations are few and far between. Eden had an immense appetite for detailed documentation and was able, when necessary, to use it to come to a view at variance with that of his advisers. Bevin not only lacked Eden's appetite for paper, but rarely crossed swords with his officials. His officials digested the material for him whilst Bevin operated by picking their brains in conversation. It was a system which could only work when there was either a weak Foreign Secretary who would do what he was told, or where there was considerable identity of view between the officials and their chief; as no one has accused Bevin of being weak, it is towards the latter explanation that this account tends. With a Foreign Office which had grown used to having to take into account the vagaries of a Great Man in the form of Churchill, the advent of Bevin posed few problems – not least because the broad ideas he entertained about the Soviet Union matched those of his predecessor.

The suave and sophisticated Oxford-educated Eden and the untidy burly trades union leader, who had left school as soon as he could, were nevertheless united in a common perception of the long rivalry between British and Russian power. Bevin had been expected to become Chancellor of the Exchequer, but doubts about Hugh Dalton, the man who was tipped for the job, and the difficulties of getting Bevin and Herbert Morrison working together on the Home Front, seem to have decided Attlee in favour of sending Bevin to the Foreign Office. From the point of view of the diplomats, the appointment was a good one. In the first place he was clearly 'the heavyweight of the Cabinet', which would mean that he would 'get his own way with them', unlike the harassed Eden; all that was necessary was that he should be 'put on the right line'.[23] But as it transpired, there was little need to put the new Foreign Secretary on 'the right line' as he was already there, at least in a general sense. Like many trades union leaders, Bevin had little liking for communists or their doctrine, having spent too much time preventing their infiltration of the unions.[24] Communists were either untrustworthy working men or intellectuals who had never done a hand's turn in their lives; either way Bevin was not sympathetic to them. Cadogan found him 'pretty sound on the whole'.[25]

Bevin shared the view generally held in the Foreign Office and elsewhere that Britain was still a Great Power and he did not intend to allow anyone to take advantage of weaknesses which he was sure were temporary. In particular he wanted to persuade America to join Britain in considering whether 'we are prepared to acquiesce' in countries like Romania, Bulgaria, Hungary, Yugoslavia, Czechoslovakia and Poland 'remaining definitely in the Soviet sphere of influence'.[26] He also took the view that 'the maintenance of our position in the Middle East remains a cardinal feature of British policy' and intended to prevent the 'incursion' of the Soviet Union into the region.[27] Willing to accept that America would play a predominant role in the treatment of Japan, Bevin regarded it as 'important that we should not play a lesser part in the control of Japan than Russia and China, as otherwise our prestige and standing as one of the Big Four Powers might suffer damage'.[28] As for India, if Labour Ministers lacked Churchill's instinctive opposition to making concessions to nationalist feeling – 'the policy which has brought us to our present miserable pass in India'[29] – that was, as the out-going Conservative Secretary of State for India, Leo Amery, observed, no bad thing.[30] Attlee, Bevin and company would bring fresh perspectives to the vexing problem of how to maintain British power in the sub-continent, but they had no intention of abandoning it.[31] It was the Viceroy, Field Marshal Lord Wavell, who best summed up 'the problem on which the British Commonwealth and the British reputation will stand in the post-war period', and he was determined to secure a settlement which would keep India 'within the Commonwealth' and safeguard 'our prestige and prospects in Burma, Malaya, China and the Far East generally'.[32] In this, at least, the Viceroy spoke for the new Government.[33]

But such a foreign and imperial policy demanded the financial resources which Keynes had insisted that 'Lady Bountiful' no longer possessed. It was hoped that with American support the burden could be shared and sustained.[34] Britain's imperial commitments were costing her a fortune she no longer had. She was spending £716.3 million for imperial military operations outside the German theatre, a sum 'about equal to our total net disinvestment throughout the world'. When the cost of maintaining an army of occupation in Germany and of contributing to the relief of liberated western Europe was taken into account, American help was imperative. The alternative to it – going it alone – was labelled by Keynes 'austerity' and would 'lead to serious political and social disruption at home and our withdrawal, for the time being, from the position of a first-class Power in the outside world. We should have to retire, as Russia did between the wars, to starve and reconstruct.'[35] The British had 'devoted our whole available productive resources to the war and counted on Lend-Lease to bridge the gap in our balance of payments';[36] Churchill's policy had left the maintenance of imperial power at the mercy of the Americans.

Possessing still the habit of mind of a great imperial race, the British were unable to conceive the realities of their situation. There was an expectation that America would take into account the 'toil, sweat, blood and tears suffered by us' when Britain asked for money.[37] This faith in American benevolence led Keynes to argue initially against a simple policy of borrowing from America on commercial terms – a policy he labelled 'temptation'. Wartime negotiations had shown, he argued, that quite independently of any commercial conditions attached to any loan, it was 'practically certain that they [the Americans] will want the main principles of commercial policy discussed and probably accepted in substance by us before they would be prepared to offer us adequate financial assistance'.[38] Keynes hoped that the Americans would be kind enough to offer the British financial assistance at little or no cost.[39] Unfortunately, with the cessation of lend-lease the British found themselves facing a 'financial Dunkirk'. In foreign affairs this would mean the 'sudden and humiliating withdrawal from our onerous responsibilities with great loss of prestige and an acceptance for the time being of the position of a second-class Power', whilst 'at home a greater degree of austerity would be necessary than we have experienced at any time during the war'.[40] Never good at resisting temptation, Keynes yielded to it.

There was, of course, resentment at the 'shabby fashion in which we were being treated by the Americans',[41] but a continuation of the foreign policy consensus formed during the Churchill coalition demanded American help and the payment of almost any price for it. As one official put it,

It would do us great harm if a current of opinion were formed that, at a time when America was ready and eager to enter into broad international commitments, we were bent on pursuing what in American eyes, was a contrary policy.... It might even affect the whole view the Americans take of us as partners in world affairs.[42]

This was to be of decisive weight when the going got tough. From the very start some Ministers were not keen to kow-tow, and Bevin, Dalton and Cripps told Attlee at the end of August that they would favour imperial 'autarchy' as an alternative to an onerous loan from America.[43] Bevin, whose own views on economics were heavily influenced by his experiences in the 1920s and 1930s, was 'anxious to be able to isolate us if there is a major economic recession in the United States', and was not, in any case, keen to see Britain adhere to the commitments entered into at Bretton Woods.[44] He would have preferred to avoid any commitments 'monetary or commercial' until 'we could see our way more clearly'.[45] The problem was that this cut across Keynes's 'Grand Design' and the need to secure American help against Russian expansionism. Keynes wanted to tie together the various strands of financial policy and to negotiate an overall settlement, and his optimism about the chances of getting 'justice' made him impatient with Bevin and others who wanted to proceed more slowly and in a piecemeal fashion.[46] Yet, as one contemporary Treasury official, Sir Richard (Otto) Clarke, later wrote, such a policy had much to commend it. Clarke wanted to sign the Bretton Woods agreement and offer a breathing space of two or three years before entering into full-scale negotiations, in the meantime raising an American loan. As it turned out, with America growing worried about the communist threat and European recovery, such a strategy 'would have been well justified by events'.[47]

Nor were Clarke's plans valid only with hindsight. He doubted whether the Americans would come across with a 'gift' of $750 million because of Congressional pressure, and with 'justice' scuppered that would leave 'temptation'. Yet it was in America's interests as much as anyone's that there should not be a dollar shortage, and this gave the British some leverage, especially if they pushed ahead with plans to develop a western European group which would be, in effect, an enlarged sterling bloc.[48] Keynes, however, with an arrogance of which he alone was capable, dismissed out of hand the notion that there would be any shortage of gold or of dollars, and his immense prestige carried the day. Britain would try for 'justice', but 'temptation' would beckon if the Americans proved inflexible.[49]

Truman indignantly denied that the abrupt cancellation of lend-lease was 'a direct blow at the British Government', telling the press on 23 August that he was 'merely living up to the promise' that lend-lease would end with the war; he even agreed after representations from Attlee to allow some provisional aid whilst negotiations were undertaken.[50] Truman's point was technically correct, but there is little doubt that the Americans had been growing increasingly irritated by British reluctance to abandon imperial tariffs, and that here was a chance of finally nailing them down.[51] American policy required a 'substantial reduction of import duties, and the eventual abolition of quotas and export controls' as well as the 'elimination of all forms of discriminatory trade treatment', 'export subsidies' and other 'restrictive international private business arrangements', along with the 'regulation and eventual elimination of exchange controls' as envisaged at Bretton Woods, and finally the establishment of 'an appropriate international trade organization'.[52] The Americans stuck to the position which they had always held, which was that the British could not discuss 'lend-lease and finance' without a commitment on commercial policy. It was made 'crystal clear . . . that the United States would not agree on financial aid to the United Kingdom without "British agreement on the type of economic world in which the financial plan would have to work itself out"'. No pleas from the British to deal with aid first because of its urgency would budge the American negotiators. The implication was 'crystal clear': it was 'up to the British Cabinet to decide how long it wants to discuss such matters in view of the urgency of its financial needs'.[53] By mid-October it began to dawn on the British that, to use Keynesian terminology, 'Uncle Sam' was not 'Uncle Sap'.[54]

The puncturing of British illusions was marked by the scaling down of their pretensions. At the beginning of the long and painful process, the British were not disposed to 'agree to anything except an out and out grant' and were determined not to link this to negotiations over commercial policy.[55] The latter point was conceded almost immediately since the Americans simply refused to countenance any other procedure.[56] By late September it was clear that there would be no 'grant in aid', or even an interest-free loan.[57] All along the line the British had to concede to American demands. The Americans even resented Keynes calling 'attention to the fact that our casualties were greater than theirs and that reverse lend-lease as proportionate to national output did not fall far short of lend-lease'.[58] From the start there was a political aspect to the loan negotiations quite beyond the narrow sphere of Anglo-American negotiations.

The Americans showed a 'keen interest' in the vast British military expenditure in the Middle East, and clearly wondered whether 'it is to their advantage to provide the cash to enable us to cut any sort of figure in the Middle East'. The British negotiators thought that it might be necessary for them to 'be brought to realise that unless they are prepared to provide the wherewithal to set us on our feet as worthy partners in world affairs, they will find themselves obliged to step in and take our place' – which reveals how little the British still understood the Americans and their world-view.[59] They would not even allow the British to conduct their own negotiations with the Commonwealth and sterling area creditors independently of the Anglo-American negotiations. Most crucially of all, in the eyes of many British imperialists, the Americans finally succeeded in carrying through their long-held intention of getting the British to abandon imperial preference – 'a substantial victory for the American delegation', as an official report on the negotiations described it.[60]

The American negotiators denied any intention of 'using a financial pistol to obtain preference concessions against our will',[61] but that was what the negotiations amounted to. Nowhere was the Churchillian myth of the 'fraternal association' more rudely shattered. The British had entered into the process fondly imagining that they could persuade the Americans to 'accept a broad and generous solution which took account of our financial sacrifices before the U.S. entered the war' and also of the 'post-war advantages to the U.S. of a settlement with us which would enable us to share world responsibilities with them free from undue financial pre-occupation'.[62] But Keynes and company discovered that 'the Americans were interested in the future, not the past,' and that 'the old soldier, showing his medals,' was not a 'persuasive advocate'.[63] The result was that the British, still failing to realise the reality of American opinion, refused a loan of $5 billion repaid over fifty years at just over 1 per cent interest,[64] only to find themselves eventually accepting one of $3.75 billion at 2 per cent over fifty years.[65]

Even a man as intelligent as Keynes had continued to believe in the possibility of an American free gift until 18 October,[66] whilst back in London Ministers continued in their infantile fantasies much later.[67] They had disregarded the warning from officials that America would 'insist, as a condition of . . . assistance, that we take positive steps to implement the undertakings on international and commercial policy already given in consideration for lend-lease',[68] and were correspondingly shocked as Keynes not only failed to produce the desired miracle, but became the conduit through which the new realities of Britain's international position were borne home.[69] American attempts to use the negotiations to persuade the British to abolish imperial preference and to make concessions over civil aviation disputes eventually led Bevin to use the word 'blackmail' to the American Ambassador. Ministers did not want to admit 'that we are in any sense dependent upon the U.S. to get ourselves out of our present difficulties',[70] but that was about the size of it.

When the Cabinet attempted to dictate terms to Keynes in late October, his reaction was fierce. 'White with rage and talking about resigning',[71] he accused Ministers of having 'fatally misunderstood' the position in Washington, and made it clear that there was no alternative to the American terms if they wanted a loan.[72] It is some testimony to how deep the belief in American benevolence ran that even after this stern message Ministers hung on, hoping that Keynes had got it wrong.[73] The American insistence on sterling being made fully convertible was particularly objectionable; as one Treasury official put it, 'If I were an American deliberately seeking to destroy Britain's financial and economic future, I could choose no better way of setting about it.'[74] Dalton thought that the American proposals were 'unacceptable, both in form and spirit,' and that their document 'reads like a moneylenders' agreement, and a bad one'. His conclusion was that 'we cannot accept such an agreement' and that 'we should say so quite plainly'.[75] He argued in this sense at a fraught meeting of the inner Cabinet on 23 November, stating that 'we had to take the risk of a break'. Bevin, who was already worried about the effect of American indifference upon his diplomacy, did not want to see a 'break', and thought that Attlee and Truman should thrash the matter out in the old Churchill–Roosevelt manner.[76] In the end the Americans accepted minor alterations in their terms, but it was enough to allow the Cabinet to swallow the bitter pill.[77]

Keynes found the experience 'exhausting and exasperating beyond experience' and concluded that the Americans 'mean us no harm – but their minds are so small, their prospect so restricted, their knowledge so inadequate, their obstinacy so boundless and their legal pedantries so infuriating'.[78] This was the reality behind smooth epigrams about being 'Greeks' in the 'new Roman Empire'. The sense of humiliation was palpable. Oliver Stanley, the Conservative spokesman on economics, spoke for many when he said:

Strange as it may seem, we are sitting here today as the representatives of a victorious people, discussing the economic consequences of victory. If a visitor were to come to London from Mars and, still more improbable, were to obtain a ticket of admission to the Gallery, he might well be pardoned for thinking that he was listening to the representatives of a vanquished people discussing the economic penalties of defeat.[79]

That this should have been so was the most devastating indictment on the conduct of British diplomacy during the war. Churchill's sacrifices had been made not only to win short-term concessions from the Americans, but also to guarantee a long-term relationship. Some Conservatives may have comforted themselves with the reflection that their leader would have secured a better deal than Labour, whose social security spending plans were the object of suspicion from Congress, but if they believed their own words they were fooling no one except themselves. The American terms were designed to secure British participation in the new American world order, and from the start there had been 'general agreement that the United States must furnish substantial financial aid to Great Britain in order to enable the latter nation to base its foreign economic policy upon multilateralism'.[80] The conditions upon which the loan were granted accomplished this objective.

The British had passed under the Caudine Forks. America wanted commercial and financial concessions, and she used the opportunity presented by

Britain's plight to gain them. As Molotov bitterly observed, the American insistence on 'equal opportunity' when it came to trade gave American capital unrestricted opportunities to buy what it wanted in devastated Europe:

Given such a situation, we would probably live to see the day when in your own country, on switching on the radio you would be hearing not so much your own language as one American gramophone record after another.... The time might come when in your own country, on going to the cinema you would be seeing American films sold for foreign consumption.[81]

And so it would come to pass. The British accepted the loan because they feared that without it they could not maintain their existing massive European and imperial commitments. But even with the loan they could hardly do so. Nor did there seem to be any sign that the Soviet threat was moving the Americans nearer to being willing to help the British out. The most worrying feature of the whole diplomatic scene for Bevin and Attlee was the lack of American reaction to complaints about the Soviets. Truman seemed content to let Secretary Byrnes find a way of 'fixing' Stalin in the way both men had 'fixed' deals in the Senate. What did Stalin want? Security? Well he could have it, if he did not snatch, and perhaps American aid would oil the wheels of diplomacy. There was no sign that the Americans were eager to make common cause with the British in their struggle for mastery with Russia. By showing their willingness to participate in the American new world order, the British were hoping to gain for themselves a privileged position. This was the main reason why the American loan was necessary. As Lord Halifax put it, 'It is obvious that this [American] concept of Britain's inferiority is likely to have unfortunate consequences upon our international prestige and commerce unless sedulous attempts are made to combat it.'[82]

This was not the view from Washington. The often-voiced protest from British sources about America ignoring the part which Britain was playing in the war,[83] like American criticism of British imperialism,[84] was not something to be explained away by saying that the Americans were naïve; they were authentic representations of American feeling. The British may have thought that the world owed them something for the hard time they had been through and for their heroism in 1940, but no one else seemed to agree. One reason for Beaverbrook's hard line on making concessions to America was his perception of the growth of anti-British sentiment in the United States.[85] Ironically, in view of his reputation as an appeaser, it was Halifax who put his finger on the root cause of this phenomenon: 'Because since 1939 we have had to seek and accept American assistance, and because lately we have seemed to be pleading poverty, the Americans have got too much into the habit of regarding us as weak.'[86] Churchill had been inclined to dismiss warnings that the Americans were 'tending to regard us as a factor of little account in world affairs for the future', but he had been wrong.[87]

Bevin and company may have hoped that fear of the Soviets would persuade the Americans to be more generous towards themselves,[88] but as the Americans did not share that fear, they saw no need to be generous in supporting the British Empire and the socialist welfare state.

As Bevin looked out from Whitehall at the end of a year which had seen Britain victorious in two wars, his mood was as melancholy as the aftermath of victory could make it. Attlee may have believed that 'the British Empire can only be defended by its membership of the United Nations Organization',[89] but Bevin had to live in the real world. He would have been 'willing to pursue this policy of working in with the United Nations Organization ... if the facts of the situation allowed us to do it', but they did not. Instead of world co-operation, 'we are rapidly drifting into spheres of influence or what can be better described as the three great Monroes'. What the Foreign Secretary called in his inimitable way 'this spheres of influence business' had left Britain uneasily poised between America and Russia, both of whom were practising 'power politics naked and unashamed'.[90] Churchill, out of power and already weaving his fantasy version of the Anglo-American alliance, told the Foreign Secretary that 'the future of the world depends upon the fraternal association of Great Britain and the Commonwealth with the United States';[91] but it did not seem as though the Americans saw things this way. Moreover, as Churchill's favourite ally, the 'march of events', was to show, it was not clear that an Anglo-American association could also accommodate Britain's imperial ambitions.

16

The 'Anglo-Saxon thesis'

Churchill's foreign and imperial policies had defied the conventional wisdom of the previous two decades, and his success consigned the ideas which had informed it to the dust-heap of history. Anxious about the chasm which separated Britain's commitments from her ability to meet them, Churchill's predecessors had sought to use diplomacy as a way of bridging it. Sceptical about the notion that there was any 'one traditional foreign policy',[1] they had tried to maintain a proper distance from Europe whilst they concentrated their efforts on imperial matters. In all of these endeavours Churchill's predecessors had scouted the notion that America could be used to prop up British power; Chamberlain had enough realism to know that American and imperial interests were not compatible.

These assumptions and the policy they produced were cast aside when their greatest critic became Prime Minister in 1940. Churchill embarked on an expansive foreign policy, the mainstay of which was an attempt to deploy American power to make up the deficiencies in Britain's armoury. Because America did enter the war, Churchill, like many of his successors, tended to forget that it was an imminent threat to American power which had produced this result, not British diplomacy. There followed from this mistaken diagnosis the assumption that since the first part of Churchill's wishes had come true – that is America had entered the war – the second part would also be fulfilled and America would support British power. At the same time, in the Middle East and in India Churchill pursued hard-line policies under the guise of wartime necessity. A major insurrection in India was suppressed, whilst the campaigns of 1944–5 had seen the reconquest of the Far Eastern Empire; indeed, more than that, the Indian army played a major role in restoring the Dutch and French Empires in the region.[2] In the Middle East Egypt had been turned into a mighty armed base, and when King Farouk had shown signs of independence in 1942, the British had surrounded his palace with tanks and forced him to concede their demands. Revolts in Iraq and dangers from Syria had been dealt with, whilst British troops had conquered the upstart Italian Empire in East and North Africa. Where Chamberlain's caution and economy had led to diplomatic humiliation, Churchill's robust assertion of the imperial will had led to military glory – or so it seemed at the time.

Churchill's legacy was, however, a considerable burden for his successors, not least because the extent of his success concealed the cost at which it had been obtained. To suggest that Churchill's effort might very well have fatally undermined the Empire which he had spent so much time trying to preserve is to be met by the charge that since the Empire was doomed anyway, this hardly matters.[3] But this is to ignore the effects of the war on the British Empire (and the other European colonial Powers). There were three ways in which wartime developments damaged the foundations of imperial rule. It raised questions about British military power, which affected her standing in areas where imperial power was exercised directly or indirectly. If Britain was not a Great Power, perhaps her clients should look to their own salvation; her opponents would certainly do so. When King Farouk in Egypt or Rashid Ali in Iraq showed signs of looking elsewhere for support, the British were able to deploy the military power provided by wartime conditions necessary to restrain or defeat them. The same was true when the Congress Party in India decided to challenge British power. But naked force would not be enough to maintain the Empire for the future thanks to two further effects of the war. Both economically and diplomatically the war created new international conditions which were inimical to the survival of British power.

The economic consequences of Britain's overstretched imperial role were considered in the last chapter. The immense sterling balances built up by India and Egypt were indications of the new economic realities of colonialism. Traditionally India had provided the British with an imperial reserve which could be used anywhere from Suez to Singapore, but even as the international situation demanded that money should be spent to modernise the Indian army for the new demands which might be made on it, 'in the interests of Indian political security', most of the additional cost was to fall upon Britain.[4] The new arrangements made in 1939 meant that the British Government had to pay for the employment of Indian troops outside the sub-continent as well as the cost of the whole capital outlay needed for industrial expansion to support the war effort. During 1941–3 the British had been spending more on the Indian army than the Government of India, and even by 1945 they were spending nearly as much.[5] The British were spending £410 million on the Services and war supplies in India, Burma and Ceylon in 1945.[6] During the loan negotiations the Americans had been anxious that the British should get their sterling area creditors to write off some of the debt they were owed by Britain, but the Government was not willing to weaken its own plans for the future of India by doing so. In military terms 'India during the war exploited Britain'.[7]

If the British could not afford the economic price of maintaining large forces in the Middle East and India indefinitely, still less could they afford the diplomatic cost. Both her major allies were clearly anti-colonial Powers. If American anti-imperialism had been muted by the demands of the wartime alliance, it was now unmuzzled. The new world order created to the American model would, through its symbol the United Nations, provide a powerful focus for anti-imperialism. It seemed unlikely that America would exercise her new-found position in the world to the advantage of the British Empire. Even had previous form not made this likely, the anti-colonial rhetoric of the Soviet Union would have ensured that America would not stand forth as the champion of the imperial mission. The Anglo-Soviet occupation of Iran in 1941 had brought a Soviet presence into the Gulf region, and at Potsdam the Soviets had been demanding a say in the affairs of Turkey, at least as far as control over the Straits at the Dardanelles were concerned. They had also expressed an unwelcome interest in the former Italian colonies in North Africa.[8] Indeed, in the immediate post-war months the major source of anti-colonial activity was the Soviet Union.[9]

The presence of two anti-colonial Powers and the prevalence at the United Nations of anti-imperialist rhetoric gave a powerful impetus to nationalist groups within the European colonial Empires, not least in Egypt and India. These new conditions made it difficult for the British to deal with such groups, and the reassertion of imperial control during the war had, far from cowing nationalist movements, given them a powerful impetus. Britain's Asiatic Empire, based as it was 'on a very low degree of mobilization and interference with the life of the people',[10] could not and did not survive the war in its old form. The demands which Churchill had made on Egypt and India in particular had helped to undermine the bases of the British position in those countries. British imperialism operated through a subtle and complex system of collaboration with local ruling elites, which allowed the Maharajahs and the Princes to continue to exploit their own subjects without having to pay the full cost of defending their position; it also kept civil peace and protected the ruling castes from foreign invasion.[11] In like manner the British had maintained their position in the Middle East.[12] In Egypt they had been able to use the antagonism between the King and the nationalist Wafd to divide and rule, whilst they had secured their position across the River Jordan with the establishment of the Hashemite emirate, whose ruler, Abdullah, looked to the British for support against republican nationalists.[13] But in all these places the British yoke had rested lightly before the war, and in some of them, most notably Iraq, Egypt and India, there had been attempts to render it more bearable by devolving power on domestic issues to local governments. The war altered this happy state of affairs. Nehru and Congress were as unforgiving of the humiliations of the war as were General Neguib and Colonel Nasser.

It was in these ways that Churchill's repudiation of the more cautious policies of his predecessors had weakened the foundations upon which the Empire stood. His simplistic attitude that 'we either govern India or are kicked out'[14] did less than justice to a complicated problem. But if his successors inherited his more robust foreign and imperial policy, they did not share his over-simplified view about the nature of imperial power. Attlee, in particular, hankered after a more distinctively Labour foreign policy.

The butt of Churchillian epigrams such as 'a modest little man with much to be modest about', the colourless and unobtrusive Attlee was, in his own way, as different from his predecessor as Bevin was from Eden. Indeed, in some ways the contrast between Churchill and Attlee went rather deeper than the largely cosmetic differences between Eden and Bevin. It was not just that Attlee was inclined to recede 'into the background by his very insignificance',[15] but that the assumptions he brought to international affairs were quite different from those of Churchill. Attlee was an internationalist: 'the essential framework of his views was always the idea of a powerful supra-national body which would not only review disputes, but which would also have an effective force to deter or stop potential aggressors'.[16] This gave him quite a different perspective, for example, on questions such as the future of Britain's position in the Middle East.

Where Bevin had no dispute with Eden's statement that 'Britain's interests in the Middle East are vitally important, and any sound British Middle Eastern policy must be based primarily on the need for preserving and safeguarding them',[17] Attlee had a fundamental objection, and it was one which he did not hesitate to press. Eden regarded the Middle East as 'one of the most important strategic areas in the world', the defence of which was 'life and death to the British Empire'. With its strategic importance and its vital oil reserves, Britain could not 'afford to resign our special position in the area'.[18] Attlee disagreed and thought that the United States and perhaps even the United Nations should be brought in to the region as active partners.[19] But Eden, as so often, was far from convinced that American interest in parts of the British *imperium* were helpful;[20] and he was quite sure that Soviet interest was malign.[21] Attlee, however, demurred once more. He thought that the policy of countering Russian pressure held the 'danger of our getting into a position where we and the Russians confront each other as rival great powers at a number of points of strategic importance'.[22] He saw Soviet demands for free egress through the Straits and the Baltic as 'not unnatural in the second greatest power in the world'. In Attlee's view air power made the 'occupation and holding of particular strategic areas' far less important than in the past, and he again proposed letting the United Nations decide such questions.[23] Eden, of course, continued to hold to his views that, whatever the cost, the Middle East was of such vital importance to Britain that it was worth spending the money.[24]

Bevin did not dissent in essentials from Eden's position, but he took a kindlier view of American interest in the Middle East. As we have seen, he shared the common Foreign Office view which Eden had come to hold that the Soviets were challenging Britain's position in areas like the Gulf and the Middle East, and that the time to combat that threat was now, before the Russians began to recover from the effects of the war.[25] Where Eden had been willing to concede, reluctantly, that the British might need temporary help, Bevin, more robustly confident in American beneficence, was anxious to see 'America brought into the Mediterranean' and agreed to American plans concerning the future of the Italian colonies in North Africa.[26] Bevin was worried about Russian penetration in the region and realised that Britain could only resist it with American support.[27] But there was the rub. It was acknowledged that 'the process of inducing the United States to support a British challenge to Russia' would 'be a very tricky one'. If the Americans got hold of the idea that 'the motive behind our policies derived from the apprehension that we were being regarded as a second-class power', there would be little chance of obtaining their help; it was hoped that the role of defender of liberal democracy against the Soviets might serve this purpose.[28] This policy, the 'Anglo-Saxon thesis', would, it was thought, secure American support.[29]

But Roosevelt's death made little difference to the American position of wishing to act as mediators between her two wartime partners.[30] Before the Conference of Foreign Ministers met in London in September, Bevin had told Secretary Byrnes that 'the time has come when we must face up to the question of whether or not we are prepared to acquiesce' in Czechoslovakia, Yugoslavia, Bulgaria, Hungary and Romania 'remaining definitely in the Russian sphere of influence', and what 'inducements, economic and cultural, we can offer these countries to look West rather than East'.[31] But Byrnes, like Truman, did not respond to British overtures for a concerted Anglo-American line. Indeed, since the Americans had already taken separate action in Bulgaria and Romania by sending their own observers in, Byrnes's assurances that he did not want to 'march out of step' with the British[32] were no more than window-dressing.

Churchill had left office convinced not only of the reality of Anglo-American collaboration, but also of its firm foundation in atomic diplomacy.[33] It was, therefore, something of a shock when Truman seemed to want to keep Britain at arm's length in this area too.[34] Attlee and Bevin had been turning over the question of whether or not Britain and America should share their knowledge with the Soviets;[35] now they were not even sure whether the Americans would share it with them.[36]

The failure to bring America along placed Bevin in a difficult position. Back in July the option of delimiting spheres of influence with the Soviets had been canvassed, only to be rejected partly on the grounds that it would 'represent the abdication of our right as a great Power to be concerned with the affairs of Europe', and partly because such 'cynical abandonment' would not get American support.[37] But the problem facing Bevin was that Truman and Byrnes did not seem to be interested in coming to the rescue of British power. Indeed, rather than America proving a help to the maintenance of British power in the Middle East, it was proving a positive handicap.

If the Middle East was 'vitally important' to the future of British power, one of the problems in maintaining Britain's position there was political instability in Palestine. Egypt may have been the key to the British position in the Middle East, but 'the situation in Palestine is one of the major factors in the internal security of the Middle East', and 'repercussions from a policy unfavourable to the Arabs in Palestine are, therefore, likely to be widespread'.[38] Churchill had hoped that Palestine might be the nexus of Anglo-American co-operation in the region and had even proposed that America might be asked to take on the Mandate,[39] but this showed not only a naïveté about American policy, but also a misunderstanding of the British position in the region. The 'military rights' which Britain had in the Arab world were 'based on the goodwill we have acquired' and upon the recognition by Arab rulers that 'they require the assistance of a major power against external attack'. To abrogate this predominant position 'would be looked upon by the world, and especially by India and other eastern countries, as an indication that we were no longer either prepared or able to accept our responsibilities'; the 'psychological effects' were 'incalculable'.[40] They certainly outweighed even the benefits to be anticipated from the fact that an American acceptance of the Mandate would directly involve them in the security of the supply-line off the British Empire. Moreover, to those with a less roseate view of America, it was by no means clear that British and American policies would be the same. American support for Zionism carried the risk of Anglo-American conflict, since it was taken for granted, at least by the military, that Britain would support the Arabs; moreover, if she did not and the Americans supported the Zionists, the Russians might 'set themselves up' as the champion of the Arab world.[41] Eden, in particular, feared this last eventuality, and he was far from convinced that American incursions into Saudi Arabia and Palestine boded well for British interests;[42] in this he was prescient.

Britain was bound to have problems with nationalists in Egypt and possibly elsewhere in the region. Bevin, as a good socialist, was aware that an imperial policy which had 'rested on too narrow a footing' of 'kings, princes and pashas' had failed to win the hearts and minds of the ordinary people, but he hoped to do so with a programme of economic aid.[43] Here again American aid would be essential, but it was not forthcoming. There were those who attributed some of this phenomenon to 'bureaucratic inefficiency', but that was not the whole story. It began to look as though British politicians were witnessing a development of the first importance in the history of the world: America was beginning to 'assume that role of leadership in relation to international problems to which America considers herself entitled'. In these circumstances Britain had to be 'constantly on the watch lest' the Americans 'indulge in embarrassing initiatives without reference to Great Britain'.[44] But this was precisely what Truman and his administration were to do to the British in the strategically vital area of Palestine.

Eden's comment that 'Palestine policy cannot be considered as an isolated problem. It is part of the whole British policy in the Middle East' was no more than the truth. British interests had been best secured by 'winning Arab goodwill', and the major impediment to that in the inter-war period had been the commitment in the 1917 Balfour Declaration to a homeland for the Jews in Palestine. Unsurprisingly, the Palestinians had been less than enamoured by this decision, and it had contributed materially to the instability of the region in the 1930s; indeed, from 1936 to 1939 the British army had been heavily occupied in dealing with what was, in effect, an Arab revolt. Eden understood the Arab position perfectly and rejected the fashionable solution of partition of Palestine on the grounds that 'to the Arabs, Palestine is, and has been for centuries, a purely Arab country' and 'partition' meant 'the establishment of a Jewish State in an Arab country for the benefit of . . . Eastern European "interlopers"'. Partition, or even Jewish immigration on a large scale, would, Eden predicted, 'permanently . . . destroy Arab goodwill towards us . . . and . . . imperil British interests throughout the Middle East'.[45]

For Attlee, with his internationalist line, all this was rather old-fashioned. One of his first comments on international affairs after becoming Prime Minister was that 'the British Empire can only be defended by its membership of the United Nations Organization', and to repeat his call for the abandonment of 'outworn conceptions' like the need to hold on to strategic bases in the Mediterranean.[46] His existing views had been strengthened by the advent of the atomic bomb, which meant that 'all considerations of strategic bases in the Mediterranean or the East Indies are obsolete'.[47] Attlee's view commended itself neither to his Chiefs of Staff nor yet to Bevin and the Foreign Office.[48] Far from seeking to disengage from the region, Bevin wished to change the nature of the engagement to ensure continued British influence. He wanted to 'broaden the base on which British influence rests' by pursuing a policy of economic and social development in partnership with the Arab countries; that this would help Britain's own economic recovery and prevent America making inroads into a market that had traditionally been dominated by the British were, of course, useful products of such a policy. The 'economic and social betterment of the people' would also provide the most effective bulwark against what looked increasingly like 'Russian political and economic penetration'.[49]

The only problem with the development of a policy that was both sensible and in keeping with the long-term interests of Britain, in a region which everyone except the Prime Minister accepted was strategically vital, was that America and the Zionists cut right across it. To write of the activities of the 'Jewish lobby' is to risk incurring the grave charge of anti-Semitism, but not to do so in this instance would be to do violence to the historical record. Roosevelt, whose interest in the region had more to do with oil than Zionism, had assured King Ibn Saud that he would 'make no move hostile to the Arab people, and would not assist the Jews as against the Arabs';[50] but Truman was to find himself under such pressure from the Zionists in the United States that these good resolutions flew out of the window. In the last days of his premiership Churchill had been pressed by Truman to admit more Jewish refugees to Palestine,[51] and in August 1945 Truman formally asked the British to admit 100,000 Jews into Palestine.[52]

No demand could have been more calculated to inflame a delicate situation. But the Truman administration was to find the Zionist lobby unyielding in its attentions, and as the President himself later commented to Chaim Weizmann, 'I don't think I ever had as much pressure and propaganda unnecessarily aimed at the White House as I have had in this instance.'[53] The fate of European Jewry shocked the conscience of western statesmen and there was a strong feeling in some quarters that the Arabs should be asked to pay the price to salve that conscience. Whether it was sensible to try to achieve the safety of the Jews by placing a substantial part of surviving Jewry in a sea of Arab hostility was not a thought which troubled the minds of the more intransigent Zionists. Indeed, some of the 'pressure and propaganda' to which Truman was subjected was counter-productive in its virulence and mendacity. On the bottom of one letter accusing him of arming a 'fascist Arab military organization' instead of helping the 'democracy-loving Jewish people of Palestine', Truman scrawled with enough irritation to send his grammar awry, 'Such silly drivels as this makes anti-semites!'[54] Of course anyone who expressed, often in even the mildest way, opposition to the idea of handing Palestine over to the Jews was branded an anti-Semite – none more so than Ernest Bevin, who throughout the crisis which followed Truman's request strove to maintain British interests in the Middle East.

Although historians have usually chosen to isolate events in Palestine from the debate over British policy in the Middle East, and although they have also tended to isolate both of these from events in the Near East and the development of the Cold War, all these problems crowded in on Bevin and the Government at once. By the end of 1945 a number of things seemed clear, but none of them boded well for the future. Assumptions that Britain could rely upon America to uphold British power were simply proving to be unfounded. The Conference of Foreign Ministers suggested such a low level of American support against what the British saw as Soviet encroachments that some diplomats began to wonder whether they should not come to a spheres of influence deal with the Soviets, after all.[55] Of the 'three great Monroes' which Bevin identified in November, the American and Soviet ones appeared quite healthy, but Britain's was looking rather sickly.

The hoped-for American support was not materialising, and the other options through which Britain might hold on to her position were proving equally unpromising. The notion of a 'western grouping' put forward by Duff Cooper in May 1944 had received endorsement from Eden in the Commons in September, and he had, as we have seen, pressed it on Churchill towards the end of the year. The Prime Minister's opposition to it and fears about the possible attitude of the Soviet Union had rather put the idea on the back-burner.[56] The first step towards such a 'grouping' would clearly be an Anglo-French pact, and this was desirable on other grounds too: British support for French and Dutch imperialism in the Far East was not only essential to the restoration of those Empires, but also helped the British to consolidate their own position in the region.[57] However, if a common interest in imperialism united Britain and France at a strategic level, it divided them at the tactical one. De Gaulle's long suspicions that the British intended to supplant France in the Levant, fanned by the crisis of 1943, blew into a full-scale inferno in 1945.[58] De Gaulle's attempt to strengthen France's position there with reinforcements in May 1945 had led to heavy clashes with the Syrians, which the French responded to by instituting 'nothing short of a reign of terror in Damascus'.[59] As long as the crisis lingered on, it effectively put an end to talks about a 'western group'. As Bevin told his French opposite number, Georges Bidault, in September, although the British were 'impressed with the need to present a common front in the Middle East' and wished to investigate the idea of a 'so-called "western Bloc"', a 'settlement of the Levant issue was an essential preliminary'.[60] In the absence of American support against Soviet encroachments, and pending solution of the Levant problem and with it the possibility of help from the French, the British decided to 'put a limit on Russian expansion in the Middle East' by building up a 'kind of "Monroe" system in that area'.[61]

It was, of course, useless to look for American support in such an endeavour, since it was unlikely that they would interpret British moves as being in support of any principle higher than that of maintaining the Empire. American policy under Byrnes continued to look for a *modus vivendi* with the Soviets in Europe and elsewhere. With American troops being demobilised and her forces in Europe being run down, her leaders looked to create the political stability which would allow them to claim that the American intervention in Europe by force was over and that the task of preserving the new world order could be handed over to the United Nations. The London Conference of Foreign Ministers in September showed once again the importance which the Soviets attached to having eastern Europe as their sphere of influence. Byrnes and his advisers were not unwilling to concede this, but everything depended upon what was meant by a 'sphere of influence'. In a paper prepared for Byrnes in October, George Kennan distinguished between the 'complete domination of the lives of the countries lying in that area' and the 'legitimate prerogatives of a great power in regard to smaller countries resulting from geographical proximity'; the former was 'incompatible with the principles of cooperation in world affairs to which the Soviet Union has adhered during this war' and could only 'lead to increasing friction with the Western Democracies', whilst the latter was no more than 'legitimate influence'.[62]

Until, and unless, the Americans decided that the Soviets were passing from the latter to the former, the British would have to pursue their struggle for mastery with the Soviets by themselves. By concentrating their challenge in the Middle East and the Gulf region, the Soviets were able to keep the Americans disarmed by pitching their actions at the level of anti-imperialist moves. Molotov told Bevin during the London conference that 'Russia had never given Great Britain any grounds for suspicion, whereas Great Britain had many times given Russia grounds for suspicion'.[63] Perhaps this was just Molotov being provocative, but if it reflected a belief that the British were out to block Soviet intentions to use the post-war situation to the fullest advantage, then the Soviet Foreign Minister was correct. Since the end of Yalta the British had been at pains to try to block what they saw as Soviet expansionism, and the fact that they had been unsuccessful in enlisting American help in this enterprise would have been no mitigation in Soviet eyes. Molotov showed the liveliest suspicion of British attempts to build up a 'western bloc' and did everything he could at the London conference to block the French from having any say in the peace settlement.[64] (Stalin had, in any event, great contempt for the French, who had 'broken the common allied front' by signing an armistice which had released 150 German divisions for the eastern front.)[65]

The British and the Soviets were engaged in another round of their century-and-a-half-long struggle for power in the region known as the 'northern tier' – from the Straits at the Dardanelles to those at Hormuz. It was, after all, as even some British diplomats were prepared to acknowledge, 'illogical' to oppose Soviet bases in the Dardanelles whilst Britain maintained 'our present position in the Suez Canal'.[66] It would have been as foolish of Stalin to have neglected the chance offered to him to advance Soviet influence in this oil-rich and strategically important region as it would have been for the British to have missed the comparable opportunity at the end of the Great War. Then, by one of those ironies with which history is so replete, the dissolution of the Tsarist Empire had prevented the Russians from capitalising upon the opportunity to realise the ambitions of a century and more. Had the old regime survived, it would have pressed for and have received its share in the division of the Ottoman Empire – as Molotov reminded Bevin during the London conference.[67] Stalin had been given what history rarely affords, a second chance. The Soviets had, as they were not slow to remind the world and their people, 'taken the main and decisive part in Germany's historic defeat'. Confident in their military prowess and enjoying the 'tremendous advantage of being guided by Marxist-Leninist theory which enabled them to understand the laws of social development and anticipate the future trend of events',[68] it was not surprising if the Soviet leader concluded that the moment was ripe for the realisation of the dreams of his Tsarist predecessors. When King Boris III had called Stalin '*Pierre le Grand – en rouge*', he had not been far off the truth.[69] Soviet policy had tended to be 'based exclusively on the pursuit of the Soviet Union's own interests'.[70] Resentful at having been 'regarded as an inferior race', the Soviets were out, also, to prove 'themselves as good as anyone else'. Not unnaturally the Soviets wished to have the same access as the British to the Gulf and the eastern Mediterranean.[71] The question for the British was whether it was worth risking a showdown to forestall it – and that depended upon whether 'in such a showdown we should be sure of American support'.[72] The fear was that the Soviets had calculated correctly that 'we cannot count fully on American support when defending our imperial interests'.[73]

The idea that American indifference could be overcome by prosecution of the 'Anglo-Saxon thesis' was, by the year's end, proving less than successful. Attlee's first visit to Washington in November drew none of the 'public enthusiasm which marked Mr Churchill's dramatic wartime visits'.[74] Perhaps it was inevitable that with the war over there would be less enthusiasm, but there were other indications which suggested that the public reaction reflected official thinking. Although the Embassy tried to put the best gloss on things – claiming that the visit had 'restored us to the headlines' and had 'reminded' the Americans that 'Great Britain is one of the Big Three' – the fact was that they had needed 'reminding'. Moreover, the administration had hardly demonstrated its support for Britain's beleaguered position. The negotiations over the loan were drawing to their painful end, and even the two outward signs of co-operation masked disagreements. An announcement that there would be 'full and effective co-operation in the field of atomic energy between the United States, the United Kingdom and Canada'[75] covered American displeasure at press reports of a 'British Plan' for the future of atomic energy. The announcement that there would be an Anglo-American commission of enquiry into Palestine was, again, not the unmixed benison it might have seemed. Walter Lippmann, the one American commentator who did point out that America was, for the first time in peace, taking on commitments in an area far beyond the western hemisphere, added that since Britain was 'deficient in the essentials of authority – prestige, military power and capital resources', it was up to the United States 'to "enter the Middle East as a power" and not merely as the ultimate support of the British position'.[76]

It was in this last phenomenon that the worm in the longed-for bud appeared. The British Government had no alternative to the Churchill strategy of relying upon America in order to retain her place as a Great Power. Their fear by the end of 1945 was that America would not come to Britain's aid, and this clouded the horizon to such an extent that they failed to perceive that if America did step in, she might do so 'as a power' and 'not merely as the ultimate support of the British position'.

17

The Winds of Change

Whilst recognising that Anglo-American relations went through a discordant patch in the period immediately after the war, most historians see them reviving after 1946 in the shadow of the Cold War. In effect the 'Anglo-Saxon thesis' worked; it just took a little longer than the British expected.[1] After the chill caused by Byrnes, there came Churchill's speech in the gymnasium on the hills of old Missouri in Fulton, and as the months passed there came the Truman doctrine, Marshall aid, the North Atlantic Treaty Organisation (NATO) and co-operation in Korea; the post-war order was created, civilisation saved, and Uncle Sam to thank for it all. The names of those 'present at the creation' – Truman the stout yeoman from Independence, Bevin the burly carter and Marshall the warrior-turned-statesman, along with those in the second rank such as Kennan and Frank Roberts, with their respective 'long telegrams' – would go down in the story which the good man would tell his grandchildren; the alliance which had defeated Hitler would now take on Stalin. Provided everyone stuck to the conventional dating and no one enquired whether what had come before 1945 may have influenced what happened thereafter, this schema worked well enough. There would always be those who asked whether there had really been a Soviet threat, but they could be dismissed as troublesome liberals and academics; the defining feature of what would pass for conservatism in America became anti-communism. Admiration for Churchill's speech at Fulton united American conservatives in looking to the British leader as an exemplar of the virtue of anti-appeasement, which neatly put their opponents into the despised category of appeasers. By inventing a Churchill purged of his anti-democratic and imperialist tendencies, American conservatives provided themselves with an American hero. That he cloaked their visceral anti-communism in grave Augustan periods was an added advantage, since he gave them a weight and historical pedigree which they would otherwise have sorely lacked.

Yet was it so? Might it not be that Churchill's famous speech had as little effect upon American policy as those he had uttered six years before? Was the Truman doctrine no more than a decision to safeguard what were beginning to be thought of as American interests? For all the mythology which surrounds it, was Marshall aid as essential to the British as the legends have it, and was it anything more than another act of self-interest by the United States? Indeed, to what extent was NATO in its origins little more than a latter-day Locarno pact which eventually grew teeth? And as for the co-operation in Korea, was it not more of a curse to a British economy which was recovering rapidly than it was a blessing for a beleaguered Great Power? Following events forward, was it perhaps not also the case that Churchill's return to power in 1951 served only to encourage the myth of the 'special relationship', at least in Britain? The aid sought in 1947 was bought at a cost which could scarcely be guessed at. American help had been solicited to preserve Britain's place among the Great Powers, but in fact it did nothing to preserve the Empire, and indeed the Americans soon came, impatiently, to want Britain to take the lead in a European federation. The 'special relationship' and the powerful historical legends which accompanied it hid these facts from the British people, as they do today. It might be argued that these things were either inevitable, or at least worth it, because Britain was preserved from the Soviet menace. But American help was to compromise Britain's independence by pushing her towards a United States of Europe, and it did not even save imperial interests in the Middle East; the American connection was the most extravagant sacrifice of the end to the means imaginable.

The attempt to use America to bolster up British power had, by the end of 1945, delivered none of the dividends which Churchill and then Bevin had imagined. The loan had been granted upon terms which had aroused widespread criticism in England; the American attitude on Palestine constituted part of the problem rather than contributing towards a solution; nor were there compensations elsewhere. The Ambassador in Ankara, Sir Maurice Peterson, warned in December 1945 that Britain's position 'in this part of the world vis-à-vis Russia is steadily deteriorating'. As the percentages agreement made by Churchill in Moscow the year before had indicated, 'we had hopes of retaining some influence in the Balkans'; now the 'percentage of control which we retain is (except in Greece) precisely nil'. It was, Peterson thought, essential to 'check the spread of this deterioration southwards'.[2] This was easier to prescribe than to contrive. Far from showing any great desire to bolster Britain's position or to co-operate closely with her, Secretary Byrnes seemed bent upon pursuing his own policy of seeking agreement with the Soviet Union. In the aftermath of the deadlock which had ended the London Conference of Foreign Ministers, the British had waited to see what would happen next, imagining that the forthcoming meeting of the General Assembly of the United Nations in London would see the next round in the diplomacy of peace-making. It was with consternation that Bevin learnt from Clark-Kerr in Moscow that Byrnes had suggested to Molotov that the next meeting of the Conference of Foreign Ministers should take place in Moscow before Christmas.[3] It was only with the greatest of 'misgivings' that Bevin allowed himself to go along with Byrnes's proposal.[4] It seemed as though Eden's fears that Britain would find herself being dragged at America's coat-tails were being realised.

Attlee, meanwhile, maintained his doomed attempt to articulate a distinctive Labour foreign policy, arguing that the atomic bomb had transformed international relations. It was not just concepts like strategic bases which had become obsolete. 'All nations must give up their dreams of realising some historic expansion at the expense of their neighbours. They must look to a peaceful future instead of to a warlike past.' What Attlee called 'the new world order' must, he thought, 'start now' and the 'whole conception of war' had to be 'banished from people's minds and from the calculations of governments'.[5] This was fairly rich coming from the head of a government which was busy limiting what its Foreign Secretary saw as Soviet expansionism, but it was indicative of the schizophrenia which affected the Labour Party when it came to foreign policy. For most of its MPs being in office was a novel experience, and the habits of mind formed in opposition were not easily shaken off. In this sense the Attlee Cabinet bore a certain resemblance to the last left-of-centre Government to hold power in Britain – the Liberal administrations of 1905 to 1915. In both cases there was a plentiful supply of MPs with Utopian views of foreign policy, and in both of them there was a Foreign Secretary who was largely left to his own devices to pursue a foreign policy which received more support from the Opposition than it did from his own party.

For the moment, however, Attlee's Utopianism could be confined to memoranda, and Bevin's main worry was not his backbenchers, but how to secure British imperial power if the Americans were not going to play the role long allotted to them. Clark-Kerr urged the virtues of a policy of total frankness with the Soviets at the Moscow conference, but the diplomats at home feared that there was a 'danger that any attempt to make a general survey ... [of problems in Anglo-Soviet relations] would crystallize into a discussion of spheres of influence'.[6] Bevin and the Foreign Office were at one in regarding Attlee's views as interesting but essentially irrelevant; their task was to preserve Britain's place in the balance of power, and that meant continuing the old task of containing Soviet expansionism. As his stance during the London conference had indicated, Bevin did not intend to be 'barged about'. Both his character and the experience of the late 1930s inclined him against appeasement. The Soviets had launched a major propaganda offensive against Britain after the London meeting.[7] There was a 'marked and growing tendency to pick upon His Majesty's Government', and upon Bevin in particular, as 'the villains of the piece who are hostile to the Soviet Union at every turn';[8] nor was this altogether unfair. The Soviets had correctly identified the British, and the Foreign Secretary in particular, as the main obstacle to their consolidating the gains to which they felt that their exertions in the war had entitled them. But if the British wished to engage in another round of the 'great game' in the wider sphere of the northern tier, the Soviets were more than willing to oblige them.

The commonest response to British criticism of the regimes in Soviet-occupied eastern Europe was to point out that the British themselves were not above criticism for their actions in Greece, and in the run up to the Moscow conference it appeared increasingly likely that the Soviets would take the opportunity to ask for a withdrawal of British troops.[9] This is hardly surprising. Stalin had always treated Greece as his touchstone. He had refused to join in the American criticism of British actions in December 1944 and had pointedly reminded Churchill that he regarded Greece, like France and Belgium, as British spheres of influence; the inference being that the British should return the favour with regard to Bulgaria, Romania and Poland. If the British were going to renege on the spirit of this piece of *realpolitik*, then the Soviets would respond in kind. Pressure was kept up on Turkey to make concessions with regards to the Straits and Kars,[10] whilst the Soviets showed no signs of keeping their oft-repeated promise to evacuate their zone of Iran by early March 1946.[11] Quite the opposite, in fact, as the Soviets lent ostentatious support to a left-wing coup in Iranian Azerbaijan in November 1945, which led to the setting up of a Kurdish republic.[12] If Bevin believed that the only language which the Soviets understood was that couched in firm tones, Stalin's actions suggested that he shared that belief with regard to the British. The key question remained the attitude of the United States. Thus far it seemed as though the British were correct to assume that they would not receive support for the maintenance of their own power; the question was whether they could persuade the Americans that what they were engaged upon was an ideological struggle rather than one to maintain a particular balance of power.

The British perception of American policy was accurate. Roosevelt's internationalism had triumphed, at least in principle, as the evolution of the position of men like Senator Vandenberg symbolised. The old isolationist who had opposed America's entry into the war had now come round to approving her participation in the United Nations, but there were caveats attached. In the first place not all Americans had come round to such a view. Bob Taft, who was certain to be a major challenger for the Republican nomination in 1948, still adhered to his view that America should not abandon her old foreign policy; much as he disliked communism, his view on it was similar to his attitude towards Nazism – that America, fortunately, did not have to choose between the two of them and should thank God for that fact. There were many Republicans who agreed with him.[13] Even amongst those Americans who characterised themselves as internationalists, there was little desire to commit major resources to the task of building the new world order. If, as late as 1951, as convinced an internationalist as Eisenhower could write: 'We cannot be a modern Rome, guarding the far frontiers with our legions if for no other reason than because these are *not*, politically, *our frontiers*',[14] then how much stronger was this feeling in 1945–6? The greatest desire of most Americans was for a return to normality, which for those in the armed forces meant demobilisation. This was backed by Congress, and when it seemed to be proceeding too slowly, there were riots overseas at military bases; from a high point of twelve million men under arms in June 1945, by 1947 America had only one and a half million.[15] The idealist strain in American foreign policy was apt to look to the United Nations to solve the problems of the new world order, whilst old-time political fixers like Jimmy Byrnes were apt to look to their own resources. Unless and until the Americans could be convinced that the British were backing an important point of principle and not just looking out for their own power, Bevin and company, for all their addiction to *realpolitik*, were as ineffectual as Attlee's Utopian ideas.

Not all Americans were ignorant of British machinations. The former Vice-President, Henry Wallace, congenitally suspicious of the British and their imperialist ambitions, warned Truman in mid-October that the primary goal of British foreign policy was to promote an 'unbreachable break' between America and Russia. According to Wallace's account Truman agreed, adding that America must not 'play her game'.[16] Whilst Wallace's view that 'British policy ... will be to try to set us in the United States against the Russians as much as possible'[17] was shared by men like Admiral Leahy, the conclusion which he drew from this was not. Wallace wanted to do everything possible to co-operate with the Soviets; Leahy, who was equally suspicious of the British, was, none the less, beginning to draw the conclusion that the Soviets, like the Nazis before them, were a menace to the whole American way of life. With the 'Munich analogy constantly before him', Leahy was one of a growing number of those around the President who were coming to this conclusion.[18] Harriman, of course, with his conviction that 'the Soviet program is the establishment of totalitarianism, ending personal liberty and democracy as we know it and respect it',[19] had long held the position that Soviet expansionism and pretensions should be met with a firm response, and his Chargé d'Affaires, Kennan, had similar opinions. But although the failure of the London conference had dented the possibility of American-Soviet co-operation, it had not ended it. As Truman told his Cabinet on 26 October, 'we were not going to let the public know the extent to which the Russians had tried our patience' and 'we were going to find some way to get along' with them.[20] His confidence that this could be done rested largely upon Secretary Byrnes, with his famed capacity to find a compromise where others found only deadlock.

Byrnes was given more freedom and responsibility by Truman than Roosevelt had accorded to any of his predecessors, but this did not seem to be quite enough for the South Carolinian. Unable to forget that he might have been sitting where Truman sat if things had worked out differently at the Chicago convention, Byrnes not only saw himself as a sort of co-President, but he made the mistake of letting Truman and others see that this was his attitude. Truman may have adopted a posture of humility on assuming the Presidency, but he was a stickler for propriety; he not only knew what deference was owed to the office he held, but was well aware that Byrnes was not paying it.[21] Those of his advisers, particularly Leahy, who were becoming anxious about Soviet behaviour and objectives, saw the Secretary of State's well-known 'flexibility' in negotiation as potentially damaging.[22] The major card in America's hand vis-à-vis the Soviets was the possession of the atomic bomb. Byrnes put this firmly on the agenda for the Moscow conference, holding out the hope of international control of atomic power. To those like Senator Vandenberg who identified Byrnes with the 'surrender at Yalta',[23] this was further evidence that the great 'fixer' was not to be trusted with America's security, and he succeeded in getting the President to tone down Byrnes's proposals.[24]

For Byrnes, the Moscow meeting was an initiative designed to prove his critics wrong. The Secretary had been facing increasing criticism in the press as the architect of a foreign policy that was at best directionless and at worst weak and vacillating.[25] It was for this reason that he brushed aside Bevin's objections to a conference which had neither formal agenda nor predetermined Anglo-American positions, even going so far as to imply that if the British were unable to go to Moscow, he would go alone.[26] Bitterly disappointed at the failure of the London meeting, Byrnes hoped that one in Moscow would, by allowing him access to Stalin, achieve a positive result.[27] The problem, however, was that it was difficult to see what compromise result would have satisfied the Americans; and no compromise would have satisfied the British.

The central problem was the American approach to international relations. The makers of American foreign policy had become internationalist without acquiring a diplomacy which allowed them to co-exist with another strong Power with quite different ideological presumptions. The British were, of course, no problem; their position of dependence meant, as Bevin's attendance at the Moscow conference showed, that in the end they could be made to go along with American desiderata. Things were quite different with the Soviet Union. Bohlen's view that a Soviet 'sphere' in eastern Europe might be accepted provided it was 'open' – that is confined to influence over foreign policy[28] – may have seemed to Truman and Byrnes an acceptable compromise, but Stalin was not impressed at being told how he might exercise the power which Soviet sacrifices had brought. As he told Harriman on 24 October, referring to the fact that the Soviets were being given no say in the future of Japan, 'the Soviet Union had its self-respect as a sovereign state. . . . In point of fact the Soviet Union had become an American satellite in the Pacific. This was a role it could not accept. . . . The Soviet Union would not be a satellite of the United States in the Far East or elsewhere.'[29] It was a remark which cut to the heart of the matter. America was only comfortable with satellite states. Despising the balance of power as a contrivance of the discredited old diplomacy, the Americans automatically rejected the concept as immoral, and the more the Soviets insisted upon maintaining their own position independently of America, the more the Americans became alarmed.

However, this is not to say that as a consequence the Americans in some way 'fell' for what Wallace called British 'intrigues'; it would be at this point that the Pyrrhic nature of the Anglo-American special relationship would become apparent. Pragmatic to the bone, British diplomacy aimed at convincing America that her struggle in the northern tier and the eastern Mediterranean was for the common cause of democracy. The problem with this approach was that once the Americans reached a not dissimilar conclusion by rather different means, what had begun as a struggle for power would become an ideological war. American foreign policy was, in its assumptions, as much a product of ideology as the foreign policy it sought to oppose; both were children of revolutions and both partook of the central characteristic of revolutionary ideology, which 'dismissed both balance and concert, and strove for hegemony and doctrinal uniformity'.[30] In seeking to conjure up American support, the British were making their own Frankenstein's monster. Once the Americans became convinced that the Soviets were not going to co-operate in their new world order, the way was open for an ideological conflict which would dwarf British objectives and catch the British up in a Manichean conflict; all Bevin had wanted was a little help until Britain could get back on her feet, but he was to find himself caught up in a crusade instead. Truman's declaration in his Navy Day speech on 27 October 1945 that America would retain her military strength and would not recognise governments imposed by force was a foretaste of what was to come.

Truman's declaration was welcomed by those in Britain who had long been hoping for a firmer line from Washington. Churchill, proclaiming the 'most lively admiration' for that 'truly great man', Stalin, and whilst disclaiming any anti-Soviet intentions, nevertheless rushed to proclaim his support for the President and his faith that the future peace of the world depended upon an Anglo-American combination. He showed how little he had learnt from his wartime experience by declaring that, 'There is often no need for policy or statement to make British and Americans agree together at an international council table. They can hardly help agreeing on three out of four things. They look at things the same way.'[31] This would form the body of his more famous discourse five months later at Westminster College, and upon both occasions it would incur odium. There were two main directions from which objections came. One was what might be called the liberal-Utopian one, represented during the Commons debate by the Liberal leader, Clement Davies. Although dubbed unkindly 'Clem the less', to distinguish him from Attlee, he shared the Prime Minister's naïve faith in the United Nations as a solution to the problems of the world, and he deplored Churchill's harking back to the language of the old diplomacy. Davies wanted 'one sovereign state in the world, to which all nations shall contribute, to which all nations shall owe allegiance' and he deprecated talk of war: 'Let there be talk only of permanent peace, mutual understanding and mutual aid.'[32] The other line of criticism came from the Labour left and the communists, and criticised both Truman's speech and Churchill for, in effect, creating an Anglo-American bloc which the Soviets would regard as unfriendly. What all those sections of opinion critical of Churchill wanted was for Bevin to repudiate his doctrine of power politics and a 'reassurance that, in some way or other, a means would be found to create a new system of international relations to match the needs of "the atomic era" and their own deeply felt idealism'.[33] Instead of reassurance they got the first public sign of the way the wind was beginning to blow.

One of the things which the political left found most objectionable in Truman's speech was his declaration that America would retain a monopoly over atomic power, sharing the knowledge with neither of her wartime allies. This policy had been opposed by Stimson before his retirement in September on the grounds that it could only increase Soviet suspicion of America; anyway, the aged statesman argued, the scientific principles underlying the bomb would become common knowledge soon enough, and whatever advantage America might possess from her lead in an atomic arms race was petty compared to the possibility of not having such a race at all.[34] Despite the fact that this view was shared not only (and predictably) by Henry Wallace, but also by Byrnes's deputy, Assistant Undersecretary Dean Acheson, opposition from Republican Senators like Vandenberg and from public opinion inclined Truman against sharing America's monopoly with the Soviets.[35] However, the invitation to Attlee and Mackenzie King to talks in Washington took some of the sting from the tail of this decision, as far as the British were concerned. This, of course, gave the left another ground for complaint. But as Bevin's speech in the Commons on 7 November made clear, atomic power was something for governments to decide upon, and not even the scientists who had invented it would have any say in its use or with whom the secret was shared.[36]

Even more alarming for those hankering after whatever a 'socialist' foreign policy might have been was Bevin's declaration that he favoured the creation of a 'western bloc'. Although he stated that this would not be for 'war purposes', his language breathed the assumptions which, although common by now in his memoranda, were none the less being contested by Attlee. He was critical of Soviet propaganda attacks on British foreign policy and, like Churchill, welcomed Truman's statement that America was determined to play her proper part in the world. Like Churchill, once again, his language acknowledged the possibility of another conflict and he would have nothing to do with Davies or others who put such unrealistic hopes in the United Nations Organisation; after all, as he reminded his colleagues, even the UN would need force, and it required little intelligence to guess who would provide it. Nor was he apologetic about the British Empire, stating bluntly that 'we gave freedom where it did not exist before, by the development of the Commonwealth'.[37] Singing 'our own song a little', Bevin made plain his determination to continue with the development of the Commonwealth – and to protect it. In this context he referred to the 'further territorial demands' being made by the Soviets, adding that he could not help 'being a little suspicious' if a 'great Power wants to come right across, shall I say, the throat of the British Commonwealth, which has done no harm to anyone'. It was not surprising that the political correspondent of the *Manchester Guardian* should have declared that Labour MPs felt 'chilled' by the content and tone of Bevin's speech, or that it should have been received with more rapture among 'the ranks of Tuscany' opposite.[38]

Bevin took a similar line at Moscow in December. His first remarks at a private meeting with Byrnes on 17 December showed both his irritation at the position he had been put in by the American and his anxiety lest (as his Private Secretary, Pierson Dixon, put it) 'the Americans . . . give away our interests to the Russians for the sake of a settlement'.[39] He told Byrnes that he found Soviet policy 'disturbing' and that 'it looked as if the Russians were attempting to undermine the British position in the Middle East'.[40] If Bevin was determined to meet what he saw as a Soviet challenge to Britain's 'Monroe', then Byrnes seemed equally unwilling to do so. He was not much interested in Soviet pressure on Turkey, nor yet in the question of the evacuation of northern Iran; indeed, he wished to drop this last topic from the agenda for fear that it might hold up an agreement.

Byrnes did not share Bevin's assessment, or his concerns for Britain's position in the northern tier. According to his briefing papers, the Soviet leaders were to be seen as 'realists' and pragmatists first and only secondly as ideologues; they could be expected to exploit opportunities which arose for expansionism, but not to the extent of risking confrontation with the Americans. The best way forward was seen as America asserting leadership to reassure the Soviets that their legitimate security concerns would not be ignored. It was this approach which Byrnes sought to follow at Moscow.[41] It was one suited to the Secretary's personality and experience, but its consequences worried Ambassador Harriman and his staff.

Harriman had come away from his meeting with Stalin in October with his hopes of Soviet-American collaboration lowered. This was not just the consequence of Stalin's declaration that Russia would be nobody's 'satellite'. The Soviet leader had spoken strongly about returning to a policy of 'isolationism',[42] whilst the relatively pro-western former Foreign Minister, Litvinov, gloomily commented that the problem with the international situation was that 'neither side knew how to behave towards the other'; he was exceedingly pessimistic about prospects.[43] Clark-Kerr thought that part of the problem with the Soviet leaders was that just when they finally imagined that they had some security of tenure, along came America with a weapon that once more put them at a disadvantage vis-à-vis the western Powers.[44] Whatever the reason for Soviet behaviour and whatever Stalin's attitude portended for the future, Harriman thought it important to keep the British alongside America. He refused to carry out Byrnes's request to tell the Soviets that delays in organising the Moscow meeting were Bevin's fault, whilst Bohlen told the British that the Secretary of State had let Bevin 'down once or twice rather badly'; in an effort to keep the British happy Bohlen went so far as to tell them to warn him if they saw 'snags' from their 'angle' in the proposals Byrnes was going to make. Harriman went even further, telling Dixon that Byrnes's 'inexperience' led to 'mistakes' which did not necessarily reflect the administration's policy.[45] One unnamed American diplomat went even further than this, in conversation with Isaiah Berlin, telling him that Byrnes was 'not clear' about the importance of 'various issues' to the British, and had arrived with a series of 'grievances' against them for impeding the preliminary stages of the conference.[46] If the conference proceedings suggested that this was the low point of the special relationship, what went on behind the scenes suggests that it was certainly the nadir of loyalty towards a Secretary of State who, whilst carrying out administration policy, was contravening that favoured by the Ambassador and his staff.

There were later to be allegations that Byrnes had in fact exceeded his mandate, but it would seem that such charges reflect the Harriman view rather than contemporary reality.[47] The fact was that Byrnes had come on a very long leash. Acheson later denied that Byrnes had 'appeased' the Russians: 'I just don't find that in the record,' he told interviewers in 1955. In his view the problem was Byrnes's method, or rather lack of it. In his day at the State Department common practice was to have a complete agenda, with positions worked out in advance and approved in principle by the President, but Byrnes just 'went off to the conference ... without telling the President what he was going to do'.[48] Back in Washington Leahy (who thought he was 'a horse's ass'),[49] Vandenberg (who thought him dangerously weak on America's monopoly of atomic secrets)[50] and Henry Wallace (who thought that Byrnes did not really understand what was going on)[51] had all unburdened themselves of their views to Truman, who was, in any case, affronted by the way in which his Secretary of State was treating him;[52] it was, after all, traditional for the President to ignore his Secretary of State, not the other way round.

The diplomatic wind was beginning to shift, and the criticisms of Byrnes were a sign of this. Once the wind was set, it would come to seem that Byrnes was guilty of 'appeasement', but Acheson's recollection was more accurate than those of Byrnes's later critics. Byrnes's major mistakes were that he failed to keep Truman properly informed of what was happening at the conference, thus wounding the President's already sensitive *amour propre*, and that he imagined that the bargaining methods which had served him so well on Capitol Hill could be employed with Molotov and Stalin. The Secretary's bargaining position was, in any case, based upon a false premise – that the Soviets would agree to an American definition of what a sphere of influence should be. Molotov dismissed Byrnes's specially commissioned report on the Romanian and Bulgarian Governments with the comment that 'no American could judge eastern style democracy'.[53]

As usual when the western Powers adverted to eastern Europe, Molotov dragged in Greece, claiming that the British were 'the masters' there and arguing for a withdrawal of British troops. He and Bevin got into an unedifying dispute over the roles of their respective countries in Greece and Bulgaria. This proved to be the prelude to a bargaining session over the areas where 'Soviet interests and British interests touched'.[54] With no support from Byrnes, all Bevin could do was to conduct a querulous *tour d'horizon*, defending Britain's role in helping the Dutch in Indonesia and her policy with regard to India, whilst pointedly asking the Russian when Soviet troops would leave northern Iran. Molotov similarly defended his Government's policies in eastern Europe, denied having any part in what was happening in Azerbaijan, and implied that the Soviets expected the same sort of understanding from the British as they themselves extended to Britain's position in India.

After this dialogue of the deaf, and with little progress being made in the plenary sessions (which were largely bogged down in disputes over which nations should be a party to which peace treaty with which defeated nations), Bevin sought to resuscitate proceedings by direct conversation with Stalin. The British, like the Americans, could never quite decide whether Molotov's diplomatic imitation of Buster Keaton's 'great stone face' was all his own invention or whether he was just his master's voice – which was a useful situation for the Soviets, who often seemed to put the unprepossessing Foreign Minister as the first act in order to allow Stalin to appear more moderate; so it proved on this occasion.[55] Stalin answered Bevin's blunt questions about Soviet intentions about Azerbaijan by denying any expansionist ambitions there; he merely 'wished to safeguard the oil of Baku against diversionary activities'. He was, he said, willing to consider proposals for defusing the situation. He was equally reasonable over Turkey, disclaiming malicious intentions and proclaiming that all he wanted was free passage through the Straits and land that had been Russian in the time of the Tsar. Stalin also accepted Bevin's assurance that any 'western bloc' would not be directed against the Soviets and his assurances that he 'would always strive to the utmost to remove every difficulty arising between the two Governments'.

It was Byrnes, however, who enjoyed the greatest success as the Soviet attitude shifted after 21 December. The first sign of the thaw was Soviet agreement to American suggestions for the future of Korea, providing for a Soviet-American commission to work with Korean democratic parties with a view to setting up a unified nation. This was followed by Molotov accepting American proposals for a Far Eastern Advisory Commission and Allied Control Council for Japan, and, most surprisingly of all, acceptance of a general peace conference to which India would be invited and from which the Baltic states would be excluded; since this latter point was one on which, to Bevin's fury, Byrnes had earlier conceded Russian demands that if India was included, the Baltic states must be,[56] this was a genuine concession. Further concessions were made on the question of broadening the Bulgarian and Romanian Governments, and Stalin himself agreed that American troops could stay in China, asking only that he should be 'kept informed'. He also agreed to the setting up of a United Nations Atomic Commission, asking only that it should be under the control of the Security Council.[57]

In the colder climate which would soon prevail it was easy to dismiss Soviet concessions as small beer, and Byrnes has consistently been criticised for his failure to support Bevin's interventions over Iran and Turkey, and for leaving 'many hostages to the future'.[58] But it is the essence of diplomatic negotiations that hostages to the future are given, and from Byrnes's point of view becoming entangled in what were obviously British attempts to maintain their own position in the northern tier was simply counter-productive. It was not just that Byrnes saw it as no part of America's business to oblige Britain in such matters, but he was too canny a politician not to have noticed what Frank Roberts told Clark-Kerr on 22 December, namely that 'feeling against Great Britain among the population of Moscow is quite strong. It is generally felt that we are opposing the Russians at every point.'[59] Soviet behaviour at the conference certainly suggested that the 'population of Moscow' included the Soviet Government. At the sixth meeting of the conference on 20 December, Molotov circulated a memorandum accusing the British of maintaining large units of armed German forces in their zone, in defiance of agreed policy.[60] Bevin angrily denied the charges and resented the proposal put forward by Molotov that the Allied Control Commission should examine the situation in the British zone; the British, he complained, 'always seemed to find themselves put in the dock'.[61] At the next plenary meeting on 22 December, Molotov blithely informed Bevin that, since Marshal Zhukov had now reported that the rumours were incorrect, there would be no need for an enquiry.[62] However, this did not stop him repeating the allegation, but this time stating that it was in Austria that the German units were situated.[63]

The Soviet allegations show how wary they were of the British, who were indeed opposing them at every point where they seemed poised to reap the advantages which they felt ought to accrue to them after their success and sacrifices in the war. The sparring between the two sides continued to the end, and indicates just why Byrnes was not anxious to spoil the chances of success by becoming involved in the points at issue between Britain and the Soviet Union. Elated by his own success, Byrnes returned home, ordering air-time to convey his good news to the American people. It represented the high point of his success and the beginning of the end. Truman, less than amused at not being told the results of the conference first, ordered the Secretary of State to report to him on board the Presidential yacht, and gave him a thorough dressing-down.[64] The wind of change had shifted and was now set to bring in colder air.

18

'On the hills of old Missouri'

Fulton has not changed radically since Churchill's visit in 1946. The road to it from Jefferson City is now a two-lane highway and the old College is no longer male only, but the City of Fulton in Callaway County has retained its charm and attraction. Westminster College, founded in 1851, still sits atop a ridge with its six Grecian columns, the only remnant of the original building burnt down earlier this century, acting as its symbol. That the columns still stand owes nothing to chance and everything to Westminster's greatest asset – its alumni, who paid for their repair and refurbishment. It is to that same source that the College owes its worldwide fame, for it was an alumnus of Westminster, Major-General Harry H. Vaughan, who helped ensure that Winston Churchill delivered his famous 'Sinews of Peace' speech in the College gymnasium on 5 March 1946. Harry Hawkins Vaughan and Harry S. Truman went back a long way, and when the latter became President, Vaughan was one of a number of so-called 'cronies' who received preferment. To the smart folk in Washington this may have been 'cronyism', but to Missouri boys like Truman and Vaughan it was common sense to have around you those whom you knew you could trust. Vaughan was a proud alumnus of the little college 'on the hills of old Missouri', and when the College President, Frank McCluer, approached him for some help, he was glad to oblige the old school.

'Bullet' McCluer, as he was known, was, like most of his kind, much preoccupied with fund-raising and publicising his College. Before the war John Raeburn Green, a prominent St Louis merchant, had given the College money to fund a series of lectures which would bear his name. This was a good way of attracting prominent men, and attention, to the College, and whilst on a fishing holiday in Minnesota, McCluer conceived the notion of asking Churchill to give the lecture. It was, he thought, probably a crazy idea: the statesman must have many such requests, and the Green fund did not pay that well. But the Vice-President of the Callaway Bank, Thomas VanSant, who was an old friend of Truman's, liked the idea. VanSant was one of those men who form the backbone of rural towns. As upright as he was forthright, he was the sort of man whose opinion carried weight, and it was not the least of the many services which the Callaway Bank has rendered to Fulton that VanSant suggested to McCluer that they call Vaughan and see if he could get the President to help out. Vaughan put the idea to Truman, who was keen on it and expressed his willingness to pen an appendix to the official letter of invitation.[1] The letter duly went off on 3 October, with Truman promising to 'introduce' Churchill if he came.[2] The rest is, as they say, history. But why was Truman willing to lend himself to McCluer's idea, and why did Churchill agree to come for a fee which was, as a later College President put it, 'less than he could have gotten elsewhere'.[3]

That Churchill's response came to McCluer through Truman himself, and the nature of that response, give some clues as to the answers to these questions.[4] Churchill's formal announcement stressed that the invitation was 'endorsed by the President . . . who will himself introduce Mr Churchill'; he let it be known that he was accepting 'no honorarium'.[5]

To understand why the speech took place it is necessary to recall the political and diplomatic climate around the time of the Moscow meeting. Truman, as we have seen, was under pressure from Leahy, Harriman, sections of the State Department, Vandenberg and some Republicans to take a harder line with the Soviets; far from lessening in the aftermath of Byrnes's return, the pressure increased. Leahy, Harriman and company found nothing in the conference to lessen their suspicion of the Soviets and much to increase their anxiety that a wedge was being driven between themselves and the British. The Republicans too began to find that there was a politically profitable line opening up in the views which had long been expressed by men like the former President, Herbert Hoover, that the Soviets were as much a menace to American values as the Nazis had been; that Truman and the Democrats could be nailed as 'soft' on the subject was a splendid weapon with which to beat them as the mid-term Congressionals approached. John Foster Dulles, a lawyer and prominent Republican, argued against the thesis that world peace required America to 'endorse alien doctrines or to abandon efforts to seek justice for the weaker peoples of the world'. This view, endorsed as it was by Vandenberg and (with some reservations) Taft, chimed well with American public opinion, and opinion polls suggested that support for the line being taken by Byrnes was decreasing.[6]

It is, of course, necessary to be careful when talking about American 'public opinion'. A survey taken in 1947 revealed that 65 per cent of American voters never discussed foreign affairs, and that 58 per cent had little or no idea as to why Wallace had just resigned from the Cabinet.* This did not mean that Truman's aide, George Elsey, was right to say 'there isn't any public opinion'; there was – that of the opinion formers and leaders. During early 1946 this began to coincide with the perception of Truman himself.[7] When the prominent columnist, Joe Alsop, told Wallace angrily that his views were a 'barrel of horse-shit' and that the Russians were 'expanding just like Germany', both

---

* See page 232.

the manner and the matter of his expression would have struck a chord with the President.[8]

Truman believed that it was important to keep your word, whether in private life or in international relations. In his eyes Stalin was like old Boss Prendergast, who had run Kansas City when he entered political life – tough and uncompromising, but a man you could deal with because he stuck to his word.[9] It made no difference that Prendergast had ended up in the penitentiary; indeed, this fact may even have strengthened the resemblance. Ever since Yalta attempts had been made to get Stalin to stick to his word on the declaration concerning liberated countries, and by the American definition he had not done so. He had made ingenious excuses and resorted to sophistry in his defence, but he had not done those things which he ought to have done; Truman might have been forgiven for concluding that 'there was no health' in him. He told his Cabinet in December that 'there is no evidence yet that the Russians intend to change their habits so far as honoring contracts is concerned'.[10] The short-fused Missourian was beginning to lose patience; he was, as he wrote on 5 January, 'tired of babying the Soviets'. He was coming to the conclusion that, 'Unless Russia is faced with an iron fist and strong language another war is in the making. . . . I do not think we should play at compromise any longer.'[11] That this was not simply the President blowing off steam (even if he may not, as he claimed, have told Jimmy Byrnes all this)[12] is shown by his reaction to the crisis over Iran which erupted at the first meeting of the General Assembly of the United Nations in London in January.*

The coincidence of the Iranian crisis and the meeting of the General Assembly was a God-send to the hard-pressed British. Conscious that even favourable American opinion viewed them as a slightly tiresome 'junior partner', the British felt frustrated by lack of support from what they regarded as a less than 'inspired' American leadership, which seemed to them to be at the mercy of the currents of public opinion.[13] This explanation, unflattering and inaccurate as it was, at least prevented the diplomats from realising the full extent to which their American policy was failing to pay dividends. The main hope was still, as it had been since the end of the war, the 'Anglo-Saxon thesis' – that is of convincing the Americans that there was no contradiction between defending British interests and defending the cause of democracy, because they were one and the same. Some Americans already accepted a version of the 'Anglo-Saxon thesis', although, as so often in this tale, it was not quite the version which the British sought to peddle. When Henry Wallace accused Chip Bohlen in January of 'pulling chestnuts out of the fire for England', the head of the Russian desk at the State Department did not deny

---

* Russia was refusing to honour a previous agreement to withdraw her troops from Iran by early 1946.

the charge; instead, he announced firmly that 'it is not in our interest to let Russia cut the lifeline of England in the Far East too thin'.[14] This was another way of expressing Harriman's consistently held and strongly pressed view that America should support England because she 'is so weak, she must follow our leadership'. England would, Harriman told his staff in January, 'do anything that we insist and she won't go out on a limb alone'.[15] As little as Bevin would have appreciated such sentiments, the fact that Harriman's views were beginning to gain ground in Washington could only help his cause. The problem was that supporting Britain in Iran, as Byrnes had made clear in Moscow, was not likely to win much approval from the American public. This difficulty was, however, gradually removed as Britain's interest there was covered by the aegis of the United Nations; there were times when liberal Utopianism had its advantages, even if they only occurred when a change of form allowed its adherents to see the world as Bevin saw it. If this is taken as implying that the 'Anglo-Saxon thesis' was a means to an end rather than the end itself, then such is the case. The British were interested in maintaining their strategic position in the northern tier because Bevin and the Foreign Office (amongst others) saw the region as essential to the recovery of British power; they were not aiming for, and would not (despite what some historians seem to imagine) have settled for, a 'junior partnership' with the United States.[16]

At the meeting of the General Assembly on 19 January, the Iranians formally alleged that the Soviets had fomented the revolt in Azerbaijan. The Soviets, convinced that the British had instigated the Iranian move, responded, as they always did, by raising the case of Greece; they asked the Security Council to indict Britain for retaining troops there.[17] Andrei Vyshinsky, who had presided over the Moscow Purge trials of the 1930s with savage ferocity, found in Bevin a man incapable of being brow-beaten, and the fat Englishman fought the stocky Slav's fire with a flame-thrower. In a speech on 1 February which Pierson Dixon described as 'the frankest and most forthright speech any Foreign Secretary has made since Palmerston', Bevin tore into Vyshinsky, accusing him of sophistry and hypocrisy in raising the Greek question, and declaring that 'the danger to the peace of the world has been the incessant propaganda from Moscow against the British Commonwealth as a means to attack the British . . . as if no friendship existed between us'.[18] Although American diplomacy, directed by Byrnes, aimed at a compromise, the note which Bevin sounded struck sympathetic chords in America, where it seemed that the robust Englishman had done more to defend the moral high ground than America's representative.

If the debate over Iran gave wide publicity to what looked like Soviet expansionism, then the report of Stalin's speech to the Soviet people on 9 February helped reinforce the impression that the old wartime ally was no longer to be trusted. It was not so much what Stalin said which aroused fears

– after all, he referred to Britain and America as 'allies' – it was more the tone and style. Beginning with a reference to 'comrades' rather than the wartime 'brothers and sisters', the body of the speech seemed to confirm a return to Marxist-Leninism and a shift from the nationalism characteristic of the period since the German invasion. He attributed the war to the 'development of world economic and political forces on the basis of modern monopoly capitalism'.[19] The use of the old Marxist jargon ought not, perhaps, to have surprised people, but for western politicians, who had grown used to thinking of 'Uncle Joe' as a sort of strong socialist, it was jarring – and it strengthened the view in parts of the State Department that Stalin thought that a clash between capitalism and communism was 'inevitable'.[20] Officials, like Truman himself, were more apt to think this was because of their own growing feeling that the Soviet system posed a threat to the American way of life – and to a new world order based upon American principles.

The most famous expression of this mistrust of the Soviets, if only because of its impact in Washington, was George Kennan's long telegram.[21] From the position which he had occupied in early 1945, that of wanting a division of spheres of influence,[22] Kennan had come to the conclusion that the Soviets had decided that 'there could be no permanent *modus vivendi*' with America and that it was 'desirable and necessary that the internal harmony of our society be disrupted, our traditional way of life be destroyed' and 'the international authority of our state be broken'. It followed from this that 'our public' should be 'educated to [the] realities of the Soviet situation, and that America should guide other countries to secure them from communism'. There could be no one more suited to the purpose of 'educating' America than that great war hero, Winston Spencer Churchill.

If Kennan's telegram influenced opinion at the State Department, then it was Vandenberg who first publicly expressed the sentiments which the diplomat thought needed to reach the public. The Senator had been unimpressed with the results of the Moscow conference and he had not thought much of Byrnes's performance in London, either. The results of his musings were delivered in a passionate oration on the floor of the Senate on 27 February.[23] Senatorial speeches are more noted for being polished up afterwards for the record than for anything else, but Vandenberg played to packed galleries and applause. He struck his theme early: 'What is Russia up to now?' He had been impressed by Bevin's remarks during the UN meeting in January that 'it was vital to stand up to Russia', and he now spoke the same language.[24] He had not lost faith in the possibility of the two 'rival ideologies' coexisting, but this could only be done 'if the United States speaks as plainly upon all occasions as Russia does'; there was, he stated firmly, 'a line beyond which compromise cannot go'. He was not, he declared, advocating power politics; indeed, his words criticised that concept, even if the sense of them seemed close to it. He lauded American 'unselfishness', which he felt gave his country 'extraordinary power'. It was, in fact, just the sort of attitude most likely to lead to clashes with the Soviets, not least because an ideological view of international relations lends itself to uncompromising public stances, which, although they might have to be modified in practice, confine their adherents to positions of rhetorical inflexibility. As it turned out the Senator had set himself in the role of John the Baptist – a blasphemous comparison which nevertheless catches something of the way in which Churchill has come to be regarded by his devotees.

The antique warhorse had not, as some of his colleagues had fervently wished, retired following his shocking defeat at the elections. The world situation which had been worrying him during his last months in office did not develop in ways which cheered him. Conscious as he had been of his own part in creating the conditions in which Soviet power could burgeon, he had, as we have seen, sought to enlist American help in saving Britain's bacon; naturally he had approved of Bevin's policy, based as it was on the same premise. He could, of course, simply have rested on his considerable laurels and devoted himself to writing his memoirs, but no one who had followed the old hero's career could have expected him to do anything of the sort. If Churchill had helped get Britain into a mess, he would help her out of the abyss into which she might yet tumble. His speech in the Commons in November had shown his continuing faith in the Anglo-American alliance, but events surrounding the loan, as well as those at the London and Moscow conferences, had impressed him with the need to rally those forces which looked to him. The invitation from Westminster College, with Truman's introduction and the promise of wide publicity it brought, gave Churchill the opportunity he had been looking for. He could speak not as leader of his Majesty's Loyal Opposition, but as the prophet of the 1930s.[25]

Although he would later deny it, Truman knew what Churchill intended to say – he saw a mimeographed copy of the speech on the train which carried the two men to Jefferson City.[26] But there seems to have been no discussion of the contents of the speech, and the two men spent most of the journey playing cards.[27] Leahy, as might have been expected, 'could find no fault' with what Churchill proposed to say, whilst Truman, wavering in his initial determination not to read the speech so that, if asked, he could say as much, gave in to curiosity and pronounced it 'admirable', saying that it 'would do nothing but good though it would make a stir'.[28] He was correct on both counts.

For all its later iconic status, the speech which Churchill delivered in the crowded gymnasium on the afternoon of 5 March got the reaction which such a strong piece of polemic might expect. It was a happy accident that the traditional Westminster processional which heralded the entry of the platform party should have been to the tune of 'How Firm a Foundation',[29] for the theme of what the great man had to say was that the 'special' Anglo-

American relationship was the only sure foundation of peace in a world troubled by threats of war and tyranny. Although it was to be his use of the phrase 'an iron curtain has descended across the continent' which was to attract the attention of historians, contemporaries were equally, if not more, struck by what was in fact the main theme of the lecture: the need for a continuation of the 'special relationship'.[30] From the moment he had finished, the controversy began over what Churchill called 'the most important speech of his career'.[31]

The St Louis Globe-Democrat, which admired Churchill's 'plain-speaking' and agreed with him that 'Russia is the world menace', picked up on the Anglo-American alliance theme and commented accurately that 'Anglo-phobes will decry it as merely another of England's attempts to have the United States become its cat's-paw'.[32] So it did. When Churchill went to New York to collect an honorary degree from Columbia, students demonstrated outside with placards reading, 'We had enough!! "Winnie" wants more war!!', and 'Churchill's Tory policy keeps Palestine, Ireland from being free'.[33] The Boston Globe took a not dissimilar line, stating that Churchill was inviting America to 'become the heir to the evils of a collapsing colonialism and inevitably their defender all the way from North Africa to the China Sea'.[34] The always anti-British Chicago-Sun derided Churchill as fighting for 'a world which no longer exists in reality', and claimed stridently that, 'to follow the standard raised by this great but blinded aristocrat would be to march to the world's most ghastly war'.[35] Initial reaction from Congress was 'strongly critical' of the proposal for a military alliance,[36] and it was no doubt this, along with hostile comments from Labour MPs, which led Truman and Bevin to deny foreknowledge of the speech and to reserve comment upon it.[37] But it was a Memphis newspaper, the Commercial Appeal, which discerned the real significance of what had happened:

Taken by itself, the Churchill denunciation and warning would be just another virile, prophetic utterance of a statesman whose antipathy for communism is historic. . . . Considered in the light of current events it represents an important piece in a mosaic now beginning to form – a pattern of fact-facing in which appeasement has been thrust aside.[38]

It is difficult to beat this as a commentary on the speech which Churchill gave on the hills of old Missouri.

American reaction fell into four categories. Only one section rejected his words totally, and even the 'Crusading Liberals' and left-wingers had to temper their criticism by commenting that this was the 'bad' (i.e. pre-1939) Churchill who was speaking.[39] Moderate liberals, although recognising 'the disagreeable facts forced on their attention', tended to shy away from Churchill's 'drastic remedy'. Those Congressmen and others who were worried about Soviet intentions, but looked to the United Nations for succour, argued that an Anglo-American alliance would 'weaken UNO and destroy all hopes of Russian cooperation'. Internationalist opinion, as represented by the *Herald Tribune*, partook of the common American doubt about supporting the British Empire, but favourable as it was towards his thesis asked interestingly whether Churchill would be willing to face 'a few of the unstated implications of his view of the contemporary world'. If America was to bear the burden of stopping Soviet expansion, would Churchill be willing to 'give the United States . . . commensurate' authority to deal with the 'seething peoples' of the British Empire? It was a good question. The *Tribune* spoke for many Republicans and southern Democrats, who were more suspicious of the Soviets than they were of the British, but who had, none the less, reservations about an Anglo-American alliance. Finally came the 'extreme right-wing', to whose ears then, as for the next forty years, Churchill's anti-Soviet line was music.

Whatever reserve the controversy demanded they adopt in public, Churchill's remarks were, as we have seen, in line with the private thoughts of Bevin and Truman. Following the sterner tone taken by Byrnes in a speech to the Overseas Press Club on 28 February,[40] and events in Iran, it was evident that there was a growing congruence between British and American official attitudes towards the Soviet Union. But although there were enough straws in the wind to make several bales of hay, not everyone concurred in the emerging consensus, and just as Bevin's hopes seemed about to be realised, he found himself engaged in conflict with a Prime Minister who remained fundamentally sceptical about his policies. At the Defence Committee meeting on 21 January, Attlee had once more questioned whether defence estimates needed to be quite so high since 'there was no one to fight',[41] and he had followed this up in February with a radical questioning of Bevin's assumptions about the importance of the Middle East. Attlee thought that rather than clash with Russia, it might be a better idea to disengage from areas where there was a risk of this happening, especially with America withdrawing into isolation. Instead of sticking to the old wartime policy of keeping the Mediterranean open, which meant staying in Greece and Egypt, at the very least, Attlee shocked the Chiefs of Staff with the notion that Britain should withdraw from these areas and 'constitute a line of defence across Africa from Lagos to Kenya'.[42]

Attlee pushed his arguments in a paper to the Defence Committee on 2 March, in which he repeated that the idea that Britain needed to command the Mediterranean was 'based on a strategy formulated in the past'. The advent of air power reduced the chances of Britain being able to hold the Mediterranean, and even this 'chance' would demand the expenditure of 'great sums of money' – something Attlee considered to be unjustifiable. 'We must', the Prime Minister warned his colleagues, 'consider very carefully how to make the most of our limited resources. We must not, for sentimental reasons based on the past, give hostages to fortune.' Just how radical Attlee was prepared to be can be gauged from his statement that: 'It may be we shall have to consider the British Isles as an easterly extension of a strategic era [sic, ? area] the centre of which is the American Continent rather than as a Power looking eastwards through the Mediterranean to India and the East';[43] the Chief of the Naval Staff, Admiral Cunningham, found the Prime Minister's attitude 'past belief'.[44]

Attlee's assumptions and the policy which flowed from them ran counter to those of Bevin and the Chiefs of Staff. Bevin's policy was based upon continuity with the Eden line that the Middle East was a vital British interest, and indeed went further than Eden had in seeing the region as one of the foundation-stones upon which Britain might base her future as a Great Power. He told Attlee on 13 March that Britain's presence in the Mediterranean involved a 'very great political issue'; it was 'vital to our position as a Great Power', and without it 'we should cut little ice with those States which would fall, like Eastern Europe, under the totalitarian yoke. We should also lose our position in the Middle East.' If 'we move out ... Russia will move in,' Bevin warned, and that would mean that, 'from the point of view of commerce and trade, economy and democracy', the Mediterranean countries 'would be finished'; it was, he argued, 'essential to maintain the Mediterranean as a trade route and as a trade area, and to maintain the principles of Western civilization in that area'. Such a sign of weakness would, in fact, cripple Bevin's whole foreign policy. It would deal a fatal blow to his hopes of building up a 'western group', and by drawing Russia into the Mediterranean it would drag America into the region to challenge her and take Britain's place: 'having forfeited our position', Britain would 'lack the power to bring conciliatory influence'.[45] Unlike Attlee, Bevin did not assume that the Americans could not be brought in to support British power.

Thus far the 'Anglo-Saxon thesis' had enjoyed little success. American reaction to Churchill's speech suggested that the Americans drew a very clear distinction between supporting the principles of the United Nations Organisation and those of the British Empire. But what if those principles should coincide? Events at the first meeting of the General Assembly back in January had suggested that Iran might prove to be the area in which this might happen, and with indications that America was now prepared to take a tougher line, the last thing Bevin wanted was for Britain to show signs of weakness. When the Soviets had announced on 1 March that their troops would not be leaving Iran, this had been followed up by reports that they were marching on Tehran and towards the Turkish border. Given Truman's view that 'there isn't a doubt in my mind that Russia intends an invasion of Turkey',[46] it was a foregone conclusion that there would be a formal American protest. On 7 March Truman told the Soviets that the United States could not 'remain indifferent' to the presence of Soviet troops in northern Iran. Nor was this the limit of his action, as Churchill told Bevin. Trying to calm some of the furore caused by his speech by telling Bevin that he had made it clear that he was speaking purely in a personal capacity, Churchill had gone on to give the Foreign Secretary reassuring news – Truman intended to send the body of the Turkish Ambassador to Washington, who had just died, back to Turkey in the USS *Missouri*, 'probably the strongest battleship afloat'. Leahy had added that the battleship would be accompanied by a 'strong task force' consisting of aircraft carriers, cruisers and destroyers, which would remain in the Sea of Marmora 'for an unspecified period'. Churchill correctly identified this as 'a very important act of State and one calculated to make Russia realise that she must come to reasonable terms of discussion with the western democracies'. His own view was that 'executive forces here are deeply distressed by the way they are being treated by Russia and that they do not intend to put up with treaty breaches in Persia or encroachments in Manchuria and Korea or pressure for Russian expansion at the expense of Turkey or Greece in the Mediterranean'.[47] Halifax confirmed that following the speeches by Vandenberg and Churchill and the fears generated by Soviet behaviour in Iran, there was growing unease in America at the international situation; there had even been rumours that demobilisation had been halted, and although this had been denied, it was an indication of the atmosphere. Churchill's speech, whatever the reaction to it, had 'given the sharpest jolt to American thinking of any utterance since the end of the war'.[48] With some real prospect of his policy finally paying dividends, and with the Americans seeming to be willing to support Britain's position in the eastern Mediterranean, it is no wonder that Bevin rejected Attlee's policy so decisively.

Other voices too suggested that the Prime Minister's scepticism about pursuing a policy which was designed to maintain Britain's imperial position vis-à-vis the Soviet Union was unlikely to prevail. The gist of Kennan's long telegram was available to the British thanks to Frank Roberts, his British counterpart in Moscow, and the American urged Roberts, who shared his views, to convey them to London;[49] this he did, in an even longer despatch on 14 March.[50] Roberts, a small wiry figure with the terrier-like temperament which so often accompanies it, diagnosed Soviet propaganda attacks on Britain as being due to 'a certain fear of our inherent strength' – that is of Britain's ability to mobilise UN opinion and possibly America against Soviet ambitions. He thought that the strident nature of the Soviet reaction to the Fulton speech (Stalin had called Churchill a 'warmonger' agitating for a war with the USSR) was due to a realisation that London and Washington were moving closer together, which would make it difficult to repeat their successes of the previous six months when they had been able to play their two allies off against each other. Roberts's despatches had laid emphasis on the renewed importance of 'Marxist-Leninist ideology as the basis for Soviet internal and foreign policy' and upon the 'abnormality of the Soviet Government in its dealings with other governments', and he now asked whether Soviet actions were purely 'tactical' or whether this represented 'the first steps in a carefully considered long-term offensive'. Such comparisons came easily to those already absorbing the so-called lessons of Munich, which included the idea that *Mein Kampf* provided a long-term blueprint for Hitler's objectives, and although Roberts hedged his bets on this occasion, the possible moral of his tale was not lost on his readers. The fact that Soviet leaders were 'incapable' of believing 'in the same thing that western democracies believe in', and that they 'believe that the ends justify the means', was hardly likely to inculcate faith in the future of Anglo-Soviet co-operation. But as a product of the pragmatic school of British diplomacy, Roberts failed to push the argument as far as many Americans were already doing. He did not draw a firm comparison between the Russians and the Germans – the latter had regarded themselves as a 'master race', destined to dominate the world, whilst the Russians had a 'fundamental streak of laziness, indiscipline and inefficiency', which would prevent them pursuing the same objective; nor did he place any great faith in the idea that the Russians wanted to spread the 'world revolution'. He saw Stalin and company as essentially 'flexible' opportunists without either the desire or the industrial base to set out to dominate the world, although as good Russians they were not averse to continuing with the 'national policy' which had existed since the time of Peter the Great.

Roberts had warned of the possibility that the world might be 'faced with the danger of a modern equivalent of the religious wars of the sixteenth century, in which Soviet Communism will struggle with Western social democracy and the American version of capitalism for domination of the world', but his own pragmatism warned him against such an outcome. The same was true of Bevin, and even Churchill. Bevin was not interested in waging an ideological war against the Soviets; he wanted to maintain Britain's position in the northern tier and the Middle East against Russian expansionism, but he was well aware that he could not do so successfully without engaging the Americans on his side. The Americans were not interested in enrolling in a campaign to maintain the balance of power, but offer them a crusade and their attitude might change; that was the assumption behind the 'Anglo-Saxon thesis'. With the changing mood in Washington there now existed the possibility that American aid would be forthcoming. There were, however, two likely drawbacks to this eventuality. If America did intervene, the struggle for influence in the Middle East would turn into the sort of ideological conflict which Roberts deprecated; the flexibility and willingness to compromise which usually accompanied policies based on the concept of the balance of power was absent from American messianism: let the Americans enter centre-stage and the war of ideologies, which took no prisoners, would begin. Nor was it clear that even if the Americans accepted Churchill's diagnosis of the Russian problem and his remedy of an Anglo-American alliance, it would work to the end Bevin wanted – namely the maintenance of the British Empire. It is this point that is missed by those historians who argue that American help was essential if Britain was to survive the Soviet menace. The British were not assuming that the security of the British Isles was threatened, and they were not asking for American help for that reason; enlisting it as they did to preserve their Empire was to sacrifice the end to the means.

III

The End of British Power

19

Consequences

It would be easy to draw a connection between Churchill's speech at West-minster College and the enunciation a year later of the Truman doctrine, but such connection as exists is one of common perceptions, rather than cause and effect. Truman and his advisers were, as we have seen, already beginning to move in the direction of suspicion of Soviet actions, and at most Churchill's speech contributed to a public debate.[1] Certainly Truman, for all the impression of impetuousness he sometimes gave, did not move precipitately. Indeed, so quiet was the President in the aftermath of the great speech that *Time* magazine stated that the real question of the day was not 'What is Russia up to?', but rather 'What is Harry Truman up to?'[2] Its own answer was not inaccurate – namely that he was pondering on the public reaction to Churchill's speech and wondering what to do next. The journalists could not be expected to know, yet, about Kennan's telegram, or about the change in attitude which Truman's own note of 5 January portended, but they were aware of differences within the administration, of a weakening in Byrnes's position and of opposition from Henry Wallace towards the line taken by Churchill; with all these things to ponder it was not surprising that it was to take a year for the new policy to form and emerge.

Eleanor Roosevelt spoke for many Americans when she criticised Churchill's suggestion of an Anglo-American alliance as a return to 'the old balance of power politics that has been going on in Europe for hundreds of years' and contrasted this discredited system with a new world order based upon the United Nations.[3] Even amongst those most fearful of Soviet intentions, desire for an alliance with the British was not widespread. For those like Wallace, who disagreed with Churchill's diagnosis, both it and his proposed remedy were simply blinds to get America to 'save the British Empire'. Wallace, like Mrs Roosevelt, opposed this both in principle and because it would destroy their hopes of the United Nations.[4] Truman cagily denied to Wallace that he had had any foreknowledge of what Churchill was going to say, and more truthfully added that 'the United States was not going to enter into an alliance with England'.[5]

But the Americans did note the intensification of the Soviet press campaign against the British which followed Churchill's speech,[6] and there was no repetition at the Paris conference in May of the distance which Byrnes had kept from the British five months earlier. There may have been no alliance, but there was a care not to get too distant from the British. Kennan's telegram was circulated to all Departments concerned with foreign affairs, and Truman asked for assessments of 'the present and future military policies of the Soviet Union' and for recommendations on future American policy.[7] The idea for the survey came directly from the White House, and even Leahy (who approved of it) was 'surprised that so large a project . . . could be assigned by the President & get underway without his knowing about it'.[8] Byrnes was 'more startled', and his position within the 'Beltway' was further weakened. Byrnes had, in fact, tried to adapt himself to the new, firmer line being taken with the Soviets, but Wallace, increasingly concerned at the way things were drifting, began to try to exert such influence as he had. Truman thought that a letter which he received from Wallace on 24 July was designed to engineer a break 'on the subject of U.S. policy towards Russia',[9] but the arguments rumbled on until September when the former Vice-President took a public stand condemning those who wanted to confront the Soviets. Wallace argued that eastern Europe was vital to the security of the Soviet Union, but such arguments only made sense to a public which accepted the concept of the balance of power, and for a man who detested it to put it forward in the climate which was beginning to prevail was simply asking for the comment which Churchill made when he called him a 'crypto-communist'. Truman was caught in a bind as he had approved the speech without reading it, but in the face of the opposition to Wallace's speech he demanded – and secured – his resignation.[10]

Truman's harder line was supported by the results of the survey he had asked for – the Clifford/Elsey report.[11] Instances of Soviet lack of co-operation with the Security Council were legion, and Soviet behaviour in eastern Europe and elsewhere condemned. It was thought that the Soviets were aiming to prevent the creation of a 'western bloc' and would try to sponsor the creation of 'leftist coalitions' in western Europe with a view to increasing communist governments; France and Italy were thought to be particularly at risk in this respect. It was assumed that 'the aim of current Soviet policy' was to prepare for the 'inevitable . . . conflict' with the 'capitalist states' by 'increasing Soviet power as rapidly as possible and by weakening all nations who could be considered hostile'. The result confirmed the 'lessons of Munich' – the Soviets had to be convinced by a firm stand that America would not allow them to extend their influence. Clark Clifford and George Elsey ignored the weakness of the Soviet Union and its economic problems, even as they ignored the effect which British and American policy since Yalta might have had upon Stalin, but in all its self-deception and double-standards it was a product of the administration and era which produced it.[12]

Thus it was that by degrees it seemed that the American and British positions on the Soviet Union were converging. This impression was confirmed when, in response to British messages in February 1947 stating that they could no longer take responsibility for the eastern Mediterranean, Truman promulgated his famous doctrine. There could hardly, it appeared, be a better example of the way in which America was picking up the torch passed by the British; indeed, some historians would go as far as to almost agree with Wallace in his assessment that the British had inveigled the Americans into the Cold War. But this is too simplistic a view. If the Americans were picking up the 'reins of world leadership' from Britain's 'competent but now very weak hands', she was doing so for her own purposes and reasons.[13]

The American conception of an alliance would, as the fifth Marquess of Salisbury pointed out, prove 'very different' from British notions. Where the British made the assumption that 'close collaboration between ourselves and the country concerned' in any alliance was, 'in itself, an important British interest' and thus strove to concert action even in cases, such as Korea, where primary British interests were not at stake, the American notion of an alliance 'seems entirely different': 'They don't say the British connection is of overriding importance, and base their policy on that. They say in respect of each individual issue, what is the purely American interest, from the narrowest local angle, and act on that.'[14] Thus, whilst perceptions of a growing threat from Russia would speed the British loan through Congress in 1946, and even precipitate Marshall aid and the formation of NATO, there would be no common front in areas which were not of 'primary American interest'. This applied in particular to the Middle East. Ironically, in view of the fact that American aid had first been solicited with a view to supporting the British position in that 'vital' area, American intervention in the region would have the opposite effect. American pressure on Palestine, far from helping the British to solve the problems there, would exacerbate them, and the creation of the State of Israel would severely damage British prestige in the Arab world. It was, Eden thought, one of the cardinal errors of post-war American foreign policy to assume that if America 'would only disassociate itself from ex-colonial powers, newly-liberated countries would support the United States against communism'.[15] The result of this perception, which became even stronger during the Eisenhower Presidency, was that whilst America would engage in a worldwide messianic struggle against communism, she would support British interests only when they happened, as they did in Europe, to coincide with that mission; the myth of the 'special relationship' blinded the British to this reality – at least until it was too late.

Churchill's vision of Anglo-American relations coloured the way in which the British regarded America. It was the fact that Bevin regarded the cooperation between 1941 and 1945 as the rule, and not as the exception to it, which led to his being disappointed at Byrnes's behaviour; Neville Chamberlain would not have found it odd at all. Distrust of communism did not mean that the much older mistrust of Britain and her imperialism had died. Congressmen, presented by Truman with the British notes on 27 February

1947, immediately asked: 'Does this mean pulling British chestnuts out of the fire?'[16] This was a reasonable question. Bevin's aim had been consistently to get America to underwrite Britain's position in strategically important areas until she should recover her strength. Although it has been suggested that Bevin may have deliberately staged the British withdrawal from the eastern Mediterranean to pull the Americans in, it appears more likely that he was reacting to another stage in his long debate with Attlee and Chancellor Dalton over the size of British defence estimates.[17] But Truman's action was not designed to support British imperialism; it was meant to support the cause of democracy. As Acheson explained to the Congressmen on 27 February, 'in the last 18 months the position of the democracies throughout the world has materially deteriorated', and the President's action was designed to stop it. It was the same line of thinking which would, a few months later, see Marshall make an equally famous speech at Harvard and would launch the European Recovery Programme (ERP) – or Marshall aid. As the note of the meeting put it, establishing the line American publicity would henceforth take for half a century:

in the public presentation the concept of individual liberty is basic, and the protection of democracy everywhere in the world. It is not a matter of vague do-goodism, it is a matter of protecting our whole way of life and of protecting the nation itself.

The emphasis would be on 'the spread of communism'.[18] But this had not been the British focus at all, and it would turn what had started off as an attempt to contain Russian expansionism into the Middle East and the Persian Gulf into a worldwide ideological crusade. The British saw these things differently from the Americans, and it was for this reason that Britain would be spared the excesses of McCarthyism. As the British struggle with the Russians had begun more than a century before Lenin, they were less likely to get upset about him. Of course, for Conservatives everywhere the renewed demonisation of Soviet communism was welcome; it had served British Conservatives well before 1941 and would now do them very nicely for another half century. But the fact remains that the objective which the British had been aiming for was lost.

The development of the doctrine of containment would put the British in a cruel dilemma. American aid, military and financial, was perceived as necessary if the British were going to maintain their position as a Great Power, but America's refusal to make common cause everywhere constantly involved the British in having to make difficult decisions about whether to sacrifice their own interests in parts of the globe to the wider cause of Anglo-American unity. The British usually chose to make that sacrifice, the most spectacular example being their participation in the Korean War, where the British economic recovery was pushed fatally off-course in order to prove to America that Britain was a faithful ally; the Americans were not to reciprocate.

Although it is conventional to write about Congressional approval of the loan as one of the first boons conferred on the British by the shadow of the Soviet menace, it would be more accurate to describe it in terms reminiscent of Salisbury's general description of the difference between British and American conceptions of alliance. If Britain 'experienced disappointments in seeking American support when the role and responsibilities she was invited to assume proved to be beyond her strength',[19] it was in the economic as well as the diplomatic sphere. By falling in with Keynes's grand design and thus agreeing to the loan on American terms, the British Government tied their hands unnecessarily in the fluid circumstances of the post-war world economy. The obligation not to discriminate against dollar sources of supply meant that on the one hand Britain ran through the loan at a faster rate than had been forecast, whilst on the other it prevented her from making bilateral trading arrangements with countries who needed British coal or with parts of the sterling area; indeed, strictly speaking, the subsidies which the British Government extended to agriculture and the newly nationalised mining industry ran counter to American doctrines of free trade.[20] The Government had, in fact, underestimated the resilience of British industry and ingenuity. Much of the British deficit was, as Keynes had shown, self-inflicted, and the decision to withdraw from the eastern Mediterranean in early 1947 had more to do with attempts to tackle this than they had with any grand design to inveigle America into the nascent Cold War.[21] The exporting industries responded magnificently to the challenge. Where forecasts had predicted that at best the figures for 1946 might come to 75 per cent of the 1939 figure, the reality was that exports very nearly matched what they had been in the last full year of peace; the Government's own programme of austerity succeeded in keeping imports down.[22] By late April 1946 the Cabinet was expecting a balance of payments on the current account. Although Labour's own disastrous experiments with nationalisation in the mining industry had its part to play in the frustration of such optimistic forecasts, the eventual wreckage of their economic programme had more to do with being tied to American apron-strings.

Convertibility of sterling, which came in 1947, proved disastrous, and within six weeks of coming into operation it was suspended. But by this time the truth of what Otto Clarke and others in the Treasury had predicted was apparent: the greatest problem facing the American economy was a shortage of dollars. In 1946 the Americans had a balance of payments surplus of $8 billion, but the enormous demand for American goods from devastated Europe and elsewhere far outstripped the supply of dollars. By 1947 the surplus had risen to $11.5 billion – a fact which had its effects on Britain when sterling became convertible. But it was clear that unless America's customers were provided with dollars, the economic boom at home would run into the sands very quickly; this fear, combined with that of western Europe going communist (which would, of course, have placed some very

good American customers in the communist system), prompted the programme for European recovery, better known as the Marshall plan.

In the Churchillian version of Anglo-American relations the Marshall plan
holds a place only slightly lower than the blessed lend-lease programme itself
as an 'unsordid' act. Yet, as we have seen, it was an act very much in America's
interest, and Britain, although the largest recipient in 1948, was the first
country to come off the programme. Once more a British Government had
underestimated its people – the economy was doing so well by 1949–50 that
even the most optimistic forecasts had been exceeded. Indeed, it might be
remarked that had it not been for Britain's overseas military commitments,
the economy would have been in even stronger shape. Such comments are,
however, anachronistic, since one of the main purposes of the Government's
economic policy was to allow the country to retain its status as a Great
Power.[23]

Bevin was anxious to 'free ourselves from financial dependence upon the
United States of America as soon as possible. We shall never be able to pull
our full weight in foreign affairs until we can do so.' In this process the
development of the African colonies and of the economic resources of the
Empire/Commonwealth were crucial.[24] Those historians who fondly imagine
that the Empire was either doomed or useless to Britain after the war ignore
Bevin's comment that, 'We have the material resources in the Colonial
Empire, if we develop them, and by giving a spiritual lead now we should be
able to carry out our task in a way which will show clearly that we are not
subservient to the United States . . . or to the Soviet Union.'[25] Bevin was not
aiming at prolonged dependence on America, just at using her as a crutch
until Britain regained her strength. Given the great shortage of dollars before
the advent of the Marshall plan, the colonies were crucial to a healthy supply
of dollars – earning $150 million a year;[26] rubber from Malaysia, cocoa from
West Africa and sugar and sisal from the West Indies had, between them,
brought in most of this amount.[27] Britain invested substantially in her African
colonies, even at a time when her own population was, as the Conservatives
so happily put it, 'shivering with Shinwell and starving with Strachey'.* At
the same time the colonies played a substantial part in the unexpectedly
speedy recovery of the British economy. Exports from the colonies were, by
the end of 1948, running at nearly 50 per cent more than before the war,
and the fact that during the first half of 1948 colonial products accounted
for 10.4 per cent of Britain's imports was saving scarce dollars on the one
hand, and providing the sterling area with its only earnings of dollars on the
other.[28]

But developing the resources of the British colonial Empire was only part
of a double-pronged strategy by which Bevin sought to assert that Britain

---

* Emmanuel Shinwell was Minister of Power and John Strachey was Minister of Food.

was not 'subservient' to America – the other prong was, of course, the development of a western European union.[29] The Dunkirk Treaty of 1947 with France was seen by the British Ambassador in Paris, Duff Cooper, as the first major step towards the western union which he had advocated back in 1944.[30] Cooper's arguments were now being made to a much more receptive audience, and his plea in February 1947 that, 'if we now succeed in identifying our interests with those of France, we shall with our two vast empires be able to remain not only one, but possibly not the least important of the Big Three',[31] coincided with Bevin's own thinking. Britain had helped both the French and the Dutch to recover their Empires in the Far East, and it was sensible to extend that co-operation into Europe, especially as the Soviets proved notably unco-operative over Germany during 1947 and 1948 – a period when they also extended their control over their satellites in eastern Europe. The old argument, first employed by Eden in response to Cooper in 1944, that such a western grouping would alienate the Soviets, no longer, according to Bevin in early 1948, applied 'in the situation in which we have been placed by Russian policy, half measures are useless'.[32] The other great obstacle to such a western bloc, American opposition, had also evaporated with the passage of time. Indeed, the Marshall plan was seen by America as the first necessary stage towards encouraging the creation of a federal Europe.[33]

In this last desire the Americans once again showed how different their conception of the nature of an alliance was compared to that entertained by the British. Bevin's grand plan was aimed at what Americans later called the 'British complex',[34] that is the whole network of interests and influences which Britain possessed around the world. His 'Eurafrican' policy, as it has been called,[35] was designed to give Britain an independent base from which to co-operate with America, but it was by no means clear that having a core of common concern with America about Soviet intentions meant that there would be a core of common approach. One constant British anxiety during this was the way in which the General Assembly of the United Nations acted as a focus for 'anti-imperialism', especially after India and Pakistan became independent in 1947. Russia, of course, had her own motives in encouraging pressure for the 'emancipation' of colonies in general,[36] and in so doing she was able to exploit the fact that the Americans saw it as no part of their 'special relationship' with Britain to defend the colonial Empires, or even the British themselves, from such attacks. Although America was coming to value the 'British complex' as an ally, she was prepared to do little outside of the European theatre to preserve it.[37]

Time and again it is clear that Salisbury's analysis of the Anglo-American connection was accurate. The British expected it to operate in favour of a common front across the board, whilst the Americans expected it to operate where definite American interests were concerned. This was even the case where Europe was concerned. Although it is conventional to regard both

Marshall aid and NATO as the last two major steps on the road to a long-term American commitment in Europe, it is by no means clear that this was the case – however much the British or believers in the 'special relationship' would have liked it to be so. In both cases America was taking what she considered emergency action to protect her own interests in western Europe; the hope was that after the Europeans had been stimulated to help themselves, America would be able to scale down the level of her support.[38] It was General Eisenhower, the first Supreme Commander of NATO, who best defined American policy when he wrote: 'There is only one angle from which to approach any international problem: that of "America first".'[39] Thus, as one of the most perceptive of British Ambassadors to Washington, Sir Roger Makins, observed in 1954, as long as Russia seemed 'to Americans to represent a real menace to the American way of life', they were willing to 'divert a considerable proportion of their resources to armaments and to military and economic aid designed to strengthen their allies around the world'.[40] However, in intention, that aid was designed to be temporary in character. As Eisenhower put it, 'It is clear that American efforts to rejuvenate in Europe a feeling of self-respect, of self-confidence, and of self-defense, are not only worthwhile, they are mandatory because of the utter bleakness of the alternative.' But although American aid had warded off the imminent prospect of communist domination, the ultimate aim of American intervention in Europe was to try to 'inspire Europe *to produce for itself those armed forces that, in the long run, must provide the only means by which Europe can be defended*'. American *material* effort had to be, Eisenhower thought, 'limited as to *length of time*'.[41]

Rather than view American policy as simply a 'democratic reflex' which united the 'Atlantic community' and democratic interests elsewhere, it might be more accurate to see in it the development of an American 'imperial' system.[42] In this system Britain and her national interests would be subordinated to those of America, although the myths of the 'special relationship' would cushion Britain from this reality. From this point of view the protagonists of the myth take on the role of collaborators, whilst 'containment' became the slogan by which European consent was obtained for American domination. The 'material' support was not to be open-ended; it was designed to achieve the creation of a 'Europe' that suited America's purposes, and generous funding was provided for ideologues like Jean Monnet and Robert Schuman in France, who put forward visions of 'European' unity and federalism which were congenial to American desires. NATO was viewed by America as not 'simply a military treaty', but as 'a vehicle for closer political, economic and security co-operation in the North Atlantic community'[43] – a vehicle with American drivers, travelling in directions determined by Washington. The ERP was to prove a powerful instrument in this purpose. As George Kennan recalled in his memoirs, 'we hoped to force the Europeans to think like Europeans, and not like nationalists';[44] 'nationalism' was evidently only to be approved of when it was American in character. The Marshall plan, in effect, projected American corporatism (and federalism) on Europe – the ultimate aim of the ERP was to create a Europe fit for America.[45]

In short, then, the consequences of Bevin's pursuit of the Churchillian vision of the 'Grand Alliance' of Britain and America were not what either he or Churchill had imagined they would be. In areas of common interest where a common approach could be followed, such as Germany, the connection worked well enough at times like the Berlin airlift, but even in Europe, as events were to show, British interests and American policy were not always reconcilable. The British certainly did their best to show a common front with America, even where British and American interests did not run parallel – Korea being a particularly good example of this, if only because of its effect on Britain's economic recovery.

Coming as it did at the same time that NATO was being transformed from a treaty into a reality, the Korean War seemed to the British Government to be a vital test of the joint commitment to the containment of communism, and in the hope of fostering Anglo-American co-operation, Attlee's Government committed Britain to a role in the war which further over-extended her commitments overseas; it was a perfect example of the way in which the British saw joint action across the board as a vital part of any alliance.[46] Indeed, that most committed of Americanophiles, Winston Churchill, wanted to go even further, arguing to Eden in November 1951 that 'we should on no account approve any separation between our policy and that of the United States on the measures to be taken against China', and if this meant 'severing diplomatic relations and withdrawing recognition' from the communist Government in Peking, then Churchill was all for it.[47] Although the Attlee Government was not willing to go that far, the lengths to which it was prepared to go were damaging enough to British interests.

With the liquidation of British military commitments in the eastern Mediterranean, India and Palestine between 1947 and 1948, the Attlee Government finally began to get the primary cause of Britain's economic weakness under control. Defence expenditure, which had stood at £7,500 million in 1945, had come down to about £750 million by 1948–9, and the economic recovery which had been one of the Government's main objectives and which was essential if Britain's remaining global interests were to be preserved seemed well under way.[48] Now the defence expenditure programme was increased to an estimated £3,400 million over the period to 1953, and in January 1951 the figure was increased to £4,700 million. The diversion of resources from the productive economy led to a slaughtering of the Government's capital investment programmes, and at a time when the economy was already under strain because of the upsurge in the price of raw materials caused by the war, the programme effectively ended the recovery. The strain of the programme fell disproportionately on the metal and engineering industries, devastating the car-making industry, and the redeployment of manpower from the building industry had the effect of slowing down a crucial part of the Government's domestic programme – to the subsequent profit of the Conservative Party. Attlee and his colleagues, having learned nothing from the loan negotiations, seem to have imagined that America would fund part of the British war effort, but once more they were to find that this was not the case. As one distinguished economist and historian has put it, 'In the spring of 1951 the government was entitled to feel that it had been led further and further up the garden path';[49] a verdict which applies, as we have seen, to more than Korea.

Had the British solidarity with America in Korea been reciprocated elsewhere, there might have been compensating advantages for the British Government, but America continued to pursue her interests in her own way when and as it suited her. Churchill was convinced that his victory at the election in October 1951 would restore Anglo-American relations to the high estate from which he imagined they had fallen,[50] but his attempts were simply to show how far the reality of Anglo-American relations differed from what Churchill liked to imagine they were.

A new world
dawning.
Churchill, Truman
and Stalin at
Potsdam.

Back at No. 10
Churchill returns
to power 1951.

Churchill receives yet another American award in 1946

Churchill on the hills of Old Missouri, 5 March 1946.

The end of Truman, 1952.

'Ike' now in charge. Churchill with the President in 1953.

Churchill and America in happier times: with Eden, Truman and Acheson.

A reward for faithful service. Ambassador Winthrop Aldrich gives Churchill an award on his 81st birthday.

In their allotted places. Churchill and Eden leaving for Washington 1954.

Unstoppable. Churchill calling for détente in Washington, June 1954.

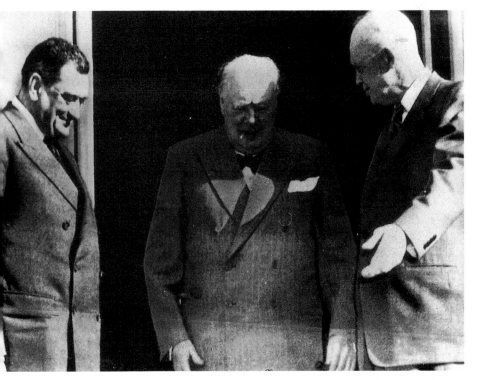

'Ike' points the way. Churchill and the French Prime Minister, Joseph Laniel, deferring to 'Ike' in Bermuda, 1953.

The labourer is worthy of his hire. Churchill gets his honorary US citizenship, 1963.

20

Churchill's 'Grand Alliance'

Eisenhower, who greatly revered Churchill, was saddened to find in late 1951 that he was 'subconsciously' trying 'to relive the days of his greatest glory' by 'struggling hard to bring about a recognition of specially close ties between America and Britain'. It seemed to him that the grand old man 'no longer absorbs new ideas'.[1] This impression was strengthened after Eisenhower became President in 1953, when he noted with evident disagreement that Churchill still seemed to imagine that 'Britain and the British Commonwealth are not to be treated just as other nations would be treated by the United States in our complicated foreign problems'. As if to confirm Salisbury's diagnosis of the different conceptions entertained by the two nations of the nature of an alliance, the new President went on to note that,

Of course, in specific instances we would be damaging our own interests if we should fail to reach prior understandings with the British; for example in most of our Asiatic problems. However, even in these cases, we will certainly be far better advised to treat publicly, every country as a sovereign equal. To do otherwise would arouse resentment and damage the understandings we are trying to promote.[2]

This was a message which Eisenhower tried to drive home to Eden in March 1952, when he told him not to 'forget the conviction we hold that our two nations will get much further along towards a satisfactory solution to our common problem if each of us preserves, consciously, an attitude of absolute equality with all other nations'.[3] Sir Roger Makins was right to warn Eden that, 'We must not be too sure that the United States would think the Prime Minister's "Grand Alliance" good enough to back.'[4]

What Makins was groping towards was the realisation that in America's new world order Britain had a place which was no more privileged than anyone else. Makins's analyses of American opinion were quite the most brilliant which any British Ambassador was to send to London, and Churchill and Eden were fortunate in having such an acute intellect in Washington, but his basic belief that 'the loss of American interest in Europe and, above all, in what is sometimes called here the "British complex" is the main thing we have to fear within the western world',[5] served in the end to reinforce the ageing Prime Minister's *idée fixe*.

Much has been written about the state of Churchill's health during his last Premiership – and much of it is nonsense. Until his stroke in June 1953 the Prime Minister may have been slower than he had been six years before – he complained to Eden in June 1952 that ' "my old brain" not working as it used to'[6] – but there is little sign that it affected his conduct of business. Even after the stroke, when Salisbury had doubts about 'whether his mind is quite as good' and about his 'capacity for prolonged work', he found that 'surprisingly, except for a short limp, he seems completely restored'.[7] But by the following year Churchill himself, although clinging fiercely on to the Premiership, was prepared, much to Salisbury's disgust, to consider 'devoting himself to a limited range of great subjects' whilst devolving 'all the rest on his deputy'.[8] Harry Crookshank, the leader of the House of Commons, was equally upset at Churchill's attitude and warned Eden that, in letting him stay on, 'we are all, I think, taking upon ourselves very great responsibilities, for we all know that he is not fit to carry on ... we have a duty to the nation which we neglect at our own and its peril'.[9] The American Ambassador, Winthrop Aldrich, told Salisbury 'very confidentially' in May 1954 that he was 'bound to say that he did not think Winston was any longer an asset from the point of view of Anglo-American relations'.[10] It would certainly seem to be the case that by 1954 most of Churchill's closest colleagues thought that he ought to resign because he was no longer up to the job.

Churchill owed his survival mainly to the unique position which he occupied in the national consciousness – and to the fastidiousness, or, as some would have it, cowardice, shown by his deputy, Anthony Eden. Eden came back to the Foreign Office in 1951 like 'a man going home'. He had spent most of his career there, and as the second man in the Government and Churchill's obvious successor, there was no question but that he should occupy the second most important office in the Cabinet. He has received heavy criticism from historians for failing to adapt himself to the changed position which Britain now occupied in the world, and he has equally been accused of not having the courage to depose Churchill; matters were, however, more complicated than such simplistic formulations allow. It was not want of courage that prevented Eden from deposing the grand old man; it was Churchill's own stubbornness. As the correspondence between them in 1954 makes clear, Churchill was quite prepared to use any excuse to dig himself in. He told Eden on 24 August that 'I have no intention of abandoning my post in the present crisis in the world',[11] despite having earlier given the impression that he would retire before the autumn Parliamentary session.[12] This was par for the course; he told Eden four times during the course of 1952 that he was going to 'go soon', whilst in March 1954 he actually put a date – May or July – on when this auspicious occasion would be.[13] It is hard to escape the conclusion that the only reason Churchill did not mention the subject during 1953 was that Eden was in such ill-health in the middle of the year that, despite his own stroke, there was no pressure on him to go. Salisbury was right to conclude that Churchill was 'much tougher than Anthony',[14] but with constant promises that the old boy would go of his own accord, Eden had every reason to hesitate over trying to remove him. Churchill clung on to office like a limpet long past the period when he was capable of exercising power, but because of his unique position it was next to impossible to remove him without his own co-operation. If this was a sign that Eden lacked guts, then he was not alone in his lack of intestinal fortitude. Harold Macmillan, who had raised the subject of the need for a new administration with Churchill in June,[15] and who kept in close touch with Eden and offered him advice during the summer of 1954 when a concerted effort was made to persuade the old man that the time had come to go gracefully,[16] nevertheless concluded fatalistically when urging Eden to 'have another shot' that, 'if he refuses ... we cannot but accept his refusal'. The best he could do was to ask whether Eden could not 'threaten him a little',[17] and to wonder whether the prospect of Eden 'and several of his colleagues' saying that they would 'prefer not to share any longer the responsibility involved' in serving under Churchill would get the old hero out.[18]

Yet the very fact that Macmillan had to suggest such strong measures is the best example of the reason why Churchill stayed. Such a move would have threatened to break up the Government, which enjoyed only a slender majority, and given Churchill's stubbornness it threatened to precipitate a general election at which a divided Conservative Party might well fail to prosper. Churchill stayed because nothing short of such a political explosion would shift him. With him stayed his outmoded conception of the Anglo-American alliance and the over-long personal letters which 'worried' Eisenhower. Much as the new President had at first welcomed the flattering attentions of the old statesman, he became increasingly anxious as Churchill tried to revive the correspondence which he had had with Roosevelt. As the American Ambassador put it, Eisenhower 'did not know where they [the letters] were going to land him'.[19]

So whilst Eden certainly refused to eject Churchill from Downing Street, it is easier to condemn him for pusillanimity than it is to suggest how such a feat might have been accomplished. But was he, nevertheless, guilty of failing to adapt to Britain's changed situation in the world? Did Churchill adapt better than Eden to the changed nature of Anglo-American relations, and did Eden's unwillngness to play the role of 'junior partner' to America inflict needless damage on the 'special relationship'?[20]

Eden's reputation has fallen so low that one eminent historian has dismissed him as 'a mediocrity held in high esteem'.[21] 'Vain, irascible' and 'overstrung', with an 'arrogant belief in his own perceptions', it has been written that 'Eden's main disability was intellectual. He had great flair but no genius.'[22] So overwhelming has the historical consensus been on Eden's shortcomings as Foreign Secretary that, despite the heroic efforts of his official biographer to tell the story straight in the hope that it will, by itself, convince the doubters,[23] it seems almost incredible that he should ever have been held in 'high esteem'. Indeed, it is so incredible that doubt must be thrown on the consensus. Pierson Dixon, who as Eden's Private Secretary in the latter part of the war had had ample exposure to his chief's idiosyncrasies of temper, and who was not given to empty flattery, wrote to him in the gloomy days of June 1954 to tell him that 'the only redeeming feature of the present situation is the fantastic height at which your stock now stands. And not only in this country.'[24] Indeed, until the disaster of Suez overtook Eden, it was the 'Dixonian' view which prevailed, and it would rather seem as though since then the pendulum has, in its usual manner, swung too hard the other way.

The notion that Eden misjudged Britain's position in the world is a subjective one, as it rather depends upon the assessment of the observer; heavily tinted with hindsight as most such judgments have been, it is easy to convict Eden of not realising what position Britain now occupied in the world. But did it make him 'less of a strategist' than Bevin to aim at a policy of using the Empire to maintain a degree of action independent of America, when this had been Bevin's own strategy? Was he less strategically gifted than his predecessor in sharing his doubts about the notion of European union which the Americans were offering? Was it really just 'vanity' and irascibility which prompted his growing impatience with America? Rhetorical questions require no answer and carry in themselves an implied one. If co-operation with America in the Middle East and the Gulf did not come easily, nor had it in the days of his predecessors, and if there was friction over how to make peace in Korea, it was perhaps because Eden actually had rather a wider vision of what British interests in the area were than his predecessors who had tied themselves to America's apron-strings. When examined closely, the criticisms of Eden often amount to the fact that he failed to follow the American line in foreign affairs – he failed, in short, to realise that after six years of war the best the British could hope for was a 'junior partnership' in the American Empire. Unlike his successor he did not want the British to be 'Greeks in the new Roman Empire', nor was he prepared to follow the American line on the question of 'European' union. Moreover, he was not prepared to play a subservient role in the Manichean view of the world which America had come to adopt. The representative of an older and more pragmatic diplomatic tradition, Eden was willing to take advantage of American preoccupations with the dangers of communism without fully sharing the same black-and-white view of the world. Naturally these things failed to recommend him to the Americans, even as they have failed to recommend him to those who have taken the view that British interests should be subordinated to American whenever they clash. But was Eden's attempt to run a British foreign policy in Britain's interests in itself a doomed anachronism? Was the era of national power and imperialism not already over, and was the path of wisdom not to follow the line of least resistance and go with the American flow? Perhaps the real moral to draw from Eden's career after 1951 is that an independent British foreign policy was no longer possible; but if that is so, then it was not for any reason more profound than an American unwillingness to support British actions in the way expected from an ally.

With the slavishness shown by sections of the Conservative Party to the American connection, and the common and politically fertile ground provided for conservatism on both sides of the Atlantic by a shared anti-communism, Eden's refusal to settle for the role of junior partner is easily represented as anachronistic. With the swift disappearance of the British Empire under the legerdemain of Macmillan and his acceptance of the European option, Eden's foreign policy becomes even more difficult to understand, and thus easier to misrepresent. He failed to sail with what his successor called 'the winds of change', but as that stout Conservative, Lord Salisbury, observed, that phrase appealed mainly to those who 'don't want to make a stand anywhere' – and such men came to dominate the Conservative Party. Still, as Salisbury noted, even before it had come to pass, 'sailors who make it a rule to run before the wind generally end up on the rocks'.[25] Eden did not run with the American wind; he attempted to tack and turn, only to end up on the rocks himself – but that, as we shall see, owed as much to sabotage as it did to bad navigation.

The policy which Eden was to carry out was, in its strategic outlines, the one which he inherited from the Attlee Government. It was, in the words of one of its most distinguished practitioners, Sir Roger Makins, 'a bold one', but it was 'the only feasible one for the United Kingdom if we are to avoid sinking to the level of a second or third class power'.[26] Makins, who had worked closely with Macmillan and Eisenhower in Algiers in 1943, was, like his mentor, rather apt to believe that British interests were largely reconcilable with the American alliance, although he did acknowledge that where there were localised conflicts, British interests might have to give way 'since American support is essential to the free world'. But this was to make the same mistake which Churchill had made in 1940 – namely to impute to British influence what in fact belonged to American perceptions. America 'defended' the 'free world' from communism because her leaders perceived it to be in America's interests to do so. Late 1945 to 1947 had shown that when American leaders perceived no such threat from Russia, they were quite capable of disregarding British interests, whatever pleas the British might make; there was no reason to suppose this situation had changed. Thus, sacrificing British interests to win American support was, literally, a meaningless activity. In the second place British and American interests were not reconcilable everywhere, and when they conflicted it was not necessarily on local and tangential matters. This was visible in three of the areas which faced Eden when he returned to the Foreign Office, and if there was conflict with the Americans in the Middle East, Europe and the Far East, it was because Eden tried to do what a British Foreign Secretary might be expected to do – defend British interests.

Oddly enough for a profession which tends to play down the importance of personality, historians have been apt to portray the difficulties which Eden had with the Americans as being the result of personal differences with Dean Acheson and John Foster Dulles.[27] But as the visit which he and Churchill made to Washington in January 1952 showed, they were, in fact, the result of real differences of opinion over substantive issues. In the Middle East, on the question of European union, as in the Far East, American wishes and British interests were not exactly matched – and, as usual, British expectations that a close relationship with America would help her interests were doomed to disappointment.

Despite the hopes which Bevin had entertained in late 1947 that America would 'do its best to support and strengthen the British strategic, political and economic position throughout the Middle East',[28] things had not quite worked out that way. Given their conception of the way an alliance should work – that is that a common front was, in itself, an important part of an alliance – the British evidently hoped that the growing congruence of views about the dangers of communism would mute American anti-colonialism; although this happened to some extent, it did not mean that America supported Britain's position in the Middle East. American pressure over Palestine had resulted in a British scuttle which had damaged her relationship with the Arab world, whilst in Arabia and Iran American oil interests had sought to entrench themselves at Britain's interests; certainly there was a feeling in some quarters that American sympathy had encouraged the Iranian leader, Dr Mossadeq, to nationalise the Anglo-Iranian Oil Company (AIOC). American fears that British colonialism would leave the way open for communism to influence nationalist movements led her policy-makers to show sympathy for such movements – and generally an offer of American patronage before the Soviets got there first. This did nothing to help the British position in a region which was still vital to her status as a Great Power. As the British Minister in Beirut put it in 1951, 'The first reason for our decline in the Middle East is our eagerness not to offend America.'[29]

If co-operation in the Middle East had not worked out to Britain's advantage, then there were signs by 1950 that even the much appreciated American aid in Europe might be turning out to have resemblances to the Trojan Horse. As Bevin put it to the Cabinet in May, just before the London meeting of Foreign Ministers, 'the United States authorities had recently seemed disposed to press us to adopt a greater measure of economic integration with Europe than we thought wise'.[30] Here again it was difficult to reconcile American objectives with British interests; and once more the operation of a latter-day 'Whig' version of recent British history distorts the historical perspective. If the triumph of anti-imperialism makes it difficult for the historian to recapture the importance which contemporary policy-makers placed upon the development and survival of the British Empire, then the fashionable consensus that missing out on joining 'Europe' in the early 1950s was one of the great 'lost opportunities' of post-war British foreign policy makes it equally difficult to appreciate the reasons behind the policy decisions which led in that direction. Indeed, so strong is this orthodoxy that in some quarters there are even fierce arguments as to whether Churchill was browbeaten by Eden into going back on the commitments which he seemed to have made in favour of a united Europe whilst he was in opposition.[31] Those who cleave to the 'lost opportunity' myth show, by so doing, an inadequate appreciation of the situation in which Britain found herself in 1950-1.

Churchill had certainly spoken about a 'united Europe', but that did not mean that he wanted the sort of federal structure that the Monnets, Schumans and Americans wanted. The common supposition that earlier British partici-pation in 'Europe' could have produced something which did not have a federal agenda is indicative of a lack of understanding of the objectives of the enterprise which the Americans were backing – it was federalist to the core. Ironically the 'loss of trust in the national state' engendered by the experience of defeat and occupation in the continent, which provided such fertile soil for the ideas of Monnet and the federalists, communicated itself at a later date to the British in the aftermath of Suez during a period of national *angst*. Naturally enough the 'born-again' adherents of what they usually choose to call the 'European Idea' hardly wish to locate their 'idealism' in such murky waters and are apt to talk profoundly about the obsolescence of nationalism and the 'nation state', as though the constant repetition of a slogan can, by dint of repetition, disguise emotional preferences as intellectual convictions. European federalism was essentially an idea of the 1930s and 1940s, which politicians who had lost faith in their own national destinies clung to as drowning men to a life-raft; since this malaise did not overcome the British political class until rather late in the day, it was natural that by the time it did its protagonists should have pointed the finger at their prede-cessors as the men responsible for missing a great opportunity; but that was political propaganda, and it is more than time that historians (and the rest of us) stopped treating the lucubrations of Gladwyn Jebb, Harold Macmillan, old uncle Ted Heath and all with respect which they scarcely deserve.

The concept of 'Europe' which was floated in the late 1940s and which the Americans backed was meant to serve two American purposes: in the first place it would lay the foundations for America to withdraw from the high-level of commitment to the defence of western Europe which the anti-communist crusade had demanded since 1947; in the second place, by providing a context in which Germany might be re-industrialised and even rearmed, it would help to solve the German problem. There was, of course, nothing wrong with either of these objectives, but equally there was no reason why Britain's failure to comply with them should be seen as a great lost opportunity.

The Americans had welcomed the creation of the Council of Europe in

1949, and most policy-makers took the view that 'no integration of Western Europe was conceivable without the full participation of the U.K.'.[32] Marshall's successor at the State Department, Dean Acheson, was less willing than his subordinates would have liked to press the British to participate fully in the move towards European federalism, but he did urge Bevin in October to take a lead in unifying Europe.[33] But the Labour Government, whilst supporting European social and cultural co-operation, was unwilling to go too far in the direction of political and economic co-operation. Willing to play a part in revivifying Europe to defend it from communism, Ministers did not want to go anywhere near as far as the Americans wanted in unifying the western part of the continent. Bevin was conscious that too discouraging an attitude by Britain would have a bad effect on French morale and might annoy the Americans, but he felt that, 'Our relationship with the rest of the Commonwealth and, almost equally important, our new relationship with the United States ensure that we must remain, as we have always been in the past, different in character from other European nations and fundamentally incapable of wholehearted integration with them.'[34] It was this same consideration which had affected Bevin's attitude towards the Schuman plan in May 1950, when Britain refused to join the European Coal and Steel Community despite pressure from the Americans to do so.

The British were aware that one of America's motives for supporting federation was a desire to be able to reduce their own commitment to the defence of Europe, but as Bevin told the Cabinet on 8 May 1950, 'To withstand the great concentration of power now stretching from China to the Oder, the United Kingdom and Western Europe must be able to rely on the full support of the English-speaking democracies of the Western Hemisphere.' In short, because Britain's commitments were global, a purely European association could not meet them, and 'for the original conception of Western Union we must now begin to substitute the wider conception of the Atlantic community'.[35] It was only in this 'wider grouping' that the 'three main pillars of our policy, the Commonwealth in some degree, Western Europe and the United States' could be brought together.[36] These assumptions were shared to the full by Eden.

Churchill's ostentatious support for the Council of Europe, and some of the rhetoric which he had used whilst in opposition, had created an expectation in America (and elsewhere) that his Government would be more sympathetic to the federalist project than his predecessor; after all, the Conservatives certainly lacked the hostility felt by English socialists for an organisation which might render the nationalisation of the coal and steel industries a nullity. But whilst a selective reading of Churchill's speeches by his admirers can seem to show that the great man was, yet again, a prescient figure,[37] a fuller reading reveals not so much ambiguities but rather an attitude typical of many of his contemporaries. In September 1946 at Zurich he had delivered what is better regarded as the European counterpart to his Fulton speech than as a harbinger of the European Community as it came to exist. Referring back to pre-war concepts of 'pan-Europeanism', Churchill had called for a 'United States of Europe' and, as a first step towards it, a Franco-German reconciliation.[38] But his idea of Britain's place in such an organisation was clearly not far removed from that of Bevin and Attlee, who were willing to participate in cultural and social matters, but less eager to become embroiled economically and politically in something from which it might be impossible to disentangle the country. In a great speech at the Albert Hall in May 1947 he took the well-worn path of eschewing precise definitions of what a 'United Europe' might consist of, speaking instead in his best vatic mode of the 'spiritual conception of Europe'.[39] His wise avoidance of detail served in this sphere, as in the wider one of Conservative policy in general, the dual purpose of keeping his own Party united whilst allowing Labour few targets at which to strike, and in retrospect it has allowed advocates of the federalist project to enlist Churchill in their ranks – some of them indeed going so far as to claim that it was Eden who obstructed the achievement of British entry into 'Europe'.[40] But this is Whig history with a vengeance, writing off, as it does, concern with the Empire/Commonwealth as somehow anachronistic and arguing, in effect, that Britain should have fallen in with American pressure. Ironically the early 1950s were, as one historian has commented, 'the time when Britain stood up to the United States as strongly as she was ever to do in the post-war world'. The same source, however, goes on to comment that, 'It was a testament to the quality of the special relationship, and the dedication of Churchill and Eden, that differences were weathered and that the underlying bond remained'; which is, in itself, testament to the capacity of historians writing about Anglo-American relations to allow sentiment to overlay their capacity for critical analysis.[41]

Because of the fall in Eden's own stock and the dearth of successors willing to attempt the same line of policy, it is easy either to miss or to ignore what he was trying to do as Foreign Secretary in the early 1950s. It is a sign of how far and fast Britain has fallen since the war that an attempt to run British foreign policy in Britain's interests should appear so esoteric. America had her priorities for Britain: in Europe, out of Empire, particularly in places where American interests suggested it was desirable, and under America's wing. Eden, however, did not think things had yet come to such a pass that British interests should be subordinated to the American great design, and he would have agreed with Sir Roger Makins that 'it must be our objective to maintain our position as a great Power' and that 'if we relaxed our grip scarcely a British interest outside the United Kingdom would survive'.[42] He saw Britain, as his Private Secretary, Sir Evelyn Shuckburgh, put it, as 'an active and enlightened European nation with a world role'.[43]

On 'Europe', Eden wanted to continue the line of policy set forth in the

September 1951 Declaration of the American, British and French Foreign Ministers, which welcomed the Schuman plan 'as a means of strengthening the economy of Western Europe', talked of the entry of a 'democratic Germany' into a 'Continental European Community', but did so as part of a 'constantly developing Atlantic Community'.[44] Whilst some 'innocent' souls such as officials in the British Treasury might have thought that the Declaration implied a 'serious change' in British policy towards Europe,[45] and those who had long hoped that Churchill's advent would signify the same thing[46] might have entertained optimistic notions, it was clear that Eden intended British policy to continue along existing lines.[47] There was the usual pressure from American sources to 'show our willingness to take over the leadership of the movement towards European integration',[48] but Eden refused to bow to it. Despite the legends perpetrated by the then Home Secretary and later Lord Chancellor, David Maxwell-Fyfe, Harold Macmillan and other Europe-enthusiasts, Eden's statement on 28 November at the end of a NATO meeting in Rome did not mark any change in British policy; indeed, it differed but little from Maxwell-Fyfe's own statement in Strasbourg.[49] Churchill himself did not support full British integration with Europe, although he had no objections to the Americans encouraging European union. As for the Schuman plan, he 'never contemplated Britain joining . . . on the same terms as Continental partners'. On this, as on plans for a European army, Churchill took a pragmatic view: 'We help, we dedicate, we play a part, but we are not merged and do not forfeit our insular or Commonwealth-wide character.' Churchill's definition of Britain's objectives did not differ from Eden's: 'Our first object is the unity and consolidation of the British Commonwealth. . . . Our second, "the fraternal association" of the English-speaking world; and third, United Europe, to which we are a separate closely- and specially-related ally and friend.'[50] It was 'only when plans for uniting Europe take a federal form that we ourselves cannot take part, because we cannot subordinate ourselves or the control of British policy to federal authorities'.[51] As for American pressure, Eden agreed with Churchill's comment that, whilst the Americans 'would like us to fall into the general line of European pensioners', he had 'no intention' of doing so.[52]

It was not just in Europe that Eden did not intend Britain to be an American 'pensioner'. During the war America had tempered her own competition with the British in the Middle East to the imperatives of common strategic interests, but 'in general, American officials remained interested in diminishing British political and commercial strength in Egypt' and elsewhere.[53] The advent of the Cold War may have moderated American policy after 1946, but that did not mean that America endorsed the British position in the Middle East. Although the Truman administration appreciated the attempts of Bevin to improve the standard of living of the Egyptian people,[54] America's own strategic interests in the region in the early Cold War dictated a policy of trying to ensure that nascent nationalist movements in the Middle East did not turn to the communists for support. Given British expectation of American support, this produced rather an awkward situation for American policy-makers, who, whilst not wanting to be seen by the nationalists to be backing Britain, did not wish to offend the British unduly by seeming not to be backing them. Although agreement was reached between the British and the Americans in 1947 that they would 'cooperate with each other in the area' and abjure 'any sense of rivalry',[55] things did not work out quite as either side would have liked. The British were apt to complain that 'our eagerness not to offend America' had compromised their position in the Arab world, without any compensating advantages.[56] It was thus evident to Eden, as he contemplated renegotiating the Anglo-Egyptian Treaty of 1936 (which he had himself signed), that he could expect little real help from America in a region still regarded as vital to Britain.

Britain's commitment to help America in Korea stemmed, as we have seen, directly from the notion that common action was, in itself, an essential part of any alliance, and, as Attlee put it in November 1950, 'If we were to withdraw our support for US strategy in the Far East, the US Government would be less willing to continue their policy of supporting the defence of Western Europe.'[57] But Bevin and Attlee had also hoped that participation in the war would give them an opportunity of counselling moderation. By the end of November 1950, with Chinese intervention having almost pushed the Americans and the UN out of South Korea, there were rumours that General MacArthur might resort to the use of nuclear weapons – which had prompted a hasty visit by Attlee to Washington to dissuade Truman from authorising their use. Eden certainly saw himself as a possible mediator in the diplomatic attempts to end the war in 1951–2, but this was not a role which the Americans were to welcome.

In short, then, Eden was perfectly conscious that Britain's commitments exceeded her ability to meet them; indeed, it would not have been possible to have been Foreign Secretary and not to have known this.[58] What was less easily diagnosed was how Britain was to fulfil her commitments. It was easy for Dean Acheson to snap at Eden that, '"You must learn to live in the world as it is"',[59] but what he actually meant was that Britain should follow America's lead. Eden had other ideas.

21

Renewing the Grand Alliance?

Anglo-American relations during the period of Churchill's second Premier-ship have been called a 'sorry and deplorable story', much of the blame for which 'can be laid at the door of Lord Avon's [i.e. Anthony Eden's] tenure of the Foreign Office and of 10 Downing Street'.[1] It is eloquent testimony to the hold which the myth of the special relationship has upon those of a certain generation that an attempt to run Britain's foreign policy in Britain's interests can be written off thus; no doubt Franco-German relations were at their best, from one point of view, in the period 1940–5, but that hardly set a desirable precedent. As Eden was to put it when reflecting upon the experi-ence of actually running policy during the early 1950s, 'The lesson may be that allies should subordinate their interests more closely to the opinions of their stronger partner, but an alliance does not gather strength that way.'[2] If Anglo-American relations were in a 'sorry' state, then the reason is not far to seek: weaned on the Churchillian version of the 'special relationship', British policy-makers (including Eden) expected America to grant them a privileged place in their new world order, and quite failed to appreciate that whether the year was 1940 or 1950, or even 1956, America would support British interests where they coincided with her own, and only then, whilst expecting the British to tow the line whenever America wanted her to do so. That was the reality of the 'special relationship'.

In the period since the (probably) temporary dissolution of the Russian Empire the comment has sometimes been heard that the Cold War may have been no bad thing in its way as it imposed a certain order on the world. It is not surprising that such comments should come from those in gainful employ in the United States, since the order was one which very much suited America.[3] With the Soviets firmly identified as the 'bad guys', full-blooded internationalism was totally reconciled with America's own interests. This was all very well in terms of mobilising American opinion, and in Europe the issue seemed similarly clear-cut, but elsewhere the situation was not quite so amenable to the simplicities of Cold War debate. The American Chiefs of Staff were aware of the strategic value of the British bases at Suez and in the Gulf, but their concern did not translate itself into diplomatic support from the State Department; the pluralistic nature of American government made life difficult for America's allies. Although a world power, America had not left behind the facile anti-imperialism which had always been an element in her attitude towards international affairs. Although American historians have tried to shy away from it, the fact remains that America's attitude towards it contributed materially to the erosion of the British Empire. In an era when unconcealed colonialism is out of fashion, it might seem unexceptionable to write that, 'So long as the British genuinely seemed to be making progress towards "colonial independence", then the colonial issue was relatively unimportant in Anglo-American relations',[4] but British politicians charged with the task of looking after British interests could hardly take such a cavalier attitude. It was not much consolation to men like Eden, trained to regard international relations as a complex interlocking web, to reflect later that, 'The Americans have a great deal to answer for. They always push out the colonial powers and get something far worse instead; and they never learn by bitter experience';[5] nor did they, although the nemesis awaiting their hubris was a terrible one. What the arrogant naïveté of American policy failed to appreciate was that even in the Cold War era the world was more complicated than their perspective allowed. The 'British complex' provided security and thus order in parts of the world where American power was unavailable. To fail to support Britain in the belief that newly independent countries would somehow be grateful to America was to prove an expensive mistake. What Americans failed to appreciate was that 'the anti-colonial movements of Asia and Africa did not merely want independence, like Washington and Bolivar, but represented a profounder revolt against the West, including the United States as the leader of the West'.[6]

The tone for the years of Churchill's final administration was set during the visit he and Eden paid to Washington in early 1952. Churchill was anxious to see a 'revival' of Britain's 'former influence and initiative among the Allied Powers',[7] and went to Washington determined to rekindle the glory days. Truman and Acheson wanted nothing more than that 'Mr Churchill should return home in a good mood' – and that on Europe, the possibility of *détente* with the Soviets, the Middle and Far East, Eden should be persuaded to come into line with America's wishes.[8] Well aware that Churchill would try to 'strengthen and re-emphasize the partnership between the United States and the United Kingdom', the Americans had no intention of being trapped into proclaiming any sort of exclusive relationship with the British in world affairs – although they wished to use their own position to influence British policy.[9] Thus, whilst Churchill tried to secure American economic aid so that Britain could play her part in 'the common cause against Communist tyranny', Truman finessed, and whilst the Prime Minister attempted to secure 'only a brigade' of American troops to help Britain in the Suez Canal zone, the President argued the merits of the European Defence Force (EDF). When Truman sought to bring Britain into line over policy towards 'Red China', Churchill asked for 'moral assistance' in Persia: 'We must both play one hand there.' Churchill was convinced that if America stood by Britain in Egypt and Iran, his own troubles in both areas would be materially lessened.[10] His remark to his doctor, Lord Moran, that 'We talked as equals',[11] spoke more of the success of Truman's tactics than it did of Churchill's perspicacity. Acheson's comment that 'the Middle East presented a picture that might have been drawn by Karl Marx himself – with the masses a disinherited and poverty-stricken proletariat, no middle class, a small and corrupt ruling class pushed about by foreigners', should have given the ageing Prime Minister an insight into America's real views on the Middle East. In Acheson's view 'Anglo-American solidarity on a policy of sitting tight offered no solution, but was like a couple in a warm embrace in a rowboat about to go over Niagara Falls. It was high time to break the embrace and take to the oars.' Churchill's response, 'a chuckle' and a repetition of 'take to the oars', may have been amusing, but hardly suggests that he took in the implications of the Secretary's comments.[12]

Indeed, surveying the visit, one of the things which struck the Americans was how out of touch the British seemed. In place of their own obsession with the global communist threat, the British seemed inclined to play it down except where British interests in the Middle and Far East were concerned. Where the Americans were attempting to construct a global strategy of containment, the British still seemed obsessed with their old-fashioned notions of spheres of influence.[13] If Churchill's age and position meant that Truman and Acheson 'went out of their way to be jolly' to him, it also meant that 'they bore down hard on poor Eden', who 'never really learned that the national interests of the European States had to take second place to America's global interests or else'.[14]

It had been American pressure which had dissuaded Attlee from taking military action against Mossadeq in Iran, and Acheson was firmly of the view that sooner or later the British would have to come to terms with him. But Eden, equally firmly, rejected the view that 'the only alternative to Mossadeq is communism', which had prompted Acheson to comment in November that the 'same incompetents who allowed AIOC to lead the United Kingdom into disaster are still the source of United Kingdom policy'.[15] Now Acheson took the opportunity to once more impress upon the British the necessity of making concessions to nationalism in the Middle East. Eden, in turn, was inclined to blame American reserve towards Britain for encouraging the likes of Mossadeq, whom he called 'little more than a rug merchant who ought to be brushed aside as he deserved'. Acheson, losing his temper, said that it was the British who 'were behaving like a bunch of rug merchants' by haggling over financial compensation for the nationalised AIOC 'when they ought to be focusing on the bigger issue of how to resolve the crisis without impairing Britain's access to the oil'.[16] As he later acknowledged, Acheson 'pressed this point on Mr Eden with such asperity and impatience as to require subsequent amends'.[17]

The British failure to appreciate the lineaments of American thinking vitiated much of Churchill's attempt to revive the great days of yore. His efforts to secure American military support for Britain in Egypt and the Middle East in return for British participation in Korea[18] simply showed how little he had appreciated the distinction which Acheson had drawn between Asia, where it was communism which was the threat, and the Middle East, where it was nationalism which had to be dealt with. In the case of the former stern resistance was the only policy; in the latter Britain, like other imperial Powers, would have to make concessions. As it was, Eden and other members of the British delegation were rather concerned at Churchill's 'readiness to give away our case, both in regard to the Far East and on raw materials'.[19] Indeed, on the latter subject, Churchill's eagerness to impress the Americans by promising to increase copper production led to the embarrassment of Eden having to politely but publicly contradict him.[20] As usual, Churchill was making unnecessary concessions to try to secure American support which would not be forthcoming; like the restored House of Bourbon, Churchill appeared to have forgotten and learnt nothing during his period in exile.

Far from being concerned to protect British interests in the Middle East or the Gulf, Truman's and Acheson's main concern seemed to be to press the British on the EDF issue. At their meeting on 5 January Churchill had been at his worst, affecting to believe that the EDF would result in a French drill sergeant having to bark orders in half-a-dozen different languages to recruits from all over the Continent.[21] He dropped this tomfoolery when he discussed the matter with Truman on 8 January. He denied being 'inconsistent', but made it clear that he drew a distinction between 'the Army question' and 'talk about unity'.[22] American anxiety to limit the length and nature of their commitment to NATO led them towards a scheme that would allow German rearmament without the resultant product being under German control. Acheson emphasised that 'we were not urging the United Kingdom to join the European Army', but expected Britain to help secure its formation. For his part, Eden asked for reassurances that 'the European Army is within the Atlantic thing and part of it'. Churchill, as usual, cut through the diplomatic fencing with bravado, emphasising that the main question was, 'Are there loyal, brave divisions ... that will stand and fight and die together?' In fact that was not the main question; Eden had put his finger on that, and the Prime Minister's intervention had let Acheson off the hook.

The difference between Churchill and Eden in their attitude to America was visible in the days which followed the formal meetings at the White House. In New York on 10 January in conversation with three leading American journalists, Churchill waxed lyrical about 'America's altruism, her sublime disinterestedness', and pleaded for 'a token American brigade, or even a battalion of marines, to be sent to the Suez Canal'.[23] Speaking to Congress on 17 January he once again sought to conjure up the atmosphere of former days by references to the common struggle against Hitler and America's great generosity. On 11 January Eden had spoken in a different tone at Columbia University. Absent was the sickly sycophancy of the Prime Minister's rhetoric, and in its place was a firm and manly assertion of Britain's independence. 'The American and British people should each understand the strong points in the other's national character. If you drive a nation to adopt procedures which run counter to its instincts, you may destroy the motive force of its action,' he told his audience, in a vein which was more prophetic than he could have known. 'We know in our bones', he declared, that Britain could not join 'a federation on the continent of Europe'. During the war he had frequently complained about American ignorance of the British effort, and he took the opportunity to remind his listeners that Britain was not only contributing to the UN forces in Korea, but she was also engaged in tackling communist insurrection in Malaya and defending the Middle East; she had 'the largest armoured force on the continent of Europe'.[24]

Here, in brief, was the reason why Eden would not tow America's line. Britain was making her own contribution to the 'common cause' and, unlike America, she was not obsessed with a global communist threat. Britain recognised what America seemed oblivious to, which was that there were more threats to British (and American) interests than communism. As Churchill's parting meeting with Truman on 18 January showed (to American dismay), the British were not wholly averse to the idea of a summit conference with the Soviets.[25] As the next few years were to show, the Americans were not only uninterested in the notion of Britain mediating between themselves and the Soviets, they were positively hostile to it.

At the start of Churchill's visit the Prime Minister had delivered himself of one of his 'powerful and emotional declarations of faith in Anglo-American co-operation', only for Truman to cut him off 'with a "Thank you, Mr Prime Minister. We might pass that to be worked on by our advisers"',[26] and by an unhappy symmetry a similar scene was to mark its end. One of the Prime Minister's main concerns during his time in Washington had been to secure American agreement to appoint a British admiral to command NATO's naval forces. The Americans had gently parried his requests, and now he delivered what Acheson remembered as 'one of . . . [his] greatest speeches':

For centuries England had held the seas against every tyrant, wresting command from Spain and then from France, protecting our hemisphere from penetration by European systems in the days of our weakness. Now, in the plenitude of our power, bearing as we did the awful burden of atomic command and responsibility for the final word of peace or war, surely we could make room for Britain to play her historic role 'upon that western sea whose floor is white with the bones of Englishmen'.[27]

It was magnificent stuff – it always was – but it got Britain nowhere. Out of deference to Churchill, personally, Truman and Acheson were prepared to make cosmetic changes which ensured that the old boy went home happy, but on all the substantive issues it was clear that America would support Britain only when her own interests were vitally involved. There was nothing wrong with that – except that Churchill's over-emotional approach to Anglo-American relations prevented him from seeing what was obvious.

The notion that Eden somehow failed to understand Britain's 'true position' in the world is one more properly directed at his critics, who seem to imagine that the objective of British foreign policy should have been to arrive at our current ignominious position by the shortest possible route. Eden recognised that 'certain fundamental factors' determined Britain's foreign policy.[28] In the first place came 'world responsibilities inherited from several hundred years as a great Power'; in the second was the fact that Britain was 'not a self-sufficient economic unit'; finally came the threat which Britain, and other countries, faced from communism. Eden recognised as clearly as his critics that 'the essence of a sound foreign policy is to ensure that a country's strength is equal to its obligations', and that current commitments were 'placing a burden on the economy which it is beyond the resources of the country to meet'; but unlike later commentators, Eden had to find a way of squaring this vicious circle. There was always the possibility of transferring some of the burden to 'other shoulders', but even so it might be that a 'choice of the utmost difficulty lies before the British people': they could either shoulder the costs of Empire or, 'by relaxing their grip in the outside world, see their country sink to the level of a second-class Power, with injury to their essential interests and way of life of which they can have little conception'. Abandoning 'major commitments' might look attractive in the short-term, but it would almost certainly mean that Russia would take over any areas Britain might withdraw from, which would mean that they would enter the Soviet economic sphere. Moreover, there was another equally cogent argument against precipitate withdrawals: 'By reducing the value of the United Kingdom as a partner and an ally, it would undermine the cohesion of the Commonwealth and the special relationship of the United Kingdom with the United States and its European partners and other allies.' These things were in addition to the economic and financial advantages which being at the centre of a worldwide trading network gave the British. There were no ways of obtaining substantial and immediate relief of the burdens on Britain's economy, and given that the defence of western Europe was a priority which could not be denied, it was only in the Middle or Far East that the possibility existed of liquidating major commitments. But given that these were areas vital to British security, it was not possible to eliminate such commitments without serious damage. Instead, Eden aimed at the 'creation of international defence organizations' for these regions: 'Our aim should be to persuade the United States to assume the real burdens in such organizations, while retaining for ourselves as much political control – and hence prestige and world influence – as we can.'

It was a story familiar to those involved in policy-making before the war: how to hang on to as many of the benefits of Empire as possible without having to incur the expense of doing so. The war had so altered the situation in India that the old policies of devolving more power to local rulers, whilst retaining control over imperial matters, had proved ineffective, and the rise of nationalism in Egypt and elsewhere made it unlikely that it could be employed elsewhere. In these circumstances it was not surprising that Britain fell back on the Churchillian concept of the Anglo-American alliance. But Eden realised the difficulties in such a strategy. Not only was it unlikely that the Americans would be unwilling to incur 'new commitments in peacetime', but 'distrust of the British and fear of becoming an instrument to prop up the British Empire are still strong'. This, alas, meant that Britain would have to 'demonstrate that we are making the maximum possible effort ourselves', which made it unclear just how the 'gradual' and 'inconspicuous' process of transferring the 'real burdens from our own to American shoulders' was going to be carried out.

But the idea was not as ridiculous as later events made it appear. By early 1952 a National Security Council (NSC) study had concluded that, 'Whatever the US can do to bolster both generally and locally the power of the UK will assist the UK in maintaining stability in the area and will reduce the need for direct action by the US'.[29] The problem, however, was that British and American estimates of how to maintain stability conflicted. Eden wished to reach agreement with the Egyptians upon the terms by which Britain might reoccupy the Canal base in an emergency, and he hoped to be able to use a renegotiated treaty as the foundation for a new Anglo-Egyptian relationship, in which Britain, Egypt and perhaps America and France would agree to a multilateral treaty to defend the Middle East from the Soviets.[30] Churchill, who wanted to 'take a stronger line with the Egyptians' than Eden,[31] so misunderstood American policy that he thought that they might be prevailed upon to help him, arguing in Cabinet on 4 April that, 'It should be made clear to the Americans that we were not prepared to go on carrying this burden alone.'[32] But far from fulfilling any such Churchillian fantasy, the Americans refused to take part in any negotiations unless requested to by the Egyptians. America's main contribution in Egypt during 1952 was, in fact, distinctly unhelpful, as it consisted of the Central Intelligence Agency playing a role in the overthrow of King Farouk and his replacement by the nationalist government of General Neguib.[33]

America proved equally unhelpful over the Iranian issue. By August, although Eden still wanted to hold out against any negotiations with Mossadeq, he feared that 'there was a real danger that the United States Government would make an offer of independent financial assistance to Persia with the object of preventing the establishment of a communist regime', and advised the Cabinet that negotiations would have to be opened.[34] When the negotiations broke down thanks to Mossadeq's rejection of British terms,[35] Eden found himself under fresh pressure from Acheson. The American proposals, which would have given the AIOC less compensation than it wanted and which would have set a precedent for the seizure of British assets elsewhere, was unacceptable to Eden and to the Cabinet, but fear of a 'visible breach' with America meant that they had to be seriously considered.[36] It took the advent of a new administration in America for a solution to the problem to emerge.

If Britain was expected to defer to American opinions, the same was not true in reverse. The British withdrawal from India and Burma had not ended her interests in the region, and one of the enduring objectives of British foreign policy in the early 1950s was to try to secure Indian co-operation in South-East Asia and avoid her drifting towards a neutralist, or even a pro-Soviet, position. As part of this enterprise, and also as a means of bringing the war in Korea to an end, Eden was disposed to support the proposals for an armistice brought before the United Nations by the Indian Foreign Minister, Krishna Menon, in November 1952. Acheson's reaction was described by Eden as 'the most disagreeable' interview 'he has ever encountered'. He accused Eden's Minister of State, the harmless and docile Selwyn Lloyd, of 'not having dealt honourably by the Americans' and, for good measure, 'of being a Welshman (!)'. Continuing in this intemperate vein for nearly an hour, Acheson told Eden and Lloyd that, 'if Britain could not make up her mind that she was with the US on this matter, it would be the end of Anglo-American cooperation'. His deputy, John Hickerson, 'had the impertinence at one point to say, "Anthony, you have got to choose between the US and India. Which will you have?"'[37] Acheson, who may well have had a few cocktails too many, talked about 'debagging that Swami', saying that he would 'tear the Indian resolution apart'.[38] As Eden's Private Secretary, Evelyn Shuckburgh, commented aptly, 'The fact is that, when you scratch this elegant and civilized Acheson, he turns out just to be another tough guy.'[39] In the end a clumsy Soviet attack on Menon provided a resolution to the crisis, but the episode had portrayed a brutally clear picture of Acheson's view of Britain's place in the alliance.

One reason for Acheson's bad temper was no doubt the fact that his period in office was coming to an end. Eden's stay in New York gave him an opportunity to talk at some length with the victor of the recent Presidential election, his old wartime acquaintance, Dwight David Eisenhower. The old image of 'Ike' as the President who spent more time on the golf course than he did in the Oval Office, the lovable 'stumble-bum' who left foreign policy in the hands of his advisers, especially John Foster Dulles, is not one which has stood the test of recent scholarship; in its place we have an able and experienced President, who had clear views on international affairs and expected to be able to implement them.[40] Churchill's reaction to the new President was less positive than that of later historians.

There were a number of reasons why Churchill was less enthusiastic than might have been supposed to the advent of an old colleague to the White House, but the chief one was that Eisenhower made no secret of the fact that he was not disposed to treat Britain differently than any of America's other allies.[41] Churchill was 'considerably disappointed' by the talks which he had with the new President and his Secretary of State, John Foster Dulles, in New York in early January 1953, and was 'much perturbed by the inclination not to show the UK any kind of preference over Portugal and other small nations'.[42] Churchill's conclusion – that Eisenhower, 'for all his qualities, did not show much political maturity' – was shockingly inadequate, but rather than take the new President at his word, Churchill insisted upon imputing political motives to him; the Republicans 'were mainly concerned', he thought, 'to take a different line to their predecessors'. Yet as a discussion with Acheson showed, the Democrats took a similar line, and the out-going Secretary tried to persuade Churchill to soften his position on Egypt and on the European Defence Community (EDC), arguing in both cases that Britain had a 'last chance'. It was all very well for Churchill to conclude that 'we would have been better off with a Stevenson victory* and with the continuance in power of the men with whom we have been through so much together', but Makins was nearer the mark when he warned Eden that, 'We must not be too sure that the US would think the Prime Minister's "Grand Alliance" good enough to back.'[43] It was a warning that Churchill would have done well to have heeded.

Eisenhower found Churchill's 'faith' that 'all of the answers' to international problems were to be 'found merely in British and American partnership' quite 'childlike'. He did not think it was possible to 'relive the days of World War II' and thought that, 'In the present international complexities, any hope of establishing such a relationship is completely fatuous.' He saw British opposition to colonial nationalism as playing into the hands of the communists and was totally opposed to being seen to join with Churchill in a combination to maintain the status quo.[44] It was clear that if the British stuck to their current foreign policy, a clash with America was, at some point, inevitable.

For all the later hostility between Eden and Dulles, the British Foreign Secretary did not, initially, share Churchill's negative view of Eisenhower – if only because, at their meeting in November, the latter had discoursed upon

---

* Adlai Stevenson, the Democratic opponent of Eisenhower in the 1952 election.

international affairs without once mentioning Churchill.[45] This assumption that Churchill would soon be retiring was, in itself, guaranteed to recommend the new President to Eden, who was becoming increasingly exasperated by the Prime Minister's interventions. Given his opposition in the 1930s and 1940s to independence to India, it was hardly surprising to find him hostile to making concessions to the Egyptians in order to secure a treaty. The problem for Eden, however, was that Churchill had 'no alternative policy whatever'; he 'just moans'.[46] But Churchill's 'moans' were, unfortunately for Eden, shared by many members of their own Party. The 'Suez group', led by Harold Macmillan's son-in-law, Julian Amery, and the Chamberlainite loyalist, Captain Charles Waterhouse, provided a vocal opposition to what they characterised as Eden's policy of 'appeasement'. Caught between this group, which he suspected may have had Churchill's tacit support, and the demands of the Americans for further concessions, Eden had a particularly unhappy time during 1953 as he slowly but tenaciously negotiated his way to a treaty. Churchillian humour hardly helped matters, with his 'I didn't know Munich was on the Nile' being a particularly cruel jibe, considering the way in which both men regarded the Munich treaty.

The one area in which America did prove of some use to the British was Iran, but her action did not exactly fill Eden with cheer. By late 1952 the Americans had come to the conclusion that 'the risks of continuing our present policy have become unacceptable', and the Defense Department started to advocate a proactive policy which would 'involve a willingness, if necessary, to displace British influence and responsibility in Iran as has occurred in Greece, Turkey and Saudi Arabia'.[47] Thus, having refused to offer the British even moral support against Mossadeq for two years, the Americans reversed their policy and sponsored a coup, which replaced him with a new Shah of Iran. British intervention would have been classed as 'colonialism' of the worst sort; only the ideologically pure Americans could intervene in the affairs of other sovereign states without risking the taint of such a label. To adapt a phrase of Metternich's, the British might well have said: 'Ah, non-intervention, a phrase signifying much the same as intervention.'

It was little wonder then that Evelyn Shuckburgh should have become 'very depressed about the world in general', with Britain's economic situation still grim, German and Japanese competition beginning to appear on the horizon, the 'destruction of British influence in the Mediterranean and the Middle East' and 'the Americans not backing us anywhere'. Indeed, far from backing Churchillian notions of the 'Grand Alliance', it seemed to Shuckburgh that 'having destroyed the Dutch empire, the United States are now engaged in undermining the French and British empires as hard as they can'.[48] In Iran, as in Saudi Arabia, there was much in what Shuckburgh said, and if America was not actively undermining the British position elsewhere in the Middle East, her ostentatious lack of support for it had much the same effect. In Europe Eisenhower's 'New Look', which envisaged a reduction of American ground troops in NATO by half a million, made the organisation 'even more obviously an instrument of American hegemony',[49] since it would leave the Europeans to take the brunt of any Soviet attack. It was testimony to the continuing influence of Britain's economic weakness, and to fears of the Soviet Union, that there was no reappraisal of the need for the American alliance; far from being the foundation of Britain's position as a Great Power, it was helping to undermine it.

22

Defeated by 'the bastard'

When approached by the Dulles Project at Princeton for 'oral reminiscences' of the great man, Salisbury told Eden in a bemused tone: 'I really do not know what to say. I personally liked him – I suppose I was almost the only person in England who did'; but 'from the point of view of England' he could not, Salisbury thought, 'be regarded as having been anything but a disaster'. Eden was a good deal more blunt. He had told the people from Princeton that he had already said everything he had to say in his memoirs, adding, for Salisbury's benefit, 'After all, the man was bitterly anti-British.'[1] Long-winded and given to preaching, the tall 'slab-faced' American was inflexibly armoured in two convictions: that America was the pre-eminent power in the free world; and that the communist threat was omnipresent and evil – and a man of his evangelical temperament did not sup with the Devil, even using the longest possible spoon.[2] From his point of view Britain was a power in decline and the British did not 'really amount to much any more', although they were 'ultra-sensitive' and had to be 'kept sweet' because they were 'important real estate'.[3] Given Eden's intuitive and pragmatic approach to diplomacy, it was hardly likely that he and Dulles would have hit it off, even if Eisenhower had not maintained that during his meeting with Eden in November 1951, the latter had advised him against making Dulles Secretary of State.[4] The large, untidy American, imbued with the spirit of 'manifest destiny', and the elegant and suave Englishman, so redolent of the effortless superiority which so annoyed Americans, were not destined to be soul-brothers – not least because each of them put his own country's interests first.

This could hardly be said of Churchill, whose 'hope for the future' was 'founded on the increasing unity of the English-speaking world',[5] but he was coming under increasing pressure by early 1953 to define when he would retire. At first it had been hoped that the coronation of Elizabeth II would provide an auspicious moment to bow out, although it was perhaps not very tactful to point out the precedent of Baldwin going in 1937 after the coronation of the old King. But when Eden temporarily retired to hospital in April to undergo what turned out to be a series of botched operations on his bile duct, Churchill told him that he would 'look after your foreign policy as well as your political interests',[6] and proceeded to supervise the Foreign Office, with Salisbury taking charge of day-to-day diplomacy. It was the death of Stalin* in March which had given the old boy not just a fresh lease of life, but also a new purpose to his remaining in power. As the only surviving member of the 'Big Three', and with his faith in personal destiny undimmed, Churchill felt that he had a perfect opportunity for trying to thaw out the Cold War.[7]

He wrote to Eisenhower on 11 March ventilating the idea of a summit meeting with the Russians,[8] but when the State Department seemed hesitant, and the Foreign Office was equally doubtful, he took advantage of Eden's absence from duty to announce in the Commons on 11 May that he wanted a 'conference at the highest level . . . between leading powers without a long delay'.[9] Eclipsing as it did a less dramatic statement by Eisenhower on 16 April, Churchill's initiative was not welcomed by a State Department which had not wanted Eisenhower to hold out anything which might be construed as an olive-branch to the Soviets. However, the American Embassy correctly interpreted the widespread support for the speech as a sign that 'Churchill the politician' had taken 'account of widespread disappointment and appre-hension which now exists among British with respect to policies [of] new United States administration'; it was noted that 'for [the] first time in [a] major address on foreign affairs Churchill did not mention Anglo-American alliance or necessary solidarity with United States'.[10]

If Churchill's initiative startled the Americans, it had a similar effect upon many of his own Cabinet. Salisbury disliked the fact that neither the Cabinet nor Britain's European allies had been consulted before the announcement had been made, and he grew increasingly to fear that it would 'sow deep distrust between us, the United States and our European allies'.[11] Anthony Nutting, one of Eden's junior Ministers at the Foreign Office, reported that the speech had, by the offence which it had given to the French (who were excluded from the idea of a conference), 'brought any momentum that remained behind the EDC virtually to a dead stop', and that it had 'given more comfort to our enemies than to our friends', with the Soviets seeking to exploit what they saw as a 'rift between us and the Americans'.[12] Such concern was understandable in view of the damage which Churchill's action threatened to inflict upon the position which Eden had painstakingly been trying to build up during months of negotiations over the future of the EDC.

Although he had remained resolutely opposed to Britain's joining the EDC, Eden refused to adopt Churchill's negative attitude towards it. Placing, as he did, all his eggs in the Anglo-American basket, Churchill appeared to imagine that western Europe would do as it was told by an Anglo-Saxon condominium; Eden was under no such illusion. As he ceaselessly pointed out, failure on the EDC question would throw the whole question of German rearmament back into the melting-pot – and with it the American commitment to the

---

* Stalin was succeeded by a diarchy, Malenkov and Bulganin.

defence of western Europe; it had, after all, been the Americans who had first demanded German rearmament. This latter consideration helped to stop Churchill making public criticisms of the scheme, but it still fell to Eden to negotiate a delicate balancing act. The French and Dutch very much wanted Britain to join the EDC, and knowing that an outright refusal might bring an end to the plan, Eden manoeuvred skilfully, promising that Britain would become 'associated' with it.[13] By such means he had secured the signature of an EDC treaty in May 1952, but given hostility to it in France and legal challenges to it in Germany, ratification proved a long and slow (and ultimately unsuccessful) process; Churchill's speech cut right across it. The German Chancellor, Dr Konrad Adenauer, was alarmed at 'reunification' becoming an issue in West German politics in election year, and equally unhappy about the prospect that Britain seemed prepared to negotiate his country's future with Russia without consulting him.[14] The French were equally annoyed at being treated as they had been at Yalta and Potsdam. Churchill's preoccupation with Anglo-American relations had upset the European apple-cart – and it had not gone down particularly well in Washington, either.

Eisenhower had done his best to dissuade Churchill from making any comment about a summit meeting. On 27 April he had warned: 'I feel we should not rush things too much with the Soviets. Premature action by us in that direction might have the effect of giving them an easy way out.' In his last letter on the subject before Churchill's speech, Eisenhower had again counselled him not to 'rush things'.[15] Dulles was furious at the British move – and with McCarthyism still in full flight, it would have been surprising had he not been.

Churchill's speech had come the day after the anniversary of his accession to the Premiership in 1940, and it was, as with much of Eden's diplomacy, an attempt to show that Britain still had a part to play in the world. But it was more than that; it was the expression of a world-view which was quite different to the one the Americans had adopted. As he told Eisenhower on 12 April, 'It ought to be possible to proclaim our unflinching determination to resist Communist tyranny and aggression and at the same time, though separately, to declare how glad we should be if we found there was a real change of heart.'[16] Although he had played such a strenuous role in trying to alert the Americans to the possible dangers of communist expansion, Churchill's mind remained flexible on the subject; it had never been part of the British diplomatic tradition to demonise other Powers with whom it might be necessary to coexist – that was reserved for wartime. Churchill saw in Stalin's death a 'precious chance' and feared that 'the judgement of future ages would be harsh and just' if he failed to try to grasp it; 'But if we strive and fail, it will be clear who has condemned humankind to this black fate.'[17] He was, if it should prove necessary, prepared to sacrifice Adenauer and West

Germany. Churchill did not share the view common at the Foreign Office and in Washington that a unified Germany would fall into the Soviet orbit. Indeed, he was even prepared to go so far as to have a meeting with the Soviets by himself, if the Americans refused to come along. Even when the Soviets put down riots in East Germany on 17 June, Churchill refused to condemn them or acknowledge that the moment was not propitious for a summit.[18]

Churchill's initiative, which opened up the prospect of an Anglo-Soviet meeting, brought home to some within the State Department the 'fissures' which existed between British and American policy in the Far and Near East. Assistant Secretary of State Livingston Merchant argued on 15 June that he did not think that 'a durable relationship can be based upon a complete surrender to us on every point which Great Britain considers important to its security and world position'. He would have found Eden in complete agreement with this as with his proposed solution, which was that in return for the British 'giving us complete support for our policies in the Far East', America would 'recognise that not only do the British have wide-spread interests and responsibilities in the Middle East, but that they in fact control the only western military forces in the area', which meant that 'we should, therefore, support them in the execution of jointly-agreed policies in the Middle East and therefore avoid finding ourselves trapped in the unwelcome role of mediator between native regimes and Great Britain'.[19] But this cut clean across 'recent policy thinking', which was expressing concern about the way in which even the limited support which had been given to the British had ended up with the Americans being tarred with the same brush by the Egyptians and others: 'To tie ourselves to the British kite in the Middle East at the present juncture . . . would be to abandon all hope of a peaceful alignment in that area with the West.' Since this was also Dulles's view, it was the one which prevailed.[20]

What prevented the great summit from coming off was the Prime Minister's physical infirmity. Carrying the Foreign Office as well as the Premiership would have been a burden for one half of his seventy-eight years, and with Eden out of action for much longer than expected due to botched operations, Churchill had to carry the load for months rather than weeks. Whether for this reason, or for some other, he had a major stroke on 23/24 June. Had Eden been in England and in good health, Churchill's Premiership would have been over, but as he was not, an unenviable dilemma faced his closest associates. Such was the old hero's extraordinary strength of will that he presided over Cabinet on the morning of 24 June without anyone noticing anything other than that he seemed a little pale. Quite what this says about Churchill's Cabinet meetings or about his colleagues is uncertain, but as his condition worsened on 25 June it became necessary to take some decisions. If a public announcement was made about Churchill's condition, he would have to go, but it was unclear who would succeed him; moreover, given his extraordinary powers of recuperation, who could tell what would happen. In the end a small group of intimates took the decision to keep the news even from the Cabinet. It was decided that in the event of the Prime Minister's condition worsening, or in the event of his death, Salisbury would be asked to be acting Prime Minister until Eden was fit enough to take over.[21] It was an extraordinary arrangement, and perhaps fortunately its ingenuity was not tested, since by 3 July the formidable old warrior seemed to be on the mend. Indeed, by 6 July he was capable of composing the trenchant memorandum on German reunification which he used as part of his argument in favour of a summit conference. But the illness, concealed as it was, still put an end to the hope of an immediate conference – although Churchill did despatch Salisbury to Washington.[22]

Salisbury brought to the Foreign Office a 'very calm and aristocratic atmosphere'.[23] His long friendship with Eden went back to the 1930s, and they had resigned together in 1938, with Cranborne (as he then was) making by far the better resignation speech. Succeeding to the Marquessate in 1947, he had no great ambitions for his own career, and he had watched the long saga of Churchill's on-off resignation with amusement and exasperation. Back in 1947 he had come to the conclusion that Churchill wanted to stay on 'because he likes power', and he had been convinced, even at that early stage, that 'nothing will budge him but a massed demonstration by his colleagues'. Having told Eden this, he found his complaints about Churchill 'futile and exasperating', and he was clear-sighted enough to see that if Eden 'wants to be regarded as a leader, he must act like one'.[24] He thought that the country owed Churchill 'a debt of gratitude such as [it] ... has seldom owed to anyone', but he was equally convinced that 'he now belongs to the past'.[25] When things failed to work out that way, Salisbury adapted himself to circumstances. He had been happy to take on the Foreign Office during Eden's absence, but Churchill's 11 May speech seriously disturbed him. Like most Cecils, the fifth Marquess had something of a hair-trigger finger when it came to thoughts of resignation, and it certainly began to itch after the speech.[26]

But much as he disagreed with the manner of Churchill's initiative, Salisbury could see that something might come of it if handled correctly; he was almost equally worried by what seemed to him 'a new and more dangerous American tendency' to interpret events behind the Iron Curtain 'as already very shaky' and to advocate 'new, although unspecified measures to encourage and even promote the early liberation of the satellite countries'. What he wanted to do was to prevent such a policy developing, but at the same time to suggest to the Americans that, with due preparation and Anglo-American consultation, a high-level conference of the sort Churchill suggested would be no bad thing.[27] In the face of this modification of the Churchill initiative, the Cabinet agreed that Salisbury should go to Washington.[28] But any Anglo-

American meeting was bound, in the nature of things, to reveal the 'fissures' between the two allies.

It had been a fear of the consequences of its failure which had so inclined Dulles against the idea of a summit conference.[29] Dulles was afraid that 'consequences other than a truly united approach to world problems would be grave'. It would give an impetus to 'isolationism' in America, whilst in Europe her prestige would suffer 'and the incipient tendency on the part of Churchill towards a position of "mediation" between the United States and the USSR could find extensive support'. Given the 'difficulty of reaching precise agreement on most of the key issues', Dulles wanted 'acceptance, tacit or otherwise,' of America's 'line of action in the Far East, particularly Korea'; indeed, he feared that 'serious disagreement' over the Far East 'could cause the beginning of disintegration of NATO'. He also wanted a 'united approach and course of action with regard to European problems' and discussion of 'a common problem toward "colonial areas", particularly the Middle East', as well as discussion of the desirability of a conference with the Soviets.

On most of these issues, however, Britain was a problem from the American point of view. Eden's tactics over the EDC had, to an extent, soothed American fears over that subject, but on Egypt, in particular, the two sides were wide apart. Eden's plans to mitigate the effects of a British withdrawal from the Canal zone by setting up a Middle Eastern Defence Organisation (MEDO), which would be underpinned by America, had met with difficulties because of American reluctance to associate themselves too closely with British imperialism.[30] Churchill's view, which was that with the end of the British commitment to India, it was up to America to help defray the costs and burdens of keeping forces in the region and thus to present an Anglo-American front to Neguib,[31] was regarded with less than wholehearted affection by the Americans. Eisenhower told Eden on 16 March that they must avoid presenting the world with 'the picture of British-American association' trying to 'dominate the Councils of the free world', and warned him not to 'forget the conviction we hold that our two nations will get much further along towards a satisfactory solution to our common problems if each of us preserves, consciously, an attitude of absolute equality with all other nations'.[32] In American eyes it was the inability of the British to carry out the spirit of this last injunction which risked prejudicing the position of the 'West' in the whole Middle East. Following a tour of the region in May, Dulles reported that 'bitterness toward West, including United States [is] such that while Arab goodwill may still be restored, time is short before loss becomes irretrievable'. He thought that the 'United Kingdom-Egypt problem' was 'most dangerous and if unsolved' might 'find [the] Arab world in open and united hostility to [the] West and in some cases receptive to Soviet aid'. He concluded that the idea of a MEDO was 'impractical' and that, unless Britain could be persuaded to make concessions, 'any hope of extending United States influence over the Near East and building at least a minimum of strength here would have to be renounced unless we would publicly disagree with Britain and thus allow accomplishment of one of primary aims of Soviet Russia'.[33] Eisenhower's advisers wanted to use the conference with the British to persuade them that, 'if they are to have any hope of preserving their commercial advantage through their crumbling world, they must allow us occasionally to take a front position'. The American idea of 'unity' was spelt out plainly:

at the apex of the triangle there must be the U.S., in the person of President Eisenhower. This role should not be sacrificed because of a very human feeling of decency and generosity towards an opinionated old gentleman who is still sufficiently sharp and selfish to grab every advantage with bland assurances of unwavering esteem.[34]

In these circumstances, with America moving away from offering the British even nominal support in the Middle East, it was hardly surprising that Salisbury's talks with Dulles in Washington were somewhat acrimonious. Salisbury, who wanted to maintain Anglo-American solidarity, still looked upon 'close collaboration' between allies as 'an important British interest' in itself, and he had not yet realised, as he was later to do, that 'the broad consideration of maintaining a common front between America and Britain never seems to weigh in the balance at all'.[35] He had no idea that the Americans were already mediating in the dispute with Egypt.

Dulles saw Egypt, and indeed just about everything else, through the spectacles of the Cold War. American policy towards the Middle East, summed up in NSC directive 155/1, adopted on 19 July,[36] provided for the gradual replacement of British influence in the region by American and led to behind-the-scenes dealings with the Egyptians which had, as their objective, the securing of the Canal base for the 'West', whilst acknowledging that 'the continuation of British forces on Egyptian soil is an impossibility'. Thus, at his meeting with Salisbury, Dulles was essentially deceiving the British on a number of levels. Far from being available as a prop to Britain's position, as he allowed the British to believe, Dulles saw their presence in Egypt as one of the obstacles to American policy. The proposals which the Egyptians had put forward in July were, in fact, based on American suggestions, and although Dulles promised Salisbury that he would urge new British proposals on Neguib, he did so only after Salisbury agreed that the only outstanding issue was whether or not the British would be able to use the base in wartime. When Dulles was told that the British believed that this agreement had revived American support for Britain in Egypt, he thought this simply reflected 'wishful thinking'. America was not '"backing" either Britain or Egypt'.[37] Indeed, she was not; she was backing America.

There was, about the American belief that the rising tide of nationalism was irresistible, a certain element of the self-fulfilling prophecy. The British belief that Anglo-American solidarity would have strengthened their negotiating position with regard to Egypt and elsewhere was, of course, never tested since the Americans never did support them; but to argue that British lack of success somehow proves that colonialism was doomed is false logic. What neither Dulles nor Eisenhower appreciated was that not every one of the world's disputes could be explained away in terms of the Cold War; nor did they appreciate that many of the nationalist movements were actively hostile to western interests in general. Their habit of seeing everything in fairly simple terms was shown most vividly to Salisbury by Dulles's attitude towards Britain's dispute with Saudi Arabia over the Buraimi oasis.

Dulles 'insisted on regarding Buraimi as a British colonial issue', which it was not, and as a consequence once more helped contribute towards a weakening of Britain's position in a vital strategic region – in this case the Persian Gulf.[38] The British position in the Gulf was based upon a series of defence treaties with the Sheikdoms and with Muscat, and when in late 1952 the Saudis occupied the oasis of Buraimi, it raised in stark form the whole question of the value of the British connection to the Gulf states. The vast increase in wealth of Saudi Arabia in the early 1950s was accompanied by an aggrandisement of her diplomatic and territorial position in the region. Eden, who did not want to confront the Saudis directly – not least because they were looked upon as a client state of the Americans – wanted the dispute to go to arbitration and looked towards the Americans for support.[39] Whilst the Saudis mounted a propaganda campaign at the UN pillorying the British as 'imperialists', the British quietly sent troops into the region, anticipating a Saudi rejection of any arbitration; but the big question was whether the Americans would support any firm British action at the oasis.[40] It should occasion little surprise that the Americans were not at all helpful when Salisbury raised the matter at the Washington meeting.

What Salisbury proposed was that Eisenhower suggest to King Ibn Saud that both sides should withdraw their forces, leaving Buraimi under the supervision of a commission of three pending the results of arbitration. The Americans suggested a course of action which the British found quite unacceptable, namely that both sides should keep their forces in place pending the arbiter's report, but that the British should lift their blockade in return for a Saudi promise to desist from suborning the local tribes. The poor Cabinet had to confront the unpalatable alternatives of either accepting the American proposal, thus 'seriously' weakening 'British influence and prestige' in an area with rich oil potential, or rejecting it and losing what they wrongly thought was the chance of American support elsewhere in the region. Salisbury did not push the point.[41]

Nor was it only in the Middle East that British hopes of American support were not realised. Despite doubts about Churchill's 11 May initiative, Salisbury pressed for his policy of a 'Potsdam' type meeting with the Russians; but with the French arguing that this would ensure the failure of the EDC by raising fears of German unification, and Dulles, for his own reasons, agreeing with Foreign Minister Georges Bidault that what was needed was a meeting in Moscow with a prepared agenda, the British were once again left with no choice.[42] Salisbury was not joking when he told Eden that he would be returning to a 'thorny legacy', especially in the Middle East.[43]

The acting Foreign Secretary was, in fact, on the verge of resignation and had actually offered to go. He was dissatisfied that Churchill was not only showing every sign of staying on as Prime Minister, but that he was obviously not even contemplating any Cabinet reshuffle to bring in younger men – he did not think that having seven septuagenarians in high office was the way to prepare for the future. Nor did he like 'the policy of May 11th'; indeed, he had come to think that talks in Moscow would 'be regarded in Europe as another Munich' and would 'sow deep distrust' with America and Europe. 'It might even go far', he told Eden, 'to destroy the rather shaky structure of western defence which you have so laboriously and so skilfully built up.' Yet 'nothing' seemed to 'budge' the Prime Minister: 'much though I love and revere him. He tends more and more to go his own way and expect his colleagues to follow him, which they always do.' So much for the 'calm' and 'aristocratic atmosphere' that Salisbury had brought to the office.

Eden's return saw the start of serious disagreements between himself and the Prime Minister, and his official biographer, the very soul of courtierly discretion, has gone so far as to admit that there 'is some truth' in the suggestion that relations between the two men 'never really recovered' from this point.[44] There was certainly greater asperity, as we shall see, in the exchanges between the two men in the middle of the following year over the question of Churchill's retirement, and Eden had every reason to feel exasperation, but at least part of his irritation stemmed from their continuing differences over foreign policy. Perhaps Eden would have been wiser to have taken the advice of those who suggested that he should not return to the Foreign Office; but for all the incessant pressures at the Foreign Office, he could not live without it.[45] Nor is it easy to see who could have taken the job on. Although Salisbury was persuaded not to resign, his feelings about 'the policy of May 11th' and his propensity for threats of resignation hardly made him the ideal candidate, and it was exceedingly unlikely that Eden, jealous as he was of his position as heir-apparent, would have let any other major political figure such as Rab Butler or Harold Macmillan take the second most senior post in the Government; to that extent, Eden had no one but himself to blame if his health suffered.

One item which remained high on the foreign policy agenda, if only because of the public expectations raised by Churchill's speech on 11 May, was the question of a meeting with the French and the Americans to consider the possibility of a conference with the Soviets.[46] Eden, unlike Churchill, 'did not regard four-power talks at the highest level as a panacea',[47] but in the face of continuing pressure from the Prime Minister he had no choice but to explore the matter. A further complication was that Churchill, who was increasingly 'anti-Frog', was not keen on having the French at any conference. Despite Eisenhower's known views on the undesirability of an Anglo-American connection, Churchill, persisting with his sentimental belief in the 'special relationship', evidently thought that a meeting between himself and 'Ike' would help put things back on the right track; indeed, misinterpreting some remarks of the American Ambassador, Winthrop Aldrich, he even had the Queen extend an invitation to Eisenhower to visit London.[49] The President showed equally little enthusiasm for a *tête-à-tête* meeting with Churchill in the Azores,[50] but following a Russian proposal in November for a Great Power conference, the Americans decided that, if only to try to ensure western unity, there had better be a conference – but with the French, as well as the British.[51]

Thus, from the start, Churchill's hopes of an Anglo-American love-*fest* were spoiled. He had told his audience at the Guildhall on 9 November that 'John Bull and Uncle Sam' were 'never closer together than they are now',[52] but the Bermuda conference provided an ironic commentary on such myth-making.

Churchill began the conference in a style familiar to Eden, who had attended most of the great wartime gatherings, but his manner must have seemed a little odd to those like Dulles and Eisenhower who had not had such a privilege. The great speech he launched into was a powerful exposition of his view of the international situation and showed him at his best. Whilst suitably sceptical about the possibility that there had been a 'change of heart' in the Soviet Union, he was eloquent on the necessity of not letting any chance for peace pass by; a 'resolute attitude' towards the Soviets was not, he declared, incompatible with holding out the hand of friendship.[53] In sharp contrast to Churchill's elevated tone, Eisenhower 'came down like a ton of bricks' and was 'rude' and 'vulgar', telling Churchill that, '"So long as you mean what I think you mean, I agree; that it is the same old woman of the streets, even if she has on a new hat."'[54] Others recorded the President's remark as referring to Russia as 'the same whore underneath' a new dress, as well as his reference to American determination to 'drive her off her present "beat" into the back streets'.[55] It was hardly an auspicious beginning, especially as the French leaked the colourful terminology to the press. When Eden asked when the next meeting would be, Eisenhower replied breezily that he did not know, adding, 'Mine is with a whisky and soda.'[56]

The tough mood continued into the following two days. Applying great pressure on the British and French to sort the EDC matter out, Dulles made it plain that there might have to be an 'agonizing reappraisal' of the American commitment to Europe if this was not done, and that he expected the British to satisfy French doubts by agreeing to join the Community if that was what it took to get the French Assembly to ratify the treaty.[57] Even more alarming was Eisenhower's declaration at dinner on 5 December that if the Chinese and the North Koreans broke the armistice in Korea, he was prepared to authorise the use of nuclear weapons. Just to add to Britain's discomfort, in the same speech to the UN in which Eisenhower proposed to make these comments, he also wanted to refer to the 'obsolete Colonial mold' which was now being 'broken'.[58]

Although the President agreed to drop what Churchill called the 'obnoxious' phrase, his comment illustrated once again the gulf which divided Britain and America. Eisenhower thought that there was, 'philosophically', much to be said for Churchill's view that 'many of the countries attempting to assume the rights of independence were unaware of the inescapable responsibilities and burdens of self-government', but he believed that 'the hard fact was that the spirit of nationalism had become rampant and often uncontrollable in the world'.[59] Or, as he put it more pithily to Churchill's Private Secretary, Jock Colville, 'to Americans liberty was more precious than good government';[60] a reassuring thought, no doubt, in view of the results which were to follow from America's policies. It should not have come as the surprise which it evidently did to Churchill to find that when he raised the subject of Egypt, the Americans refused to back his idea that for the troops withdrawn from Egypt there should be an Anglo-American plan to redeploy them from within the NATO system.

By the end of the conference Churchill was inveighing against Dulles, whom he regarded as the ventriloquist behind Eisenhower, and he declared angrily: 'Ten years ago I could have dealt with him. Even as it is I have not been defeated by this bastard, I have been humiliated by my own decay.'[61] However, the lachrymose Prime Minister was wrong: what had 'defeated' him were his own sentimental misconceptions as to the real nature of the Anglo-American relations; but he was too old a dog for new tricks.

23

'They like to give orders'

According to Britain's representative at the United Nations, Eden's former Private Secretary, Sir Pierson Dixon, what was at the heart of the Bermuda conference was 'whether the Allies are to go serenely on with the Bevin–Acheson policy of Atlantic defence (streamlined) or whether something different is required' in view of three recent developments. The first of these was the possibility of a 'Russian change of heart', and Churchill's evident desire to find out if there had been one; the second development which suggested the need for a re-think was the 'American itch to get the boys home', as the French saw the American pressure for ratification of the EDC; the third was the American impatience with what they saw as the 'French inability to face up to rearmed Germany'.[1] There were two ways of looking at all these events: one was to ignore them, saying that it was important that the western allies stood together and did nothing to let Russia divide them; the other was to explore the possibilities for thawing the Cold War. The Americans preferred the first approach; the British, on the whole, the latter. If 1954 was seen in retrospect as Eden's *annus mirabilis* after the problems of 1953, the reason is not far to seek: a multi-polar diplomatic structure gave Eden a chance to exercise his diplomatic skills, just as it gave Britain a chance to play a mediatory role; Eden took the opportunity he was offered.

As a preparation for the meeting with the Russians in Berlin in February, the Bermuda conference had been less than helpful. Not only had no common position on the possibility of a summit meeting evolved, but it had become clear that the Americans were becoming seriously irritated by the failure of their European allies to put through the EDC treaty. At a meeting of the NATO Council on 14 December, Dulles assured his listeners that the formation of the EDC would not be the first step in American disengagement from Europe – and then startled them by saying that failure to do so might have this result; America, he warned, might have to have an 'agonizing reappraisal' of her 'basic policy'.[2] There were some who dismissed this as an American bluff, but Eden was not so sure. Dulles told him that Britain and America 'were approaching a parting of the ways with regard to American policy' and that, 'if things went wrong, the United States might swing over to a policy of western hemispheric defence'.[3] There had been fears from the start that the Republicans 'would not be prepared to take the same positive lead in international affairs or take the same risks in foreign policy which the Democrats had been willing to do',[4] and the evidence suggests that Dulles's remarks should have been taken seriously. Despite his own commitment to the Atlantic alliance, Eisenhower could not but be worried about the costs not only to the American economy, but to the American way of life, by the escalating price of the Cold War.[5] As he put it to Churchill's old friend, Bernie Baruch, in March 1953, 'To accustom our population to living indefinitely under such [governmental] controls will gradually bring a new conception of the relation of the individual to the state – a conception that would change in revolutionary fashion the kind of government under which we live.'[6] The President was a true Republican in his feeling that 'in permitting the incessant growth of the Federal Government, we have already drifted a long way from the philosophy of Jefferson'.[7] The EDC would, he hoped, play a crucial role in reducing American defence costs, and despite Dulles's disclaimer that its formation would not have been the first step towards an American withdrawal, the most recent study of American policy shows that this was 'deceit' and that the administration did, indeed, intend to pull troops out if the EDC had succeeded.[8] Unaware of possible American deceit, but aware of the possibility of an American return to isolation, Eden took Dulles's bluff – if bluff it was[9] – seriously, and whilst continuing to press the French to ratify the EDC treaty, he began to explore the option of associating a rearmed Germany with NATO.[10]

Eden was well aware that the Soviets might try to use their first meeting with the western alliance to probe its weak points and to try and disrupt it. The EDC was the obvious target, along with the whole question of the future of Germany, of any such Soviet attempt. Adenauer, who had never liked the idea of a five-Power conference, feared that the Soviets might make a negotiable offer on a reunified but disarmed Germany, which, given Churchill's attitude the previous year, might, by attracting the British, disrupt the western partnership and leave his own hopes of a Federal German state as part of NATO in ruins.[11] Eden shared some of the anxiety that the Prime Minister's hankerings after a summit meeting might lead to problems in Berlin, but when it came to European questions, he was determined to line up with Dulles; he did not want to give the Americans any excuse for opting for 'hemispheric defence'.[12]

Although Dulles was worried by 'some slight sign of Eden's desire to play intermediary role with Molotov' at the conference,[13] western unity held, not least thanks to the clumsy Soviet offer of a neutralised and unified Germany after elections held on the model of those in the Soviet zone – a prospect which appealed to no one. By carefully preparing the ground at home against the possibility that the conference would produce little, and by skilful diplomacy in Berlin, Eden ensured that the western alliance remained unimpaired – and paved the way for a further conference at Geneva in May.[14]

One of the main obstacles in the way of a five-Power conference had been the Soviet insistence that China should participate in any gathering designed to thaw the Cold War; after all, the situation in Korea and Indo-China was an essential part of international tension, and both the Soviets and the Americans were involved directly, and by proxy, in the region. However, the Americans not only had no diplomatic relations with 'Red China', but Dulles bitterly resented the fact that Britain had recognised it and had no intention of following suit. What he would have liked was a British commitment to agree to a Korean-like intervention in the event of the French losing their long and bitter struggle against the Viet-Minh communists. Eden was anxious to avoid any such expensive commitment, but he was also aware of the need, if only on grounds of imperial solidarity, to support the French.[15] Before the Berlin conference it had been agreed that if, as expected, the Soviets raised the subject of a conference over the Far East, Eden should side with what was expected to be the American objection; but given French desperation at their situation in Indo-China, Eden changed his tactics at the conference.[16]

On 27 January the British delegation came up with what was to be the germ of the Geneva meeting: 'We were wondering whether we could get Dulles to agree to spike Molotov's guns by actually agreeing to a five-power meeting *on Korea*, or even "on the Far East beginning with Korea".'[17] Dulles turned the idea down, but it soon became clear that whatever the Americans wanted, the French were in such a desperate plight that they were likely to agree to a conference at which the Chinese were represented; as the French Foreign Minister, Bidault, put it, *'séparez la France ... ajoutez la Chine; et là vous avez 3 contre 2'.*[18] Molotov, well aware of this fact, attempted to play the 'we are all Europeans' card to divide the colonial Powers from the Americans, which gave Eden the opportunity he needed.[19] On 28 January a 'very excited' Bidault spoke emotionally of his 'duty' to consider any Soviet proposals for a conference. He convinced himself, but no one else. What Dulles did now begin to appreciate was Eden's argument that the only way to maintain western solidarity was to seize the initiative by suggesting a conference on the Far East, which would include Korea and Indo-China on the agenda.[20] Eden grasped instinctively and from his own experience what Dulles saw only fitfully, if at all, that not all international questions could be reduced to the massive simplicities of the rivalry between East and West. He saw that America's non-recognition of 'Red China' was one of the ties which 'hold China and Russia together', and wanted to try to alter American policy, if possible.[21] On the vexed question of Germany, however, Eden played the straightest of bats, using procedural devices to circumvent the Soviets and putting forward his own plan for German unification after free and fair elections.[22]

By siding with the French in their desire for a conference at which the Chinese were represented, whilst at the same time maintaining solidarity with the Americans over European matters, Eden presented Dulles with a dilemma;

since it was clear that the French would break allied unity on the Far Eastern question anyway, Dulles risked being isolated if he turned the Soviet suggestion for a conference down. By linking the Indo-China question to the still unresolved Korean peace settlement – where Dulles knew that he would have to deal with China – Eden managed to secure his agreement to a proposal to the Russians for a conference limited to Far Eastern questions.[23] Dulles had reckoned that the Soviets would not agree, but he had underestimated Eden's persuasiveness.[24] As Eden told Churchill on 28 January, he had a 'very intense meeting' with Molotov, in which he 'pulled no punches'.[25] Despite the fears of his Private Secretary that he was pushing Dulles too hard,[26] Eden's mediation with Molotov smoothed away the diplomatic niceties which it had appeared might stymie the proposed conference, and the Soviets left Berlin having agreed to attend a conference in Geneva in May. Although he had used the Indo-China/Korea link as a diplomatic device to move Dulles, Eden had not been keen to see Indo-China on the agenda for the Geneva meeting, but given the role Bidault had played in resisting Soviet attempts to undermine the EDC, he felt that he had no alternative but to give him some public compensation for his stand.[27]

Eden's achievement had been possible because the format of the conference had allowed him to exercise his 'great speciality', which was 'to remember always the third and the fourth parties in . . . international confrontations'.[28] He may, at times, have tended to overestimate what 'charm and sweet reason' could achieve with Molotov,[29] but he had succeeded at least in preparing the way for the Americans and the Chinese to meet, and his policy had had the full support of the Prime Minister, who was still hankering after his summit meeting.[30] Unfortunately for Eden, not all the Prime Minister's instincts were quite so helpful to his diplomacy.

Historians have the luxury (if such it be) of being able to disentangle the various problems confronting their principal characters; indeed, without that it is doubtful whether diplomatic history would make much sense. But even as Eden was trying to juggle with the EDC, Germany and the unity of the western alliance in Berlin, he was embroiled in fresh problems over Egypt.

With negotiations with the Egyptians deadlocked and the Americans refusing to lend the British any help beyond suspending promised economic aid to Neguib's regime, the Cabinet was forced to consider a number of options in early 1954; no one was in much doubt about the Prime Minister's preferences.[31] As Salisbury told Eden on 14 February, Churchill wanted to take the hardest line possible, even if that meant breaking off negotiations and keeping troops in the Canal zone under the 1936 treaty – and this despite the fact that a report by the Lord Chancellor had specifically stated that such an option was only possible on the last count with co-operation from the Egyptians. Salisbury thought that Churchill's reasons were largely 'political':

It is bitter for him with his past record to have to sponsor an agreement with the Egyptians on the withdrawal of British troops from Egypt, and he feels that to stand on the Treaty would be a more acceptable line with the Tory Party, even if it in fact came to much the same thing in the end [as the results of negotiation].

Salisbury, who liked the prospect as little as Churchill himself, and took the view that either a negotiated treaty or a contested withdrawal 'will be generally regarded as a blow to our prestige', thought that that was 'a fact we have just got to face, since it seems we have no longer either the money or the manpower to stay there'.[32] Selwyn Lloyd thought that Churchill was 'longing for the Egyptians to break off negotiations',[33] whilst his Parliamentary Private Secretary, Robert Carr, reported even more worryingly that there were press comments to the effect that Churchill 'and some other members of the Cabinet are secretly on the side of the rebels and not supporting your policy'.[34] The fact that Lloyd, who was looking after the Egyptian negotiations whilst Eden was in Berlin, had given dinner to one of the leading 'rebels' on 3 February, gave substance to Carr's story, and Eden began to fear that he had been 'got at' by Churchill.[35]

Given that the substantive points at issue had now narrowed down to whether British technicians in the Canal zone should be in uniform, whether the provisions for reoccupation should apply in the event of an attack on Turkey by a third power, and how long they should apply, Eden was hoping that American mediation could finally induce the Egyptians to settle.[36] He was moving away from the old policy of basing Britain's position in the Middle East on Cairo; Baghdad would be the new centre of gravity. Aware of American moves to initiate discussions with Pakistan and Turkey with a view to reaching a defence pact, Eden was not keen on the idea of the Americans muscling into a region where, in the absence of co-operation from Egypt, he intended to base British interests.[37] Makins did not think that America was 'consciously trying to substitute their influence for ours in the Middle East',[38] which was a somewhat optimistic reading of events. But Eden, who had been building up towards his new policy since 1953, did not like the possible implications of America's interest in the northern tier. However, the Americans took the British by surprise[39] and on 2 April signed a pact for military aid with Turkey, following it up with one with Iraq on 21 April and Pakistan on 19 May.[40] So much for Makins's suppositions about American policy. In fact, having decided, as we have seen, to distance themselves from Britain's stand in Egypt and to abandon the idea of basing their strategy in the Middle East there, the Americans had moved in the same direction as Eden, only rather more speedily.[41] It was hardly the background Eden would have chosen for the Geneva conference – especially as negotiations with the Egyptians were still stalled, with a revolt against Neguib at the end of February seeming to leave Colonel Nasser in power in Cairo.

As matters turned out, it was as well that Eden had agreed at Berlin that

Indo-China should appear on the agenda for Geneva, for by the time the conference met it was the most pressing problem on his desk, not least because of the chasm between American policy and his own. As the French position deteriorated, Dulles became increasingly anxious to take steps to prevent the spread of communism, but he was aware that adding another commitment to those already undertaken by America might prove difficult to sell to Congress – which was where the British came in.[42] On 4 April Eisenhower asked Churchill to co-operate in the formation of an anti-communist coalition in the Far East, and a week later Dulles arrived in England to follow up this initiative, reporting back happily that he had moved the British away from their original position that nothing could be done before Geneva. He was, however, concerned that the British did not share his views about the importance of the loss of northern Vietnam, and he doubted their willingness to commit ground forces to the region.[43] Eisenhower found the British position almost incomprehensible and supposed it had something to do with their fear of losing Hong Kong if the Chinese turned nasty.[44] In fact, there was far more to it than that.

Eden thought that American policy on China lacked any sense of realism and feared that the creation of such a coalition would simply end up exporting the Cold War to Indo-China. As he told Lloyd later, 'we do not want to bring a greater disaster on our head by trying to avert the immediate one'.[45] He feared that Dulles's clumsiness might even provoke a '3rd world war'.[46] Eden had correctly divined that American hubris was beginning to take a dangerous form. As one historian has put it, 'There was, then, at this time, what looks like an increasing and self-induced American conviction that something was almost in their grasp which would change the course of the Indo-China war.'[47] Nor was he over-impressed by deliberately misleading statements fed to Makins to the effect that a refusal to back full-blooded American participation in the region might 'call into question the whole concept of alliances'.[48]

The whole business showed the problem with the American connection: they expected Britain to answer 'how high?' when they said 'jump', but were quite unwilling to help the British in areas where they considered their own vital interests were at stake. Eden did not consider that the fall of northern Vietnam would be the end of the world, but he did like the idea of a Far Eastern security pact which might take in Britain's possessions in the region, and so during Dulles's visit he tried to distinguish between the two objectives.[49] There has been a considerable controversy over exactly what Eden did say to Dulles, not least because the latter appears to have thought later that he had been 'betrayed' by the British Foreign Secretary.[50] Eden himself later acknowledged that their joint communiqué of 13 April 'could bear the interpretation [Dulles] ... put upon' it,[51] and it was unwise to leave Dulles with the impression that he was willing to open talks on a security pact immediately. But as we have seen, Dulles left London telling Eisenhower that he had doubts whether the British would commit ground forces to Vietnam, so any sense of 'betrayal' stemmed more from the fact that Dulles expected unquestioning obedience from America's allies than from anything else. Indeed, the speed with which Dulles moved to try to convene a security pact suggests that he was uncertain how far the British would back him.

Eden's patience with Dulles was, by late April, close to snapping. As his telegram to Makins rejecting calls for the British to participate in a meeting in Washington shows, he had had enough of what passed for diplomacy on the banks of the Potomac:

Americans may think the time passed when they need consider the feelings or difficulties of their allies. It is the conviction that this tendency becomes more pronounced every week that is creating difficulties for anyone in this country who wants to maintain close Anglo-American relations. [52]

For those who shared Dulles's views about the need for intervention to prevent the 'free world' from falling to communism, Eden's attitude naturally looked rather like appeasement.[53] Eden, however, genuinely believed that he was preventing America dragging everyone into a third world war, as he told Dulles on 23 April.[54]

Dulles was in Paris for a meeting of the NATO council, which provided the French with the perfect opportunity to press him for aid as the situation at their stronghold, Dien Bien Phu, became critical. The NATO Supreme Commander reported on 24 April that he had 'never seen French morale so low',[55] and both he and Dulles were inclined to grant the French request for immediate military aid. Whether this last was genuine, or whether it was designed to put pressure on the British, it certainly alarmed Eden, who went to bed that night 'a troubled man'.[56]

There is a certain irony in the Americans pressing the British to intervene to help the French in Indo-China when they had spent much of the war wanting to keep the French from returning to the region – but, of course, the crusade against communism excused and explained everything. Eisenhower thought that the British were 'frightened ... by two things': a 'morbid obsession that any positive move on the part of the free world may bring upon us World War III' and concern for 'the safety of Hong Kong'.[57] It was only the need 'to produce collective security in this world' which prevented the President from showing his 'impatience & frustrations' rather more directly.[58] When Churchill invited himself to Washington on 22 April, Eden tried to deflect a positive response from the administration by telling Dulles that it was 'quite general in character', but the President wrote breezily: 'You tell Churchill to "come along".'[59] He perhaps hoped to get something firmer out of the man of 1940.

Eden's dilemma by the evening of 24 April was as acute as any faced since he had come to office. The Americans seemed determined to go ahead with intervention in Vietnam to help the French. If the British refused to go along with the plan, they risked wrecking the alliance with America as well as alienating the French; if they played along, they might be entering World War III. He decided that before proceeding to Geneva, he had better return to London for consultation.[60]

Churchill was in one of his more discursive moods when he saw Eden that evening. Lamenting the fact that 'We have thrown away our glorious Empire, our wonderful Indian Empire', he seemed disinclined to help the French save theirs.[61] As he told his doctor on 28 April, 'I don't see why we should fight for France in Indo-China when we have given away India.'[62]

At a specially convened meeting on the morning of 25 April, senior Ministers and the Service Chiefs agreed with Eden's suggestion that Britain should not commit herself to supporting immediate military action. Eden wanted to leave the opportunity open for negotiations at Geneva and was willing to pledge not only diplomatic support for the French, but also a guarantee that if a settlement was reached Britain would join in any security pact to enforce it. As a fall-back position he was willing to 'consider with our Allies the action to be taken jointly' if negotiations failed, but he was not willing to give any assurances about what the British would do. As a sop to the Americans he was ready to 'study . . . measures to ensure the defence of Siam and the rest of South-East Asia'.[63] But no sooner had Ministers agreed to back Eden than it became apparent that the Americans had another shot in their locker. The French Ambassador, René Massigli, arrived at the Foreign Office with a message from Bidault saying that the Americans had agreed to mount a 'massive air strike' and to seek support for further action from Congress, provided the British agreed to join in an undertaking to 'resist communism by force if necessary' and build up a common front in Indo-China.[64] In the face of a blatant attempt to either bounce him into action or to land him with the role of scapegoat, Eden summoned another meeting of Ministers – which simply confirmed the earlier endorsement of his policy; it just remained to tell Dulles that if he was not bluffing, he would be fighting his crusade alone.

Distressed as he was at the British decision, Bidault accepted it with a show of good grace, which was more than could be said for Dulles and company.[65] If Dulles did not like Eden's news, Eden was none too pleased to be told by him that there could be no question of an immediate air-strike since the political groundwork for one had not been laid – which made the earlier American manoeuvre totally transparent. It was little wonder that the following morning Eden was in a violently 'anti-American' mood.[66] Dulles told Eden that it was a 'serious error to write off the loss of all of Indochina and assume that the rest of Southeast Asia could be held', and repeated the arguments in favour of an immediate joint attempt to work out plans to help the French hang on to most of the country. But Eden, admitting there was a 'gap' between Britain and America, stood by British policy.[67]

Dulles told Eisenhower that it was the 'increasing inability of Winston to lead his Cabinet' which was responsible for the British 'unwillingness to face up to [the] Indo-China issue' – which is a sign of the extent to which the Americans had grown used to being able to rely on Churchill to secure immediate compliance with their wishes.[68] Admiral Radford reported from London that the British Chiefs of Staff did not 'relate the implications of the situation . . . to the future of the EDC and effects on NATO', adding that he would raise these points, and the effect on Congress and American opinion of the British failure to 'stand . . . firmly' with America on the issue.[69] Having failed to make the British play the game according to their rules, the Americans were ready to hint that they might have to take their ball home. It all made for a most difficult start to the Geneva conference, as well as putting the Indo-China question at the head of the agenda.

That Eden managed to pluck success from such a thorn-bush owed everything to his unwillingness to identify British policy too closely with that of the Americans. It was a strategy which appalled his Private Secretary, Evelyn Shuckburgh, who tried to warn him about the dangers of 'too great a split with the Americans'.[70] Eden's temper, never totally reliable, was strained to breaking-point, what with Dulles, panicking Frenchmen, continued rumblings from Churchill over Egypt and anxieties over his own political future – and the fact that his hotel was 'noisy, smelly and uncomfortable'; but however much he ranted at his subordinates, when it came to the business of the conference he was calm, controlled and persuasive.

The Americans imagined that the British attitude might leave them isolated, and Eisenhower speculated about the possibility of forming a 'coalition' with Australia, New Zealand, the Philippines, France and Indo-China, 'to the complete exclusion of the British', deciding that although it was a 'tough one', he would 'go along with the idea because I believe that the British Government is showing a woeful unawareness of the risks we run in that region'.[71] Condemning the 'increasing weakness' of the British, Dulles urged Eisenhower to 'take the leadership in what we think is the right course' – once they had decided what that was.[72] But there, of course, was the rub. It was by no means clear that Congress would authorise military action, and the Joint Chiefs were by no means agreed in any case on what that action should be; it was all very well being leader of the free world, but the difference between possessing potential power and employing it was something which the Americans were just beginning to get some glimmer of.

A grim-faced Dulles complained to Eden on 30 April that 'nobody was supporting the U.S.';[73] it evidently had not occurred to him that there might be good reasons why. It had been, of course, 'particularly galling' for him to hear America attacked as 'being an "imperialist" power', and it is some measure of the sheer arrogance of the man that he should have told Eden that,

the United States was eager to beat the Communists at their own game and to sponsor nationalism in the independent colonial areas, which was in accordance with our historic tradition, but that we were restrained from doing so by a desire to cooperate with Britain and France in Asia, in North Africa and in the Near and Middle East. . . .

However, this did not seem to 'be paying dividends because when the chips were down', there was 'no cohesion between us'. After restraining himself at this fine piece of sanctimonious humbuggery, it is no wonder that Eden needed to shout at his subordinates; it was lucky there was no cat available. Dulles droned on in the same vein, warning that if he had to report to Washington 'under present conditions', the 'consequences would be disastrous for the close United Kingdom–United States relations which we wanted to maintain'.[74]

Eden thought the idea of his making the sort of anti-communist rant favoured by the American was 'mad' (although Dulles left under the impression that he might make such a speech),[75] and by this stage he could hardly bear to talk to him,[76] but diplomacy required an effort to calm the Americans down and to prevent their going off in a huff. The British were still anxious to form a Far Eastern version of NATO, but they were far more aware than the Americans of the complexity of the situation in the region. What Eden wanted to do was to try to win political support from India, Burma and other Asian countries, to ensure that any military pact would have a firm grounding. Pakistan and Ceylon had already agreed to do so, and even Nehru had been diverted from his original intention of condemning the pact root and branch. He suggested that British and American representatives should begin to discuss the nature, purpose, membership and scope of such a defence pact. Dulles took note of what was said, but did not appear any happier by the end of the meeting.[77] He told Eden on 1 May that 'he was not asking us for any military assistance but only for our moral support in any action that they might take', but when quizzed as to what action he had in mind, 'Mr Dulles replied that it had not yet been decided.' Eden, naturally, refused to give him a blank cheque, but noted that Dulles was 'deeply aggrieved'. The American went back to Washington on 3 May.[78]

Salisbury heard from Aldrich that Dulles felt that he had been 'double-crossed, not by you' but by Lloyd's and Churchill's statements in the Commons on 22 April, which had said that no agreement had been reached with America over policy in the Far East; in view of the fact that Dulles felt that he had been let down by everyone, most of all Eden, this was probably a fine example of diplomatic tact. But what worried the Ambassador was the mood he had found in Washington, which was that America should go it alone –

an attitude, it seemed, shared by the President himself, whom Salisbury described as a 'well-meaning' but 'prize noodle'.[79]

The whole episode had left Eden with the conviction that 'all the Americans want to do is to replace the French and run Indo-China themselves'. He told Shuckburgh just before Dulles's departure that: '"They want to replace us in Egypt too. They want to run the world."'[80] He felt so strongly about the matter that, despite pleas from Shuckburgh and others, he refused to consider Dulles's compromise proposal, which would have involved immediate discussions with other countries over a security pact; Eden felt that such a move, before the conference had had its first plenary session, would be to prejudice the chance of a settlement. His twin objectives – 'to give the Geneva Conference a chance of success without doing grave damage to Anglo-United States relations' and 'not to lose the chance of making defensive arrangements with the United States for South-East Asia at the proper stage' – were not easily achieved;[81] indeed, it might be argued that the deterioration in his relationship with Dulles had already done 'grave damage' to Anglo-American relations.

Dulles's replacement by Eisenhower's old Chief of Staff, Walter Bedell Smith, cleared the atmosphere. Eden's attempts to find a way forward included frank discussions with Molotov – so frank, in fact, that when Eden's Private Secretary's diaries were edited for publication, Sir Evelyn (as he was by then) toned down his account of what happened. In the version of Eden's conversation with Molotov on 5 May which appeared in print, Shuckburgh describes Eden as having 'played up to Molotov',[82] but the diary itself describes how Eden hardly 'touched upon the bad conduct of the other side' and how 'All the ills of the world, as Molotov was only too glad to confirm, came from the Americans.' Eden explained how he had avoided making any commitment to intervention in Indo-China and, 'in fact, he went straight to the bosom of Auntie Mol'.[83]

From the point of view of Shuckburgh, who worried throughout at the distance which Eden seemed willing to put between himself and the Americans, Eden's reported conduct was shocking enough to expunge from the published record, but far from reflecting (as the loyal Sir Evelyn feared) badly on Eden, the incident shows his technique at its most effective. He managed to make it clear to Molotov that there would be no immediate allied intervention in Indo-China, and he emphasised his own willingness to reach a negotiated settlement, but he also told the Russian that there was a possibility that the Americans might take matters into their own hands and that a world war might be the result.[84] Shuckburgh thought that Eden was playing the 'prima donna', but he was taking a calculated risk based upon his own assessment of the situation – which is, after all, one of the functions of a Foreign Secretary. He calculated that Molotov had no more desire to see a war in the Far East than he had himself, and that (rather as he was himself) the Russian was anxious lest the Americans or his own protégés, the Chinese, should do something to spark a general conflagration.[85] He was aware that Molotov's unexpectedly helpful attitude might be 'a deliberate exercise in dividing us from Americans',[86] but he thought that the risk was worth taking; after all, there were differences between the British and the Americans, and unless some room could be found for manoeuvre, the conference was doomed to failure.

The conference lasted from 8 May to 12 July, with Eden playing the major role throughout. By not appearing simply as an American puppet, he gave himself the room to bring along the Asian countries whose support would be essential for the success of a Far Eastern NATO. Even Australia, which after the 1951 ANZUS pact looked to America for help against the spread of communism, did not want to find herself isolated from the Asian countries and participating in a war whose objectives were uncertain, and so backed Eden's line.[87] The solution which he played for was a partition of Indo-China on acceptable terms and then negotiations for a security pact. From Washington, Makins warned that although the Americans were 'moving slowly to a historic decision to accept far-reaching commitments on the mainland of Asia', British refusal to open negotiations on a security pact before an agreement had been reached at Geneva might jeopardise Anglo-American relations. But Eden refused to be moved, telling Makins on 26 May that 'we could defeat this object if we are not clear what part of the mainland we are going to defend and with whom'. He was, he said, as aware as the Americans of the dangers of communist expansion in South-East Asia: 'But we have, and are entitled to have, our own ideas of how this can best be done.'[88]

Despite underhand attempts by the Americans to discuss with the French the terms on which they might intervene in Indo-China,[89] and criticisms in the British and American press, Eden laboured on. But even as he was being accused of 'appeasement' over Indo-China, the 'Suez revolt' raised its head again and the rebels began demanding assurances that there would be no fresh negotiations with the Egyptians without the Commons being informed first.[90] It was not the best background for taking over from the ailing Prime Minister. Eden told Churchill on 7 June that a new administration would have to have at least two weeks to face the Commons before the recess.[91] As ever, faced with the prospect of losing his beloved red boxes, Churchill temporised, telling Eden on 11 June that, whilst he was 'most anxious' to prepare for an election at the end of 1955 and to 'establish the repute and efficiency of yr. Administration', he had to offer 'wider reasons than this to history'.[92] Despite efforts from Macmillan and others to budge the old boy, it was plain to Eden that, in addition to carrying the burden of Geneva and Egypt, he would have to carry the old man of the sea as well.

But none of these things, even Churchill's sudden decision in June that he wanted a summit conference, put the Foreign Secretary off his stroke and he was able to bring off a remarkable success, with armistices in all the

Indo-Chinese countries and an agreement to partition Vietnam. He might have taken some comfort from the comment of his former Private Secretary, Bob Dixon, who wrote just before the end of the conference to say that 'the only redeeming feature of the present situation is the fantastic height at which your own stock now stands'.[93]

Any man, even one not so given to vanity as Eden, would have felt elated by the press which greeted his success at Geneva, and the Order of the Garter which he was awarded was well-merited. But he had been given a disturbing insight into America's attitude: 'They like to give orders, and if they are not at once obeyed they become huffy. That is their conception of an alliance – or Dulles' anyway.'[94] This was not Eden's conception of Britain's position in the world, despite her financial difficulties, and the conferences at Berlin and Geneva had vindicated him. The question was whether the Americans would rest happy with it when – and if – he succeeded the Grand Old Man at 10 Downing Street.

24

The Act of Succession

Churchill did not like the tension which had come to dominate Anglo-American relations by mid-1954. His entire career since 1940 had been devoted to the unity of the 'English-speaking alliance' and now, 'at the end of the long day, nothing else seems to matter'.[1] He could not see 'why anyone should want to quarrel with America. She stands alone in the world against Communism.'[2] He feared that the Americans 'might become impatient' and resort to a showdown with the Soviets.[3] Nor was this without reason. It was not just Dulles's belligerence in April which suggested that the Americans needed restraining. Back in February Churchill had received a worrying letter from Eisenhower, in which the President had called for a strong 'association of free nations' to convince the 'evil and savage individuals in the Kremlin' that their cause could not prevail.[4] Eden had been at 'a loss' to understand Eisenhower's rather vague references to carrying on the 'struggle' and encouraged Churchill to send him a soothing letter. But Churchill, who still hankered after a summit meeting with the Soviets, began to turn his mind towards the possibility of improving Anglo-American relations at the same time as promoting his longed-for summit.[5] It was against this background, and with the Geneva conference seemingly stalled in early June, that Churchill decided that it was his duty to 'history' to stay on.

Churchill concluded that a visit to Washington was just the thing to improve Anglo-American relations. Impatient at the delays in Geneva, he saw his visit as providing an opportunity to discuss the Far Eastern version of NATO, as well as the Middle East and the future of the EDC. It would be just the sort of *tour d'horizon* which he loved – and which Eden hated.[6] Eden had managed, in sharp contrast to his previous spell at the Foreign Office, to keep the reins of foreign policy mainly in his own hands, and he was less than pleased with the notion of the Prime Minister going off to Washington and disrupting the progress which was being made in Geneva. Naturally, he resented the fact that Churchill's mission meant that the old boy was not going to retire in the near future after all.[7] He also had the strongest objections to asking for American help in the Middle East. The latest telegrams from Makins seemed to confirm what Dulles's bad-tempered remarks on 30 April had suggested – namely that America was going to pursue a 'more independent policy in the Middle East'; the fact that the words reported by the press were so similar to those Dulles himself had used – America being 'handicapped by a tendency to support British and French "colonial" views' – gave the reports great credence in Eden's mind.[8] He warned Churchill of this on 21 June, adding that he was worried about the effect it would have on Britain's position in Iraq and the Gulf if it seemed that Britain could not settle the Egyptian matter without American aid.[9] Eden was now fully aware that the Americans were setting out to replace British influence in the area with their own, and he was determined to push on with his own policies in the northern tier; he wanted co-operation with America, but he would not have been fooled by the euphemism 'competitive-cooperation' – competition was competition, whatever you called it.

Churchill, however, was unconcerned about Eden's opposition to his visit. He resented the way in which Eden 'keeps me out of foreign affairs' and was quite prepared to go on his own.[10] Eden, however, opposed the idea, and Ministers were less than happy at the idea of the Prime Minister being allowed to go to Washington unsupervised, and so it was agreed at Cabinet on 5 June that Eden should accompany him when he went to Washington on 18 June.[11] But what neither the Cabinet nor Eden was aware of was that the Prime Minister intended to use this visit – perhaps his last official one – to launch his final attempt at making peace with Moscow.

The Americans saw the visit as a sign that the British wanted to 'restore harmony' to Anglo-American relations.[12] Eisenhower was 'not sure that anything good would come of it', but he 'decided to let the old man come over' anyway.[13] Much as they admired Churchill for what he had done in the past, the Americans no longer took the ageing hero very seriously as a political force. Aldrich warned Dulles that the 'real danger' in the meeting was 'Churchill and his repetition of old ideas which don't have the support of Eden or basically of the Cabinet'. He thought that Churchill's 'extreme' ideas about a new Locarno with the Soviets and a summit meeting were not shared by the Cabinet, but that 'Eden is O.K. and that if he were on his own we would have much less difficulty'. Aldrich was well aware, however, of the residual influence which Churchill could still exercise by use of the weapon of his retirement, and he warned Washington that Eden did not dare quarrel too bitterly with Churchill for fear of risking his claim to the Premiership. But he advised Dulles to support Eden because his views 'would be considerably closer to our own than those of Mr Churchill on many matters'.[14]

Churchill's hopes that the trip would do something to restore Anglo-American harmony were fulfilled. Eisenhower had a great affection for the old man, even if he did think he was beginning to fail, and from their very first meeting on 25 June the atmosphere between the two leaders was cordial, with them swapping anecdotes, views about painting and the evils of communism.[15] On more substantive matters the ground was cleared early on. The Americans were exceedingly anxious that Britain and France should support their stand at the UN against a left-wing regime in Guatemala, so much so that Eisenhower wanted them to know that if they did not, 'it would mean we would feel entirely free without regard to their position in relation to any such matters as any of their colonial problems in Egypt, Cypress [*sic*] etc.'.[16] Eden, after a little hesitation, gave the Americans the support they required, and, as always when they had their own way, the Americans were gracious in return.[17]

Eden's views on Indo-China naturally raised some comment, with Eisenhower coming under pressure from some Congressmen to distance himself from British and French colonialism,[18] whilst others complained about the British unwillingness to support the American position.[19] Churchill, for his part, embarked upon 'a prolonged and rather emotional discussion of Egypt' at the meeting on the afternoon of 25 June, but Eisenhower, at his most conciliatory, drew discussion back to the more general topic of the need to align Anglo-American policy more closely. It was agreed to set up joint study groups to look at problems of mutual interest – including atomic matters.[20] Detailed discussion on policy in Indo-China between Dulles and Eden produced agreement on the way forward at Geneva,[21] whilst Churchill did his best to mend relations between Dulles and Eden.

Churchill's attitude towards the coolness between Dulles and Eden reveals much about his attitude towards Anglo-American relations – and the difference between himself and Eden on the matter. At their meeting on 26 June, he told Eisenhower that Dulles had 'said a couple of things to Eden that need not have been said', and the following day informed Dulles that Eden regarded him very 'highly'.[22] Churchill was concerned lest Eden 'upset' the Americans, who were, he told his doctor, Lord Moran, with his habitual naïveté on this score, 'so kind and generous to their friends'.[23] He could not understand 'why Anthony should go out of his way to find faults in the Americans'; as he told Moran, 'Does he not realize that without the United States Britain is alone?'[24] He feared that the two men might quarrel during the visit, and when Eden returned slightly late from a long meeting with Dulles, he joked: '"Christ! I hope they haven't quarrelled and killed each other."'[25] In fact, the two men got on reasonably well, coming to broad agreement over Indo-China and policy towards the EDC.[26] What Churchill failed to see was that the main reason that Eden and Dulles tended to differ was that they held quite different views of the character of an alliance: Dulles wanted obedience after discussion, Eden wanted a dialogue. The Prime Minister's almost slavish willingness to follow the American line 'right or wrong' was shown when he argued with Bob Dixon over American backing for the rebels in Guatemala. When Dixon condemned it as just the sort of thing the Americans disliked about Soviet policy in Korea and Greece, Churchill dismissed Guatemala as a 'bloody place' he'd 'never heard of' and, calling for a 'sense of proportion', refused to 'jeopardize our relations with the United States, for on them the safety of the world might depend'.[27]

One reason for the Prime Minister's disregard for the sort of moral considerations which could make him wax so lyrical when the occasion arose was that he was an old man in a hurry – to get to Moscow. In conversation with Eisenhower on 26 June and again with Dulles on the 27th, Churchill raised the subject of his meeting with the Russian leaders without the Americans, promising Eisenhower that, 'I will not compromise you in the slightest', and telling a highly sceptical Dulles that 'he would not be going in any sense as an intermediary ... but representing the spirit and purpose of "our side"'.[28] The first Eden picked up of all this was when Dulles told him about Churchill's idea that afternoon.[29] But it was not until the jollifications and the discussions were over, and they were embarked for England on the *Queen Mary*, that Churchill struck.

Eden had been greatly disappointed when Churchill put it to him that if he would sanction the idea of a Prime Ministerial visit to Moscow, he would stand down after it had taken place – which should, he thought, mean that Eden could take over in September.[30] It was not Eden's finest hour. He actually had grave doubts about the effect which sending the telegram might have on opinion in America and Europe, and he particularly disliked the fact that Churchill had not consulted the Cabinet. Churchill, however, would not be balked and talked about resigning. At his most ruthless – Eden could hardly resign at a crucial point in the Geneva conference and at a time when he was so close to the succession – Churchill extracted a 'compromise' out of the Foreign Secretary: he would send the telegram to the Cabinet, provided Eden agreed to say that he concurred in it in principle. But having given way about consulting the Cabinet, Churchill then evaded doing so by sending another message to the acting Prime Minister, Rab Butler, telling him that he need not show the Russian message to the Cabinet as it did not commit them to anything.[31]

The result was a major Cabinet crisis.[32] Salisbury, with bitter memories of 11 May 1953, threatened to resign and was only dissuaded from doing so when the Americans did not immediately repudiate Churchill.[33] Churchill, for his part, threatened to resign if he did not get his way, and Eden, who was heavily occupied with Geneva, spent his time trying to temporise.[34] Even though he had been told by Churchill what was in his mind, Eisenhower was taken aback by the speed with which Churchill had acted – but he could hardly put the toothpaste back into the tube.[35] As Churchill pressed his case during July and Eden awaited the results of Geneva, it seemed that the Cabinet might split, but with Eden's ultimate success, and the Soviet suggestion on 24 July of a five-Power conference, the main crisis passed without political fatalities.[36] The one good thing to come out of the furore was that, whilst the Cabinet and Churchill were at loggerheads on the Russian issue, a final settlement of the treaty with Egypt passed with relatively little dissent – apart from the odd complaint from Churchill.[37] However, by this stage Eden had his hands full with the French rejection of the EDC treaty in which was to plunge him into a fresh round of hectic European diplomacy, culminating in the new year in an agreement to let the German army come under NATO command, along with a British commitment to closer military co-operation.

Salisbury's threats to resign over Churchill's Russian initiative had as much to do with 'resentment at Winston's methods' as they did with his fears of the effect which it would have on American opinion.[39] In Eden's view the ageing Prime Minister could not, or would not, believe that 'the era of Stalin' was over.[40] But the whole episode, and his continuing hope that he could be 'of help to the cause of "peace through strength"', prompted Churchill to stay on, trusting, as he told Eden on 24 August, that he could count on 'your loyalty and friendship'.[41] Provoked almost beyond endurance by Churchill's antics, Eden had a 'stiff' interview with him on 27 August. Churchill protested that he 'felt better' and argued that he ought not to go until 'he fell ill again'. Eden argued that the Government's prestige was suffering and that senior Ministers were working under an intolerable strain: 'If I was not fit to stand on my own two feet now and choose an administration now, I should probably be less so a year from now'; he even hinted that he might have to resign himself. Churchill asked him what the hurry was, adding that the Party would never forgive him if he did resign – although, of course, he could always lead a rebellion. Even by Churchill's by now rather cruel standards where Eden was concerned, this was a little much; had Eden been that sort of man, he would have led a rebellion years before – and Churchill must have known it.[42] The most the old man would agree to was a reshuffle, with Eden perhaps taking control on the home front, leaving foreign policy to someone like Macmillan.[43] It is a sign of how much Churchill had used the succession issue to blackmail Eden over his Russian initiative that it was at this time that Eden told Salisbury that 'the solitary pilgrimage is off';[44] even Churchill must have realised that he could not get that one past the Cabinet again. With the old boy determined to stay on as long as possible, even the resourceful Macmillan was reduced to suggesting to Eden that they perhaps hinted to him that he should resign in November when he was eighty; but if he refused, 'and we cannot but accept his refusal', then all he could advise was: 'Could you not threaten him a little . . . ?'[45] Although it is usually Eden who is criticised for not pushing Churchill, Salisbury had it right when he pointed out that all the senior Ministers were being 'put in the unhappy dilemma of either acquiescing in things with which we do not disagree or being accused of breaking up the Party', adding that, 'to sit in a Government which is becoming something very like a dictatorship is an experience which few of us can relish unless we are very ambitious, which I am not'.[46] But Eden was ambitious, and so was Macmillan – so after further desultory attempts to shift the old barnacle, they resolved to soldier on for a while;[47] and even Salisbury did not resign.

By December, with an election due in late 1955 at the latest, Eden renewed his attempts to secure a retirement date out of Churchill, and was horrified to discover that he was thinking of hanging about until June or July. Churchill did agree to a meeting between himself and senior Ministers, including Macmillan, but added as a Parthian shot that the latter was 'very ambitious'.[48] Eden was tempted to write to Churchill telling him that since any new government would not have proper time to establish itself, 'I could not myself feel justified in taking on the task. In that event I would hope to be allowed to complete my work at the Foreign Office. . . . After this I would propose to retire into private life.'[49] At the meeting on 22 December, Churchill inveighed against those who 'wanted me out', but Ministers held their nerve and told him that he was being utterly selfish and ought to go soon; but once more he refused to give a firm date.[50] It was not until late February that Eden could finally feel that the Premiership would soon be his.

Churchill's departure from office did not necessarily portend the end of his approach to what Makins had called the 'Grand Alliance'; Bevin and Attlee had continued with it, minus much of the rhetoric which Churchill had kept from the hey-day of 'Anglo-Saxonism' at the turn of the century. There had been other differences too. Churchill tended to see the alliance as an end in itself – or, rather, to see Anglo-American 'unity' in an almost mystical sense, as an objective. Bevin and Attlee took a more hard-headed view, seeing in the American connection a way of propping up Britain's crumbling position in the Middle East in the face of Russian encroachment; American money would play the role it had during the war, of allowing Britain to maintain commitments which she could not afford. As the threat of Soviet expansion came to Europe in the late 1940s, Bevin had striven to secure an American military commitment to the security of western Europe. But the connection had been bought at a price – as Korea showed. But there was another sort of price to be paid. The American approach to foreign policy was ideological. Once the Soviet Union had been identified as a threat, it also became the 'enemy', in rather the same way as Nazism had, and the techniques which had been used to arouse popular support for the war in Europe were now used to mobilise the American public behind a policy of 'containment'. By the early 1950s American rhetoric about rolling back communism and 'liberating' the Soviet satellites had actually served to put some distance between British and American attitudes – a phenomenon which worried some of the more thoughtful observers on both sides of the Atlantic.

In 1951 Ambassador Walter Gifford discounted 'anti-Americanism' as having a negligible influence upon British attitudes towards America, perceptively noting that much of the resentment which manifested itself at times stemmed from the 'fear' that Britain 'may have lost control over her own destiny', and that American actions might drag Britain into a war with the Soviet Union. There was also a strain in British opinion which thought that American policy in the Far East lacked 'realism' – but that was part of a more generalised feeling that America lacked the diplomatic experience to carry the role of world leadership which had fallen upon her shoulders. The British were also less apt to demonise the Soviet Union than Americans might like.[51] The 'growing self-confidence' which Gifford had noticed in 1951 – the feeling that Britain was not simply 'dependent' but could, and should, 'deal on a more equal basis' with America[52] – had increased markedly by 1954, and Eden's diplomacy was a reflection of this fact. Churchill may have remained locked into the 'dependent' relationship which his own Americanophilia and the experience of the war had inculcated, but Eden reflected the 'appreciable decline in British confidence in American leadership and in American prestige in the UK generally', noted by Ambassador Aldrich in 1953.[53] It was not that Eden did not realise the value of the American connection or that he was 'anti-American' – such broad and condemnatory phrases do little justice to the complexity of his attitudes, all of which may be found in Aldrich's penetrating analysis of the changing British attitudes towards America. Aldrich noted a 'marked lessening of confidence' in America's ability to provide 'sound and constructive leadership for the west', as well as the 'essential military and economic support'. Britain, like many of America's allies, was concerned that America did not give 'proper weight to their legitimate interests and concerns in the formulation of our own policy'; all these things were features of Eden's diplomacy. His attitude was not far removed from Aldrich's conclusion that, 'there has been no change in the basic awareness that successful leadership of the Free World can only come from the US; there has certainly been a marked falling-off in the willingness to follow whole-heartedly that lead'.[54] Eden reflected this development in a way Churchill was incapable of doing. But there was more to his policy than that.

As Makins noted in a perceptive despatch at the end of 1954, Soviet and American attitudes towards foreign policy were 'imbued with a messianic spirit', and the Americans, with their tendency to 'divide the world into big and small powers and two "superpowers"', were inclined to give insufficient attention to the nuances of the world situation. Makins thought that this was, on the whole, a great advantage for Britain because as long as the Russian threat 'seems to Americans to represent a real menace to the American way of life, they will be prepared to devote a considerable proportion of their resources to armaments and to military and economic aid destined to strengthen their allies around the world'; put bluntly, 'there was less money for other countries in a state of co-existence than in a state of emergency'. In Makins's judgment 'the loss of American interest in Europe, and above all in what is sometimes called here "the British complex", is the main thing we have to fear within the western world'.[55] It was an acute, even brilliant analysis, but it had two main weaknesses. If there would be 'less money still' if a *modus vivendi* were ever reached' between America and Russia, then it was presumably in Britain's interests for the Cold War to go on indefinitely, and moves, like those Churchill wanted to make, towards what a later generation would call *détente* were to be deprecated; this was another example of a rather extravagant sacrifice of end to means. On this argument American aid was a means to the end of maintaining British independence of the Soviet Union, but since this involved, in practice, sacrificing it to America instead, it was perhaps more sensible to have sought *détente* wherever and whenever possible; but, of course, the shadow of 'appeasement' hung heavily over any such moves. The second fault in Makins's analysis was its belief that America was interested in maintaining the 'British complex' – that is the agglomeration of British interests in the Middle East, the Gulf and the Far East. Shaken by the criticisms that America was 'imperialist', Dulles and Eisenhower were moving away from even the vestigial support which America had given to British interests in such areas. The logic employed, which was that in the Cold War it was better that colonial nations should look towards America rather than to the Soviets, was impeccable, wrong and hardly in Britain's interests. It was wrong because it assumed that Nasser and company were in some sense the spiritual descendants of George Washington and would look towards the Great Republic for inspiration. The only resemblance between Nasser and Washington was that they both led anti-British rebellions. The Pandora's box which the Americans so blithely opened was to produce regimes which regarded them as the 'Great Satan' rather than as the great redeemer. That nemesis lay far in the future, but it was clear enough to Eden that American policy in the Middle East was not likely to be of much help in maintaining the British position there.

The word most often used to describe Eden's approach to diplomacy is 'intuitive'; he operated, it was often said, more by his 'antennae' than by logic, and seeking to impose a grand strategy on his diplomacy is perhaps dangerous on that account. But because he has so often been accused of having little or no strategic vision, or of being obsessed with tactics rather than having a longer-term vision, it is necessary to point out that there was, indeed, a strategy behind his diplomacy, and it was the one inherited from Bevin: he wished to maintain as much of Britain's place in the world as could be managed. He was not so much anti-American as pro-British, and when the interests of the two countries clashed, he put his own country first – a policy which perhaps only seems odd in the light of that of his successor. Where co-operation with America was to be had, he was happy to go along with America, as he was to do in 1955 and 1956 with plan 'Alpha', which was designed to reduce the friction between the Arab world and Israel. But where it was not possible, or not forthcoming, as with his attempt to re-establish Britain's position in the Middle East on the basis of the Baghdad pact,* then he felt free to pursue Britain's interests by his own means. He

* See page 302.

may have been vain – but few enter politics out of an overwhelming sense of personal humility – but his policy was not based upon that characteristic. If he came to distrust and even dislike John Foster Dulles, that was not the reason for his policy towards America; the distrust came out of long experience of dealing with the Americans in parts of the world where Britain's interests were more vitally concerned than were America's.

Eisenhower once described Churchill as 'completely Victorian' in his 'attitude towards "independent peoples"', but the same could not be said of Eden.[56] On the other hand, he did not share Eisenhower's belief that 'colonialism should be militantly condemned by the colonial powers, especially Britain and France'.[57] It was not simply that this was hardly practical politics – although the bitterness with which he was assailed by the 'Suez group' for appeasing the Egyptians suggests that it was not – it was not in Britain's interests to dismantle the Empire; nor was it in the interests of the western alliance, as the Americans were to discover too late and at great cost to themselves. Often identified as something of a liberal because of his early association with the League of Nations, Eden was certainly a believer in international co-operation, but again not at the expense of Britain's interests. He did not doubt the necessity of making concessions to nationalism in places like India and Egypt, but he believed in trying to do so in ways which allowed the maintenance of British influence. The Persian Gulf and Saudi Arabia were economically vital to the continued prosperity of the western world. History had handily placed the British in a position to protect the region, and if that involved backing regimes which did not come up to the standard required by the United Nations whenever countries which were not behind the Iron Curtain were discussed, well that was too bad; as the Americans were already discovering in Guatemala, protecting your own interests was not always compatible with democracy. The Soviets, like the British, had long been aware of this simple fact; it took the Americans a long series of expensive lessons to become aware of it. Eden did not share the 'Victorian' distaste felt by Captain Waterhouse and Julian Amery for concessions made to the Egyptians, and ironically he found himself placed by them in the role his old mentor Baldwin had been placed in by Churchill – that of 'appeaser'. But Eden was a realist. He did not really need Selwyn Lloyd to tell him that, 'if we are to maintain our position of leadership, we must produce a little more money';[58] his own diplomacy in Egypt and elsewhere was influenced by Britain's financial weakness. But there were also strengths to Britain's diplomatic position, something which had tended to be ignored by the 'declinologists' in their haste to chronicle her decline from power. Some of those strengths had been demonstrated in Eden's diplomacy at Geneva. Britain still possessed 'influence', a quality more easily defined in its absence than when it is present, but at Geneva, and in the long negotiations to repair the damage done by the failure of the EDC, as well as in the creation of the Baghdad pact, it can be seen at work. There perhaps even existed, as Churchill had tried to prove in 1953 and again in 1954, the possibility of Britain playing a role in ameliorating the asperities of the Cold War.

The temptation of this role still, in fact, had one small act to play in the seemingly endless saga of the succession to the Premiership. When he heard in early March 1955 that Eisenhower might be coming over to Europe to 'lay plans for a meeting with the Soviets', Churchill told Eden that this must 'be regarded as creating a new situation which will affect our personal plans and time-tables'.[59] As the Prime Minister had only recently let Eden into the secret that he was intending to retire in April,[60] the latter was less than pleased. He told Churchill frostily that, 'I was not aware that anything I had done in my public life would justify the suggestion that I was putting party before country or self before either'; Churchill denied that he had made any such imputation, but continued to hold out for a later retirement date.[61] Sadly, as the date for his retirement approached, Churchill began to regret his decision and to go back on it. As his Private Secretary put it, Churchill began 'to form a cold hatred of Eden', whom he said had 'done more to thwart him and prevent him pursuing the policy he thought right than anyone'. He saw no reason to go: 'he was only doing it for Anthony'.[62] It was a melancholy spectacle, but it was part of the same characteristics which had made him such a great man: he never gave in, he never knew when he had had enough. Allied to the right circumstances this stubborn egocentricity became resolution of purpose and heroism of a high order; in the wrong circumstances they shrank back to their less commendable basic elements. Failure had not broken him, but nor had success mellowed him very much. It was plain to his intimates, and to many who were not, that however glorious his past, he was adding nothing to his laurels by staying on; but he could not go gracefully – indeed, he could hardly be prevailed upon to go at all. Only at the end of March, when it was clear that there would be no summit before the period in which a general election would have to take place in Britain, did the grand old barnacle release his hold. On the morning of 6 April 1955 Sir Anthony Eden finally ascended to the position which had awaited him for a decade. There were those who wondered about his capacity to deal with the domestic front, but when it came to foreign affairs the country could hardly be in safer hands. Had anyone predicted that within two years Eden would be gone, brought down tragically by a crisis in Egypt, he would hardly have been believed. That this was to be so owed much to the fact that Eden believed that co-operation with America involved the Americans taking account of Britain's legitimate interests when they were threatened.

25

Tensions and Disagreements

From the moment the guns stopped firing at Suez, the historians opened their barrage, and there have been few without a vested interest who have defended Eden's actions during the Suez crisis; defeat, as ever, remains an orphan. But it was the crucial point in defining the real nature of the Anglo-American connection. Before Suez there seemed to be a relationship and, Eden assumed, the give and take which characterises any alliance. Just as the Americans expected the British to back them in Korea and Guatemala, even though their own interests were hardly vitally concerned, so the British expected the Americans to support them when the 'chips were down'. Had the Americans done so, the subsequent history of the Middle East might have been very different; but they did not do so. Eden had known since 1954 that the Americans were wary of being identified with British and French 'colonialism', but it was only in 1956 that he realised quite how far they were willing to go in this direction. He acted on the assumption that the alliance founded by Churchill operated in both directions; he discovered that this was a mistake: it operated in the direction the Americans wanted.

This American attitude had already created tensions in the last year of Eden's period as Foreign Secretary, and it continued to do so after he became Prime Minister. In his first letter as Prime Minister to Eisenhower, Eden invoked the 'memory of all the work done together with you in utter confidence and trust', which was 'always an inspiration to my great predecessor', and he looked forward to 'the closest co-operation with you and your administration at all times';[1] there was a certain irony in this in view of the differences between the two partners in Europe, Asia and the Middle East. But why did the breakdown in Anglo-American relations come over a crisis in the Middle East and not in the other two areas?

On both Europe and the Empire Eden was less than satisfactory from the American point of view. They had, as it were, tolerated Churchill's 'Victorian' attitudes on both subjects almost as a mark of respect for the old boy; moreover, like everyone else, they had hardly expected him to last quite as long as he did. But under the younger Eden they expected something a little more progressive. What they got instead was the man of Geneva – that is a diplomat who, whilst wishing to preserve the solidarity of the western alliance, had his own ideas about what Britain's place within it should be.

Eden was not, as some of his detractors have alleged, anti-European; no one who laboured as hard as he did to rescue something from the ruins of the EDC deserved such a label. Even before the French Assembly rejected the EDC in September 1954, and at a time when the Americans did not want to treat the scheme as 'finally dead',[2] Eden had already come up with a viable alternative.[3] The prospect of the EDC meeting such a fate had been discussed during the Washington visit in June, and the suggestions which Eden had fed into the discussion then now moved centre-stage. The essential thing was German rearmament, and if it could not be achieved through the EDC, then the best alternative was for West Germany to become a sovereign state and adhere to the 1948 Brussels pact with Britain, France, Holland and Belgium, before entering NATO – with suitable safeguards to reassure the French, to whom the very notion of German rearmament was, understandably enough, anathema. But before this could be achieved, someone would have to win French acceptance and soothe the anxieties which a juxtaposition of the words 'Germany' and 'rearmament' tended to induce in western Europe. Speed was essential, if only to take advantage of the confusion left by the demise of the EDC. Between 11 and 17 September Eden visited every major western European capital and convened a conference in London on 28 September. Agreement in principle was reached, and the detailed agreements were signed in Paris in October. As a feat of diplomacy it was a considerable achievement.[4] As Paul-Henri Spaak, the Belgian Foreign Minister, put it, 'Eden saved the Atlantic alliance.'[5]

This, however, was not quite in the way that Dulles had wanted. He was disappointed at the absence of any supranational element in the plans which might give a further impetus to European union, progress towards which had been, from the American point of view, disappointingly slow.[6] But Eden had been at great pains to manoeuvre so that although the British did finally give the commitment to maintaining troops on the continent which the French had long demanded, she did so in a way which avoided encouraging the European federalists. As his success came only months before the Messina meeting at which the federalist phoenix rose once more, it was to win him, in retrospect, only criticism for somehow failing to grab yet another opportunity. But Eden's priorities remained those propounded by Churchill in November 1951: 'the unity and the consolidation of the British Commonwealth and what is left of the former British Empire' and the '"fraternal association" of the English-speaking world'; a 'United Europe' came third.[7] Like Churchill, Eden did not want to join with the rest of America's 'pensioners' in an American-sponsored federation.[8] Britain was prepared to encourage the 'integration movement', although mindful of the possibility that if 'Germany emerges as the predominant economic partner', there would be disadvantageous consequences for Britain; what she was not prepared to do was to risk compromising her position as a 'world power' with independence vis-à-vis America by joining a United States of Europe.[9] Half of Britain's trade was with the sterling area, only a quarter of it was with western Europe, and although this pattern of trade was slowly changing, economically there was little point in joining a federalist project.[10] Eden and the Government wanted to 'cultivate the Atlantic Community'.[11] Britain was prepared to co-operate in inter-governmental organisations to promote European co-operation, such as the Organisation of European Economic Co-operation (OEEC) and the EDC, but federalism was not on the agenda, and if that upset the Americans then, as far as Eden was concerned, that was just too bad.[12]

Much of the writing on the subject of 'Europe' takes the form of laments for 'lost opportunities';[13] like the 'special relationship', it is one of those subjects upon which there exists a consensus so universal as to create the impression of immutable Truth. Ironically, because Eden refused to go along with American desires on the issue of the common market, he can be attacked for being at once short-sighted on 'Europe' and as failing to sponsor an issue which would have helped the 'special relationship'. Dulles and Eisenhower wanted a 'unification' of Europe because it would thereby 'achieve a strength to balance the Soviet part of Europe'.[14] A 'United States of Europe' would allow German energies to be channelled in a constructive direction, which, in turn, would pave the way for America to reduce her military commitment on the Continent.[15] From this point of view the lack of interest in the federal enterprise shown by the new Eden Government was disappointing.

Eden was quite happy with the existing collaboration provided by the OEEC.[16] Britain was invited to associate herself with the Messina proposals, but fears about the protectionist nature of the common market prescribed caution in that sphere, whilst the notion of becoming involved in an atomic energy authority had few attractions since the Six 'had much to gain and little to give'.[17] Eden stuck to his long-held view on 'Europe'.[18] Nor, despite the later myth-making of those who were to lament 'lost opportunities', were so-called 'Europeans' like Harold Macmillan prepared to go further than Eden. As the latter had acknowledged in February 1952, 'It was, of course, clear from the start that our membership of the Commonwealth and our special relationship with the United States would preclude us from joining a European *Federation*'; but what he and other enthusiasts for other visions of Europe never explained was how their views on 'confederation' would have been any more acceptable to Monnet and the federalists than were Eden's.[19]

'European unity' remained a 'basic objective of US policy', despite the collapse of the EDC, and despite fears that the Coal and Steel Community might become a 'cartel', and from this point of view the British attitude was a nuisance.[20] Dulles told Macmillan in December 1955 that America had decided to give her full support to the 'closer unity' approach favoured by the 'Six', and encouraged Britain to join in. 'I cannot but feel', he told Macmillan, 'that the resultant increased unity would bring in its wake greater responsibility and devotion to the Common welfare of Western Europe.'[21] It was another sign of how badly the British were now misjudging their status in the eyes of Washington that they should have imagined that staying out of the 'Six' would enable them to keep their 'special relationship' with America. As Dulles told the West German Foreign Minister, Heinrich von Brentano, in September 1955, America 'took a deep interest in this topic of integration in Europe. He thought there was perhaps no aspect of foreign policy which had more unanimous support in this country.'[22] Both Dulles and Eisenhower warned the British, in the gentlest possible way, of course, not to obstruct the movement towards unity.[23] Thus, British attempts to block the 'closer unity' option was frustrated and the movement towards unity on the model favoured by America was stimulated. But whatever the differences between Britain and America on the subject of European integration, security matters in the region bulked too large for any real schism to occur in that region. However, with Eden victorious at the election in 1955, it appeared that America's hopes for British participation in 'Europe' would be in vain.

If Eden was not likely to be 'misled by the kind of mysticism which appeals to European catholic federalists', then the same was not true of his Foreign Secretary, Harold Macmillan.[24] If one of Eden's biggest mistakes on becoming Prime Minister was not to have a major clear-out from the Churchill era, then the appointment which most prevented him from establishing his hold on the Government was Macmillan's. He had wanted to appoint his old friend, Salisbury, who, whilst far from being a malleable figure, was someone with whom he could have discussed matters freely; he would also have given disinterested advice and would not have been afraid to tell Eden when he was wrong. But Eden let the consideration that Salisbury was a member of the House of Lords dissuade him – perhaps the fact that his own replacement in 1938, Lord Halifax, had been a peer influenced him – but for whatever reason, the appointment was a mistake from his own point of view.[25] Ironically enough Macmillan was to make the fourteenth Earl of Home Foreign Secretary in 1959, and he gaily scouted the furore which greeted the move; one followed, incidentally, by Edward Heath in 1970, also with Home, and Mrs Thatcher in 1979 with Lord Carrington.

Now fifty-nine, Macmillan had been languishing on the backbenches when Eden had been the golden boy of the Tory Party in the 1930s. When Eden had been Churchill's right-hand man, Macmillan had held a series of undistinguished posts; it was not until he was sent to North Africa as Minister Resident in late 1942 that the shy, retiring and bookish figure known to Westminster in the 1930s began the transformation into the ruthless political operator familiar in the 1950s.[26] Designated to the lowly post of Minister of Housing and Local Government by Churchill in 1951, Macmillan had tried to make his voice heard on topics like Europe, where it was not welcomed by Eden. It was thought significant by some that his son-in-law, Julian Amery, was one of the leaders of the 'Suez group', and Churchill himself had warned Eden in 1954 that Macmillan was 'ambitious'.[27] So he was; promotion to Minister of Defence in 1955, with Churchill breathing down his neck, was not quite what he wanted. In the normal course of events, if Eden's Premiership lasted until the next election, Macmillan's chances of getting the top job would vanish. He was only two years younger than Eden, whilst the even younger Rab Butler, who had already served as Chancellor, would have been the obvious successor. Macmillan had long experience of dealing with the Americans and he and Eisenhower were on familiar terms, as Macmillan had been responsible for getting the future President out of a good deal of hot water during the war when he had served as his political adviser. Macmillan's views on the American alliance were closer to Churchill's than they were to Eden's. In some ways, however, his wartime experience was not necessarily an advantage. He easily fell into his old role vis-à-vis Eisenhower and the Americans, assuming that they were the 'Romans' who needed cunning 'Greeks' like himself to guide their apprentice footsteps in the great world of international diplomacy; but Eisenhower, like the country he led, had grown out of the habit of looking to the British for tutelage.

The result of placing a strong and ambitious figure at the Foreign Office was not successful, and Eden proved temperamentally incapable of leaving Macmillan to run his own show.[28] 'Europe' apart, there were two other areas where Macmillan found himself at odds with the Americans and carefully watched by Eden: the Far East and the Middle East.

Amongst the oddest of the manifestations of America's visceral anti-communism was the need to pretend that Chiang Kai-shek was President of China, and that Formosa and other offshore islands which he controlled, like Quemoy, were the whole of China. This American obligation to defend 'China' threatened a rupture in Anglo-American relations in late 1954 and early 1955, when the rulers of the real China began to bombard some of the islands of America's imaginary China. Eisenhower wanted to try to use the failure of the EDC to emphasise the importance of close Anglo-American relations, with a view of getting Churchill to withdraw recognition from Mao's China and come into line with America and take common action[29] – if necessary including the use of atomic weapons.[30] Talk along these lines naturally alarmed Eden thoroughly.[31]

In January 1955 the Americans suggested that they were prepared to give a provisional guarantee to Quemoy and wanted to raise the matter at the UN; once again the British were expected to give their support.[32] Eden took the view that this was another example of Dulles's penchant for 'tough guy' tactics. His advisers thought that Quemoy was far from vital to the security of Formosa, and his own view was that the Americans were, as so often in the Far East, running the risk of igniting a wider conflict for ill-thought-out ends. He tried hard to persuade the Americans against giving any guarantee to Quemoy,[33] and endeavoured to use Britain's contacts with Russia and China to bring the matter to a peaceful resolution at the UN.[34] But there really were times when being allied to the Americans was like being the registered keeper of a lunatic – especially given Churchill's susceptibility to their blandishments.

Eisenhower told Churchill on 10 February that America had to back Chiang, who they believed would one day 'go back to the mainland'. This involved protecting him from the communists – by the tactical use of nuclear weapons if necessary, although the President did not think it would be necessary because he did not think the Russians wanted a war.[35] Eden feared that it might become necessary to reveal publicly his disagreements with the Americans, if that was the only way of restraining them,[36] but Eisenhower's reference to a Far Eastern 'Munich'[37] evidently had its effect on Churchill, who tried to persuade Eden that there was something to be said for the American point of view. Eden, however, with the Premiership in his sights, held firm; indeed, he was even, at one point in March, prepared to have talks with Chou En-lai in an effort to defuse the situation. For his part, Eisenhower did his best to use Churchill to bring British policy into line with American wishes, but without success.[38] Here again, Eden was prepared to hold out and to take an independent line, as he had done ever since 1954. Had the Americans pushed much further on the offshore islands issue, a breach might well have come in Anglo-American relations – but it would not have been over an issue where vital British interests were concerned.

The Middle East was different. Here the British felt very strongly that absolutely vital interests were at stake. As Eden put it to the Cabinet in October 1955,

Our interests in the Middle East were greater than those of the United States because of our dependence upon Middle East oil, and our experience of the area was greater than theirs. We should not therefore allow ourselves to be restricted overmuch by reluctance to act without full American concurrence and support. We should frame our own policy in the light of our interest in the area and get the Americans to support it to the extent we could induce them to do so.[39]

Here, then, there was real potential for a schism. British policy had two main aims. One was to construct a viable basis for exercising continuing influence in the region following the withdrawal from Egypt, and the chosen basis for this was what became known as the Baghdad pact: that is a series of security pacts linking Britain's allies in the northern tier – Turkey, Pakistan and perhaps even Iran – with her Arab friends, particularly Iraq and perhaps even Jordan. The second aim was to reduce tension and perhaps even broker an Arab-Israeli settlement. Only on this last point was there harmony with America.

American policy in the region followed three lines after 1954: a political line, in which priority was given to the settlement of the Arab-Israeli problem; an economic line, in which, in addition to an annual programme of $75 million to the area, money was to be made available, on the right conditions, for major projects such as the Aswan High Dam; finally, there was a military line, which was embodied in the support given to collective security among the northern tier states.[40] Worried as Eden had been since Geneva about American 'identification with countries pursing colonial policies not compatible with our own',[41] at least two of these lines of policy involved substituting American influence for British in the region. On the first line of policy, that of trying to resolve the Arab-Israeli dispute, Anglo-American policy converged, and there was a joint initiative, plan 'Alpha', designed to relieve tension by Israel making territorial concessions to Egypt and Jordan in return for concessions for the Arabs.[42]

The British supported the initiative for two reasons: in the first place, with an American administration finally prepared to put some pressure on Israel, there existed an opportunity to undo at least some of the damage done by the creation of the State of Israel;[43] in the second place Eden's hopes of expanding the Baghdad pact into a regional defence alliance depended upon *détente* between the Arabs and the Israelis. The problem, however, as the British discovered, was that the two aims were not wholly compatible. The Americans were happy to work for an Arab-Israeli settlement, but disliked the Baghdad pact, which Dulles saw as an 'instrument of Arab intrigue' rather than the 'instrument for collective defense against the Soviet Union', which his own actions had been designed to achieve.[44] The pact was certainly an instrument of Iraqi intrigue, but the mistake which Dulles made was in not realising that, as far as the Middle East was concerned, everyone was intriguing; to adapt an inelegant American phrase, if Nuri and the Iraqis were 'sons of bitches', they were at least western ones. Dulles's belief that Nasser could be used to support western interests vis-à-vis the Soviets should have been thoroughly shaken by Egypt's hostile response to the Iraqi-American arms deal in April 1954, but American illusions lingered long in the Nile delta. Nuri's initiative in August 1954 in proposing a security pact offered the British two things: a way out of what threatened to be an impasse over the negotiation of a new treaty with Iraq, and a way of asserting her own interests. As Eden told the Cabinet on 6 May 1954, there was a risk that otherwise the Iraqis might believe that America had been left to 'make the running of that part of the world'.[45]

The Americans saw the Middle East through their usual Cold War lenses, and as ever, when that focus proved inadequate, their policy was somewhat myopic. Dulles's pacts with Iraq, Pakistan and Turkey served as a barrier against the Soviets, but Nuri's main concern was not the Soviets. He wanted to challenge the position Nasser was seeking to build up for himself in the Arab world – and Dulles's lack of interest in linking the northern tier arrangements with the Arab League failed to give Nuri any help in his enterprise; British adherence to the pact, which he signed with Turkey in January 1955, did give him this assistance. America, far from condemning the pact (as Dulles did privately), gave the impression that they had no objections to it – which led the British on a wild-goose chase for the next few months as they sought to secure American adhesion to it.[46] But if the Americans seemed to have no problems with it, the same was not true of Nasser, as Eden found at his one and only meeting with the Egyptian leader in February 1954.

When Eden arrived in Cairo on 20 February, Britain had not yet signed the pact, and one of his objectives was to persuade Nasser that the Egyptians should adhere to it. The meeting was not a success at any level. Eden's wife Clarissa found Nasser's informality unmannerly and insulting, whilst her husband objected to the way Nasser grabbed his hand when a photographer appeared.[47] Eden's attempt to break the ice by speaking in classical Arabic and discoursing on Islamic civilisation, subjects in which he had some expertise and long experience, seems to have backfired, with the Egyptians feeling that he had set out to make them feel their inferiority; he had done nothing of the sort, but it was the impression which he made on the Egyptians which counted, unfortunately.[48] On the political level Nasser was adamant in his refusal to have anything to do with the Turkish-Iraqi pact. Eden was correct to predict that he would denounce it when news of Britain's adherence got out.[49] Indeed, Nasser went further than this, telling the American Ambassador in March 1955 that, because he feared that Nuri was out to isolate him, he would endeavour to construct an Arab pact against the Iraqis.[50] By refusing to join the pact themselves because it would have identified them with British policy and 'colonialism', the Americans paved the way for the defeat of that policy. At another level, the Americans did not want to upset Nasser at a time when they were proceeding with 'Alpha', but they failed to win him over by offering the arms he wanted. The Americans were also anxious not to upset the Israelis. But their policy brought no one save Nasser any gains. By not adhering to the pact the Americans handed him a cheap propaganda victory, but they failed to get any rewards. It might have been, as much of the current wisdom had it, that the future lay with Nasser's brand of pan-Arabism, but by displaying weakness and leaving the alternative to it, Nuri, isolated, the Americans did their best to ensure that it became a self-fulfilling prophecy. What they failed to see was that whatever else he may have represented, Nasser stood for something profoundly antipathetic to western interests; it is seldom a good idea to sacrifice your friends to your enemies – as the West was to discover once Nuri, and the Hashemite kingdom he had served so long, were no more.

If Anglo-American interests were seriously diverging over the best way to defend the Middle East, it was not surprising as they were, in fact, doing two different things. The Americans were seeking to guard against Soviet penetration – even if their refusal to supply Nasser with arms except on their own terms was to invite it – whilst the British were trying to implement the policy decided on back in 1953. Given that Britain could no longer rely upon Egypt, and given that she could no longer afford the cost of defending the region, she hoped that pacts like the one signed in Baghdad in April 1955 would spread the burden. In Europe, the Far East and the Middle East the theme of British policy was the same when it came to defence: 'unity by consent'.[51] However, the problem in the Middle East was, and remained, Israel. As long as the Arab states did not recognise Israel, and as long as Britain was identified with America and her backing for Israel, then it was always possible for Nasser to play the 'Arab card' against any security arrangements for the region which involved Britain. As Shuckburgh put it in December 1954, 'the state of tension with Israel and the sufferings of the refugees keep anti-Western feeling continuously aflame'.[52] A necessary pre-condition of any relaxation of this tension was a settlement of the Arab-Israeli dispute.

After a six-week tour of the Middle East in late 1954, Shuckburgh (now head of the Middle East Department) felt that Britain could play a leading role in reaching such a settlement. He found that there were 'certain general expectations from British diplomatic skill', and that Eden's successes in Geneva and in negotiating a treaty with Egypt had inspired hopes in 'many people on both sides' that it was his 'purpose and within his power to bring about a solution which will satisfy them'.[53] It is partly from this background that the Anglo-American plan 'Alpha' evolved in late 1954. Much, however, would depend upon Washington's willingness to put pressure on the Jews to make concessions.

Dulles and the Americans responded well, at first, to the British initiative, but as the Secretary of State explained to Makins on 29 January 1955, 'the Truman Administration had gone far in the direction of favouring the Israelis. The present Administration had changed this and had favoured the Arabs. But the Israeli position had been deflated as far as it could in terms of American opinion and politics.' It was, he warned, 'inevitable, particularly as the Presidential election approached, that rather more weight should be given to the Israeli case'.[54] The actual text of the Anglo-American proposals is still withheld from public scrutiny by the benevolent hand of bureaucracy. Shuckburgh's initial optimism did not survive a week in Washington.[55] By 3 February he felt 'no great optimism as to chance of success';[56] he was right. The Americans refused to bring the French or anyone else in on the talks,[57] and insisted that they remain an Anglo-American initiative.

But the British had misjudged the effect which Nuri's actions and the Baghdad pact would have on the Egyptians.[58] Nasser proved, as we have seen, quite impervious to Eden's persuasions in late February, and the Egyptians spread the story in Jordan that the pact was designed to divide that country between Israel and Iraq, whilst the Saudis, according to the Jordanian Ambassador, were doing their bit to scupper the chances of Jordan joining the pact by bribing everyone from the Queen of Jordan downwards.[59] These were unpromising waters into which to launch the product of extensive Anglo-American discussions – plan 'Alpha' – and they were soon to become even rougher. The plan provided for Arab recognition of Israel's borders in return for Israeli territorial concessions which would allow for land communication between Egypt and Jordan – with America, Britain and France guaranteeing the treaty; it was, in effect, a Middle Eastern 'Locarno'.[60] But by the time the scheme was ready, in early March, massive Israeli retaliation for minor Arab attacks in the Gaza Strip had effectively soured any slim chances the plan might have had.[61]

The British realised that the renewed Arab-Israeli conflict meant a postponement of their initiative,[62] but they went ahead with their plans to adhere to the Baghdad pact. Then they learned in late March that the Americans were discouraging Jordan from joining the pact because that would 'have unfavourable repercussions in Egypt and influence Nasser against cooperation with us over Alpha'; Eden's marginal comment, 'Amazing!', summed up the British reaction to American policy. If the pact was to become the base for a regional defence system, it needed Syrian, Lebanese and Jordanian accession, and of these countries Jordan, with its strong links with Britain (symbolised by the presence of Sir John Glubb as commander of Jordanian forces), was by far the easiest from the British point of view. The British feared that if it became known that Jordan was being discouraged by the Americans, that would not only scupper the chance of Syria and Lebanon joining, but it would also do damage inside Iraq and Turkey, where it would be represented as a triumph for Nasser. Far from sharing the American belief that it would help 'Alpha', the British feared that the American action might well kill it.[63]

If America's policy was blocking the achievement of one of Britain's objectives, it also seemed to be bent on getting all the credit for pursuit of the other – the Arab-Israeli settlement. In early April the Americans put 'Alpha' to the Egyptians, thus seizing the initiative from the British.[64] The British notion of the way to get Nasser's agreement – by pressing Israel for greater territorial concessions – clearly did not appeal to the Americans.[65] With the American Presidential election in mind, Dulles preferred to make a public announcement of the principles upon which 'Alpha' was based rather than risk the wrath of the Jewish lobby by seeming to put pressure on the Israelis.[66] The British fought a long rearguard action to avoid having any public statement, but the Americans persevered – insisting that when it came in July, it should be a purely American one.[67] This put the British in a difficult position. If they refused their assent, they risked losing what they still regarded as valuable co-operation with America; but if they allowed Dulles to go ahead, all manner of evils might follow: the Arabs would regard it as another attempt to force them to come to terms with Israel, which might, in turn, 'throw away the progress we have made over the Northern Tier defence and even endanger our treaty with Iraq', as well as undermining Nuri's position by making it appear as though he was some sort of 'stooge'. It is testimony to how little the British understood the mainsprings of American policy that Macmillan should have thought that he could avert these dangers by persuading the Americans to supply arms to Iraq and to say that they would join the pact if 'Alpha' was successful. He even thought that 'since we are in effect being exposed to possible embarrassments and dangers in the Middle East on account of American internal politics . . . we should ask the Americans to consider what physical support they would be ready to give us' if Britain found herself involved in hostilities through her defence pacts with Jordan and with Iraq.[68] As evidence that the British still believed that alliances worked by reciprocity, this could not be beaten.

The first meetings which Eden had as Prime Minister with Eisenhower in July revealed how far apart the two allies were. Telling the President that the 'British Government would always hope to be on the American side in every quarrel', Eden nevertheless made it clear that he did not support the hard line which America was taking in the Far East.[69]

When it came to the Middle East, the two sides were no closer together. Macmillan had put the British concerns to Dulles on 14 July and asked for American aid to Iraq, but without committing himself, the American had made it clear that he needed to make an announcement for 'political reasons'.[70] In order to bring the British along Dulles did commit himself to telling the Iraqis that, 'if the Palestine settlement could be achieved the United States would be prepared' to join the Baghdad pact;[71], although this appeared to give the British what they wanted, it was, in fact, window-dressing to keep them following America. The whole thrust of Dulles's policy since at least April was that America should take the initiative in the Middle East, and he had little, if any, intention of joining the Baghdad pact – whatever he said.[72]

Reassured by Dulles's comments, Macmillan told Eden on 16 July that the crucial question now was whether the Americans would help fund arms supplies to Iraq so that Nuri could get the 'reward for his courage in joining the Northern Tier defence'.[73] When Eden talked with the President at Geneva on 19 July, Eisenhower was reluctant to take on the 'full financial responsibility' for supplying Centurion tanks, but he did say that America might 'participate' if the British carried a 'satisfactory proportion' of the costs; privately, however, the President did not see why the Iraqis and the British could not pick up most of the tab.[74]

But no sooner did the British think that they had persuaded the Americans to postpone any statement until September than they found themselves once again left in the wake of a new initiative. On 19 August the Foreign Office discovered that Dulles intended to make his statement within the week. Eden thought the Americans were 'behaving disgracefully'. A public statement of the principles upon which 'Alpha' was based, without any equally public reward for Nuri, would weaken his position; but the most Eden could do was to be 'prepared to have a row with the Americans'.[75] American policy was now being driven by the desire to keep the initiative, and British interests had little place. Dulles was concerned by evidence that the Arabs would only negotiate collectively with Israel and that Nasser was looking to the Soviets for the arms supplies which the Americans would not give him without attaching conditions.[76] Thus, his announcement on 26 August that America was prepared, in effect, to mediate in the Arab-Israeli quarrel was a sign that, whatever the Soviets offered in terms of arms, only the Americans were prepared to take the trouble to broker and finance a peace settlement. All the British could do was to rather feebly issue their own statement in support of the Americans. There was little enthusiastic response, and Eden took a little satisfaction, noting that, 'Mr Dulles started all of this and, if he has gotten himself into trouble, it is not for us to help him out.'[77]

'Alpha' had little further to go, with an increase in tension between Israel and Egypt making its prospects dimmer than ever towards the end of the year. Far from the Baghdad pact and 'Alpha' working in tandem, and Britain and America doing the same, the one had worked against the other. The Americans had no time for 'Arab intrigues' and were quite prepared to leave the British floundering if it suited their purposes. Diplomacy in the Middle East had not brought the Prime Minister the rewards he had hoped.

This was all the more important to Eden because there were no bouquets coming his way from anywhere else. The summit conference at Geneva in July had not produced an opening for a thaw in the Cold War, and in contrast with the previous year, Eden returned with no laurels. In September long-standing disputes between the Greek and Turkish communities on Cyprus erupted into something very akin to civil war, whilst at home the tax cuts made in the spring budget had to be clawed back in an autumn one. To make matters worse, the rumours already current in parts of Whitehall about the Prime Minister's capacity began to gain wider circulation.[78] Eden's habit of telephoning Ministers to check on their progress did not give the impression of a Prime Minister who was on top of his job, and inevitably this filtered out – not least perhaps because the Minister who suffered most was Harold Macmillan at the Foreign Office. In view of Eden's resentment at Churchill's interference, it was ironic that his own successor should have been declaring by late August that, 'I might as well give up and let him run the shop.'[79] But Macmillan was no political *ingénue* to be pushed around at a Prime Minister's whim, and there was a steady market for anti-Eden gossip in the form of Churchill's son, Randolph, and the newspapers owned by the Berry family.

Lady Pamela Berry, the daughter of the great Lord Birkenhead, had her father's capacity for forming settled views on matters – and one of these was Eden's lack of fitness for the Premiership. As far back as December 1953 she had announced at a lunch party that Eden's health was so bad that he could never become Prime Minister. Duff Cooper (by now Lord Norwich), who was a good friend of Clarissa Eden's, warned her, in what proved to be one of his last letters, that Lady Pamela was no 'friend'.[80] Whilst it might be going too far to assert that the *Daily Telegraph*'s attacks on Eden owed their existence to the subsequent rift between Lady Pamela and Lady Eden, it certainly did not help matters when Eden's prestige began to slump in the autumn of 1955.[81] It was no doubt coincidence that Randolph Churchill, another vociferous and bitter critic of the Prime Minister, was a close acquaintance of both Lady Pamela and Macmillan himself. Coincidence or not, the attacks increased in intensity as the Prime Minister reshuffled his Cabinet on 20 December – when the main 'victim' was Macmillan, who was moved to the Exchequer. It was a sign either of Eden's weakness, or of Macmillan's strength, or of the strength of the latter's friends in the press, that this move was accompanied by a statement that the move did not mean any demotion for Macmillan.[82]

The relationship between Macmillan and Eden had not been a happy one. Macmillan regarded the Prime Minister as too 'nervy' and highly strung, and resented his interference, whilst Eden, with his vast experience of diplomacy, could not leave his Foreign Secretary alone to get on with the job.[83] That Macmillan's replacement should have been the less senior and infinitely more malleable Selwyn Lloyd was as clear a sign as anyone could want that Eden intended, in fact, to be his own Foreign Secretary. When the *Daily Telegraph* caustically remarked on 6 January 1956 that what the country needed was the 'smack of firm government', Eden reacted as if stung.[84] It was not surprising that a Prime Minister with Eden's background should have looked towards foreign affairs for something to bolster his position, but what 'Alpha' and the Baghdad pact had shown was that, at least in the Middle East, he could not afford to wait and rely on American help. It was a lesson which helped dictate how the beleaguered Prime Minister would act in the climacteric of his career.

26

'Misguided sentimental investments'

The fundamental premise upon which British foreign policy had been based since 1940 was the necessity of the Anglo-American alliance: Churchill had schemed for it, rejoiced in it, cultivated it and finally tried to reinvigorate it when, in 1945, its bonds had seemed to slacken. Its existence was the central pillar of the post-war consensus in foreign affairs, and Churchill had sought to renew it during his peacetime Premiership. Of all the assumptions underlying the alliance, none was more firmly fixed than that it could be used to underwrite Britain's position as a Great Power. What had dawned but slowly was that this assumption contained a number of what were, at best, half-truths. If, in the larger sphere encompassed by the Cold War, Anglo-American interests coincided, a core of common interest did not mean a core of common approach; the question of how far divergent approaches could be pursued before threatening the common core interest had been neither posed nor answered. Was Britain anything more than a satellite state of the United States of America? What had Britain's victory in 1945 signalled – the triumphant assertion of the independence of Britain and the survival of her Empire, or her subservience to the Americans? If asked, no doubt the vast majority of Britons would much have preferred to have been the forty-ninth state (as things stood before the entry of Hawaii and Alaska into the Union) than a German *gau* – even if that had not been the alternative which they had been confronted with – but the fact was that an even greater majority had assumed that there was no contradiction between independence and the American alliance; indeed, it was widely assumed that the former depended upon the latter.

Yet the post-war period had not quite worked out the way in which a victorious people had the right to expect. There had been peace, but it soon became overshadowed by the mushroom cloud. Leftist sensitive intellectuals (and others) feared lest a new and more terrible war might succeed in destroying civilisation itself; 'hot' war was so speedily overtaken by 'cold' war that it became easy to forget that there had been anything between them, as memoir-writers tried hard to show that they had anticipated the shadow that was to come. So ideologically charged did life become for some that even the simple task of writing history became rather an expression of ideological choice. Churchill's wartime 'Grand Alliance' had been succeeded by an even grander one, even if one of the original partners became the enemy. Britain was overshadowed. Austerity reigned under the Attlee Government, and it was claimed that the 'people' had opted for socialism, even though more votes were cast against Attlee than for him;[1] on such slender foundations are baroque historical legends constructed.

The loss of Palestine could have been borne easily enough were it not for the manner of its going. Indian independence was in like case, although there were more Britons with a stake in the Raj, and its ending in civil war and the loss of Indian unity made it a more emotional issue; and of course, once the King ceased to be an 'Emperor', the flashy 'Empire' dreamed up by Disraeli and Queen Victoria as a riposte to the King of Prussia becoming Emperor of Germany ceased to exist. This was hardly what those who had fought in the war had expected. This sense that the post-war world was in some way 'unfair' to Britain was most readily articulated on the imperial right-wing of the Conservative Party. The 'Anglo-Saxonism' which Churchill so personified had at its heart a racial assumption: the Anglo-Saxon races were superior to the 'lesser breeds without the Law', and it was their duty and destiny to rule. The legendary inarticulacy of the Conservative right prevents the sensibilities of a later age being assaulted by the ripeness of the vocabulary which was used to cover those of lesser racial stock engaged in twisting the tail of the imperial lion; but the violence of the feelings thus represented was all the more forceful for being inarticulate. Eden had become an object of hatred to the imperialist wing of the Conservative Party; the anti-appeaser had become the appeaser; the 'Anthony Eden' hat swapped for the wing-collar and umbrella of Mr Chamberlain. For a man who prided himself on the legend of his role in the 1930s retailed by Churchill in *The Gathering Storm*, this was a bitter fate; it was not to be expected that he would bear with it for long. Nasser's nationalisation of the Suez Canal in July 1956 provided him with a challenge which he could not side-step; it also provided the first occasion upon which the British asked the Americans to support them in an area where they felt their own interests were being challenged. The American response demonstrated clearly the exact nature of the Anglo-American relationship. If the defining characteristic of a slave is that he is not free to do what he will but must obey the command of another, then Macmillan's old analogy was correct – the British were indeed the 'Greeks in the new Roman Empire'; in the old Roman Empire, as now, the Greeks were slaves.

At the root of the American action was Dulles's comment in April 1956 that the British had 'made a number of mistakes in the area and we are most reluctant publicly to identify ourselves in the area with the U.K.'.[2] Although both the British and the Americans referred to 'western interests' in the Middle East, they meant different things by this. The British meant the whole delicate structure of 'Empire by treaty', which they were building up to replace their formal presence in the region; the Americans did not acknowledge this fact. For the Americans, the main 'western' interest was to prevent Soviet penetration of the region. Although this last point formed part of a joint Anglo-American 'position paper' drawn up at Geneva in November, the British were not to know just what meaning the Americans attached to it until it was too late. The paper was part of a reconsideration of policy towards Egypt in the light of the revelation in September that Nasser was prepared to accept arms from the Soviets. Both the British and the Americans decided to give diplomacy another chance.

American action in the Middle East was based upon the premise that 'colonialism was ended', and the belief that the British and French failed to appreciate this fact.[3] The existence of the British and the French Empires was an affront to what Eisenhower called 'the kind of world we are trying to establish'. In the effort to 'promote the rights of all, and observe the equality of sovereignty as between the great and small', it was, he thought, inevitable that 'we ... give to the little nations opportunities to embarrass us greatly'; but he believed that 'in the long run such faithfulness will produce real rewards'.[4] Impeccable though such sentiments are to the modern liberal, as a prescription for policy they were fatally flawed. In the first place no foreign policy could be carried out on such a woolly basis, and American foreign policy was no exception; but then as Eden had put it a decade earlier, 'American foreign policy is exaggeratedly moral, at least where American interests are not concerned'. Where they were vitally engaged, as in Iran or Guatemala, then 'little nations' were given no opportunity to 'embarrass' America; they had to do as they were told. This, of course, was observable by others and came to give American pronouncements that unmistakable air of hypocrisy. In the second place it was based upon a false assumption. The notion that 'such faithfulness will produce real rewards' was an act of faith unwarranted by observable facts, and it seems to have meant no more than the hope that if America supported colonial liberation movements, they would not then look to the Soviets for support; yet, as America was already discovering in Egypt, what was most likely to happen was that any intelligent leader would play the two blundering superpowers off against each other. In the third place it was the Americans, and not the British, who were being 'old-fashioned' about imperialism.

The British position in the Middle East did not rest, and had never rested, on formal imperialism. The occupation of Egypt in 1882 had been an aberration in British imperial policy, and the country had never been formally part of the Empire. The British position in the Middle East was imperialism by treaty, and Eden had been carrying through the policies he had inherited from the past. From the National Governments of the 1930s he had inherited a commitment to a variety of informal rather than formal imperialism, which Attlee and Bevin had also followed; the massive presence of Churchill obscures the essential continuity of British imperial policy between the 1930s and the

1950s. From Attlee and Bevin, Eden had inherited a massive commitment to colonial development and the nurturing of democratic structures in areas where these seemed possible. The old Empire was evolving into the modern Commonwealth. This is not to posit an uncomplicated process whereby a benign metropolitan authority conferred self-government on grateful natives out of a recognition that 'imperialism' was no longer acceptable. Reality was, as always, a great deal messier, but after the traumas of India and Palestine, the process of retreat from one form of Empire to another had been managed with some skill. In Malaysia the threat of communist insurgence had been contained, whilst in Egypt a satisfactory treaty had been negotiated. The British had avoided anything like the problems being faced by the French in Indo-China and Algeria, or by the Dutch in Indonesia.

The British did not ignore the forces of nationalism; indeed, their policy during the twentieth century had been one of ruling by reaching accommodation with such forces.[5] One of the dangers posed to the British Empire by the rise of American power and by the United Nations was that nationalist leaders were given leverage thereby in their struggle for self-rule. In the 1930s accommodation with nationalist leaders was easier because they often had no alternative other than to reach agreement with the British; now, with the Americans and the United Nations, they could see less reason to settle for anything less than their full demands. The attempts of the General Assembly of the United Nations to 'establish control and supervision over *all* dependent territories', and not just those governed under a UN mandate, had long been a cause of concern to British Governments.[6] America's desire to 'cast a succulent fly' over the uncommitted Arab–Asian bloc at the UN meant, as British officials gloomily recognised, that they could expect no help from their 'ally' on this score.[7] The British hoped that the Americans would realise that 'the grant of premature self-government to colonial peoples', and attempts to 'apply in practice such catchwords as "self-determination"', would merely increase the areas of political instability in the world',[8] but this failed to take into account the extraordinary thinking created by the combination of traditional American anti-colonialism with the new obsession with communism.

Eisenhower did indeed recognise that the British had a case, but it was not one he was prepared to do anything to advance. He saw that 'Nationalism is on the march' and feared that 'world communism is taking advantage of that spirit of nationalism to cause dissension in the free world'. In this situation 'the free world's hopes of defeating the communist aims does not include objecting to national aspirations. We must show the wickedness of purpose in the communist promises and convince dependent peoples that their only hope of maintaining independence, once attained, is through cooperation with the free world.'[9] He wanted the colonial Powers to 'militantly' condemn 'colonialism' and announce a twenty-five-year term to the continuation of colonial rule.[10] This, like his other pronouncements on the subject, demonstrated an alarming level of simplicity. It suggested that the President regarded French actions in Indo-China as the 'norm' and not as the exception to it. The notion that such an announcement would have done anything save encourage every demagogue to demand complete independence much sooner similarly suggests an understanding of the problems involved which was somewhat less than completely informed. Finally, of course, American objections to colonialism offered no solution to the problem of how to maintain 'western' interests in the Middle East, where the British were not actually directly ruling the important countries concerned. The British were not a 'colonial' Power in this region; they were attempting to maintain the political influence which was necessary to ensure the security of western oil supplies. American policy not only failed to recognise this fact, but by a combination of maladroit tactics and mistaken strategy, it contributed materially to a weakening of not just the British position, but also of western interests.

It was not that the Americans failed to see that important western interests were involved, but rather that their strategy for achieving this end was fatally flawed. The Americans thought that their studied neutrality over the Anglo-Egyptian treaty, combined with promises of aid, would be enough to win over Nasser and perhaps even bring an end to the Arab-Israeli conflict; this delusion that 'aid' could solve any problem would die hard – if indeed it died at all. They also thought that the best way to preserve western influence was to build up Saudi Arabia.[11] No doubt this was entirely unconnected with the fact that the Americans regarded the Saudis as their clients, but it did lead them to share the Saudi objection to the Baghdad pact as 'an instrument of the extension of British and Hashemite influence'. It was these differences of tactics and of strategy which lay behind the Suez fiasco.

Eden's one and only visit to Washington as Prime Minister in early 1956 failed to reconcile the perceptual differences over the Middle East, producing only the by now customary rhetoric which concealed more than it revealed. Eden warned the Americans that 'if Egypt should succeed in undermining the Baghdad Pact the Western Powers would be in terrific trouble in the Middle East', and the Americans, for their part, talked about the fact that their public opinion was 'not accustomed to looking upon the Middle East as a vital area' and recognised that 'security matters were usually a British responsibility'.[12] Eden told Dulles that although he had not completely lost confidence in being able to work with Nasser, it was 'difficult to evaluate . . . a man of limitless ambition', an assessment the Americans were prepared to accept. In just the same way, it appeared, they were prepared to offer 'moral support' for the Baghdad pact.[13] So, publicly, a united front was proclaimed, whilst privately Nasser was to be given more time to show whether he would co-operate.

But by March 1956 Eden was telling the Americans that 'the time has come for a reappraisal of the situation'. Comparing Nasser to Mussolini (and by implication the Soviets to Hitler), Eden thought that he was 'beholden to a ruthless power'. He was a threat to Israel and his propaganda attacked 'the Western position in all parts of the Middle East and Africa'. The Egyptian attitude 'towards our relations with Iraq, Jordan, Saudi Arabia, the Persian Gulf states and Libya suggests that they are determined to eliminate British and other Western influences from the whole area'. Eden had a very clear idea of how to combat this: 'increased support should be given to the Baghdad Pact and its members, notably Iraq', which should include America at least declaring her intention to join the pact. Moves should also be made to draw Iraq and Jordan together and to detach Saudi Arabia and Libya from Egypt's orbit.[14] Although the American documents, like their British counterparts, have been doctored to conceal what 'other policy' was under consideration, it is perhaps not unreasonable to assume that its spirit was captured in Eden's remark to Shuckburgh on 12 March: 'He was quite emphatic that Nasser must be got rid of. "It is either him or us, don't forget that."'[15] Nutting, then Minister of State at the Foreign Office, has gone so far as to say that Eden wanted Nasser 'murdered' – although it might be significant that he waited until both Eden and Lloyd were dead to make this claim.[16]

What had particularly aroused Eden's ire was the dismissal on 1 March of Sir John Glubb from his position in Jordan. Eden's immediate reaction had been to consider the 're-occupation of Suez to counteract the blow to our prestige which Glubb's dismissal means'.[17] Shuckburgh's inclination was to do quite the opposite – 'to get out of some of these untenable positions', in particular to withdraw from the pact, from the commitment to Jordan, and to declare a 'solution of the Palestine problem on the basis of giving the Negev back to Egypt'; he was, in fact, almost at the end of his tether. Ever since he had taken over the Middle Eastern Desk in July 1954, none of his initiatives had enjoyed any success, and now it seemed as though things were going from bad to worse.

Dulles and Eisenhower were reluctant to 'conclude that it is impossible to do business with Nasser' and even more so to actually join the Baghdad pact,[18] but Nasser's failure to follow up American initiatives for a peace with Israel, combined with his dealings with the Soviets, inclined Eisenhower towards a policy of isolating the Egyptians. In his view, if Egypt found herself 'with no ally in sight except Soviet Russia, she would very quickly get sick of that prospect and would join us in the search for a just and decent peace in that region'.[19] This was, in itself, a highly questionable judgment, but in the short-term it led to what looked like a closer alignment of British and American policies. On 28 March, five days after Eden's telegram arrived in Washington, Dulles submitted a memorandum suggesting an adjustment of American policy: 'The primary purpose would be to let Colonel Nasser realize that he cannot cooperate as he is doing with the Soviet Union and at the same time enjoy most-favoured-nation treatment from the United States.' However, although there would be a joint hardening of rhetoric which would mislead the British into thinking that a common approach implied a common objective, this was far from being the case.

If Eden's objective was to 'get' Nasser by means of strengthening the Baghdad pact, neither in his objective nor in his methods was Dulles at one with the British. The Americans wanted to 'avoid any open break which would throw Nasser irrevocably into a Soviet satellite status' – at 'least for the time being' – and Dulles also wanted to leave him with 'a bridge back to good relations with the West if he so desires'. Thus, where Eden thought about withholding 'all military supplies' and withdrawing 'our offer of support over the Aswan dam', Dulles thought of controlling export licences and of delaying 'the conclusion of current negotiations on the high Aswan Dam'.[20] When it came to the Baghdad pact, he told Eisenhower that America might 'give increased support . . . without actually adhering to the Pact or announcing our intention of doing so'. The package of measures against Nasser, Operation 'Omega', had as its centrepiece the building up of another 'prospective leader of the Arab world',[21] but instead of backing the obvious choice, Iraq, the Americans opted for their own client, Saudi Arabia. It was a sign of how little the Americans understood the Middle East that Eisenhower thought that King Saud could be 'built up, possibly, as a spiritual leader' – as though Nasser's secular nationalism, with its deep anti-western hue, could be challenged by Islam, and as though devout Muslims would have accepted Saud in such a role. This of course leaves out the question of whether backing Islamic fundamentalism would be a very clever move from the western point of view. For a Power with such an obsession about 'western interests' wherever the Soviets were concerned, the Americans had a very odd idea of what was in 'western interests' in the Middle East. Building up the Saudis, who were still in dispute with the British over Buraimi, and whom the British regarded as under Nasser's influence,[22] would hardly suggest to Nasser that his western opponents were united.

Because there were measures on which the British and Americans could agree, such as delaying the negotiations on the loan for the Aswan High Dam, and because the British never had spotted the basic duplicity in American policy, they continued to live in the fairy-tale land of the 'special relationship'. But then British policy towards the Middle East was hardly being conducted with any degree of calm foresight. Shuckburgh, who had ideas about what should be done, was too tired and depressed to push them, and before the summer was out he would be moved to 'lighter duties'.[23] Anthony Nutting, the Minister of State with oversight of the problem, was entering the throes of a stressful, unpleasant, and distracting divorce.[24] The new Foreign Secretary, Selwyn Lloyd, was regarded as 'a cypher',[25] who, when he was not acting as Eden's voice, was overly secretive and seldom sought advice.[26] There was, of course, nothing intrinsically wrong in having a 'cypher' for a Foreign Secretary, and being the Prime Minister's 'voice' was no bad thing – if the Prime Minister was saying sensible things – but at a time when there was a real need for Prime Ministerial grip, Eden's seemed to be slipping. At lunch at Chequers on 3 March Eden talked 'loud and excitedly' with 'many histrionic remarks', comparing Nasser to Mussolini and speaking 'darkly . . . of having a good mind to revise the evacuation of Suez'.[27] He wanted to 'destroy' Nasser,[28] and his judgment seemed less sound than it had been. The result was described thus by Shuckburgh:

> We have now got to a state where each telegram that comes in causes Ministers to meet, telephone one another, draft replies and curse everybody. Not only does each one of our telegrams contradict the one before, but each paragraph in each telegram contradicts the paragraph before.[29]

Even making allowances for the depression which was beginning to overwhelm the diarist, this was hardly the context out of which to expect a foreign policy which would realise what America was up to – especially when even the most sympathetic commentator admits that Dulles 'seemed to be speaking at two levels';[30] for Eden it was rather simpler: 'the man was bitterly anti-British'.[31]

Retrospection made Dulles seem the villain of the piece for Eden and Salisbury, but in truth Eisenhower was quite as much to blame – indeed, more so if one takes the now fashionable view that he was firmly in control of American policy.[32] What both men were was anti-colonialist – a viewpoint shared by most historians and, therefore, not usually the subject of much comment. But there were some contemporary Americans who saw how short-sighted such views were, and in May 1956 Eisenhower was exposed to a powerful critique of the motive force of the policy he and Dulles were following. Eisenhower's friend, Jerry Bermingham, passed him a letter from an acquaintance which lamented the 'Roosevelt days when, through misguided conceptions of so-called "traditional anti-colonialism", the U.S., with short-sighted and unjustified precipitation, deprived its major allies of their colonial possessions'. America had then, 'almost hysterically, supported the claims of colonial nations in the name of "self-determination"', but 'what did our country gain', Eisenhower was asked (in a manner which would have won him the disapproval of those historians who contend that America did no such thing),[33] 'from having thrown the Dutch out of Indonesia? The British out of India, Suez and Ceylon?' Had 'Mr Nehru or Colonel Nasser ever demonstrated to us their gratitude for the support we gave them?'[34] It was not as if the 'colonial empires could have been expected to last forever', but he did think that,

> in the midst of a cold war with Russia, we should have, if anything, temporarily put

the brakes on the colonial liberation process, or should have at least helped both sides arrive at a modus vivendi, where the interests of our major allies would have been preserved, at least until a loosening of the world tension could have enabled our allies to face a gradual transfer of sovereignty without endangering the position of the Free World in the cold war.

The letter described it as 'pure folly on our part . . . to believe for a moment that the colonial nations of Asia and Africa, who hate all "whites", would ever develop into reliable allies, no matter what promises they gave'. America was 'paying, and very dearly,' for her 'misguided sentimental investments', because the only thing 'in which all the "liberated" countries are uniform' was 'their blackmailing of the US into more and more aid, under the open threat of deserting into the enemy's camp':

> The time has come – and I only hope it isn't too late – for us to re-evaluate completely our foreign policy; and in order to be constructive and not merely negative or opportunistic (which a world leader cannot indefinitely afford), we must, before anything else, learn to distinguish between our long-range enemies and friends.

It was a great shame that Eisenhower did not take on board the message of this letter. Unfortunately, America continued with her 'misguided sentimental investments' and failed totally to 'distinguish' between her 'long-range enemies and friends'.

By late July the Americans had come to the conclusion that the best way to teach Nasser a lesson was to withdraw the offer of finance for the Aswan High Dam, which Dulles did on 19 July – without informing the British in advance.[35] Six days later Nasser seized the Suez Canal and the crisis erupted.

Eden's response was determined by the conclusions which he had come to in March about the need to replace Nasser. He told Eisenhower on 27 July: 'We cannot afford to allow Nasser to seize control of the canal in this way. If we take a firm stand over this now, we shall have the support of all the maritime powers. If we do not, our influence and yours throughout the Middle East will, we are convinced, be irretrievably undermined.'[36] From this point onwards American policy was, to put it at its mildest, less than straight with the British. Whilst using the rhetoric of firmness and allowing the British to proceed on the assumption of Anglo-American co-operation which had obtained since 1941, Eisenhower and Dulles set out to prevent them from taking any firm action – imagining that there was some negotiated settlement which might bring the dispute to an end. In the belief that 'Asian and African' opinion could be won over to support America and thus snatched from the Soviets if only the Americans disowned British and French 'colonialist policies', Eisenhower and Dulles decided to sacrifice their friends.[37]

What the crisis caused by Nasser's actions did was to expose the gulf between Britain and America over policy towards the Middle East. From the start the Americans recognised that 'the basic problem is that the British will want to move very drastically in this matter'.[38] As early as 28 July Eisenhower stressed the 'importance of keeping this Government clear of any precipitate action with the French and the British'.[39] Yet, at the same time, Dulles's deputy, Herbert Hoover Jr, son of the only surviving Republican former President, argued that 'we must move strongly in the Middle East – otherwise the whole Western position will be quickly challenged'.[40] This ambivalence was to have dire results. If the administration failed to convey a clear sense of its policy to the British and the French, this was because it had no coherent line.

Deputy Undersecretary Robert Murphy was despatched to London to try to calm the British down. Murphy was not the best choice for the job. Although he had known Macmillan well when they had both been on Eisenhower's staff in Algiers in 1943, he had the reputation of being anti-British. If his job was to press moderation on the British, Macmillan took the opportunity to emphasise the extreme seriousness of the situation from the British point of view. He was 'left in no doubt that the British Government believed that Suez was a test which could only be met by the use of force', and Macmillan told him that unless Britain succeeded here she would 'sink to the rank of a second-rate power like the Netherlands'.[41] As the Chancellor recorded in his diary, 'It seems that we have succeeded in thoroughly alarming Murphy. He must have reported in the sense we wanted. . . .'[42]

Murphy's reports certainly did alarm his masters. Dulles told Vice-President Richard Nixon on 30 July that the situation was 'bad. The British and French are really anxious to start a war and get us into it.'[43] Murphy told Dulles that the British had 'decided to drive Nasser out of Egypt'. Both Eden and Macmillan had expressed the hope that America 'would be with them in this determination, but if we could not they would understand and our friendship would be unimpaired'.[44] The British attitude was clear, and it was taken seriously in Washington, but the Americans declined now, or later, to make it clear that they would actively seek to block any such British action.

Eisenhower thought that the British were 'unwise' to consider such 'out of date' action, but, instead of telling Eden this, decided to send Dulles to London to press for the convening of an international conference. Dulles was concerned that British military action would 'unite in opposition' the 'whole Arab world', whilst Eisenhower went even further and thought it would 'unite' the 'whole Moslem world'. If the British had seemed 'calm' and unhysterical to Murphy, the same could hardly be said of his own leaders. Whilst Eisenhower and Dulles tried to outdo each other in making the flesh creep, Admiral Arleigh H. Burke, the Chief of Naval Operations, stated bluntly the view of the Joint Chiefs: 'Nasser must be broken', by sanctions if possible, but if the British had to resort to arms, then 'we should declare ourselves in support of their action'. But the former Supreme Commander had now thoroughly alarmed himself. Nasser embodied 'the emotional demands of the people of the area for independence and for "slapping the white man down"'. This massive misjudgment was followed by another: 'We must consider what the end could be. It might array the world from Dakar to the Philippine Islands against us.' Clearly the military and political might thus conjured up was too much for poor Eisenhower. Burke reminded him laconically that what he was suggesting was a way of isolating Nasser from other Muslim groups. At this point the President and Secretary Dulles vanished off into a world of their own wish-fulfilment. Dulles 'thought we could make Nasser disgorge what he had seized, and agree to internationalize the canal', although, perhaps wisely, he did not say how this remarkable feat could be achieved without at least implying the use of force. But the American leaders had now taken themselves off into a scenario of fear of their own imagining. Dulles thought that a British attack on Egypt would encourage an Israeli attack on Jordan, 'with the result of inflaming the whole Arab world'. But perhaps it would not stop there, for, as the tremulous Secretary recalled, 'the British went into World War I and World War II without the United States, on the calculation that they would be bound to come in'. (This was as fine a piece of American egotism as could be imagined, since neither Asquith nor Chamberlain had included such a calculation in their decisions in 1914 and 1939.) But having thus frightened themselves, American policy-makers once more veered in their course. Whilst arguing that 'we must let the British know how gravely we view this matter' and 'what an error we think their decision is', Allen Dulles of the CIA recalled how 'worked up' the British were, and Eisenhower, thinking of America's position in Panama, determined that 'we must not let Nasser get away with this action'.[45] But once again, it was by no means clear that the administration knew how it wanted to achieve this objective; as so often in American diplomacy, the statement of an objective was taken as tantamount to its being achieved.

Eisenhower's message to Eden on 31 July reflected this fatal ambivalence and confusion of thought – as did the fact that the final version of the document was handed to Dulles 'barely in time for the Secretary to make his scheduled departure'.[46] Eisenhower recognised the 'transcendent worth of the Canal to the free world and the possibility that eventually the use of force might become necessary in order to protect international rights', but called for a conference to try to settle the problem peacefully before resorting to 'such drastic means'. Although he waffled on interminably about 'our peoples' feelings' being against military action, he nowhere stated that America would not only not condone such action, but would also actively oppose it. Perhaps he really supposed that a conference would solve the problem; perhaps he thought that the 'whole Moslem world' was about to rise in arms and be joined by the Soviets. It was evidently too much to hope that a man who was incapable of giving a clear view on whether or not he wanted Nixon to run again as his Vice-President would give a lead to his allies.

In the short-term this ambiguity achieved one of the main American objectives: it persuaded the British to go along with Dulles's suggestion of a conference. After all, they already had Eisenhower's assurance that if diplomacy failed, a resort to arms was not ruled out, and since there could be no military action for at least six weeks, there was nothing to lose by seeking to follow America's advice.

British and French reaction to Nasser's actions owed much to the perceived 'lessons of Munich'. The British referred to the episode as being analogous to Hitler's occupation of the Rhineland in 1936[47] and described Nasser as 'a paranoiac like Hitler',[48] whilst the French Premier, Guy Mollet, declared that 'Nasser's deal with the Soviets for arms is the parallel to the Hitler–Stalin pact of 1939';[49] even the Hampstead intellectual and leader of the Labour Party, Hugh Gaitskell, likened the Egyptian leader to 'Hitler and Mussolini'.[50] Churchill's version of the 1930s as portrayed in the best-selling and influential *Gathering Storm* made such analogies common intellectual currency – and, of course, prescribed firm action as the remedy. American intelligence sources recognised that if Nasser succeeded in 'getting away with it', there would be a 'further erosion of Western prestige' and an increase in his influence in the Middle East',[51] but this did not lead to support for the Anglo-French line. Between the fears of an inflamed Middle East and the shadow of World War III, American policy amounted to little more than letting her allies twist slowly in the wind.

On the evening that the news of Nasser's actions had come through, Nuri es Said had told Eden that the 'only' course of action was to 'hit' Nasser: 'hit now and hit hard', otherwise 'he will finish all of us'.[52] Unfortunately, the state of Britain's armed forces had ruled out any such action, and the Defence Staff threatened to resign if Eden disregarded their advice that no immediate military strike was possible.[53] It was this which opened the way for American diplomacy, but acceptance of Dulles's mediation did not rule out the use of force, and the Americans themselves gave the impression that they understood this.

Dulles told the British on 1 August that 'a way had to be found to make Nasser disgorge what he was attempting to swallow. Force was the last method to be tried to accomplish this, but the United States Government did not exclude the use of force if all other methods failed.'[54] Although Dulles qualified this by stating that if force was to be used it must 'be backed by world opinion', it was the word 'disgorge' which 'rang' in Eden's 'ears for months', and he 'felt a great sense of relief that evening' as it seemed to him that British and American policy was converging.[55] In fact, Dulles's visit was the prelude to a period of 'phoney diplomacy' reminiscent of the 'phoney war'; but, as Karl Marx observed, when history repeats itself, it does so the second time as farce.

27

Schism

That matters turned out the way they did owed much to Eden's belief, encouraged by Macmillan, that in the final analysis America would support Britain. Although doubt has been cast upon Eden's statements of belief in the firm line which Dulles propounded at their meeting on 2 August, there would appear to be little warrant for this; if Eden was prepared to consider a two-pronged strategy of diplomacy and preparations for military action, there is no reason to suppose that he should have doubted America's willingness to pursue similar tactics.[1] The problem for Eden was that the longer he followed the will-o'-the-wisp of a diplomatic settlement, the more difficult did it become to find a *casus belli* for military intervention.

As Eden and the British military knew from the last war, amphibious and airborne operations are the most difficult ones to mount; in the case of Egypt this situation was exacerbated by uncertainty as to the purpose of the operation. If the objective was to seize the Canal, then landings at Port Said and in the Canal zone would be necessary; but if Nasser was to be brought down, as Eden wanted, then it was to Alexandria and perhaps Cairo that troops should be directed. But what pretext could be adduced for this? On 14 August the First Sea Lord, Mountbatten, asked what steps were being taken to ensure that an Egyptian Government could be found which would both endorse British action and have popular support, but Eden appeared unwilling to pursue this line of discussion.[2] Such difficulties made both the planning of operations and their ultimate success problematic, and they certainly disposed Eden to try to keep in step with America; but there were limits to how far he could go.

Once he had accepted Dulles's proposal for a conference, Eden wrote to Eisenhower commending this 'display to Nasser and to the world' of 'a United Front between our two countries and the French', but he also made it clear that 'we have . . . gone to the very limits of the concessions which we can make'.[3] Aware that the conference might have an inconclusive result, Eden wanted to use the concessions which he had made to America as leverage to ensure that Eisenhower would stand by him if a resort to force was necessary. Although the language which he and Macmillan used to the Americans was undoubtedly meant to make their flesh creep, there can be no doubt of the seriousness with which they viewed the situation. If Nasser 'got away with it', then his position would be greatly strengthened and the Baghdad pact and everything that went with it would be weakened; Britain's friends, from Amman through to Baghdad and the Gulf, would be discredited and the anti-western propaganda spewed forth by Cairo radio would undermine those regimes which had backed Britain.[4] But Macmillan's hope that by keeping the Americans 'really frightened' they would 'help us to get what we want, without the necessity for force', shows the extent to which a decade and a half of mythology about the 'special relationship' had clouded his judgment.[5]

The tortuous nature of American policy was aptly reflected in Dulles's statement to the President on 12 August that,

it is necessary for us to convey to Egypt and the other Arab nations our own convictions relative to the impossibility of the Western World tolerating the kind of a situation that confronts us as a result of Nasser's action. At the same time he feels we must not let the British and the French believe that we are willing to support any kind of precipitous action they may take.[6]

If words are an accurate expression of mental state, Dulles was confused. He had told Eisenhower on 2 August that he was 'not sure' that the British and French could be 'blamed' for taking action 'as they feel, probably with reason, that if Nasser gets away with his action' it would be the beginning of a process 'which will end British and French positions in Middle East and North Africa, respectively'.[7] Senate majority leader and future President, Lyndon B. Johnson, told Eisenhower on 12 August that the proper response was to tell the British and French that 'they have our moral support' and to 'go on in', whilst at the same meeting Dulles described Nasser as a 'Hitlerite personality'.[8] Examination of Nasser's writings revealed him to be something more dangerous than a Soviet 'stooge'. He clearly had ambitions to become the focus of an anti-western 'third force'.[9] Dulles saw the seizure of the Canal not as an 'erratic or an isolated action but an integral part of a long-term program'; a generation accustomed to regard Hitler's *Mein Kampf* as a blueprint for conquest was readily disposed to see Nasser's *Revolution* in the same light.[10] Nasser's actions were designed to 'reduce Western Europe to subservience to Arab control' – the achievement of which objective would 'jeopardize' those sought by America through the Marshall plan. It is some indication of the mental paralysis which afflicted the Americans in areas unamenable to the stark simplicities of the Cold War that in the face of such an analysis they were unable to decide on the spot whether or not to give 'moral' and 'economic' support to the British and the French – especially since it was already clear to them that Nasser was unlikely to accept any proposal from the forthcoming conference which would put the Canal under international control.[11] Eisenhower even went so far as to say that if Nasser was successful, 'there will be chaos in the Middle East for a long time', and to declare that Europe could not 'be expected to remain at the mercy of the whim of a dictator',[12] but still American diplomacy floundered between visceral anti-colonialism and common sense. The only hope was that the conference would produce a solution; unfortunately, American diplomacy helped to ensure that this would not happen.

The eighteen-Power conference which met at Lancaster House from 16 to 23 August duly came up with a proposal to allow an international board to run the Canal. Eisenhower thought it unlikely that Nasser would accept and had wanted to water down the proposals to suggest that there should be international 'supervision', rather than 'control', but neither the British nor the French would accept this.[13] Dulles himself calmed Eden's fears of a rift. In conversation on 15 August Eden recorded Dulles as seeming to be 'quite as firm as before. . . . He also seemed not to exclude possibility of joint use of force.'[14] But if Eden and Macmillan were convinced that the Americans would be with them if diplomacy failed, the Secretary of State was coming to equally erroneous conclusions about the British attitude. Noticing that the atmosphere was 'much more composed than two weeks ago', Dulles thought that there was a 'growing realization of the magnitude of the task of military intervention and of the inadequacies of their military establishments'.[15] Eden tried to disabuse Dulles of his growing conviction that 'the British public would not support the use of force', telling him on 19 August that 'this view was incorrect' and that, although he had 'refrained from building up public sentiment for the use of force', he was absolutely confident that when the chips were down, the Government would have 'the full backing of the public'.[16] Dulles, however, was more impressed by what he took to be the dwindling of 'domestic support', and he interpreted Macmillan's 'hard-line' threats to resign if Nasser was not coerced as evidence that his favoured policy 'can scarcely be carried through', and that in the event of Nasser rejecting the conference's proposals, 'some form of governmental crisis may result'.[17]

Having come so far to meet the Americans, Eden and Macmillan now expected Dulles to put the conference's proposals to Nasser, taking the view that he was unlikely to be impressed with anyone less.[18] However, it seems as if it was not only the British who were using language more for effect than for communication. On the question of who should take the good news from Lancaster House to Cairo, Dulles told Eisenhower on 20 August that, 'I am disinclined to do so as this might engage me for a considerable time. Also while the US has played a dominant role in the conference so far, I think it is preferable that we should become less conspicuous, if this can be done without jeopardizing the whole affair.'[19]

If the British were wrong in thinking that Dulles was prepared to support military action, the Americans were equally wrong in supposing that the idea of military action had faded from the minds of the British. Although he misinterpreted their import, Dulles was quite correct in discerning political undercurrents at work. He might have picked something up from the very strong hint which Macmillan gave him on 21 August that he hoped to return to the Foreign Office soon.[20]

It was the future leader of the Labour Party, Harold Wilson, who summed up Macmillan's role in the Suez crisis best: 'first in, first out' – and the more that is known about his role, the more accurate does Wilson's summary seem. From the very first Macmillan was unequivocal in advocating the use of force, and on 2 August he argued that Britain might collaborate with Israel in bringing down Nasser – something which Selwyn Lloyd and Eden both rejected.[21] But whilst even the usually staunchly imperialist Salisbury was rabbiting on about the United Nations and the divisions in the Cabinet,[22] Macmillan was briefing Churchill and eliciting his support for a project which would involve a major assault on Alexandria as well as Israeli support.[23] Eden suspected a 'conspiracy', and certainly for him to have shown himself irresolute faced with a Churchill–Macmillan axis would have been to have invited major press criticism. But the problem with Macmillan's scheme was not only that it would ruin Britain's relations with other Arab states, but it would also be impossible to disguise the fact that the objective of British policy was to drive Nasser from power. Nor was it easy to see where what Macmillan called 'a popular *casus belli*' would come from.[24] Cabinet on 24 August suggested that several Ministers were beginning to have severe doubts whether force would work or be popular, but Macmillan countered this mood with a powerful paper on the 26th arguing that the defeat of Nasser was imperative.[25]

It was, in part, the need to find a 'moral basis' for military action which had brought the British along with Dulles's proposals, but this was on the assumption that force could be employed if the conference failed to solve the problem, as Eden and Macmillan made plain to the Cabinet on 24 August. Although the Minister of Defence, the ever emollient Walter Monckton, sought to argue for further delay, Eden, supported by Macmillan and Salisbury, took the view that 'we had no alternative. We must secure the defeat of Nasser, by one method or another.'[26] Military planning went ahead, but as the Cabinet Secretary, Sir Norman Brook, made clear to Eden on 25 August, there was a substantial minority of Ministers, including Rab Butler, who wanted to postpone force until genuine negotiations had been exhausted.[27] Given this situation, and the need to bring the Americans along, it was agreed on 28 August that if the Menzies mission* failed, the matter would be taken to the United Nations.[28]

Eden raised the question of what to do if Nasser proved obdurate when he wrote to Eisenhower on 27 August, and the tenor of his letter bears witness both to the seriousness with which the Prime Minister regarded the situation – 'the most hazardous that our country has known since 1940' – and to the

---

* A mediation mission led by the Australian Prime Minister, Sir Robert Menzies.

tactics which he deemed necessary to keep the Americans interested – 'the bear is using Nasser'. Given Russian interference, and the tremendous western interests which were at stake, 'the firmer the front we show together, the greater the chance that Nasser will give way without the need for any resort to force', Eden told Eisenhower.[29]

If it was difficult to interpret Dulles's mind, that was hardly surprising, since his mood vacillated so. He saw both the Menzies mission and a resort to the UN as leading to a situation where the British 'would have to accept a result which, while reasonably safeguarding the Canal, would not give the blow to Nasser's prestige which the British and French felt was indispensable',[30] and did his best to encourage the British to take the dispute to the UN and to refrain from military action in the interim period.[31] But at the same time he found it 'extremely difficult to take a strong stand against the British and French views', since 'after all' they would be 'finished as first-rate powers if they didn't somehow manage to check Nasser and nullify his schemes'. Having said that, he could not see 'how they could successfully carry through a war against Egypt'. Of course, the British were assuming that they could do so with American help, but from this prospect Dulles recoiled, as there rose before his eyes the image of the 'whole Arab world . . . pitted against them'.[32] The Joint Chiefs were less vacillating than Secretary Dulles and thought that the 'most desirable course of action . . . would be strong public, political and logistic support for Great Britain and France, without direct military intervention by the United States'. But both Dulles and Eisenhower recoiled from this, or any other clear policy, taking refuge in the hope that a diplomatic 'fudge' might yet be had.

Eden had been able to gain some inkling of the way the President's mind was moving in a letter from him on 2 September, which Macmillan described as 'a very hesitating and defeatist message, urging caution and appeasement'.[33] Eisenhower's letter was a plea for a diplomatic solution, and he made it clear that this demanded 'overwhelming' public support' in Britain and America – something which was being eaten away by news of military preparations; he doubted whether Congress would give authority 'even for the lesser support for which you might have to look for us'.[34] But even if this warned Eden and Macmillan that they could not, as they assumed, rely on American support, it did state that Nasser should be 'under no misapprehension as to the firm interest of the nations primarily concerned with the Canal in safeguarding their rights in that waterway', and that the 'highest skill' would be required in the negotiation; Eisenhower's intervention on 5 September was inconsistent with either of these desiderata.

It is not easy to imagine what positive result Eisenhower expected to follow from his statement on 5 September that 'we are committed to a peaceful settlement of this dispute, nothing else', but whatever slim chance Menzies had of success vanished. The British now pressed for a perfunctory referral to the UN followed by military action, whilst Dulles sought a way of postponing any possible resort to arms, coming up with the idea of forming a Suez Canal Users' Association (SCUA).[35]

In his memoirs Macmillan referred to the implicit 'confidence in the good faith of our American allies' and the assumption that 'in a real crisis we could rely on the at least tacit assistance of our American friends';[36] both these characteristics were present in the letter which Eden sent to Eisenhower on 6 September, as was a further Churchillian assumption that 'appeasement' did not pay.[37] Expressing his willingness to consider Dulles's new scheme, Eden embarked upon the exposition of the pure milk of the Churchillian version of the 1930s: Hitler had started with the Rhineland and had been excused all the way up to Poland; the allies had learned from this and had stopped the Soviets before it was too late: 'Similarly the seizure of the Suez Canal is, we are convinced, the opening gambit in a planned campaign by Nasser to expel all western influence and interests from Arab countries.' Although he stated that 'the difference which separates us today appears to be a difference of assessment of Nasser's plans and intentions and of the consequences of military action against him', Eden was only partly correct. As we have seen, some of the estimates which Dulles and Eisenhower had made of Nasser's intentions were similar to those being made by Eden; the real difference was over the 'consequences of military action'. Eden made plain his determination not to allow Britain and 'all western Europe' to be 'held to ransom by Egypt', and ended on a Churchillian note: 'We have many times led Europe in the fight for freedom. It would be an ignoble end to our long history if we tamely accepted to perish by degrees.' He might have done better to have recalled that it was the last great heroic stand which had led to the current situation.

Eisenhower caught the Churchillian echo, but neither he nor Dulles was overly impressed with Eden's analysis and conclusions, which were 'intemperate' and 'not thought through'.[38] The problem was that the American analysis was equally half-baked. Eisenhower and Dulles accepted the basic premises of the British position – that Nasser was a 'Hitlerian personality' whose triumph would not only mean the end of Britain and France as Great Powers, but would also damage western interests – but they feared the consequences if the 'Arab world' should be 'pitted against' them. They took no account of the view so energetically propagated by one of the President's correspondents that 'the Arabs are on Nasser's side today because they are led to believe that the western powers are weak and cowardly and incapable of any reaction', but that if this should be proved false, then the reaction would be much as it had been for Mossadeq. It was not unknown for Middle Eastern crowds to shout 'hossana!' one day and 'crucify him!' the next.[39] What the American analysis ignored was the consequences of a British and French failure. If they accepted Eden's view that it would lead to the destruction of pro-western regimes in the region,[40] then their refusal to back a strong diplomatic line with an implication that they would not prevent Anglo-French military action if this failed was as extraordinary a piece of pusillanimity as one could wish to see – except on the assumption that what Dulles and Eisenhower were looking towards was American influence replacing that of the discredited colonial Powers; on this reading the whole crisis was the climax of the policy pursued since 1953. That it also removed a Prime Minister who refused to let British interests suffer simply to win nebulous American 'goodwill' was a bonus.

For the next month and a half the Americans did their best to prevent the British and the French from resorting to military action. Their favoured technique in this endeavour was the one already tried with such success – that of starting numerous diplomatic hares in the hope that, embroiled in the toils of diplomacy and with British domestic opinion divided, Eden would be unable to resort to war; it was an ignoble strategy, but one almost attended with success. The reason it almost succeeded was that it played on British reluctance to take action without America, which in turn fed off the assumption that America was tacitly behind Britain and would do nothing that was not in Britain's interest.

The problem for Eden, faced as he was with pressure from the French and from his own 'hawks', was that Eisenhower's strategy was, on the surface, unexceptionable. The President nowhere stated that America was unalterably opposed to the use of force and would not allow it; instead, he obfuscated with the perfectly unassailable proposition that there should be no resort to force 'without thoroughly exploring and exhausting every possible peaceful means of settling the issue'; it was his caveat to this – 'regardless of the time consumed' – which contained the sting in the tail for Eden.[41] The idea of SCUA was designed to give the impression that something was being done, without allowing the British an excuse to resort to force. Clever as this tactic was, it ignored the fact that a Prime Minister under pressure could not afford an infinite number of failed diplomatic initiatives.

At the same time that he put forward the SCUA initiative, Dulles also tried to reassure the British that, as he put it to Makins on 8 September, 'We could not let Nasser win a victory.'[42] The British Ambassador's report of the conversation had Dulles using even firmer language: 'The President did not exclude the use of force in the last resort. Between us we could get Nasser down, and the U.S. Administration was quite determined that this should happen.'[43] The difference between the American record of the conversation and that of the British is crucial, for the former has Dulles holding to the sort of language which was used in Eisenhower's letter to Eden, whilst the British record has him using language which was calculated to appeal to Eden and the British. He certainly succeeded in this last objective. The comments in Eisenhower's letter about 'alternative measures' to topple Nasser, Dulles's comments to Makins on 8 September, and promises that America would help Britain with emergency oil shipments and economic sanctions against Egypt,[44] all encouraged even the 'hawkish' Permanent Under-secretary, Sir Ivone Kirk-patrick, to believe that there was 'a large measure of identification of views between' Britain and America.[45] Eden told Churchill on 10 September that 'the Americans seem very firmly lined up with us'.[46] Indeed, so close did the British now believe the two sides were that the Americans were shown advance copies of, and given the chance to comment on, the major speech which Eden had to deliver on 12 September in the Commons.[47]

Thus, when he delivered his long-awaited statement, Eden was able to strike a confident note. He surprised the Opposition and delighted his own side of the House by announcing the Users' Association, and by giving the clear impression that if this initiative too was spurned by Nasser, the Govern-ment would be 'free to take such further steps, either through the United Nations or by other means, for the assertion of their rights'. For once, he was greeted with a 'thunderous Conservative ovation'.[48] Not even the 'Suez group' could complain about his tone, the Opposition had been left flounder-ing, and nothing in his statement was inconsistent with what he took the American view to be. For the first time since the crisis began, it seemed as though Eden had the situation if not under control, then at least on the way there.

Dulles had told Makins that there must be no implication that America would join in any military action, but privately he had told Eisenhower that he thought Eden's speech 'goes somewhat too far'.[49] However, he had not mentioned this to Makins at their conversation on 11 September.[50] His first reaction to Eden's statement was that the Prime Minister 'went a little out of bounds', and he suspected that he was trying to 'justify war' – which was 'where our policy splits'.[51] The consequence was that at a press conference on 13 September Dulles went out of his way (departing from the prepared text) to assure reporters that 'we do not intend to shoot our way through' the Canal. He denied that SCUA amounted to a boycott of the Canal or that it would be in a position 'to guarantee anything to anybody'.[52]

The Secretary of State's comments put Eden in a difficult position. It was clear that the Americans would not support any immediate recourse to the United Nations, and that they would be disposed to resent a British rejection of SCUA. Moreover, for a man so used to maintaining an 'Anglo-American front', the prospect of breaking it was so unappealing as to be almost unthink-able. As Eden himself was later to see, it was the constant need to keep in line with America, even on an issue where 'American interest was secondary', which hamstrung his policy.[53] He had thought that Anglo-American policy was aligned, but Dulles had unilaterally driven the modern equivalent of a coach and horses through any such notion (assuming that such a metaphor is admitted). As Eden later put it, 'Such cynicism towards allies destroys true partnership. It leaves only the choice of parting, or a master and vassal relationship in foreign policy';[54] the true price of Churchill's 'Grand Alliance' was now apparent, and the time had come to pay it.

Eden was now close to having to make a choice which had been avoided since 1940, and which could yet be evaded by pursuing the usual policy of appeasement towards Washington. On the one hand, a vital British interest was being threatened, and whatever America would or would not do, Britain faced a choice between the 'use of force or surrender to Nasser'.[55] On the other, there was the consideration pressed by Makins, which was that to attempt military action 'without full American moral and material support could easily lead to disaster'.[56] The British electorate, under the natural assumption that they had elected a government of an independent Great Britain, expected that government to act as it saw the nation's best interests, but it was not open to Eden to point out that he could not do so because the Americans would not let him. Still unable to believe that the Americans would let him down, Eden proceeded with his two-pronged policy of following America's lead in diplomacy whilst preparing, as a final resort, military plans.

Unfortunately, there was quite as much confusion on the military front as there was on the diplomatic. The revised version of Operation 'Musketeer' reverted to the original plan of occupying Port Said, but only after two initial stages which would see air attacks, psychological warfare and the seizure of key positions, which would, it was hoped, destabilise the Nasser regime.[57] A stunned Eden argued against the new scheme with 'considerable rudeness and anger'.[58] After all the preparations that had been made, the Chiefs of Staff had changed their minds, and this was their only response to the furious Prime Minister.[59] Of course 'Musketeer Revise' fulfilled the ostensible desideratum, which was that it allowed for the seizure of the Canal, but it would impose further delays on the date for military action and would not necessarily meet Eden's wider objectives. It would seem as though the reasons for the changes were primarily political,[60] but even Churchill, faced with a united team of Chiefs of Staff and Defence Minister, would have hesitated to overrule them;[61] the same applied to Eden, and he agreed to the adoption of the new plan.

Eden thus found himself in a position where SCUA had to be tried, not only in order to appease the Americans, but because the British and the French were in no position to take military action until October at the earliest. However, the longer the diplomatic quadrille went on, the more difficult it would become to find a *casus belli*. With international pressure on sterling increasing – $170 million was lost from the British reserves during the first three weeks in September[62] – with dangerous divisions beginning to appear in the Cabinet,[63] and with an Opposition hounding him as a warmonger, what was left of Eden's formerly great prestige was insufficient to allow him to assert the authority necessary for Party unity. The former Chief Whip,

Patrick Buchanan-Hepburn, reported that there was a 'good deal of trouble in the Party' and that the Tory group who were opposed to the use of force, even as a 'last resort', was perhaps large 'enough to put us in a minority in a division'; but for Eden it was '1938 over again, and he could not be a party to it'.[64] 'Appeasement', the 'special relationship', all the shadows of the past were reaching out to cloud judgment in the present.

The problem which British Ministers refused to face was the one they had been taught by Churchill did not exist: what to do when British interests and American intentions did not coincide? It is this, rather than some form of deep-seated conspiracy, which most probably accounts for Macmillan's misreading of the situation in late September. Before leaving for Washington on 20 September for a meeting of the IMF, he did his 'best to convince Dulles of the need to take a very firm line'.[65] Once in Washington he continued to interpret what the Americans told him through the star-spangled spectacles customarily donned by Churchillian acolytes when observing America. Thus, when he and Dulles discussed the Suez affair again on 25 September and the American began by complaining that Britain and France had taken a unilateral decision to refer the matter to the UN, Macmillan still interpreted his remarks as embodying an implicit commitment to support Britain. According to Macmillan's account of the conversation, Dulles talked about 'different methods of getting rid of Nasser', even if these took 'six months'. When Macmillan protested that Britain did not have that long in view of the increase in Nasser's prestige, Dulles said that 'he quite realised that we might have to act by force', and that he thought 'our threat of force was vital, whether we used it or not, to keep Nasser worried'. The only caveat he seemed to impose was one dictated by the Presidential election in November: 'Could we not . . . try to hold things off until after November 6th?'[66] With knowledge of the real position taken up by Eisenhower and Dulles, American historians have tended to regard this as wilful misinterpretation,[67] but if this was what Macmillan thought he heard, then from the angle of someone used to assuming that common action was, in itself, an important component of any alliance, it is not surprising that he should have interpreted it as tacit agreement that in the last resort the British might well use force. This was one of the results of the long appeasement of the United States.

Dulles was warned on 19 September that 'both Macmillan and Salisbury still regard military action as the only satisfactory solution to the Suez problem', and that 'the way might be prepared for action in about a month' after the British had 'arranged' a 'grave incident in Egypt'.[68] Yet at his meeting with Eden on 20 September, Dulles did not warn him that America could not back any military action.[69] Thus, Dulles's anger that Eden did not tell him that Britain was intending to take the Suez dispute to the Security Council pales into insignificance when compared to American duplicity. Dulles's own account of his conversation with Macmillan on 25 September varies so drastically from Macmillan's that it is hard to believe that they were describing the same event[70] – a symbol, if ever there was one, of the growing schism. If Macmillan left Washington convinced that the Americans would not obstruct British action, Dulles and Eisenhower finished their meetings with him convinced that 'the British didn't know how they were proceeding themselves' and that Macmillan himself was 'far less bitter than he had been a few weeks ago'.[71] If the British could not conceive of the Americans not acting in concert with them, from their side the Americans had much the same conviction; the scene was being set for the veil which had long obscured the reality of the Anglo-American relationship to be stripped away. It was not an instance of two countries united by one language, but of two countries blinded by mythology.

28

Macmillan's Metamorphosis

The denouement to the drama was swift and shocking. Macmillan knew better than anyone else how much British action depended for its success on American acquiescence. On 7 September the Treasury had emphasised to him 'the vital necessity from the point of view of our currency and our economy of ensuring that we do not go it alone, and that we have the maximum U.S. support'.[1] By 21 September there were warnings that the drain on Britain's foreign reserves was such that the 'floor' of $2 billion was in sight, and confidence in sterling would not 'survive a war followed by protracted negotiations, resulting even in the fall of Nasser and the corresponding restoration of our prestige in the Middle East'. Treasury officials even warned Macmillan before Dulles did that it was 'unlikely' that America would join in any 'far-reaching actions in the Middle East prior to the elections' – predictions which Macmillan described as 'gloomy, but very likely correct'.[2] But not only did this seem to make no difference to Macmillan's views, but his reports from Washington, as we have seen, contained no implication that the Americans were extremely unlikely to back action by the British and the French. Indeed, in his report to Eden on his conversations with Eisenhower, Macmillan wrote that 'Ike is really determined somehow or another to bring Nasser down'.[3]

Makins, who had been present at the meeting, was 'astounded' that Macmillan had said 'nothing' about Suez.[4] Eisenhower's comment on the meeting, whilst not going quite so far, confirms that Macmillan had said nothing to alarm him. Talking to Dulles on the morning of 25 September, Eisenhower said he had had a 'nice chat' with his old friend, who had talked 'much more moderately (about the Suez) than he had anticipated'.[5] How was it then that Macmillan, in his detailed reports to Eden, had the President talking about the need to, in effect, revive the 'old Concert of Europe in a new form' and holding firm language about the need to 'get Nasser down'? How did the Chancellor persuade himself that he had had 'an important and sympathetic exchange of views about Suez and Nasser',[6] when 'Ike' thought that they had had a 'nice chat'? As Macmillan's official biographer acknowledges, parts of the report read more like comments made to Eisenhower than by him, which perhaps reflects the fact that when they had been in Algiers Macmillan had got into the habit of projecting his own views on Eisenhower, who usually followed his advice. He certainly reported in bullish mood to Eden on 1

October, who was so encouraged that he wrote to Eisenhower stressing the need to show joint 'firmness' to Nasser in the wake of Soviet warnings about the consequences of military intervention.[7]

It was perhaps no accident that the most 'hawkish' member of the Cabinet should have given such an up-beat report, for in his absence his colleagues had been moving towards a diplomatic solution. Selwyn Lloyd recommended to the Egypt Committee on 25 September that they should consider a plan brought forward by the Indians, which would have permitted a 'system of guarantees, controlled by arbitrators' between the Egyptians and SCUA.[8] Eden himself acknowledged that the resort to the Security Council might well mean further negotiations,[9] and it was this which led to a distinctly difficult meeting with the French on 26 September, when Foreign Minister Christian Pineau pressed for military action before the end of October.[10] The French were so disgusted by what they took to be British spinelessness that they reopened unofficial talks which they had been having with the Israelis. Pineau suggested to the latter on 30 September that if Israel attacked Egypt, Britain and France could intervene as 'peace-keepers' – but of course, with the British now apparently moving towards a negotiated settlement, the odds on this happening were lengthening.[11]

Thus, the perils and the possible profits of the American approach of stringing the British along were now in plain view: the diplomatic road still seemed open, but instead of the long delay ruling military action out, it had provided the opportunity for French ingenuity to find a way of ruling it in. Dulles himself was well aware of French bellicosity (although not of the contacts with the Israelis), and of their view that he had 'snatched the British from their clutches', but he was not sure 'where the balance of power' lay in the 'divided' British Cabinet.[12] He did feel, however, that 'events were working towards a settlement',[13] although he recognised that relations with both Britain and France had deteriorated because of their feeling that 'we were [not] backing them fully'. Both he and Eisenhower rejected any plans the British were floating for covert action against Nasser, but neither of them had any fixed ideas on how to deal with a man who had 'dangerous tendencies'. Eisenhower's great contribution to American policy was to stress the need to 'maintain an independent position as regards the British and French until we knew definitely what they were up to'.[14]

Quite how firm pressure was to be kept up on Nasser whilst America was distancing herself from her two NATO partners was not apparent, but matters were certainly not helped when Dulles announced at a press conference on 3 October that SCUA had 'no teeth'. In pursuance of Eisenhower's desire to put 'distance' between America and the British and French, Dulles declared that America could not be expected to 'identify itself 100 per cent either with the colonial Powers or the Powers uniquely concerned with the problem of getting independence as rapidly, and as fully as possible'. Colonial regimes should, he said, be dismantled, and America's role was to facilitate that process and to see that it moved forwards 'in a constructive' and 'evolutionary way'.[15]

Dulles's comments, repeating as they did publicly some of the comments that he and Eisenhower had made privately, reveal once more the effect of puerile and visceral American anti-colonialism. The Suez dispute was not about 'colonialism' because Egypt was not a 'colony'. Nasser, of course, had been winning support at the talking-shop in New York by claiming that it was a 'colonial' dispute – and now the American Secretary of State had seemingly come down upon his side. To call this a 'catastrophic failure of judgement'[16] hardly does it justice. The words used by Eden's official biographer to sum up the whole SCUA episode seem particularly well adapted to apply to Dulles's actions on this occasion: 'In the unhappily long saga of Anglo-American duplicity, this ranks very high.'[17] But even this is not quite enough, for it treats the incident as though it were one of a series of atypical occurrences which marred the smooth working of an otherwise amicable relationship. The point about Dulles's words is that they express the reality of the American conception of the nature and purpose of the Anglo-American alliance.

As far as the Americans were concerned the crisis showed how essential 'increased European unity' was. Dulles, indeed, was so far gone in his American-centred view of the world as to imagine that the 'Western European nations have been preserving their political divisions which keep them weak, partly because they feel that they could afford this luxury so long as they had more or less a blank check on the US'. But of course, as Suez revealed only too well, 'they cannot count upon us outside the North Atlantic Treaty area automatically'. Dulles saw this as helping the American goal of a federal western Europe.[18] Britain, in short, was a useful partner in NATO, although she would be a more useful one if she came in with the movement towards European union. The Empire lessened Britain's attractiveness as an ally: it kept her out of 'Europe' and gave her illusions of grandeur. The Anglo-American alliance was applicable only when it worked in the way America wanted. These things the British had refused to see, preferring the roseate picture conjured up by Churchill's powerful rhetoric. For America, the Suez crisis was about keeping the support of the Arab–Asia bloc at the United Nations, and about electoral considerations; British and French interests came a very poor third to these. Eisenhower had 'not any very definite views' of what he 'might do either now or in the future in order to prevent the Suez business getting out of hand'.[19] He thought about perhaps issuing a statement which declared that America 'will not support a war or warlike moves in the Suez area' and insisted that negotiations 'must be continued until a peaceful but just solution is reached – regardless of how long it takes'. In the meantime Britain and France were expected to sit still and behave themselves until Uncle Sam told them otherwise.

This was an intolerable position, and Dulles's words on 3 October made the achievement of American aims more, not less, difficult; after all, the essence of a policy of duplicity is that it should be pursued in secret. Dulles's preference for microphone diplomacy gave a whole new dimension to the old American penchant for open diplomacy.

Much of the 'lack of nerve' of Eden's diplomacy during the crisis has been put down to ill-health or lack of capacity for the job,[20] but surely the real explanation of his failure is that for so long he tried to follow the Churchillian policy of appeasing America. His failure was due to the fact that unlike Churchill and Macmillan, he was not prepared to go to any lengths to keep in with the Americans. The American alliance was, after all, a means to an end, not an end in itself, and as it became clear that far from fulfilling the purpose of maintaining British power in the Middle East, it was helping to undermine it, Eden determined to act as though Britain was an independent Power. As he warned Selwyn Lloyd on 7 October, 'In the last resort action will be necessary. It is therefore very important that, while appearing reasonable, we shall not be inveigled away in negotiation from the fundamentals to which we have held all along and that we should not be parted from the French.'[21] With one stroke Dulles had provided Nasser and Eden with good reasons not to seek a negotiated settlement.

His intervention had certainly not helped those like Lloyd who looked towards the United Nations and further negotiations for a solution. The UN discussed the matter almost continuously from 5 to 13 October, and Lloyd worked hard to find a diplomatic settlement. Disturbed by reports of Anglo-American differences, he asked Dulles on 7 October what these were so that he could answer them. Dulles, the model of emollience, denied that America had any plans to go behind Britain's back – which was true only in so far as America had no 'plans' at all, simply a desire to prevent the British and the French from resorting to military action.[22]

Eden had been furious at Dulles's action on 3 October, which was, coincidentally, the date at which he told the Cabinet that 'the Jews have come up with an offer'.[23] The Cabinet 'hawks', led by Macmillan, were opposed to any settlement of the dispute which left Nasser's 'influence undiminished throughout the Middle East'. Pineau had told Eden that the Israelis were going to attack Egypt 'within three weeks' and had asked what the western Powers were going to do about it. Lloyd and the Foreign Office had already imposed a prohibition on negotiations with Israel, so the matter was taken no further – but Eden warned that if the Egyptians 'continued to be obdurate, world opinion might be ready to support a recourse to forceful measures'.[24]

On the surface the discussions between Dulles and Lloyd in New York finally did something to clear the air, with Dulles saying that he was unsure whether the negotiations were a real attempt to find a peaceful solution or just a blind: 'there must be a real understanding as to what is planned. None of us can take for granted that the other will go along blindly. The issues are too momentous for that.'[25] The problem was that the two sides were not agreed on how momentous the 'issues' were. As both Lloyd and Pineau attempted to explain to Dulles on 5 October, what was at stake was nothing less than 'all the Middle East' – and the Frenchman was not above dragging in the question of the future of NATO, if only to say that he would never be part of a government which agreed to give it up; the implication that there were others who would do so was clear to anyone who recalled the tall inhabitant of Colombey-les-deux-Eglises.* Dulles responded with his usual formulation designed to reassure the Europeans without alarming them into taking military action: 'the US would not want to say that circumstances would not arise where the only alternative would be the use of force' – but America would, of course, want to see all the resources of diplomacy tried before then. It was, in fact, the usual dialogue of the deaf: the European warning the Americans that they might have to resort to force in the near future without specifying a date, whilst the Americans agreed that force might one day be used – before postponing that eventuality to the Greek calends.

Nevertheless, in the hands of the emollient Lloyd, the negotiations at the United Nations eventually produced some progress. The Americans came to regard Lloyd as a 'serious' negotiator, who, unlike Pineau, was making a real effort to find a diplomatic solution.[26] Indeed, Lloyd was actually willing to open negotiations with the Egyptians, but Macmillan and the 'hawks' on the Egypt Committee put an end to that scheme.[27] Nevertheless, it seemed by 13 October that the bases for an agreement had been reached, and despite another maladroit piece of microphone diplomacy when Eisenhower announced that it 'looks like here is a very great crisis behind us',[28] Eden agreed on 14 October that further negotiations should be pursued.[29] Thus, for all the legend of a seriously unbalanced Prime Minister unalterably determined to break Nasser spread by some historians, and for all Eden's own presentation of himself as the man who would make no concessions, Eden was still pursuing the two-pronged strategy he had pursued from the start; but even as it looked like Lloyd might produce some results, the balance of policy shifted towards war.

Originally the Egypt Committee had not wanted to prolong negotiations beyond 12 October, and it was getting very late in the year to launch military operations. The French were unhappy with the course of the negotiations. With their own problems in Algeria, they were anxious to make an example of Nasser; so too, to judge from the Conservative Party conference, were many of Eden's supporters. On 14 October, the day he returned from the conference, Eden received a French mission. Exactly what transpired at that meeting remains a cause of controversy, and since Eden determined that no

---

* Charles de Gaulle.

minutes were taken, the exact course of events will never be conclusively established; nevertheless, enough evidence has now emerged for the crucial points to be clear. General Challe put forward the essence of what would later be called 'collusion': supposing Israel attacked Egypt, would Britain and France be willing to intervene in order to safeguard the Canal?[30]

With tension between Egypt and Israel and Israel and Jordan increasing, there was a very strong likelihood that the British might find themselves being called upon to honour their agreement to defend Jordan. The Jordanians had already sought help from Britain's major protégé in the region, Iraq, and on 1 October, in a bid to keep the Baghdad pact on its feet, the Egypt Committee had agreed to provide aid for Jordan in the event of an Israeli attack.[31] Unfortunately for the British, their major partner, France, was also Israel's main supplier of Mystère fighters.[32] The prospect that would be opened up by an Israeli-Jordanian conflict hardly bore thinking about, as Britain and France, instead of supporting each other over Suez, supported different sides in a regional conflict which would effectively get Nasser off the hook. After his meeting with Challe, Eden put pressure on Nuri to postpone the deployment of Iraqi troops in Jordan.[33]

No official record exists of the meeting of the Egypt Committee on 16 October,[34] but according to Nutting, who was present, it was at this meeting that Eden expounded the essence of the French plan to those colleagues present. Lloyd did not turn up until lunchtime, having been warned by Nutting what was afoot, but despite initial hostility, he gave way to Eden's arguments in favour of the French plan.[35] Later that day both men flew to Paris, where details of the 'collusion' were discussed with the French.[36] The decision had been taken: diplomacy, with all its possibilities of dragging the matter out for months, had been abandoned in favour of an Anglo-French scheme to destroy Nasser by hiding behind the Israelis. This truth was known to very few in the British Government and was kept from the Americans. Eden had determined to act without them; after all, he had no warrant for believing that they would actively intervene to stop him.

To Dulles, peering through the fog of obfuscation, the British position now appeared 'equivocal. They seemed at times really to be seeking a peaceful settlement . . . at other times they seemed to feel that any settlement would not eliminate Nasser fast enough and that they must have a more rapid time schedule.' But he did not think that the British would resort to overt or covert action against Nasser before the election.[37] This was to underestimate the frustration induced by America's restraints on British action. Even the 'six points' which Lloyd hoped would provide the basis for a settlement seemed likely to prove inadequate, given the American interpretation that SCUA was not an 'instrument of coercion'.[38] For a decade and a half the British had hoped that they would be able to use the American connection to bolster their position as a Great Power, but now it seemed as though it was being used by the Americans to curb action designed to protect British interests. 'Collusion' with the Israelis and the French offered Eden a road to independent action – and he took it.

But for that action to be successful it was essential that the military strike should be swift and sure. The secret protocol signed at Sèvres on 24 October, at the house of the parents of the man who had assassinated Admiral Darlan in 1942, provided the *casus belli* so long required.[39] On 29 October Israel would attack Egypt; the following day the British and French would call for a cease-fire and for both sides to withdraw ten miles from the Canal and to accept an Anglo-French occupation of the zone. If Egypt rejected this call – which was in effect an invitation to the Israelis to advance to within ten miles of the Canal – then she would be faced with Anglo-French military operations on the morning of 31 October. The Cabinet was not informed of the protocol, and both Eden and Lloyd would deny to the end of their lives that there had been 'collusion'.

There were a number of problems with the course of action Eden and Lloyd had decided upon: in the first place, because the reasons behind it had to be concealed, it came as a great shock to many diplomats and politicians, which made it difficult to secure widespread support for the military action; in the second place, because the military could not be informed of the collusion, it slowed down their plans; in the third place, the Israeli attack would so obviously look like what it was, a transparent excuse for Anglo-French intervention, that Britain's role would be suspected in the Arab world and her prestige would suffer thereby; and finally, it assumed that the Americans would do nothing to prevent the operation from taking place.

The final two objections were raised forcibly at Cabinet on 25 October, when Eden outlined his plans – without, however, revealing just how he was so sure that the Israelis were going to attack.[40] Some Ministers argued that it would 'do lasting damage to Anglo-American relations' and that it would bring Britain into odium at the UN. But Macmillan had no doubts that Eisenhower would not let him down. Some time before the Cabinet meeting, Macmillan forcibly reminded Lloyd that although he had been in America more recently than himself, he had neither seen Eisenhower, nor did he have the long relationship with him that Macmillan enjoyed: 'I don't think there is going to be any trouble from Ike – he and I understand each other – he's not going to make any real trouble if we have to do something drastic.'[41] Not for the last time, Macmillan's opinion said more about his self-confidence than it did about his judgment.

The Americans were totally surprised by the Israeli invasion of Egypt – they had been assuming that Jordan was the intended target of the military build-up which their intelligence sources had identified.[42] Initially Eisenhower could not 'believe Britain would be dragged into this', and Dulles was anxious lest the Arab world assumed that America had foreknowledge.[43] Even by 29

October Eisenhower was still so unconvinced that the British had been 'in' on the Franco-Israeli action that he wondered whether to warn them that the French 'may be playing us false'. But unlike his old friend Macmillan, Eisenhower had correctly read the mind of his ally; he thought that the British were 'calculating that we must go along with them'. However, he had no intention of doing so. Whatever the merits of the British case, 'nothing justifies double-crossing us'. Assistant Secretary of State Hoover spoke for many American policy-makers when he voiced the view that 'if we were to side with the French and British we would find the USSR lined up with the Arabs and in fact with all of Africa'. Dulles, who said that there 'has been a struggle between the French and ourselves to see who will have the British allied with them in the tense situations in the Middle East and North Africa', thought that America ought to take the 'bare chance' which existed to 'unhook' the British.[44] The British Chargé d'Affaires, John Coulson, was then hauled in and given a lecture about abiding by the 1950 Tripartite Declaration, which pledged both Britain and America to maintain stability in the Middle East. Poor Coulson, who had no idea of what was going on, promised support for taking the matter to the UN in the morning.[45]

During the night, however, the British seemed to change their minds about what form of resolution to support at the Security Council, and the motive behind this became clear on the morning of 30 October, when the news came through of Anglo-French 'landings'. Dulles 'pointed to the danger of our being drawn into the hostilities as we were in World Wars I and II with the difference that this time it appears that the British and French might well be considered the aggressor in the eyes of the world, engaged in an anti-Arab, anti-Asian war'. Hoover wondered whether the British and French were trying to force America to choose 'between themselves and the Arabs'. That was, of course, in effect, exactly what the British were doing, but they would have been disabused of the Churchillian illusions about America sooner than they were had they been present at the meeting. Eisenhower, who did not think the British and French 'have an adequate cause for war', wondered 'if the hand of Churchill might not be behind this – inasmuch as this action is in the mid-Victorian style'. The Americans had now been presented with a choice, and they made it. Eisenhower 'said he did not see much value in an untrustworthy and unreliable ally and that the necessity to support them might not be as great as they believed'.[46]

Everything now depended upon the speed with which the Anglo-French military option was carried out. Formally there could be no doubt about the line the Americans would take in public, but it would be some time before that line could be publicly expressed. Indeed, it rather seems as though Eisenhower, assuming that the British had gone 'too far to reconsider' and that their 'plan is all worked out', was prepared to accept a *fait accompli*. After receiving explanatory cables from Eden, he drafted a response which, although cool in tone, ended by saying, 'I think I faintly understand and I certainly deeply sympathize with you in the problem you have to solve. Now we must pray that everything comes out both justly and peacefully.' These were the kindest sentiments he was to express for quite a while – and it is significant that on 31 October he postponed sending the message; it was never sent.[47]

The reason why Eisenhower withdrew his message was the hardening of the American attitude on 30 October as it became clear just how heavily involved the British were in what was happening in the Middle East. The American representative at the UN, Cabot Lodge, reported that his British counterpart, Sir Pierson Dixon, who was 'normally an agreeable fellow', had been 'virtually snarling' at him when he had put forward the American request that they should live up to the Tripartite Declaration. It was, he told Dulles, as though 'a mask had fallen off, he was ugly and not smiling', and when Lodge had spoken of living up to the Declaration, Dixon had snapped, '"Don't be silly and moralistic. We have got to be practical."'[48] Eisenhower was less than impressed by Eden's tardy and obviously incomplete explanation, telling Dulles on the afternoon of 30 October that America should adopt a 'hands off' policy. 'After all', America was not going to 'fight them', but he saw no reason to call a 'special session of our people to get money to help them out'. He felt strongly about a situation in which 'our friends & allies ... suddenly ... put us in a hole & expect us to rescue them'. He wanted Eden to 'know that we are a Government of honor'.[49] Thus it was he despatched a formal telegram telling Eden that their two Governments 'hold somewhat different attitudes toward the Tripartite Declaration of 1950' and that America could not 'violate our pledged word'.[50] Brushing aside British objections, Lodge asked the Security Council to consider steps to bring about an immediate cessation of hostilities.[51] Although the use of the veto could postpone action by the UN, it would further alienate American opinion and further divide opinion in Britain; only a swift military victory could avert disaster. As Shuckburgh recorded in his diary, 'If it is successful, the damage to our prestige and reputation and to our relations with Asia and the other Arabs, though serious, may not be so terrible. If it fails to get a result in two or three days ... God help us';[52] it did not, and He did not.

Eisenhower thought that the British had made 'the biggest error of our time', and although he did not want to condemn them 'too bitterly',[53] that was, in effect, what he allowed to happen. As Dulles explained at the NSC meeting on the morning of 1 November, with the Anglo-French veto of action at the Security Council, the matter would come before the UN General Assembly, and if 'we were not now prepared to assert our leadership', then the Soviets would.

For many years now the United States has been walking a tightrope between the effort to maintain our old and valued relations with our British and French allies on the one hand, and on the other trying to assure ourselves of the friendship and understanding of the newly independent countries who have escaped from colonialism.

It seemed to Dulles 'that in view of the overwhelming Asian and African pressure upon us, we could not walk this tightrope much longer'. His visceral anti-colonialism coming to the surface, Dulles declared in apocalyptic tones that, 'In short, the United States would survive or go down on the basis of colonialism if the United States supports the French and the British on the colonial issue. Win or lose, we will share the fate of Britain and France.'[54] It was vintage Dulles, and exposed the fault-lines in the policy of those in Britain who had long held the view that only the American alliance could secure the future of British power.

Dulles's views on 'colonialism' were 'shared widely by his countrymen',[55] so were his views about the Soviets, but the Suez crisis was not about 'colonialism' and could be viewed only in distorted fashion if seen through the lenses of the Cold War and American obsessions with 'colonialism'. His comment that 'win or lose, we will share the fate of Britain and France', applied *mutatis mutandis* whatever America did, for as Eden constantly tried to point out to uncomprehending Americans, what the British were up to was not 'harking back to the old Colonial and occupational concepts', but rather an attempt to maintain western interests.[56] The British had plenty of information which suggested that Nasser's successful defiance of British and French opinion was having a deleterious effect upon the position of Britain's allies in the Baghdad pact, and the Americans themselves had long accepted that he was a threat to western interests. But because he was not a major threat to direct and vital American interests, the Americans had not only failed to take action against him themselves, but they had pursued a line of action designed to prevent their NATO partners from doing so. Quite what American interests were going to be served by the collapse of the British and French positions – which were not, on the whole, 'colonial' – neither Dulles nor Eisenhower asked. But then they had no need to ask, for they had long operated on the assumption, which would become known as the 'Eisenhower doctrine' from January 1957, that America would become the leading western Power in the Middle East, replacing the decadent 'colonialism' with benign American influence – Coca-Cola and crooners for the Arabs, oil for the Americans. It had never been clear quite how Britain and France would be removed to make way for this epiphany – Suez provided the answer. This is not to say that the Americans designed matters this way, any more than they designed them so that Eden would fall, but when events put the attainment of these things into Eisenhower's lap, he took full advantage, not from opportunism or chance, but because ever since 1953 he and Dulles had been aiming to replace British power in the Middle East with American power.[57]

But there was more in heaven and earth than such calculations allowed for. The notion that former 'colonial' people were just out there longing for a 'lead' from Washington and would be eternally grateful for one was optimistic neo-colonialism; newly independent people wanted independence, not direction from Washington – and, as the example of the British showed, following Washington's leadership was something you did with total obedience, and if you failed to do so, you could and would be pulled into line. It was an odd conception of independence, and even odder that the Americans should have thought that it would appeal to newly emerging nations. In their bloc the Soviets did things with their accustomed crudity, and one of Eisenhower's concerns during the Suez crisis was the Soviet invasion of Hungary, which America condemned roundly. America had no need of such vulgar tactics to bring their British ally to heel; moreover, there existed, in the form of the myth of the 'special relationship', an antidote to the anti-Americanism which America's actions during the crisis caused. All that was needed was to bring the British into line first.

Britain was vulnerable to American pressure on a number of levels, and most of them were, alas, Britain's own fault. At Cabinet on 30 October the 'hawkish' Macmillan showed the first signs of his startling metamorphosis into 'dove'. Confident as he was in at least American acquiescence, and reluctant to reveal the full extent of 'collusion', Macmillan had made no preparations for the economic consequences of military action. Where the French had taken the precaution of seeking an advance from the IMF before operations commenced, Macmillan had done nothing. At Cabinet he warned that 'our reserves of gold and dollars were still falling at a dangerously rapid rate' and that 'in view of the extent we might have to rely on American economic assistance we could not afford to alienate the US Government more than was absolutely necessary'.[58] By failing to take precautionary measures, Macmillan had left Britain totally vulnerable not only to a run on sterling, but also to American pressure exerted through the IMF. Dulles was confident that the British and French would soon come to heel because 'there would be a strain on the Br[itish] and Fr[ench] and it will be economic and quickly – the oil problem will be acute pretty soon'.[59] In the first two days of November the Bank of England lost $50 million, and after taking the necessary measures to safeguard the exchange rate, Britain's dollar reserves were falling close to the lowest level that was considered safe.[60] Undersecretary Hoover, who took control of the State Department on 2 November when Dulles was rushed to hospital, told Eisenhower that same morning that there were '3 possibilities' when it came to putting pressure on the British and French: 'Economic pressure, military pressure, & moral pressure'. Although he ruled out the first two, there was no need for America actively to do anything to undermine an economic position which was deteriorating daily. The moral pressure, applied through the UN, combined with the failing nerve of Macmillan, were

343

enough to bring the British into line. But that was not enough. As Hoover put it, 'this is a group in British Gov[ernmen]t that does not represent [the] British people. [It] would be a good thing if we could put them out.'[61]

Eisenhower was inclined to believe those who said that 'this is nothing except Eden trying to be bigger than he is'. His own view was that 'Eden and his associates have become convinced that this is the last straw and Britain simply had to react in the manner of the Victorian period'.[62] He wondered whether to 'get in touch with Eden, so as to keep the channel open', but it was decided to, in effect, put 'Eden and his associates' into diplomatic quarantine, until it was seen how they reacted to the initiative taken by the United Nations.[63]

On 2 November the UN adopted an American resolution calling for a complete cease-fire in the region, a withdrawal of British, French and Israeli troops, and the opening of the Canal. Naturally enough the Egyptians immediately announced their compliance, and on 3 November, under great economic pressure from Washington, the Israelis did the same.[64] In an effort to provide the British and the French with a face-saving device, the Canadian Foreign Minister, Lester Pearson, introduced a resolution providing for the establishment of a UN Emergency Force (UNEF) to ensure that the cease-fire was carried out.[65] The 'moral pressure' on Britain was now as intense as the economic strain.

The notion of a UNEF had first been bruited by Eden himself in the commons on 1 November, and it was difficult for him to turn it down without looking even more of a hypocrite than he was beginning to appear. Moreover, the French were pressing for immediate airborne landings, despite Eden's doubts, and acceptance of Pearson's motion would put the whole Anglo-French military operation at risk. On the morning of 4 November Eden faced a stormy Cabinet.[66] He had decided that operations should go ahead and should be speeded up as the French wanted, but rumours of an Israeli cease-fire brought something of a Cabinet revolt. Quite what happened is the subject of some dispute. According to Rab Butler, he 'took the line that were the news correct, we could not possibly continue with our expedition'; after all, if the ostensible purpose of the Anglo-French intervention was to stop Egyptian-Israeli hostilities, what would its purpose be if those hostilities had stopped? According to Butler, this argument 'nonplussed' Eden, who threatened to 'consider his position'.[67] Eden's official biographer, despite disputing this version of events, provides one which is not dissimilar, except on his telling of the story Eden only made this threat privately to Butler, Macmillan and Salisbury.[68] Either way, it was a fraught meeting, at which Eden did threaten to consider his position if his senior colleagues did not back him. Macmillan's metamorphosis went a stage further when news came through from Dixon in New York that the UN was considering oil sanctions. At this news, which came to the meeting of the Egypt Committee, the great 'unflappable' one 'threw his hands in the air and said, "Oil sanctions! That finishes it!" '⁶⁹

The motion to create a UNEF was passed on 4 November, and the following morning British and French troops landed in Egypt. In an effort to avert the wrath that was to come, Eden wrote a long and anguished letter to Eisenhower on 5 November in which he reiterated the basic British position, which was that, 'if we had allowed things to drift, everything would have gone from bad to worse'. Nasser would have become 'a kind of Moslem Mussolini and our friends in Iraq, Jordan, Saudi Arabia, and even Iran would gradually have been brought down'.⁷⁰ Whilst willing to pay lip-service to the professions of Anglo-American amity contained in Eden's letter, Eisenhower's prime concern was to 'bring him into an acceptable position in this matter'.⁷¹ Having been informed privately by the French of the extent of 'collusion', he was not likely to have been impressed by Eden's professions of innocence.⁷² As he warned in a letter which was not sent because it was overtaken by events, 'Harold's financial problem is going to be a serious one, and this in itself I think would dictate a policy of the least possible provocation.'⁷³

But even whilst the Americans frowned and the Soviets decided to involve themselves, the military operations were going very successfully, and Hoover warned the President on the evening of 5 November that 'Nasser's position is wobbly'.⁷⁴ The Soviet message to Eden spoke of a full 'determination to use force to crush the aggressors and to restore peace in the East. We hope you will show the necessary prudence and will draw from this the appropriate conclusions';⁷⁵ with Soviet tanks in Budapest, there was little doubt as to the 'appropriate conclusion'. Eisenhower was anxious lest this portended a 'wild adventure' on the part of the Soviets,⁷⁶ and the Cabinet took the threat seriously when it met on 6 November.

Macmillan's metamorphosis was completed at the Cabinet meeting. The Americans were refusing to do anything to expedite oil supplies, and Treasury Secretary George Humphrey had told Macmillan that 'only a cease-fire by midnight would secure US support' of a British request for a loan from the IMF. The run on Britain's gold reserves in the past week had reduced holdings by an eighth, and he was convinced that the run on sterling had been orchestrated from Washington. Although he later denied doing any such thing, Lloyd described how Macmillan threatened to resign unless there was a cease-fire.⁷⁷ He had become, in Brendan Bracken's trenchant phrase, 'the leader of the bolters'.⁷⁸ A cease-fire was declared from midnight.

29

The Strange End of Anthony Eden

Looking back on events when he was composing his memoirs, Eden 'came to the conclusion that the Americans behaved much worse after the cease-fire than before'; he was quite correct in this assumption, but he knew only the half of it.[1] The hope that the British would get immediate relief from their problems by agreeing to a cease-fire was not fulfilled, because what the Americans wanted was not just a cease-fire, but an unconditional British withdrawal – and the end to the whole strand of policy which Eden represented.

It is significant that the strongest criticisms of Eden in the Foreign Office and by historians with close links to it should have centred upon the fact that he acted without being sure of American backing and that he kept America in the dark. So deep-seated is the habit of appeasing the Americans in such quarters that the Americans were not blamed for frustrating the actions of an independent state, but rather Eden was held culpable for 'embarking upon an action which the Americans would wish to frustrate'.[2] Eden had committed the great sin against the Churchillian conception of the alliance, which at bottom meant accepting that Britain was a satellite state, arguing that there was no purpose to be served by dwelling on this fact, and moving on quickly to claim that the relationship brought Britain immense advantages. Eden, as we have seen, had been both more sceptical about American benevolence and motives, and less inclined to defer to American wishes in areas where they seemed to conflict with his conception of British interests. No doubt it was unfortunate of the electorate to vote for such a man. If what happened to the British over the few weeks after the cease-fire had occurred in Latin America, then its true nature would have been clearer, for in her own back-yard America acted with less circumspection. Leaders who were adjudged unsuitable for America's purposes were overthrown by freedom-fighters who usually turned out to have American sponsorship, and the foreign policy of the country concerned was realigned to suit America's purposes. In the case of Britain there were no freedom-fighters, but Eden was overthrown quite as effectively as any Latin American President, as the Americans first wrecked his policy, put him into diplomatic quarantine, and then made it plain to Macmillan and Butler that there would be no help from America until Eden's policy was gone.

Questions must certainly be raised about whether Britain needed to have knuckled down quite so readily to America as Macmillan, the foremost advocate of the cease-fire (and the major beneficiary of the end of Eden's policy), claimed. It was not simply that Macmillan had failed to take any precautionary measures to guard against a run on sterling; the actual figures which he gave to his colleagues on 6 November were incorrect. His statement that Britain's gold reserves had fallen by $270 million overestimated the real figure of $85 million by more than three times; indeed, it was not until 16 November that the losses reached $200 million.[3] Moreover, if the Treasury and the Bank of England had not been so determined not to resort to it, a devaluation of sterling would have slowed down the drain on the reserves. Indeed, it was this self-imposed strait-jacket which increased British vulnerability to American pressure: by the end of the month an announcement would have to be made on the state of Britain's reserves, and unless something was done to relieve the pressure, then a forced devaluation might be on the cards. Macmillan seems to have hoped that the cease-fire would be the prelude to American help – a view shared by Eden; both men soon discovered how wrong they had been.

The day after the cease-fire, 7 November, Eden noted that his priority was to 'get US support' to 'tackle an Anglo-US policy for a long-term settlement in the Middle East'.[4] When he had telephoned Eisenhower on 6 November to tell him about the cease-fire, he had put out feelers for co-operation.[5] He telephoned again the following morning to congratulate 'Ike' on his victory in the Presidential election, and to suggest that he and Mollet might come to Washington for discussions. he was encouraged to hear the President describe what had happened as 'like a family spat'.[6] Eden was anxious to comply with Eisenhower's wishes to bring about an end to the crisis, but even *in extremis* he was not willing to surrender unconditionally. He wanted the Anglo-French forces to be part of the UNEF, something the Americans were not prepared to allow.[7] Hoover thought that it would be unwise to allow an immediate visit lest it give rise to suspicion that America was going to act independently of the UN: 'we must be very careful not to give the impression that we are teaming with the British and French'. Eisenhower, who had 'really looked forward to talking with Eden', postponed the visit.[8] The Americans too wanted to establish a basis for a long-term policy, but their ideas did not include a joint Anglo-American one.[9] The Americans were prepared to use any intelligence information which the British had about Soviet intentions in the Middle East, and they expected the British to support their position in the region, but nothing would be done until the British and French troops had gone – 'as soon as possible'.[10] The big freeze had begun.

Not only did Eden not get his visit to Washington, but the drain on sterling and the gold reserves continued. On 8 November Macmillan predicted that the dollar balances would fall below the critical $2 billion level by the beginning of January, and Britain would be unable to meet the interest due on the 1946 loan. Only an American-sanctioned loan from the IMF would help, but whilst there were British and French troops in Egypt, this was not forth-coming.[11] Nor was help in the form of oil. At a meeting of the NSC on 8 November, Robert Anderson, the President's special adviser on the Middle East, advised against helping the British for fear of alienating the Arabs, and in discussing the general situation, Treasury Secretary Humphrey commented that, 'if the United Kingdom did not look out, it would bust itself to a point of bankruptcy and of no return'.[12] Who then would maintain order and security in this vital region? From the NSC records and from the comments which the President made to a bipartisan Congressional delegation on 9 November,[13] there can be no doubt that the answer to this was America.

With Soviet actions in Hungary stamping them indelibly as 'imperialist' and giving 'every weak country' firm evidence of what it meant to fall under Russian control, Eisenhower hoped that countries in the Middle East would now look to America. Egypt could be supplied with arms 'in return for an agreement that it will never accept any Soviet offer'; America could supply 'training missions' and even cash for the Aswan Dam. Loans could likewise be offered to Israel, Jordan and others, whilst the Tripartite Declaration could be turned into a series of bilateral agreements between America and the nations of the Middle East.[14] America would take over the Baghdad pact,[15] and in general American money would supply the space left vacant by the fall of British and French power.

It was ironic that Dulles should have 'thought that the British having gone in should not have stopped until they had toppled Nasser',[16] because American pressure not only secured that result, but it also ensured that the British retreated from Suez with as little in the way of compensation as possible. It may have taken a monumental lack of tact to have repeated this sentiment to Selwyn Lloyd, but Dulles was undoubtedly correct in stating that, 'as it was', the British 'now had the worst of both worlds'.

Eden's prestige, as well as his health, had been badly shaken by the crisis, and an early meeting with Eisenhower might well have helped him, but as it was the President almost disregarded him. Eden had never played the part expected of a British politician by the Americans, but there were plenty of alternatives who would do so. Aldrich reported on 12 November that both Butler and Macmillan were anxious to mend Anglo-American relations, with the former saying how 'greatly disturbed' he had been by 'the course followed by the majority' of his colleagues, and advising Aldrich to talk to Macmillan.[17] Doubt has been cast on the notion that one of the 'implicit conditions attached to a normal resumption of Anglo-American relations' was that Eden should be ditched,[18] and given Eisenhower's view that the importance of personal relationships could be 'exaggerated',[19] it might be thought to be going too far to say that the Americans wanted Eden himself to leave. But the real object of American displeasure was the independent policy which Eden had attempted to follow; provided that was dropped, the Americans did not really care, or need to care, who was Prime Minister of what would be, in effect, not so much a forty-ninth state as a satellite state.

It is, of course, unlikely that Eisenhower ever said to anyone, 'Get rid of Eden', but his view of the Prime Minister was certainly a poor one: 'one of the most disappointing things was to start with an exceedingly high opinion of a person and then have continually to downgrade this estimate on the basis of succeeding contacts with him. . . . Eden fell into this category.'[20] On 20 November the President telephoned Aldrich and 'told him to let Butler and Macmillan know simultaneously that we are sympathetic with their troubles and interested in helping them out'.[21] It may, of course, have been pure coincidence that this first friendly gesture since turning down Eden's request for a visit came just as the latter was about to stand down, but this seems unlikely. Unbeknown to Eden, both Butler and Macmillan were engaged in an exercise to find terms on which the Americans might save Britain's face; the fact that success in this enterprise would help the man concerned to succeed Eden was no doubt a secondary consideration.

Certainly the British faced an unenviable dilemma, summed up by Secretary Hoover as, 'they will either have to withdraw from Egypt, & have their Cabinet fall – or else they would have to renew hostilities, taking over [the] entire Canal'.[22] This was certainly the way Macmillan presented the matter to Aldrich in a long conversation on 18 November. The Chancellor tried to frighten the Ambassador with tales of hardliners in the Cabinet being willing to 'go down fighting' rather than agree to the American condition that British and French troops should play no part in UNEF and should be withdrawn from the Canal zone. Of course, this dire prospect, or its equally unpleasant alternative, the fall of the Government, could be averted if America would step in and ensure that the Canal was cleared and operated by an international agency. Aldrich correctly divined that Macmillan's plea, like his anxiety to get to Washington, was the result of Britain's 'desperate financial position'. Macmillan had spoken of going as 'Eden's deputy', and Aldrich wondered whether his hints about Eden's health were not a sign 'that some sort of movement is on foot in the Cabinet to replace Eden'.[23]

Aldrich's speculation, of course, is evidence only of itself, not of Macmillan's intentions, or yet of any American 'plot'. But the fact that Macmillan followed this up on 19 November with the news that due to ill-health Eden was going on 'vacation' and would soon be retiring, and the suggestions he then made to Aldrich, are signs that he was prepared to bargain about the terms on which Eden would be replaced – especially when Eden himself was unaware that he was going to retire. The Prime Minister's health had broken down, but even in early January he was genuinely doubtful about whether he would go or stay.[24] Yet Macmillan, predicting that he might be the next Prime Minister, told Aldrich that the first thing that would happen when Eden went would be the total and unconditional withdrawal of British troops, and he asked for an American 'fig-leaf to cover our nakedness'. No sooner had it been decided that Eden would leave the country than Macmillan was presenting himself to the Americans as the candidate who would offer them their solution.[25]

Eisenhower was certainly prepared to offer either Butler or Macmillan what he had denied to Eden, instructing Aldrich to tell them that 'they would have the necessary support from us' – by which Eisenhower's Secretary assumed he meant 'financial aid during the next couple of months'.[26] Although impartial, Eisenhower himself preferred Macmillan to Butler; he had, after all, long experience of him and described him as 'the outstanding one of the British he served with during the war'. The 'day the British agree to start withdrawing at once' was, Hoover and Eisenhower thought, the day that the British would be offered economic aid. As Secretary Humphrey put it, 'the key point in his mind was that we *are* in a position to supply the "fig leaf" which the British say they need to cover their nakedness. ... We can furnish dollars to meet stringent needs, providing they start to get out of the Suez at once.' There could hardly be a more naked statement of American intent. No one said that Eden himself had to go – just his policy. A more complaisant Prime Minister could expect to be clothed in American 'fig leaves' – a variant upon the usual new clothing ascribed to emperor's in fairy-tales. Not only would kindly Uncle Sam supply these garments, but he had even discerned some 'blessings in disguise coming to Britain out of this affair, in the form of impelling them to accept the common market'.[27]

The central theme of this book, that America wanted a compliant, non-imperial Britain as part of a European federation, and that that was what the worshippers at the golden shrine of the 'special relationship' were, unwittingly, signing up to, may strike some as strange, but there, in Eisenhower's words on the eve of Eden's departure for Jamaica, is evidence as hard and fast as anyone could want. If the British were prepared to forget their imperial pretensions and settle down as part of an Americanised Europe, then all manner of good things would be theirs; the consequences of failure were writ large in the fate which was befalling the man who, as Foreign Secretary and then Prime Minister, had attempted to plough a British furrow.

It seems almost inevitable that at this point, with Eden out of the way, the icon of the myth of the 'special relationship' should have been wheeled out by the British, almost as a token of their willing surrender. The concept was, after all, Churchill's, and it was fitting that the old boy should be brought into play as the British sought to get what terms they could from America. In a touching and emotional letter on 25 November the aged appeaser once more declared his 'unfaltering conviction' that the 'theme of the Anglo-American alliance is more important today than at any time since the war'.[28] It was not true, of course, but then since about 1941 it never had been, and even then it could have been less important had Churchill not chosen to hitch his star to it. Eisenhower had not believed it was true in 1953, and Suez was hardly likely to have changed his mind, but in bringing on the chief proponent of the myth, efforts were already being made to ensure its continuance. Given the right Prime Minister, Suez could be written off as an aberration, and the reality which had been glimpsed so vividly in 1956 could once again be covered by veils of mythology and evocations of the good old days of the war.

But the Americans would not yield, even to the blandishments of Churchill; the British had to agree to withdraw from the Canal zone before the 'fig leaves' would be provided. None of Macmillan's scare stories about last-ditch stands, nor Butler's pleas for help, were of any avail. On 24 November the General Assembly censured Britain and France and demanded that they withdraw their troops; the Americans not only supported it, but voted against an amendment from Belgium designed to give the Anglo-French forces more time. Despite more than a hundred Conservative MPs supporting an 'early day' motion censuring America, Butler and Macmillan surrendered. Macmillan told the Cabinet bluntly on 28 November that 'the goodwill of the United States Government was necessary' if the strain on the reserves was to be eased, 'and it was evident that this goodwill could not be obtained without an immediate and unconditional undertaking to withdraw the Anglo-French force from Port Said'.[29] As he put it in his memoirs, 'It was, of course, a little wounding to feel that we were to be given a "reward" for our submission to American pressure. Nevertheless, I was not foolish enough to refuse, even though the conditions were somewhat distasteful';[30] he was obviously well-suited to the coming age.

If what was required was, in effect, a surrender disguised as something else, Macmillan was your man. As Enoch Powell has said, 'It was not in his nature to believe or hope that men and nations can be led by reason or fired by sincerity: success and the surmounting of difficulties and dangers were the reward of dexterity and illusionism.' The old 'actor-manager' was the man to act 'Britain's attempt to humbug away the loss of its Empire', as well as to articulate the belief, shared by so many of his generation, that 'decline' had 'doomed' Britain 'to embodiment in Europe and subordination to America'.[31] He was a formidable political operator, as the manner in which he had changed from 'hawk' to 'dove' without destroying his career had shown. He liked to model himself on Churchill, and his actions in 1956 are indeed reminiscent of the manner in which his hero had managed to stage the Norway fiasco and get Chamberlain to carry the can. There was, of course, the problem of Butler, but not only did he lack Macmillan's advantages when it came to kow-towing to the Americans, he lacked the keen political skills which had already taken Macmillan to sounding out Aldrich. As deputy leader in Eden's absence, it fell to him to explain the British withdrawal to the House and to pay the price of the policy which Macmillan was advocating.

Talking to the 1922 Committee on the evening of 22 November, Butler made a business-like speech, whilst Macmillan pulled out all the stops, in a performance which Enoch Powell described as 'one of the most horrible things I remember in politics'. The 'skill of the old actor manager', and the 'sheer devilry of it, verged upon the disgusting'.[32] Macmillan clearly possessed all the qualities required to lead Britain into the brave new world of American domination.

Whilst Macmillan manoeuvred for the succession, the Americans planned for the future in the Middle East. Of course, British experience and advice would be useful to America, but Secretary Hoover thought it 'might be necessary for us to approach the British and say that it looks as though they are "through" in the area, and ask if they want us to try to pick up their commitments'. It was not as kindly a thought as Eisenhower's notion of giving the British 'every chance to work their way back into a position of influence and respect in the Middle East'.[33] It was perhaps wise of the President not to speculate upon how this remarkable feat was to be achieved.

Once Butler and Macmillan had opened informal negotiations, the Americans were prepared to give them the time they needed to persuade the Cabinet that withdrawal was necessary,[34] and to make it clear that America approved of the actions taken.[35] Lloyd informed the Commons on 3 December that withdrawals would begin at once; the operation was completed by Christmas. An IMF loan was sanctioned on 10 December, and two days later the British received $250 million, getting the rest of the $561,470,000 the following week, as well as a stand-by credit for $738,530,000; appeasement paid well.[36]

As Hoover had put it at the NSC on 30 November, 'what we were witnessing ... was a very rare phenomenon for the United Kingdom. It was nothing less than a decision for complete reversal of a disastrous policy in the middle of a crisis and without involving any change of the Party at the head of that Government.' Hoover's comment, that it would be a 'masterful stroke by Butler' if it worked, was altogether too modest in disclaiming the major share of the credit. Of course, there was some concern that 'anti-Americanism' was growing in Britain and France, but those two countries were in a 'highly psychopathic state', and it was only the British Conservative Party that seemed to be genuinely tinged with anti-Americanism.[37] Given the anxiety of Butler and Macmillan to come to terms with America, then Eisenhower need have no concern for the long-term consequences; the British would come to heel and the French could be disregarded.

Eden remembered Baldwin 'telling me years ago, how very lonely it was at the top. I didn't know what he meant then, I do now.'[38] His decision to depart for Jamaica was a mistake if he wanted to remain in power. In his absence his influence on policy was negligible, and although he felt to the end of his days that Macmillan had caved in too cravenly to the Americans, he could not stop him.[39] Whatever the state of his health, and however much he would like to have carried on, it was always unlikely that he could have done so, if only because it is difficult to imagine him following the new policy. Loyal friends urged him to persevere and to recover 'his hold' on an 'utterly demoralized' Party,[40] but given the new line of total subservience to America, Eden was hardly the man for the task. That this was so was clear from the statement which Eden wished to make on his return to London on 14 December, which not only reiterated Eden's case against Nasser as a Russian puppet, but also referred to the lessons of the 1930s and criticised the United Nations. This was not the language of the new order. He was told that 'people' were 'looking forward rather than back' and that there was a 'growing wish to end the breach with the United States'; nor must there be any harsh references to Nasser. Eden chafed, but it was a sign of the power of the new order that he was overruled by Macmillan, Butler and Salisbury.[41] Ill-health was not an excuse for resigning; Eden's health was genuinely fragile, but it did provide a dignified reason for an action which would, in any event, have been necessary.

The policy for which Eden has stood for so long, which was for an alliance with America which was a genuine partnership in which mutual co-operation was an integral part of what the alliance was for, had been broken. It had been broken on the rock of the American perception that an anti-colonial stand would win them friends in the Arab–Asian bloc at the United Nations, and would allow their more wholesome influence to replace that of the British and the French in the Middle East. Although he did not believe as fervently as Macmillan, Eden had operated long enough in Churchill's shadow for it to be difficult for him not to assume that the Americans had Britain's best interests at heart; it was, after all, at the heart of the Churchillian conception of the 'Grand Alliance' that the 'English-speaking peoples' shared a great common interest. Like all political mythologies, it had its uses, but for many years it had been more useful to the Americans than it had to the British. America had a tendency, as Dulles noted to Eisenhower on 3 December, to sacrifice her friends for her own interests:

I mentioned that while we did not seek it, we in fact did tend by our anti-colonial policies gradually to replace British, French and Dutch interests in what had been their particular spheres and that there was a tendency on the part of these colonial countries to attribute this motivation to us.

Dulles's only remedy for this situation was, in effect, to do what America was already doing with the British:

we must recognize that just as we expect other members of the free world to allow their positions to be eroded at least temporarily to give ... [our] policies time to work, so too we must make a contribution and that should not be regarded as charity or 'give-away' but a 'fair-sharing' of a common burden.[42]

Eden had not wanted Britain's position to be 'eroded', even 'temporarily'.

Eden, the last representative of the old order, resigned on 9 January 1957. Eisenhower wrote to express his regret: 'To me it seems only yesterday that you and I and others were meeting with Winston almost daily – or nightly – to discuss the next logical move of our forces in the war.'[43] His replacement, inevitably enough, was Macmillan, who lost no time in establishing personal contact with his 'dear friend', as he addressed him from the start of their correspondence.[44] The meeting which had been denied to Eden was readily accorded to Macmillan, and with the Bermuda conference it seemed as though the 'special relationship' was back on course. With Eden out of the way and a Prime Minister who knew how to flatter both Eisenhower and his successor, Britain could revert to the role of the 'old retainer', more especially since the policies which Macmillan was to follow, both in the rapid liquidation of much of the Empire and in applying for membership of the Common Market, were fully in accord with American desiderata; there would be no distressing shows of independence from London.

The Eisenhower declaration of January 1957 established American influence in the Middle East, and only nine months later they found themselves having to send troops to the Lebanon. Macmillan hoped that 'the Americans are learning their lesson and are realizing the vital importance of the Middle East. I only hope it is not too late';[45] Eden rather thought it was. As he told Salisbury in December 1957, 'The Americans have a great deal to answer for. They always push out the colonial powers and get something far worse instead; and they never learn by bitter experience';[46] nor did they. Nuri and the young King of Iraq were slaughtered in scenes of unspeakable barbarity in 1958, and the British position in the Gulf continued to weaken, until, in 1968, Britain retreated from the region altogether. American 'influence' proved little substitute for troops on the ground, and the triumph of anti-western feeling in the region brought the Americans less profit than they had imagined. As Eden (by now Lord Avon) commented to Macmillan in September 1965, it had been a cardinal 'error' for the Americans to suppose that if the 'US would only disassociate itself from ex-colonial powers, newly-liberated countries would support the US against communism'.[47]

As for Macmillan's policy, Eden looked back at the end of 1957 and concluded that whether he intended it to or not, it 'has had the effect of making us the 49th state'.[48] But that had been implicit from the moment Macmillan and Butler had taken up the running when Eden had gone to Jamaica. Eden has been accused of suffering from *folie de grandeur*, oddly enough by a critic who wisely refuses to regard the history of Britain after 1945 as one of inevitable decline,[49] yet his only *folie* was not to believe that Britain could, by herself, assert her interests in the Middle East and elsewhere, but rather to believe that the American alliance was an instrument for this purpose; but that had been the view in Whitehall from Churchill's time onwards. It was that acutest of observers of the international scene, Lord Salisbury, who identified the problem which had brought Eden down: 'I really don't know what is to be done with the Americans, their idea of an alliance is so different from ours.' The British expected 'close collaboration between ourselves and the country concerned', and indeed regarded such co-operation as 'in itself an important British interest'. In Korea and Guatemala the British had followed America's lead, because although 'neither was of the first importance to us . . . it *was* of the first importance to support our American allies'; but the same did not apply in reverse. Salisbury had spotted what Dulles told Eisenhower in December 1956 about America's allies being expected to sacrifice their interests for the 'purely American interest' in any particular problem: 'the broad consideration of maintaining a common front never seems to weigh in the balance at all. As a result we never know where we are vis-à-vis them, either in the UN or elsewhere.'[50]

The effect of the Suez crisis on the end of the British Empire will always be open to debate, but it seems somewhat perverse to believe that African nationalists learned nothing from it, or that the speeding up of the decolonisation progress in London owed nothing to the revelation of British weakness and the strength of American anti-colonialism. It is not argued that Suez 'caused' the decline – that, as Eden knew better than most, was already happening – but it did put an end to the process of managing it gracefully and with some attempt to leave behind viable political entities. Africa paid a high price, on this reading, for Eden's failure. It may, again, have been entirely coincidental that save for the action of General de Gaulle, Britain would have fulfilled Eisenhower's wishes by 1963 and would have been in the Common Market.

There had, of course, been genuine co-operation in wartime, but this had blinded many in Britain to the reality that this 'cordial intimacy in the common task did not preclude an ultimate divergence in aims'.[51] As long as Britain served the purpose of a virtually unsinkable aircraft carrier off the European coast, there would be a special defence relationship, but de Gaulle recognised this for what it was after the Kennedy/Macmillan meeting at Nassau in 1962; he rejected the British application to join the Common Market because he regarded her as little more than an American satellite. He had, after all, spent 1943 in Algiers with Macmillan and Eisenhower, and had seen Macmillan put into practice his notion of being a 'Greek' in the 'new Roman Empire'. His stubborn independence had won him the dislike of both Roosevelt and Churchill, but it had not damaged the interests of France – nor would it after 1958. As Eden recognised, looking back, it was the Frenchman who had had the sounder instincts when it came to America. If de Gaulle had seemed 'contumacious, especially to our American allies, perhaps we should have learnt from it. Some of the faults of later years might have been avoided if we had shown more of the same spirit.'[52]

Epilogue

The French word *l'histoire*, with its connotation of 'story', reminds us that history is a version of events. No historian can include everything which happened in his account. All history is selective. The period and theme which have been considered here have usually been described from a very different viewpoint, and it is some indication of how much history is influenced by current politics that the version offered here seems to provoke intemperate outbursts from otherwise sensible people; their seeming claim to infallibility for the orthodox version of events is a reminder that it is not an immutable historical truth, but rather a point of view disguised as such.

The Americans did not ensure that the Nazis were defeated, that honour belonged to the Soviet Union; Britain was more willing to pay the price demanded by the Americans than it was Russia's bill. The main reason for this was that Churchill and those who thought like him did not imagine that there was much of a price to pay for the American alliance. America would pick up Britannia's torch and the 'English-speaking peoples' would bring order to the world; that she would also defend the Empire was a bonus. This ignored the fact that the War of Independence had achieved its objective: America was a free country with an agenda all of its own. For Churchill, the defeat of the Nazis was the final objective; long-term planning, whether on the home front or in foreign affairs, held little attraction. This left Britain at the mercy of those who did have war aims which encompassed a view of what the future of the international order would look like. It might be argued that even had Churchill had some strategic vision, he could have done little to implement it as the smallest and weakest of the 'Big Three'. This may be so, but it may also be false. Perspective is a treacherous guide. At what point was Britain the 'weakest' of the 'Big Three'? Was her economy really worse off than its Soviet counterpart? Until 1944 she had more men under arms than the Americans. To what extent did lend-lease make Britain more economically dependent upon America than she need have been? Were there really no levers which could have been pushed by the Power which was contributing most to the war effort in the west until after D-Day? It may be that historians have mistaken Churchill's unwillingness to act for an inability to do so; this is not a mistake which those who have studied de Gaulle are apt to make. When tasked by Churchill in November 1942 with being stubborn and ungrateful to the allies to whom he owed everything, the great Frenchman replied that it was precisely because he had nothing save his independence and integrity left that he exercised them both so often. Eden was correct to wonder whether the British could not have learned something from de Gaulle.

During the war the British gave every impression that they would be willing to pay the price which Stalin would demand. From 1941, at the latest, it was clear to everyone who thought about it that an allied victory would depend upon the fortunes of Soviet arms. It was equally clear what the Soviets would take as the price of their success – the frontiers of June 1941. This meant that the defeat of Nazism would find eastern Poland, the Baltic republics, Bessarabia and parts of Finland under Soviet rule; the nationalities inhabiting these regions could not expect the Second World War to deliver them from totalitarianism. The Soviets were also bound to wish to protect themselves from a German war of revenge, which meant, at the least, that the rest of Poland, Czechoslovakia, Romania and Bulgaria would all need to be in the hands of governments approved by the Soviets; given the nature of the Soviet regime, this was hardly likely to mean that 'free and fair elections' would be allowed in the states which bordered Mother Russia. Again the British implicitly, and at Moscow in October 1944 explicitly, agreed to pay this price. Stalin had a vision of the future and he so manoeuvred during the war that by its end he was in a position to realise his ambitions.

The Americans resembled the Soviets in that they had war aims which went beyond the one enunciated by Churchill in 1940; for both Powers war was the pursuit of political ends by other means. Roosevelt's charm and insouciance, like his rhetoric, served a number of purposes – most of them obfuscatory. He may not have known how he was going to reach his destination, but he knew where he was going. Internationalising the 'New Deal' may sound a vague and incoherent objective, but like the original 'New Deal' it was a protean force which FDR could mould as circumstances dictated. There would be a world fit for Americans to live in. There would be 'democracy', 'free trade' and an end to 'imperialism'. Because Churchill and the British supported the first of these things, they signed up for the other two, which did not necessarily suit them at all.

Like most junior partners in a Faustian bargain, Churchill wished to welch on it when the time for payment fell due, and he looked towards the American connection to make this feat possible. There were many reasons not to pay the Soviet price for victory once it was in sight. How could the scourge of the 'Municheers' agree to hand over eastern Poland against the wishes of the Polish Government-in-exile? Lest Churchill should forget this dilemma, there were many Conservatives to remind him of it. But in truth he needed no such promptings; his anti-communism and his liberal faith in the virtues of nationalism (for European peoples, of course) predisposed him to seek to bilk Stalin. He also wished to preserve the strategically and economically important northern tier against Soviet incursions; here too the American alliance would, it was hoped, pay dividends. Historians who have discovered traces of these things in the archives have sometimes been led by them to suppose that Churchill was trying to inveigle Truman into the Cold War, but that is to ignore what Churchill supposed to be the lessons of Munich.

In 1938 Churchill had argued the merits of a 'Grand Alliance', which would, he declared, deter Hitler; now he hoped that a version of it would deter Stalin. On both occasions he overestimated the interventionist instincts of his potential partners. America did not enter what became known as the Cold War because of Churchill or the British, and had the Truman administration not come to believe that the Soviets posed a threat to the achievement of a world fit for Americans to live in, they would have left the British to face the Soviets as best they could – as they did in late 1945 and 1946. From the point at which the Americans decided to oppose the Soviets, the new war became an ideological one in which the old conservative virtues of pragmatism were discarded. When Churchill tried to revive them in 1953 and 1954, he was told firmly to shut up and keep to his place.

This is the reason why this particular version of events does not dwell upon the heroic days of 1947–50 and the founding of NATO or the Korean War. By 1947 a variation on Churchill's 'Grand Alliance' was in place. If it is believed that the Soviets intended to invade Great Britain or western Europe, then that alliance contributed to Britain's safety – although it was worth pointing out that it had been the formulation of that partnership that had contributed to the alienation of the Soviets and thus helped create the eventuality which it had been designed to avert. Eden had been correct to warn Duff Cooper in 1944 that a 'western bloc' might, indeed, create a Soviet threat. If American saved Europe, then it was for American purposes. Prosperity also brought America cultural colonisation.

Churchill's attempt to revive his vision of the old wartime alliance was sad and revealed how little substance there had been to it. The Americans had some use for the British, but not very much. Eden's attempt to act in defence of British interests revealed how vulnerable the British were to American pressure. Economically Eden could, perhaps, have toughed it out, but the British political establishment was so locked into its vision of the 'special relationship' that psychological dependence dictated submission. Indeed, so deeply rooted in the story of the last fifty years is the notion of the centrality of the Anglo-American alliance that even today a version of events such as the one provided here is apt to provoke Pavlovian responses about 'anti-Americanism'. Yet there is not much here which merits that epithet. The Americans acted sensibly to promote and protect what they conceived of as their interests; that some of these actions damaged Britain was not a proper concern for an American President: he was not elected to serve the interests of Great Britain. The foregoing narrative is only 'anti-American' in so far as it conflicts with the benign legend which has been used to make the British feel better about the way in which successive Governments have subordinated British interests to American desires.

With the end of the long period of expansion which began at the same time as Great Britain itself was created in the early eighteenth century, the centrifugal forces holding the latter together began to weaken. Unable to be partners in the great imperial enterprise, the Scots and even the Welsh would begin to argue that the logic of the triumph of nationalism was that they should themselves become free and independent nations. At the same time, losing faith in their special destiny, those who ruled Great Britain would seek to submerge her independence into that of a greater Europe. It was all very odd. The British had fought two world wars to prevent Germany from dominating Europe, and they had still ended up in a German-dominated Europe. They had fought to preserve their independence, but they had lost it all the same. The words of the great Duke of Wellington seem apposite: 'the only thing worse than such a victory is a defeat'.

So, at the end we have a version of events which casts doubts not only on the need for 'their finest hour' and the necessity for Britain to have stayed in the war, but one which also portrays American policy as the product of calculation and not sentiment, the results of which were not beneficent for Great Britain. It is consistent (perhaps wrongly so) in arguing for accommodation with Hitler and Stalin; balances of power are usually to be preferred to the imbalance which results from one or two Powers dominating the world. It does not locate the Cold War in an Anglo-Soviet dispute, but rather places the latter in the pre-history of the former. It is a version which queries the results of the unwillingness of the western allies to live up to the promises they had made to the Soviets, and which asks what Britain and America supposed Russia wanted for the scores of millions of lives lost in the great patriotic war? Contrary to what some reviewers might suppose, it does not argue that the British Empire would have still been with us today if Churchill had not thrown it all away. As Paul Kennedy has remarked, the historiography of the British Empire

runs the risk of becoming a curious variant of . . . 'the Whig interpretation of history'. That is to say, instead of assuming the inexorable rise of constitutional freedom and democracy, and categorizing historical events and personalities as they fitted that teleology . . . one was assuming here the inevitable decline of the British Empire and then searching out the evidence of weakness.[1]

The sudden end of the Empire and the fact that Churchill himself viewed the 1930s as a period of imperial retreat has obscured the signs of a vigorous and subtle imperial strategy at work during that decade, dividing and ruling, making concessions where necessary, but none which undermined the Empire. Churchill's abandonment of that policy certainly overstrained the resources of the Empire, as it did the loyalty of those in India upon whom the Raj depended, but it was the triumph of American anti-imperialism which put paid to the imperial mission.

In this version of events Churchill's reputation as a seer seems very much overrated; if he had a vision, it was a backward-looking one. That was why he was so successful in 1940. During that long, perilous summer he was able to articulate a sense of English history which stiffened the sinew of his fellow countrymen; for the first, but also the last time, Churchill and the English people were at one (the Welsh and the Scots, not to mention the Irish, seem to have been less susceptible to his appeal, which was, after all, to an imperial race). If he had overestimated British power, so did the people whom he led. He used the political capital accrued in 1940 to prolong his career at the top, and he genuinely believed that English history was leading to the Anglo-American union which he had espoused at Harvard in 1943 and Fulton in 1946. Because it was not leading there, historians have tended to ignore the first speech and have concentrated on what was, at best, a lesser theme in the misnamed 'Iron Curtain' speech. The Fulton speech is, as Churchill entitled it, about the 'Sinews of Peace', and the foremost of those was the Anglo-American alliance.

Anthony Eden, by contrast, emerges with an unsuspected reputation as a seer. He foresaw the shape of the future better than anyone. In December 1941 he warned Churchill that if Soviet territorial demands were not satisfied, there would be no stability in Europe at the end of the German war; he was right. He saw that if the war was ever won, it would be because the Soviets had crossed the June 1941 frontiers, and he argued that Britain should concede this in advance and try to win Russia's trust. Of course there are historians, heavily influenced by the Cold War and the so-called 'lessons of Munich', who would see this as nothing more than another manifestation of appeasement. It was, in fact, classic diplomatic wisdom. Palmerston may have been apt to lecture Metternich upon the virtues of the constitutional form of government, but he had never made it a precondition of coexistence. It had been the British habit to stick to Castlereagh's line in 1815 that countries should decide their own form of governance; only the autocratic Holy Alliance powers believed that it was right to interfere in the internal affairs of other countries. Eden, the last of the classic diplomatists, saw that salvation lay in recreating a balance of power in Europe, independent of America, and that for this to happen, Russia's demands would have to be granted – as they had been in 1815. He was not apocalyptic about Russia; Stalin's demands seemed a good deal more limited than Hitler's, and there were historical justifications for them (as there had been for Hitler before 1939). If Russia would stick to her sphere, Britain would reciprocate. There would be rivalry in the Middle East and throughout the northern tier, but that had always been the case; there would also be rivalry with America. What Eden appreciated was that without the pragmatism to give Russia her territorial desiderata, the war would end in diplomatic and political instability.

Eden was correct. He was also acute in discerning the challenge to British power posed by America. But where he failed was in getting Churchill to act. Those historians who allege that the line of argument pursued here is the product of hindsight have clearly not immersed themselves in the thinking of Anthony Eden, who saw these things when they still lay in the mists of the future. Churchill received excellent advice about how to deal with the Soviets, and with the French, but he ignored it because it conflicted with his fantasy about an Anglo-American union. Thereafter he tried to make up the lost ground, but it was too late. The onset of the Cold War and the triumph of a version of Churchill's 'Grand Alliance' locked Britain into a junior partnership with the Americans, which in the Far East overstrained the British economy and brought the risk of nuclear war. In the Middle East it resulted in the British being forced to subordinate their own policy to American desiderata, whilst in western Europe its result was pressure to join a federation.

The Second World War will always fascinate historians, but they have hardly begun to get to grips with its wider significance. There are a number of these, ranging from the rise of American power (to a position which would prove and will prove unsustainable), to the road opened to the rise of Islam by the collapse of the European Empires, which had, in the late nineteenth century, arrested it. This narrative has attempted to deal with one part of one of those wider themes – what might be called the war of the British succession. Which Powers would succeed to the power and influence in those regions of the world where the British had once exercised them? Eden saw something of this. He recognised that if there was no balance of power in Europe, then an Empire of global compass would find itself unable to cope. Much of Britain's Empire had been acquired as a by-product of wars in Europe, and her most acute Foreign Secretaries had recognised the importance of a balance of power in Europe to imperial security. The results of the decision to fight in 1939 hardly suggested that Britain should end the German war by beginning one against the Soviet Union. Eden had come to recognise the wisdom contained in Halifax's homely aphorism that 'the world is a strangely mixed grill of good and evil and for good or ill we have to do our best to live in it'.[2] So it was. Roosevelt's purpose was, in Henry Kissinger's words, 'to remove Hitler as the obstacle to a cooperative international order based on harmony, not on equilibrium'.[3] It was at this deeper level that British and American war aims clashed. A balance of power, not a preponderance of it, suited British interests best; the same was not true of America.

Churchill's 'misguided sentimental investment' paid few dividends for Britain, but it made the road to world power for America smoother. It is, therefore, appropriate that whilst his fellow countrymen have named a college after him, it should be the Americans who have raised a shrine to Winston Leonard Spencer Churchill.

Notes

1: Special Relationships

1 A. L. Frieberg, *The Weary Titan: Britain and the Experience of Relative Decline* (Princeton, 1988), for the debates
2 S. Anderson, *Race and Rapprochement: Anglo-Saxonism and Anglo-American Relations, 1895–1904* (NJ, 1981), p. 12
3 *Ibid.*, p. 13
4 C. S. Campbell, *Anglo-American Understanding, 1898–1903* (CT, 1980 edn), p. 27
5 R. G. Neale, *Great Britain and the United States Expansion: 1898–1900* (Michigan, 1966), pp. 1–3
6 Randolph S. Churchill, *Winston S. Churchill, vol. I, companion vol. 2: 1896–1900* (1967), letter to Lady Randolph, 22 May 1898, p. 937
7 Randolph S. Churchill, *Winston S. Churchill, vol. I, companion vol. 1: 1874–1896* (1967), pp. 604–21
8 PRO, Hankey Papers, Cab. 63/40, Paper by Sir Maurice Hankey, 'The origins and present position of the decision to make no defensive preparations against America as a possible enemy', May 1929, fo. 137
9 D. C. Watt, *Succeeding John Bull* (1984), pp. 30–2
10 *Ibid.*, p. 32, quoting Wilson to House, 21 July 1917
11 R. Blake, *The Unknown Prime Minister* (1955), pp. 490–6
12 Donald A. Yerxa, *Admirals and Empire: The United States Navy and the Caribbean 1898–1945* (South Carolina, 1991), p. 94
13 M. Gilbert, *Winston S. Churchill, vol. V, companion vol. 2* (1979), pp. 899–901
14 Philip Williamson (ed.), *The Modernisation of Conservative Politics: The Diaries and Letters of William Bridgeman 1904–1935* (1990), diary, June–August 1927, p. 207
15 *Ibid.*, p. 205
16 British Library, Balfour Papers, Add. MSS. 49704, Hankey to Balfour, 29 June 1927
17 PRO, Cab. 63/40, Hankey memo., May 1929, fo. 134
18 Gilbert, *op. cit.*, WSC memo., 19 November 1928, pp. 1380–2
19 Birmingham University Library, Neville Chamberlain MSS., diary, NC 2/1, December 1927, for Baldwin, and NC 18/1/1032, Neville to Hilda Chamberlain, 19 December 1937
20 Winston S. Churchill, *The Second World War, vol. I: The Gathering Storm* (1948), pp. 158, 160

21 This argument is explored in detail in my *Chamberlain and the Lost Peace* (1989)
22 A. J. P. Taylor, *The Italian Problem in European Diplomacy 1847–1849* (Manchester, 1934), p. 3
23 C. Hill, *Cabinet Decisions on Foreign Policy, October 1938–June 1941* (Cambridge, 1991), pp. 156–8; D. Reynolds, 'Churchill and the British "Decision" to fight on in 1940: Right Policy, Wrong Reasons', in D. Langhorne (ed.), *Diplomacy and Intelligence during the Second World War* (Cambridge, 1983), pp. 147–67
24 Ralph F. de Bedts, *Ambassador Joseph Kennedy 1938–40* (NY, 1985), p. 44
25 The most recent assault on Kennedy comes in Nigel Hamilton's biography of JFK. See also M. R. Beschloss, *Kennedy and Roosevelt* (NY, 1980)
26 Donald B. Schewe (ed.), *Franklin D. Roosevelt and Foreign Affairs: Second Series, vol. 16: July–August 1939* (NY, 1969), Kennedy to Roosevelt, 21 July 1939, p. 108
27 Churchill Memorial, State Department (hereinafter SD) Microfilm, Roll 22, European War 1939/3487 4/10, Kennedy to State Department, 10 June 1940
28 Churchill Memorial, SD Microfilm, Roll 22, 740.0011, European War 1939/3487 6/10, Kennedy to State Department, 12 June 1940
29 John Charmley, *Churchill: The End of Glory* (1993), p. 413
30 W. Kimball (ed.), *Churchill and Roosevelt: The Complete Correspondence, vol. 1: The Alliance Emerging, October 1939–November 1942* (hereinafter *Churchill and Roosevelt I*) (Princeton, 1984), p. 42
31 SD Microfilm, Roll 22, 740.0011, European War 1939/3485 7/10, Kennedy to FDR, 14 June 1940
32 *Loc. cit.*, Roosevelt to Kennedy, 14 June 1940
33 *Ibid.*
34 de Bedts, *op. cit.*, p. 206

2: Churchill's Roosevelt

1 James MacGregor Burns, *Roosevelt: The Lion and the Fox* (NY, 1956), and *Roosevelt: The Soldier of Freedom* (1970), remain the best biographical studies. Warren Kimball, *The Juggler: Franklin Roosevelt as Wartime Statesman* (Princeton, 1992), gathers together, in revised form, a series of brilliant essays; it is essential reading
2 Kimball, *ibid.*, p. 7
3 Story told to me by Professor Elliot A. Rosen of Rutgers in 1980

4 MacGregor Burns, *Roosevelt: The Lion and the Fox*, esp. chap. V; Geoffrey C. Ward, *A First Class Temperament: The Emergence of Franklin Roosevelt* (NY, 1989), chaps 13–16

5 Hugh G. Gallagher, *FDR's Splendid Deception* (NY, 1985)

6 Keith D. McFarland, *Harry H. Woodring* (Kansas, 1975), p. 140

7 R. Sherwood, *Roosevelt and Hopkins: An Intimate History* (NY, 1948), pp. 135–6

8 McFarland, *op. cit.*, p. 140

9 Kimball, *op. cit.*, p. 14

10 This picture of FDR is drawn from a variety of sources, the most important being Sherwood, Kimball, Ward and MacGregor Burns

11 Max Beloff, 'Roosevelt and Stalin', in *Purnell's History of the Twentieth Century*, p. 2024

12 J. Harvey (ed.), *The War Diaries of Oliver Harvey 1941–5* (hereinafter *Harvey diary*) (1978), 12 August 1941, p. 31

13 McFarland, *op. cit.*, pp. 201–3

14 PRO, Foreign Office, General Correspondence, FO 371/30653, contains many examples of this during 1942

15 See the evidence cited in Watt, *op. cit.*, pp. 40–2

16 de Bedts, *op. cit.*, p. 16

17 Arthur H. Vandenberg Jr (ed.), *The Private Papers of Senator Vandenberg* (Boston, 1952), 15 September 1939, pp. 2–3

18 R. J. Maddox, *William E. Borah and American Foreign Policy* (Baton Rouge, 1969), p. 59

19 *Ibid.*, p. 229

20 W. L. Langer and S. Gleason, *The Challenge to Isolation* (NY, 1952), and also *The Undeclared War* (NY, 1953). MacGregor Burns, *Roosevelt: The Soldier of Freedom*, sympathises but criticises

21 C. Tansil, *Back Door to War* (Chicago, 1952); Harry Elmer Barnes (ed.), *Perpetual War for Perpetual Peace* (Idaho, 1953)

22 R. Divine, *The Reluctant Belligerent* (NY, 1965), and R. Dallek, *Franklin D. Roosevelt and American Foreign Policy 1932–1945* (NY, 1979), combine both lines

23 SD Microfilm, Roll 22, 740.0011, European War 1939/3487 2/10, Kennedy to FDR, 6 June 1940

24 Maddox, *op. cit.*, p. 239

25 Vandenberg (ed.), *op. cit.*, 27 October 1939, p. 3

26 Franklin D. Roosevelt Library, Hyde Park, New York (hereinafter FDRL), Harry L. Hopkins Papers, Sherwood Collection, Box 304, FDR Mss. note, c. 2 August 1940

27 SD Microfilm, Roll 22, 740.0011, European War 1939/3625, Heath (Berlin) to SD (sent to FDR), tel. 1754, 9 June, 8 a.m. (recd 10.19 a.m.), marked that both FDR and CH saw it

28 R. T. Thomas, *Britain and Vichy* (1978)

29 Halifax Papers, diary, 27 May 1940

30 PRO, Kew, Prime Minister's Papers, PREM[IER] (hereinafter PREM.) 3/476/10, Halifax to WSC, 28 May 1940, fo. 537

31 PREM. 3/476/10, Sir D. Scott, 28 May 1940, fos 539–40

32 *Loc. cit.*, Mr Whitehead minute, 30 May 1940, fos 533–5

33 *Loc. cit.*, Churchill to Lothian, 9 June (sent 10th), fos 560–1

34 T. J. McCormick, *America's Half-Century* (Baltimore, 1989), p. 5

35 *Ibid.*, p. 33

36 See Charmley, *Churchill*, pp. 456–8, 525–9, 537–8

37 FDRL, Harry L. Hopkins Papers, Box 298, file 'Footnotes: Jan.–Aug. 1941'

38 *Loc. cit.*, Eden minute, 29 December 1940

39 Elliot Roosevelt (ed.), *The Roosevelt Letters, vol. 3: 1928–1945* (hereinafter *FDR letters 3*) (1953), FDR to David Walsh, 22 August 1940, pp. 329–30

40 *Churchill and Roosevelt I*, WSC to FDR, 27 October 1940, p. 80

41 *FDR letters 3*, FDR to Hull, 11 January 1941, pp. 347–8

42 Kimball, *op. cit.*, pp. 46–8

43 *Ibid.*, p. 46

44 *Ibid.*, p. 49

45 *Churchill and Roosevelt I*, WSC to FDR, 7 December 1940, p. 108

46 J. M. Blum (ed.), *From the Morgenthau Diaries: Years of Urgency 1938–1941* (hereinafter *Morgenthau diary*) (Boston, 1965), pp. 199–201

47 MacGregor Burns, *Roosevelt: The Soldier of Freedom*, pp. 24–9

48 Churchill Memorial, Morgenthau microfilm, frame 0748, diary, 23 December 1940

49 PREM. 4/17/1, fos 92–4

50 *Churchill and Roosevelt I*, WSC to FDR, 2 January 1941, pp. 123–4

51 A. J. P. Taylor, *Beaverbrook* (1972), p. 439; the original is at PREM. 4/17/1, fos 104–6

52 *Morgenthau diary*, p. 204

53 PREM. 4/17/2, Wood to WSC, 15 March 1941, fos 169–73

54 PREM. 4/17/1, Cherwell to WSC, December 1940, fos 82–5

55 *Loc. cit.*, Wood to WSC, 30 December 1940, fos 79–81

56 PREM. 4/17/1, Beaverbrook to WSC, 19 February 1941, fos 49–50

3: *Alliances*

1 PREM. 4/17/2, WSC to EH, 15 March 1941, fos 166–7

2 *Loc. cit.*, M 325/1, WSC to Wood, 20 March 1941, fo. 156

3 L. Pressnell, *External Economic Policy since the War, vol. I* (1987), chap. 3; Kimball, *op. cit.*, pp. 52–5; FDRL, Morgenthau diary, vol. 404, fos 240, 246, 276

4 Kimball, *op. cit.*, p. 50

5 A. Hitler, *Mein Kampf* (1975 edn)

6 John Erickson, *The Road to Stalingrad* (1975), chap. 2; C. Andrew and O. Gordievsky, *KGB: The Inside Story* (1990), pp. 209–17

7 B. A. Leach, *German Strategy against Russia 1939–1941* (Oxford, 1973), pp. 5–9 and chap. 1. See also A. Bullock, *Hitler: A Study in Tyranny* (1962), p. 594, and *Hitler and Stalin: Parallel Lives* (NY,

1992); H. R. Trevor-Roper (ed.), *Hitler's War Directives, 1939–1945* (1964)

8 G. Gorodetsky, *Sir Stafford Cripps' Mission to Moscow 1940–42* (Cambridge, 1984), pp. 172–4

9 For three different views of Cripps, see S. Miner, *Between Churchill and Stalin* (1988); Gorodetsky, *ibid.*; and H. Hanak, 'Sir Stafford Cripps as British Ambassador in Moscow, May 1940 to June 1941', *English Historical Review*, 1979

10 S. Lawlor, 'Britain and the Russian entry into the war', in Langhorne (ed.), *op. cit.*; Gorodetsky, *op. cit.*, pp. 174–7

11 Gorodetsky, *op. cit.*, pp. 180–1

12 W. H. McNeil, *America, Britain and Russia 1941–1946* (1953), pp. 20–1

13 Sherwood, *op. cit.*, pp. 264–5

14 *Ibid.*, p. 305

15 George C. Herring, *Aid to Russia, 1941–1946* (Columbia, 1973), p. 8

16 Sherwood, *op. cit.*, pp. 306–8

17 MacGregor Burns, *Roosevelt: The Soldier of Freedom*, p. 111

18 Herring, *op. cit.*, p. 9

19 MacGregor Burns, *Roosevelt: The Soldier of Freedom*, pp. 112–15; Sherwood, *op. cit.*, pp. 327–43; Herring, *op. cit.*, pp. 11–13

20 G. Ross (ed.), *The Foreign Office and the Kremlin 1941–45* (Cambridge, 1984), pp. 10–11

21 Gorodetsky, *op. cit.*, p. 187, citing Cripps's diary and his reports to London; see also Ross, *ibid.*, pp. 10–14; Miner, *op. cit.*, pp. 131, 143

22 Miner, *op. cit.*, p. 141

23 V. Mastny, 'Stalin and the prospects of a separate peace in World War II', *American Historical Review*, December 1972, pp. 1366–7

24 Earl of Avon, *The Eden Memoirs, vol. II: The Reckoning* (hereinafter *Eden II*) (1965), pp. 318–19

25 Winston S. Churchill, *The Second World War, vol. III: The Grand Alliance* (1975 edn), WSC to Eden, 8 January 1942, pp. 453–5

26 On Eden, see R. R. James, *Anthony Eden* (1987); D. Carlton, *Anthony Eden* (1981). V. Rothwell, *Anthony Eden* (1992), adds little

27 Charmley, *Chamberlain*, chap. 5 and the references given there

28 *Ibid.*, pp. 11, 28–36, 40–52, 152, 177–8

29 PRO, Halifax MSS., FO 800/328, Hal/38/39, EH to Sir Roger Lumley, 21 March 1938

30 I owe this reference to my former student, Richard Grayson, who is writing a thesis on Sir Austen Chamberlain's foreign policy

31 *Eden II*, pp. 318–20

32 Birmingham University Library, Avon Papers (hereinafter AP), Eden diary, AP 20/1/21, 2 January 1941

33 AP 20/39/151, Cranborne to Eden, 16 February 1941

34 *Harvey diary*, 14 November 1941, p. 63

35 PRO, Avon Papers, FO 954/24, SU/41/1, AE to Cripps, 17 January 1941

36 Gorodetsky, *op. cit.*, p. 187

37 *Eden II*, p. 319

38 Miner, *op. cit.*, p. 68

39 FO 954/24, SU/41/24, Eden to Cripps, 30 June 1941

40 *Loc. cit.*, SU/41/48, Cripps to AE, 26 July 1941

41 Churchill, *op. cit.*, vol. *III*, WSC to Eden, 8 January 1942, pp. 453–5

42 FDRL, Adolf A. Berle Papers, diary, Welles to Berle, 4 April 1942

43 *Ibid.*, diary, 3 April 1942; Jordan A. Schwarz, *Liberal: Adolf A. Berle and the Vision of an American Era* (NY, 1987), p. 187; C. Hull, *The Memoirs of Cordell Hull, vol. II* (hereinafter *Hull memoirs II*) (1948), pp. 1167–71

44 *Eden II*, p. 318

45 FDRL, Private Secretary's File (hereinafter PSF), Safe File, Great Britain, Box 3, aide memoire, 25 February 1942

46 FDRL, PSF, Navy, Frank Knox, Box 62, FDR to Knox, 4 May 1942

47 FO 954/25, SU/42/21, Beaverbrook to Eden, 3 March 1942, and enclosure

48 *Loc. cit.*, SU/42/26 Butler to Eden, 13 March 1942

49 *Churchill and Roosevelt I*, FDR to WSC, 18 March 1942, p. 421

50 Bullock, *Parallel Lives*, pp. 634–8, 641–3; Roy Medvedev, *Let History Judge: The Origins and Consequences of Stalinism* (NY, 1989 edn), chaps 9 and 12, esp. pp. 541–51

51 FO 954/25, SU/42/33, Cripps to Eden, 27 March 1942

4: Uncle Sam and the Brave New World

1 D. Moggridge (ed.), *The Collected Writings of John Maynard Keynes, vol. XXIII: Activities 1940–1943* (hereinafter *Keynes XXIII*) (1979), JMK to Sir Kingsley Wood, 2 June 1941, p. 109

2 Ambassador Smith Hempstone, delivering the 139th Commencement Address, at Westminster College, Fulton, Missouri, 9 May 1993

3 Schwarz, *op. cit.*, pp. 201–6

4 *Ibid.*, p. 211

5 FDRL, PSF, Diplomatic Correspondence, Great Britain: Churchill, Winston, 1940–2, Box 37, Berle to FDR, 9 July 1941

6 *Ibid.*, Berle to FDR, 8 July 1941

7 *Churchill and Roosevelt I*, FDR to WSC, 14 July 1941, pp. 221–2

8 FDRL, PSF, Winant, John G., Box 6, Winant to FDR, 1 August 1941

9 *Harvey diary*, 12 August 1941, p. 31

10 D. Dilks (ed.), *The Diaries of Sir Alexander Cadogan 1938–1945* (hereinafter *Cadogan diary*) (1971), p. 401

11 *Ibid.*, p. 400, for the text

12 Sherwood, *op. cit.*, pp. 359–60

13 *FDR letters 3*, 'Pa' Watson to FDR, 16 May 1941, pp. 369–70

14 *Ibid.*, pp. 354–5

15 FDRL, Box 37, Hopkins to FDR, 21 February 1942

16 PRO, War Cabinet Meetings, Cab. 65/19, WM 84 (41) 1, annexe, for this and WSC's other statements

17 *Keynes XXIII*, JMK to Sir Kingsley Wood, 2 June 1941, p. 108
18 D. Reynolds, *The Creation of the Anglo-American Alliance 1937-41* (1981), pp. 214–16
19 FDRL, PSF, Safe File, Atlantic Charter (1), Box 1, WSC to Hopkins, 29 August 1941
20 Sherwood, *op. cit.*, p. 369
21 James T. Patterson, *Mr Republican: A Biography of Robert A. Taft* (1972), p. 247, quoting from a letter written in September 1941
22 *Ibid.*, p. 243
23 *Ibid.*, p. 245
24 FDRL, Hopkins Papers, Box 308, 'Shoot on Sight', memo., 2 September 1941
25 *Keynes XXIII*, p. 112
26 PREM. 3/474/1, Beaverbrook to WSC, 13 September 1941, fos 11–12
27 S. I. Rosenman (ed.), *The Public Papers of Franklin D. Roosevelt 1941* (NY, 1950), p. 463
28 PREM. 3/476/10, note by Malcolm MacDonald, 3 November 1941, fos 413–14
29 MacGregor Burns, *Roosevelt: The Soldier of Freedom*, pp. 133–7
30 *Churchill and Roosevelt I*, WSC to FDR, FDR to WSC, 5, 8 November 1941, pp. 266–7
31 MacGregor Burns, *op. cit.*, p. 156
32 *Churchill and Roosevelt I*, FDR to WSC, 24 November 1941, pp. 275–6
33 Reynolds, *op. cit.*, p. 361
34 *Churchill and Roosevelt I*, WSC to FDR, 26, 30 November 1941, pp. 277–9
35 *Hull memoirs II*, p. 1082
36 MacGregor Burns, *op. cit.*, p. 157
37 *Ibid.*
38 Reynolds, *op. cit.*, pp. 243–6
39 FO 371/35957, F2602/751/23, WSC minute, 19 September 1943
40 PREM. 3/476/3, T 794 to Smuts, 8 November 1941, fos 30–1
41 James Rusbridger and Eric Nave, *Betrayal at Pearl Harbor: How Churchill Lured Roosevelt into World War II* (NY, 1991), for one example. A more serious case is advanced by David Irving, 'Churchill and US entry into World War II', *Journal of Historical Review*, vol. 9, no. 3, Fall 1989, pp. 261–86
42 Reynolds, *op. cit.*, pp. 219–21
43 *Churchill and Roosevelt I*, p. 281
44 *Keynes XXIII*, p. 106
45 MacGregor Burns, *op. cit.*, p. 172
46 PREM. 3/120/7, WSC minutes, 11 April, 30 May 1942, fos 285, 283
47 Cab. 65/43, WM (43) 93, 14 July 1943
48 PREM. 4/17/3, Martin to Halifax, 6 January 1942, fo. 365; WSC to Halifax, 10 January 1942, fos 363–4

5: The Empire at Bay

1 *Eden II*, pp. 316–20, 341, 370–4, 398, for examples of Eden's thinking; Carlton, *op. cit.*, pp. 192–5, 209–12, 220–1
2 Sir L. Woodward, *British Foreign Policy in the Second World War, vol. V* (1976), pp. 2–18. For

Foreign Office thinking along the same lines, see FO 371/36118, Z1648/5/69, Mr Strang minute, February 1942, and other papers
3 PREM. 4/100/7, WP (42) 516, Eden memo., The 'Four Power' Plan, 8 November 1942
4 PREM. 4/30/8, WSC to Eden, 31 December 1944
5 *Churchill and Roosevelt I*, pp. 373–4, 400–1, and especially FDR to WSC, 10 March 1942, pp. 402–4, and Churchill's comment in *The Second World War, vol. IV*, p. 214
6 PREM. 4/17/3, Halifax to WSC, 4 January 1942, fos 366–8
7 *Loc. cit.*, WSC to Halifax, 10 January 1942, fo. 363
8 *Loc. cit.*, WSC to Halifax, 10 January 1942, fo. 364
9 J. Barnes and D. Nicholson (eds), *The Empire at Bay: The Leo Amery Diaries 1929–1955* (hereinafter *Amery diary*) (1988), 2 February 1942, p. 767
10 *Churchill and Roosevelt I*, WSC draft, 5 February 1942, not sent; also at PREM. 417/3, fos 299–302, where it can be seen that the phrase about 'tutelage' was Churchill's own, added in his own hand to the prepared draft
11 *Foreign Relations of the United States 1942, vol. I* (hereinafter *FRUS 1942, I*) (Washington, 1960), Winant to Acheson, 3 February 1942, pp. 527–8
12 Dean Acheson, *Present at the Creation: My Years in the State Department* (NY, 1969), p. 28
13 *FRUS 1942, I*, Welles memo., 7 February 1942, pp. 533–5; Acheson memo., 11 February 1942, pp. 533–4, and the draft given in *Churchill and Roosevelt I*, pp. 356–7. See also PREM. 4/17/3, fos 276–7
14 *Churchill and Roosevelt I*, FDR to WSC, 11 February 1942, pp. 357–8
15 R. J. Moore, *Churchill, Cripps and India 1939–1945* (Oxford, 1979), p. 42
16 PREM. 4/48/9, WSC draft, 2 March 1942, fos 766–8
17 *FRUS 1942, I*, Berle to Welles, 17 February 1942, pp. 602–3
18 *Ibid.*, pp. 604–6
19 Nicholas Mansergh (ed.), *The Transfer of Power in India, 1942–1947, vol. III* (hereinafter *Transfer III*) (1971), Mudaliar to Sir G. Laithwaite, 21 September 1942, p. 3
20 *Ibid.*, Linlithgow to Amery, 3, 10 October 1942, pp. 82, 120, for examples. FO 371/30659, 30660, contain 122 files on British reactions to the Cripps mission; FO 371/30660/A7216/122/45 for FO attitudes to the US on India, August 1942
21 Kimball, *op. cit.*, p. 66
22 *Ibid.*, p. 64
23 J. M. Blum (ed.), *The Price of Vision: The Diary of Henry A. Wallace 1942–1946* (hereinafter *Wallace diary*) (1973), p. 29
24 FO 371/30653/A5948/31/45, tel. 3381, Halifax to FO, 22 June 1942
25 FO 371/30653/A5574/31/45, Sir D. Scott, 17 June 1942
26 *Churchill and Roosevelt I*, FDR draft, 25 February 1942, pp. 400–2
27 *Ibid.*, pp. 402–5

28 Charmley, *Churchill*, pp. 489 foll., for details

29 *Transfer III*, Amery to Linlithgow, 26 September 1942, p. 50

30 Moore, *op. cit.*, pp. 67–83, for the details

31 *Ibid.*, pp. 109–16. See also Sherwood, *op. cit.*, p. 524

32 Sherwood, *op. cit.*, p. 524. See also *FRUS 1942, I*, HH to FDR, 9 April 1942, pp. 629–30

33 Moore, *op. cit.*, p. 117

34 *FRUS 1942, I*, pp. 631–2

35 *Churchill and Roosevelt I*, FDR to WSC, 11 April 1942, pp. 446–7

36 *Ibid.*, p. 447, editorial note

37 Sherwood, *op. cit.*, p. 531. See also *Churchill and Roosevelt I*, pp. 447–8

38 Sherwood, *op. cit.*, p. 533

39 *Churchill and Roosevelt I*, WSC to FDR, 12 April 1942, pp. 448–9

40 *Transfer III*, Eden and Halifax, 10 October 1942, pp. 118–19

41 *Ibid.*, Eden to Amery, 23 September 1942, p. 28

42 *Ibid.*, Linlithgow to Amery, 10, 12 October, 11 November 1942, pp. 120–1, 125–6, 231–2

43 FO 371/30652/A4741/31/45, Mr Ronald minute, 21 May 1942, and other FO minutes

44 *Ibid.*, Ronald minute, 24 May 1943

45 *Ibid.*, Halifax to FO, 14 May 1942, para. 10

46 FO 371/30652/A5312/31/45, Mr Evans minute, 6 June 1942

47 FO 371/30652/A5312/31/45, Mr Butler to Sir D. Scott, 22 May 1942

48 PREM. 3/478/6, Dill to WSC, 7 March 1942, fo. 27

49 *Transfer III*, note by Mr Patrick, 25 September 1942, p. 30

50 *Ibid.*, Amery to Linlithgow, 19 October 1942, p. 139

51 FO 371/30653/A5574/31/45, Eden minute, 17 June 1942

52 FO 371/30685/A5545/1684/54, Mr King minute, 26 June 1942

53 FO 371/30653/A5575/31/45, Eden to WSC, 15 June 1942; FO 371/30685/A5545/1684/45, 'American tendencies subversive of the British Empire', Mr Newton, 10 June 1942; A/7112/1684/45, 'America and the British Colonial Empire', Mr Newton, July 1942

54 FO 371/30653/A7567/31/45, Mr King, 18 August 1942

55 FO 371/34114/A444/32/45, Mr Butler, 16 October 1942

56 *Loc. cit.*, Gladwyn Jebb minute, 18 October 1942

57 *Transfer III*, pp. 252–5, for Law's report

58 PREM. 3/476/11A, F 4320/4320/61, Ashley Clarke to Eden, 11 June 1942, fo. 660

59 *Ibid.*, para. 8. On these things, see also C. Thorne, *Allies of a Kind* (1978)

60 *Ibid.*, para. 12, fo. 661

61 *Amery diary*, 4 March 1942, p. 783

62 PREM. 4/100/7, WP (42) 516, 'The "Four Power" Plan', AE memo. 8 November 1942

63 *Harvey diary*, October, November 1942

64 PREM. 4/100/7, WP (42) 516, 'The "Four Power" Plan'

65 PREM. 4/100/7, M 474/2, WSC to Eden, 21 October 1942, fos 265–7

66 J. Colville, *The Fringes of Power: The Downing Street Diaries, 1939–1955* (hereinafter *Colville diary*) (1985), 13 December 1940

67 PREM. 4/100/7, PM/42/229, AE to WSC, 19 October 1942, fos 268–9

68 *Loc. cit.*, M 461/42, WSC to AE, 18 October 1942, fos 271–2

69 *Amery diary*, 3 November 1942, p. 840; *Harvey diary*, 3 November 1942, p. 175

70 *Harvey diary*, 3 November 1942, p. 176

6: The 'mad house' and the Kremlin

1 *Harvey diary*, 23 October 1942, p. 171

2 PREM. 4/100/7, WP (42) 516, 'The "Four Power" Plan', fos 285–323

3 *Ibid.*, fo. 292

4 *Ibid.*, fo. 293

5 *Ibid.*, fo. 306

6 FO 954/26, SU/43/70, PM/43/258, AE to WSC, 31 July 1943

7 W. F. Kimball (ed.), *Churchill and Roosevelt: The Complete Correspondence, vol. II: Alliance Forged, 1942–1944* (hereinafter *Churchill and Roosevelt II*) (1984), pp. 244–5

8 FO 954/26, SU/43/17A, Bob Boothby to Eden, 25 February 1943: SU/43/52, PM/43/160, AE to WSC, note of WSC/Maisky conversation, 10 June 1943; *Churchill and Roosevelt II*, pp. 244–5

9 *The Times*, 11 November 1942

10 FO 371/34114/A444/32/45, Mr Montgomery minute, and other FO minutes, October 1942; FO 371/34115/A3361/32/45, Prof. Whitehead memo., 9 April 1943

11 FO 954/29, US/42/194, 195, FO minutes, October 1942

12 FO 954/29, US/42/61, FO minutes, April 1942; FO 954/29, US/42/202, 230, Halifax to AE, 12 October, AE to Halifax, 15 October 1942; FO 371/34114/A72/45, FO minutes, January 1943

13 FO 954/29, US/42/225, 226, Halifax to AE, 30 October 1942; US/42/227, Halifax to AE, 29 October 1942; *Transfer III*, Amery to Linlithgow, 13 December 1942, pp. 362–3.

14 FO 954/29, US/42/202, Halifax to AE, 12 October 1942

15 *Transfer III*, Linlithgow to Amery, 25, 30 November 1942, pp. 299–300, 324; Amery to Linlithgow, 25 November 1942, pp. 299–300, 306–7

16 *Loc. cit.*, Halifax to Linlithgow, 11 December 1942, p. 359

17 *Loc. cit.*, Halifax to AE, 14 November 1942, pp. 260–1

18 Kimball, *op. cit.*, pp. 70–2

19 FDRL, PSF, Diplomatic Correspondence: India, Box 39, Phillips to FDR, 23 February 1943

20 *Ibid.*, Phillips to FDR, 3 March 1943

21 *Ibid.*, FDR to Hopkins, 19 March 1943

22 *Harvey diary*, 13 March 1943, p. 229

23 *Eden II*, p. 374

24 *Foreign Relations of the United States 1943, vol. III*:

The British Commonwealth, Eastern Europe, the Far East (hereinafter *FRUS 1943, III*) (Washington, 1965), Welles memo., 30 November 1942; FO 954/29, US/42/203, AE to Halifax, 15 October 1942

25 FO 954/29, US/42/202, Halifax to AE, 12 October 1942

26 FO 954/29, US/42/176, Halifax to AE, 14 September 1942

27 *Loc. cit.*, US/42/214, Halifax to AE, 25 October 1942

28 FO 371/30660/A7216/122/45, Campbell to FO, 4 August 1942; A7709, Mr Newton minute, 20 August 1942; Sir Alexander Cadogan to Radcliffe, 29 September 1942

29 FO 371/30685/A9422/1684/45, Radcliffe to Sir Alexander Cadogan, 9 October 1942; A9423, 9424, 9610, 9700, 9726, 10067, 10263, 10059, correspondence, October to December 1942

30 FO 371/30654/A9668/31/45, FO minute, 22 October 1942

31 FO 371/34114/A711/32/45, Mr Price reporting Alf Landon, 6 December 1942

32 FO 954/29, US/42/225, 226, Halifax to AE, 30 October 1942

33 FO 371/34114/A72/32/43, extract from WP (42) 591, 16 December 1942

34 FO 371/34114/A72/32/43, Mr Malcolm minute, 4 January 1943

35 *Loc. cit.*, marginalia by Eden, Mr Butler minute, 5 January 1943

36 FO 954/29, US/42/227, Halifax to Eden, 29 October 1942

37 FO 954/29, US/42/260, notes by Oliver Lyttelton, 24 November 1942

38 *FRUS 1943, III*, Hopkins memo., 15, 22 March 1943, pp. 13–18, 34–6, for the American record; FO 954/29, US/43/24, AE to FO and WSC, 14 March 1943; FO 954/22, PWP/43/12, AE to FO and WSC, 29 March 1943, for Eden's record

39 FO 954/29, US/42/227, Halifax to AE, 29 October 1942

40 *Eden II*, pp. 372–5

41 *FRUS 1943, III*, Welles memo., 30 November 1942, p. 2

42 *Loc. cit.*, Hull to FDR, 15 February 1943, p. 3

43 *Ibid.*, Welles memo., 22 February 1943, pp. 4–5

44 FO 954/22, PWP/43/12, AE to WSC, 29 March 1943

45 *Transfer III*, Amery to WSC, 1 December 1942, p. 327

46 Sherwood, *op. cit.*, pp. 715, 719–20

47 FO 371/36118/Z1648/5/69, minutes by Mr Dixon, Mr Strang, 27 January 1943

48 A. L. Funk, 'The Anfa Memorandum', *Journal of Modern History*, 1954, pp. 252–4; FO 371/36117/Z1336/5/69, tels STRATAGEM 317, 361, 1, 6 February 1943

49 FO 371/35993/Z2576/2/17, Halifax to FO, February 1943

50 *FRUS 1943, III*, Hull memo., 15 March 1943

51 FO 371/36118/Z1648/5/69, FO minutes, February, March 1943

52 FO 371/36199/Z1760/117/69, Eden minute, 12 February 1943

53 FO 371/36013/Z2913/51/17, M 72/3, WSC to AE, 3 March 1943

54 *Harvey diary*, 11 March 1943, p. 228

55 *FRUS 1943, III*, Hopkins memo., 22, 27 March 1943, pp. 35–6, 38–9

56 *The Times*, 22 March 1943, quoting a speech given on 21 March

57 FO 954/22, PWP/43/12, WSC to AE, 29 March 1943

58 *Loc. cit.*, PWP/43/13, WSC to AE, 30 March 1943

59 FO 954/26, SU/43/17A, Bob Boothby to AE, 25 February 1943

60 FO 954/32, W(g)/43/18, Stalin to WSC and FDR, 16 February 1943

61 *Loc. cit.*, W(g)/43/19, Eden memo., 17 February 1942

62 FO 954/26, SU/43/70, PM/43/258, AE to WSC, 31 July 1943

63 FO 954/32, W(g)/43/22, Mr Warner minute, 24 February 1943

64 FO 954/20, SU/43/41, WSC to Clark-Kerr, 2 May 1943

65 FO 954/20, SU/43/47, Clark-Kerr to WSC, 8 May 1943

66 FO 954/29, US/42/5, Halifax to WSC, 11 January 1942

67 FO 954/26, SU/43/17A, Bob Boothby to Eden, 25 February 1943

68 FO 954/19, POL/43/1, Halifax to AE, 14 January 1943

69 FO 954/26, SU/43/61, Clark-Kerr to WSC, 22 June 1943

70 *Loc. cit.*, SU/43/64, Clark-Kerr to WSC, 1 July 1943

71 Ross (ed.), *op. cit.*, O'Malley despatch, 30 April 1943, pp. 127–30

72 R. Nadeau, *Stalin, Churchill and Roosevelt Divide Europe* (NY, 1990), chap. 4

73 Carlton, *op. cit.*, pp. 215–16; *Cadogan diary*, p. 521

74 FO 954/19, POL/43/12, minute of WSC/Maisky meeting, 23 April 1943

75 *Loc. cit.*, POL/43/13, Stalin to WSC, 21 April 1943

76 POL/43/14, 15, WSC to Stalin, 24 April 1943

77 POL/43/16, Stalin to WSC, 25 April 1943

78 FDRL, Oscar Cox Papers, Hopkins, Harry L. (October 1942–July 1943), Cox to Hopkins, 26 April 1943

79 PREM. 4/30/3, WP (43) 233, WSC memo., 10 June 1943, fos 126–30

80 PREM. 4/30/3, WSC to Halifax, 26 May 1943, fos 141–2

81 Charles de Gaulle, *Mémoires de Guerre, vol. II* (Paris, 1956), p. 123

82 Cab. 65/38, WM (43) 75, 23 May 1943, and annexes

83 FO 371/36047/Z6026/148/17, PENCIL 224, WSC to AE, 24 May 1943

84 AP 20/1/23, diary, 25 April, 14 June 1943; *Harvey diary* for this period is full of this subject.

7: *Anglo-Saxon Attitudes*

1 FO 371/36301/Z8225/6504/69, draft memo., 12 July 1943
2 *The Times*, 7 September 1943, quoting a speech given on 6 September.
3 FO 371/34114/A132/32/45, Col. B. W. Rowe, 22 August 1942
4 FO 371/34114/A670/32/45, Ministry of Information survey, 14 January 1943
5 FO 371/34114–19, January–August 1943, are full of bright ideas for doing this
6 FO 371/34120/A9559/32/45, BIS Report No. 82, 12 September 1943, survey of American press and radio reaction to Churchill's Harvard speech
7 FO 954/29, US/43/65, Halifax to FO, 20 June 1943
8 *Loc. cit.*, US/43/66, Halifax to WSC, 21 June 1943
9 FO 371/38544/AN2253/20/45, Political Summary, June 1943
10 FO 371/34139/A8438/57/45, Gore-Booth to FO, 6 September 1943
11 PREM. 3/476/6, fo. 266
12 *Ibid.*, fos 234–5
13 *Ibid.*, fo. 245
14 McNeill, *op. cit.*, p. 323
15 Nadeau, *op. cit.*, is a recent example
16 Warren Kimball, 'Eden in Washington', paper given at the Foreign Office/University of East Anglia Seminar in Atlantic Studies, 17–19 September 1993, p. 35
17 McNeill, *op. cit.*, p. 322
18 I owe this reference to Jonathan Haslam of Cambridge, who tells me that there is a record of it in the files of the former Soviet Ministry of Foreign Affairs
19 Sir L. Woodward, *British Foreign Policy in the Second World War, vol. II* (hereinafter Woodward II) (1971), p. 557
20 FO 954/26, SU/43/67, Clark-Kerr to WSC, 13 June 1943
21 *Loc. cit.*, SU/43/58, draft to Clark-Kerr, 16 June 1943
22 Woodward II, pp. 558–9
23 McNeill, *op. cit.*, p. 324; see also V. Mastny, *Russia's Road to the Cold War* (1979)
24 FO 954/32, W(g)/43/111, WSC to Clark-Kerr, 29 June 1943
25 Colonel David Glantz's figures, given at the UEA/FCO seminar, 18 September 1993. See fns 51–4
26 *Churchill and Roosevelt II*, WSC to FDR, 24 June 1943, pp. 278–9
27 Elizabeth Kimball Maclean, *Joseph E. Davies*, unpublished Ph.D. thesis, University of Michigan, 1986, p. 293
28 *Ibid.*, p. 294
29 *Ibid.*, pp. 338–9
30 *Ibid.*, p. 340, citing Davies journal, 13 May 1945
31 *Churchill and Roosevelt II*, FDR to WSC, 28 June 1943, pp. 283–4
32 Ross, *op. cit.*, FO minutes, July 1943, pp. 130–2
33 *Loc. cit.*, SU/43/100, E. L. Spears to Eden, 9 October 1943

34 FO 954/29, US/42/7, AE to Halifax, 22 January 1942
35 *Loc. cit.*, SU/43/115, AE to WSC, 29 October 1943
36 W. Averell Harriman and Elie Abel, *Special Envoy to Churchill and Stalin 1941–6* (NY, 1975), p. 236
37 Ross (ed.), *op. cit.*, pp. 139–41
38 FO 954/32, W(g)/43/175, Cadogan (Washington) to FO, 14 September 1943
39 *Churchill and Roosevelt II*, WSC to FDR, 20 October 1943, pp. 543–4
40 K. Sainsbury, *The Turning Point* (Oxford, 1985), pp. 124–34
41 Harriman, *op. cit.*, Harriman to FDR, 5 November 1943, pp. 248–51
42 *Documents on Polish-Soviet Relations, vol. II* (hereinafter *Polish-Soviet Relations II*) (The Sikorski Institute, 1967), Chip Bohlen's record of FDR/Stalin conversation, 1 December 1943; Harriman, *op. cit.*, pp. 278–9. The British record at PREM. 3/136/8, WP (44) 9, WSC paper, 7 January 1944, fos 18–21, is less explicit about what FDR said, but I have preferred the American record
43 Randall B. Woods and Howard Jones, *Dawning of the Cold War: The United States' Quest for Order* (Georgia, 1993), p. 23
44 Harriman, *op. cit.*, p. 279; McNeill, *op. cit.*, pp. 329–30
45 PREM. 3/136/8, WSC's WP (44) 9, 7 January 1944, fos 2–5
46 Harriman, *op. cit.*, p. 273
47 Lord Moran, *Churchill: The Struggle for Survival 1940–65* (1966), diary, 29 November 1943, pp. 139–40
48 McNeill, *op. cit.*, p. 355
49 J. W. Wheeler-Bennett, *Action This Day* (1967), p. 96
50 *Polish-Soviet Relations II*, notes of conversation between Eden and Mikolajczyk, 11 January 1944, pp. 134–6
51 *Ibid.*, p. 735
52 Woodward II, p. 657
53 *Ibid.*, pp. 660–2
54 *Polish-Soviet Relations II*, p. 735
55 FO 954/20, POL/44/9, record of conversation, 20 January 1944
56 FO 954/20, POL/44/10, O'Malley to Eden, 22 January 1944
57 PRO, Halifax MSS., FO 800/328, Hal/38/101, EH to Mrs Lindsay, November 1938
58 PRO, Halifax Papers, FO 800/328, Hal/38/38, Halifax to Sir Roger Lumley, 21 March 1938
59 *Loc. cit.*, POL/44/14, Eden to O'Malley, 26 January 1944
60 FO 954/20, POL/44/28, record of Churchill/Mikolajczyk conversation, 6 February 1944; also at *Polish-Soviet Relations II*, pp. 165–71
61 Sir L. Woodward, *British Foreign Policy in the Second World War, vol. III* (hereinafter Woodward III) (1971), pp. 106–7
62 FO 954/26, SU/44/26, WSC to Stalin, 24 January 1944
63 FO 954/20, POL/44/34, O'Malley minute, 13 February 1944

64 *Loc. cit.*, POL/44/35, M. 117/4, WSC to AE, 15 February 1944
65 POL/44/37, record of conversation, 16 February 1944; also at *Polish-Soviet Relations II*, pp. 180–7
66 POL/44/43, FO to Moscow, 21 February 1944; also at *Polish-Soviet Relations II*, pp. 191–3
67 *Hansard*, H. C. Deb. 5th Series, vol. 397, cols 697–9
68 FO 954/20, POL/44/50, O'Malley minute, n.d. but c. 25/26 February 1944
69 *Loc. cit.*, POL/44/53, FO to Moscow, 25 February 1944
70 POL/44/53, Clark-Kerr to FO, 28 February 1944
71 *Polish-Soviet Relations II*, pp. 196–7
72 *Ibid.*, WSC to Stalin, 7 March 1944, pp. 199–200
73 FO 954/20, POL/44/61, Clark-Kerr to WSC, 8 March 1944
74 POL/44/69, Clark-Kerr to WSC, 19 March 1944
75 POL/55/75, WSC to Stalin, 21 March 1944
76 POL/44/80, Stalin to WSC, 23 March (received 25 March) 1944
77 *Loc. cit.*, SU/44/102, M. 338/4, WSC to AE, 1 April 1944

8: A Suitable America?

1 FO 371/38523/AN1538/16/42, 'The Essentials of an American Policy' by Mr Dudley, 21 March 1944
2 FO 371/38523/AN1577/16/45, FO paper 'American relations with the British Empire'
3 FO 954/30, US/44/18, Halifax to WSC, 13 February 1944
4 PREM. 4/42/9, Attlee to WSC, 16 June 1944, fo. 1114
5 PREM. 4/42/9, PMM (44) 1, 1 May 1944, fo. 802; the quotation is from the first draft
6 PREM. 4/42/9, WP (42) 544, 5 December 1942, 'Colonial Policy', fo. 1096 foll.; WP (43) 6, 6 January 1943, 'Colonial Policy'
7 PREM. 4/42/9, WP (43) 9, Linlithgow to Amery, 2 January 1943, fo. 1057 foll.
8 FDRL, PSF, Box 75, Hull, Cordell, CH to FDR, 30 September 1944
9 *Morgenthau Diary*, pp. 232–3
10 L. S. Pressnell, *External Economic Policy since the War, vol. I* (1987), pp. 118–19
11 *Morgenthau diary*, pp. 238–40
12 Donald Moggridge (ed.), *The Collected Writings of John Maynard Keynes, vol. XXVI: Activities 1941–1946. Shaping the Post-War World. Bretton Woods and Reparations* (hereinafter *Keynes XXVI*) (1980), p. 3
13 FO 954/30, US/43/99A, M. Petherick to AE, 16 August 1943
14 PREM. 3/332/6, Beaverbrook to WSC, 24 February 1944, fo. 236
15 Michael B. Stoff, *Oil, War and American Security* (New Haven, 1980), pp. 4–6, 58–61; David Sidney Painter, *The Politics of Oil, Multi-National Oil Corporations and United States Foreign Policy*, unpublished Ph.D. thesis, University of North Carolina, 1982, *ibid.*, pp. 150–6
16 Painter, *ibid.*, pp. 153–4; Stoff, *ibid.*, pp. 57–61
17 Stoff, *ibid.*, pp. 81–4
18 Painter, *op. cit.*, p. 160
19 Stoff, *op. cit.*, p. 106, quoting FO 371, E6164/545/43
20 PREM. 4/52/1, Eden draft Cabinet Paper on Palestine, May 1944
21 PREM. 3/332/6, R. K. Law to WSC, 19 February 1944, fos 273–9
22 PREM. 3/332/6. Halifax to AE, 21 February 1944, fo. 255
23 PREM. 3/332/6, Beaverbrook to WSC, 14 February 1944
24 Stoff, *op. cit.*, p. 130
25 *Churchill and Roosevelt II*, WSC to FDR, 20 February 1944, p. 734
26 PREM. 4/17/5, Anderson to WSC, 11 November 1943, fos 733–7
27 *Churchill and Roosevelt II*, FDR to WSC, 22 February 1944, p. 744
28 *Ibid.*, p. 744, editor's comment. The telegram, 22 February, is on pp. 744–5
29 *Ibid.*, FDR to WSC, 23 February 1944, pp. 748–9
30 R. B. Woods, *A Changing of the Guard: Anglo-American Relations, 1941–1946* (1990), p. 31
31 PREM. 4/17/10, WP (44) 95, Beaverbrook paper, 9 February 1944
32 PREM. 4/17/5, Anderson to WSC, 24 February 1944, fos 723–4
33 PREM. 4/17/8, WP (44) 121, 18 February 1944
34 PREM. 4/17/11, M 220/4, WSC to AE, 4 March 1944, fo. 1207
35 *Ibid.*, PM/44/133, AE to WSC, 6 March 1944, fos 1204–6
36 W. F. Kimball (ed.), *Churchill and Roosevelt: The Complete Correspondence: Alliance Declining, 1944–1945* (hereinafter *Churchill and Roosevelt III*) (1984), WSC to FDR, 9 March 1944, p. 35
37 *FRUS 1944, III*, Morgenthau and Crowley to FDR, 4 January 1944, pp. 33–5
38 *Churchill and Roosevelt III*, FDR to WSC, 24 March 1944, pp. 65–6
39 *FRUS 1944, III*, Stettinius to Hull, 22 May 1944, pp. 1–2
40 PREM. 3/332/6, Halifax to AE, 21 February 1944, fo. 256
41 *FRUS 1944, III*, Stettinius to FDR, 22 February 1944, pp. 43–4
42 Woods, *op. cit.*, p. 18
43 *Churchill and Roosevelt III*, FDR to WSC, 3 March 1944, p. 3
44 *Ibid.*, WSC to FDR, 4 March 1944, pp. 17–18
45 *Ibid.*, pp. 3–7
46 Painter, *op. cit.*, pp. 165–95
47 PREM. 4/17/10, WP (44) 95, 'Anglo-American Discussions Under Article VII', Beaverbrook, 9 February 1944; Beaverbrook to WSC, 'British policy towards the United States', 24 February 1944; WP (44) 148, 'Discussions under Article VII...', Beaverbrook, 6 March 1944; Amery to WSC, 10 March 1944
48 Woods, *op. cit.*, pp. 58–62
49 Cab. 66/53, WP (44) 419, 31 July 1944, 'Supplies

from North America in Stage II', esp. pp. 6–9 and Annexe 5

50 PREM. 4/17/8, fo. 882 foll., WM (44) 49, 14 April 1944, Beaverbrook's comments, amplifying on what Cherwell had warned WSC on 17 March at PREM. 4/17/11, fo. 1196

51 Donald Moggridge (ed.), *The Collected Writings of John Maynard Keynes, vol. XXIV: Activities 1944–1946. The Transition to Peace* (hereinafter *Keynes XXIV*) (1979), JMK to Stettinius, 18 April 1944, pp. 28–9

52 Woods, *op. cit.*, p. 72

53 *Morgenthau diary*, p. 123

54 *Ibid.*, p. 133

55 PREM. 4/17/10, Cherwell to WSC, 15 March 1944, fo. 1135

56 *Amery diary*, 27 February 1944, p. 969

57 PREM. 4/17/12, Amery to Law, 5 April 1944, fo. 1271

58 PREM. 4/17/12, Amery to WSC, 13 April 1944, fos 1272–5

59 *Loc. cit.*, M 413/4, WSC to Amery, 13 April 1944, fo. 1265. See also *Amery diary*, 14 April 1944, p. 978

60 PREM. 4/17/8, WM (44) 49, 14 April 1944; *Amery diary*, 14 April 1944, p. 978

61 PREM. 4/17/12, P 13/44, Amery to WSC, 14 April 1944, fos 1263–4

9: Seeking a Suitable Stalin

1 Terry H. Anderson, *The United States, Great Britain and the Cold War 1944–1947* (Missouri, 1981); Robert Frazier, 'Did Britain start the Cold War? Bevin and the Truman Doctrine', *Historical Journal*, 1984, pp. 715–27; Fraser J. Harbutt, *The Iron Curtain: Churchill, America and the Origins of the Cold War* (1986); H. B. Ryan, *The Vision of Anglo-America* (1987); V. Rothwell, *Britain and the Cold War 1941–1947* (1982); H. Thomas, *Armed Truce* (1988); Anne Deighton (ed.), *Britain and the First Cold War* (1990), and numerous others. See also Walter Lacqueur, 'Visions and Revisions', *TLS*, 5 March 1982, pp. 243–4

2 T. E. Utley, 'Stockton, the Times and the Anglo-Soviet Alliance', *Spectator*, 30 August 1986, p. 6

3 Henry L. Stimson and McGeorge Bundy, *On Active Service in Peace and War* (NY, 1947), p. 527

4 Woodward III, M 497/4, WSC to AE, 4 May 1944

5 M. Gilbert, *Winston S. Churchill, vol. VII: The Road to Victory 1941–5* (hereinafter *Churchill VII*) (1986), M 483/4, WSC to AE, 2 May 1944, p. 754

6 Woodward III, M 498/4, WSC to AE, 4 May 1944, p. 116

7 FO 954/20, POL/44/90, M 537/4, WSC to AE, 8 May 1944

8 PREM. 4/42/5, PMM (44) 6, 4 May 1944, fo. 490

9 Cab. 65/53, WP (44) 436, 9 August 1944, 'Soviet Policy in Europe'

10 Woodward III, p. 116

11 *Churchill and Roosevelt III*, WSC to FDR, 31 May 1944, pp. 153–4

12 FDRL, PSF, Departmental file State: Hull, Janu-

ary–August 1944, Box 74, CH to FDR, 5 May 1944

13 *Hansard*, House of Commons, 21 April 1944

14 FDRL, PSF, Departmental file State: Hull, January–August 1944, Box 74, CH to FDR, 5 May 1944

15 *Churchill and Roosevelt III*, FDR to WSC, 10 June 1944, p. 177

16 *Ibid.*, editor's note, p. 178

17 *Ibid.*, WSC to FDR, 11 June 1944, pp. 178–80

18 *Ibid.*, FDR to WSC, 12 June 1944, p. 182

19 FDRL, Special Files, Box 31, 051 – Balkans – Spheres of Influence, British and Russian, MacVeagh to Hull, 26 June 1944

20 *Foreign Relations of the United States 1944, vol. V: The Near East, S. Asia and Africa* (hereinafter *FRUS 1944, V*) (Washington, 1965), CH to FDR, 17 June 1944, pp. 124–5

21 *Churchill and Roosevelt III*, FDR to WSC, 22 June 1944, p. 201

22 *Ibid.*, WSC to FDR, 23 June 1944, pp. 202–3

23 *Ibid.*, FDR to WSC, 26 June 1944, p. 207

24 FDRL, Special Files, Box 31, 051 – Balkans – Spheres of Influence, British and Russian, CH to FDR, 29 June 1944

25 *Churchill and Roosevelt III*, FDR to WSC, 26 June 1944, p. 209

26 Cab. 66/53, WP (44) 409, Cooper to AE, 30 May 1944

27 PRO, Post-Hostilities Planning Committee, Cab. 81/45, 'Basic Assumptions for Staff Studies of Strategical Problems', 7 June 1944, extracts of which are at Ross (ed.), *op. cit.*, pp. 166–8

28 Rothwell, *op. cit.*, pp. 117–20; Ross (ed.), *op. cit.*, pp. 50–1

29 PREM. 4/42/9, AE to WSC, 29 March 1943, fo. 1004

30 FO 954/22/, PWP/44/17, 18, Eden to Cooper, Eden to Bland, Oliphant and Collier, 12 July 1944

31 Cab. 66/59, WP (44) 735, 12 December 1944, 'Policy towards Spain'

32 F. S. Northedge and Audrey Wells, *Britain and Soviet Communism* (1982), p. 97

33 *Churchill VII*, 8 September 1944, p. 945

34 Lest it be thought that this is simply a perverse view held by the author, sceptics are directed to Harbutt, *op. cit.*, pp. 74–9, and Lloyd C. Gardner, *Spheres of Influence* (1993), pp. 203–6, who substantially agree

35 Harbutt, *op. cit.*, p. 73

36 PREM. 3/66/7, M 813/4, WSC to AE, 9 July 1944, fo. 194

37 *Churchill VII*, 8 September 1944, p. 945

38 *Polish-Soviet Relations II*, p. 413. The following paragraph is taken from the account given on pp. 405–15

39 Winston S. Churchill, *The Second World War, vol. VI: Triumph and Tragedy* (1954), p. 205

40 *Churchill VII*, p. 1011

41 *Ibid.*, pp. 1011–12

42 *Polish-Soviet Relations II*, record of conversations with WSC, 14 October 1944, p. 417

Notes

43 *Ibid.*, record of conversations with WSC, 14 October 1944, 3.40–4.20, p. 423
44 Cited in Nadeau, *op. cit.*, p. 128
45 *Polish-Soviet Relations II*, conversation with AE, 17 October 1944, p. 429
46 *Ibid.*, Mikolajczyk to FDR, 26 October 1944, p. 437
47 The account which follows is taken from *ibid.*, pp. 450–7, and FO 954/20, POL/44/323, Eden to O'Malley, 6 November 1944
48 *Polish-Soviet Relations II*, p. 457
49 *Ibid.*
50 *Ibid.*, p. 462
51 Harriman, *op. cit.*, p. 357
52 *Foreign Relations of the United States 1944*, vol. IV (hereinafter *FRUS 1944*, IV) (1965), Harriman to FDR, 10 October 1944, p. 1006
53 *Ibid.*, FDR to Harriman, 11 October 1944, p. 1009
54 *Churchill and Roosevelt III*, WSC to FDR, 11 October 1944, p. 353
55 Churchill, *Second World War*, VI, p. 231; Harriman, *op. cit.*, p. 358
56 *Churchill VII*, p. 1056
57 FO 371/38551/AN4642/20/45, FO minute, 16 December 1944
58 Nadeau, *op. cit.*, p. 119

10: *'Lady Bountiful' and Uncle Sam*

1 FO 371/38550/AN4451/20/45, Michael Wright letter, 14 November 1944
2 FO 954/30, US/44/254, Halifax to AE, 20 November 1944
3 FO 954/30, US/44/262, Halifax to FO, 27 November 1944
4 FO 954/30, US/44/268, Winant to AE, 7 December 1944
5 FO 371/38551/AN4618/20/45, Halifax to FO, 10 December 1944
6 *Ibid.*, pp. 1–2
7 FO 371/38551/AN4642/20/45, FO minute, 18 December 1944
8 *Loc. cit.*, AN4685/20/45, Halifax to FO, 19 December 1944
9 *FRUS 1944*, V, Stettinius to FDR, 13 December 1944, p. 149
10 *Churchill and Roosevelt III*, p. 450
11 *Ibid.*, WSC to Hopkins, 10 December 1944, p. 451
12 PREM. 3/212/5, draft WSC to FDR, 10 December 1944
13 Sherwood, *op. cit.*, p. 840
14 *Ibid.*, p. 841
15 *Churchill and Roosevelt III*, FDR to WSC, 13 December 1944, pp. 455–6
16 Charmley, *Churchill*, pp. 599–603
17 H. G. Nicholas (ed.), *Washington Despatches 1941–1945* (1981), 24 December 1944, p. 483
18 FO 954/30, US/44/272, Hopkins to WSC, 16 December 1944
19 US/44/273, WSC to HLH, 17 December 1944
20 R. Frazier, *Anglo-American Relations with Greece* (1957), p. 67 and the evidence cited there
21 Linda McClain, *The Role of Admiral W. D. Leahy in United States Foreign Policy*, Ph.D. thesis, University of Virginia, 1984, pp. 67–8, 86, 194. See also *Churchill VII*, p. 969, for Mrs Churchill's view of Leahy's influence
22 FO 371/38550/AN4451/20/45, Michael Wright minute, 14 November 1944
23 Harbutt, *op. cit.*, p. 73
24 FO 371/34119/A8047/32/45, 'Anglo-American Relations: United States attitude towards the British Empire', August/September 1943; FO 371/34121/A10579/32/45, 'Essentials of an American Policy', 8 November 1943: FO 371/38523/AN1538/16/45, 'The Essentials of an American Policy', 21 March 1944
25 FO 371/38523/AN1538/16/45, 'The Essentials of an American Policy', 21 March 1944
26 FO 371/38547/AN3570/20/45, 'United States Memorandum no. 226', 4 September 1944
27 Anderson, *op. cit.*, p. 24
28 *Keynes XXIV*, JMK to T. Padmore, 7 August 1944, p. 92
29 Cab. 66/53, WP (44) 360, 'The Problem of Our External Finances in the Transition' by JMK, 1 July 1944
30 PREM. 4/18/6, Cherwell to WSC, 'Lend/lease in Stage II', 7 September 1944
31 Cab. 66/53, WP (44) 360, 'The Problem of Our External Finances in the Transition' by JMK, 1 July 1944
32 *Ibid.*
33 *Keynes XXIV*, JMK memo., c. August 1944, p. 125
34 FO 371/40405/U5799/130/74, FO minutes, 13 June, on a draft of JMK's paper
35 Cab. 65/43, WM (44) 93, 18 July 1944
36 *FRUS 1944*, III, Stettinius memo., 19 April 1944
37 J. M. Blum (ed.), *From the Morgenthau Diaries: Years of War 1941–1945* (hereinafter *Morgenthau diary II*) (1967), pp. 308–9
38 Woods, *op. cit.*, pp. 253–6
39 Harry S. Truman Library, Independence, Missouri (hereinafter HSTL), Dean Acheson Papers, Box 27, Acheson to Stettinius and Hull, 27 January 1944
40 PREM. 4/18/6, Sir R. Campbell to AE, 25 July 1944, reporting conversation with Hopkins; *Morgenthau diary II*, pp. 305–6
41 PREM. 4/18/6, Cherwell to WSC, 26 July 1944
42 PREM. 4/18/6, Lyttelton to WSC, 4 August 1944
43 PREM. 4/18/6, Cherwell to WSC, 7 September 1943
44 *Churchill VII*, p. 962
45 *Colville diary*, 14 September 1944, p. 515
46 *Churchill VII*, p. 965
47 *Hull memoirs II*, pp. 1603–9
48 *Morgenthau diary III*, p. 314; FDRL, PSF, Box 75, Hull, Cordell, CH to FDR, 2 October 1944; *Hull memoirs II*, pp. 1613–14
49 *Ibid.*, p. 1614
50 Gardner, *op. cit.*, p. 179
51 *Hull memoirs II*, pp. 1617–20
52 FDRL, PSF, Box 75, Hull, Cordell, FDR to CH, 29 September 1944

371

53 FO 954/30, US/44/277, Halifax to WSC, 20 December 1944
54 PREM. 3/396/14, Halifax to FO, 29 March 1944
55 FDRL, PSF, Poland 1944–5, Harriman to FDR, 15 August 1944
56 *Loc. cit.*, Harriman to FDR, 17 August 1944
57 PREM. 3/396/4, Harriman to Hopkins, 11 September 1944
58 *Churchill VII*, p. 189; G. Ross, 'Operation Bracelet: Churchill in Moscow, 1942', in D. Dilks (ed.), *Retreat from Power, vol. II* (1981), pp. 118–19
59 Mastny, *Russia's Road to the Cold War*, p. 72
60 *Ibid.*, p. 107
61 *Ibid.*, pp. 129–33, 144, 162–4
62 Quoted in Woods, *op. cit.*, p. 250
63 George Kennan, *Memoirs* (1967), p. 211
64 Gardner, *op. cit.*, pp. 178–81
65 Wilson S. Miscamble, *George F. Kennan and the Making of American Foreign Policy 1947–1950* (Princeton, 1992), pp. 21–2 and references given there
66 Quoted in Mastny, *op. cit.*, p. 108
67 George C. Herring, *Aid to Russia, 1941–1946*, pp. 136–7; Harriman, *op. cit.*, pp. 342–5
68 Harriman, *op. cit.*, p. 345
69 On these things, see Gardner, *op. cit.*, pp. 181–7
70 Gardner, *op. cit.*, pp. 181–2, 225–9; Warren F. Kimball, 'Naked Reverse Right: Roosevelt, Churchill and Eastern Europe from TOLSTOY to Yalta – and a Little Beyond', *Diplomatic History*, vol. 9, no. 1, Winter 1985, and reprinted in his *The Juggler*
71 FDRL, PSF, Box 66, Poland, September–December 1944, Stettinius to FDR, 31 October 1944

11: Roosevelt's Last Throw

1 McGregor Burns, *Roosevelt: The Soldier of Freedom*, p. 550
2 Paterson, *op. cit.*, p. 288
3 *Ibid.*, p. 289
4 G. Paterson Thomas (ed.), *On Every Front* (NY, 1979), p. 31
5 Moran, *op. cit.*, 3 February 1945, p. 218
6 Hugh Gregory Gallagher, *FDR's Splendid Deception* (1985), pp. 178–81
7 *Ibid.*, pp. 182–90; MacGregor Burns, *op. cit.*, pp. 448–50
8 MacGregor Burns, *op. cit.*, p. 450
9 *Ibid.*, p. 451
10 *Eden II*, p. 513
11 Harriman, *op. cit.*, pp. 388–90. This is also the conclusion of Nadeau, *op. cit.*, pp. 134–6
12 FO 954/30, US/45/26, M 110/5, WSC to AE, 25 January 1945
13 FO 954/20, POL/45/5, WSC to Stalin, 5 January 1945
14 FO 954/20, POL/45/14, PM/45/61, AE to WSC, 28 January 1945
15 FO 954/20, POL/45/16, PM (A) 2, AE to WSC, 1 February 1945

16 Thomas M. Campbell and George C. Herring (eds), *The Diaries of Edward R. Stettinius Jr 1943–1946* (hereinafter *Stettinius diary*) (NY, 1975), 18 December 1944, p. 200
17 *Ibid.*, p. 201
18 MacGregor Burns, *op. cit.*, p. 550
19 PRO, Halifax Papers, FO 800/328, Hal/38/101, draft letter, November 1938
20 Vandenberg (ed.), *op. cit.*, p. 125
21 *Ibid.*, p. 128
22 *Ibid.*, pp. 133–9
23 Thomas (ed.), *On Every Front*, pp. 14–18, for the figures
24 Harry S. Truman, *Memoirs, vol. I: Years of Decisions* (hereinafter *Truman memoirs I*) (1955), p. 341
25 Mastny, *op. cit.*, p. 249
26 Nadeau, *op. cit.*, p. 135
27 Halifax Papers, FO 800/328, Hal/38/101, draft letter, November 1938
28 FDRL, Hopkins Papers, Box 170, political memoranda for Yalta conference, February 1945, 'British Plan for a Western European Bloc'
29 *Loc. cit.*, 'The necessity of the three principal Allies arriving at a common political program for liberated countries'
30 *Foreign Relations of the United States: The Conferences at Malta and Yalta, 1945* (hereinafter *FRUS, Yalta*) (Washington, 1955), for the American texts; R. Beitzell (ed.), *Tehran, Yalta, Potsdam: The Soviet Protocols* (Mississippi, 1970), for the Soviet texts. The British account is unpublished and is at PREM. 3/51/10
31 Harriman, *op. cit.*, pp. 390–1
32 *Eden II*, diary, 4 January 1945, p. 504
33 *Stettinius diary*, 4 February 1945, pp. 240–1
34 Charles E. Bohlen, *Witness to History* (NY, 1973), p. 181.
35 Mastny, *op. cit.*, p. 242
36 *Churchill VII*, p. 1180
37 Moran, *op. cit.*, p. 224
38 *Stettinius diary*, 6 February 1945, p. 243
39 *Ibid.*, pp. 245–7; Harriman, *op. cit.*, pp. 406–9; Sherwood, *op. cit.*, pp. 857–8
40 Beitzell, *op. cit.*, pp. 87–8
41 *Ibid.*, p. 89
42 McClain, *op. cit.*, p. 229
43 *Churchill VII*, p. 1184; Beitzell, *op. cit.*, p. 84
44 *FRUS, Yalta*, pp. 727–8
45 Mastny, *op. cit.*, p. 246
46 *Stettinius diary*, 7 February 1945, p. 246
47 *Ibid.*, pp. 247–8, where the discussions on the UN are the dominant topic throughout the conference; Mastny, *op. cit.*, pp. 246–7; *FRUS, Yalta*, pp. 716–18
48 Beitzell, *op. cit.*, p. 97
49 Edward R. Stettinius Jr, *Roosevelt and the Russians: The Yalta Conference* (NY, 1949), p. 184
50 Beitzell, *op. cit.*, p. 106
51 Cab. 65/51, WM (45) 22, minute 1, 19 February 1945
52 McClain, *op. cit.*, p. 232
53 PREM. 3/192/3, M (Arg)7/5, WSC to AE, 8 February 1945

12: The End of FDR

1 *Public Papers of the Presidents of the United States: Ronald Reagan, 1985, book 1* (Washington, 1988), p. 119
2 McClain, *op. cit.*, p. 231
3 Walter Isaacson and Evan Thomas, *The Wise Men* (NY, 1986), pp. 246–7
4 *Polish-Soviet Relations II*, p. 424
5 McNeill, *op. cit.*, pp. 466–71
6 PREM. 3/192/3, M (Arg)7/5, WSC to AE, 8 February 1945
7 Henry Kissinger, *A World Restored* (1959), chaps 1 and 2
8 B. Pimlott (ed.), *The Second World War Diary of Hugh Dalton, 1940–1945* (1986), 23 February 1945, p. 835
9 *Colville diary*, 23 February 1945, pp. 562–3
10 *Hansard*, House of Commons, 27 February 1945
11 *Churchill and Roosevelt III*, WSC to FDR, 28 February 1945, p. 539
12 *Colville diary*, 28 February 1945, p. 565
13 FO 954/23, AE to WSC, 5 March 1945
14 Kimball, 'Naked Reverse Right . . .', p. 17 and references there
15 *Churchill and Roosevelt III*, WSC to FDR, 8 March 1945, pp 547–51
16 Woodward III, p. 496
17 *Churchill and Roosevelt III*, WSC to FDR, 8 March 1945, p. 549
18 FO 954/20, POL/45/17, Cranborne memo., 5 February 1945
19 FO 954/20, POL/45/20, Eden memo., 20 February 1945
20 FO 954/20, POL/45/21, Eden memo., 21 February 1945
21 FO 954/20, POL/45/25, FO to Moscow, 28 February 1945
22 FDRL, Hopkins Papers, Microfilm, Roll 20, personal letters, Beaverbrook to HLH, 1 March 1945
23 Robert L. Messer, *The End of an Alliance: James F. Byrnes, Roosevelt, Truman and the Origins of the Cold War* (Chapel Hill, 1982), pp. 28–35
24 *Ibid.*, p. 37
25 *Ibid.*, pp. 55–7
26 Harriman, *op. cit.*, pp. 426–8
27 FO 954/30, US/45/39, Halifax to FO, 9 March 1945
28 *FRUS 1945, V*, Grew to Harriman, 8 March 1945, pp. 150–2
29 *Churchill and Roosevelt III*, WSC to FDR, 10 March 1945, p. 552
30 *Ibid.*, WSC to FDR, 10 March 1945, pp. 553–8
31 *Ibid.*, FDR to WSC, 11 March 1945, pp 560–2
32 *Ibid.*, pp. 562–3; McClain, *op. cit.*, pp. 253–4
33 *Churchill and Roosevelt III*, FDR to WSC, 12 March 1945, p. 563
34 *Ibid.*, FDR to WSC, 15 March 1945, pp 568–9
35 FO 954/20, POL/45/45, EH to FO, 14 March 1945
36 Quoted in Gardner, *op. cit.*, p. 238
37 *Churchill and Roosevelt III*, FDR to WSC, 15 March 1945, pp. 568–9
38 *Ibid.*, WSC to FDR, 16 March 1945, pp 571–2

39 Anderson, *op. cit.*, p. 45
40 PREM. 3/356/9, WSC to AE, 24 March 1945
41 *Churchill and Roosevelt III*, WSC to FDR, 27 March 1945
42 *Churchill VII*, WSC to Stalin, 21 March 1945, p. 1259
43 Ross (ed.), *op. cit.*, Clark-Kerr, 27 March 1945, pp. 192–9
44 FO 954/22, PWP/45/33, Cranborne to Eden, 26 March 1945
45 FO 954/20, POL/45/65, Petherick to AE, 30 March 1945
46 Ross (ed.), *op. cit.*, Sir Orme Sargent minute, 2 April 1945, pp. 199–203
47 Harriman, *op. cit.*, p. 434
48 FO 954/32, W(g)45/47, M 262/5, WSC to AE, 25 March 1945
49 *Loc. cit.*, W(g)45/60, WSC to Stalin, 6 April 1945
50 Ross (ed.), *op. cit.*, p. 200
51 *Churchill and Roosevelt III*, WSC to FDR, 27 March 1945, p. 588
52 Ross (ed.), *op. cit.*, p. 203
53 Edward M. Bennett, *Franklin D. Roosevelt and the Search for Victory* (Wilmington, 1990), pp. 166–7
54 *Churchill and Roosevelt III*, FDR to WSC, 29 March 1945, pp. 593–4
55 *Ibid.*, pp. 595–7
56 FO 954/20, POL/45/74, WSC to Stalin, 1 April 1945
57 *Churchill and Roosevelt III*, WSC to FDR, 5 April 1945, p. 613
58 *Ibid.*, FDR to WSC, 6 April 1945, p. 617
59 Cab. 65/50, WM (45) 39, 3 April 1945
60 McClain, *op. cit.*, pp. 250, 251–2; see also Kimball's editorial comments, *Churchill and Roosevelt III*, p. 617
61 McClain, *op. cit.*, p. 254
62 *Churchill and Roosevelt III*, FDR to WSC, 11 April 1945, p. 630

13: Enter Mr Truman

1 R Crockatt, *The Cold War* (1991), surveys the literature. The chief works used here are: H. Feis, *Churchill, Roosevelt, Stalin* (NJ, 1957); Anderson, *The United States, Great Britain and the Cold War*; Harbutt, *The Iron Curtain*. The last two generally agree with the line taken here. For a contrary view (in more senses than one), see Arthur M. Schlesinger Jr, 'The Origins of the Cold War', *Foreign Affairs*, October 1967
2 Wilson D. Miscamble, 'Anthony Eden and the Truman–Molotov Conversations, April 1945', *Diplomatic History*, vol. 2, no. 2, 1978, p. 167
3 Warren F. Kimball (ed.), *America Unbound* (NY, 1992), p. 15
4 B. B. Berle and T. B. Jacobs (eds), *Navigating the Rapids, 1918–1971: From the Papers of Adolf A. Berle* (NY, 1973), memo., 26 September 1944, p. 461
5 *Ibid.*, pp. 460–1
6 *Ibid.*, p. 464
7 HSTL, HST papers, Post-Presidential, Memoirs, Box 5, 'Illness and death of President Roosevelt'

8 PREM. 4/27/10, Halifax to WSC, 16 April 1945
9 McClain, *op. cit.*, p. 261 and references given there
10 Robert H. Ferrell (ed.), *Off the Record: The Private Papers of Harry S. Truman* (NY, 1980), p. 19
11 On this see Anderson, *op. cit.*, pp. 54–6, and Harbutt, *op. cit.*, pp. 98–100; McClain, *op. cit.*, chap. VII
12 PREM. 4/27/10, Berlin report, May 1945
13 PREM. 3/473, HST to WSC, 14 April 1945, desp. to Stalin the 15th, fos 254–6, no. 2
14 FO 954/20, POL/45/94, M 315/5, WSC to AE, 8 April 1945
15 FO 954/20, POL/45/113, M 335/5, WSC to Sir A. Cadogan, 14 April 1945
16 FO 954/20, POL/45/115, WSC to AE, 15 April 1945
17 PREM. 3/473, WSC to HST, 18 April 1945, fos 239–40, no. 7
18 *Churchill VII*, p. 1299, although the draft which he quotes was not actually sent to Truman
19 A. D. Chandler et al. (eds), *The Papers of Dwight David Eisenhower, vol. IV: The War Years* (Baltimore, 1970), p. 2624
20 There is, of course, considerable and passionate debate over this matter. The question of whether the western allies should have gone for Berlin is rehearsed most conveniently in S. Ambrose, *The Supreme Commander: The War Years of General Dwight David Eisenhower* (NY, 1970), chap. 20, which gives the Eisenhower view, and N. Hamilton, *Monty: The Field Marshal, 1944–1976* (1986), which does not!
21 *Churchill VII*, p. 1302
22 *Cadogan diary*, p. 728
23 Miscamble, *op. cit.*
24 *Stettinius diary*, 13 April 1945, p. 318
25 David McCullough, *Truman* (NY, 1992), p. 324
26 A terribly subjective judgment, based upon the author having lived in the middle of Missouri for ten months
27 McCullough, *op. cit.*, p. 325
28 McClain, *op. cit.*, p. 277
29 McCullough, *op. cit.*, pp. 370–2; Harriman, *op. cit.*, pp. 448–50; McClain, *op. cit.*, pp. 275–8
30 *Foreign Relations of the United States 1945, vol. V* (hereinafter *FRUS 1945, V*) (Washington, 1967), Harriman to Stettinius, 4 April 1945, p. 818
31 *Ibid.*, Minutes of the Secretary of State's Staff Committee, 21 April 1945, p. 843
32 Harriman, *op. cit.*, p. 448
33 *FRUS 1945, V*, Harriman to Stettinius, 4 April 1945, p. 819
34 *Ibid.*, Minutes of the Secretary of State's Staff Committee, 21 April 1945, p. 843
35 *Ibid.*, p. 452
36 McClain, *op. cit.*, pp. 278–9
37 Harriman, *op. cit.*, p. 452
38 McClain, *op. cit.*, p. 278
39 *Stettinius diary*, 21 April 1945, pp. 326–8; FO 954/20, POL/45/140, AE to WSC, 22 April 1945
40 *Stettinius diary*, memo. of conversation with Eden, 21 April 1945, pp. 326–7

41 *Cadogan diary*, 23 April 1945, p. 732
42 FO 954/20, POL/45/143, tel. 2804, AE to WSC, 23 April 1945
43 FO 954/20, POL/45/144, tel. 2805, AE to WSC, 23 April 1945
44 *Cadogan diary*, 23 April 1945, p. 732
45 FO 954/20, POL/45/144, tel. 2805, AE to WSC, 23 April 1945
46 *Cadogan diary*, 23 April 1945, p. 732
47 FO 954/20, POL/45/146, AE to WSC, 23 April 1945
48 FO 954/20, POL/45/148, AE to WSC, 23 April 1945
49 *FRUS 1945, V*, Charles E. Bohlen memo., 23 April 1945, pp. 252–5
50 Miscamble, *op. cit.*, p. 180
51 *Truman memoirs I*, pp. 79–82. See also Miscamble, *op. cit.*
52 MacLean, *op. cit.*, p. 136
53 McCullough, *op. cit.*, pp. 375–6
54 Harriman, *op. cit.*, pp. 453–4
55 Mastny, *Russia's Road to the Cold War*, p. 261
56 *Ibid.*, p. 48
57 *Ibid.*, p. 265
58 McCormick, *op. cit.*, p. 17
59 Mastny, *op. cit.*, p. 271
60 *Ibid.*, p. 272
61 MacLean, *op. cit.*, p. 136

14: 'Diplomatic language' or 'a baseball bat'?

1 *FRUS 1945, V*, Minutes of the Secretary of State's Staff Committee, 20 April 1945, Harriman's comment, p. 841
2 *Ibid.*, Bohlen memo., 19 April 1945, pp. 832–8
3 MacLean, *op. cit.*, pp. 136–8
4 Woods and Jones, *op. cit.*, pp. 49–52
5 MacLean, *op. cit.*, p. 141
6 Ross (ed.), *op. cit.*, Cadogan minute, 4 April 1945, p. 203
7 FO 954/20, POL/45/154, Stalin to WSC, 24 April 1945
8 PREM. 3/430/1, T 675/5, WSC to Stalin, 28/29 April 1945, fos 125–30, which differs slightly from the draft at FO 954/20, POL/45/162, 26 April 1945
9 McNeill, *op. cit.*, p. 535
10 PREM. 3/473, WSC to HST, 30 April 1945, fo. 205, no. 22
11 *Loc. cit.*, no. 24, WSC to HST, 30 April 1945
12 *Loc. cit.*, no. 25, WSC to HST, 30 April 1945
13 On this, see Timothy Garton Ash, 'From World War to Cold War', *The New York Review of Books*, 11 June 1987, pp. 47–9
14 Martin Kitchen, 'Winston Churchill and the Soviet Union during the Second World War', *Historical Journal*, 30, 2 (1987), p. 434
15 FO 954/20, POL/45/175, FO to AE, 2 May 1945
16 FO 954/20, POL/45/177, tel. 321, WSC to AE, 4 May 1945
17 Ross (ed.), *op. cit.*, Sir Orme Sargent minute, 2 April 1945, p. 202
18 FO 954/20, POL/45/177, fo. 711

19 *Ibid.*, fo. 713
20 PREM. 3/484, T 875/5, WSC to AE, 11 May 1945, fo. 41
21 FO 954/20, POL/45/180, tel. 363, WSC to AE, 11 May 1945
22 PREM. 3/473, WSC to HST, 6 May 1945, fo. 179, tel. 34
23 PREM. 3/473, HST to WSC, 9 May 1945, fo. 166, tel. 31
24 PREM. 3/484, T 875/5, WSC to AE, 11 May 1945, fo. 41
25 PREM. 3/473, WSC to HST, 11 May 1945, fo. 159, no. 41 (T 877/5)
26 PREM. 3/430/1, draft telegram, WSC to HST, 10 May 1945 (not sent), fos 106–7
27 PREM. 3/473, WSC to HST, 12 May 1945, fo. 147, no. 44
28 PREM. 3/473, WSC to HST, 12 May 1945, fo. 145, no. 46
29 PREM. 3/430/1, HST to WSC, 12 May 1945, no. 36 (T 898/5)
30 Winston Churchill Memorial and Library, Fulton, Missouri (hereinafter WCML), Microfilm relating to the Potsdam Conference, reel 1, frame 0123. Although this is dated 16 March, it is evident from the extract quoted in *Foreign Relations of the United States: The Conference of Berlin (The Potsdam Conference), 1945, vol. I* (hereinafter, *FRUS, Potsdam I*) (Washington, 1960), p. 256, that 'March' should be 'May'
31 *FRUS, Potsdam I*, 'Briefing Book Paper', quoting Joint Chiefs of Staff to HST, 16 May 1945
32 WCML, Potsdam microfilm, reel 1, frames 0123–4, JCS to HST, 16 May 1945
33 Anderson, *op. cit.*, p. 64
34 HSTL, PSF, Box 321, personal – Mrs Roosevelt, HST to Eleanor Roosevelt, 10 May 1945
35 PREM. 3/473, HST to WSC, 16 May 1945, no. 42 (T 954/5)
36 PREM. 3/473, WSC to HST, 19 May 1945, no. 52 (T 968/5)
37 PREM. 3/430/1, AE to WSC, 14 May 1945
38 Ferrell (ed.), *op. cit.*, 22 May 1945, p. 35
39 *Ibid.*, 19 May 1945, p. 31
40 *FRUS 1945*, V, p. 24
41 Ferrell (ed.), *op. cit.*, p. 35
42 MacLean, *op. cit.*, pp. 137–8
43 *Ibid.*, pp. 140–1
44 Sherwood, *op. cit.*, pp. 887–913, and *FRUS, Potsdam I*, pp. 21–62
45 Sherwood, *op. cit.*, pp. 898–900
46 PREM. 3/430/1, M 529/5, WSC to AE, 28 May 1945
47 *FRUS, Potsdam I*, pp. 64–78, for Davies's report
48 *Ibid.*, p. 77; see also p. 69
49 *Ibid.*, p. 77; see also MacLean, *op. cit.*, p. 144
50 *Ibid.*, p. 68
51 *Ibid.*, p. 70
52 *Ibid.*, p. 73
53 MacLean, *op. cit.*, p. 145
54 McNeill, *op. cit.*, p. 588
55 Ferrell (ed.), *op. cit.*, 7 June 1945, p. 44

56 See the draft at PREM. 3/430/1, WSC to HST, 29 May 1945
57 PREM. 3/194/4, M 554/5, WSC to AE, 1 June 1945, fo. 5
58 PREM. 3/473, no. 72, WSC to HST, 4 June 1945
59 PREM. 3/473, no 61, HST to WSC, 6 June 1945
60 Ferrell (ed.), *op. cit.*, 13 June 1945, p. 45
61 PREM. 3/473, no. 81, WSC to HST, 9 June 1945
62 PREM. 3/473, no. 70, HST to WSC, 12 June 1945
63 *Eden II*, p. 525
64 Sir Arthur Bryant (ed.), *The Triumph in the West, 1943–1945* (1959), Alan Brooke's diary, 11 June 1945, pp. 470–1
65 *FRUS, Potsdam I*, pp. 790–804
66 *Ibid.*, 'Briefing Book Paper', 28 June 1945, pp. 257–9
67 *Ibid.*, p. 264
68 *Ibid.*, 'Lend Lease during the Second Year of Phase II', 6 July 1945, p. 809
69 *Ibid.*, 'The Need for Discussion with the British . . .', undated, p. 810
70 WCML, Potsdam microfilm, 'Briefing Book. Phase II Commitments to the British', frame 0469
71 *FRUS, Potsdam I*, p. 811

15: *The Great Game*

1 Ross (ed.), *op. cit.*, Bevin/Molotov conversation, 23 September 1946, p. 239. See also Kenneth M. Jensen (ed.), *Origins of the Cold War: The Novikov, Kennan, and Roberts 'Long Telegrams' of 1946* (Washington, 1993), Novikov's telegram, 27 September 1946, pp. 14–16, and Steven Miner's commentary, p. 90
2 Ross (ed.), *op. cit.*, Sargent minute, 2 April 1945, p. 199
3 Quoted in Woods, *op. cit.*, p. 261
4 Ross (ed.), *op. cit.*, O'Malley minute, 22 May 1945, p. 209
5 R. Butler and M. Pelly (eds), *Documents on British Policy Overseas, Series 1, vol I: The Conference at Potsdam, 1945* (hereinafter *DBPO 1/1*) (1984), doc. 176, PM/45/2T, AE to WSC, 17 July 1945, pp. 352–4
6 *Ibid.*, doc. 111, PM/45/324, AE to WSC, 12 July 1945, p. 212
7 R. Smith and J. Zametica, 'The Cold Warrior: Clement Attlee Reconsidered 1945–7', *International Affairs*, vol. 61, no. 3, Spring 1985
8 *DBPO 1/1*, doc. 179, Attlee to Eden, 18 July 1945, pp. 365–6
9 Lord Hankey, *The Supreme Command 1914–1918, vol. I* (1961), quoting from the First Report of the Committee of Imperial Defence, 1904, p. 46
10 *DBPO 1/1*, doc. 102, 'Stocktaking after VE-Day', Sir Orme Sargent, 11 July 1945, p. 182
11 On this, see R. F. Holland, *The Pursuit of Greatness* (1991); John Darwin, 'Imperialism in Decline? Tendencies in British Imperial Policy between the Wars', *Historical Journal*, 1980, pp. 657–79; and particularly, Jack Gallagher, *The Decline, Rise and Fall of the British Empire* (Cambridge, 1982)

12 B. R. Tomlinson, *The Political Economy of the Raj, 1914–1947* (1979), for this

13 Gallagher, *op. cit.*, p. 75

14 *Ibid.*, p. 78

15 *Colville diary*, 23 February 1945, p. 563

16 *Cadogan diary*, p. 764

17 PRO, PSF, Terminal Conference, FO 800/416, T 63/11, Cadogan to WSC, 2 July 1945; *DBPO I/I*, docs 77, 111, 176, PM/45/322, AE to WSC, 10 July, PM/45/324, AE to WSC, 12 July, PM/45/2T, AE to WSC, 17 July

18 British Library, Paul Emrys Evans MSS., Harvey to Emrys Evans, 26 August 1945

19 Alan Bullock, *Ernest Bevin: Foreign Secretary 1945–1951* (1983); R. Ovendale (ed.), *The Foreign Policy of the Labour Governments, 1945–1951* (1984); Kenneth Morgan, *Labour in Power* (1986)

20 British Library of Political and Economic Science, Papers of Sir Charles Webster, 1/28, Lord Cecil to Webster, 20 December 1948

21 Frank K. Roberts, 'Ernest Bevin as Foreign Secretary', in Ovendale (ed.), *op. cit.*, pp. 21–42

22 *Ibid.*, p. 25

23 *Cadogan diary*, 28 July 1945, p. 776

24 Bullock, *Bevin*, pp. 75–7, 90–1, 105–7

25 *Cadogan diary*, 29 July 1945, p. 776

26 R. Bullen and M. Pelly (eds), *Documents on British Policy Overseas, Series I, vol. II: Conferences in London, Washington and Moscow, 1945* (hereinafter *DBPO I/II*) (1985), no. 9, Bevin to Balfour, 25 August 1945, p. 16

27 *Ibid.*, no. 12, Bevin and Mr Hall memo., 25 August 1945, pp 33–4

28 *Ibid.*, no. 37, Far Eastern Department memo., 10 September 1945, p. 99

29 H. Tinker (ed.), *Burma: The Struggle for Independence 1944–1948, vol. I* (1983), no. 60, WSC to James Stuart, 3 December 1944, p. 117

30 N. Mansergh (ed.), *The Transfer of Power in India, 1942–1947, vol. V: The Simla Conference* (hereinafter *Transfer V*) (1974), Amery to Wavell, 28 July 1945, p. 1299

31 N. Mansergh (ed.), *The Transfer of Power in India, 1942–1947, vol. VI: The Post-War Phase* (1976), no. 50, Lord Pethick-Lawrence to F. M. Lord Wavell, 21 August 1945, p. 112. See also R. J. Moore, *Escape from Empire: The Attlee Government and the Indian Problem* (Oxford, 1983), pp. 29–40

32 *Transfer V*, Wavell to WSC, 24 October 1944, p. 64

33 Moore, *op. cit.*, esp. pp. 29–45, 63–7

34 *Keynes XXIV*, 'Overseas Financial Policy in Stage III, 15 May 1945, pp. 256–95, for this and the following paragraph. See also L. S. Pressnell, *External Economic Policy since the War, vol. I* (1987), pp. 237–41.

35 *Keynes XXIV*, p. 275

36 R. Bullen and M. Pelly (eds), *Documents on British Policy Overseas, Series I, vol. III: Britain and America: Negotiation of the United States Loan 3 August–7 December 1945* (hereinafter *DBPO I/III*) (1986), doc. 10, FO memo. on Anglo-American relations, 16 August 1945, pp. 49–53

37 *Hansard*, 5th series, vol. 417, col. 645 (Sir Thomas Moore), 13 December 1945

38 *DBPO I/III*, doc. 6, fn. 4, Sir Stafford Cripps to Hugh Dalton, 13 August 1945

39 *Keynes XXIV*, p. 277

40 *Ibid.*, 'Our Overseas Financial Prospects', 13 August 1945, para. 28. Circulated to the Cabinet as CP (45) 112, at PRO, Cab. 129/1, and reproduced at *DBPO I/III*, no. 6

41 *DBPO I/III*, no. 12, meeting at Bevin's room, 21 August 1945, p. 56

42 *Ibid.*, no. 1, Mr Hall-Patch memo., 3 August 1945, p. 3

43 *Ibid.*, no. 17, fn. 2, Bevin, Dalton and Cripps to Attlee, 22 August 1945, p. 72

44 *Ibid.*, no. 1, Mr Hall-Patch minute, 9 August 1945

45 *Keynes XXIV*, JMK to Sir Wilfrid Eady, 16 August 1945, p. 412

46 *DBPO I/III*, no. 17, meeting of Ministers, 23 August 1945, p. 73, for Keynes's optimism

47 Sir Richard Clarke, *Anglo-American Collaboration in War and Peace 1942–1949* (Oxford, 1982), p. 57; his memo. is doc. 7, pp. 126–35

48 *Ibid.*, doc. 7

49 *Ibid.*, pp. xviii–xix, JMK memo., doc. 8, 9 July 1945; also at *Keynes XXIV*, pp. 366–7

50 HSTL, Official File 48, note on lend-lease; *DBPO I/III*, no. 15, Balfour to Bevin, 22 August 1945, p. 67; no. 23, British Mission to Cabinet Office, 5 September 1945, pp. 111–13

51 HSTL, Official File 356, 'The negotiations leading to the Anglo-American Joint Statement ...', Research Project no. 23, April 1947, pp. 15–27

52 *Loc. cit.*, pp. 20–1

53 *Loc. cit.*, p. 31

54 *Keynes XXIV*, p. 279

55 *DBPO I/III*, no. 17, record of meeting at 10 Downing St, 23 August 1945, p. 73

56 *Loc. cit.*, nos 27, 31, 9, 13 September 1945; HSTL, Official File 356, 'The negotiations leading to the Anglo-American Joint Statement ...', Research Project no. 23, April 1947, pp. 34–5

57 *DBPO I/III*, no. 44, Halifax to Bevin, 26 September 1945, p. 153

58 *Loc. cit.*, no. 39, Calendar, ii, Keynes to Sir Wilfrid Eady, 22 September. Dalton marked this '!'

59 *Loc. cit.*, no. 34, Hall-Patch to Butler, 15 September 1945, p. 137

60 HSTL, Official File 356, 'The negotiations leading to the Anglo-American Joint Statement ...', Research Project no. 23, April 1947, p. 38

61 *DBPO I/III*, no. 69, Halifax to Bevin, 12 October 1945, p. 216

62 *Loc. cit.*, no. 74, Keynes to Dalton, 18 October 1945, p. 228. That this had been Dalton's assumption from the start can be seen from his paper to the Cabinet on 17 August 1945 at *ibid.*, Calendar to no. 6, i (a)

63 Clarke, *op. cit.*, p. 61

64 *DBPO I/III*, no. 67, Halifax to Bevin, 9 October 1945, pp. 210–14

65 *Loc. cit.*, no. 78, Keynes to Dalton, 20 October 1945, pp. 243–7

66 *Loc. cit.*, no. 51, fn. 1, telephone conversation Eady/Keynes, 1 October 1945, p. 168; Calendar to no. 51, i, Keynes to Dalton, 1 October 1945; no. 64, British Missions to Cabinet Office, 9 October 1945, pp. 200–5; no. 67, Halifax to Bevin, 9 October 1945, pp. 210–14; no. 74, Keynes to Dalton, 18 October 1945, p. 227–35

67 *Loc. cit.*, no. 56, Bevin to Halifax, 3 October 1945, pp. 185–7; Calendar to no. 74, ii, Lord Catto to Keynes, 20 October 1945; Calendar to no. 78, i, Brief by Economic Relations Department, 20 October 1945; PREM. 8/35, Jay to Attlee, 19 October 1945

68 *Loc. cit.*, Calendar to no. 6, i (b), J. M. Fleming memo., 22 August 1945

69 *Loc. cit.*, no. 62, Bevin to Halifax, 8 October 1945, pp. 196–9; also Calendar to no. 62, i, meeting of Ministers, 5 October 1945; no. 71, Bevin to Halifax, 13 October 1945, pp. 219–23

70 *Keynes XXIV*, Sir Wilfrid Eady to JMK, 12 October 1945, pp. 544–5

71 *Ibid.*, p. 568

72 *DBPO I/III*, no. 85, Keynes to Dalton, 28 October 1945, pp. 269–71

73 *Loc. cit.*, no. 117, note by Mr Coulson, 23 November 1945, pp. 352–3

74 *Ibid.*, Calendar to no. 117, i, Mr Rowe-Dutton to Sir Wilfrid Eady, 21 November 1945

75 *Ibid.*, ii, Gen. 89/13, Dalton memo., 22 November 1945

76 *Ibid.*, Calendar to no. 118, i, Gen. 89/6th meeting, 23 November 1945

77 *Ibid.*, nos 145, 146, Halifax to Bevin, 3 December 1945, pp. 419–22; no. 161, Cabinet Offices to British Missions, 5 December 1945, pp. 440–1

78 *Keynes XXIV*, JMK to F. A. Keynes, 21 November 1945, p. 593

79 *Hansard*, 5th series, vol. 417, cols 652–3, 13 December 1945

80 HSTL, PSF, Box 172, 'The Negotiation of the Anglo-American Financial Agreement of December 6 1945', State Department report, April 1947, p. 13

81 Martin Walker, *The Cold War* (1993), p. 46

82 *DBPO I/III*, Calendar to no. 3, ii, Halifax to Bevin, 14 September 1945

83 FO 371/34119/A8165/32/45, FO minutes, August 1943; FO 371/38523/AN1665/20/45, British Information Services Report, 18 April 1944; PREM. 4/27/9, Halifax to Eden, 13 February 1944

84 FO 371/34119/A8047/32/45, meeting of officials, 28 July 1943; FO 371/38524/AN3519/16/45, meeting of officials, 5 September 1944

85 House of Lords Record Office, Beaverbrook Papers, BBK. D/182, Beaverbrook to Halifax, 29 August 1944

86 Woods, *Changing of the Guard*, p. 250

87 PREM. 4/27/10, R. Law to WSC, 11 May 1945, and WSC's minute, 11 May

88 Peter G. Boyle, 'The British Foreign Office View of Soviet-American Relations, 1945–46', *Diplomatic History*, vol. 3, no. 3, 1979, p. 317

89 *DBPO I/II*, no. 18, Attlee memo., 1 September 1945, pp. 42–3

90 *DBPO I/III*, no. 99, Bevin memo., 8 November 1945, pp. 310–13

91 *Loc. cit.*, no. 102, WSC to Bevin, 13 November 1945, pp. 316–18

16: *The 'Anglo-Saxon thesis'*

1 Trinity College, Cambridge, R. A. Butler Papers, RAB G. 9/13, Butler to Ian Black, 21 April 1938

2 John Darwin, *Britain and Decolonisation* (1988), pp. 42–4; D. A. Low, *Eclipse of Empire* (Cambridge, 1991), pp. 137–42

3 Such was the burden of the song of several reviewers of my last book

4 Gallagher, *op. cit.*, p. 138

5 Tomlinson, *op. cit.*, p. 93, for the figures

6 *Keynes XXIV*, p. 408

7 Gallagher, *op. cit.*, p. 139

8 *DBPO I/I*, no. 78, Clark-Kerr to AE, 10 July 1945, pp. 142–8; no. 176, AE to WSC, 17 July 1945, pp. 352–4; no. 207, Molotov to Clark-Kerr, 20 July 1945, pp. 457–8

9 Bruce R. Kuniholm, *The Origins of the Cold War in the Near East* (Princeton, 1980), chap IV

10 Jean van der Poel (ed.), *Selections from the Smuts Papers, vol. VI* (Cambridge, 1973), Amery to Smuts, 13 February 1942, pp. 353–4

11 Gallagher, *op. cit.*, pp. 100–2, 109–14

12 J. Charmley, *Lord Lloyd and the Decline of the British Empire* (1987), pp. 114–19; Peter L. Hahn, *The United States, Great Britain and Egypt 1945–1956* (Chapel Hill, 1991), pp. 10–13; W. R. Louis, *The British Empire in the Middle East 1945–1951* (Oxford, 1984), pp. 25–7

13 Avi Schlaim, *Collusion across the Jordan* (Oxford, 1988), pp. 37–9

14 Gallagher, *op. cit.*, p. 140

15 *Cadogan diary*, 29 July 1945, p. 176

16 Smith and Zametica, *op. cit.*, p. 239

17 Cab. 66/64, WP (45) 229, 'Palestine', AE memo., 10 April 1945

18 Cab. 66/64, WP (45) 256, 'Defence of the Middle East', AE memo., 13 April 1945

19 Cab. 66/64, WP (45) 197, Attlee memo., 20 March 1945

20 Cab. 66/64, WP (45) 229, 'Palestine', AE memo., 10 April 1945, para. 10

21 *DBPO I/I*, no. 176, AE to WSC, 17 July 1945, pp. 352–4

22 *Ibid.*, no. 179, Attlee to AE, 18 July 1945, pp. 363–4

23 *Ibid.*, no. 237, Attlee to WSC, 23 July 1945, pp. 573–4

24 *Ibid.*, no. 238, AE to Attlee, 23 July 1945, pp. 575–6

25 *Ibid.*, no. 102, 'Stocktaking after VE-Day' by Sir Orme Sargent, pp. 183–5

26 *DBPO I/II*, no. 62, record of conversation, 16 September, 1945, p. 191

27 *Ibid.*, no. 102, pp. 26–34

28 *Ibid.*, Calendar to no. 102, i, N. M. Butler minute, 30 July 1945

29 *Ibid.*, no. 193, FO memo., 11 September 1945, p. 533

30 FO 371/44538/AN3159/4/45, J. Donnelly minute, 17 October 1945

31 *DBPO I/II*, no. 9, Bevin to Balfour, 25 August 1945, p. 16

32 *Ibid.*, no. 10, Balfour to Bevin, 25 August 1945, pp. 18–19

33 *Ibid.*, no. 186, Sir R. Campbell memo., 8 August 1945, pp. 516–20

34 *Presidential Papers, Harry S. Truman, 1945*, pp. 381–8

35 *DBPO I/II*, no. 190, FO memo., 18 August 1945, pp. 524–6; no. 200, minute from Mr Butler to Bevin, 12 October 1945, pp. 559–62

36 *Ibid.*, no. 212, Mr Butler memo., 4 November 1945; Bullock, *Bevin*, pp. 184–5

37 *DBPO I/I*, no. 102, Annexe *II*, p. 189; Calendar to no. 10.2, i, minutes by Gladwyn Jebb, 20 July, by N. M. Butler, 30 July, and Sir Orme Sargent, 31 July 1945

38 *Ibid.*, Calendar to no. 109, i, JP (45) 167 (Final), 'Future control of Palestine', paras 2 and 3

39 *Ibid.*, no. 15, WSC to Oliver Stanley, 6 July 1945, p. 25

40 *Loc. cit.*, Calendar to no. 109, i, JP (45) 167 (Final), 'Future control of Palestine', para. 3

41 *Ibid.*, para. 9; see also no. 109, Annexe I, Ismay to WSC, 12 July 1945

42 Cab. 66/64, WP (45) 229, 'Palestine', AE memo., 10 April 1945

43 PRO, Bevin Papers, FO 800/484/PA45/13, Bevin to Halifax, 12 October 1945

44 *DBPO I/II*, no. 26, Balfour to Bevin, 6 September 1945, p. 67

45 Cab. 66/64, WP (45) 229, 'Palestine', AE memo., 10 April 1945

46 *DBPO I/II*, no. 18, Attlee memo., 1 September 1945, pp. 42–3

47 *Ibid.*, no. 192, Attlee memo., circulated 28 August 1945, pp. 529–31; see also no. 213, Attlee memo., 5 November 1945, pp. 583–7

48 *Ibid.*, no. 33, Bevin memo., 10 September 1945; Smith and Zametica, *op. cit.*, pp. 243–4

49 Ronald Hyam (ed.), *British Documents on the End of Empire, Series A, vol. 2* (1992), Cab. 129/2, CP (45) 174, 'Middle East Policy' by Bevin, 17 September 1945, pp. 210–13

50 HSTL, PSF, Box 184, file 'Palestine 1945–1947', Joseph C. Grew to HST, 1 May 1945

51 *DBPO I/I*, No. 480, Bevin to Attlee (with enclosures), 30 July 1945, pp. 1042–3

52 Louis, *op. cit.*, p. 386; Nicholas Bethell, *The Palestine Triangle* (NY, 1979), pp. 205–7

53 HSTL, PSF, Box 184, file 'Palestine 1945–1947', HST to Weizmann, 1 December 1947

54 *Loc. cit.*, HST to Niles, 23 August 1947, attaching a letter from a Chicago lawyer, Joseph J. Abbell, 19 August 1947

55 FCO Historical Branch, Occasional Papers No. 4, *Eastern Europe*, Keith Hamilton, 'The Quest for a

Modus Vivendi: The Danubian Satellites in Anglo-Soviet Relations 1945–6', pp. 12–16

56 *DBPO I/I*, no. 119, brief for UK Potsdam delegation, 12 July 1945, also Annexes 1, 1 (g), pp. 234–51

57 *Ibid.*, no. 102, 'Stocktaking after VE-Day' by Sir Orme Sargent, 11 July 1945, pp. 186–7

58 Sir L. Woodward, *British Foreign Policy in the Second World War, vol. IV* (1975), pp. 255–81, for the background

59 *Ibid.*, p. 336, fn. 1, Mr Shone to AE, 30 May 1945

60 *DBPO I/II*, no. 62, note of conversation after dinner, 16 September 1945, p. 191

61 M. Pelly and H. J. Yasamee (eds), *Documents on British Policy Overseas, Series I, vol. VI: Eastern Europe 1945–1946* (1991), no. 63, Sir Orme Sargent to Houston-Boswall, 26 November 1945

62 Eduard Mark, 'Charles E. Bohlen and the Acceptable Limits of Soviet Hegemony in Eastern Europe: A Memorandum of 18 October 1945', *Diplomatic History*, vol. 3, no. 2, Spring 1979, p. 208

63 *DBPO I/II*, no. 99, note of discussion between Bevin and Molotov, 22 September 1945, p. 296

64 *Ibid.*, no. 107, Sir Orme Sargent minute, 23 September 1945, pp. 314–16

65 *DBPO I/I*, no. 495, 11th Plenary Meeting, 31 July 1945, p. 1077

66 *Ibid.*, no. 459, Gladwyn Jebb memo., 29 July 1945, p. 993

67 *DBPO I/II*, no. 108, note of Bevin/Molotov conversation, 23 September 1945, pp. 317–18

68 *DBPO I/I*, no 580, F. K. Roberts to Bevin, 1 August 1945, p. 1224

69 Churchill College, Cambridge, Lord Lloyd of Dolobran Papers, GLLD 20/6, Balkan diary, 21 November 1939

70 *DBPO I/II*, no. 193, FO memo., 11 September 1945, p. 537

71 *Ibid.*, no. 108, note of Bevin/Molotov conversation, 23 September 1945, p. 317; see also no. 120, Pierson Dixon memo., 24 September 1945, pp. 349–50, and no. 163, Pierson Dixon memo., pp. 473–4

72 *DBPO I/I*, no. 459, Gladwyn Jebb memo., 29 July 1945, p. 993

73 *DBPO I/II*, no. 120, Pierson Dixon memo., 24 September 1945, p. 349

74 *Ibid.*, Calendar to no. 242, i, Halifax to FO, 17 November 1945

75 *Ibid.*, no. 239, minute, 16 November 1945, p. 627

76 *Ibid.*, Calendar to no. 242, i, Halifax to FO, 17 November 1945

17: *The Winds of Change*

1 R. Edmonds, *Setting the Mould: The United States and Great Britain 1945–50* (Oxford, 1986), pp. 151–61; Bradford Perkins, 'Unequal Partners: The Truman Administration and Great Britain', in Bull and Louis (eds), *The Special Relationship*, pp. 43–64

2 *DBPO* I/II, no. 278, Peterson to Bevin, 12 December 1945, p. 691

3 *Ibid.*, no. 244, Clark-Kerr to Bevin, 24 November 1945, pp. 636–7

4 *Ibid.*, no. 249, Bevin to Halifax, 28 November 1945, p. 645

5 *Ibid.*, no. 192, undated memo. by Attlee on the atomic bomb, pp. 529–31

6 *Ibid.*, nos 263–5, Clark-Kerr to Bevin, 8 December 1945, FO brief, 8 December 1945, pp. 665–8

7 James L. Gormly, *From Potsdam to the Cold War: Big Three Diplomacy 1945–1947* (Delaware, 1990), pp. 89–90; Harbutt, *op. cit.*, pp. 133–5

8 *DBPO* I/II, no. 250, Clark-Kerr to Bevin, 29 November 1945, p. 646

9 *Ibid.*, no. 268, Clark-Kerr to Bevin, 10 December 1945, p. 671

10 *Ibid.*, no. 278, Peterson to Bevin, 12 December 1945, p. 691; Harbutt, *op. cit.*, pp. 135–6; no. 288, brief for UK delegation at Moscow, December 1945, pp. 719–21

11 *DBPO* I/II, nos 85, 90, 98, 99, 102, 112, 119, meetings between Bevin and Molotov, 19, 20, 22, 23, 24 September 1945, pp. 248–9, 264–5, 295–6, 302, 327, 348, for Iran

12 Harbutt, *op. cit.*, pp. 135–6; Kuniholm, *op. cit.*, pp. 304–26

13 For Taft, see Patterson, *op. cit.*

14 Louis Galambos et al. (eds), *The Papers of Dwight David Eisenhower, vol. XII: NATO and the Campaign of 1952* (hereinafter *Eisenhower papers XII* (Baltimore, 1989), DDE to Edward John Bermingham, 26 February 1951, p. 77

15 Robert A. Pollard, 'The national security state reconsidered', in Michael J. Lacey (ed.), *The Truman Presidency* (Cambridge, 1989), p. 208

16 *Wallace diary*, 15 October 1945, p. 490

17 *Ibid.*, 13 November 1945, p. 513

18 McClain, *op. cit.*, p. 469; Woods and Jones, *op. cit.*, pp. 90–1, 98–103; Isaacson and Thomas, *op. cit.*

19 *FRUS 1945*, V, Harriman to Stettinius, 4 April 1945, p. 819

20 *Wallace diary*, 26 October 1945, p. 502

21 Messer, *op. cit.*, pp. 148–51; Alonzo Hamby, 'The Mind and Character of Harry S. Truman', in Lacey (ed.), *op. cit.*, p. 43; Woods and Jones, *op. cit.*, pp. 86–7; Isaacson and Thomas, *op. cit.*, p. 299

22 McClain, *op. cit.*, pp. 467–9

23 Vandenberg (ed.), *op. cit.*, undated letter, 1945, p. 225

24 *Ibid.*, pp. 232–5; Messer, *op. cit.*, pp. 143–4

25 Anderson, *The United States, Great Britain and the Cold War*, p. 99; Harbutt, *op. cit.*, pp. 132–3

26 Anderson, *ibid.*, pp. 99–100

27 Woods and Jones, *op. cit.*, p. 91

28 Mark, *op. cit.*, pp. 205, 207–9; Isaacson and Thomas, *op. cit.*, pp. 340–1

29 Harriman, *op. cit.*, p. 514

30 Elie Kedourie, 'A New International Disorder', in *The Crossman Confessions and Other Essays* (1984), p. 98

31 *Hansard*, House of Commons, 5th series, col. 1294, 7 November 1945

32 *Ibid.*, cols 1300–7

33 Bullock, *Bevin*, p. 191

34 Isaacson and Thomas, *op. cit.*, pp. 319–22

35 *Ibid.*, pp. 325–7

36 *Hansard, loc. cit.*, col. 1334

37 *Ibid.*, col. 1342

38 Bullock, *Bevin*, pp. 192–3

39 Diary of Sir Pierson Dixon (in the possession of his son, Mr Piers Dixon), 7 December 1945

40 *DBPO* I/II, no. 294, record of Bevin/Byrnes conversation, 17 December 1945, pp. 733–4

41 Gormly, *op. cit.*, pp. 92–4

42 Harriman, *op. cit.*, pp. 516–17

43 *Ibid.*, p. 518

44 *DBPO* I/II, no. 253, Clark-Kerr to Bevin, 3 December 1945, pp. 650–2; Harriman, *op. cit.*, pp. 521–2, says similar things, which makes it likely that both reports had a common Soviet source

45 *DBPO* I/II, no. 318, note by Dixon of conversation with Bohlen and Harriman, 20 December 1945, pp. 803–4

46 *Ibid.*, Calendar to no. 318, i

47 Messer, *op. cit.*, pp. 149–55, rehearses the arguments

48 HSTL, Post-Presidential Papers, Box 1, interview with Dean Acheson, 18 February 1955, pp. 22, 23

49 McCullough, *op. cit.*, p. 479

50 Vandenberg (ed.), *op. cit.*, pp. 230–3

51 *Wallace diary*, 28 November 1945, pp. 523–4

52 Messer, *op. cit.*, pp. 147–8

53 Gormly, *op. cit.*, p. 96

54 *DBPO* I/II, no. 300, Bevin/Molotov meeting, 18 December 1945, pp. 748–55

55 *Ibid.*, no. 308, Bevin/Stalin meeting, 19 December 1945, pp. 779–84

56 *Ibid.*, no. 312, Bevin to FO, 20 December 1945, p. 787

57 Gormly, *op. cit.*, pp. 97–8

58 Harbutt, *op. cit.*, p. 140, joins a host of critics from Truman onwards

59 *DBPO* I/II, no. 328, Roberts to Clark-Kerr, 22 December 1945, p. 837

60 *Ibid.*, no. 315, Annexe 797

61 *Ibid.*, no. 320, informal meeting of the three Foreign Ministers, pp. 807–8

62 *Ibid.*, no. 326, 9th formal meeting, p. 833

63 *Ibid.*, no. 322, Soviet memo., 21 December 1945, pp. 818–19

64 Messer, *op. cit.*, pp. 156–8; McCullough, *op. cit.*, pp. 478–80

18: 'On the hills of old Missouri'

1 Westminster College, Missouri, archives. *The Columns*, 2 May 1969, 'The Christening of the "Iron Curtain"' by Dr William E. Parrish, p. 3. I am indebted to the College archivist, Warren M.

Hollrah, and my former research assistant, Kevin S. Mathis, for pointing out this source to me

2 WCML, 'Churchill's visit', Box 1, F. L. McCluer to WSC, 3 October 1945

3 The comment is that of the man responsible for the Churchill Memorial, Dr Larry Davidson

4 WCML, Box 1, HST to McCluer, 10 December 1945

5 *Ibid.*, note in archives

6 Woods and Jones, *op. cit.*, pp. 99–100; Thomas G. Paterson, 'Presidential Foreign Policy, Public Opinion and Congress: The Truman Years', *Diplomatic History*, vol. 3, no. 1, 1979; Harbutt, *op. cit.*, pp. 152–3

7 Paterson, *ibid.*, p. 6

8 *Wallace diary*, 2 January 1946, p. 536. See also Mervyn P. Leffler, *A Preponderance of Power: National Security, the Truman Administration and the Cold War* (Stanford, 1992), pp. 51–5

9 John Lewis Gaddis, 'The Insecurities of Victory', in Lacey (ed.), *op. cit.*, pp. 250–1

10 Walter Mills (ed.), *The Forrestal Diaries* (NY, 1951), 4 December 1945, p. 124

11 Ferrell, *op. cit.*, pp. 79–80

12 Messer, *op. cit.*, pp. 158–61, provides good reasons for supposing this

13 *DBPO I/IV*, no. 1, enclosure, Mr Balfour memo., 28 November 1945, pp. 2–11

14 *Wallace diary*, 2 January 1946, p. 537

15 Harriman, *op. cit.*, p. 531

16 See chap. 21 above and also John Kent, 'The Empire and the Origins of the Cold War', in Anne Deighton (ed.), *Britain and the First Cold War* (1990), pp. 168–70

17 Kuniholm, *op. cit.*, pp. 304–6

18 Bullock, *Bevin*, pp. 220–1

19 Thomas, *Armed Truce*, pp. 9–11

20 HSTL, Papers of George M. Elsey, Box 63, Moscow to State, 29 January 1946; PSF, Box 187, undated paper (but c. January–March 1946 from internal evidence), 'Why are the Russians slow to trust the Western Powers?'

21 Jensen (ed.), *op. cit.*, pp. 17–21

22 See above, and also W. W. Rostow, *The Division of Europe after World War II: 1946* (Texas, 1982), pp. 39–40

23 Vandenberg (ed.), *op. cit.*, pp. 246–9, for the text

24 *DBPO I/IV*, no. 18, Bevin/Vandenberg/Foster Dulles conversation, 18 January 1946, pp. 67–9; see also Leffler, *op. cit.*, pp. 102–10, for domestic backdrop

25 On the background to this, see Martin Gilbert, 'The Origins of the "Iron Curtain" Speech', the first Crosby Kemper Memorial Lecture, given at Westminster College, Fulton, Missouri, 26 April 1981. I am greatly indebted to my friend Warren M. Hollrah for giving me his copy of this scarce publication – and for much else besides

26 *Ibid.*, p. 17

27 HSTL, Ross papers, Box 21, diary, March 1946

28 Harbutt, *op. cit.*, p. 180

29 *The Columns*, 2 May 1969, Parrish article, p. 6

30 Winston S. Churchill, 'The Sinews of Peace', text published by Westminster College, which is based on the copy of the text taken by a shorthand stenographer present at the time. It differs only marginally from the version in Robert Rhodes James (ed.), *Winston S. Churchill: His Complete Speeches 1897–1963, vol. VII: 1943–1949* (hereinafter *Churchill Speeches*) (NY, 1974), pp. 7285–93

31 HSTL, Ross Papers, Box 21, diary, 7 March 1946, p. 22

32 WCML, *St Louis Globe-Democrat*, 6 March 1944, main leader. All other quotations from newspapers are from the fine collection at the Churchill Memorial, unless otherwise indicated. I am grateful to Warren M. Hollrah and Kevin S. Mathis for helping me through the great mass of material

33 *St Louis Post-Dispatch*, 19 March 1946

34 *Boston Globe*, 6 March 1946

35 *Chicago-Sun*, 6 March 1946

36 FO 371/51624/AN649/4/45, American press summary, para. 15

37 FO 371/51624/AN675/4/45, Halifax to Bevin, 9 March 1945, for Truman and Byrnes; Bullock, *Bevin*, p. 225

38 *Commercial Appeal* (Memphis, Tennessee), 6 March 1946

39 FO 371/51624/AN649/4/45, Isaiah Berlin's report, 8 March 1945. The rest of this paragraph is based partly upon this report, partly upon Halifax's despatch at AN656, which is in *DBPO I/IV*, no. 49, and partly on a reading of the press comment. It takes account of, but does not quite coincide with, Harbutt's perceptive categorisation on pp. 197–8

40 Messer, *op. cit.*, pp. 188–91

41 PRO, Defence Committee Meetings, Cab. 131/1, DO (46), 3rd meeting, 21 January 1946

42 B. Pimlott (ed.), *The Political Diary of Hugh Dalton, 1918–40, 1945–60* (1986), p. 368

43 R. Hyam (ed.), *British Documents on the End of Empire, Series A, vol. 2, pt III: Strategy, Politics and Constitutional Change* (hereinafter *BDEE A/2/III*) (1992), no. 276, DO (46) 27 by Attlee, 2 March 1946, pp. 213–15

44 Smith and Zametica, *op. cit.*, p. 245

45 *BDEE A/2/III*, no. 277, DO (46) 40 by Bevin, 13 March 1946, pp. 215–18

46 Ferrell (ed.), *op. cit.*, p. 80

47 *DBPO I/IV*, no. 48, WSC to Attlee and Bevin, 7 March 1946, pp. 150–1

48 *Ibid.*, no. 49, Halifax to Bevin, 10 March 1946, pp. 152–9

49 F. K. Roberts, *Dealing with Dictators* (1991), p. 108

50 Jensen (ed.), *op. cit.*, pp. 33–69

19: Consequences

1 Leffler, *op. cit.*, pp. 109–14

2 *Time*, 25 March 1946

3 *St Louis Post-Dispatch*, syndicated column, 13 March 1946

4 *Wallace diary*, 5 March 1946, p. 556

5 *Ibid.*, 12 March 1946, p. 558–9

6 HSTL, Elsey Papers, Box 63, tel. 1143 from State, 11 April 1946

7 *Ibid.*, Clark Clifford to Leahy (copies to other Departments), 18 July 1946

8 *Ibid.*, longhand notes, 18 July 1946

9 *Ibid.*, 24 July 1946

10 Woods and Jones, *op. cit.*, pp. 126–7

11 HSTL, Papers to Clark M. Clifford, 'Outline of the Report', 26 July 1946; see also Elsey Papers, Box 63, 'Soviet Foreign Policy: A Summation'. See Leffler, *op. cit.*, pp. 135–40, for a critique

12 Leffler, *op. cit.*, p. 133

13 *Ibid.*, p. 143, quoting William Clayton of the State Department in 1947

14 AP 23/60/7A, Salisbury to AE, 31 August 1957

15 AP 23/48/60A, notes on Vietnam, enclosed in a letter, AE to Macmillan, 2 September 1965

16 HSTL, Papers of Joseph M. Jones, Box 2, draft note of meeting, February 1947

17 R. Frazier, 'Did Britain start the Cold War? Bevin and the Truman Doctrine', *Historical Journal*, 1984, pp. 715–27

18 Jones Papers, *loc. cit.*

19 Sir Alec Cairncross, *Years of Recovery: British Economic Policy 1945–51* (1985), p. 76

20 *Ibid.*, pp. 81–3

21 Frazier, *op. cit.*, Woods, *Changing of the Guard*

22 Cairncross, *op. cit.*, pp. 80–1

23 R. Hyam (ed.), *British Documents on the End of Empire, Series A, vol. 2: The Labour Government and the End of Empire 1945–1951: pt I: High Policy* (1992), no. 68, 'Projection of Britain Overseas', 17 August 1946, pp. 308–9

24 R. Hyam (ed.), *British Documents on the End of Empire, Series A, vol. 2: The Labour Government and the End of Empire 1945–1951: pt II: International Relations* (hereinafter *BDEE A/2/II*) (1992), no. 140, Bevin to Attlee, 16 September 1946, p. 314

25 *Ibid.*, no. 142, 'The first aim of British foreign policy', Bevin memo., 4 January 1948, p. 318

26 *Ibid.*, no. 91, Colonial Office memo. on colonial development, 19 August 1948, p. 86

27 *Ibid.*, 'Prices of Colonial Export Products', March 1947, p. 39

28 *Ibid.*, 'Practical achievements in the colonies since the war', Creech-Jones memo., 7 December 1948, pp. 111–15

29 *Loc. cit.*, no. 142, 'The first aim of British foreign policy', Bevin memo., 4 January 1948, pp. 317–18

30 J. Charmley, 'Duff Cooper and Western European Union, 1944–47', *Review of International Studies*, vol. 11, 1985, pp. 53–64

31 FO 371/67670/Z1215, Cooper to Oliver Harvey, 7 February 1947

32 *BDEE A/2/II*, no. 142, 'The first aim of British foreign policy', Bevin memo., 4 January 1948, p. 318

33 A. Rappaport, 'The United States and European Integration: The First Phase', *Diplomatic History*, vol. 5, no. 2, Spring 1981, pp. 121–49; Charles S. Maier, 'Alliance and Autonomy: European Identity and US Foreign Policy Objectives in the Truman Years', in Lacey (ed.), *op. cit.*, pp. 273–98

34 AP 20/17/30, Makins to AE, 2 December 1954

35 HSTL, Geoffrey Warner, unpublished paper on 'The Special Relationship', p. 2; see also Ronald Hyams, *BDEE A/2/I*, pp. i–li of the introduction

36 *BDEE A/2/II*, no. 174, 'International aspects of colonial policy – 1947', J. S. Bennet, p. 411

37 *Ibid.*, no. 184, J. Fletcher-Cooke memo., 10 December 1949, pp. 449–451; no. 186, 'United States attitude towards colonial and trusteeship matters at the UN', Sir Oliver Franks to FO, 22 December 1949, pp. 457–8; no. 187, 'Relations with the United States and the UN', CO minutes, 9 February–14 April 1950, pp. 459–65

38 *Foreign Relations of the United States 1950, vol. I: National Security Affairs; Foreign Economic Policy* (Washington, 1977), JSC report to Truman, approved 14 December 1950, pp. 467–77

39 *Eisenhower papers XII*, no. 51, DDE to John Bermingham, 28 February 1951, p. 75

40 AP 20/17/30, Makins to AE, 2 December 1954

41 *Eisenhower papers XII*, no. 51, DDE to John Bermingham, 28 February 1951, pp. 76–7, emphases in the original

42 Maier, *op. cit.*, pp. 274–5

43 HSTL, PSF, Box 132, Acheson to Truman, 5 January 1951

44 George Kennan, *Memoirs* (Boston, 1967), p. 337

45 Michael J. Hogan, *The Marshall Plan: America, Britain and the Reconstruction of Western Europe 1947–1952* (NY, 1987), chap. 1, for this argument. For a review of the recent scholarship, see William Diebold Jr, 'The Marshall Plan in Retrospect', *International Affairs*, vol. 41, 1988, pp. 430–5

46 Pelling, Morgan, MacDonald here

47 AP 19/1/67, WSC to AE, 8 January 1951

48 Cairncross, *op. cit.*, pp. 207–25; J. C. R. Dow, *The Management of the British Economy, 1945–1960* (Cambridge, 1968), pp. 29–54, upon which these paragraphs are based

49 Cairncross, *op. cit.*, p. 224

50 AP 20/16/23, Makins to AE, 9 January 1953, for a retrospective example

20: Churchill's 'Grand Alliance'

1 R. H. Ferrell (ed.), *The Eisenhower Diaries* (hereinafter *Eisenhower diary*) (1981), 21 December 1951, p. 208

2 *Ibid.*, 6 January 1953, p. 222

3 AP 20/16/25A, DDE to AE, 16 March 1953

4 AP 20/16/23, Makins to AE, 9 January 1953

5 AP 20/17/30, Makins to AE, 2 December 1954

6 AP 20/1/28, Eden diary, 4 June 1952

7 AP 20/16/142, Salisbury to AE, 14 August 1953

8 AP 20/17/191, Salisbury to AE, 31 August 1954

9 AP 20/17/208, Crookshank to AE, 12 October 1954

10 AP 20/17/118, Salisbury to AE, 9 May 1954

11 AP 20/17/179, WSC to AE, 24 August 1954

12 AP 20/17/138, WSC to AE, 11 June 1954

13 J. Charmley (ed.), *Descent to Suez: The Diaries of Sir Evelyn Shuckburgh 1951–1956* (hereinafter *Shuckburgh diary*) (1987), 30 April, 28 November, 2, 8 December 1952, 11 March 1954, pp. 42, 62, 63, 66, 145

14 *Ibid.*, 28 July 1953, p. 93

15 AP 20/17/141A, copy to AE of HM to WSC, 18 June 1954

16 AP 20/17/200, 202, 202A, for a digest by HM of the correspondence between WSC and AE and letter to WSC, 2 October 1954, urging the need for reconstruction of the Government

17 AP 20/17/192, HM to AE, 9 September 1954

18 AP 20/17/195, mss. notes, 24 September 1954, not signed, but in Macmillan's hand

19 AP 20/17/118, Salisbury to AE, 9 May 1954

20 For these charges, see Carlton, *op. cit.*, pp. 209–302, and also Peter Boyle, 'The "Special Relationship" with Washington', in John W. Young (ed.), *The Foreign Policy of Churchill's Peacetime Administration 1951–1955* (Leicester, 1988), pp. 29–51; also Anthony Adamthwaite's introduction to this volume, pp. 1-27, and the longer article on which it is based, 'Overstretched and Overstrung: Eden, the Foreign Office and the making of policy, 1951–1955', *International Affairs*, vol. 64, no. 2, Spring 1988, pp. 241–59

21 Christopher Thorne's review of Carlton in the *TLS*, 1983

22 Adamthwaite, *op. cit.*, p. 250

23 Robert Rhodes James, *Anthony Eden* (1987)

24 AP 20/17/2, Dixon to AE, 22 June 1954

25 AP 23/60/46, Salisbury to AE, 26 February 1960

26 *BDEE A/2/II*, no. 162, 'Some notes on British foreign policy', Sir Roger Makins, 11 August 1950, p. 378

27 Carlton, *op. cit.*, pp. 295–307

28 *BDEE A/2/II*, no. 141, 'Anglo-American relations in the Middle East . . .', Bevin, 9 December 1947, pp. 315–16

29 *Ibid.*, no. 163, 'Foreign Policy in the Middle East', E. A. Chapman-Andrews, 17 September 1951, pp. 379–84

30 *Ibid.*, no. 156, 'Anglo-American relations', Bevin, 8 May 1950, p. 357

31 Correspondence with Richard Lamb, Clarissa Avon and myself in the *Daily Telegraph*, 1993

32 *Foreign Relations of the United States, 1949, vol. IV* (1975), record of meeting of US Ambassadors in Paris, 21–22 October 1949, pp. 472–96

33 Bullock, *Bevin*, p. 733

34 *BDEE A/2/II*, no. 153, CP (49) 204, 'Council of Europe', Bevin, 24 October 1949, pp. 348–53

35 R. Bullen and M. Pelly (eds), *Documents on British Policy Overseas, Series 2, vol. II: The London Conferences: Anglo-American Relations and Cold War Strategy January–June 1950* (1987), no. 74, CM (50) 29, pp. 257–61

36 *Ibid.*, Calendar to no. 74, Bevin's brief, 7 May 1950

37 Lord Gladwyn, 'Europe, Dreams and Realities', the eighth Winston Churchill Memorial Lecture, February 1974, *Schweitzer Montatshefte*, 1975

38 *Churchill Speeches, vol. 7*, pp. 7379–82

39 *Ibid.*, pp. 7483–8

40 The Earl of Kilmuir, *Political Adventure* (1964), pp. 185–7; Harold Macmillan, *Tides of Fortune, 1945-1955* (1969), pp. 463–6; James, *op. cit.*, p. 614

41 Anthony Seldon, *Churchill's Indian Summer* (1981), pp. 395–6

42 *BDEE A/2/II*, no. 162, 'Some notes on British foreign policy', p. 374

43 *Shuckburgh diary*, p. 18

44 R. Bullen and M. Pelly (eds), *Documents on British Policy Overseas, Series 2, vol. I: The Schuman Plan, the Council of Europe and Western European Integration 1950-1952* (hereinafter *DBPO 2/I*) (1986), no. 375, 14 September 1951, pp. 723–4

45 *Ibid.*, no. 377, Mr Butt to Mr Robertson, 15 September 1951, pp. 725–6

46 *Ibid.*, Calendar to no. 98, i, Sir Oliver Harvey to FO, 27 April 1950

47 *FCO Historical Branch, Occasional Papers, no. 1*, November, 1987, H. J. Yasamee, 'Anthony Eden and Europe, November 1951', pp. 39–50, for an excellent account

48 *DBPO 2/I*, no. 403, Maxwell-Fife to AE, 28 November 1951, p. 765; see also Calendar to no. 402, i, Boothby to AE and WSC, 30 November, 11 December 1951

49 See Yasamee, *op. cit.*, pp. 42–4, for a brilliant dissection of Kilmuir's and Macmillan's claims

50 *DBPO 2/I*, Calendar to no. 402, C (51) 32, WSC note for Cabinet, 29 November 1951

51 *Ibid.*, no. 409, AE to Strasbourg, 6 December 1951, p. 775

52 *Ibid.*, no. 314, M, 153C/51, WSC to AE, 13 December 1951, p. 781

53 Peter L. Hahn, *The United States, Great Britain and Egypt 1945–1956* (Chapel Hill, 1991), p. 14

54 Anderson, *The United States, Great Britain and the Cold War*, pp. 121–5; Louis, *British Empire in the Middle East*, pp. 242–4

55 *BDEE A/2/II*, no. 141, 'Anglo-American relations in the Middle East . . .', draft letter by Bevin, 9 December 1947, pp. 315–16

56 *Ibid.*, no. 163, Chapman-Andrews to FO, 17 September 1951, pp. 379–84

57 Cab. 128/18, CM (50) 79, 11 November 1950

58 *Shuckburgh diary*, p. 17

59 *Ibid.*, 4 November 1951, p. 27

21: Renewing the Grand Alliance?

1 D. C. Watt, 'Demythologizing the Eisenhower Era', in Louis and Bull (eds), *op. cit.*, p. 75

2 Earl of Avon, *The Eden Memoirs, vol. III: Full Circle* (hereinafter *Eden III*) (1960), p. 64

3 Sir Michael Howard, 'The barbarian solution', *TLS*, 11 February 1994

4 William Roger Louis, 'American anti-colonialism', in Louis and Bull (eds), *op. cit.*, p. 273

5 AP 23/60/13A, AE to Salisbury, 15 December 1957

6 Adam Watson, 'Cushioning the fall', *TLS*, 31 May 1985
7 M. Gilbert, *Winston S. Churchill, vol. VIII: Never Despair 1945–65* (hereinafter *Churchill VIII*) (1988), p. 661
8 Acheson, *op. cit.*, p. 595
9 *Foreign Relations of the United States 1952–1954, vol. VI* (hereinafter *FRUS 1952–1954, VI*) (Washington, 1979), 'Approaches and Objectives for the Churchill talks', 21 December 1951, pp. 709–17
10 *Ibid.*, meeting, 5 January 1952, pp. 730–42; Cab. 21/3057, note of conversation between the Prime Minister and the President, 5 January 1952; Acheson, *op. cit.*, pp. 598–600
11 Moran, *op. cit.*, diary, 5 January 1952, p. 356
12 Acheson, *op. cit.*, p. 600
13 David S. McLellan, *Dean Acheson: The State Department Years* (NY, 1976), p. 358
14 *Ibid.*, p. 358
15 *Ibid.*, p. 390
16 *Ibid.*
17 Acheson, *op. cit.*, p. 600
18 HSTL, PSF, Box 115, meeting of HST and WSC, 8 January 1952
19 *Shuckburgh diary*, 5 January 1952, p. 32
20 HSTL, PSF, Box 115, meeting 8 January, 11 a.m.
21 Acheson, *op. cit.*, p. 598
22 HSTL, PSF, Box 115, meeting 8 January, 5.30 p.m.
23 Moran, *op. cit.*, diary, 10 January 1952, p. 362
24 *Eden III*, pp. 36–7
25 HSTL, PSF, Box 115, meeting 18 January 1952, 3.10 p.m.
26 *Shuckburgh diary*, 5 January 1952, p. 32
27 Acheson, *op. cit.*, p. 602
28 Cab. 129/53, C (52) 202, 'British Overseas Obligations', AE memo., cited in full in D. Goldsworthy (ed.), *British Documents on the End of Empire, Series A, vol. 3: The Conservative Government and the End of Empire 1951–1957, pt I: International Relations* (hereinafter *BDEE A/3/I*) (1994), no. 3, pp. 4–12
29 W. Scott Lucas, *Divided We Stand: Britain, the US and the Suez Crisis* (1991), p. 14
30 Cab. 129/51, C (52) 122, 'Anglo-Egyptian Negotiations', AE memo., 8 April 1952; Cab. 128/24, CC (52) 35th conclusions, 1 April 1952. Also *BDEE A/3/I*, no. 31, C (52) 267, 'Suez Canal', AE memo., 28 July 1952, pp. 111–17; no. 33, C (52) 269, 'Egypt: defence negotiations', AE memo., 27 October 1952, pp. 118–22
31 *Colville diary*, 8 April 1952, p. 645
32 Cab. 128/24, CC (52) 37th conclusions, 4 April 1952
33 Lucas, *op. cit.*, pp. 15–17
34 Cab. 128/25, CC (52) 76th conclusions, 7 August 1952
35 Cab. 128/25, CC (52) 79th conclusions, 11 September 1952
36 Cab. 128/25, CC (52) 89th conclusions, 23 October 1952; Cab. 129/56, C (52) 354, 'United States Ideas for a Settlement of the Oil Dispute', AE memo., 23 October 1952
37 AP 20/15/18A, Shuckburgh to Oliver Franks, 22 November 1952

38 *Shuckburgh diary*, 19 November 1952, p. 54
39 *Ibid.*, 22 November 1952, pp. 56–7
40 The key work here was Robert A. Divine, *Eisenhower and the Cold War* (1981). A good summary of the present situation can be found in Richard H. Innerman's 'Confessions of an Eisenhower Revisionist: An Agonizing Reappraisal', *Diplomatic History*, vol. 14, no. 3, Summer 1990, pp. 319–42
41 *Eisenhower diary*, 6 January 1953, pp. 222–3
42 AP 20/16/23, Makins to AE, 9 January 1953
43 *Ibid.*, Makins to AE, 9 January 1953
44 *Eisenhower diary*, 6 January 1953, p. 223
45 *Shuckburgh diary*, 20 November 1952, p. 55
46 AP 20/1/28, Eden diary, 22 December 1952
47 Lucas, *op. cit.*, p. 12
48 *Shuckburgh diary*, 2 December 1952, p. 63
49 D. C. Watt, *Succeeding John Bull* (1984), p. 128; see Divine, *op. cit.*, pp. 360–7

22: *Defeated by 'the bastard'*

1 AP 23/60/115, 115A, Salisbury to AE and AE to S, 6, 8 April 1964
2 See Townsend Hoopes, *The Devil and John Foster Dulles* (Boston, 1973); Herman Finer, *Dulles over Suez* (Chicago, 1964)
3 Lucas, *op. cit.*, p. 22
4 Dwight D. Eisenhower, *The White House Years: Mandate for Change 1953–1956* (NY, 1963), p. 142
5 Peter G. Boyle (ed.), *The Churchill-Eisenhower Correspondence 1953–1955* (hereinafter *WSC-DDE Corr.*) (Chapel Hill, 1990), WSC to DDE, 5 April 1953, p. 34
6 AP 19/1/76, WSC to AE, 6 April 1953
7 *Churchill VIII*, pp. 805–7
8 *WSC-DDE Corr.*, WSC to DDE, 11 March 1953, p. 31
9 John W. Young, 'Churchill, the Russians and the Western Alliance: the three-power conference at Bermuda, 1953', *English Historical Review*, October 1986, pp. 898–912
10 *FRUS 1952–1954, VI*, Aldrich to State, 12 May 1953, pp. 985–6
11 AP 20/16/145, Salisbury to AE, 6 September 1953
12 AP 20/16/127, Nutting to AE, May 1953
13 *Eden III*, pp. 37–47; John W. Young, 'German Rearmament and the European Defence Community', in Young (ed.), *The Foreign Policy of Churchill's Peacetime Administration*, pp. 82–4
14 Anthony Glees, 'Winston's Last Gambit', *Encounter*, vol. LXIV, no. 4, April 1985, pp. 30–1
15 *WSC-DDE Corr.*, DDE to WSC, 25 April, 5 May 1953, pp. 47, 49
16 *Ibid.*, WSC to DDE, 12 April 1953, pp. 43–4
17 Glees, *op. cit.*, p. 30, quoting from an undated memo. by WSC
18 *Ibid.*, pp. 32–4. Churchill's views are at Cab. 129/61, C (53) 194, Salisbury to Cabinet, 7 July 1953, circulating WSC's memo. of 6 July
19 *FRUS 1952–1954, VI*, Merchant to Dulles, 15 June 1953, pp. 991–2

20 *Ibid.*, Jernegan to Dulles, 17 June 1953, pp. 992–3
21 John Grigg, 'Churchill, Crippled Giant', *Encounter*, vol. XLVIII, no. 7, April 1977, pp. 10–11; Moran, *op. cit.*, 24 June–3 July, pp. 408–18; *Churchill VIII*, pp. 846–57
22 Young, 'Churchill, the Russians . . .', pp. 896–7
23 *Shuckburgh diary*, 21 July 1953, p. 89
24 British Library, Paul Emrys-Evans Papers, ADD. MSS. 58240, fos 191–3, Cranborne to Evans, 9 January 1947
25 AP 20/43/1, Cranborne to AE, 8 January 1946
26 AP 20/16/145, Salisbury to AE, 6 September 1953
27 Cab. 129/61, C (53) 187, Salisbury memo., 3 July 1953
28 Cab. 128/26, CC (53) 39th conclusions, 6 July 1953
29 D. D. Eisenhower Library, Abilene, Kansas (hereinafter DDEL), Ann Whitman File, Dulles/Herter Series, Box 1, Dulles, June 1953 (2), JFD to DDE
30 Cab. 128/26, CC (53) 12th conclusions, 17 February 1953; Cab. 129/59, C (53) 65, 'Egypt: The Alternatives', AE memo., 16 February 1953
31 *WSC–DDE Corr.*, WSC to DDE, 25 February 1953, pp. 28–9
32 AP 20/16/25A, DDE to AE, 16 March 1953
33 DDEL, Whitman File, Dulles/Herter Series, Box 1, JFD to DDE, 18 May 1953
34 DDEL, Papers of C. D. Jackson, Box 37, General Robert Cutler, Jackson to Cutler, 11 May 1953
35 AP 23/60/7A, Salisbury to AE, 31 August 1957
36 Steven Z. Freiberger, *Dawn over Suez* (Chicago, 1992), pp. 52–4
37 Lucas, *op. cit.*, p. 27
38 AP 23/60/154A, Salisbury to AE, 15 April 1969
39 Cab. 129/56, C (52) 383, 'Saudi Arabian Frontier Dispute', AE memo., 4 November 1952
40 Cab. 129/60, C (53) 103, 'Saudi Arabian Frontier Dispute', Salisbury memo., 16 March 1953
41 Cab. 128/26, CC (53) 42nd conclusions, 13 July 1953
42 *FRUS 1952–1954, VI*, pp. 1607–96, for a full record of the meetings
43 AP 20/16/145, Salisbury to AE, 6 September 1953
44 James, *op. cit.*, p. 373
45 *Shuckburgh diary*, 1 October 1953, pp. 102–3
46 *Ibid.*, 5 October 1953, p. 105
47 AP 20/1/29, Eden diary, 1 October 1953
48 Moran, *op. cit.*, diary, 2 December 1953, p. 501
49 *WSC–DDE Corr.*, WSC to DDE, 3 August 1953, p. 88
50 *Ibid.*, WSC to DDE, 7 October 1953, p. 89; *Shuckburgh diary*, 7, 9 October 1953, pp. 106–8
51 Young, 'Churchill, the Russians . . .', pp. 900–2; *WSC–DDE Corr.*, DDE to WSC, 7 November 1953, p. 95; *Shuckburgh diary*, p. 110
52 *Churchill VIII*, p. 911
53 *Colville diary*, 4 December 1953, pp. 682–3; Moran, *op. cit.*, diary, 4 December 1953, p. 505
54 *Shuckburgh diary*, 4 December 1953, p. 113
55 *Colville diary*, 4 December 1953, p. 683
56 *Ibid.*
57 *Ibid.*, 6 December 1953, pp. 685–7; *Eden III*, p. 55;

Shuckburgh diary, 5–6 December 1953, pp. 113–15
58 *Colville diary*, 6 December 1953, p. 685; *Shuckburgh diary*, 5 December 1953, p. 114
59 Eisenhower, *op. cit.*, p. 247
60 *Colville diary*, 6 December 1953, p. 686
61 Moran, *op. cit.*, diary, 7 December 1953, p. 508

23: *'They like to give orders'*

1 Author's files, Dixon to Shuckburgh, 16 November 1953
2 *FRUS 1952–1954, VI*, pp. 462–3
3 *Eden III*, pp. 57–8
4 AP 20/16/23, Makins to AE, 9 January 1953; see also Peter Boyle 'The Special Relationship with Moscow', in Young (ed.), *op. cit.*, pp. 34–5
5 Brian R. Duchin, 'The "Agonizing Reappraisal": Eisenhower, Dulles and the European Defense Community', *Diplomatic History*, vol. 16, no. 2, Spring 1992, pp. 201–21; also, James G. Hershberg, ' "Explosion in the Offing": German Rearmament and American Diplomacy, 1953–1955', *Diplomatic History*, vol. 16, no. 4, Fall 1992, pp. 511–49
6 DDEL, Whitman File/DDE Diary Series, Box 4, DDE to Baruch, 10 March 1953
7 Robert W. Griffith (ed.), *Ike's Letters to a Friend, 1941–1958* (Lawrence, Kansas, 1984), letter, 20 July 1954, p. 130
8 Marc Trachtenberg, *History and Strategy* (Princeton, 1991), pp. 167–8; Hershberg, *op. cit.*, p. 532; see also *Foreign Relations of the United States 1952–1954, vol. II* (Washington, 1983), NSC meeting, 10 December 1953, p. 450
9 Duchin, *op. cit.*, p. 212
10 *Eden III*, p. 58
11 Hershberg, *op. cit.*, p. 545
12 *Eden III*, pp. 58–9; *Shuckburgh diary*, 18 and 19 January 1954, p. 128, also entries for late January in the unpublished Shuckburgh diaries, copy in author's possession
13 DDEL, Whitman File, Dulles/Herter Series, Box 2, Dulles to DDE, 26 January 1954
14 Kevin Ruane, 'Anthony Eden, British Diplomacy and the Origins of the Geneva Conference of 1954', *Historical Journal*, 1994, pp. 153–72
15 Geoffrey Warner, 'The Settlement of the Indochina War', in Young (ed.), *op. cit.*, pp. 237–40
16 Unpublished Shuckburgh diary, 26 January 1954, copy in the author's collection
17 *Ibid.*, 27 January 1954
18 *Ibid.*
19 *Ibid.*
20 *Ibid.*, 28 January 1954
21 *Ibid.*
22 *Ibid.*, 29 January 1954
23 *Ibid.*, 7, 8, 17 February 1954
24 Ruane, *op. cit.*, pp. 157–63, for this line of argument; *Eden III*, pp. 87–8
25 AP 20/45/39, AE to WSC, 27 January 1953; *Eden III*, p. 88
26 *Shuckburgh diary*, 17 February 1953, p. 133

27 Ruane, *op. cit.*, p. 168, for this line. See also Macmillan's comment in Cabinet, Cab. 128/27, CC (54) 8th conclusions, 10 February 1954 (minute 5)
28 *Shuckburgh diary*, p. 15, a comment which Sir Evelyn repeated many times to me when I was editing his diaries
29 Unpublished Shuckburgh diary, 3 February 1954
30 Cab. 128/27, CC (54) 8th conclusions, 10 February 1954
31 Cab. 128/27, CC (54) 1st conclusions, 7 January, 8th conclusions, 10 February 1954; Cab. 128/65, C (54) 45, 'Egypt' by Lord Simonds, 9 February 1954
32 AP 20/17/157, Salisbury to AE, 15 February 1954
33 AP 20/17/10, Lloyd to AE, 3 February 1954
34 AP 20/17/163, Carr to AE, 5 February 1954
35 *Shuckburgh diary*, 3, 7 February 1954, pp. 131, 132
36 Cab. 129/65, C (54) 6, 'Middle East policy', AE memo., 7 January 1954
37 Cab. 128/27, CC (54) 1st conclusions; Cab. 129/65, C (54) 4, AE memo., 7 January 1954
38 Cab. 129/65, C (54) 53, Lloyd to Cabinet, 12 February 1954
39 Cab. 129/66, C (54) 58, Lloyd to Cabinet, 16 February 1954
40 Lucas, *op. cit.*, p. 32
41 Freiberger, *op. cit.*, pp. 86–9
42 *Eden III*, pp. 92–3; *WSC–DDE Corr.*, DDE to WSC, 4 April 1954, pp. 136–9
43 DDEL, Whitman File, Dulles/Herter Series, Box 2, JFD to DDE, 13 April 1954
44 DDEL, Whitman File, DDE Diary Series, Box 5, telephone call, 25 April 1954
45 AP 20/17/15A, AE to Lloyd, 21 May 1954
46 Ruane, *op. cit.*, p. 171
47 Anthony Short, *The Origins of the Vietnam War* (1989), p. 115
48 Quoted in *ibid.*, p. 137
49 *Eden III*, pp. 95–6
50 Carlton, *op. cit.*, pp. 343–6, rehearses the evidence
51 Cab. 120/68, C (54) 196, 'South-East Asia', AE memo., 11 June 1954
52 *Eden III*, p. 99
53 Carlton, *op. cit.*, p. 345, seems to take this view
54 DDEL, Whitman File, Dulles/Herter Series, Box 2, message from JFD, 24 April 1954, recording conversation with Eden and Bidault, 23 April 1954
55 DDEL, Whitman File, DDE Diary Series, Box 5, telephone calls, 24 April 1954
56 *Eden III*, p. 102
57 Griffith (ed.), *op. cit.*, letter, 27 April 1954, pp. 125–6
58 DDEL, Whitman File, DDE Diary Series, Box 5, telephone calls, 27 April 1954
59 DDEL, Whitman File, Dulles/Herter Series, Box 2, JFD to DDE, 24 April 1954, DDE manuscript annotation
60 *Eden III*, p. 104
61 *Shuckburgh diary*, 24 April 1954, p. 173
62 Moran, *op. cit.*, diary, 28 April 1954, p. 543

63 Cab. 129/68, C (54) 155, 'Indo China', record of meeting on 25 April 1954
64 *Ibid.*, record of 2nd meeting, 25 April 1954; *Shuckburgh diary*, 25 April 1954, p. 175
65 *Shuckburgh diary*, 25 April 1954, p. 176
66 *Ibid.*, 26 April 1954, p. 176
67 DDEL, Whitman File, Dulles/Herter Series, Box 2, Dulles memo., 25 April 1945
68 *Loc. cit.*, tel. DULTE 4, JFD to DDE, midnight, 25 April 1954
69 *Loc. cit.*, Radford to JFD, 26 April 1954
70 *Shuckburgh diary*, 26 April 1954, p. 178
71 DDEL, Whitman File, Dulles/Herter Series, Box 2, Dulles, April 1954, DDE memo., 17 April 1954
72 *Ibid.*, tel. DULTE 21, JFD to DDE, 29 April 1954
73 *Shuckburgh diary*, 30 April 1954, p. 183
74 DDEL, Whitman File, Dulles/Herter Series, Box 2, tel. DULTE 33, JFD to DDE, 30 April 1954
75 *Ibid.*
76 *Shuckburgh diary*, 30 April 1954, p. 185
77 *Eden III*, pp. 110–11
78 Cab. 129/68, C (54) 196, 'South-East Asia', AE memo., 11 June 1954
79 AP 20/17/118, Salisbury to AE, 9 May 1954
80 *Shuckburgh diary*, 2 May 1954, p. 187
81 Cab. 129/68, C (54)177, 'The Geneva Conference', Eden memo., 24 May 1954
82 *Shuckburgh diary*, 5 May 1954, p. 193
83 Unpublished Shuckburgh diary, 5 May 1954, xeroxed typescript in author's possession
84 *Ibid.*, 5 May 1954
85 *Ibid.*
86 Eden's Geneva diary, quoted in James, *op. cit.*, p. 378, where the text (as in the original) differs from the version Eden gives in *Eden III*, p. 117
87 Cab. 129/68, C (54) 199, AE memo., 15 June 1954
88 AP 20/17/18A, Makins to AE, 21 May 1954; 18B, AE to Makins, 26 May 1954
89 Cab. 129/68, C (54) 177, 'The Geneva Conference', AE memo., 24 May 1954
90 AP 20/17/126, Carr to AE, 30 May 1954
91 AP 20/17/200, summary of correspondence with Churchill, summer 1954
92 AP 20/17/138, mss. letter, WSC to AE, 11 June 1954
93 AP 20/17/2, Dixon to AE, 22 June 1954
94 AP 20/17/118A, AE to Salisbury, 16 May 1954

24: *The Act of Succession*

1 Moran, *op. cit.*, diary, 24 June 1954, p. 559
2 *Ibid.*, 27 May 1954, p. 552
3 *Ibid.*, 4 May 1954, p. 545
4 *WSC–DDE Corr.*, DDE to WSC, 9 February 1954, pp. 120–1
5 John W. Young, 'Churchill's Bid for Peace with Moscow, 1954', *History*, vol. 73, no. 239, October 1988, pp. 428–33
6 *WSC–DDE Corr.*, WSC to DDE, 21 June 1954, pp. 147–8
7 *Shuckburgh diary*, 24 April, 14 June 1954, pp. 173, 220
8 AP 20/17/19, Makins to AE, 18 June 1954

9 *BDEE A/3/I*, no. 40, AE to WSC, 21 June 1954, pp. 128–9.
10 Moran, *op. cit.*, diary, 2 June 1954, p. 553
11 *Ibid.*, 4 June 1954, p. 554; Cab. 128/27, CC (54) 39th conclusions, 5 June 1954 (minute 3)
12 DDEL, Whitman File, Dulles/Herter Series, Box 3, Aldrich to JFD, 18 June 1954
13 *FRUS 1952–1954, VI*, Hagerty diary, 14 June 1954, p. 1064
14 *Loc. cit.*, no. 462, memo. by Mr Raynor to Mr Merchant, reporting Aldrich's views, 24 June 1954, pp. 1073–4
15 DDEL, Whitman Diary Series, Box 2, ACW diary, 25 June 1954
16 DDEL, Whitman File, Dulles/Herter Series, Box 5, memo. for the record, 24 June 1954
17 *FRUS 1952–1954, VI*, no. 464, record of meeting on Guatemala, 25 June 1954, pp. 1075–6
18 DDEL, Whitman Diary Series, Box 2, ACW diary, 25 June 1954
19 *FRUS 1952–1954, VI*, no. 467, record of meeting, 25 June 1954, pp. 1077–8
20 *Ibid.*, pp. 1079–84
21 *Ibid.*, pp. 1086–96
22 *Ibid.*, p. 1098, for WSC's remark to Eisenhower on 26 June 1954; DDEL, Whitman File, International Series, Box 18, JFD to DDE, 28 June 1954, for the record of his meeting on 27 June
23 Moran, *op. cit.*, diary, 24 June 1954, p. 560
24 *Ibid.*, 26 June 1954, p. 564
25 *Ibid.*, 27 June 1954, p. 566
26 *FRUS 1952–1954, VI*, nos 466, 470, 478, 481, JFD/AE meetings, 27–29 June 1954, pp. 1076–7, 1086–94, 1112–14, 1115–22
27 Moran, *op. cit.*, diary, 28 June 1954, p. 568
28 *FRUS 1952–1954, VI*, p. 1098; DDEL, Whitman File, International Series, Box 18, JFD to DDE, 28 June 1954
29 DDEL, Whitman File, International Series, Box 18, JFD to DDE, 28 June 1954, Dulles note
30 *Shuckburgh diary*, 5 July 1954, p. 221; Young, 'Churchill's Bid for Peace', p. 435
31 *Colville diary*, 2 July 1954, pp. 697–8; Moran, *op. cit.*, diary, 2 July 1952, pp. 572–3
32 Cab. 128/27, confidential annexe to CC (54) 48th conclusions, 8 July 1954; 49th conclusions, 9 July; 50th conclusions, 13 July; 52nd conclusions, 23 July; and 53rd conclusions, 26 July, give a sanitised version
33 *Shuckburgh diary*, 7 July 1954, pp. 222–3
34 Young, 'Churchill's Bid for Peace', pp. 438–40
35 *WSC–DDE Corr.*, correspondence, July 1954, pp. 152–66
36 Young, 'Churchill's Bid for Peace', pp. 442–3, for the details
37 *Shuckburgh diary*, 7, 20 July 1954, pp. 222–3, 226–7; Cab. 128/27, CC (54) 47th conclusions, 7 July; 51st conclusions, 20 July
38 Cab. 128/27, 61st conclusions, 21 September 1954
39 AP 20/17/144, Macmillan to AE, 15 July 1954; AP 20/17/144, 175, Salisbury to AE, 15 July, 20 August 1954

40 AP 20/17/173, Eden to Lyttelton, 10 August 1954
41 AP 20/17/179, WSC to AE, 24 August 1954
42 AP 20/1/30, Eden diary, 27 August 1954
43 AP 20/17/186, 188, WSC to AE, 26, 30 August 1954
44 AP 20/17/191, Salisbury to AE, 31 August 1954
45 AP 20/17/192, Macmillan to AE, 9 September 1954
46 AP 20/17/193, Salisbury to AE, 9 September 1954
47 AP 20/17/195, Macmillan notes, 24 September 1954
48 AP 20/1/30, Eden diary, 21 December 1954
49 AP 20/17/218, draft letter from AE to WSC, December 1954; although undated, it must be about 21/22 December
50 AP 20/1/30, Eden diary, 22 December 1954
51 *Foreign Relations of the United States 1951, vol. IV, pt I* (hereinafter *FRUS 1951, IV/I*) (Washington, 1985), no. 420, Gifford to Acheson, 20 January 1951, pp. 894–9
52 *Ibid.*, p. 898
53 *FRUS 1952–1954, VI*, Aldrich to Dulles, 12 August 1954, pp. 997–1002
54 *Ibid.*, p. 998
55 AP 20/17/30, Makins to AE, 2 December 1954
56 DDEL, Whitman File, DDE Diary Series, Box 8, DDE diary, November 1954, DDE to General Al Greunther, 30 November 1954
57 *Ibid.*
58 AP/20/17/27, Lloyd to AE, 4 October 1954
59 AP 20/18/5, WSC to AE, 12 March 1955
60 *Churchill VIII*, pp. 1102–3
61 AP 20/18/5A, 6, AE to WSC and WSC's reply, 12 March 1955
62 *Colville diary*, 29 March 1955, p. 706

25: Tensions and Disagreements

1 DDEL, Whitman File, International Series, Box 20, AE–DDE, AE to DDE, 7 April 1956
2 DDEL, Whitmore File, DDE Diary Series, Box 8, JFD to DDE, 24 August 1954
3 Cab. 129/70, C (54) 276, 'Alternatives to the EDC', AE memo., 27 August 1954
4 *Eden III*, pp. 151–74; Young, 'German Rearmament and the EDC', in Young (ed.), *op. cit.*, pp. 95–100
5 Young, *ibid.*, p. 101
6 Pascaline Winand, *Eisenhower, Kennedy, and the United States of Europe* (1993), pp. 62–3
7 Cab. 129/48, C (51) 32, 'United Europe', WSC memo., 29 November 1951; David Goldsworthy, (ed.), *BDEE A/3/I*, mistakenly has 'European-speaking' for 'English-speaking', p. 4, which rather spoils the sense
8 *DBPO 2/I*, fn. 3 to no. 413, p. 781; for the Americans, see Winand, *op. cit.*, pp. 75–6, 78–82
9 *Ibid.*, no. 414, memo. by FO committee, 12 December 1951, pp. 781–8
10 *BDEE A/3/III*, no. 381, pp. 80–8, FO Research Department Paper, 20 July 1954, for the changing figures

11 *DBPO 2/I*, no. 416, AE telegram, 15 December 1951, pp. 780–93

12 *Ibid.*, no. 417, PM/51/148, AE to WSC, 15 December 1951, pp. 794–5

13 See the excellent survey by Jan Melissen and Bert Zeeman, 'Britain and Western Europe, 1945–51: Opportunities Lost?', *International Affairs*, vol. 63, no. 1, 1986/7, pp. 80–95; and also see Stuart Croft, 'British Policy towards Western Europe, 1947–9', *International Affairs*, vol. 64, no. 4, 1988, pp. 617–29

14 *Foreign Relations of the United States 1955–1957, vol. IV* (hereinafter *FRUS 1955–1957, IV*) (Washington, 1986), no. 97, memo. of conversation, Dulles/Erhard, 7 June 1955, pp. 291–2

15 Winand, *op. cit.*, pp. 79–81

16 Cab. 129/76, Annexe B, meeting in Chancellor's rooms, 21 June 1955

17 Simon Burgess and Geoffrey Edwards, 'The Six plus One: British policy-making and the question of European economic integration, 1955', *International Affairs*, vol. 64, no. 3, 1988, pp. 393–9

18 *DBPO 2/I*, chap. IV, esp. nos 428, C (52) 40, 'Future of the Council of Europe' by AE, 15 February 1955, pp. 826–7; no. 435, AE to Sir Oliver Harvey, 17 March, pp. 842–3; *Eden III*, pp. 47–8. See also Young, *op. cit.*, pp. 119–23

19 *DBPO 2/I*, no. 426, C (52) 56, Macmillan memo., 29 February 1952, pp. 828–30

20 *FRUS 1955–1957, IV*, no. 84, report by the Department of State to the Council on Foreign Economic Policy, 16 March 1955, pp. 263–7

21 *Ibid.*, no. 135, Dulles to Macmillan, 10 December 1955, pp. 362–3

22 *Ibid.*, p. 330

23 *Ibid.*, no. 139, JFD to DDE, 17 December 1955, p. 369; no. 140, JFD to State, 17 December 1955, fn. 4, p. 370; DDEL, Whitman File, International Series, Box 20, Eden visit (4), memo. of conversation, 30 January 1956, 2.15–4.00 p.m.

24 Sir E. Bridges to Rab Butler, 20 September 1956, quoted in Burgess and Edwards, *op. cit.*, p. 404

25 *Eden III*, p. 273

26 J. Charmley, 'Macmillan and the making of the French Committee of Liberation', *International History Review*, 1982; see also A. Horne, *Harold Macmillan, vol. I: 1894–1957* (1988)

27 See above, chapter 24, note 48

28 *Shuckburgh diary*, 31 August 1955, p. 277

29 DDEL, Whitman File, DDE Diary Series, Box 8, DDE to Bedell-Smith, 7 September 1954

30 *FRUS 1952–1954, XIV*, pp. 608–10

31 Cab. 129/72, C (54) 364, 367, AE memos on Formosa, September 1954

32 Cab. 128/28, CC (55) 5th conclusions, 20 January 1955

33 Cab. 128/28, CC (55) 6th conclusions, 24 January 1955

34 Cab. 128/28, CC (55) 8th conclusions, 31 January 1955

35 *WSC–DDE Corr.*, DDE to WSC, 10 February 1955, pp. 190–2

36 Cab. 129/74, C (55) 82, 25 March 1955, 'Quemoy and Formosa', note by AE, 24 March 1955

37 *WSC–DDE Corr.*, DDE to WSC, 18 February 1955, pp. 195–8

38 PREM. 11/879, for the correspondence between Eisenhower, Churchill and Eden in early 1955

39 Cab. 128/29, CC (55) 34th conclusions, 4 October 1955

40 *Foreign Relations of the United States 1955–1957, vol. XV: Arab-Israeli Dispute, Jan. 1–July 25 1956* (hereinafter *FRUS 1955–1957, XV*) (Washington, 1989), Mr Wilkins memo., 14 March 1956, pp. 352–3

41 DDEL, Whitman File, DDE Diary Series, Box 19, memo. of conference with the President, 30 October 1956

42 Freiberger, *op. cit.*, chap. 7

43 David Carlton, *Britain and the Suez Crisis* (1988), pp. 26–7; Lucas, *op. cit.*, pp. 46–7

44 *FRUS 1955–1957, XV*, O'Connor memo., 10 April 1955, pp. 506–7

45 Freiberger, *op. cit.*, p. 94

46 *Ibid.*, pp. 100–2

47 James, *op. cit.*, pp. 398–9

48 *Ibid.*, p. 399; Lucas, *op. cit.*, pp. 40–1

49 Lucas, *op. cit.*, pp. 41–2

50 *Foreign Relations of the United States 1955–1957, vol. XIV* (1989), Byroade to Dulles, 11 March 1955, pp. 78–9

51 Unpublished Shuckburgh diary, 1 November 1954

52 FO 371/111095/VR1079/10, 'Notes on Arab-Israel dispute', 15 December 1954

53 *Ibid.*

54 FO 371/115865/VR1076/20, Makins's record, 29 January 1955

55 *Shuckburgh diary*, ES to Kirkpatrick, 22 January 1955, pp. 246–7

56 FO 371/115864/VR1076/9, Makins to London, 3 February 1955

57 *Shuckburgh diary*, 22 January 1955, p. 246

58 *Ibid.*, 11 February 1955, p. 249

59 Unpublished Shuckburgh diary, 14 February 1954; for fairly obvious reasons the Foreign and Commonwealth Office insisted that this passage should be omitted from the published version

60 FO 371/115865/VR1076/25, draft treaty, 17 February 1955

61 Freiberger, *op. cit.*, p. 115; Lucas, *op. cit.*, pp. 43–4

62 FO 371/115866/VR1076/36, Shuckburgh to Kirkpatrick, 8 March 1955

63 FO 371/115866/VR1076/48, Sir Harold Beely to Shuckburgh, 24 March 1955; E. M. Rose minute, 30 March 1955, AE's marginalia

64 FO 371/115867/VR1076/52, Shuckburgh minute, 5 April 1955

65 *Ibid.*, VR1076/69, Geoffrey Arthur minute, 20 April 1955; VR1076/74, Shuckburgh to Kirkpatrick, 4 May 1955; unpublished Shuckburgh diary, 25 April 1955

66 FO 371/115870/VR1076/115, Shuckburgh minute, 13 June 1955

67 FO 371/115871/VR1076/131, Shuckburgh min-

utes, 8, 11 July 1955; Cab. 129/76, CP (55) 75, Macmillan memo., 12 July 1955

68 Cab. 129/76, CP (55) 75, Macmillan memo., 12 July 1955

69 DDEL Whitman File, DDE Diary Series, Box 11, DDE diary, July 1955 (1), record of meeting, 17 July 1955

70 FO 371/115872/VR1076/143, memo. of conversation, 14 July 1954

71 FO 371/115871/VR1076/134, Shuckburgh memo., 15 July 1955

72 Freiberger, *op. cit.*, pp. 120–1

73 FO 371/115871/VR1076/134, PM/55/1(G), Macmillan to AE, 16 July 1955

74 DDEL, Whitman File, DDE Diary Series, Box 11, DDE diary, July 1955 (1), record of meeting, 17 July 1955; FO 371/115876/VR1076/141, AE memo., 17 July 1955

75 FO 371/115874/VR1076/185, A. A. Stark to Sir Ivone Kirkpatrick, 19 August 1955

76 Freiberger, *op. cit.*, pp. 120–2

77 FO 371/115876/VR1076/218, AE minute, 31 August 1955

78 Carlton, *Eden*, pp. 384–9

79 *Shuckburgh diary*, 31 August 1955, p. 277

80 Author's collection, copy of Lord Norwich to Clarissa Eden, 24 December 1953

81 Randolph Churchill, *The Rise and Fall of Sir Anthony Eden* (1959), p. 211

82 Horne, *op. cit.*, p. 377

83 *Ibid.*, pp. 374–6

84 Carlton, *Eden*, p. 389

26: 'Misguided sentimental investments'

1 11,995,152 for Labour, 9,988,306 Conservative, 2,248,226 Liberal, 854,294 'other'

2 FRUS 1955–1957, XV, O'Connor memo., 10 April 1956, pp. 506–7

3 DDEL, Whitman Diary Series, Box 5, ACW diary, May 1955 (2), DDE conversation

4 Griffith (ed.), *op. cit.*, DDE letter, 3 August 1956, p. 165

5 Darwin, *Britain and Decolonisation*, pp. 168–72

6 BDEE A/2/II, no. 183, Creech-Jones to Bevin, October 1949, pp. 442–8; no. 184, J. Fletcher-Cooke memo., 10 December 1949, pp. 448–54

7 BDEE A/3/I, no. 102, Colonial Office minutes, 28 October 1952, p. 268

8 *Ibid.*, no. 105, notes from WSC and AE, June 1954, pp. 277–8

9 *Eisenhower diary*, 6 January 1953, p. 223

10 DDEL, Whitman File, DDE Diary Series, Box 8, DDE diary, DDE to General Greunther, 30 November 1954

11 DDEL, Whitman File, International Series, Box 20, Eden visit, briefing paper on Middle Eastern matters, 30 January–1 February 1956

12 *Loc. cit.*, memo. of conversations on 30 January, 2.15–4.00 p.m., 7 February 1956

13 *Loc. cit.*, conversations on 30 January, 4.00 p.m. 7 February 1956

14 DDEL, Dulles Papers, subject files 5, Hoover folder, Makins to Dulles, 23 March 1956

15 *Shuckburgh diary*, 12 March 1956, p. 346

16 W. R. Louis, 'Dulles, Suez and the British', in Richard H. Immerman (ed.), *John Foster Dulles and the Diplomacy of the Cold War* (Princeton, 1990), p. 145

17 *Shuckburgh diary*, 3 March 1956, p. 341

18 DDEL, Whitman File, International Series, Box 19, Anthony Eden (5), Herbert Hoover Jr to DDE, 6 March 1956

19 *Eisenhower diary*, 8 March 1956, p. 319

20 DDEL, Dulles Papers, subject files 5, Hoover folder, JFD to DDE, 28 March 1956

21 *Eisenhower diary*, 28 March 1956, p. 323

22 *Shuckburgh diary*, 12 March 1956, p. 346

23 *Ibid.*, 23, 29 March 1956, pp. 349–50

24 Private information

25 *Shuckburgh diary*, 24 January, 17 February 1956, pp. 325, 334

26 Unpublished Shuckburgh diary, 22 March 1956

27 *Shuckburgh diary*, 3 March 1956, p. 341

28 *Ibid.*, 8 March 1956, p. 341

29 *Ibid.*, 15 March 1956, p. 347

30 Louis, 'Dulles, Suez and the British', p. 147

31 AP 23/60/115A, AE to Salisbury, 8 April 1964

32 Louis, 'Dulles, Suez and the British', pp. 134–5; Richard A. Melanson and David Mayers (eds), *Reevaluating Eisenhower: American Foreign Policy in the 1950s* (Chicago, 1987), esp. Kenneth W. Thompson, 'The Strengths and Weaknesses of Eisenhower's Leadership', pp. 13–28, and William Stivers, 'Eisenhower and the Middle East', pp. 192–220

33 See Louis in *The Special Relationship*

34 DDEL, Bermingham/Eisenhower correspondence, October 1948–February 1958, Box 1, vol. 4 (3), Alex Makinsky to Bermingham, 4 May 1956

35 Robert Bowie, 'Eisenhower, Dulles and the Suez Crisis', in Wm. Roger Louis and Roger Owen (eds), *Suez 1956: The Crisis and its Consequences* (1989), pp. 192–6; Ambrose, *Eisenhower, vol. II*, pp. 328–30

36 DDEL, Whitman File, International Series, Box 19, Eden, July 1956 (1), AE to DDE, 27 July 1956

37 FRUS 1955–1957, XVI, p. 907

38 DDEL, Whitman File, DDE Diary Series, Box 16, July 1956, staff memos, Goodpaster memo., 27 July 1956

39 FRUS 1955–1957, XVI, no. 15, Goodpaster memo., 28 July 1956, p. 26

40 DDEL, Whitman File, DDE Diary Series, Box 16, July 1956, staff memos, Goodpaster memo., 30 July 1956

41 Robert Murphy, *Diplomat among Warriors* (1964), p. 463; see n. 44 below for the text

42 Harold Macmillan, *Riding the Storm, 1956–1959* (1971), diary, 31 July 1956, p. 105

43 DDEL, Dulles Papers, Telephone Calls Series, Box 5, conversation with Nixon, 30 July 1956

44 FRUS 1955–1957, XVI, no. 33, tel. 550, Murphy to State, 31 July 1956, pp. 60–2

45 DDEL, Whitman File, DDE Diary Series, Box 16, July 1956, staff memos, Goodpaster memo., 31 July 1956
46 *FRUS 1955–1957, XVI*, no. 35, DDE to AE, 31 July 1956, fn. 1, p. 69
47 DDEL, Whitman File, DDE Diary Series, Box 16, July 1956, staff memos, Goodpaster memo., 31 July 1956
48 *FRUS 1955–1957, XVI*, no. 41, meeting at the Foreign Office, 1 August 1956, p. 91
49 *Ibid.*, no. 38, Embassy Paris to State, 31 July 1956, p. 75
50 Philip M. Williams, *Hugh Gaitskell* (1979), pp. 420–1
51 *FRUS 1955–1957, XVI*, no. 40, Special National Intelligence Estimate, 31 July 1956, pp. 78–93
52 Lucas, *op. cit.*, p. 142
53 Philip Ziegler, *Mountbatten* (1985), pp 538–40; R. Lamb, *The Failure of the Eden Government* (1987), pp. 198–200
54 PREM. 11/1098, Lloyd–Foster Dulles meeting, 1 August 1956; the American version, at *FRUS 1955–1957, XVI*, no. 41, pp. 94–7, uses different words
55 *Eden III*, pp. 437–8

27: Schism

1 Carlton, *Eden*, p. 412; Lucas, *op. cit.*, pp. 154–5
2 Ziegler, *op. cit.*, p. 540
3 DDEL, Whitman File, International Series, Box 19, July 1956 (1), AE to DDE, 5 August 1956
4 *Ibid.*; *FRUS 1955–1957, XVI*, no. 42, memo. of JFD/AE conversation, 1 August 1956, pp. 98–100; no. 46, memo. of JFD/HM conversation, 1 August 1956, pp. 108–9; also Macmillan, *Riding the Storm*, pp. 102–3; *Eden III*, pp. 421–32
5 Macmillan, *ibid.*, diary, 1 August 1956, p. 106
6 DDEL, Whitman File, DDE Diary Series, Box 17, August 1956, diary, staff memos, memo. for record, 12 August 1956
7 *FRUS 1955–1957, XVI*, no. 48, JFD to DDE, 2 August 1956, pp. 110–11
8 Ambrose, *op. cit.*, pp. 333–4; *FRUS 1955–1957, XVI*, no. 79, record of meeting, 12 August 1956, pp. 188–96
9 *FRUS 1955–1957, XVI*, no. 62, 'US Policies towards Nasser', 4 August 1956, p. 142
10 *Ibid.*, no. 71, memo. of DDE/JFD conversation, 8 August 1956, pp. 163–76, esp. p. 167. See also *Eden III*, p. 431
11 *FRUS 1955–1957, XVI*, no. 59, Byroade (Cairo) to State, 4 August 1956, pp. 133–5
12 *Ibid.*, no. 71, DDE/JFD conversation, 8 August 1956, p. 174
13 DDEL, Whitman File, DDE Diary Series, Box 17, August 1956, Misc. (2), DDE to JFD, 19, 20 August 1956; *FRUS 1955–1957, XVI*, no. 100, JFD to DDE, 20 August 1956, p. 236
14 James, *op. cit.*, p. 501
15 *FRUS 1955–1957, XVI*, no. 86, JFD to DDE, 16 August 1956, pp. 210–11
16 *Ibid.*, no. 99, memo. of JFD/AE conversation, 19 August 1956, pp. 233–5
17 *Ibid.*, no. 97, JFD to DDE, 19 August 1956, pp. 231-2
18 *Ibid.*, no. 109, McCardle memo., 21 August 1956, pp. 249–50
19 *Ibid.*, no. 101, JFD to DDE, 20 August 1956, p. 237
20 *Ibid.*, no. 108, memo of JFD/HM conversation, 21 August 1956, pp. 245–6
21 PRO, Egypt Committee, Cab. 134/1216, EC (56) 9th meeting, 2 August 1956; Horne, *op. cit.*, pp. 400–1; James, *op. cit.*, pp. 484–5; D. R. Thorpe, *Selwyn Lloyd* (1989), p. 220
22 James, *op. cit.*, pp. 483–4, Salisbury to AE, 2 August 1956
23 *Churchill VIII*, p. 1203; Horne, *op. cit.*, pp. 402–3
24 Horne, *op. cit.*, p. 405; Lucas, *op. cit.*, pp. 156–61, for British plans
25 Horne, *op. cit.*, pp. 410–11
26 Cab. 134/1216, EC (56) 21st meeting, 24 August 1956
27 PREM. 11/1152, Brook to AE, 25 August 1956
28 Cab. 134/1216, EC (56) 23rd meeting, 28 August 1956
29 *FRUS 1955–1957, XVI*, no. 137, AE to DDE, 27 August 1956, pp. 304–5
30 *Ibid.*, no. 144, memo. of DDE/JFD conversation, 29 August 1956, pp. 314–15
31 *Ibid.*, no. 148, memo. of conversation, 29 August 1956, pp. 322–4
32 *Ibid.*, no. 149, 295th meeting of the NSC, 30 August 1956, pp. 324–34
33 Horne, *op. cit.*, p. 412
34 *FRUS 1955–1957, XVI*, no. 163, DDE to AE, 2 September 1956, pp. 355–8
35 *Ibid.*, no. 179, memo. of conversation, 6 September 1956, pp. 396–8
36 Macmillan, *Riding the Storm*, p. 119
37 *FRUS 1955–1957, XVI*, no. 181, AE to DDE, 6 September 1956, pp. 400–3
38 *Ibid.*, no. 182, memo. of DDE/JFD conversation, 7 September 1956, pp. 403–4
39 DDEL, Bermingham Papers, Bermingham–Eisenhower Corr., Box 1, letter from Makinsky, 8 September 1956
40 *FRUS 1955–1957, XVI*, no. 190, draft message, DDE to AE, 8 September 1956, pp. 431–3
41 *Ibid.*, no. 192, DDE to AE, 8 September 1956, pp. 435–7
42 *Ibid.*, no. 193, memo. of conversation, 8 September 1956, pp. 438–40
43 PREM. 11/1100, Makins to FO, 8 September 1956
44 *FRUS 1955–1957, XVI*, no. 197, memo. of conversation, 9 September 1956, pp. 448–51
45 Lucas, *op. cit.*, p. 191
46 James, *op. cit.*, p. 516
47 *FRUS 1955–1957, XVI*, nos 205, 208, records of conversations, 10, 11 September 1956, pp. 469–72, 476–9
48 James, *op. cit.*, p. 514
49 *FRUS 1955–1957, XVI*, no. 205, memo. of JFD/Makins conversation, 10 September 1956,

pp. 469–72; and DDEL, JFD Papers, Telephone Calls Series, Box 5

50 *Ibid.*, no. 208, memo. of JFD/Makins conversation, 11 September 1956, pp. 476–9

51 DDEL, JFD Papers, Telephone Calls Series, Box 5, memo. of call from Dr Flemming, 12 September 1956, 5:54 p.m.

52 Westminster College, Reeves Library, Department of State *Bulletin*, 24 September 1956, pp. 476–83; excerpts are at *FRUS 1955–1957, XVI*, no. 218, fn. 2

53 *Eden III*, p. 481

54 *Ibid.*, p. 484

55 PRO, Private Papers, Selwyn Lloyd, FO 800/740, draft telegram, Kirkpatrick to Makins, 10 September 1956

56 *Loc. cit.*, Makins to Lloyd, 9 September 1956

57 PREM. 11/1105, EC (56) 43, 6 September 1956

58 James, *op. cit.*, p. 509

59 Cab. 134/1216, EC (56) 25th Meeting, 7 September 1956; for Eden's reactions, see AP 20/1, Eden diary, 7 September 1956

60 Carlton, *Eden*, pp. 420–1, rehearses the evidence

61 James, *op. cit.*, p. 509

62 Macmillan, *Riding the Storm*, p. 128; Diane B. Kunz, 'The Economic Diplomacy of the Suez Crisis', in Louis and Owen (eds), *Suez 1956*, p. 222

63 Macmillan, *Riding the Storm*, p. 125; Carlton, *Eden*, p. 425; Lamb, *op. cit.*, pp. 206–8

64 Horne, *op. cit.*, p. 418, quoting Macmillan's diary, 20 September 1956

65 Macmillan, *Riding the Storm*, p. 127

66 PREM. 11/1102, note of a private talk with Mr Dulles, 25 September, by HM, 26 September 1956

67 Bowie, pp. 204–5, and Kunz, p. 222, in Louis and Owen (eds), *Suez 1956*; Louis, pp. 147–8, in Immerman (ed.), *op. cit.*; it is perhaps significant than none of these commentators dwell on Macmillan's account of the meeting – which would rather spoil their story

68 *FRUS 1955–1957, XVI*, no. 233, Douglas Dillon to JFD, 19 September 1956, pp. 521–2

69 *Ibid.*, no. 245, memo. of JFD/AE conversation, 20 September 1956, pp. 545–6

70 *Ibid.*, nos 263, 265, memos of conversations, 25 September 1956, pp. 577–81

71 DDEL, Whitman File, DDE Diary Series, Box 18, September 1956, telephone calls, conversation DDE/JFD, 11.20 a.m., 25 September 1956

28: Macmillan's Metamorphosis

1 PRO, Treasury Papers, T 236/4188, Sir Edward Bridges to Macmillan, 7 September 1956

2 *Loc. cit.*, Sir Leslie Rowan to Macmillan, 21 September 1956

3 PREM. 11/1102, HM to AE, 25 September 1956

4 Horne, *op. cit.*, p. 421

5 DDEL, Whitman File, DDE Diary Series, Box 18, September 1956, telephone calls, DDE/JFD conversation, 11.20 a.m., 25 September 1956

6 Horne, *op. cit.*, p. 421

7 James, *op. cit.*, p. 525

8 Cab. 134/1216, EC (56) 31st meeting, 25 September 1956

9 PREM. 11/1102, Bishop minutes and AE corrections, 25 September 1956

10 PREM. 11/1102, Embassy, Paris, to FO, 26 September 1956

11 Lucas, *op. cit.*, p. 215, and sources cited there

12 DDEL, JFD Papers, Telephone Calls Series, Box 5, memoranda, telephone conversations – general, 1 October 1956–29 December 1956 (4), telephone call from Ambassador Lodge, 2 October 1956

13 *FRUS 1955–1957, XVI*, no. 271, memo. of conversation, 27 September 1956, p. 591

14 *Ibid.*, no. 291, memo. of conversation, 2 October 1956, pp. 625–7

15 *Ibid.*

16 Lucas, *op. cit.*, p. 216

17 James, *op. cit.*, p. 515

18 *FRUS 1955–1957, XVI*, no. 298, State to Embassy in France, 4 October 1956, pp. 634–7

19 DDEL, Whitman File, DDE Diary Series, Box 18, October 1956, Misc. (4), DDE to Herbert Hoover Jr, 8 October 1956

20 Frederick W. Marks III, *Power and Peace: The Diplomacy of John Foster Dulles* (1993), p. 91

21 PREM. 11/1102, FO (AE) to New York (Lloyd), 7 October 1956

22 Thorpe, *op. cit.*, pp. 228–9; *FRUS 1955–1957, XVI*, no. 307, memo. of JFD/Lloyd conversation, 7 October 1956, pp. 656–7

23 Horne, *op. cit.*, p. 427

24 Cab. 128/30, C (56) 68th meeting, 3 October 1956

25 *FRUS 1955–1957, XVI*, no. 300, memo. of conversation, 5 October 1956, p. 640

26 DDEL, JFD Papers, Telephone Calls Series, Box 5, memoranda, telephone conversations – general, 1 October 1956–29 December 1956 (4), telephone call from Ambassador Lodge, 11 October 1956, 8.45 a.m.; *FRUS 1955–1957, XVI*, no. 302, JFD to DDE, 5 October 1956, pp. 648–50

27 Cab. 134/1216, EC (56) 33rd meeting, 8 October 1956

28 Selwyn Lloyd, *Suez 1956: A Personal Account* (1976), p. 160

29 PREM. 11/1102, AE to Lloyd, 14 October 1956

30 James, *op. cit.*, pp. 527–8, substantially confirms the account in A. Nutting, *No End of a Lesson* (1967), pp 90–6

31 Cab. 134/1216, EC (56) 32nd meeting, 1 October 1956; *FRUS 1955–1957, XVI*, no. 277, editorial note, pp. 599–600; no. 288, memo. of conversation, 1 October 1956, pp. 620–2

32 *FRUS 1955–1957, XVI*, no. 253, memo., 21 September 1956, pp. 559–60; no. 305, Herbert Hoover Jr memo., 6 October 1956, pp. 653–4

33 Lucas, *op. cit.*, pp. 237–8

34 Carlton, *Britain and the Suez Crisis*, pp. 59–60, for the circumstances

35 Thorpe, *op. cit.*, pp. 231–2

36 *Ibid.*, pp. 232–3; James, *op. cit.*, pp. 528–9

37 DDEL, JFD Papers, WHD, Box 4, meetings with

the President, August–December 1956 (4), memo. of JFD/DDE conversation, 21 October 1956, 11.00 a.m.

38 *FRUS 1955–1957, XVI*, no. 351, State to Embassy, London, 17 October 1956, pp. 744–5

39 For this controversial episode, see Thorpe, *op. cit.*, pp. 241–3; James, *op. cit.*, pp. 520–31; Lloyd, *op. cit.*, pp. 186–8; Christian Pineau, *Suez, 1956* (Paris, 1976), pp. 149–52; Moshe Dayan, *Story of My Life* (1976), pp. 231–2; Nutting, *op. cit.*, pp. 101–5

40 Cab. 128/30, C (56) 74th meeting, 25 October 1956

41 Horne, *op. cit.*, p. 433

42 *FRUS 1955–1957, XVI*, no. 378, memo. of discussion at 301st meeting of the NSC, 26 October 1956, p. 784; no. 391, Special Watch report, 28 October 1956, pp. 798–9

43 DDEL, Whitman File, DDE Diary Series, Box 18, October 1956, telephone calls, Sunday, 28 October 1956, 5.38 p.m.

44 *Ibid.*, Box 19, October 1956 diary, staff memos, memo. of conference, 29 October 1956, 7.15 p.m.

45 *Ibid.*, memo., 29 October 1956, 8.15 p.m.

46 *Ibid.*, memo., 30 October 1956

47 *Ibid.*, International Series, Box 19, Eden 7/18/56–11/7/56, draft dated 10/30/56, 5.05 p.m., final revise dated 31 October, marked 'Do *not* send' in DDE's hand

48 *Ibid.*, DDE Diary Series, Box 18, October 1956, telephone calls, 30 October 1956, 8.40 a.m., where Dixon's words are deleted, but they are left uncensored in JFD Papers, Telephone Calls Series, Box 5, memoranda, telephone conversations – general, 1 October 1956–29 December 1956 (3), memo. of conversation, 29 October 1956, 10.00 p.m. Since their sense is also given at *FRUS 1955–1957, XVI*, no. 413, editorial note, p. 841, it might be time for the archivists at Abilene to clear it in the DDE diary series too!

49 DDEL, Whitman File, DDE Diary Series, Box 18, October 1956, telephone calls, 30 October 1956, conversation with Dulles, 3.40 p.m.

50 *Ibid.*, International Series, Box 19, Eden (6), DDE to AE, 30 October 1956

51 *FRUS 1955–1957, XVI*, no. 423, Lodge to State, 30 October 1956, pp. 858–60

52 *Shuckburgh diary*, 1 November 1956, p. 364

53 DDEL, Whitman File, DDE Diary Series, Box 18, October 1956, telephone calls, 9.47 p.m., 31 October 1956

54 *FRUS 1955–1957, XVI*, no. 455, minutes of 302d meeting of the NSC, 1 November 1956, p. 906

55 Louis, 'Dulles, Suez and the British', in Immerman (ed.), *op. cit.*, p. 158

56 DDEL, Whitman File, International Series, Box 19, Eden (4), AE to DDE, 30 October 1956

57 Freiberger, *op. cit.*, pp. 186–7, appears to agree with this analysis, but may well not

58 Horne, *op. cit.*, p. 437

59 DDEL, JFD Papers, Telephone Calls Series, Box 5, telephone call to Allen Dulles, 1 November 1956

60 Kunz, *op. cit.*, p. 226

61 DDEL, Whitman File, DDE Diary Series, Box 19, November 1956, telephone calls, 2 November 1956, conversation with Hoover, 11.16 a.m.

62 *Ibid.*, 1956, misc. (4), Box 20, DDE to General Greunther, 2 November 1956

63 *FRUS 1955–1957, XVI*, no. 477, memo. of conversation, 3 November 1956, pp. 947–9

64 *Ibid.*, no. 467, editorial note, pp. 932–3

65 *Ibid.*, no. 473, memo. of conversation, 2 November 1956, pp. 940–2

66 Cab. 128/30, C (56) 79th meeting, 4 November 1956

67 R. A. Butler, *The Art of the Possible* (1971), p. 193

68 James, *op. cit.*, p. 567; Carlton, *Britain and Suez*, pp. 74–5, rehearses the evidence

69 Lloyd, *op. cit.*, p. 206; Horne, *op. cit.*, p. 439

70 DDEL, Whitman File, International Series, Box 19, AE to DDE, 5 November 1956, where, once again, the text is heavily censored but available in print at *FRUS 1955–1957, XVI*, no. 499, pp. 984–6. Another one for the archivists at Abilene?

71 *FRUS 1955–1957, XVI*, no. 500, memo. of conference with the President, 5 November 1956, pp. 986–8

72 *Ibid.*, no. 459, Dillon (Paris) to State, 1 November 1956, pp. 919–22

73 *Ibid.*, no. 502, draft DDE to AE, 5 November 1956, pp. 989–90

74 *Ibid.*, no. 509, memo. of conference, 5 November 1956, pp. 1000–1

75 *Eden III*, p. 554

76 *FRUS 1955–1957, XVI*, no. 509, memo. of conference, 5 November 1956, pp. 1000–1

77 Horne, *op. cit.*, p. 440; Lloyd, *op. cit.*, p. 209; Cab. 128/30, C (56) 80, 6 November 956, naturally contains little of this drama

78 Horne, *op. cit.*, p. 441

29: The Strange End of Anthony Eden

1 AP 23/60/41A, AE to Salisbury, 14 December 1959

2 M. Beloff, 'The Special Relationship: An Anglo-American Myth', in Gilbert (ed.), *op. cit.*, p. 167

3 Diane Kunz, 'Did Macmillan lie over Suez?', *Spectator*, 3 November 1990, p. 23

4 PREM. 11/1105, Eden minute, 7 November 1956

5 *FRUS 1955–1957, XVI*, no. 525, transcript of DDE/AE conversation, 6 November 1956, pp. 1025–7

6 *Ibid.*, no. 536, memo. of conversation, 7 November 1956, p. 1040

7 *Ibid.*, no. 527, DDE to AE, 6 November 1956, pp. 1028–9

8 *Ibid.*, no. 539, Goodpaster memo., 7 November 1956, pp. 1043–4

9 *Ibid.*, no. 541, memo. of conversation with Hoover, 7 November 1956, pp. 1047–8

10 *Ibid.*, no. 542, memo. of conversation with Dulles and Hoover, 7 November 1956, p. 1049–53

11 Freiberger, *op. cit.*, pp. 195–8; Kunz, *op. cit.*, pp. 228–30

12 *FRUS 1955–1957, XVI*, no. 554, memo. of 303d

meeting of the NSC, 8 November 1956, pp. 1070-8

13 DDEL, Whitman File, DDE Diary Series, Box 20, 1956, Misc. Bipartisan legislative meeting, 9 November 1956

14 *Eisenhower diary*, 8 November 1956, pp. 333-4

15 DDEL, JFD Papers, Telephone Calls Series, Box 5, JFD/Hoover telephone call, 9 November 1956

16 *FRUS 1955-1957, XVI*, no. 570, memo. of DDE/JFD conversation, 12 November 1956, pp. 1112-14

17 *Ibid.*, no. 571, Aldrich to State, 12 November 1956, pp. 1115-16

18 A. Howard, *RAB: The Life of R. A. Butler* (1987), p. 242

19 DDEL, Whitman Diary Series, Box 8, additional diary, 13 November 1956

20 DDEL, JFD Papers, WHM Box 4, meetings with the President, August–December 1956 (3)

21 *Eisenhower diary*, 20 November 1956, p. 336

22 DDEL, DDE Diary Series, Box 19, November 1956, telephone calls, conversations with Aldrich and Hoover, 19 November 1956

23 *FRUS 1955-1957, XVI*, no. 588, Aldrich to State, 19 November 1956, pp. 1150-3

24 AP 20/33/19, Lord Coleraine to Lady Eden, 5 January 1957

25 *FRUS 1955-1957, XVI*, no. 593, Aldrich to State, 19 November 1956, p. 1163

26 DDEL, Whitman Diary Series, Box 8, diary, 20 November 1956

27 DDEL, Whitman File, DDE Diary Series, Box 19, Goodpaster memo. of conference, 20 November 1956, 5.30 p.m.

28 DDEL, Whitman File, International Series, Box 18, Churchill, 8 April 1955–31 December 1957 (1), WSC to DDE, 25 November 1956

29 Cab. 128/30 C (56) 90th meeting, 28 November 1956

30 Macmillan, *Riding the Storm*, p. 177

31 Enoch Powell, 'Macmillan: The Case Against', *Spectator*, 10 January 1987, p. 15

32 Howard, *op. cit.*, p. 241

33 DDEL, Whitman File, DDE Diary Series, Box 19,

34 *FRUS 1955-1957, XVI*, no. 618, memo. of conversation, 27 November 1957, pp. 1202-3

35 *Ibid.*, no. 622, Aldrich to State, 29 November 1956, pp. 1232-3

36 Kunz, *op. cit.*, p. 231

37 *FRUS 1955-1957, XVI*, no. 626, memo. of discussion at 305th meeting of the NSC, 30 November 1956, pp. 1218-29

38 AP 20/33/8A, AE to Irene Ward, 28 December 1956

39 James, *op. cit.*, pp. 585-9

40 AP 20/33/19, Lord Coleraine to Lady Eden, 5 January 1957

41 James, *op. cit.*, pp. 590-1

42 DDEL, WHD, Box 4, meetings with the President, August–December 1956 (2), memo., 3 December 1956

43 DDEL, Whitman File, International Series, Box 20, Eden 11/7/56 (3), DDE to AE, 10 January 1957

44 *Ibid.*, Macmillan (1), HM to DDE, 16 January 1957

45 AP 23/48/9, HM to AE, 29 September 1957

46 AP 23/60/13, AE to Salisbury, 9 December 1957

47 AP 23/48/60A, Avon to Macmillan, 2 September 1965

48 AP 23/60/14A, AE to Salisbury, 28 December 1957

49 Watt, *Succeeding John Bull*, p. 131

50 AP 23/60/7A, Salisbury to AE, 31 August 1957

51 Beloff, *op. cit.*, p. 169

52 *Eden II*, p. 250

Epilogue

1 Paul Kennedy, 'Why did the British Empire last so long?', in Paul Kennedy (ed.), *Strategy and Diplomacy 1870-1945* (1983), p. 202

2 FO 800/328, Hal/38/38, Halifax to Sir Roger Lumley, 21 March 1938

3 Henry Kissinger, *Diplomacy* (1994), p. 395

Bibliography

I. ARCHIVAL SOURCES

British Archives

Public Record Office,
Kew

Cab. 65. War Cabinet Meetings
Cab. 66. War Cabinet Memoranda
Cab. 128. Cabinet Minutes, 1945–56
Cab. 129. Cabinet Memoranda, 1945–56
Cab. 134. Records of the Egypt Committee
Foreign Office. General Correspondence, FO 371 Series, various 1940–56
Foreign Office. Private Papers, FO 800, Ernest Bevin, Selwyn Lloyd
Avon Papers, FO 954
Prime Minister's Papers. PREM. 3 series, 1940–5
Prime Minister's Papers. PREM. 4 series, 1940–5
Prime Minister's Papers. PREM. 8 series, 1945–51
Prime Minister's Papers. PREM. 11 series, 1951–7

Birmingham
University Library

Avon Papers

American Archives

Franklin D. Roosevelt
Library, Hyde Park,
New York

Papers of President Franklin D. Roosevelt
  Map Room Papers
  Official Files
  Private Secretary's File
Papers of Adolf A. Berle
Papers of Oscar Cox
Papers of Harry L. Hopkins
Papers of Tyler Kent
Papers of Isadore Lubin
Papers of Henry J. Morgenthau (microfilm)

Harry S. Truman
Library,

Papers of President Harry S. Truman
  Naval Aide's Files

Independence, Missouri	Official Files
	Private Secretary's Files
	Post-Presidential Files
	White House Confidential Files
	Papers of Dean Acheson
	Papers of Clark M. Clifford
	Papers of George M. Elsey
	Papers of Henry F. Grady
Dwight David Eisenhower Library, Abilene, Kansas	Papers of President Dwight D. Eisenhower
	Ann Whitman Files, Diary Series, 1953–61
	Ann Whitman Files, DDE Diary Series
	Ann Whitman Files, International Series
	Ann Whitman Files, Dulles/Herter Series
	Ann Whitman Files, Legislative Meetings Series
	Ann Whitman Files, Name Series
	Ann Whitman Files, National Security Council Series
	Papers of John Foster Dulles
	General Correspondence and Memoranda Series
	JFD Chronological Series
	Special Assistant's Chronological Series
	Subject Series – Alphabetical subseries
	Telephone Conversation Series
	White House Memoranda Series
	Bermingham Papers
	Greunther Papers
	Oral Histories
	Winthrop Aldrich
	Robert R. Bowie
	William H. Draper
	Dwight David Eisenhower
	Andrew J. Goodpaster
	Alfred M. Greunther
	Robert Murphy
	Vernon Walters
Winston Churchill Memorial and Library, Westminster College, Fulton, Missouri	Papers relating to Churchill's visit, 5 March 1946
	Newspaper files relating to Churchill's visit
	Crosby Kemper Memorial Lectures, 1981–93
	Microfilm of State Department Files, 1938–45
	Microfilm of British Documents from the PRO
	State Department Bulletins

2. PRINTED PRIMARY SOURCES

Documents on British Policy Overseas, Series 1

Butler, R., and Pelly, M. (eds), *vol. I: The Conference at Potsdam, 1945* (1984)

Bullen, R., and Pelly, M. (eds), *vol. II: Conferences in London, Washington and Moscow, 1945* (1985)

Bullen, R., and Pelly, M. (eds), *vol. III: Britain and America: Negotiation of the United States Loan, 3 August–7 December 1945* (1986)

Bullen, R., and Pelly, M. (eds), *vol. IV: Britain and America* (1987)

Pelly, M., and Yasamee, H. J. (eds) *vol. VI: Eastern Europe 1945–1946* (1991)

Documents on British Policy Overseas, Series 2

Bullen, R., and Pelly, M. (eds), *vol. I: The Schuman Plan, the Council of Europe and Western European Integration 1950–1952* (1986)

Bullen, R., and Pelly, M. (eds), *vol. II: The London Conferences: Anglo-American Relations and Cold War Strategy January–June 1950* (1987)

British Documents on the End of Empire, Series A, vol. 2

Hyam, Ronald (ed.), *The Labour Government and the End of Empire 1945–1951: pt I: High Policy* (1992)

Hyam, Ronald (ed.), *The Labour Government and the End of Empire 1945–1951: pt II: International Relations* (1992)

Hyam, Ronald (ed.), *The Labour Government and the End of Empire 1945–1951: pt III: Strategy, Policies and Constitutional Change* (1992)

British Documents on the End of Empire, Series A, vol. 3

Goldsworthy, David (ed.), *The Conservative Government and the End of Empire 1951–1957: pt I: International Relations* (1994)

Goldsworthy, David (ed.), *The Conservative Government and the End of Empire 1951–1957: pt. II: Politics and Administration* (1994)

Goldsworthy, David (ed.), *The Conservative Government and the End of Empire 1951–1957: pt. III: Economic ... Policies* (1994)

Mansergh, Nicholas (ed.), *The Transfer of Power in India, 1942–1947, vol. III* (1971)

Mansergh, Nicholas (ed.), *The Transfer of Power in India, 1942–1947, vol. V: The Simla Conference* (1974)

Mansergh, Nicholas (ed.), *The Transfer of Power in India, 1942–1947, vol. VI: The Post-War Phase* (1976)

Tinker, Hugh (ed.), *Burma: The Struggle for Independence 1944–1948, vol. I* (1983)

Foreign Relations of the United States 1942, vol. I (1960)

Foreign Relations of the United States 1943, vol. II (1963)

Foreign Relations of the United States 1944, vol. III: The British Commonwealth, Eastern Europe, The Far East (1965)

Foreign Relations of the United States 1944, vol. IV (1965)

Foreign Relations of the United States 1944, vol. V: The Near East, S. Asia and Africa (1965)

Foreign Relations of the United States 1945, vol. V (1966)

Foreign Relations of the United States: The Conferences at Malta and Yalta, 1945 (1955)

Foreign Relations of the United States: The Conference of Berlin (The Potsdam Conference), 1945, vols I and II (1960)

Foreign Relations of the United States 1949, vol. IV (1975)

Foreign Relations of the United States 1950, vol. I: National Security Affairs: Foreign Economic Policy (1977)

Foreign Relations of the United States 1951, vol. IV, pt I (1985)

Foreign Relations of the United States 1952–1954, vol. II (1983)

Foreign Relations of the United States 1952–1954, vol. VI (1979)

Foreign Relations of the United States 1955–1957, vol. IV: Western European Security (1986)

Foreign Relations of the United States 1955–1957, vol. XIV (1989)

Foreign Relations of the United States 1955–1957, vol. XV: Arab-Israeli Dispute, January 1–July 25 1956 (1989)

Foreign Relations of the United States 1955–1957, vol. XVI: The Suez Crisis (1990)

Barnes, J., and Nicholson, D. (eds), *The Empire at Bay: The Leo Amery Diaries 1929–1955* (1988)

Beitzell, R. (ed.), *Tehran, Yalta, Potsdam: The Soviet Protocols* (1970)

Berle, B. B., and Jacobs, T. B., *Navigating the Rapids, 1918–1971: From the Papers of Adolf A. Berle* (1973)

Bland, Larry I. (ed.), *The Papers of George Catlett Marshall, vol. 3: Dec. 7, 1941–May 31, 1943* (1991)

Blum, John Morton (ed.), *From the Morgenthau Diaries: Years of Urgency 1938–1941* (1965)

Blum, John Morton (ed.), *From the Morgenthau Diaries: Years of War 1941–1945* (1967)

Blum, John Morton (ed.), *The Price of Vision: The Diary of Henry A. Wallace 1942–1946* (1973)

Blumenson, M. (ed.), *The Patton Papers 1940–45* (1974)

Boyle, P. G. (ed.), *The Churchill–Eisenhower Correspondence 1953–1955* (1990)

Bryant, Sir Arthur (ed.), *The Turn of the Tide, 1939–1943* (1957)

Bryant, Sir Arthur (ed.), *The Triumph in the West, 1943–1945* (1959)

Campbell, T., and Herring, G. C. (eds), *The Diaries of Edward R. Stettinius Jr, 1943–1946* (1975)

Chandler Jr, Alfred D., et al. (eds), *The Papers of Dwight David Eisenhower: The War Years I* (1970)

Chandler Jr, Alfred D., et al. (eds), *The Papers of Dwight David Eisenhower: The War Years II* (1970)

Chandler Jr, Alfred D., et al. (eds), *The Papers of Dwight David Eisenhower: The War Years III* (1970)

Chandler Jr, Alfred D., et al. (eds), *The Papers of Dwight David Eisenhower: The War Years IV* (1970)

Chandler Jr, Alfred D., et al. (eds), *The Papers of Dwight David Eisenhower: The War Years V* (1970)

Charmley, John (ed.), *Descent to Suez: The Diaries of Sir Evelyn Shuckburgh 1951–56* (1987)

Churchill, Winston S., *Maxims and Reflections* (1992)

Cockett, Richard (ed.), *My Dear Max: Letters of Brendan Bracken to Lord Beaverbrook* (1990)

Colville, Sir John, *The Fringes of Power: The Downing Street Diaries, 1939–1955* (1985)

Dilks, D. (ed.), *The Diaries of Sir Alexander Cadogan 1938–1945* (1971)

Dixon, Piers (ed.), *Double Diploma: The Life of Sir Pierson Dixon* (1968)

Eisenhower, J. S. D. (ed.), *Letters to Mamie* (1978)

Ferrell, Robert H. (ed.), *The Eisenhower Diaries* (1981)

Ferrell, Robert H. (ed.), *Off the Record: The Private Papers of Harry S. Truman* (1980)

Galambos, Louis, et al. (eds), *The Papers of Dwight David Eisenhower: NATO and the Campaign of 1952 XII* (1989)

Galambos, Louis, et al. (eds), *The Papers of Dwight David Eisenhower: NATO and the Campaign of 1952 XIII* (1989)

Griffith, Robert W. (ed.), *Ike's Letters to a Friend, 1941–1958* (1984)

Harvey, J. (ed.), *The War Diaries of Oliver Harvey 1941–5* (1978)

James, Robert Rhodes (ed.), *Chips: The Diaries of Sir Henry Channon* (1967)

James, Robert Rhodes (ed.), *Winston S. Churchill: His Complete Speeches, vol. VII: 1943–1949* (1974)

Jensen, Kenneth J. (ed.), *Origins of the Cold War: The Novikov, Kennan, and Roberts 'Long Telegrams' of 1946* (1993)

Kimball, W. F. (ed.), *Churchill and Roosevelt: The Complete Correspondence: The Alliance Emerging, October 1939–November 1942* (1984)

Kimball, W. F. (ed.), *Churchill and Roosevelt: The Complete Correspondence: Alliance Forged, 1942–1944* (1984)

Kimball, W. F. (ed.), *Churchill and Roosevelt: The Complete Correspondence: Alliance Declining, 1944–1945* (1984)

Macmillan, H., *War Diaries* (1984)

Martin, J., *Downing Street: The War Years* (1991)

Mills, W. (ed.), *The Forrestal Diaries* (1951)

Moggridge, D. (ed.), *The Collected Writings of John Maynard Keynes, vol. XXI* (1980)

Moggridge, D. (ed.), *The Collected Writings of John Maynard Keynes, vol. XXII* (1980)

Moggridge, D. (ed.), *The Collected Writings of John Maynard Keynes, vol. XXIII: Activities 1940–1943* (1979)

Moggridge, D. (ed.), *The Collected Writings of John Maynard Keynes, vol. XXIV: Activities 1944–1946. The Transition to Peace* (1979)

Moggridge, D. (ed.), *The Collected Writings of John Maynard Keynes, vol. XXVI: Activities 1941–1946. Shaping the Post-War World. Bretton Woods and Reparations* (1980)

Moon, Penderel (ed.), *The Viceroy's Journal* (1973)

Moran, Lord, *Churchill: The Struggle for Survival 1940–65* (1966)

Nicholas, H. G. (ed.), *Washington Despatches* (1981)

Nicolson, Nigel (ed.), *Harold Nicolson: Diaries and Letters, vol. 2: 1939–45* (1966)

Nicolson, Nigel (ed.), *Harold Nicolson: Diaries and Letters, vol. 3: 1945–62* (1968)

Noakes J., and Pridham, G. (eds), *Nazism, vol. 2* (1988)

Pimlott, B. (ed.), *The Political Diary of Hugh Dalton, 1918–40, 1945–60* (1986)

Pimlott, B. (ed.), *The Second World War Diary of Hugh Dalton, 1940–45* (1986)

Poel, J. van der (ed.), *Selections from the Smuts Papers, vol. VI* (1973)

Roosevelt, Elliot (ed.), *The Roosevelt Letters, vol. 3: 1928–1945* (1953)

Roper, H. Trevor- (ed.), *Hitler's War Directives, 1939–1945* (1964)

Rose, N. (ed.), *Baffy: The Diaries of Blanche Dugdale* (1973)

Ross, G. (ed.), *The Foreign Office and the Kremlin 1941–45* (1984)

Vandenberg Jr, Arthur H. (ed.), *The Private Papers of Senator Vandenberg* (1952)

Williamson, Philip (ed.), *The Modernisation of Conservative Politics: The Diaries and Letters of William Bridgeman 1904–1935* (1990)

Young, K. (ed.), *The Diaries of Sir Robert Bruce Lockhart, vol. II: 1939–65* (1980)

Ziegler, P. (ed.), *Personal Diary of Admiral The Lord Louis Mountbatten 1943–47* (1988)

3. MEMOIRS

Acheson, Dean, *Present at the Creation: My Years in the State Department* (1969)

Avon, Earl of, *The Eden Memoirs, vol. III: Full Circle* (1960)

Avon, Earl of, *The Eden Memoirs, vol. II: The Reckoning* (1965)

Bohlen, Charles E., *Witness to History* (1973)

Butler, R. A., *The Art of the Possible* (1971)

Carter, Violet Bonham-, *Churchill as I Knew Him* (1966)

Clarke, Sir Richard, *Anglo-American Collaboration in War and Peace 1942–1949* (1982)

Dyan, Moshe, *The Story of My Life* (1976)

Eisenhower, Dwight D., *The White House Years: Mandate for Change 1953–1956* (1963)

Eisenhower, Dwight D., *The White House Years: Waging Peace 1956–1961* (1965)

Harriman, W. Averell, and Abel, E., *Special Envoy to Churchill and Stalin, 1941–6* (1975)
Hull, Cordell, *The Memoirs of Cordell Hull, vol. II* (1948)
Ismay, Lord, *The Memoirs of General The Lord Ismay* (1960)
Kennan, George, *Memoirs* (1967)
Lloyd, Selwyn, *Suez, 1956: A Personal Account* (1976)
Macmillan, Harold, *Tides of Fortune, 1945–1955* (1969)
Macmillan, Harold, *Riding the Storm, 1956–1959* (1971)
Nutting, Anthony, *No End of a Lesson* (1967)
Pineau, Christian, *Suez, 1956* (1976)
Roberts, F. K., *Dealing with Dictators* (1991)
Stettinius Jr, Edward R., *Roosevelt and the Russians: The Yalta Conference* (1949)
Stimson, Henry L., and Bundy, M., *On Active Service in Peace and War* (1947)
Truman, Harry S., *Memoirs, vol. I: Years of Decisions* (1955)
Truman, Harry S., *Memoirs, vol. II: Years of Trial and Hope, 1946–1953* (1956)

4. BIOGRAPHY

Addison, Paul, *Churchill* (1992)
Ambrose, Stephen E., *The Supreme Commander: The War Years of General Dwight David Eisenhower* (1970)
Ambrose, Stephen E., *Eisenhower, vol. I: Soldier, General of the Army, President Elect 1890–1952* (1983)
Ambrose, Stephen E., *Eisenhower, vol. II: The President* (1984)
Ashley, Maurice, *Churchill as Historian* (1968)
Bedts, Ralph de, *Ambassador Joseph Kennedy 1938–40* (1985)
Beschloss, M. R., *Kennedy and Roosevelt* (1980)
Birkenhead, Earl of, *Halifax: The Life of the Earl of Halifax* (1965)
Birkenhead, Earl of, *Churchill 1874–1922* (1989)
Bullock, Alan, *Ernest Bevin: Foreign Secretary, 1945–1951* (1983)
Bullock, Alan, *Hitler and Stalin: Parallel Lives* (1992)
Burns, James MacGregor, *Roosevelt: The Soldier of Freedom* (1970)
Carlton, David, *Anthony Eden* (1981)
Charmley, John, *Duff Cooper* (1986)
Charmley, John, *Lord Lloyd and the Decline of the British Empire* (1987)
Charmley, John, *Churchill: The End of Glory* (1993)
Finer, H., *Dulles over Suez* (1973)
Gilbert, Martin, *Winston S. Churchill, vol. V: 1922–39* (1976)
Gilbert, Martin, *Winston S. Churchill, vol. VI: Their Finest Hour 1939–41* (1983)
Gilbert, Martin, *Winston S. Churchill, vol. VII: The Road to Victory 1941–5* (1986)
Gilbert, Martin, *Winston S. Churchill, vol. VIII: Never Despair 1945–65* (1988)
Hamilton, Nigel, *Monty: The Field Marshal, 1944–1976* (1986)
Hamilton, Nigel, *JFK: Reckless Youth* (1992)

Hoopes, Townsend, *The Devil and John Foster Dulles* (1973)

Hoopes, T., and Brinkley, D., *Driven Patriot: The Life and Times of James Forrestal* (1992)

Horne, Alistair, *Harold Macmillan, vol. I: 1894–1957* (1988)

Howard, Anthony, *RAB: The Life of R. A. Butler* (1987)

Isaacson, W., *Kissinger: A Biography* (1992)

James, Robert Rhodes, *Churchill: A Study in Failure* (1970)

James, Robert Rhodes, *Anthony Eden* (1987)

James, Robert Rhodes, *Bob Boothby: A Portrait* (1991)

Kimball, W. F., *The Juggler: Franklin Roosevelt as Wartime Statesman* (1992)

Louis, W. R., *In the Name of God Go! Leo Amery and the British Empire* (1992)

Lysaght, Charles, *Brendan Bracken* (1979)

Maddox, R. J., *William E. Borah and American Foreign Policy* (1969)

McCullough, David, *Truman* (1992)

McFarland, Keith D., *Harry H. Woodring* (1975)

McLellan, David S., *Dean Acheson: The State Department Years* (1976)

Patterson, James T., *Mr Republican: A Biography of Robert A. Taft* (1972)

Pimlott, B., *Hugh Dalton* (1985)

Roskill, Stephen, *Hankey: Man of Secrets, vol. 3: 1931–63* (1974)

Sainsbury, Keith, *Churchill and Roosevelt at War* (1994)

Schwarz, Jordan A., *Liberal: Adolf A. Berle and the Vision of an American Era* (1987)

Soames, Mary, *Clementine Churchill* (1979)

Taylor, A. J. P., *Beaverbrook* (1972)

Thorpe, D. R., *Selwyn Lloyd* (1989)

Ward, Geoffrey C., *A First-Class Temperament: The Emergence of Franklin Roosevelt* (1989)

Ziegler, P., *Mountbatten: The Official Biography* (1985)

5. MONOGRAPHS

Addison, Paul, *The Road to 1945* (1975)

Anderson, S., *Race and Rapprochement: Anglo-Saxonism and Anglo-American Relations, 1895–1904* (1981)

Anderson, Terry H. *The United States, Great Britain, and the Cold War 1944–1947* (1981)

Andrew, C., and Gordievsky, O., *KGB: The Inside Story* (1990)

Barker, Elizabeth, *Churchill and Eden at War* (1978)

Barnett, C., *The Audit of War* (1986)

Bartlett, C. J., *British Foreign Policy in the Twentieth Century* (1989)

Beaumont, J., *Comrades in Arms* (1986)

Bell, P. M. H., *A Certain Eventuality: Britain and the Fall of France* (1974)

Bennett, Edward M., *Franklin D. Roosevelt and the Search for Victory* (1990)

Bethell, N., *The Palestine Triangle* (1979)

Bridge, C., *Holding on to the Empire* (1986)

Butler, J. R. M., *Grand Strategy, vol. II* (1957)

Cairncross, Sir Alec, *Years of Recovery: British Economic Policy 1945–51* (1985)

Callahan, Raymond, *Churchill: Retreat from Empire* (1984)

Campbell, C. S., *Anglo-American Understanding, 1898–1903* (1980)

Carlton, D., *Britain and the Suez Crisis* (1988)

Charmley, John, *Chamberlain and the Lost Peace* (1989)

Churchill, W. S., *The Second World War, 6 vols* (1948–54)

Cohen, Michael J., *Palestine and the Great Powers 1945–1948* (1982)

Cook, Don, *Forging the Alliance: NATO 1945–1950* (1989)

Costello, John, *Ten Days to Destiny* (1991)

Crockatt, R., *The Cold War* (1991)

Dallek, Robert, *Franklin D. Roosevelt and American Foreign Policy 1932–1945* (1979)

Darwin, John, *Britain and Decolonisation* (1988)

Day, David, *Menzies and Churchill at War* (1986)

Deighton, A. (ed.), *Britain and the First Cold War* (1990)

Deist, W., et al. (eds), *Germany and the Second World War, vol. I* (1990)

Dilks, D., and Andrew, C., *The Missing Dimension: Governments and Intelligence Communities in the Twentieth Century* (1984)

Divine, Robert, *The Reluctant Belligerent* (1965)

Divine, Robert, *Eisenhower and the Cold War* (1981)

Dobson, A. P., *US Wartime Aid to Britain* (1986)

Dobson, A. P., *The Politics of the Anglo-American Economic Special Relationship* (1988)

Dow, J. C. R., *The Management of the British Economy 1945–1960* (1968)

Edmonds, R., *Setting the Mould: The United States and Great Britain 1945–50* (1986)

Edmonds, R., *The Big Three: Churchill, Roosevelt and Stalin* (1991)

Eggleston, G. T., *Roosevelt, Churchill, and the World War II Opposition* (1979)

Ehrman, John, *Grand Strategy, vol. V* (1956)

Erickson, John, *The Road to Stalingrad* (1975)

Feis, Herbert, *Churchill, Roosevelt and Stalin* (1957)

Frazier, R., *Anglo-American Relations with Greece* (1991)

Freiberger, Steven Z., *Dawn over Suez* (1992)

Frieberg, A. L., *The Weary Titan: Britain and the Experience of Relative Decline* (1988)

Gallagher, Hugh G., *FDR's Splendid Deception* (1985)

Gallagher, J., *The Decline, Rise and Fall of the British Empire* (1982)

Gardner, Lloyd C., *Spheres of Influence* (1993)

Garlinski, J., *Poland in the Second World War* (1979)

Gilbert, Martin, *Churchill's Political Philosophy* (1981)

Gillingham, John, *Coal, Steel, and the Rebirth of Europe, 1945–1955* (1991)

Gormly, James L., *From Potsdam to the Cold War: Big Three Diplomacy 1945–1947* (1990)

Gorodetsky, Gabriel, *Sir Stafford Cripps' Mission to Moscow 1940–42* (1984)

Hahn, Peter L., *The United States, Great Britain and Egypt 1945–1956* (1991)

Hamby, Alonzo L., *Beyond the New Deal: Harry S. Truman and American Liberalism* (1973)

Hankey, Lord, *The Supreme Command 1914–1918, vol. I* (1961)

Harbutt, Fraser, *The Iron Curtain: Churchill, America and the Origins of the Cold War* (1986)

Hartmann, Susan M., *Truman and the 80th Congress* (1971)

Herring, George C., *Aid to Russia, 1941–1946* (1973)

Hogan, Michael J., *The Marshall Plan: America, Britain and the Reconstruction of Western Europe 1947–1952* (1987)

Holland, R. F., *The Pursuit of Greatness* (1991)

Howard, Michael, *Grand Strategy, vol. IV* (1972)

Howard, Michael, *The Continental Commitment* (1972)

Irving, David, *Churchill's War* (1987)

Isaacson, Walter, and Thomas, Evan, *The Wise Men* (1986)

Jefferys, K., *The Churchill Coalition and Wartime Politics, 1940–45* (1991)

Kaspi, A., *La Mission de Jean Monnet à Algers* (1971)

Kaufman, Burton I., *Trade and Aid: Eisenhower's Foreign Economic Policy, 1953–1961* (1982)

Kennedy, P. M., *The Rise and Fall of Great Powers* (1988)

Kersaudy, François, *Churchill and de Gaulle* (1981)

Kimball, W. F., *The Most Unsordid Act: Lend-Lease, 1939–1941* (1969)

Kissinger, Henry, *Diplomacy* (1994)

Kitchen, M., *British Policy towards the Soviet Union during the Second World War* (1986)

Kolko, G., *The Politics of War: Allied Diplomacy and the World Crisis of 1943–5* (1969)

Kuniholm, Bruce R., *The Origins of the Cold War in the Near East* (1980)

Lamb, Richard, *The Failure of the Eden Government* (1987)

Lamb, Richard, *Churchill as War Leader* (1991)

Langer, W. L., and Gleason, S., *The Challenge to Isolation* (1952)

Langer, W. L., and Gleason, S., *The Undeclared War* (1953)

Langhorne, R. (ed.), *Diplomacy and Intelligence during the Second World War* (1983)

Lash, Joseph P., *Roosevelt and Churchill 1939–1941* (1976)

Leach, B. A., *German Strategy against Russia 1939–1941* (1973)

Leffler, Melvyn P., *A Preponderance of Power: National Security, the Truman Administration and the Cold War* (1992)

Louis, W. R., *The British Empire in the Middle East 1945–1951* (1984)

Low, D. A., *Eclipse of Empire* (1991)

Lucas, W. Scott, *Divided We Stand: Britain, the US and the Suez Crisis* (1991)

Marks III, Frederick W., *Power and Peace: The Diplomacy of John Foster Dulles* (1993)

Mastny, Vojtech, *Russia's Road to the Cold War* (1979)

McCormick, Thomas J., *America's Half-Century* (1989)

McNeill, William H., *America, Britain and Russia 1941–1946* (1953)

Medvedev, Roy, *Let History Judge: The Origins and Consequences of Stalinism* (1989)

Messer, Robert L., *The End of an Alliance: James F. Byrnes, Roosevelt, Truman and the Origins of the Cold War* (1982)

Miner, S., *Between Churchill and Stalin* (1988)

Miscamble, Wilson S., *George F. Kennan and the Making of American Foreign Policy 1947–1950* (1992)

Moore, R. J., *Churchill, Cripps and India 1939–1945* (1979)

Moore, R. J., *Escape from Empire: The Attlee Government and the Indian Problem* (1983)

Morgan, K. O., *Labour in Power* (1986)

Nadeau, Remi, *Stalin, Churchill, and Roosevelt Divide Europe* (1990)

Neale, R. G., *Great Britain and the United States Expansion: 1898–1900* (1966)

Ovendale, R., *The English Speaking Alliance 1945–51* (1985)

Parker, R. A. C., *Struggle for Survival: The History of the Second World War* (1989)

Paterson, Thomas G., *On Every Front: The Making of the Cold War* (1979)

Pelling, Henry, *The Labour Governments of 1945–1951* (1986)

Ponting, C., *1940: Myth and Reality* (1990)

Porter, David L., *The Seventy-sixth Congress and World War II, 1939–1940* (1979)

Pressnell, L. S., *External Economic Policy since the War, vol. I* (1987)

Read, A., and Fisher, D., *The Deadly Embrace: Hitler, Stalin and the Nazi–Soviet Pact 1939–1941* (1988)

Reynolds, David, *The Creation of the Anglo-American Alliance 1937–41* (1981)

Rock, William R., *Chamberlain and Roosevelt: British Foreign Policy and the United States, 1937–1940* (1988)

Rostow, W. W., *The Division of Europe after World War II: 1946* (1982)

Rothwell, Victor, *Britain and the Cold War 1941–1947* (1982)

Rusbridger, James, and Nave, E., *Betrayal at Pearl Harbor: How Churchill Lured Roosevelt into World War II* (1991)

Ryan, H. B., *The Vision of Anglo-America* (1987)

Sainsbury, K., *The Turning Point* (1985)

Schlaim, Avi, *Collusion across the Jordan* (1988)

Schoenfeld, D., *The War Ministry of Winston Churchill* (1972)

Seldon, A., *Churchill's Indian Summer 1951–1955* (1981)

Sherwood, Robert, *Roosevelt and Hopkins: An Intimate History* (1948)

Smith, Bradley F., *The Ultra–Magic Deals: And the Most Secret Special Relationship 1940–46* (1993)
Stoff, Michael B., *Oil, War and American Security* (1980)
Tansil, C., *Back Door to War* (1952)
Thomas, H., *Armed Truce* (1988)
Thomas, R. T., *Britain and Vichy* (1978)
Thompson, K. W., *Cold War Theories, vol. 1* (1982)
Thorne, C., *Allies of a Kind* (1978)
Tomlinson, B. R., *The Political Economy of the Raj, 1914–1947* (1979)
Trachtenberg, Marc, *History and Strategy* (1991)
Ulam, Adam B., *The Rivals: America and Russia since World War II* (1971)
Walker, Martin, *The Cold War* (1993)
Watt, D. C., *Succeeding John Bull* (1984)
Weber, Frank G., *The Evasive Neutral* (1985)
Weinberg, G., *The Foreign Policy of Hitler's Germany, vol. 2* (1970)
Winand, Pascaline, *Eisenhower, Kennedy, and the United States of Europe* (1993)
Woods, Randall Bennett, *A Changing of the Guard: Anglo-American Relations, 1941–1946* (1990)
Woods, Randall B., and Jones, H., *Dawning of the Cold War: The United States' Quest for Order* (1993)
Woodward, Sir L., *British Foreign Policy in the Second World War, 5 vols* (1970– 6)
Yerxa, Donald A., *Admirals and Empire: The United States Navy and the Caribbean 1898–1945* (1991)

6. COLLECTIONS OF ESSAYS

Barnes, Harry Elmer (ed.), *Perpetual War for Perpetual Peace* (1953)
Blake, R., and Louis, W. R. (eds), *Churchill* (1993)
Deighton, Anne (ed.), *Britain and the First Cold War* (1990)
Dilks, David (ed.), *Retreat from Power, vol. II* (1981)
Gilbert, Martin (ed.), *A Century of Conflict* (1967)
Heller, F. H., and Gillingham, J. (eds), *NATO: The Founding of the Atlantic Alliance* (1992)
Immerman, Richard H. (ed.), *John Foster Dulles and the Diplomacy of the Cold War* (1990)
Kedourie, Elie (ed.), *The Crossman Confessions and Other Essays* (1984)
Kimball, Warren F. (ed.), *America Unbound* (1992)
Lacey, Michael J. (ed.), *The Truman Presidency* (1989)
Langhorne, R. (ed.), *Diplomacy and Intelligence during the Second World War* (1985)
Langworth, Richard (ed.), *Proceedings of the Churchill Societies 1988–1989* (1990)

Laqueur, Walter (ed.), *The Second World War: Essays in Military and Political History* (1982)

Louis, W. R., and Bull, H. (eds), *The Special Relationship: Anglo-American Relations since 1945* (1986)

Louis, W. R., and Owen, R. (eds), *Suez 1956: The Crisis and its Consequences* (1989)

Melanson, R. A., and Mayers, D. (eds), *Reevaluating Eisenhower: American Foreign Policy in the 1950s* (1987)

Ovendale, R. (ed.), *The Foreign Policy of the Labour Governments, 1945–1951* (1984)

Taylor, A. J. P. (ed.), *Churchill: Four Faces and the Man* (1969)

Wheeler-Bennett, J. (ed.), *Action This Day: Working with Churchill* (1968)

Young, John W. (ed.), *The Foreign Policy of Churchill's Peacetime Administration 1951–1955* (1988)

7. ARTICLES

Adamthwaite, Anthony, 'Suez Revisited', *International Affairs* (1988)

Ash, Timothy Garton, 'From World War to Cold War', *New York Review of Books*, 11 June 1987

Beloff, Max, 'The Special Relationship: An Anglo-American Myth', in Gilbert (ed.), *op. cit.* (1967)

Boyle, Peter, 'The British Foreign Office View of Soviet-American Relations, 1945–46', *Diplomatic History* (1979)

Burgess, S., and Edwards, G., 'The Six plus One: British policy-making and the question of European economic integration, 1955', *International Affairs* (1988)

Charmley, John, 'Macmillan and the making of the French Committee of Liberation', *International History Review* (1982)

Charmley, John, 'Duff Cooper and Western European Union, 1944–47', *Review of International Studies* (1985)

Croft, Stuart, 'British Policy towards Western Europe, 1947–9', *International Affairs* (1988)

Darwin, John, 'Imperialism in Decline? Tendencies in British Imperial Policy between the Wars', *Historical Journal* (1980)

Darwin, John, 'British Decolonization since 1945', *Journal of Imperial and Commonwealth History* (1984)

Deighton, Anne, 'The "frozen front" ... Labour ... and the origins of the Cold War', *International Affairs* (1987)

Diebold Jr, William, 'The Marshall Plan in Retrospect', *International Affairs* (1988)

Duchin, Brian R., 'The "Agonizing Reappraisal": Eisenhower, Dulles and the European Defense Community', *Diplomatic History* (1992)

Fish, M. Steven, 'After Stalin's Death: The Anglo-American Debate . . .',
  Diplomatic History (1986)

Frazier, R., 'Did Britain Start the Cold War? Bevin and the Truman
  Doctrine', *Historical Journal* (1984)

Gaddis, John Lewis, 'The Emerging Post-Revisionist Synthesis on the
  Origins of the Cold War', *Diplomatic History* (1983)

Gerber, Larry G., 'The Baruch Plan and the Origins of the Cold War',
  Diplomatic History (1982)

Glees, Anthony, 'Winston's Last Gambit', *Encounter*, vol. LXIV, no. 4
  (1985)

Gormly, James L., '. . . Anglo-American Atomic Diplomacy, 1945–46',
  Diplomatic History (1984)

Grigg, John, 'Churchill, Crippled Giant', *Encounter*, vol. XLVIII, no. 7 (1977)

Hanak, H., 'Sir Stafford Cripps as British Ambassador in Moscow', *English
  Historical Review* (1979)

Harbutt, Fraser J., 'Cold War Origins: An Anglo-European Perspective',
  Diplomatic History (1989)

Heinrichs, Waldo, 'FDR's intervention in the Battle of the Atlantic, 1941',
  Diplomatic History (1986)

Hershberg, James G., '"Explosion in the Offing": German Rearmament
  and American Diplomacy, 1953–1955', *Diplomatic History* (1992)

Hogan, M. J., 'The Search for a "Creative Peace" . . . the origins of the
  Marshall Plan', *Diplomatic History* (1982)

Holland, R. F., 'The Imperial Factor in British Strategies from Attlee to
  Macmillan', *Journal of Imperial and Commonwealth History* (1984)

Holland, R. F., 'Controversy: Did Suez Hasten the End of Empire?',
  Contemporary Record, vol. 1, no. 4 (1988)

Innerman, Richard H., 'Confessions of an Eisenhower Revisionist: An
  Agonizing Reappraisal', *Diplomatic History* (1990)

Irving, D., 'Churchill and US entry into World War II', *Journal of Historical
  Review*, vol. 9, no. 3 (1989)

Kaplan, Lawrence S., 'Western Europe in "The American Century"',
  Diplomatic History (1982)

Kavanagh, D., 'Crisis, charisma and British political leadership', in D.
  Kavanagh (ed.), *Politics and Personalities* (1990)

Kimball, W. F., and Bartlett, Bruce, 'Roosevelt and Prewar Commitments
  to Churchill . . .', *Diplomatic History* (1981)

Kimball, W. F., 'Naked Reverse Right: Roosevelt, Churchill and Eastern
  Europe . . .', *Diplomatic History* (1985)

Kitchen, Martin, 'Winston Churchill and the Soviet Union during the
  Second World War', *Historical Journal* (1987)

Knight, Jonathan, 'The Great Power Peace: The US and the Soviet Union
  since 1945', *Diplomatic History* (1982)

Knight, Wayne, 'Laborite Britain: America's "Sure Friend"?', *Diplomatic History* (1983)

Kunz, Diane, 'Did Macmillan lie over Suez?', *Spectator*, 3 November 1990

Laqueur, Walter, 'Visions and Revisions', *TLS*, 5 March 1982

Louis, W. R., 'American anti-colonialism and the dissolution of the British Empire', *International Affairs* (1985)

Low, D. A., and Lapping, B., 'Controversy: Did Suez Hasten the End of Empire?', *Contemporary Record*, vol. 1, no. 2 (1987)

Maclean, Elizabeth Kimball, 'Joseph E. Davies and Soviet-American Relations, 1941–43', *Diplomatic History* (1980)

Mark, Eduard, 'Charles E. Bohlen and the Acceptable Limits of Soviet Hegemony', *Diplomatic History* (1979)

Mastny, V., 'Stalin and the prospects of a separate peace in World War II', *American Historical Review* (1972)

McFarland, Stephen L., 'A peripheral view of the origins of the Cold War', *Diplomatic History* (1980)

Melissen, J., and Zeeman, B., 'Britain and Western Europe, 1945–51: Opportunities Lost?', *International Affairs* (1986)

Miscamble, Wilson D., 'Anthony Eden and the Truman–Molotov Conversations, April 1945', *Diplomatic History* (1978)

Paterson, Thomas G., 'Presidential Foreign Policy, Public Opinion and Congress: The Truman Years', *Diplomatic History* (1979)

Pollock, Fred E., 'Roosevelt . . . and the British Fleet: All Done with Mirrors', *Diplomatic History* (1981)

Powell, Enoch, 'Macmillan: The Case Against', *Spectator*, 10 January 1987

Rappaport, A., 'The United States and European Integration: The First Phase', *Diplomatic History* (1981)

Reynolds, D., 'Eden the Diplomatist, 1931–1956: Suezide of a Statesman?', *History*, vol. 74, no. 240 (1989)

Ruane, Kevin, 'Anthony Eden, British Diplomacy and the Origins of the Geneva Conference of 1954', *Historical Journal* (1994)

Schlesinger Jr, Arthur M., 'The Origins of the Cold War', *Foreign Affairs* (1967)

Smith, R., 'British officials and the development of British Soviet policy, 1945–7', *International Affairs* (1988)

Smith, R., and Zametica, J., 'The Cold Warrior: Clement Attlee Reconsidered 1945–47', *International Affairs* (1985)

Utley, T. E., 'Stockton, the Times and the Anglo-Soviet Alliance', *Spectator*, 30 August 1986

Warner, G., 'The Anglo-American Special Relationship', *Diplomatic History* (1989)

Warner, G., 'The United States and the Suez Crisis', *International Affairs* (1991)

Watt, D. C., 'Britain and the Historiography of the Yalta Conference and the Cold War', *Diplomatic History* (1989)

Watt, D. C., '1939 Revisited: on theories on the origins of wars', *International Affairs* (1989)

Yasamee, H. J., 'Anthony Eden and Europe, November 1951', *FCO Occasional Papers*, no. 1 (1987)

Young, John W., 'Churchill, the Russians and the Western Alliance . . . 1953', *English Historical Review* (1986)

Young, John W., 'Churchill's Bid for Peace with Moscow, 1954', *History*, vol. 73, no. 239 (1988)

8. THESES

Maclean, Elizabeth Kimball, 'Joseph E. Davies', Ph.D. thesis, University of Michigan (1986)

McClain, Linda, 'The Role of Admiral W. D. Leahy in United States Foreign Policy', Ph.D., University of Virginia (1984)

Painter, David Sidney, 'The Politics of Oil, Multi-National Oil Corporations and United States Foreign Policy', Ph.D., University of North Carolina (1982)

Index

Churchill, Winston Spencer – *cont.*
  and de Gaulle 46, 48, 65, 70–1
  hopes from Anglo-American
    cooperation 46–7
  lack of foresight 48
  and India 50–1, 53
  irritation with Roosevelt 53–4
  and China 56, 65, 70
  reliance on US 57–8, 60
  comparison with Eden 57–8
  and Europe 58, 65
  and Soviet Union 58, 66, 67, 68,
    102–13, 133, 143, 144–5, 153,
    160–1, 170–1, 179, 184, 288,
    290, 357
  and British Empire/
    Commonwealth 49, 60, 62,
    183–4, 193–4
  on postwar reconstruction 65–6
  and Poland 69, 81–6, 103, 108,
    109–12, 117, 138–41, 145, 167,
    170–1, 172–3
  and Sikorski 69–70
  visit to US May 1943 76–7
  and Roosevelt 70, 96
  and France 70
  and United Nations 74, 137–8,
    140
  and Stalin 68, 69, 75, 76, 80,
    82–3, 84–6, 102–13, 144, 146,
    151, 172, 184
  Tehran conference 79
  belief in himself as
    Anglo-American mediator 89
  and Middle East oil 92, 93–4, 97
  and US economic policy 95
  views on economics 100
  to Moscow 1944 103
  and Balkans 103, 104
  'naughty document' to Stalin 109
  and Greek uprising 115, 116, 117
  critical of US 117
  troubles at home 118–19, 120
  faith in USA 121

  and treatment of Germany 122
  and Yalta conference 127–8,
    129, 133, 136, 146, 147
  and France/Germany 137
  tackles Roosevelt on Soviet
    Union 143, 146–7, 149
  and Romania 146
  under Parliamentary pressure
    147, 149
  on Britain's future role 155
  after Roosevelt, pursues Truman
    159
  attitude to Soviet Union 160–1,
    179, 184
  gets Anglo-American
    cooperation, briefly 162, 169
  and the occupation of Germany
    162
  and Cold War 162
  and Poland 167, 170–1, 172–3
  General Election 1945 168
  encouragement of Truman 170,
    171, 173–4, 180
  the Munich precedent 172
  wish for US intervention 172–3
  and Third World War 173
  meets Joseph Davies 177–9
  wish to preserve UK status 178
  depressed over US relations
    180–1
  and British Empire 183–4, 193–4
  out of office, dreams of
    Anglo-American alliance 192
  and Palestine and USA 198
  against Western grouping 201
  Fulton (Missouri) speech 204,
    217–18, 222–6, 360
  back in power 1951 205, 240, 241
  pro Truman and USA 210
  but objects to his views of
    Anglo-American relationship
    210–11
  not retiring 222, 242–3, 263, 271,
    296